Microsoft®

Exploring

Excel 2002

Microsoft®

Exploring

Excel 2002

Robert T. Grauer

University of Miami

Maryann Barber

University of Miami

Prentice
Hall

PRENTICE HALL   *Upper Saddle River, New Jersey 07458*

Senior Acquisitions Editor: David Alexander
VP/Publisher: Natalie Anderson
Managing Editor: Melissa Whitaker
Assistant Editor: Kerri Limpert
Editorial Assistant: Maryann Broadnax
Technical Editor: Cecil Yarbrough
Media Project Manager: Cathleen Profitko
Marketing Assistant: Jason Smith
Production Manager: Gail Steier de Acevedo
Project Manager: Lynne Breitfeller
Production Editor: Greg Hubit
Associate Director, Manufacturing: Vincent Scelta
Manufacturing Buyer: Lynne Breitfeller
Design Manager: Pat Smythe
Interior Design: Jill Yutkowitz
Cover Design: Blair Brown
Cover Illustration: Marjorie Dressler
Composition: GTS
Printer/Binder: Banta Menasha

Microsoft and the Microsoft Office User Specialist logo are trademarks or registered trademarks of Microsoft Corporation in the United States and/or other countries. Prentice Hall is independent from Microsoft Corporation, and not affiliated with Microsoft in any manner. This publication may be used in assisting students to prepare for a Microsoft Office User Specialist Exam. Neither Microsoft Corporation, its designated review company, nor Prentice Hall warrants that use of this publication will ensure passing the relevant Exam.

Use of the Microsoft Office User Specialist Approved Courseware Logo on this product signifies that it has been independently reviewed and approved in complying with the following standards:

Acceptable coverage of all content related to the expert level Microsoft Office Exam entitled, "Excel 2002," and sufficient performance-based exercises that relate closely to all required content, based on sampling of text.

1 0 9 8 7 6 5
ISBN 0-13-092435-0

To Marion —
my wife, my lover, and my best friend

Robert Grauer

To Frank —
for giving me the encouragement, love, and the space

Maryann Barber

APPROVED COURSEWARE

What does this logo mean?

It means this courseware has been approved by the Microsoft® Office User Specialist Program to be among the finest available for learning **Excel 2002**. It also means that upon completion of this courseware, you may be prepared to become a Microsoft Office User Specialist.

What is a Microsoft Office User Specialist?

A Microsoft Office User Specialist is an individual who has certified his or her skills in one or more of the Microsoft Office desktop applications of Microsoft Word, Microsoft Excel, Microsoft PowerPoint®, Microsoft Outlook® or Microsoft Access, or in Microsoft Project. The Microsoft Office User Specialist Program typically offers certification exams at the "Core" and "Expert" skill levels.[*] The Microsoft Office User Specialist Program is the only Microsoft approved program in the world for certifying proficiency in Microsoft Office desktop applications and Microsoft Project. This certification can be a valuable asset in any job search or career advancement.

More Information:

To learn more about becoming a Microsoft Office User Specialist, visit www.mous.net

To purchase a Microsoft Office User Specialist certification exam, visit www.DesktopIQ.com

To learn about other Microsoft Office User Specialist approved courseware from Prentice Hall, visit http://www.prenhall.com/phit/mous_frame.html

---

[*]The availability of Microsoft Office User Specialist certification exams varies by application, application version and language. Visit www.mous.net for exam availability.

Microsoft, the Microsoft Office User Specialist Logo, PowerPoint and Outlook are either registered trademarks or trademarks of Microsoft Corporation in the United States and/or other countries.

CONTENTS

4

GRAPHS AND CHARTS: DELIVERING A MESSAGE 167

5

CONSOLIDATING DATA: 3-D WORKBOOKS AND FILE LINKING 217

6

A FINANCIAL FORECAST: WORKGROUPS, AUDITING, AND TEMPLATES 261

ESSENTIALS OF MICROSOFT® WINDOWS®

INDEX

PREFACE

Continuing a tradition of excellence, Prentice Hall is proud to announce the latest update in Microsoft Office texts: the new Exploring Microsoft Office XP series by Robert T. Grauer and Maryann Barber.

The hands-on approach and conceptual framework of this comprehensive series helps students master all aspects of the Microsoft Office XP software, while providing the background necessary to transfer and use these skills in their personal and professional lives.

WHAT'S NEW IN THE EXPLORING OFFICE SERIES FOR XP

The entire Exploring Office series has been revised to include the new features found in the Office XP Suite, which contains Word 2002, Excel 2002, Access 2002, PowerPoint 2002, Publisher 2002, FrontPage 2002, and Outlook 2002.

In addition, this revision includes fully revised end-of-chapter material that provides an extensive review of concepts and techniques discussed in the chapter. Many of these exercises feature the World Wide Web and application integration.

Building on the success of the Web site provided for previous editions of this series, Exploring Office XP will introduce the MyPHLIP Companion Web site, a site customized for each instructor that includes on-line, interactive study guides, data file downloads, current news feeds, additional case studies and exercises, and other helpful information. Start out at www.prenhall.com/grauer to explore these resources!

Organization of the Exploring Office Series for XP

The new Exploring Microsoft Office XP series includes four combined Office XP texts from which to choose:

- **Volume I** is MOUS certified in each of the major applications in the Office suite (Word, Excel, Access, and PowerPoint). Three additional modules (Essential Computer Concepts, Essentials of Windows, and Essentials of the Internet) are also included.

- **Volume II** picks up where Volume I left off, covering the advanced topics for the individual applications. A VBA primer has been added.

- The **Brief Microsoft Office XP** edition provides less coverage of the individual applications than Volume I (a total of 8 chapters as opposed to 14). The supplementary modules (Windows, Internet, and Concepts) are not included.

- A new volume, **Getting Started with Office XP**, contains the first chapter from each application (Word, Excel, Access, and PowerPoint), plus three additional modules: Essentials of Windows, Essentials of the Internet, and Essential Computer Concepts.

Individual texts for Word 2002, Excel 2002, Access 2002, and PowerPoint 2002 provide complete coverage of the application and are MOUS certified. For shorter courses, we have created brief versions of the Exploring texts that give students a four-chapter introduction to each application. Each of these volumes is MOUS certified at the Core level.

To complete the full coverage of this series, custom modules on Microsoft Outlook 2002, Microsoft FrontPage 2002, Microsoft Publisher 2002, and a generic introduction to Microsoft Windows are also available.

This book has been approved by Microsoft to be used in preparation for Microsoft Office User Specialist exams.

APPROVED COURSEWARE

The Microsoft Office User Specialist (MOUS) program is globally recognized as the standard for demonstrating desktop skills with the Microsoft Office suite of business productivity applications (Microsoft Word, Microsoft Excel, Microsoft PowerPoint, Microsoft Access, and Microsoft Outlook). With a MOUS certification, thousands of people have demonstrated increased productivity and have proved their ability to utilize the advanced functionality of these Microsoft applications.

By encouraging individuals to develop advanced skills with Microsoft's leading business desktop software, the MOUS program helps fill the demand for qualified, knowledgeable people in the modern workplace. At the same time, MOUS helps satisfy an organization's need for a qualitative assessment of employee skills.

Customize the Exploring Office Series with Prentice Hall's Right PHit Binding Program

The Exploring Office XP series is part of the Right PHit Custom Binding Program, enabling instructors to create their own texts by selecting modules from Office XP Volume I, Volume II, Outlook, FrontPage, and Publisher to suit the needs of a specific course. An instructor could, for example, create a custom text consisting of the core modules in Word and Excel, coupled with the brief modules for Access and PowerPoint, and a brief introduction to computer concepts.

Instructors can also take advantage of Prentice Hall's Value Pack program to shrinkwrap multiple texts together at substantial savings to the student. A value pack is ideal in courses that require complete coverage of multiple applications.

INSTRUCTOR AND STUDENT RESOURCES

The **Instructor's CD** that accompanies the Exploring Office series contains:

- Student data disks
- Solutions to all exercises and problems
- PowerPoint lectures
- Instructor's manuals in Word format enable the instructor to annotate portions of the instructor manual for distribution to the class
- A Windows-based test manager and the associated test bank in Word format

Prentice Hall's New MyPHLIP Companion Web site at www.prenhall.com/grauer offers current events, exercises, and downloadable supplements. This site also includes an on-line study guide containing true/false, multiple-choice, and essay questions.

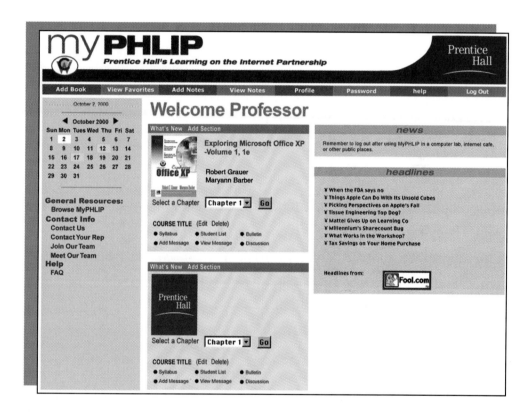

WebCT www.prenhall.com/webct

 GOLD LEVEL CUSTOMER SUPPORT available exclusively to adopters of Prentice Hall courses, is provided free-of-charge upon adoption and provides you with priority assistance, training discounts, and dedicated technical support.

Blackboard www.prenhall.com/blackboard

 Prentice Hall's abundant on-line content, combined with Blackboard's popular tools and interface, result in robust Web-based courses that are easy to implement, manage, and use—taking your courses to new heights in student interaction and learning.

CourseCompass www.coursecompass.com

 CourseCompass is a dynamic, interactive on-line course management tool powered by Blackboard. This exciting product allows you to teach with marketing-leading Pearson Education content in an easy-to-use customizable format.

Exploring Microsoft Office XP assumes no prior knowledge of the operating system. A 64-page section introduces the reader to the Essentials of Windows and provides an overview of the operating system. Students are shown the necessary file-management operations to use Microsoft Office successfully.

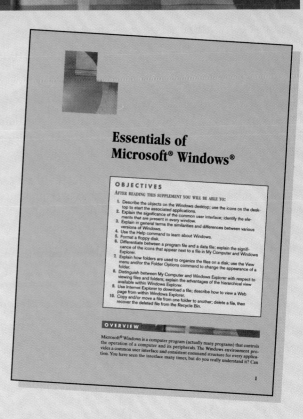

In-depth tutorials throughout all the Office XP applications enhance the conceptual introduction to each task and guide the student at the computer. Every step in every exercise has a full-color screen shot to illustrate the specific commands. Boxed tips provide alternative techniques and shortcuts and/or anticipate errors that students may make.

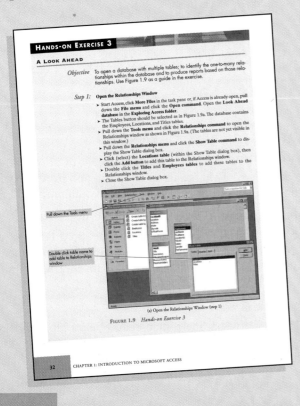

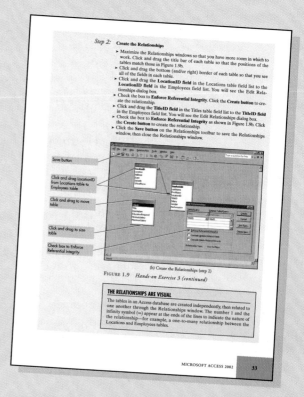

The authors have created an entirely new set of end-of-chapter exercises for every chapter in all of the applications. These new exercises have been written to provide the utmost in flexibility, variety, and difficulty.

Web-based Practice Exercises and On Your Own Exercises are marked by an icon in the margin and allow further exploration and practice via the World Wide Web.

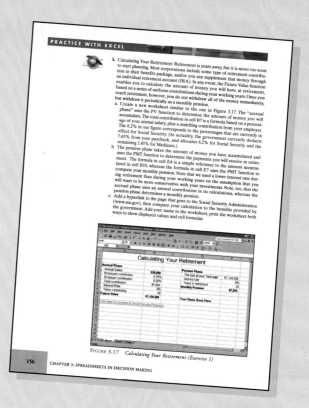

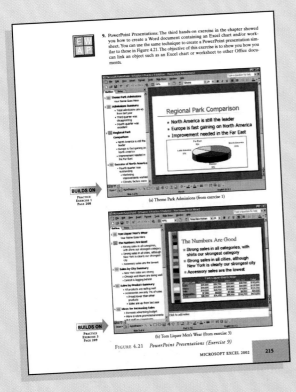

Integration Exercises are marked by an icon in the margin. These exercises take advantage of the Microsoft Office Suite's power to use multiple applications in one document, spreadsheet, or presentation.

Builds On Exercises require students to use selected application files as the starting point in later exercises, thereby introducing new information to students only as needed.

The end-of-chapter material includes multiple-choice questions for self-evaluation plus additional "on your own" exercises to encourage the reader to further explore the application.

ACKNOWLEDGMENTS

We want to thank the many individuals who have helped to bring this project to fruition. David Alexander, senior editor at Prentice Hall, has provided new leadership in extending the series to Office XP. Cathi Profitko did an absolutely incredible job on our Web site. Melissa Whitaker coordinated the myriad details of production and the certification process. Greg Christotterson was instrumental in the acquisition of supporting software. Lynne Breitfeller was the project manager and manufacturing buyer. Greg Hubit has been masterful as the external production editor for every book in the series. Cecil Yarbrough did an outstanding job in checking the manuscript for technical accuracy. Chuck Cox did his usual fine work as copyeditor. Kerri Limpert was the supplements editor. Cindy Stevens, Tom McKenzie, and Michael Olmstead wrote the instructor manuals. Patricia Smythe developed the innovative and attractive design. We also want to acknowledge our reviewers who, through their comments and constructive criticism, greatly improved the series.

Lynne Band, Middlesex Community College
Don Belle, Central Piedmont Community College
Stuart P. Brian, Holy Family College
Carl M. Briggs, Indiana University School of Business
Kimberly Chambers, Scottsdale Community College
Alok Charturvedi, Purdue University
Jerry Chin, Southwest Missouri State University
Dean Combellick, Scottsdale Community College
Cody Copeland, Johnson County Community College
Larry S. Corman, Fort Lewis College
Janis Cox, Tri-County Technical College
Martin Crossland, Southwest Missouri State University
Paul E. Daurelle, Western Piedmont Community College
Carolyn DiLeo, Westchester Community College
Judy Dolan, Palomar College
David Douglas, University of Arkansas
Carlotta Eaton, Radford University
Judith M. Fitspatrick, Gulf Coast Community College
James Franck, College of St. Scholastica
Raymond Frost, Central Connecticut State University
Midge Gerber, Southwestern Oklahoma State University
James Gips, Boston College
Vernon Griffin, Austin Community College
Ranette Halverson, Midwestern State University
Michael Hassett, Fort Hays State University
Mike Hearn, Community College of Philadelphia
Wanda D. Heller, Seminole Community College
Bonnie Homan, San Francisco State University
Ernie Ivey, Polk Community College
Mike Kelly, Community College of Rhode Island
Jane King, Everett Community College

Rose M. Laird, Northern Virginia Community College
John Lesson, University of Central Florida
David B. Meinert, Southwest Missouri State University
Alan Moltz, Naugatuck Valley Technical Community College
Kim Montney, Kellogg Community College
Bill Morse, DeVry Institute of Technology
Kevin Pauli, University of Nebraska
Mary McKenry Percival, University of Miami
Delores Pusins, Hillsborough Community College
Gale E. Rand, College Misericordia
Judith Rice, Santa Fe Community College
David Rinehard, Lansing Community College
Marilyn Salas, Scottsdale Community College
John Shepherd, Duquesne University
Barbara Sherman, Buffalo State College
Robert Spear, Prince George's Community College
Michael Stewardson, San Jacinto College—North
Helen Stoloff, Hudson Valley Community College
Margaret Thomas, Ohio University
Mike Thomas, Indiana University School of Business
Suzanne Tomlinson, Iowa State University
Karen Tracey, Central Connecticut State University
Antonio Vargas, El Paso Community College
Sally Visci, Lorain County Community College
David Weiner, University of San Francisco
Connie Wells, Georgia State University
Wallace John Whistance-Smith, Ryerson Polytechnic University
Jack Zeller, Kirkwood Community College

A final word of thanks to the unnamed students at the University of Miami, who make it all worthwhile. Most of all, thanks to you, our readers, for choosing this book. Please feel free to contact us with any comments and suggestions.

Robert T. Grauer
rgrauer@miami.edu
www.bus.miami.edu/~rgrauer
www.prenhall.com/grauer

Maryann Barber
mbarber@miami.edu
www.bus.miami.edu/~mbarber

CHAPTER 1

Introduction to Microsoft® Excel: What Is a Spreadsheet?

OBJECTIVES

AFTER READING THIS CHAPTER YOU WILL BE ABLE TO:

1. Describe a spreadsheet and suggest several potential applications; explain how the rows and columns of a spreadsheet are identified.
2. Distinguish between a formula and a constant; explain the use of a predefined function within a formula.
3. Open an Excel workbook; insert and delete rows and columns of a worksheet; save and print the modified worksheet.
4. Describe the three-dimensional nature of an Excel workbook; distinguish between a workbook and a worksheet.
5. Print a worksheet to show either the displayed values or the cell contents; use the Page Setup command to modify the appearance of the printed worksheet.
6. Copy and/or move cells within a worksheet; differentiate between relative, absolute, and mixed references.
7. Format a worksheet to include boldface, italics, shading, and borders; change the font and/or alignment of a selected entry.

OVERVIEW

The spreadsheet is the PC application that is used most frequently by business managers and executives. This chapter provides a broad-based introduction to spreadsheets in general and to Microsoft Excel in particular. A spreadsheet (also called a worksheet) is stored within a workbook, which in turn may contain multiple worksheets. The chapter discusses how the rows and columns of a spreadsheet are labeled and the difference between a formula and a constant.

1

All of the illustrations in this chapter are set in the context of a professor's grade book that computes the semester averages for his or her students. You will learn how students can be inserted or removed from the worksheet and how changing a student's grade automatically recalculates the dependent values in the worksheet. We also show you how to create a new workbook, how to move and copy formulas within the worksheet, and how to format the worksheet.

The hands-on exercises in the chapter enable you to apply all of the material at the computer, and are indispensable to the learn-by-doing philosophy we follow throughout the text. As you do the exercises, you may recognize many commands from other Office applications, all of which share a common user interface and consistent command structure.

INTRODUCTION TO SPREADSHEETS

A *spreadsheet* is the computerized equivalent of an accountant's ledger. As with the ledger, it consists of a grid of rows and columns that enables you to organize data in a readily understandable format. Figures 1.1a and 1.1b show the same information displayed in ledger and spreadsheet format, respectively.

"What is the big deal?" you might ask. The big deal is that after you change an entry (or entries), the spreadsheet will, automatically and almost instantly, recompute all of the formulas. Consider, for example, the profit projection spreadsheet shown in Figure 1.1b. As the spreadsheet is presently constructed, the unit price is $20 and the projected sales are 1,200 units, producing gross sales of $24,000 ($20/unit × 1,200 units). The projected expenses are $19,200, which yields a profit of $4,800 ($24,000 − $19,200). If the unit price is increased to $22 per unit, the spreadsheet recomputes the formulas, adjusting the values of gross sales and net profit. The modified spreadsheet of Figure 1.1c appears automatically.

With a calculator and bottle of correction fluid or a good eraser, the same changes could also be made to the ledger. But imagine a ledger with hundreds of entries and the time that would be required to make the necessary changes to the ledger by hand. The same spreadsheet will be recomputed automatically by the computer. And the computer will not make mistakes. Herein lie the advantages of a spreadsheet—the ability to make changes, and to have the computer carry out the recalculation faster and more accurately than could be accomplished manually.

					Initials	Date
					Prepared by:	
					Approved by:	
	1	2	3	4	5	6

		1	2	3	4	5	6	
1	UNIT PRICE		2 0					1
2	UNIT SALES		1 2 0 0					2
3	GROSS PROFIT		24 0 0 0					3
4								4
5	EXPENSES							5
6	PRODUCTION		10 0 0 0					6
7	DISTRIBUTION		1 2 0 0					7
8	MARKETING		5 0 0 0					8
9	OVERHEAD		3 0 0 0					9
10	TOTAL EXPENSES		19 2 0 0					10
11								11
12	NET PROFIT		4 8 0 0					12

(a) The Accountant's Ledger

FIGURE 1.1   *The Accountant's Ledger*

Unit price is increased to $22

Formulas recompute automatically

	A	B
1	Profit Projection	
2		
3	Unit Price	$20
4	Unit Sales	1,200
5	Gross Sales	$24,000
6		
7	Expenses	
8	Production	$10,000
9	Distribution	$1,200
10	Marketing	$5,000
11	Overhead	$3,000
12	Total Expenses	$19,200
13		
14	Net Profit	$4,800

(b) Original Spreadsheet

	A	B
1	Profit Projection	
2		
3	Unit Price	$22
4	Unit Sales	1,200
5	Gross Sales	$26,400
6		
7	Expenses	
8	Production	$10,000
9	Distribution	$1,200
10	Marketing	$5,000
11	Overhead	$3,000
12	Total Expenses	$19,200
13		
14	Net Profit	$7,200

(c) Modified Spreadsheet

FIGURE 1.1 *The Accountant's Ledger (continued)*

The Professor's Grade Book

A second example of a spreadsheet, one with which you can easily identify, is that of a professor's grade book. The grades are recorded by hand in a notebook, which is nothing more than a different kind of accountant's ledger. Figure 1.2 contains both manual and spreadsheet versions of a grade book.

Figure 1.2a shows a handwritten grade book as it has been done since the days of the little red schoolhouse. For the sake of simplicity, only five students are shown, each with three grades. The professor has computed class averages for each exam, as well as a semester average for every student. The final counts *twice* as much as either test; for example, Adams's average is equal to (100+90+81+81)/4 = 88. This is the professor's grading scheme and it is incorporated into the manual grade book and equivalent spreadsheet.

Figure 1.2b shows the grade book as it might appear in a spreadsheet, and is essentially unchanged from Figure 1.2a. Walker's grade on the final exam in Figure 1.2b is 90, giving him a semester average of 85 and producing a class average on the final of 75.2 as well. Now consider Figure 1.2c, in which the grade on Walker's final has been changed to 100, causing Walker's semester average to change from 85 to 90, and the class average on the final to go from 75.2 to 77.2. As with the profit projection, a change to any entry within the grade book automatically recalculates all other dependent formulas as well. Hence, when Walker's final exam was regraded, all dependent formulas (the class average for the final as well as Walker's semester average) were recomputed.

As simple as the idea of a spreadsheet may seem, it provided the first major reason for managers to have a personal computer on their desks. Essentially, anything that can be done with a pencil, a pad of paper, and a calculator can be done faster and far more accurately with a spreadsheet. The spreadsheet, like the personal computer, has become an integral part of every type of business. Indeed, it is hard to imagine that these calculations were ever done by hand. The spreadsheet has become an integral part of corporate culture.

Final counts twice so average is computed as (100 + 90 + 81 + 81)/4

	TEST 1	TEST 2	FINAL	AVERAGE
ADAMS	100	90	81	88
BAKER	90	76	87	85
GLASSMAN	90	78	78	81
MOLDOF	60	60	40	50
WALKER	80	80	90	85
CLASS AVERAGE	84.0	76.8	75.2	
NOTE: FINAL COUNTS DOUBLE				

(a) The Professor's Grade Book

Walker's original grade is 90

	A	B	C	D	E
1	Student	Test 1	Test 2	Final	Average
2					
3	Adams	100	90	81	88.0
4	Baker	90	76	87	85.0
5	Glassman	90	78	78	81.0
6	Moldof	60	60	40	50.0
7	Walker	80	80	90	85.0
8					
9	Class Average	84.0	76.8	75.2	

(b) Original Grades

Grade on Walker's final is changed to 100

Formulas recompute automatically

	A	B	C	D	E
1	Student	Test 1	Test 2	Final	Average
2					
3	Adams	100	90	81	88.0
4	Baker	90	76	87	85.0
5	Glassman	90	78	78	81.0
6	Moldof	60	60	40	50.0
7	Walker	80	80	100	90.0
8					
9	Class Average	84.0	76.8	77.2	

(c) Modified Spreadsheet

FIGURE 1.2   *The Professor's Grade Book*

Row and Column Headings

A spreadsheet is divided into rows and columns, with each row and column assigned a heading. Rows are given numeric headings ranging from 1 to 65,536 (the maximum number of rows allowed). Columns are assigned alphabetic headings from column A to Z, then continue from AA to AZ and then from BA to BZ and so on, until the last of 256 columns (column IV) is reached.

The intersection of a row and column forms a *cell*, with the number of cells in a spreadsheet equal to the number of rows times the number of columns. The professor's grade book in Figure 1.2, for example, has 5 columns labeled A through E, 9 rows numbered from 1 to 9, and a total of 45 cells. Each cell has a unique *cell reference*; for example, the cell at the intersection of column A and row 9 is known as cell A9. The column heading always precedes the row heading in the cell reference.

Formulas and Constants

Figure 1.3 is an alternate view of the professor's grade book that shows the cell contents rather than the computed values. Cell E3, for example, does not contain the number 88 (Adams's average for the semester), but rather the formula to compute the average from the exam grades. Indeed, it is the existence of the formula that lets you change the value of any cell containing a grade for Adams (cells B3, C3, or D3), and have the computed average in cell E3 change automatically.

To create a spreadsheet, one goes from cell to cell and enters either a constant or a formula. A *constant* is an entry that does not change. It may be a number, such as a student's grade on an exam, or it may be descriptive text (a label), such as a student's name. A *formula* is a combination of numeric constants, cell references, arithmetic operators, and/or functions (described below) that displays the result of a calculation. You can *edit* (change) the contents of a cell by returning to the cell and reentering the constant or formula.

A formula always begins with an equal sign. Consider, for example, the formula in cell E3, =(B3+C3+2*D3)/4, which computes Adams's semester average. The formula is built in accordance with the professor's rules for computing a student's semester average, which counts the final twice as much as the other tests. Excel uses symbols +, −, *, /, and ^ to indicate addition, subtraction, multiplication, division, and exponentiation, respectively, and follows the normal rules of arithmetic precedence. Any expression in parentheses is evaluated first, then within an expression exponentiation is performed first, followed by multiplication or division in left to right order, then finally addition or subtraction.

The formula in cell E3 takes the grade on the first exam (in cell B3), plus the grade on the second exam (in cell C3), plus two times the grade on the final (in cell D3), and divides the result by four. Thus, should any of the exam grades change, the semester average (a formula whose results depend on the individual exam grades) will also change. This, in essence, is the basic principle behind the spreadsheet and explains why, when one number changes, various other numbers throughout the spreadsheet change as well.

A formula may also include a *function*, or predefined computational task, such as the AVERAGE function in cells B9, C9, and D9. The function in cell B9, for example, =AVERAGE(B3:B7), is interpreted to mean the average of all cells starting at cell B3 and ending at cell B7 and is equivalent to the formula =(B3+B4+B5+B6+B7)/5. You can appreciate that functions are often easier to use than the corresponding formulas, especially with larger spreadsheets (and classes with many students). Excel contains a wide variety of functions that help you to create very powerful spreadsheets. Financial functions, for example, enable you to calculate the interest payments on a car loan or home mortgage.

Constant (entry that does not change)

Function (predefined computational task)

Formula (displays the result of a calculation)

	A	B	C	D	E
1	Student	Test 1	Test 2	Final	Average
2					
3	Adams	100	90	81	=(B3+C3+2*D3)/4
4	Baker	90	76	87	=(B4+C4+2*D4)/4
5	Glassman	90	78	78	=(B5+C5+2*D5)/4
6	Moldof	60	60	40	=(B6+C6+2*D6)/4
7	Walker	80	80	90	=(B7+C7+2*D7)/4
8					
9	Class Average	=AVERAGE(B3:B7)	=AVERAGE(C3:C7)	=AVERAGE(D3:D7)	

FIGURE 1.3   *The Professor's Grade Book (cell formulas)*

Figure 1.4 displays the professor's grade book as it is implemented in Microsoft Excel. Microsoft Excel is a Windows application, and thus shares the common user interface with which you are familiar. (It's even easier to learn Excel if you already know another Office application such as Microsoft Word.) You should recognize, therefore, that the desktop in Figure 1.4 has two open windows—an application window for Microsoft Excel and a document window for the workbook, which is currently open.

Each window has its own Minimize, Maximize (or Restore), and Close buttons. Both windows have been maximized and thus the title bars have been merged into a single title bar that appears at the top of the application window. The title bar reflects the application (Microsoft Excel) as well as the name of the workbook (Grade Book) on which you are working. A menu bar appears immediately below the title bar. Two toolbars, which are discussed in depth on page 8, appear below the menu bar. Vertical and horizontal scroll bars appear at the right and bottom of the document window. The Windows taskbar appears at the bottom of the screen and shows the open applications. The Ask a Question list box appears to the right of the menu bar and provides instant access to the Help facility.

The terminology is important, and we distinguish between spreadsheet, worksheet, and workbook. Excel refers to a spreadsheet as a **worksheet**. Spreadsheet is a generic term; *workbook* and *worksheet* are unique to Excel. An Excel **workbook** contains one or more worksheets. The professor's grades for this class are contained in the CIS120 worksheet within the Grade Book workbook. This workbook also contains additional worksheets (CIS223 and CIS316) as indicated by the worksheet tabs at the bottom of the window. These worksheets contain the professor's grades for other courses that he or she is teaching this semester.

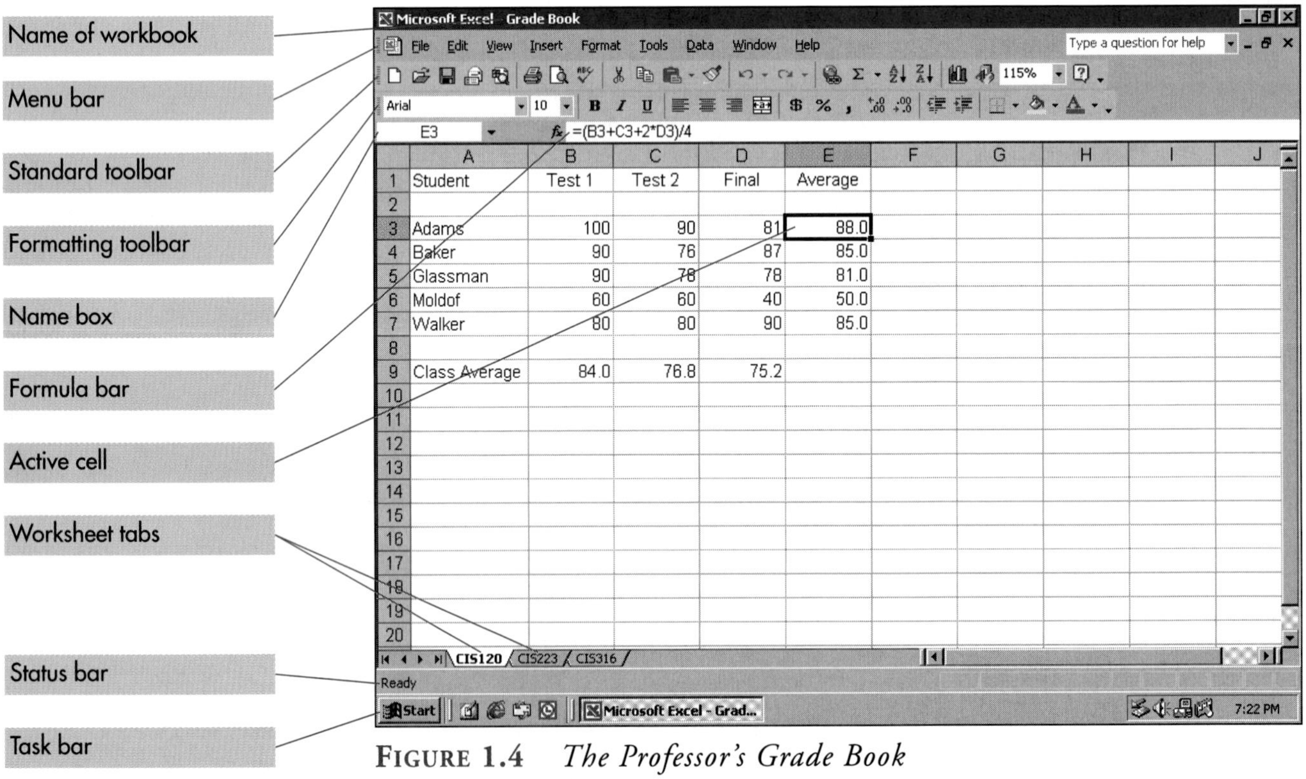

Name of workbook
Menu bar
Standard toolbar
Formatting toolbar
Name box
Formula bar
Active cell
Worksheet tabs
Status bar
Task bar

FIGURE 1.4   *The Professor's Grade Book*

Figure 1.4 resembles the grade book shown earlier, but it includes several other elements that enable you to create and/or edit the worksheet. The heavy border around cell E3 indicates that it (cell E3) is the *active cell*. Any entry made at this time is made into the active cell, and any commands that are executed affect the contents of the active cell. The active cell can be changed by clicking a different cell, or by using the arrow keys to move to a different cell.

The displayed value in cell E3 is 88.0, but as indicated earlier, the cell contains a formula to compute the semester average rather than the number itself. The contents of the active cell, $=(B3+C3+2*D3)/4$, are displayed in the *formula bar* near the top of the worksheet. The cell reference for the active cell, cell E3 in Figure 1.4, appears in the *Name box* at the left of the formula bar.

The *status bar* at the bottom of the worksheet keeps you informed of what is happening as you work within Excel. It displays information about a selected command or an operation in progress.

THE EXCEL WORKBOOK

An Excel workbook is the electronic equivalent of the three-ring binder. A workbook contains one or more worksheets (or chart sheets), each of which is identified by a tab at the bottom of the workbook. The worksheets in a workbook are normally related to one another; for example, each worksheet may contain the sales for a specific division within a company. The advantage of a workbook is that all of its worksheets are stored in a single file, which is accessed as a unit.

Toolbars

Excel provides several different ways to accomplish the same task. Commands may be accessed from a pull-down menu, from a shortcut menu (which is displayed by pointing to an object and clicking the right mouse button), and/or through keyboard equivalents. Commands can also be executed from one of many *toolbars* that appear immediately below the menu bar. The Standard and Formatting toolbars are displayed by default. The toolbars appear initially on the same line, but can be separated as described in the hands-on exercise that follows.

The *Standard toolbar* contains buttons corresponding to the most basic commands in Excel—for example, opening and closing a workbook, printing a workbook, and so on. The icon on the button is intended to be indicative of its function (e.g., a printer to indicate the Print command). You can also point to the button to display a *ScreenTip* showing the name of the button.

The *Formatting toolbar* appears under the Standard toolbar, and provides access to common formatting operations such as boldface, italics, or underlining. It also enables you to change the alignment of entries within a cell and/or change the font or color. The easiest way to master the toolbars is to view the buttons in groups according to their general function, as shown in Figure 1.5.

The toolbars may appear overwhelming at first, but there is absolutely no need to memorize what the individual buttons do. That will come with time. Indeed, if you use another office application such as Microsoft Word, you may already recognize many of the buttons on the Standard and Formatting toolbars. Note, too, that many of the commands in the pull-down menus are displayed with an image that corresponds to a button on a toolbar.

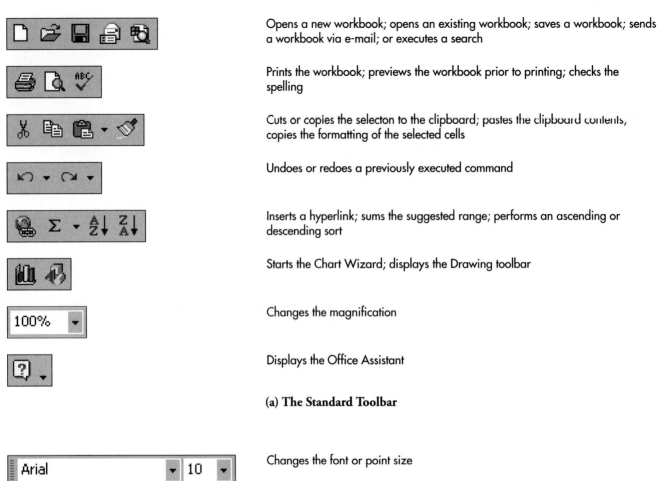

Opens a new workbook; opens an existing workbook; saves a workbook; sends a workbook via e-mail; or executes a search

Prints the workbook; previews the workbook prior to printing; checks the spelling

Cuts or copies the selecton to the clipboard; pastes the clipboard contents, copies the formatting of the selected cells

Undoes or redoes a previously executed command

Inserts a hyperlink; sums the suggested range; performs an ascending or descending sort

Starts the Chart Wizard; displays the Drawing toolbar

Changes the magnification

Displays the Office Assistant

(a) The Standard Toolbar

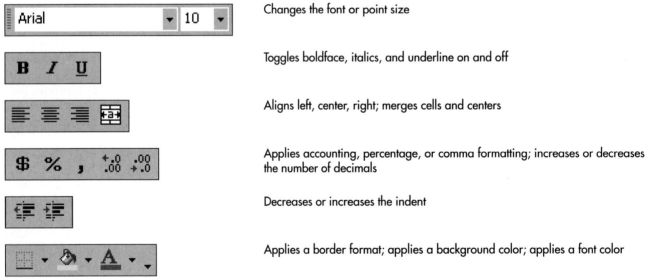

Changes the font or point size

Toggles boldface, italics, and underline on and off

Aligns left, center, right; merges cells and centers

Applies accounting, percentage, or comma formatting; increases or decreases the number of decimals

Decreases or increases the indent

Applies a border format; applies a background color; applies a font color

(b) The Formatting Toolbar

FIGURE 1.5   *Toolbars*

The *File menu* is a critically important menu in virtually every Windows application. It contains the Save and Open commands to save a workbook on disk, then subsequently retrieve (open) that workbook at a later time. The File menu also contains the *Print command* to print a workbook, the *Close command* to close the current workbook but continue working in the application, and the *Exit command* to quit the application altogether.

The *Save command* copies the workbook that you are working on (i.e., the workbook that is currently in memory) to disk. The command functions differently the first time it is executed for a new workbook, in that it displays the Save As dialog box as shown in Figure 1.6a. The dialog box requires you to specify the name of the workbook, the drive (and an optional folder) in which the workbook is to be stored, and its file type. All subsequent executions of the command save the workbook under the assigned name, replacing the previously saved version with the new version.

The *file name* (e.g., My First Spreadsheet) can contain up to 255 characters including spaces, commas, and/or periods. (Periods are discouraged, however, since they are too easily confused with DOS extensions.) The Save In list box is used to select the drive (which is not visible in Figure 1.6a) and the optional folder (e.g., Exploring Excel). The *Places bar* provides shortcuts to any of its folders without having to search through the Save In list box. Click the Desktop icon, for example, and the file is saved on the Windows desktop. You can also use the Favorites folder, which is accessible from every application in Office XP.

The *file type* defaults to an Excel 2002 workbook. You can, however, choose a different format to maintain compatibility with earlier versions of Microsoft Excel. You can also save any Excel workbook as a Web page or HTML document.

The *Save As command* saves a copy of an existing workbook under a different name, and/or a different file type, and is useful when you want to retain a copy of the original workbook. The Save As command results in two copies of the workbook. The original workbook is kept on disk under the original name. A copy of the workbook is saved on disk under the new name and remains in memory.

The *Open command* is the opposite of the Save command as it brings a copy of an existing workbook into memory, enabling you to work with that workbook. The Open command displays the Open dialog box in which you specify the file name, the drive (and optionally the folder) that contains the file, and the file type. Microsoft Excel will then list all files of that type on the designated drive (and folder), enabling you to open the file you want.

The Save and Open commands work in conjunction with one another. The Save As dialog box in Figure 1.6a, for example, saves the file My First Spreadsheet in the Exploring Excel folder. The Open dialog box in Figure 1.6b loads that file into memory so that you can work with the file, after which you can save the revised file for use at a later time.

The toolbars in the Save As and Open dialog boxes have several buttons in common that facilitate the execution of either command. The Views button lets you display the files in one of four different views. The Details view shows the file size as well as the date and time a file was last modified. The Preview view shows the beginning of a workbook, without having to open the workbook. The List view displays only the file names, and thus lets you see more files at one time. The Properties view shows information about the workbook including the date of creation and number of revisions.

Other buttons provide limited file management without having to go to My Computer or Windows Explorer. You can, for example, delete a file, create a new folder, or start your Web browser from either dialog box. The Tools button provides access to additional commands that are well worth exploring.

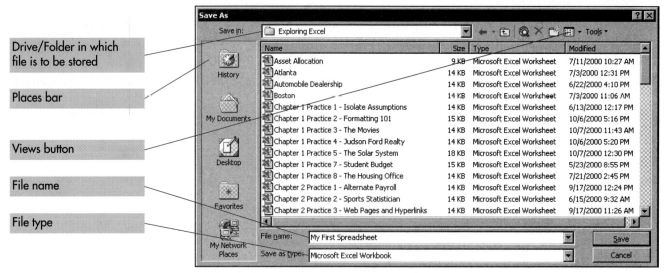

Drive/Folder in which
file is to be stored

Places bar

Views button

File name

File type

(a) Save As Dialog Box (Details View)

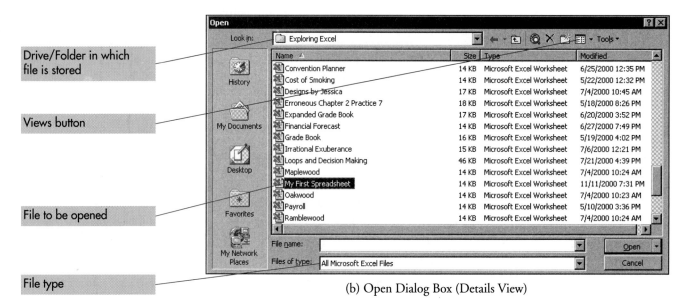

Drive/Folder in which
file is stored

Views button

File to be opened

File type

(b) Open Dialog Box (Details View)

FIGURE 1.6   *The Save and Open Commands*

SORT BY NAME, DATE, OR FILE SIZE

The files in the Save As and Open dialog boxes can be displayed in ascending or descending sequence by name, date modified, or size. Change to the Details view, then click the heading of the desired column; for example, click the Modified column to list the files according to the date they were last changed. Click the column heading a second time to reverse the sequence—that is, to switch from ascending to descending, and vice versa.

INTRODUCTION TO MICROSOFT EXCEL

Objective To start Microsoft Excel; to open, modify, and print an existing workbook. Use Figure 1.7 as a guide in the exercise.

Step 1: **Welcome to Windows**

> Turn on the computer and all of its peripherals. The floppy drive should be empty prior to starting your machine. This ensures that the system starts by reading from the hard disk, which contains the Windows files, as opposed to a floppy disk, which does not.

> Your system will take a minute or so to get started, after which you should see the desktop in Figure 1.7a. Do not be concerned if the appearance of your desktop is different from ours.

> You may also see a Welcome to Windows dialog box with commands to take a tour of the operating system. If so, click the appropriate button(s) or close the dialog box.

> You should be familiar with basic file management and very comfortable moving and copying files from one folder to another. If not, you may want to review the material in the Essentials of Windows section of this text.

> You are ready to download the practice files you will need for the hands-on exercises that appear throughout the text.

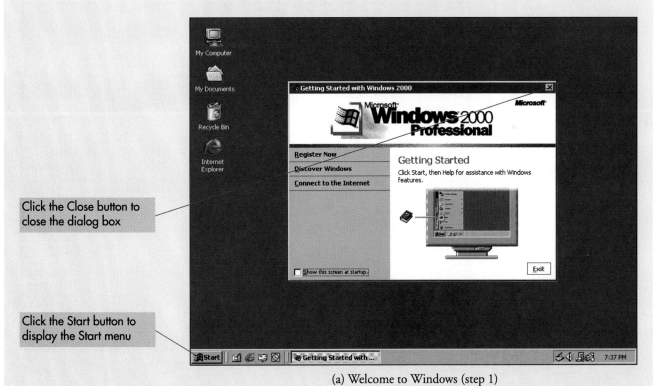

Click the Close button to close the dialog box

Click the Start button to display the Start menu

(a) Welcome to Windows (step 1)

FIGURE 1.7 *Hands-on Exercise 1*

Step 2: **Obtain the Practice Files**

➤ We have created a series of practice files (also called a "data disk") for you to use throughout the text. The files may be on a network drive, in which case you use Windows Explorer to copy the files from the network to a floppy disk.

➤ You can also download the files from our Website provided you have an Internet connection. Start Internet Explorer, then go to the Exploring Windows Series home page at **www.prenhall.com/grauer**.

   • Click the book for **Office XP**, which takes you to the Office XP home page. Click the **Student Resources tab** (at the top of the window) to go to the Student Resources page as shown in Figure 1.7b.

   • Click the link to **Student Data Disk** (in the left frame), then scroll down the page until you can select Excel 2002. Choose **Exploring Excel 2002** if you have the individual Excel text. Choose **Excel 2002 Volume I** if you are using *Exploring Microsoft Office Volume I*. Click the link to download the file.

   • You will see the File Download dialog box asking what you want to do. The option button to save this program to disk is selected. Click **OK**. The Save As dialog box appears.

   • Click the down arrow in the Save In list box to select the drive and folder where you want to save the file. It's best to save the file to the Windows desktop or to a temporary folder on drive C.

   • Double click the file after it has been downloaded to your PC, then follow the onscreen instructions.

➤ Check with your instructor for additional information.

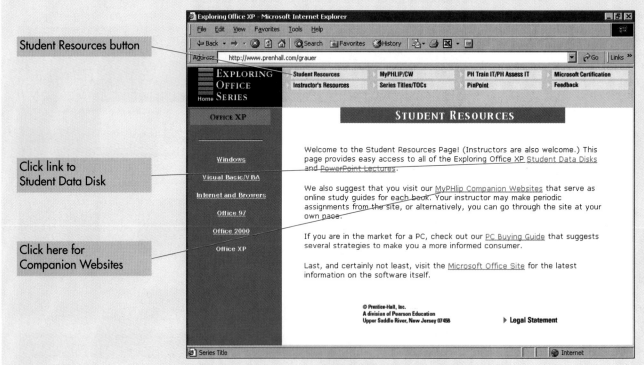

(b) Obtain the Practice Files (step 2)

FIGURE 1.7   *Hands-on Exercise 1 (continued)*

Step 3: **Start Excel**

➤ Click the **Start button** to display the Start menu. Click (or point to) the **Programs menu**, then click **Microsoft Excel** to start the program. Close the task pane if it is open.

➤ Click and drag the Office Assistant out of the way. (The Office Assistant is illustrated in step 8 of this exercise.)

➤ If necessary, click the **Maximize button** in the application window so that Excel takes the entire desktop as shown in Figure 1.7c. Click the **Maximize button** in the document window (if necessary) so that the document window is as large as possible.

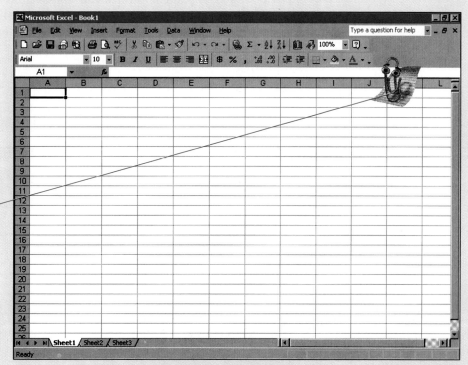

Click and drag Office Assistant out of way

(c) Start Excel (step 3)

FIGURE 1.7   *Hands-on Exercise 1 (continued)*

ABOUT THE ASSISTANT

The Assistant is very powerful and hence you want to experiment with various ways to use it. To ask a question, click the Assistant's icon to toggle its balloon on or off. To change the way in which the Assistant works, click the Options button within the balloon and experiment with the various check boxes to see their effects. If you find the Assistant distracting, click and drag the character out of the way or hide it altogether by pulling down the Help menu and clicking the Hide the Office Assistant command. Pull down the Help menu and click the Show the Office Assistant command to return the Assistant to the desktop.

Step 4: **Open the Workbook**

➤ Pull down the **File menu** and click **Open** (or click the **Open button** on the Standard toolbar). You should see a dialog box similar to the one in Figure 1.7d.

➤ Click the **drop-down arrow** on the Views button, then click **Details** to change to the Details view. Click and drag the vertical border between two columns to increase (or decrease) the size of a column.

➤ Click the **drop-down arrow** on the Look In list box. Click the appropriate drive, drive C or drive A, depending on the location of your data. Double click the **Exploring Excel folder** to make it the active folder (the folder from which you will retrieve and into which you will save the workbook).

➤ Click the **down scroll arrow** if necessary in order to click **Grade Book** to select the professor's grade book. Click the **Open command button** to open the workbook and begin the exercise.

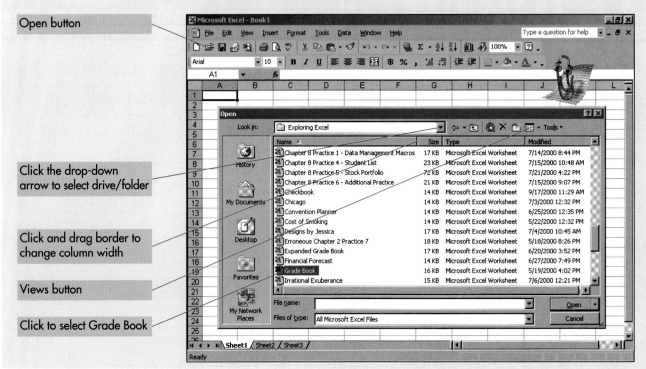

(d) Open the Workbook (step 4)

FIGURE 1.7   *Hands-on Exercise 1 (continued)*

SEPARATE THE TOOLBARS

You may see the Standard and Formatting toolbars displayed on one row to save space within the application window. If so, we suggest that you separate the toolbars, so that you see all of the buttons on each. Click the down arrow at the end of any visible toolbar to display toolbar options, then click the option to show the buttons on two rows. Click the down arrow a second time to show the buttons on one row if you prefer this configuration.

Step 5: **The Save As Command**

> ➤ Pull down the **File menu**. Click **Save As** to display the dialog box shown in Figure 1.7e.
> ➤ Enter **Finished Grade Book** as the name of the new workbook. (A file name may contain up to 255 characters. Spaces and commas are allowed in the file name.)
> ➤ Click the **Save button**. Press the **Esc key** or click the **Close button** if you see a Properties dialog box.
> ➤ There are now two identical copies of the file on disk: "Grade Book" and "Finished Grade Book," which you just created. The title bar shows the latter name, which is the workbook currently in memory.
> ➤ You will work with "Finished Grade Book," but can always return to the original "Grade Book" if necessary.

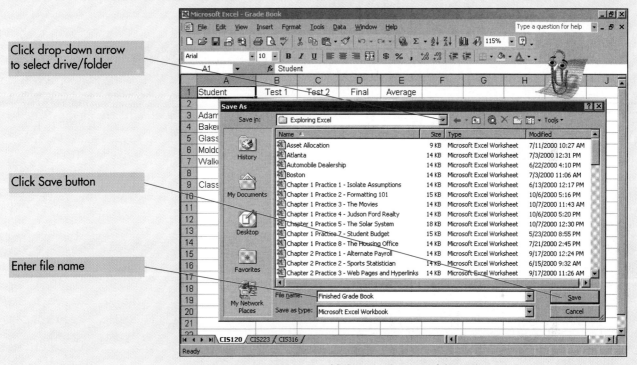

Click drop-down arrow to select drive/folder

Click Save button

Enter file name

(e) Save As Command (step 5)

FIGURE 1.7 *Hands-on Exercise 1 (continued)*

QUIT WITHOUT SAVING

There will be times when you do not want to save the changes to a workbook—for example, when you have edited it beyond recognition and wish you had never started. The Undo command, useful as it is, reverses only the last operation and is of no use if you need to cancel all changes. Pull down the File menu and click the Close command, then click No in response to the message asking whether to save the changes. Pull down the File menu, click the file's name at the bottom of the menu to reopen the file, then begin all over.

Step 6: **The Active Cell, Formula Bar, and Worksheet Tabs**

> ➤ You should see the workbook in Figure 1.7f. Click in **cell B3**, the cell containing Adams's grade on the first test. Cell B3 is now the active cell and is surrounded by a heavy border. The Name box indicates that cell B3 is the active cell, and its contents are displayed in the formula bar.
>
> ➤ Click in **cell B4** (or press the **down arrow key**) to make it the active cell. The Name box indicates cell B4 while the formula bar indicates a grade of 90.
>
> ➤ Click in **cell E3**, the cell containing the formula to compute Adams's semester average; the worksheet displays the computed average of 88.0, but the formula bar displays the formula, =(B3+C3+2*D3)/4, to compute that average based on the test grades.
>
> ➤ Click the **CIS223 tab** to view a different worksheet within the same workbook. This worksheet contains the grades for a different class.
>
> ➤ Click the **CIS316 tab** to view this worksheet. Click the **CIS120 tab** to return to this worksheet and continue with the exercise.

Name box indicates address of active cell

Formula bar displays cell contents (a formula)

Active cell displays result of a formula

Click tab to view CIS223 worksheet

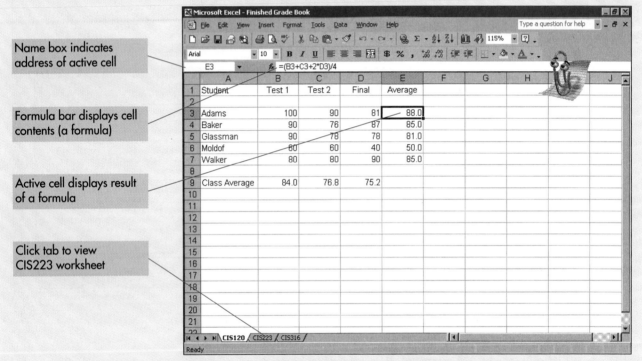

(f) The Active Cell, Formula Bar, and Worksheet Tabs (step 6)

FIGURE 1.7 *Hands-on Exercise 1 (continued)*

THE MENUS MAY CHANGE

Office XP gives you the option of displaying short menus (ending in a double arrow to show additional commands) as opposed to complete menus with all commands. We prefer the complete menus because that is the way you learn an application, but the settings may be different on your system. Pull down the Tools menu, click the Customize command to display the Customize dialog box, click the Options tab, and clear the box that menus show recently used commands first.

Step 7: **Experiment (What If?)**

➤ Click in **cell C4**, the cell containing Baker's grade on the second test. Enter a corrected value of **86** (instead of the previous entry of 76). Press **enter** (or click in another cell).

➤ The effects of this change ripple through the worksheet, automatically changing the computed value for Baker's average in cell E4 to 87.5. The class average on the second test in cell C9 changes to 78.8.

➤ Change Walker's grade on the final from 90 to **100**. Press **enter** (or click in another cell). Walker's average in cell E7 changes to 90.0, while the class average in cell D9 changes to 77.2.

➤ Your worksheet should match Figure 1.7g. Save the workbook.

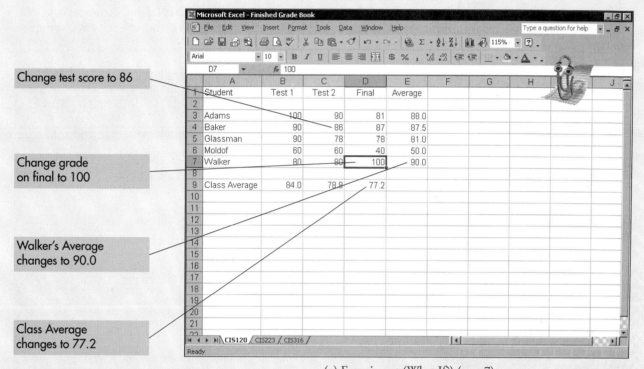

Change test score to 86

Change grade on final to 100

Walker's Average changes to 90.0

Class Average changes to 77.2

(g) Experiment (What If?) (step 7)

FIGURE 1.7 *Hands-on Exercise 1 (continued)*

THE UNDO AND REDO COMMANDS

The Undo Command lets you undo the last several changes to a workbook. Click the down arrow next to the Undo button on the Standard toolbar to display a reverse-order list of your previous commands, then click the command you want to undo, which also cancels all of the preceding commands. Undoing the fifth command in the list, for example, will also undo the preceding four commands. The Redo command redoes (reverses) the last command that was undone. It, too, displays a reverse-order list of commands, so that redoing the fifth command in the list will also redo the preceding four commands.

Step 8: **The Office Assistant**

➤ If necessary, pull down the **Help menu** and click the command to **Show the Office Assistant**. You may see a different character than the one we have selected. Click the Assistant, then enter the question, **How do I use the Office Assistant?** as shown in Figure 1.7h.

➤ Click the **Search button** in the Assistant's balloon to look for the answer. The size of the Assistant's balloon expands as the Assistant suggests several topics that may be appropriate.

➤ Select (click) any topic, which in turn displays a Help window with multiple links associated with the topic you selected.

➤ Read the displayed information and explore Help, then close the Help window when you are finished.

➤ Pull down the **File menu** and click **Exit** to close Excel if you do not wish to continue with the next exercise at this time. Save the workbook if you are prompted.

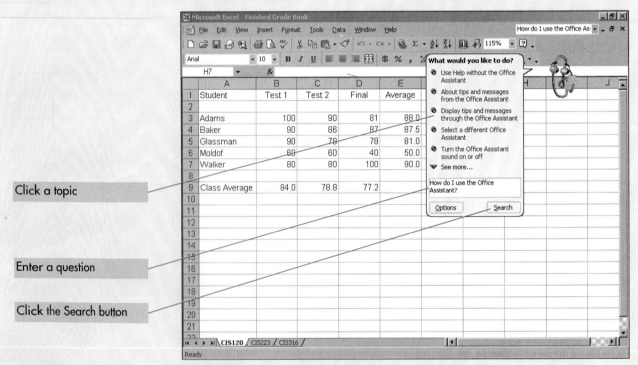

(h) The Office Assistant (step 8)

FIGURE 1.7 *Hands-on Exercise 1 (continued)*

ABOUT MICROSOFT EXCEL

Pull down the Help menu and click About Microsoft Excel to display the specific release number as well as other licensing information, including the Product ID. This Help screen also contains two very useful command buttons, System Info and Technical Support. The first button displays information about the hardware installed on your system, including the amount of memory and available space on the hard drive. The Technical Support button provides information on obtaining technical assistance.

We trust that you completed the hands-on exercise without difficulty and that you are more confident in your ability than when you first began. The exercise was not complicated, but it did accomplish several objectives and set the stage for a second exercise, which follows shortly.

Consider now Figure 1.8, which contains a modified version of the professor's grade book. Figure 1.8a shows the grade book at the end of the first hands-on exercise and reflects the changes made to the grades for Baker and Walker. Figure 1.8b shows the worksheet as it will appear at the end of the second exercise. Several changes bear mention:

1. One student has dropped the class and two other students have been added. Moldof appeared in the original worksheet in Figure 1.8a, but has somehow managed to withdraw; Coulter and Courier did not appear in the original grade book but have been added to the worksheet in Figure 1.8b.
2. A new column containing the students' majors has been added.

The implementation of these changes is accomplished through a combination of the *Insert command* (to add individual cells, rows, or columns) and/or the *Delete command* (to remove individual cells, rows, or columns). Execution of either command automatically adjusts the cell references in existing formulas to reflect the insertion or deletion of the various cells. The Insert and Delete commands can also be used to insert or delete a worksheet. The professor could, for example, add a new sheet to a workbook to include grades for another class and/or delete a worksheet for a class that was no longer taught. We focus initially, however, on the insertion and deletion of rows and columns within a worksheet.

	A	B	C	D	E
1	Student	Test 1	Test 2	Final	Average
2					
3	Adams	100	90	81	88.0
4	Baker	90	86	87	87.5
5	Glassman	90	78	78	81.0
6	Moldof	60	60	40	50.0
7	Walker	80	80	100	90.0
8					
9	Class Average	84.0	78.8	77.2	

Moldof will be dropped from class

(a) After Hands-on Exercise 1

	A	B	C	D	E	F
1	Student	Major	Test 1	Test 2	Final	Average
2						
3	Adams	CIS	100	90	81	88.0
4	Baker	MKT	90	86	87	87.5
5	Coulter	ACC	85	95	100	95.0
6	Courier	FIN	75	75	85	80.0
7	Glassman	CIS	90	78	78	81.0
8	Walker	CIS	80	80	100	90.0
9						
10	Class Average		86.7	84.0	88.5	

A new column has been added (Major)

Two new students have been added

Moldof has been deleted

(b) After Hands-on Exercise 2

FIGURE 1.8   *The Modified Grade Book*

Figure 1.9 displays the cell formulas in the professor's grade book and corresponds to the worksheets in Figure 1.8. The "before" and "after" worksheets reflect the insertion of a new column containing the students' majors, the addition of two new students, Coulter and Courier, and the deletion of an existing student, Moldof.

Let us consider the formula to compute Adams's semester average, which is contained in cell E3 of the original grade book, but in cell F3 in the modified grade book. The formula in Figure 1.9a referenced cells B3, C3, and D3 (the grades on test 1, test 2, and the final). The corresponding formula in Figure 1.9b reflects the fact that a new column has been inserted, and references cells C3, D3, and E3. The change in the formula is made automatically by Excel, without any action on the part of the user other than to insert the new column. The formulas for all other students have been adjusted in similar fashion.

Some students (all students below Baker) have had a further adjustment to reflect the addition of the new students through insertion of new rows in the worksheet. Glassman, for example, appeared in row 5 of the original worksheet, but appears in row 7 of the revised worksheet. Hence the formula to compute Glassman's semester average now references the grades in row 7, rather than in row 5 as in the original worksheet.

Finally, the formulas to compute the class averages have also been adjusted. These formulas appeared in row 9 of Figure 1.9a and averaged the grades in rows 3 through 7. The revised worksheet has a net increase of one student, which automatically moves these formulas to row 10, where the formulas are adjusted to average the grades in rows 3 through 8.

Formula references grades in B3, C3, and D3

Function references grades in rows 3–7

	A	B	C	D	E
1	Student	Test1	Test2	Final	Average
2					
3	Adams	100	90	81	=(B3+C3+2*D3)/4
4	Baker	90	86	87	=(B4+C4+2*D4)/4
5	Glassman	90	78	78	=(B5+C5+2*D5)/4
6	Moldof	60	60	40	=(B6+C6+2*D6)/4
7	Walker	80	80	100	=(B7+C7+2*D7)/4
8					
9	Class Average	=AVERAGE(B3:B7)	=AVERAGE(C3:C7)	=AVERAGE(D3:D7)	

(a) Before

	A	B	C	D	E	F
1	Student	Major	Test1	Test2	Final	Average
2						
3	Adams	CIS	100	90	81	=(C3+D3+2*E3)/4
4	Baker	MKT	90	86	87	=(C4+D4+2*E4)/4
5	Coulter	ACC	85	95	100	=(C5+D5+2*E5)/4
6	Courier	FIN	75	75	85	=(C6+D6+2*E6)/4
7	Glassman	CIS	90	78	78	=(C7+D7+2*E7)/4
8	Walker	CIS	80	80	100	=(C8+D8+2*E8)/4
9						
10	Class Average		=AVERAGE(C3:C8)	=AVERAGE(D3:D8)	=AVERAGE(E3:E8)	

Function changes to reference grades in rows 3–8 (due to addition of 2 new students and deletion of 1)

Formula changes to reference grades in C3, D3, and E3 due to addition of new column

(b) After

FIGURE 1.9 *The Insert and Delete Commands*

The **Page Setup command** gives you complete control of the printed worksheet as illustrated in Figure 1.10. Many of the options may not appear important now, but you will appreciate them as you develop larger and more complicated worksheets later in the text.

The Page tab in Figure 1.10 determines the orientation and scaling of the printed page. **Portrait orientation** ($8\frac{1}{2} \times 11$) prints vertically down the page. **Landscape orientation** ($11 \times 8\frac{1}{2}$) prints horizontally across the page and is used when the worksheet is too wide to fit on a portrait page. The option buttons indicate mutually exclusive items, one of which *must* be selected; that is, a worksheet must be printed in either portrait or landscape orientation. Option buttons are also used to choose the scaling factor. You can reduce (enlarge) the output by a designated scaling factor, or you can force the output to fit on a specified number of pages. The latter option is typically used to force a worksheet to fit on a single page.

The Margins tab not only controls the margins, but will also center the worksheet horizontally and/or vertically. The Margins tab also determines the distance of the header and footer from the edge of the page.

The Header/Footer tab lets you create a header (and/or footer) that appears at the top (and/or bottom) of every page. The pull-down list boxes let you choose from several preformatted entries, or alternatively, you can click the appropriate command button to customize either entry.

The Sheet tab offers several additional options. The Gridlines option prints lines to separate the cells within the worksheet. The Row and Column Headings option displays the column letters and row numbers. Both options should be selected for most worksheets. Information about the additional entries can be obtained by clicking the Help button.

The Print Preview command button is available from all four tabs within the Page Setup dialog box. The command shows you how the worksheet will appear when printed and saves you from having to rely on trial and error.

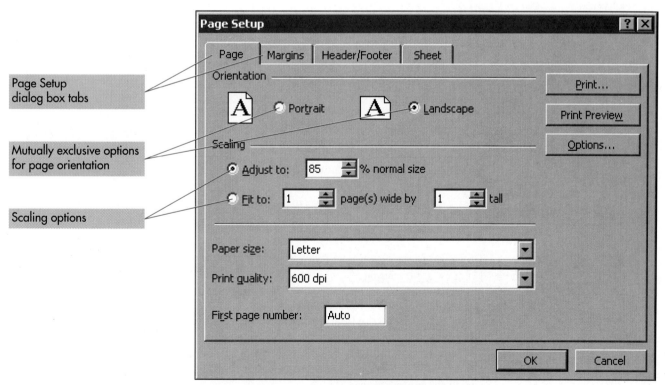

FIGURE 1.10   *The Page Setup Command*

MODIFYING A WORKSHEET

Objective To open an existing workbook; to insert and delete rows and columns in a worksheet; to print cell formulas and displayed values; to use the Page Setup command. Use Figure 1.11 as a guide.

Step 1: **Open an Existing Workbook**

➤ Start Excel. If necessary, pull down the **View menu** and click the **Task Pane command** to display the task pane as shown in Figure 1.11a. You should see the Finished Grade Book from the previous exercise since the most recently used workbooks are listed automatically.

➤ Click the link to the **Finished Grade Book workbook**. (Click the link to **More Workbooks** if the workbook is not listed to display the Open dialog box where you can select the drive and folder to locate your workbook.)

➤ The task pane closes automatically after the workbook has been opened.

Ask a Question list box

Task pane

Click link to Finished Grade Book

Click to display the open dialog box

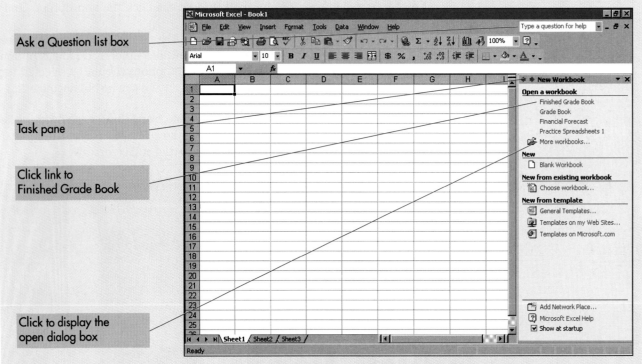

(a) Open an Existing Workbook (step 1)

FIGURE 1.11 *Hands-on Exercise 2*

ASK A QUESTION

Click in the "Ask a Question" list box to the right of the menu bar, type a question, press enter, and Excel returns a list of Help topics. Click any topic that appears promising to open the Help window with detailed information. You can ask multiple questions during an Excel session, then click the down arrow in the list box to return to an earlier question, which will return you to the Help topics.

Step 2: **Delete a Row**

➤ Click any cell in **row 6** (the row you will delete). Pull down the **Edit menu**. Click **Delete** to display the dialog box in Figure 1.11b. Click **Entire row**. Click **OK** to delete row 6.

➤ Moldof has disappeared from the grade book, and the class averages (now in row 8) have been updated automatically.

➤ Pull down the **Edit menu** and click **Undo Delete** (or click the **Undo button** on the Standard toolbar) to reverse the last command.

➤ The row for Moldof has been put back into the worksheet.

➤ Click any cell in **row 6**, and this time delete the entire row for good.

➤ Save the workbook.

Undo button

Click a cell in row 6

Click Entire row

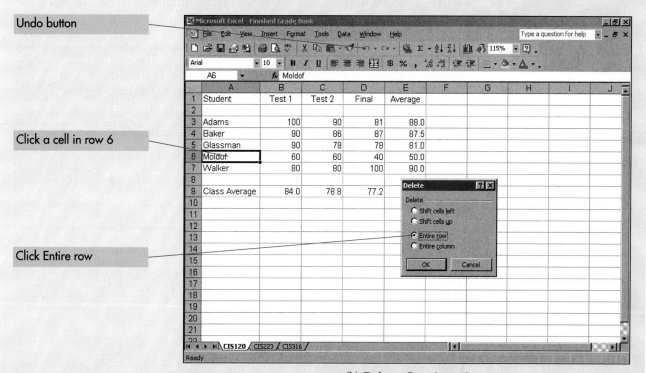

(b) Delete a Row (step 2)

FIGURE 1.11   *Hands-on Exercise 2 (continued)*

INSERT COMMENT COMMAND

You can add a comment, which displays a ScreenTip when you point to the cell, to any cell in a worksheet to explain a formula or other piece of information associated with that cell. Click in the cell that is to hold the comment, pull down the Insert menu, and click Comment to display a box in which you enter the comment. Click outside the box when you have completed the entry. Point to the cell (which should have a tiny red triangle) and you will see the comment you just created.

Step 3: **Insert a Row**

➤ Click any cell in **row 5** (the row containing Glassman's grades). Pull down the **Insert menu**. Click **Rows** to add a new row above the current row.
➤ A new row is inserted into the worksheet with the same formatting as in the row above. (Thus, you can ignore the Format Painter button, which allows you to change the formatting.) Row 5 is now blank, and Glassman is now in row 6.
➤ Enter the data for the new student in row 5 as shown in Figure 1.11c. Click in **cell A5**. Type **Coulter**. Press the **right arrow key** or click in **cell B5**. Enter the test grades of 85, 95, 100 in cells B5, C5, and D5, respectively.
➤ Enter the formula to compute the semester average, **=(B5+C5+2*D5)/4**. Be sure to begin the formula with an equal sign. Press **enter**.
➤ Click the **Save button** on the Standard toolbar, or pull down the **File menu** and click **Save** to save the changes made to this point.

Save button

Enter data for new student (Coulter)

Glassman is now in row 6

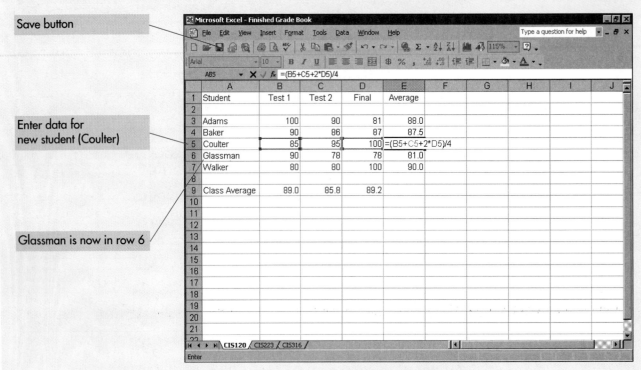

(c) Insert a Row (step 3)

FIGURE 1.11 *Hands-on Exercise 2 (continued)*

CORRECTING MISTAKES

The fastest way to change the contents of an existing cell is to double click in the cell in order to make the changes directly in the cell rather than on the formula bar. Use the mouse or arrow keys to position the insertion point at the point of correction. Press the Ins key to toggle between insert and overtype and/or use the Backspace or Del key to erase a character. Press the Home and End keys to move to the first and last characters in the cell, respectively.

Step 4:   **The AutoComplete Feature**

➤ Point to the row heading for **row 6** (which now contains Glassman's grades), then click the **right mouse button** to select the row and display a shortcut menu. Click **Insert** to insert a new row 6, which moves Glassman to row 7 as shown in Figure 1.11d.

➤ Click in **cell A6**. Type **C**, the first letter in "Courier," which also happens to be the first letter in "Coulter," a previous entry in column A. If the AutoComplete feature is on (see boxed tip), Coulter's name will be automatically inserted in cell A6 with "oulter" selected.

➤ Type **ourier** (the remaining letters in "Courier," which replace "oulter."

➤ Enter Courier's grades in the appropriate cells (75, 75, and 85 in cells B6, C6, and D6, respectively). Click in **cell E6**. Enter the formula to compute the semester average, **=(B6+C6+2*D6)/4**. Press **enter**.

Click in A6 and type C

oulter is selected and will be replaced if you continue to type

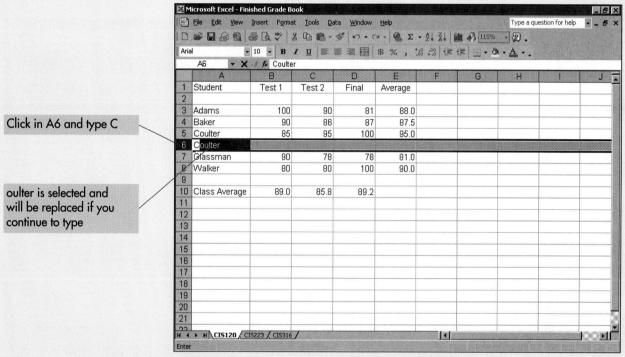

(d) The AutoComplete Feature (step 4)

FIGURE 1.11   *Hands-on Exercise 2 (continued)*

AUTOCOMPLETE

As soon as you begin typing a label into a cell, Excel searches for and (automatically) displays any other label in that column that matches the letters you typed. It's handy if you want to repeat a label, but it can be distracting if you want to enter a different label that just happens to begin with the same letter. To turn the feature on (off), pull down the Tools menu, click Options, then click the Edit tab. Check (clear) the box to enable the AutoComplete feature.

Step 5: **Insert a Column**

➤ Point to the column heading for column B, then click the **right mouse button** to display a shortcut menu as shown in Figure 1.11e.

➤ Click **Insert** to insert a new column, which becomes the new column B. All existing columns have been moved to the right.

➤ Click in **cell B1**. Type **Major**.

➤ Click in **cell B3**. Enter **CIS** as Adams's major. Press the **down arrow** to move automatically to the major for the next student.

➤ Type **MKT** in cell B4. Press the **down arrow**. Type **ACC** in cell B5. Press the **down arrow**. Type **FIN** in cell B6.

➤ Press the **down arrow** to move to cell B7. Type **C** (AutoComplete will automatically enter "IS" to complete the entry). Press the **down arrow** to move to cell B8. Type **C** (the AutoComplete feature again enters "IS"), then press **enter** to complete the entry.

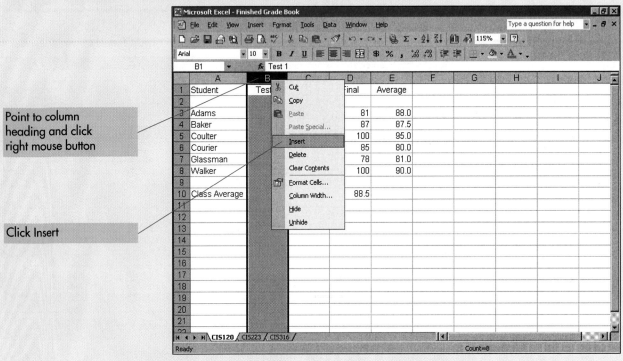

Point to column heading and click right mouse button

Click Insert

(e) Insert a Column (step 5)

FIGURE 1.11 *Hands-on Exercise 2 (continued)*

INSERTING AND DELETING INDIVIDUAL CELLS

You can insert and/or delete individual cells as opposed to an entire row or column. To insert a cell, click in the cell to the left or above where you want the new cell to go, pull down the Insert menu, then click Cells to display the Insert dialog box. Click the appropriate option button to shift cells right or down and click OK. To delete a cell or cells, select the cell(s), pull down the Edit menu, click the Delete command, then click the option button to shift cells left or up. See practice exercise 2 at the end of the chapter.

Step 6:   **Display the Cell Formulas**

➤ Pull down the **Tools menu**. Click **Options** to display the Options dialog box. Click the **View tab**. Check the box for **Formulas**. Click **OK**. (You can also press Ctrl+~ to toggle between cell formulas and displayed values.)

➤ The worksheet should display the cell formulas as shown in Figure 1.11f. If necessary, click the **right scroll arrow** on the horizontal scroll bar until column F, the column containing the formulas to compute the semester averages, comes into view.

➤ If necessary (i.e., if the formulas are not completely visible), double click the border between the column headings for columns F and G. This increases the width of column F to accommodate the widest entry in that column.

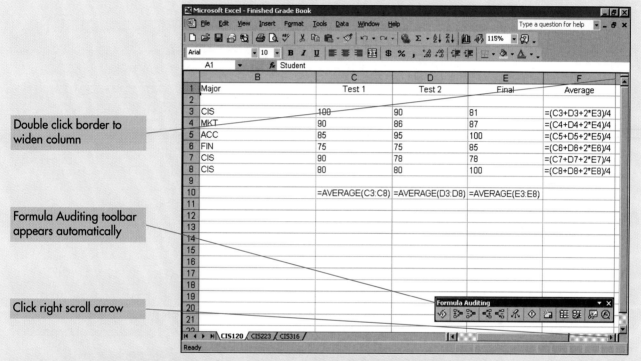

Double click border to widen column

Formula Auditing toolbar appears automatically

Click right scroll arrow

(f) Display the Cell Formulas (step 6)

FIGURE **1.11**   *Hands-on Exercise 2 (continued)*

THE FORMULA AUDITING TOOLBAR

The Formula Auditing Toolbar appears automatically any time the display is changed to show cell formulas rather than displayed values. The toolbar is designed to help you detect and correct errors in cell formulas. Click in any cell, then click the Trace Precedents button to show the cells that are used to evaluate the formula in the selected cell. You can also click in any cell and use the Trace Dependents button to show those cells whose formula references the selected cell. Click the Remove All Arrows button to erase the arrows from the display.

Step 7: **The Page Setup Command**

➤ Pull down the **File menu**. Click the **Page Setup command** to display the Page Setup dialog box as shown in Figure 1.11g.
  • Click the **Page tab**. Click the **Landscape option button**. Click the option button to **Fit to 1 page**.
  • Click the **Margins tab**. Check the box to center the worksheet horizontally.
  • Click the **Header/Footer tab**. Click the **drop-down arrow** on the Footer list box. Scroll to the top of the list and click **(none)** to remove the footer.
  • Click the **Sheet tab**. Check the boxes to print Row and Column Headings and Gridlines.
➤ Click **OK** to exit the Page Setup dialog box.
➤ Save the workbook.

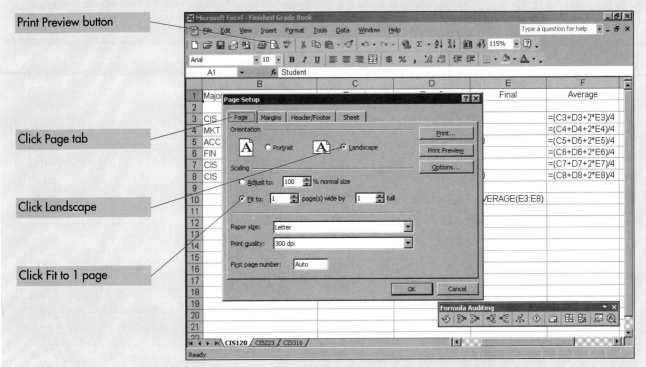

(g) The Page Setup Command (step 7)

FIGURE 1.11   *Hands-on Exercise 2 (continued)*

KEYBOARD SHORTCUTS—THE DIALOG BOX

Press Tab or Shift+Tab to move forward (backward) between fields in a dialog box, or press the Alt key plus the underlined letter to move directly to an option. Use the space bar to toggle check boxes on or off and the up (down) arrow keys to move between options in a list box. Press enter to activate the highlighted command button and Esc to exit the dialog box without accepting the changes. These are universal shortcuts and apply to any Windows application.

Step 8: **The Print Preview Command**

➤ Pull down the **File menu** and click **Print Preview** (or click the **Print Preview button** on the Standard toolbar).

➤ Your monitor should match the display in Figure 1.11h. (The Page Setup dialog box is also accessible from this screen.)

➤ Click the **Print command button** to display the Print dialog box, then click **OK** to print the worksheet.

➤ Press **Ctrl+~** to switch to displayed values rather than cell formulas. Click the **Print button** on the Standard toolbar to print the worksheet without displaying the Print dialog box.

Click Print command button

Click Setup to display the Page Setup dialog box.

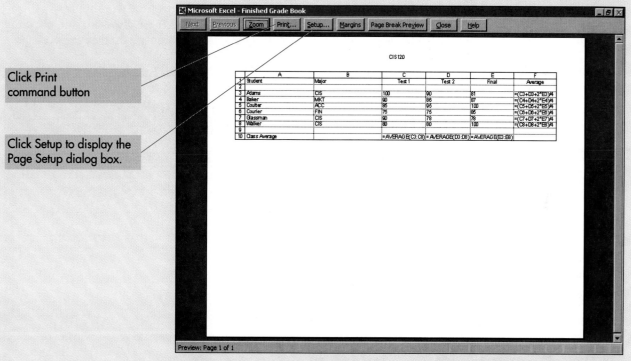

(h) The Print Preview Command (step 8)

FIGURE 1.11   *Hands-on Exercise 2 (continued)*

FIND AND REPLACE

Anyone familiar with a word processor takes the Find and Replace command for granted, but many people are surprised to learn that the same commands are also found in Excel. The commands are found in the Edit menu and provide the same options as in Microsoft Word. You can replace text and/or formatting throughout a worksheet. See practice exercise 4 at the end of the chapter.

Step 9: **Insert and Delete a Worksheet**

➤ Pull down the **Insert menu** and click the **Worksheet command** to insert a new worksheet. The worksheet is inserted as Sheet1.

➤ Click in cell **A1**, type **Student**, and press **enter**. Enter the labels and student data as shown in Figure 1.11i. Enter the formulas to calculate the students' semester averages in column D. (The midterm and final count equally.)

➤ Enter the formulas in row 7 to compute the class averages on each exam. If necessary, click and drag the column border between columns A and B to widen column A.

➤ Double click the name of the worksheet (Sheet1) to select the name. Type a new name, **CIS101**, to replace the selected text and press **enter**. If necessary, click and drag the worksheet tab to the beginning of the workbook.

➤ Click the worksheet tab for **CIS223**. Pull down the **Edit menu** and click the **Delete Sheet command**. Click **Delete** when you are warned that the worksheet will be permanently deleted.

➤ Save the workbook. Print the new worksheet. Exit Excel.

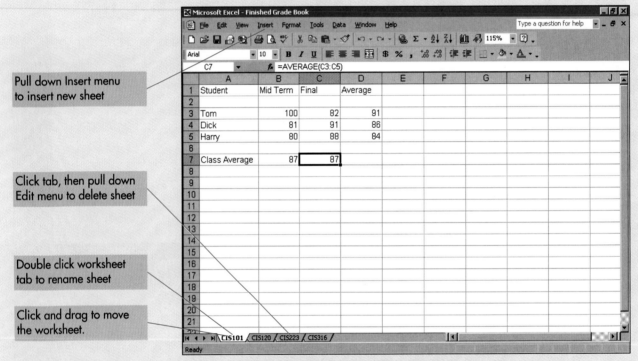

Pull down Insert menu to insert new sheet

Click tab, then pull down Edit menu to delete sheet

Double click worksheet tab to rename sheet

Click and drag to move the worksheet.

(i) Insert and Delete a Worksheet (step 9)

FIGURE 1.11 *Hands-on Exercise 2 (continued)*

MOVING, COPYING, AND RENAMING WORKSHEETS

The fastest way to move a worksheet is to click and drag the worksheet tab. You can copy a worksheet in similar fashion by pressing and holding the Ctrl key as you drag the worksheet tab. To rename a worksheet, double click its tab to select the current name, type the new name, and press the enter key.

Figure 1.12 contains a much improved version of the professor's grade book. The most *obvious* difference is in the appearance of the worksheet, as a variety of formatting commands have been used to make it more attractive. The exam scores and semester averages are centered under the appropriate headings. The exam weights are formatted with percentages, and all averages are displayed with exactly one decimal point. Boldface and italics are used for emphasis. Shading and borders are used to highlight various areas of the worksheet. The title has been centered over the worksheet and is set in a larger typeface.

The most *significant* differences, however, are that the weight of each exam is indicated within the worksheet, and that the formulas to compute the students' semester averages reference these cells in their calculations. The professor can change the contents of the cells containing the exam weights and see immediately the effect on the student averages.

The isolation of cells whose values are subject to change is one of the most important concepts in the development of a spreadsheet. This technique lets the professor explore alternative grading strategies. He or she may notice, for example, that the class did significantly better on the final than on either of the first two exams. The professor may then decide to give the class a break and increase the weight of the final relative to the other tests. But before the professor says anything to the class, he or she wants to know the effect of increasing the weight of the final to 60%. What if the final should count 70%? The effect of these and other changes can be seen immediately by entering the new exam weights in the appropriate cells at the bottom of the worksheet.

Title is centered in larger font size; it is also in boldface and italics

Formatting includes boldface, shading, and borders

Exam weights are used to calculate the semester average

	A	B	C	D	E
1	*CIS120 - Spring Semester*				
2					
3	**Student**	**Test 1**	**Test 2**	**Final**	**Average**
4	Costa, Frank	70	80	90	82.5
5	Ford, Judd	70	85	80	78.8
6	Grauer, Jessica	90	80	98	91.5
7	Howard, Lauren	80	78	98	88.5
8	Krein, Darren	85	70	95	86.3
9	Moldof, Adam	75	75	80	77.5
10					
11	**Class Averages**	**78.3**	**78.0**	**90.2**	
12					
13	**Exam Weights**	25%	25%	50%	

FIGURE 1.12 *A Better Grade Book*

ISOLATE ASSUMPTIONS

The formulas in a worksheet should always be based on cell references rather than on specific values—for example, B13 or $B$13 rather than .25. The cells containing these values should be clearly labeled and set apart from the rest of the worksheet. You can then vary the inputs (or *assumptions* on which the worksheet is based) to see the effect within the worksheet. The chance for error is also minimized because you are changing the contents of a single cell rather than changing the multiple formulas that reference those values.

Every command in Excel operates on a rectangular group of cells known as a *range*. A range may be as small as a single cell or as large as the entire worksheet. It may consist of a row or part of a row, a column or part of a column, or multiple rows and/or columns. The cells within a range are specified by indicating the diagonally opposite corners, typically the upper-left and lower right corners of the rectangle. Many different ranges could be selected in conjunction with the worksheet of Figure 1.12. The exam weights, for example, are found in the range B13:D13. The students' semester averages are found in the range E4:E9. The student data is contained in the range A4:E9.

The easiest way to select a range is to click and drag—click at the beginning of the range, then press and hold the left mouse button as you drag the mouse to the end of the range where you release the mouse. Once selected, the range is highlighted and its cells will be affected by any subsequent command. The range remains selected until another range is defined or until you click another cell anywhere on the worksheet.

COPY COMMAND

The *Copy command* duplicates the contents of a cell, or range of cells, and saves you from having to enter the contents of every cell individually. Figure 1.13 illustrates how the command can be used to duplicate the formula to compute the class average on the different tests. The cell that you are copying from, cell B11, is called the *source range*. The cells that you are copying to, cells C11 and D11, are the *destination range*. The formula is not copied exactly, but is adjusted as it is copied, to compute the average for the pertinent test.

The formula to compute the average on the first test was entered in cell B11 as =AVERAGE(B4:B9). The range in the formula references the cell seven rows above the cell containing the formula (i.e., cell B4 is seven rows above cell B11) as well as the cell two rows above the formula (i.e., cell B9). When the formula in cell B11 is copied to C11, it is adjusted so that the cells referenced in the new formula are in the same relative position as those in the original formula; that is, seven and two rows above the formula. The formula in cell C11 becomes =AVERAGE(C4:C9). The formula in cell D11 becomes =AVERAGE(D4:D9).

	A	B	C	D	E
1			*CIS120 - Spring Semester*		
2					
3	**Student**	**Test 1**	**Test 2**	**Final**	**Average**
4	Costa, Frank	70	80	90	=$B$13*B4+$C$13*C4+$D$13*D4
5	Ford, Judd	70	85	80	=$B$13*B5+$C$13*C5+$D$13*D5
6	Grauer, Jessica	90	80	98	=$B$13*B6+$C$13*C6+$D$13*D6
7	Howard, Lauren	80	78	98	=$B$13*B7+$C$13*C7+$D$13*D7
8	Krein, Darren	85	70	95	=$B$13*B8+$C$13*C8+$D$13*D8
9	Moldof, Adam	75	75	80	=$B$13*B9+$C$13*C9+$D$13*D9
10					
11	**Class Averages**	=AVERAGE(B4:B9)	=AVERAGE(C4:C9)	=AVERAGE(D4:D9)	
12					
13	**Exam Weights**	25%	25%	50%	

Formula was entered in B11

Relative addresses adjust when formula is copied

Absolute addresses stay the same when formula is copied

Relative addresses adjust when formula is copied

FIGURE 1.13 *The Copy Command*

Figure 1.13 also illustrates how the Copy command is used to copy the formula for a student's semester average, from cell E4 (the source range) to cells E5 through E9 (the destination range). This is slightly more complicated than the previous example because the formula is based on a student's grades, which vary from one student to the next, and on the exam weights, which do not. The cells referring to the student's grades should adjust as the formula is copied, but the addresses referencing the exam weights should not.

The distinction between cell references that remain constant versus cell references that change is made by means of a dollar sign. An ***absolute reference*** remains constant throughout the copy operation and is specified with a dollar sign in front of the column and row designation, for example, $B$13. A ***relative reference***, on the other hand, adjusts during a copy operation and is specified without dollar signs; for example, B4. (A ***mixed reference*** uses a single dollar sign to make the column absolute and the row relative; for example, $A5. Alternatively, you can make the column relative and the row absolute as in A$5.)

Consider, for example, the formula to compute a student's semester average as it appears in cell E4 of Figure 1.13:

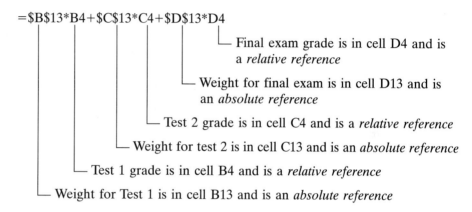

=$B$13*B4+$C$13*C4+$D$13*D4

    Final exam grade is in cell D4 and is a *relative reference*

    Weight for final exam is in cell D13 and is an *absolute reference*

    Test 2 grade is in cell C4 and is a *relative reference*

    Weight for test 2 is in cell C13 and is an *absolute reference*

    Test 1 grade is in cell B4 and is a *relative reference*

    Weight for Test 1 is in cell B13 and is an *absolute reference*

The formula in cell E4 uses a combination of relative and absolute addresses to compute the student's semester average. Relative addresses are used for the exam grades (found in cells B4, C4, and D4) and change automatically when the formula is copied to the other rows. Absolute addresses are used for the exam weights (found in cells B13, C13, and D13) and remain constant.

The copy operation is implemented by using the ***clipboard*** common to all Windows applications and a combination of the Copy and Paste commands from the Edit menu. (Office 2002 also supports the Office Clipboard that can hold 24 separate items. All references to the "clipboard" in this chapter, however, are to the Windows clipboard.) The contents of the source range are copied to the clipboard, from where they are pasted to the destination range. The contents of the clipboard are replaced with each subsequent Copy command but are unaffected by the Paste command. Thus, you can execute the Paste command several times in succession to paste the contents of the clipboard to multiple locations.

MIXED REFERENCES

Most spreadsheets can be developed using only absolute or relative references such as $A$1 or A1, respectively. Mixed references, where only the row ($A1) or column (A$1) changes, are more subtle, and thus are typically not used by beginners. Mixed references are necessary in more sophisticated worksheets and add significantly to the power of Excel.

The ***move operation*** is not used in the grade book, but its presentation is essential for the sake of completeness. The move operation transfers the contents of a cell (or range of cells) from one location to another. After the move is completed, the cells where the move originated (that is, the source range) are empty. This is in contrast to the Copy command, where the entries remain in the source range and are duplicated in the destination range.

A simple move operation is depicted in Figure 1.14a, in which the contents of cell A3 are moved to cell C3, with the formula in cell C3 unchanged after the move. In other words, the move operation simply picks up the contents of cell A3 (a formula that adds the values in cells A1 and A2) and puts it down in cell C3. The source range, cell A3, is empty after the move operation has been executed.

Figure 1.14b depicts a situation where the formula itself remains in the same cell, but one of the values it references is moved to a new location; that is, the entry

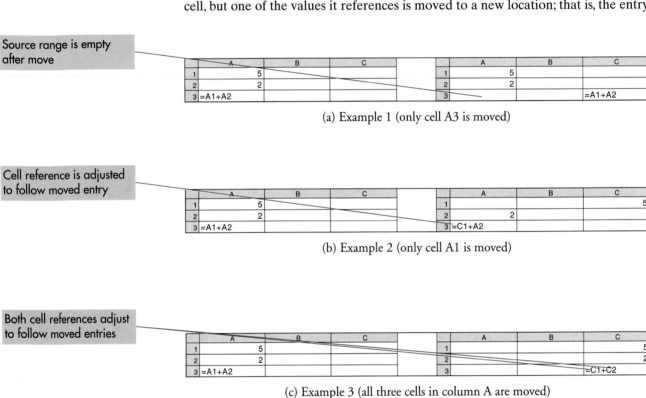

(a) Example 1 (only cell A3 is moved)

(b) Example 2 (only cell A1 is moved)

(c) Example 3 (all three cells in column A are moved)

(d) Example 4 (dependent cells)

FIGURE 1.14 *The Move Command*

	A	B	C			A	B	C
1	5	=$A$3*4			1		=$C$3*4	5
2		2			2			2
3	=$A$1+$A$2				3			=$C$1+$C$2

(e) Example 5 (absolute cell addresses)

FIGURE 1.14   *The Move Command (continued)*

in A1 is moved to C1. The formula in cell A3 is adjusted to follow the moved entry to its new location; that is, the formula is now =C1+A2.

The situation is different in Figure 1.14c as the contents of all three cells—A1, A2, and A3—are moved. After the move has taken place, cells C1 and C2 contain the 5 and the 2, respectively, with the formula in cell C3 adjusted to reflect the movement of the contents of cells A1 and A2. Once again the source range (A1:A3) is empty after the move is completed.

Figure 1.14d contains an additional formula in cell B1, which is *dependent* on cell A3, which in turn is moved to cell C3. The formula in cell C3 is unchanged after the move because *only* the formula was moved, *not* the values it referenced. The formula in cell B1 changes because cell B1 refers to an entry (cell A3) that was moved to a new location (cell C3).

Figure 1.14e shows that the specification of an absolute reference has no meaning in a move operation, because the cell addresses are adjusted as necessary to reflect the cells that have been moved. Moving a formula that contains an absolute reference does not adjust the formula. Moving a value that is specified as an absolute reference, however, adjusts the formula to follow the cell to its new location. Thus all of the absolute references in Figure 1.14e are changed to reflect the entries that were moved.

The move operation is a convenient way to improve the appearance of a worksheet after it has been developed. It is subtle in its operation, and we suggest you think twice before moving cell entries because of the complexities involved.

The move operation is implemented by using the Windows clipboard and a combination of the Cut and Paste commands from the Edit menu. The contents of the source range are transferred to the clipboard, from which they are pasted to the destination range. (Executing a Paste command after a Cut command empties the clipboard. This is different from pasting after a Copy command, which does not affect the contents of the clipboard.)

LEARNING BY DOING

As we have already indicated, there are many different ways to accomplish the same task. You can execute commands using a pull-down menu, a shortcut menu, a toolbar, or the keyboard. In the exercise that follows we emphasize pull-down menus (the most basic technique) but suggest various shortcuts as appropriate.

Realize, however, that while the shortcuts are interesting, it is far more important to focus on the underlying concepts in the exercise, rather than specific key strokes or mouse clicks. The professor's grade book was developed to emphasize the difference between relative and absolute cell references. The grade book also illustrates the importance of isolating assumptions so that alternative strategies (e.g., different exam weights) can be considered.

Objective   To create a new workbook; to copy formulas containing relative and absolute references. Use Figure 1.15 as a guide in doing the exercise.

Step 1:   **Create a New Workbook**

> ➤ Click the **Start button**, click (or point to) the **Programs command,** then click **Microsoft Excel** to start the program. If Excel is already open, click the **New button** on the Standard toolbar (or click **Blank Workbook** in the task pane) to open a new workbook.
>
> ➤ Click and drag the Office Assistant out of the way or hide it altogether. (Pull down the **Help menu** and click **Hide the Office Assistant.**)
>
> ➤ If necessary, separate the Standard and Formatting toolbars. Pull down the **View menu**, click **Toolbars**, click **Customize**, and click the **Options tab.** Check the box that indicates the Standard and Formatting toolbars should be displayed on two rows.
>
> ➤ Close the task pane. Click in cell **A1.** Enter the title of the worksheet, **CIS120 - Spring Semester.**
>
> ➤ Enter the column headings in row 3 as in Figure 1.15a. Click in cell **A3** and type **Student,** then press the **right arrow key** to move to cell **B3.** Type **Test 1.**
>
> ➤ Press the **right arrow key** to move to cell **C3.** Type **Test 2.** Enter the words **Final** and **Average** in cells D3 and E3, respectively. Your worksheet should match Figure 1.15a.

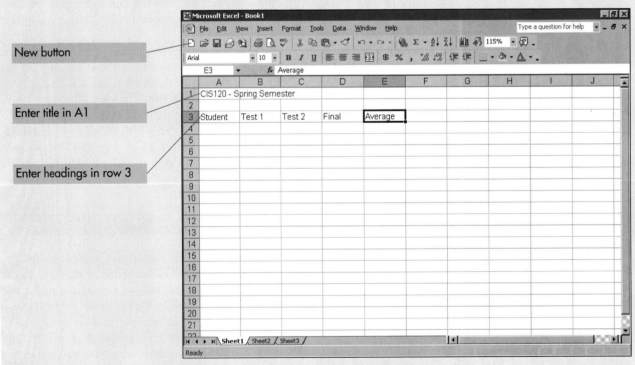

New button

Enter title in A1

Enter headings in row 3

(a) Create a New Workbook (step 1)

FIGURE 1.15   *Hands-on Exercise 3*

Step 2: **Save the Workbook**

➤ Pull down the **File menu** and click **Save** (or click the **Save button** on the Standard toolbar) to display the Save As dialog box as shown in Figure 1.15b. (The Save As dialog box always appears the first time you save a workbook, so that you can give the workbook a name.)

➤ Click the **drop-down arrow** on the Save In list box. Click the appropriate drive, drive C or drive A, depending on where you are saving your Excel workbooks.

➤ Double click the **Exploring Excel folder** to make it the active folder (the folder in which you will save the document).

➤ Click and drag **Book1** (the default entry) in the File name text box to select it, then type **Better Grade Book** as the name of the workbook. Click **Save** or press the **enter key**. The title bar changes to reflect the name of the workbook.

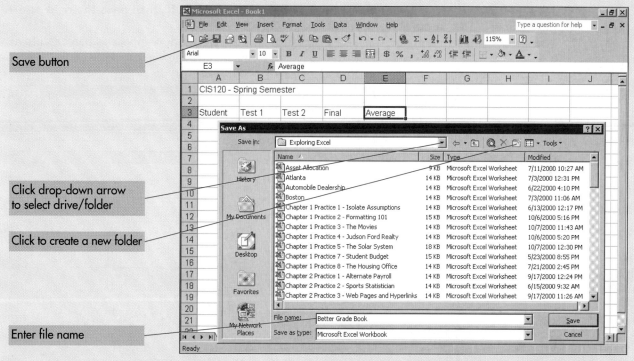

Save button

Click drop-down arrow to select drive/folder

Click to create a new folder

Enter file name

(b) Save the Workbook (step 2)

FIGURE 1.15 *Hands-on Exercise 3 (continued)*

CREATE A NEW FOLDER

Do you work with a large number of different workbooks? If so, it may be useful to store those workbooks in different folders, perhaps one folder for each subject you are taking. Pull down the File menu, click the Save As command to display the Save As dialog box, then click the Create New Folder button to display the associated dialog box. Enter the name of the folder, then click OK. Once the folder has been created, use the Look In box to change to that folder the next time you open that workbook. See practice exercise 7 at the end of the chapter.

Step 3:   **Enter Student Data and Literal Information**

➤ Click in cell **A4** and type **Costa, Frank**, then enter Frank's grades on the two tests and the final as shown in Figure 1.15c. Do *not* enter Frank's semester average in cell E4 as that will be entered as a formula.

➤ If necessary, click and drag the border between columns A and B so that you can read Frank Costa's complete name. Check that you entered the data for this student correctly. If you made a mistake, return to the cell and retype the entry.

➤ Enter the names and grades for the other students in rows 5 through 9. Do *not* enter the student averages.

➤ Complete the entries in column A by typing **Class Averages** and **Exam Weights** in cells **A11** and **A13**, respectively.

➤ Enter the exam weights in row 13. Click in cell **B13** and enter **.25**, press the **right arrow key** to move to cell **C13** and enter **.25**, then press the **right arrow key** to move to cell **D13** and enter **.5**. Press **enter**.

➤ Do *not* be concerned that the exam weights do not appear as percentages as they will be formatted in a later exercise. Save the workbook.

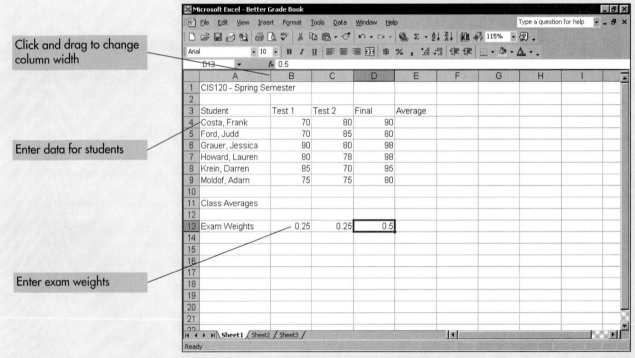

(c) Enter Student Data and Literal Information (step 3)

FIGURE 1.15   *Hands-on Exercise 3 (continued)*

COLUMN WIDTHS AND ROW HEIGHTS

Drag the border between column headings to change the column width; for example, to increase (decrease) the width of column A, drag the border between column headings A and B to the right (left). Double click the right boundary of a column heading to change the column width to accommodate the widest entry in that column. Use the same techniques to change the row heights. See practice exercise 2 at the end of the chapter.

Step 4:   **Compute the Student Semester Averages**

➤ Click in cell **E4** and type the formula **=$B$13*B4+$C$13*C4+$D$13*D4** to compute the semester average for the first student. Press **enter**. Check that the displayed value in cell E4 is 82.5 as shown in Figure 1.15d.

➤ Click in cell **E4** to make this the active cell, then click the **Copy button** on the Standard toolbar. A moving border will surround cell E4 indicating that its contents have been copied to the clipboard.

➤ Click and drag to select cells **E5** through **E9** as the destination range. Click the **Paste button** to copy the contents of the clipboard to the destination range. Ignore the Paste Options button that appears automatically any time the Paste command is executed.

➤ Press **Esc** to remove the moving border around cell E4. The Paste Options button also disappears.

➤ Click in cell **E5** and look at the formula. The cells that reference the grades have changed to B5, C5, and D5. The cells that reference the exam weights—$B$13, $C$13, and $D$13—are the same as in cell E4.

➤ Save the workbook.

Copy button

Paste button

Formula bar displays formula

Click in E4 and enter formula; cell displays computed result

(d) Compute the Student Semester Averages (step 4)

FIGURE 1.15   *Hands-on Exercise 3 (continued)*

THE PASTE OPTIONS BUTTON

The Paste Options button (includes options from the Paste Special command and) provides flexibility when you paste the contents of the clipboard into a worksheet. Press Esc to ignore the options and you automatically paste both the cell formulas and associated formatting. Alternatively, you can click the down arrow to display options to copy values rather than formulas with or without formatting, Formatting is discussed in detail later in the chapter.

Step 5: **Compute the Class Averages**

➤ Click in cell **B11** and type the formula **=AVERAGE(B4:B9)** to compute the class average on the first test. Press the **enter key** when you have completed the formula.

➤ Point to cell B11, then click the **right mouse button** to display a context-sensitive menu, then click the **Copy command**. You should see a moving border around cell B11, indicating that the contents of this cell have been copied to the clipboard.

➤ Click and drag to select cells **C11** and **D11** as shown in Figure 1.15e. Click the **Paste button** on the standard toolbar to copy the contents of the clipboard to the destination range. Press **Esc** to remove the moving border.

➤ Click anywhere in the worksheet to deselect cells C11 through D11. Cells C11 and D11 should contain 78 and 90.16667, the class averages on Test 2 and the Final, respectively. Do not worry about formatting at this time.

➤ Save the workbook.

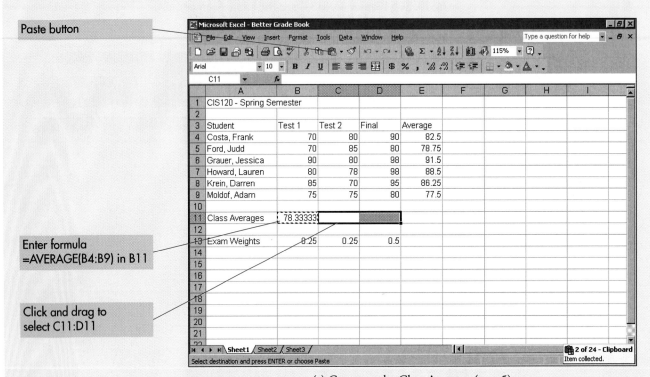

(e) Compute the Class Averages (step 5)

FIGURE 1.15 *Hands-on Exercise 3 (continued)*

TWO DIFFERENT CLIPBOARDS

The Office clipboard holds a total of up to 24 objects from multiple applications, as opposed to the Windows clipboard, which stores only the results of the last Cut or Copy command. Thus, each time you execute a Cut or Copy command, the contents of the Windows clipboard are replaced, whereas the copied object is added to the objects already in the Office clipboard. To display the Office clipboard, open the task pane, click the down arrow and select clipboard. Leave the clipboard open as you execute multiple cut and copy operations to observe what happens.

Step 6: **Change the Exam Weights**

➤ Change the entries in cells **B13** and **C13** to **.20** and the entry in cell **D13** to **.60**. The semester average for every student changes automatically; for example, Costa and Moldof change to 84 and 78, respectively, as shown in Figure 1.15f.

➤ The professor decides this does not make a significant difference and wants to go back to the original weights. Click the **Undo button** three times to reverse the last three actions. You should see .25, .25, and .50 in cells B13, C13, and D13, respectively.

➤ Click in cell **A15** and type the label **Grading Assistant**. Press **enter**. Type your name in cell **A16**, so that you will get credit for this assignment.

➤ Save the workbook. You do not need to print the workbook yet, since we will do that at the end of the next exercise, after we have formatted the workbook.

➤ Exit Excel if you are not ready to begin the next exercise at this time.

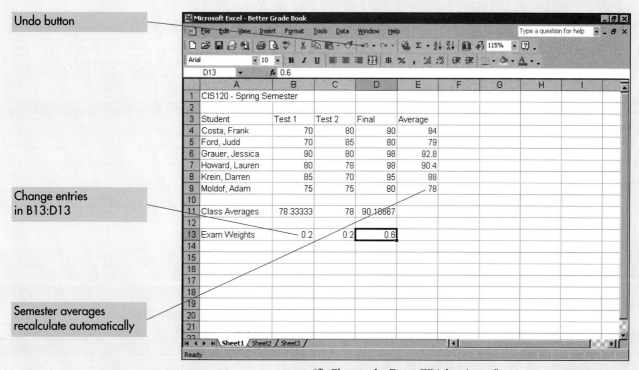

(f) Change the Exam Weights (step 6)

FIGURE 1.15 *Hands-on Exercise 3 (continued)*

CHANGE THE ZOOM SETTING

You can increase or decrease the size of a worksheet as it appears on the monitor by clicking the down arrow on the zoom box and selecting an appropriate percentage. If you are working with a large spreadsheet and cannot see it at one time on the screen, choose a number less than 100%. Conversely, if you find yourself squinting because the numbers are too small, select a percentage larger than 100%. Changing the magnification on the screen does not affect printing; that is, worksheets are always printed at 100% unless you change the scaling within the Page Setup command.

Figure 1.16a shows the grade book as it exists at the end of the third hands-on exercise, without concern for its appearance. Figure 1.16b shows the grade book as it will appear at the end of the next exercise after it has been formatted. The differences between the two are due entirely to formatting. Consider:

- The exam weights are formatted as percentages in Figure 1.16b, as opposed to decimals in Figure 1.16a. The class and semester averages are displayed with a single decimal place in Figure 1.16b.
- Boldface and italics are used for emphasis, as are shading and borders.
- Exam grades and computed averages are centered under their respective headings, as are the exam weights.
- The worksheet title is centered across all five columns.

Class Averages are not uniformly formatted

Percentages are not formatted

	A	B	C	D	E
1	CIS120 - Spring Semester				
2					
3	Student	Test 1	Test 2	Final	Average
4	Costa, Frank	70	80	90	82.5
5	Ford, Judd	70	85	80	78.75
6	Grauer, Jessica	90	80	98	91.5
7	Howard, Lauren	80	78	98	88.5
8	Krein, Darren	85	70	95	86.25
9	Moldof, Adam	75	75	80	77.5
10					
11	Class Averages	78.33333333	78	90.16666667	
12					
13	Exam Weights	0.25	0.25	0.5	

(a) At the End of Hands-on Exercise 3

Title is centered across columns; font is larger and both bold and italics

Shading, borders, and boldface are used for emphasis

Test grades are centered in columns

Uniform number of decimal places

Percent formatting has been applied

	A	B	C	D	E
1		*CIS120 - Spring Semester*			
2					
3	**Student**	**Test 1**	**Test 2**	**Final**	**Average**
4	Costa, Frank	70	80	90	82.5
5	Ford, Judd	70	85	80	78.8
6	Grauer, Jessica	90	80	98	91.5
7	Howard, Lauren	80	78	98	88.5
8	Krein, Darren	85	70	95	86.3
9	Moldof, Adam	75	75	80	77.5
10					
11	**Class Averages**	78.3	78.0	90.2	
12					
13	**Exam Weights**	25%	25%	50%	

(b) At the End of Hands-on Exercise 4

FIGURE 1.16 *Developing the Grade Book*

The ***Format Cells command*** controls the formatting for numbers, alignment, fonts, borders, and patterns (color). Execution of the command produces a tabbed dialog box in which you choose the particular formatting category, then enter the desired options. All formatting is done within the context of ***select-then-do***. You select the cells to which the formatting is to apply, then you execute the Format Cells command (or click the appropriate button on the Formatting toolbar).

Once a format has been assigned to a cell, the formatting remains in the cell and is applied to all subsequent values that are entered into that cell. You can, however, change the formatting by executing a new formatting command. You can also remove the formatting by using the Clear command in the Edit menu. Note, too, that changing the format of a number changes the way the number is displayed, but does not change its value. If, for example, you entered 1.2345 into a cell, but displayed the number as 1.23, the actual value (1.2345) would be used in all calculations involving that cell. The numeric formats are shown in Figure 1.17a and described below.

- ***General format*** is the default format for numeric entries and displays a number according to the way it was originally entered. Numbers are shown as integers (e.g., 123), decimal fractions (e.g., 1.23), or in scientific notation (e.g., 1.23E+10) if the number exceeds 11 digits.
- ***Number format***, which displays a number with or without the 1000 separator (e.g., a comma) and with any number of decimal places. Negative numbers can be displayed with parentheses and/or can be shown in red.
- ***Currency format***, which displays a number with the 1000 separator and an optional dollar sign (which is placed immediately to the left of the number). Negative values can be preceded by a minus sign or displayed with parentheses and/or can be shown in red.
- ***Accounting format***, which displays a number with the 1000 separator, an optional dollar sign (at the left border of the cell, which vertically aligns the dollar signs within a column), negative values in parentheses, and zero values as hyphens.
- ***Date format***, which displays the date in different ways, such as March 4, 2001, 3/4/01, or 4-Mar-01.
- ***Time format***, which displays the time in different formats, such as 10:50 PM or the equivalent 22:50 (24-hour time).
- ***Percentage format***, whereby the number is multiplied by 100 for display purposes only, a percent sign is included, and any number of decimal places can be specified.
- ***Fraction format***, which displays a number as a fraction, and is appropriate when there is no exact decimal equivalent. A fraction is entered into a cell by preceding the fraction with an equal sign—for example, = ⅓.
- ***Scientific format***, which displays a number as a decimal fraction followed by a whole number exponent of 10; for example, the number 12345 would appear as 1.2345E+04. The exponent, +04 in the example, is the number of places the decimal point is moved to the left (or right if the exponent is negative). Very small numbers have negative exponents.
- ***Text format***, which left aligns the entry and is useful for numerical values that have leading zeros and should be treated as text, such as ZIP codes.
- ***Special format***, which displays a number with editing characters, such as hyphens in a Social Security number or parentheses around the area code of a telephone number.
- ***Custom format***, which allows you to develop your own formats.

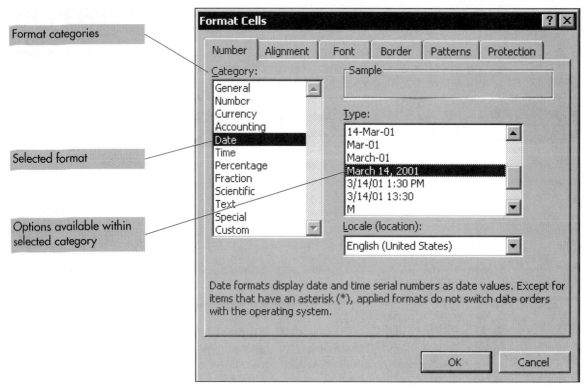

Format categories

Selected format

Options available within
selected category

(a) The Number Tab

FIGURE 1.17 *The Format Cells Command*

Alignment

The contents of a cell (whether text or numeric) may be aligned horizontally
and/or vertically as indicated by the dialog box of Figure 1.17b. The default horizontal *alignment* is general, which left-aligns text and right-aligns date and numbers. You can also center an entry across a range of selected cells (or *merge cells*),
as in the professor's grade book, which centered the title in cell A1 across columns
A through E. Clear the box to merge cells if you want to *split cells* that have been
previously merged. The Fill option duplicates the characters in the cell across the
entire width of that cell.

   Vertical alignment is important only if the row height is changed and the characters are smaller than the height of the row. Entries may be vertically aligned at the
top, center, or bottom (the default) of a cell.

   It is also possible to wrap the text within a cell to emulate the word wrap of a
word processor. You select multiple cells and merge them together. And finally, you
can achieve some interesting effects by rotating text up to 90° in either direction.

Fonts

You can use the same fonts in Excel as you can in any other Windows application.
All fonts are WYSIWYG (What You See Is What You Get), meaning that the
worksheet you see on the monitor will match the printed worksheet.

   Any entry in a worksheet may be displayed in any font, style, or point size as
indicated by the dialog box of Figure 1.17c. The example shows Arial, Bold Italic,
and 14 points, and corresponds to the selection for the worksheet title in the
improved grade book. Special effects, such as subscripts or superscripts, are also
possible. You can even select a different color, but you will need a color printer to
see the effect on the printed page. The Preview box shows the text as it will appear
in the worksheet.

Horizontal alignment options

Vertical alignment options

Click to wrap text in cell

Click to merge selected cells; clear to split cells

Enter degrees to rotate text

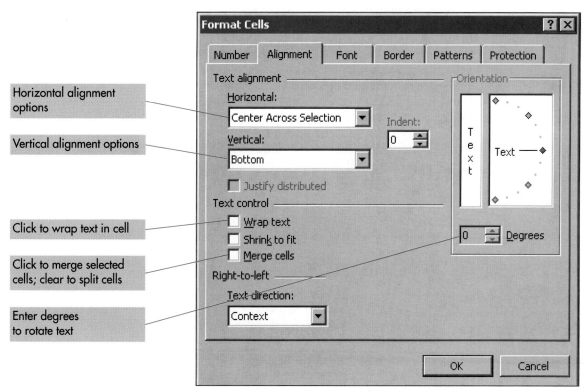

(b) The Alignment Tab

List of available styles

List of available fonts

List of available sizes

Preview of font

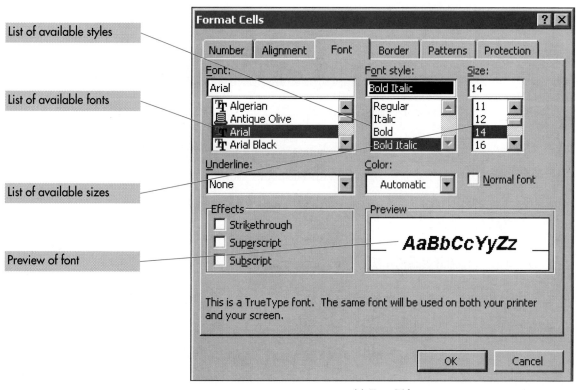

(c) Font Tab

FIGURE 1.17   *The Format Cells Command (continued)*

Borders, Patterns, and Shading

The **Border tab** in Figure 1.17d enables you to create a border around a cell (or cells) for additional emphasis. You can outline the entire selection, or you can choose the specific side or sides; for example, thicker lines on the bottom and right sides produce a drop shadow, which is very effective. You can also specify a different line style and/or a different color for the border, but you will need a color printer to see the effect on the printed output.

The **Patterns tab** (not shown in the figure) lets you choose a different color in which to shade the cell and further emphasize its contents. The Pattern drop-down list box lets you select an alternate pattern, such as dots or slanted lines.

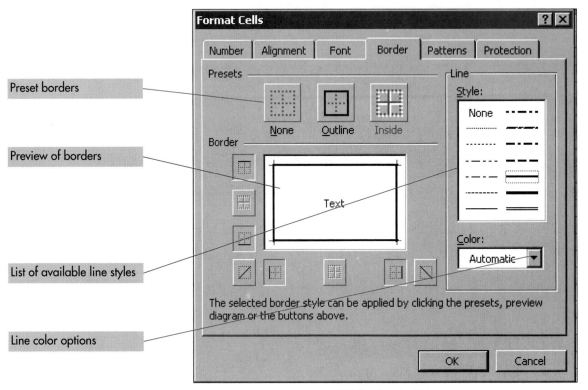

(d) The Border Tab

FIGURE 1.17 *The Format Cells Command (continued)*

USE RESTRAINT

More is not better, especially in the case of too many typefaces and styles, which produce cluttered worksheets that impress no one. Limit yourself to a maximum of two typefaces per worksheet, but choose multiple sizes and/or styles within those typefaces. Use boldface or italics for emphasis, but do so in moderation, because if you emphasize too many elements, the effect is lost.

FORMATTING A WORKSHEET

Objective To format a worksheet using boldface, italics, shading, and borders; to change the font and/or alignment of a selected entry. Use Figure 1.18 as a guide in the exercise.

Step 1: **Center the Title**

➤ Open **Better Grade Book** from the previous exercise. Click in cell **A1** to select the cell containing the title of the worksheet. Click the **Bold button** on the Formatting toolbar to boldface the title. Click the **Italics button** to italicize the title.

➤ Click in cell **A15** and click the **Bold button**. Click the **Bold button** a second time, and the boldface disappears. Click the **Bold button** again, and you are back to boldface. The same is true of the Italics button; that is, the Bold and Italics buttons function as toggle switches.

➤ Click in cell **A1**. Click the **down arrow** on the Font size list box and change the size to **14** to further accentuate the title.

➤ Click and drag to select cells **A1** through **E1**, which represents the width of the entire worksheet. Click the **Merge and Center button** on the Formatting toolbar as shown in Figure 1.18a to center the title across the width of your worksheet.

➤ Save the workbook.

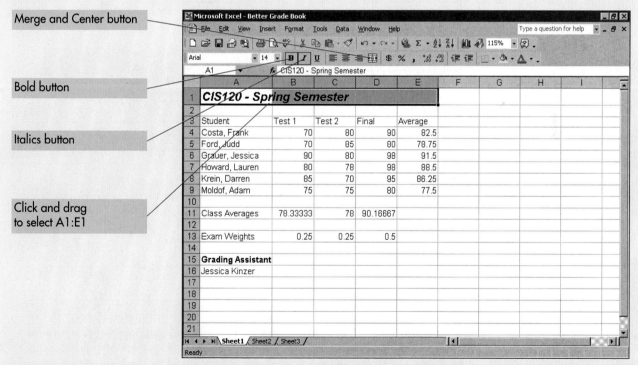

(a) Center the Title (step 1)

FIGURE 1.18 *Hands-on Exercise 4*

Step 2:   **Format the Exam Weights**

> ➤ Click and drag to select cells **B13** through **D13**. Pull down the **Format menu**, then click the **Cells command** to display the dialog box in Figure 1.18b.
> ➤ If necessary, click the **Number tab**. Click **Percentage** in the Category list box. Click the **down spin arrow** in the Decimal Places box to select **zero decimals**, then click **OK**. The exam weights are displayed with percent signs and no decimal places.
> ➤ You can also use the buttons on the Formatting toolbar to accomplish the same formatting. First remove the formatting by clicking the **Undo button** on the Standard toolbar to cancel the formatting command.
> ➤ Check that cells B13 through D13 are still selected. Click the **Percent Style button** on the Formatting toolbar. (You can also pull down the **Format menu**, click the **Style command**, then choose the **Percent Style** from the Style Name list box.) Once again cells B13 through D13 are displayed in percent.
> ➤ Save the workbook.

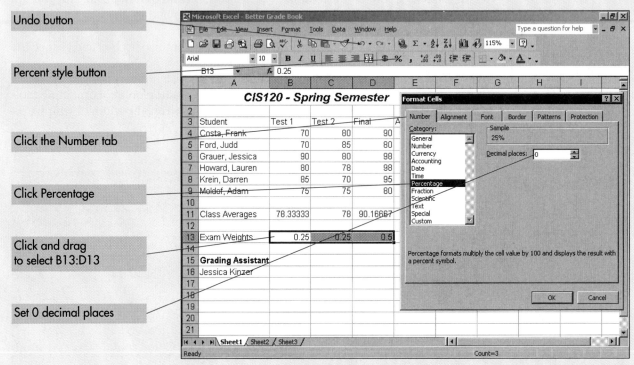

Undo button

Percent style button

Click the Number tab

Click Percentage

Click and drag to select B13:D13

Set 0 decimal places

(b) Format the Exam Weights (step 2)

FIGURE 1.18   *Hands-on Exercise 4 (continued)*

THE MENU OR THE TOOLBAR

The Formatting toolbar is often the easiest way to implement a variety of formatting operations. There are buttons for boldface, italics, and underlining (each of which functions as a toggle switch). There are also buttons for alignment (including merge and center), currency, percent, and comma formats, together with buttons to increase or decrease the number of decimal places. You can find various buttons to change the font, point size, color, and borders.

Step 3: **Format the Class Averages**

➤ Click and drag to select cells **B11 through D11**. Now press and hold the **Ctrl key** as you click and drag to select cells **E4 through E9**. Using the Ctrl key in this way allows you to select noncontiguous (nontouching) cells as shown in Figure 1.18c.
➤ Format the selected cells using the Formatting toolbar or the Format menu:
  • To use the Format menu, pull down the **Format menu**, click **Cells**, click the **Number tab**, then click **Number** in the Category list box. Click the **down spin arrow** in the Decimal Places text box to reduce the decimal places to one. Click **OK**.
  • To use the Formatting toolbar, click the appropriate button repeatedly to increase or decrease the number of decimal places to one.
➤ Click and drag to select cells **B3 through E13**. Click the **Center button** to center the numeric data in the worksheet under the respective column headings.
➤ Save the workbook.

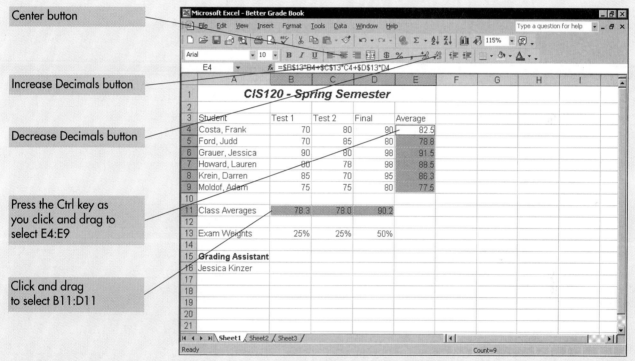

(c) Format the Class Averages (step 3)

FIGURE 1.18 *Hands-on Exercise 4 (continued)*

CLEAR THE FORMATS, BUT KEEP THE CONTENTS

You can clear the formatting in a cell and retain the contents, and/or you can clear contents but retain the formatting. Click and drag over the cell(s) for which the command is to apply, then pull down the Edit menu, click the Clear command, and choose the appropriate option—for example, the option to clear Formats. Click the tiny square immediately below the name box (to the left of the header for column A) to select the entire worksheet, then clear the formats for the worksheet. You can then repeat the steps in this exercise to practice the various formatting commands.

Step 4:   **Borders and Color**

> ➤ Click and drag to select cells **A3 through E3**. Press and hold the **Ctrl key** as you click and drag to select the range **A11:E11**.
> ➤ Continue to press the **Ctrl key** as you click and drag to select cells **A13:E13**. All three cell ranges should be selected, which means that any formatting command you execute will apply to all of the selected cells.
> ➤ Pull down the **Format menu** and click **Cells** (or point to any of the selected cells and click the **right mouse button** to display a shortcut menu, then click **Format Cells**). Click the **Border tab** to display the dialog box in Figure 1.18d.
> ➤ Choose a line width from the Style section. Click the **Top** and **Bottom** boxes in the Border section. Click **OK** to exit the dialog box.
> ➤ Check that all three ranges are still selected (A3:E3, A11:E11, *and* A13:E13). Click the **down arrow** on the **Fill Color button** on the Formatting toolbar. Click **yellow** (or whatever color appeals to you).
> ➤ Click the **Bold button** on the Formatting toolbar. Click outside the selected cells to see the effects of the formatting change. Save the workbook.

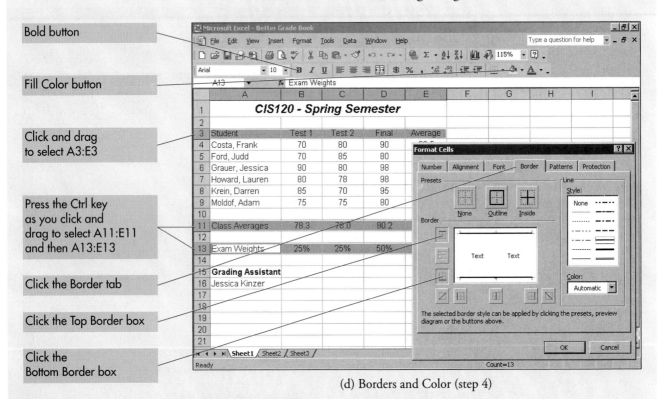

(d) Borders and Color (step 4)

FIGURE 1.18   *Hands-on Exercise 4 (continued)*

USE A PEN TO DRAW THE BORDER

You can draw borders of any thickness or color around the cells in a worksheet using a "pen" as opposed to a menu command. Click the down arrow on the Borders button on the Standard toolbar, then click the Draw Borders command to change the mouse pointer to a pen and simultaneously display the Borders toolbar. Click the Line Color or Line Style buttons to change the appearance of the border, then draw the borders directly in the worksheet. Close the Borders toolbar when you are finished.

Step 5: **The Completed Worksheet**

➤ Check that your worksheet matches ours as shown in Figure 1.18e. Pull down the **File menu**. Click **Page Setup** to display the Page Setup dialog box.
  • Click the **Margins tab**. Check the box to center the worksheet horizontally.
  • Click the **Sheet tab**. Check the boxes to print Row and Column Headings and Gridlines.
  • Click the **Header/Footer tab**. If necessary, click the **drop-down arrow** on the Header list box. Scroll to the top of the list and click **(none)** to remove the header. Click the **drop-down arrow** on the Footer list box. Scroll to the top of the list and click **(none)** to remove the footer. Click **OK**.
➤ Click the **Print Preview button** to preview the worksheet before printing:
  • If you are satisfied with the appearance of the worksheet, click the **Print button** within the Preview window, then click **OK** to print the worksheet.
  • If you are not satisfied with the appearance of the worksheet, click the **Setup button** within the Preview window to make the necessary changes.
➤ Save the workbook.

Print Preview button

Your name goes here

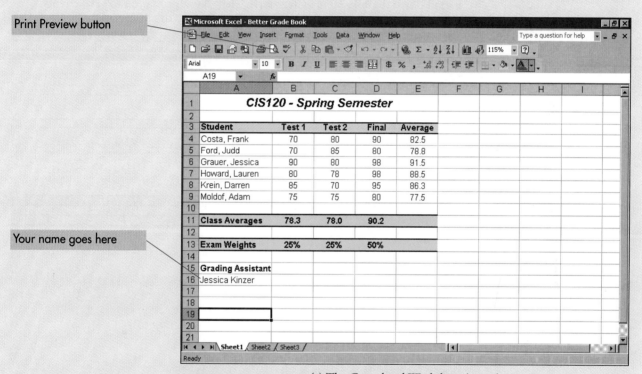

(e) The Completed Worksheet (step 5)

FIGURE 1.18   *Hands-on Exercise 4 (continued)*

FIND-AND-REPLACE FORMATTING

You can use the Find and Replace command to replace formatting as well as text. Pull down the Edit menu and click the Replace command to display the Find and Replace dialog box, then click the options button to display a Format button next to both text boxes. Click the Format button next to the Find text box and specify Bold as the Font style. Click the Format button next to the Replace text box and choose Italic. Now click the Replace All button to replace all bold with Italics. Try this within the grade book. See practice exercise 4 at the end of the chapter.

Step 6: **Print the Cell Formulas**

➤ Pull down the **Tools menu**, click **Options**, click the **View tab**, check the box for **Formulas**, then click **OK** (or use the keyboard shortcut **Ctrl+˜**). The worksheet should display the cell formulas.

➤ If necessary, click the arrow to the right of the horizontal scroll box so that column E, the column containing the cell formulas, comes into view.

➤ Double click the border between the column headings for columns E and F to increase the width of column E to the widest entry in the column.

➤ Pull down the **File menu**. Click **Page Setup** to display the Page Setup dialog box. Click the **Page tab**. Click the **Landscape** orientation **button**. Click the option button to **Fit to 1 Page**. Click **OK** to exit the Page Setup dialog box.

➤ Click the **Print Preview button** to preview the worksheet before printing as shown in Figure 1.18f. Click the **Zoom button** to increase/decrease the size of the worksheet as necessary. If you are not satisfied with the appearance of the worksheet, click the **Setup button** within the Preview window to make the necessary changes. Print the worksheet.

➤ Pull down the **File menu**. Click **Exit**. Click **No** if prompted to save changes.

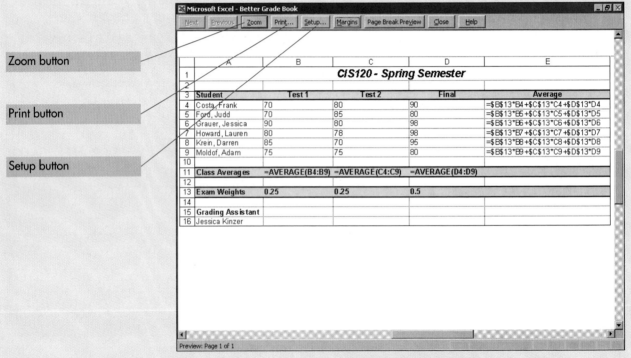

(f) Print the Cell Formulas (step 6)

FIGURE 1.18 *Hands-on Exercise 4 (continued)*

CLICK AND DRAG TO CORRECT A CELL FORMULA

Press Ctrl+˜ to display the cell formulas, then click in any cell that contains a formula. Look closely and you will see that each cell reference in that formula appears in a different color that corresponds to the border color of the referenced cell. To change a cell reference in the formula (e.g., from A4 to B4), drag the color-coded border surrounding cell A4 (the reference you want to change) to cell B4 (the new reference).

A spreadsheet is the computerized equivalent of an accountant's ledger. It is divided into rows and columns, with each row and column assigned a heading. The intersection of a row and column is a cell. Spreadsheet is a generic term. Workbook and worksheet are specific. An Excel workbook contains one or more worksheets. Every cell in a worksheet (spreadsheet) contains either a formula or a constant. A formula begins with an equal sign and is a combination of numeric constants, cell references, operators, and/or functions. A constant is an entry that does not change; it is numeric or descriptive text.

The Insert and Delete commands add or remove individual cells, rows, or columns of a worksheet. The commands are also used to insert or delete worksheets within a workbook. The Open command brings a workbook from disk into memory. Save stores the workbook in memory to disk.

The Page Setup command provides complete control over the printed page, enabling you to print the worksheet with or without gridlines or row and column headings. The Page Setup command also controls margins, headers and footers, centering the worksheet on a page, and orientation. The Print Preview command shows the worksheet as it will print and should be used prior to printing.

All formatting commands operate on a cell or group of cells known as a range. A range is selected by dragging the mouse to highlight the range; the range remains selected until another range is selected or you click another cell in the worksheet. Noncontiguous ranges may be selected in conjunction with the Ctrl key. The contents of a range of cells may be copied or moved anywhere within a worksheet. An absolute reference remains constant throughout a copy operation whereas a relative address is adjusted for the new location. Absolute and relative references have no meaning in a move operation.

Formatting is done within the context of select-then-do; that is, select the cell or range of cells, then execute the appropriate command. The Format Cells command controls the formatting for numbers, alignment, font, borders, and patterns (colors). The Formatting toolbar simplifies the formatting process.

KEY TERMS

Absolute reference (p. 33)
Accounting format (p. 43)
Active cell (p. 7)
Alignment (p. 44)
Assumptions (p. 31)
Border tab (p. 46)
Cell (p. 4)
Cell reference (p. 4)
Clipboard (p. 33)
Close command (p. 9)
Constant (p. 5)
Copy command (p. 32)
Currency format (p. 43)
Custom format (p. 43)
Date format (p. 43)
Delete command (p. 19)
Destination range (p. 32)
Edit (p. 5)
Exit command (p. 9)
File menu (p. 9)
File name (p. 9)
File type (p. 9)

Format Cells command (p. 43)
Formatting toolbar (p. 7)
Formula (p. 5)
Formula bar (p. 7)
Fraction format (p. 43)
Function (p. 5)
General format (p. 43)
Insert command (p. 19)
Landscape orientation (p. 21)
Merge cells (p. 44)
Mixed reference (p. 33)
Move operation (p. 34)
Name box (p. 7)
Number format (p. 43)
Office Assistant (p. 18)
Open command (p. 9)
Page Setup command (p. 21)
Patterns tab (p. 46)
Percentage format (p. 43)
Places bar (p. 9)
Portrait orientation (p. 21)

Print command (p. 9)
Range (p. 32)
Relative reference (p. 33)
Save command (p. 9)
Save As command (p. 9)
Scientific format (p. 43)
Select-then-do (p. 43)
Source range (p. 32)
Special format (p. 43)
Split cells (p. 44)
Spreadsheet (p. 2)
Standard toolbar (p. 7)
Status bar (p. 7)
Task pane (p. 22)
Text format (p. 43)
Time format (p. 43)
Toolbars (p. 7)
Undo command (p. 17)
Workbook (p. 6)
Worksheet (p. 6)

1. Which of the following is true?
   (a) A worksheet contains one or more workbooks
   (b) A workbook contains one or more worksheets
   (c) A spreadsheet contains one or more worksheets
   (d) A worksheet contains one or more spreadsheets

2. The cell at the intersection of the second column and third row is cell:
   (a) B3
   (b) 3B
   (c) C2
   (d) 2C

3. What is the effect of typing F5+F6 into a cell *without* a beginning equal sign?
   (a) The entry is equivalent to the formula =F5+F6
   (b) The cell will display the contents of cell F5 plus cell F6
   (c) The entry will be treated as a text entry and display F5+F6 in the cell
   (d) The entry will be rejected by Excel which will signal an error message

4. The Open command:
   (a) Brings a workbook from disk into memory
   (b) Brings a workbook from disk into memory, then erases the workbook on disk
   (c) Stores the workbook in memory on disk
   (d) Stores the workbook in memory on disk, then erases the workbook from memory

5. The Save command:
   (a) Brings a workbook from disk into memory
   (b) Brings a workbook from disk into memory, then erases the workbook on disk
   (c) Stores the workbook in memory on disk
   (d) Stores the workbook in memory on disk, then erases the workbook from memory

6. In the absence of parentheses, the order of operation is:
   (a) Exponentiation, addition or subtraction, multiplication or division
   (b) Addition or subtraction, multiplication or division, exponentiation
   (c) Multiplication or division, exponentiation, addition or subtraction
   (d) Exponentiation, multiplication or division, addition or subtraction

7. Cells A1, A2, and A3 contain the values 10, 20, and 40, respectively, what value will be displayed in a cell containing the cell formula =A1/A2*A3+1?
   (a) 1.125
   (b) 21
   (c) 20.125
   (d) Impossible to determine

8. The entry =AVERAGE(A4:A6):
   (a) Is invalid because the cells are not contiguous
   (b) Computes the average of cells A4 and A6
   (c) Computes the average of cells A4, A5, and A6
   (d) None of the above

9. Which of the following was suggested with respect to printing a workbook?
   (a) Print the displayed values only
   (b) Print the cell formulas only
   (c) Print both the displayed values and cell formulas
   (d) Print neither the displayed values nor the cell formulas

10. Which options are mutually exclusive in the Page Setup menu?
    (a) Portrait and landscape orientation
    (b) Cell gridlines and row and column headings
    (c) Left and right margins
    (d) All of the above

11. What is the end result of clicking in a cell, then clicking the Italics button on the Formatting toolbar twice in a row?
    (a) The cell contents are displayed in Italics
    (b) The cell contents are displayed in ordinary (nonitalicized) type
    (c) The cell contents are unchanged and appear exactly as they did prior to clicking the Italics button twice in a row
    (d) Impossible to determine

12. Which of the following best describes the formula used to compute a student's semester average, when the weights of each exam are isolated at the bottom of a spreadsheet?
    (a) The student's individual grades are entered as absolute references and the exam weights are entered as relative references
    (b) The student's individual grades are entered as relative references and the exam weights are entered as absolute references
    (c) All cell references are relative
    (d) All cell references are absolute

13. Cell B11 contains the formula, =SUM (B3:B9). What will the contents of cell C11 be if the formula in cell B11 is copied to cell C11?
    (a) =SUM (C3:C9)
    (b) =SUM (B3:B9)
    (c) =SUM ($B$3:$B$9)
    (d) =SUM ($C$3:$C$9)

14. Cell E6 contains the formula, =B6*$B$12+C6*$C$12+D6*$D$12. What will be the formula in cell E7 if the contents of cell E6 are copied to that cell?
    (a) =B7*$B$12+C7*$C$12+D7*$D$12
    (b) =B7*$B$13+C7*$C$13+D7*$D$13
    (c) =B6*$B$13+C6*$C$13+D6*$D$13
    (d) None of the above

15. A formula containing the reference =D$5 is copied to a cell one column over and two rows down. How will the entry appear in its new location?
    (a) =E5
    (b) =E$5
    (c) =E$6
    (d) =$E5

ANSWERS

1. b	**6.** d	**11.** c
2. a	**7.** b	**12.** b
3. c	**8.** c	**13.** a
4. a	**9.** c	**14.** a
5. c	**10.** a	**15.** b

1. Isolate Assumptions: Figure 1.19 displays a new grade book with a different grading scheme. Students take three exams worth 100 points each, submit a term paper and various homework assignments worth 50 points each, then receive a grade for the semester based on their total points. The maximum points possible is 400. A student's semester average is computed by dividing his or her total points by this number.
   a. Open the partially completed workbook, *Chapter 1 Practice 1*, in the Exploring Excel folder. Click in cell G4 and enter a formula to compute Anderson's total points. Click in cell H4 and enter a formula that will compute Anderson's semester average. Be sure this formula includes an absolute reference to cell B16.
   b. Click and drag to select the formulas in cells G4 and H4, then copy these formulas to cells G5 through H12.
   c. Click in cell B14 and enter a formula that will compute the class average on the first exam. Copy this formula to cells C14 to H14.
   d. Format the worksheet appropriately. (You need not copy our formatting exactly.) Add your name as the grading assistant, then print the worksheet twice, once to show displayed values and once to show the cell formulas. Use landscape printing and be sure that the worksheet fits on one sheet of paper.
   e. The professor is concerned about the grades being too low and wants to introduce a curve. He does this by reducing the point threshold on which the students' semester averages are based. Click in cell B16 and change the threshold to 350, which automatically raises the average of every student.
   f. Print the displayed values that reflect the change in part (e). Can you see the value of isolating the assumptions within a worksheet?
   g. Add a cover page, then submit the complete assignment (four pages in all counting the cover page) to your instructor.

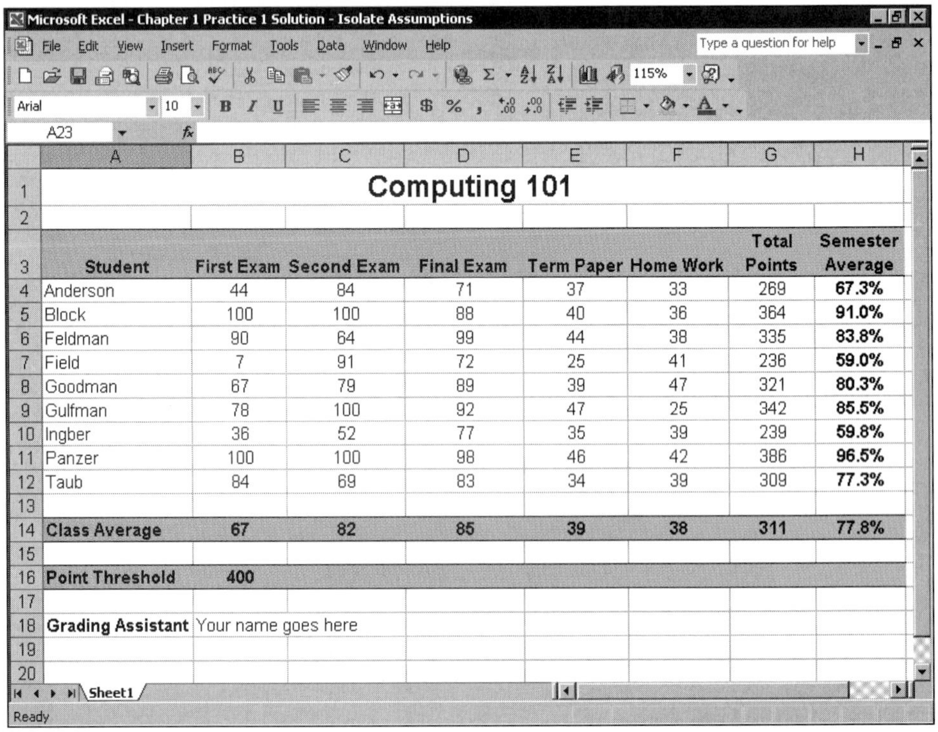

Microsoft Excel - Chapter 1 Practice 1 Solution - Isolate Assumptions

Computing 101

Student	First Exam	Second Exam	Final Exam	Term Paper	Home Work	Total Points	Semester Average
Anderson	44	84	71	37	33	269	67.3%
Block	100	100	88	40	36	364	91.0%
Feldman	90	64	99	44	38	335	83.8%
Field	7	91	72	25	41	236	59.0%
Goodman	67	79	89	39	47	321	80.3%
Gulfman	78	100	92	47	25	342	85.5%
Ingber	36	52	77	35	39	239	59.8%
Panzer	100	100	98	46	42	386	96.5%
Taub	84	69	83	34	39	309	77.3%
Class Average	67	82	85	39	38	311	77.8%
Point Threshold	400						
Grading Assistant	Your name goes here						

FIGURE 1.19 *Isolate Assumptions (Exercise 1)*

2. Formatting and Cell Movement: Figure 1.20 provides practice with formatting and basic cell operations (inserting and deleting cells, moving cells, splitting and/or merging cells). Open the partially completed *Chapter 1 Practice 2 workbook*, then follow the instructions in the individual cells to create the workbook in Figure 1.20. Cell B3, for example, asks you to italicize the text in green. The formatting is easy, but inserting and deleting cells is a little trickier since it can affect cells that have been merged together. You will find it easier, therefore, if you follow the instructions to split the cells first (cell A14 in the finished workbook), then merge the cells at the end of the exercise. Print the completed workbook for your instructor. Use landscape orientation so that the worksheet fits on one page.

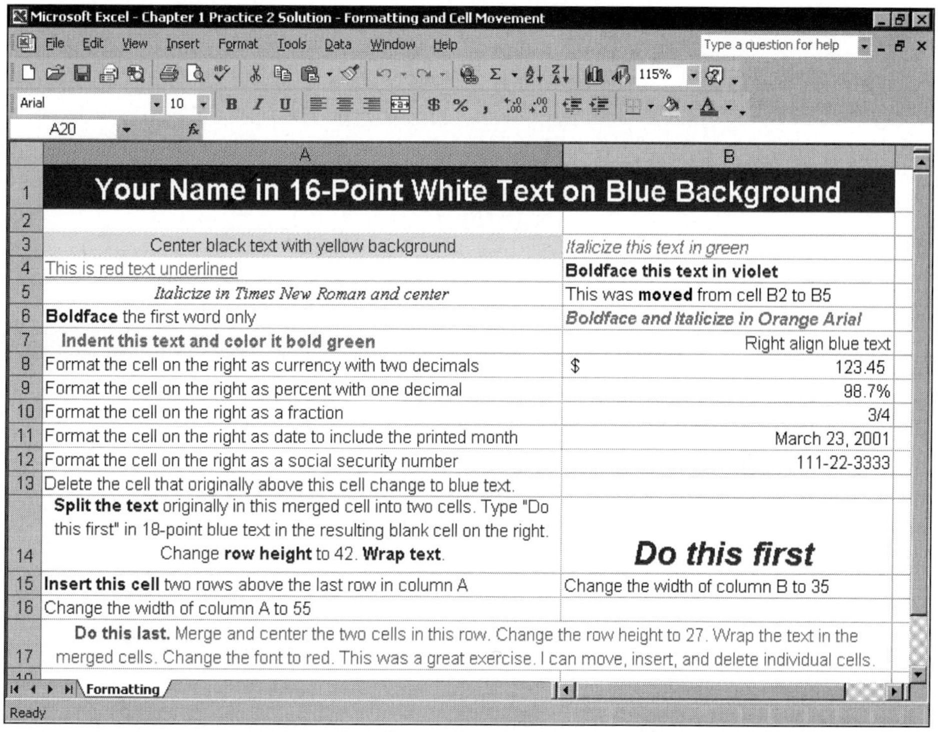

FIGURE 1.20   *Formatting and Cell Movement (Exercise 2)*

3. The Movies: Figure 1.21 displays a spreadsheet that is used to compute the weekly revenue for a chain of movie theatres. Open the partially completed version of this spreadsheet in *Chapter 1 Practice 3*, then proceed as follows:
   a. Click in cell D4 and enter a formula, using a combination of relative and absolute references, to compute the ticket revenues for the first theatre.
   b. Click in cells E4 and F4 to enter the appropriate formulas in these cells for the first theatre. Copy the formulas in cells D4, E4, and F4 to the appropriate rows for the other theatres.
   c. Click in cell B9 and enter the function to compute the total number of evening tickets that were sold. Copy this formula to the appropriate cells in row 9 to compute the other totals.
   d. Format the completed worksheet as appropriate. Print the worksheet twice, once to show the displayed values and once to show the cell contents. Submit both printouts to your instructor as proof you did this exercise.

4. Judson Ford Realty: The worksheet in Figure 1.22 displays the sales for Judson Ford Realty for the month of October. You can open a partially completed version of this worksheet in *Chapter 1 Practice 4*, but it is up to you to complete the worksheet so that it matches Figure 1.22..
   a. The price per square foot is the selling price divided by the square feet.

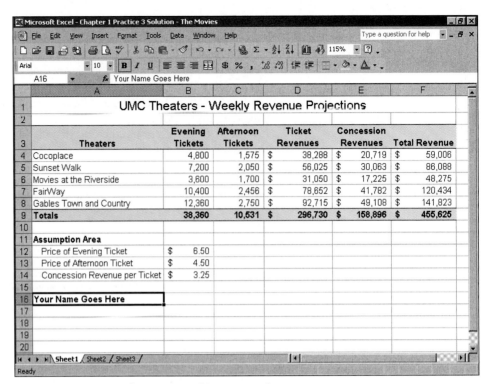

FIGURE 1.21 *The Movies (Exercise 3)*

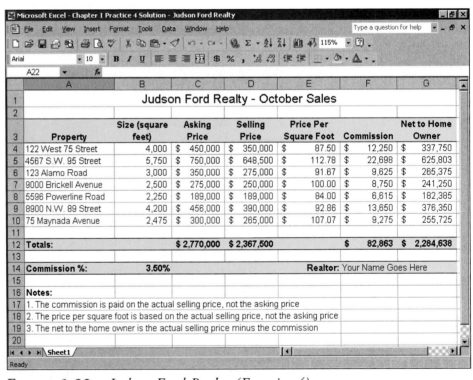

FIGURE 1.22 *Judson Ford Realty (Exercise 4)*

The MyPHLIP Web Site

Every text in the *Exploring Office XP* series has a corresponding MyPHLIP (Prentice Hall Learning on the Internet Partnership) Web site, where you will find a variety of student resources as well as online review questions for each chapter. Go to www.prenhall.com/myphlip and follow the instructions. The first time at the site you will be prompted to register by supplying your e-mail address and choosing a password. Next, you choose the discipline (CIS/MIS) and a book (e.g., *Exploring Microsoft Office XP, Volume I*). Your professor will tell you whether he or she has created an online syllabus, in which case you should click the link to find your professor after adding the book. Either way, the next time you return to the site, you will be taken directly to your text. Select any chapter, click "Go", then use the review questions as directed.

Residential Colleges

Congratulations! You have been recommended for a work-study assignment in the Office of Housing. Your supervisor has collected data on the number of students living in each dorm, and further, has divided that data according to the year in school. Your job is to open the partially completed *Residential Colleges* workbook, and compute the total number of students living in each dorm, as well as the total number of students for each year. In addition, you are to determine the percentage of the dormitory population for year in school.

The Cost of Smoking

Smoking is hazardous to your health as well as your pocketbook. A one-pack-a-day habit, at $3/pack, will cost you more than $1,000 per year. For the same money you could buy 20 concert tickets at $50 each, or more than 700 gallons of gas at $1.50 per gallon. Open the partially completed *Cost of Smoking* workbook and compute the number of various items that you could buy over the course of a year in lieu of cigarettes.

Accuracy Counts

The *Underbid* workbook on the data disk was the last assignment completed by your predecessor prior to his unfortunate dismissal. The worksheet contains a significant error, which caused your company to underbid a contract and assume a subsequent loss of $100,000. As you look for the error, don't be distracted by the attractive formatting. The shading, lines, and other touches are nice, but accuracy is more important than anything else. Write a memo to your instructor describing the nature of the error.

Two Different Clipboards

The Office clipboard is different from the Windows clipboard, but both clipboards share some functionality. Thus, whenever you copy an object to the Windows clipboard, it can also be copied to the Office clipboard, where the last 24 copied objects are retained. This is in contrast to the Windows clipboard, where each copy operation replaces the clipboard in its entirety. Experiment with the Office clipboard from different applications, then summarize your findings in a brief note to your instructor. Explain how the Office clipboard can be accessed from the task pane in Excel and/or an icon that appears on the Windows taskbar.

The Office Assistant

The Office Assistant monitors your work and offers advice throughout a session. You can tell that the Assistant has a suggestion when you see a light bulb on the Office Assistant button on the Standard toolbar or in the Office Assistant window. You can read the suggestions as they occur and/or review them at the end of a session. Redo one or more of the exercises in this chapter, but this time pay attention to the Assistant. Write a brief note to your instructor describing three tips (shortcuts) offered by the Assistant. (You should, however, reset the Assistant before you begin, or else the Assistant will not repeat tips that were offered in a previous session.) Start the Assistant, click the Options button, click the Options tab, then click the button to Reset tips.

Planning for Disaster

This case has nothing to do with spreadsheets per se, but it is perhaps the most important case of all, as it deals with the question of backup. Do you have a backup strategy? Do you even know what a backup strategy is? You had better learn, because sooner or later you will wish you had one. You will erase a file, be unable to read from a floppy disk, or worse yet suffer a hardware failure in which you are unable to access the hard drive. The problem always seems to occur the night before an assignment is due. Describe in 250 words or less the backup strategy you plan to implement in conjunction with your work in this class.

The Threat of Virus Infection

A computer virus is an actively infectious program that attaches itself to other programs and alters the way a computer works. Some viruses do nothing more than display an annoying message at an inopportune time. Most, however, are more harmful, and in the worst case erase all files on the disk. Use your favorite search engine to research the subject of computer viruses in order to answer the following questions: When is a computer subject to infection by a virus? What precautions does your school or university take against the threat of virus infection in its computer lab? What precautions, if any, do you take at home? Can you feel confident that your machine will not be infected if you faithfully use a state-of-the-art antivirus program that was purchased in January 2001?

CHAPTER 2

Gaining Proficiency: The Web and Business Applications

OBJECTIVES

AFTER READING THIS CHAPTER YOU WILL BE ABLE TO:

1. Gain proficiency in the use of relative and absolute references to create a spreadsheet; explain the importance of isolating the assumptions in a worksheet.
2. Use the fill handle to copy a cell formula to a range of adjacent cells.
3. Use pointing to enter a formula; explain the advantage of pointing over explicitly typing cell references.
4. Insert a hyperlink into an Excel worksheet.
5. Save a worksheet as a Web page; explain how the concept of "round trip HTML" applies to editing a Web page.
6. Import data from a Web query into an Excel workbook; explain how to refresh the query to obtain current information.
7. Describe the Today( ) function and its use in date arithmetic.

OVERVIEW

This chapter provides practice in creating a variety of spreadsheets using combinations of relative, absolute, and mixed references. The distinction between the different types of references, coupled with the importance of isolating the assumptions on which a worksheet is based, are two of the most basic concepts in spreadsheet design. You simply cannot use Excel effectively unless you are comfortable with this material.

The chapter also introduces several new capabilities to increase your proficiency in Excel. We begin with pointing, a preferred way to enter a cell formula, and present the fill handle to facilitate copying a formula to other rows or columns within a worksheet. We introduce the Today( ) function and the use of date arithmetic. We also discuss the various Web capabilities that are built into Excel. You will learn how to add a hyperlink to a worksheet and how to save a worksheet as a Web page for viewing in a browser such as Internet Explorer or Netscape Navigator. You will also learn how to create a Web query to download information from the Web directly into an Excel worksheet.

All of this is accomplished through three diverse examples, each of which is a typical illustration of how spreadsheets are used in business. As always, the hands-on exercises provide the opportunity to apply the concepts at the computer.

EMPLOYEE PAYROLL

The spreadsheet in Figure 2.1 shows how Excel can be used to compute a simple payroll. Figure 2.1a shows the displayed values and Figure 2.1b contains the underlying formulas. The concepts necessary to develop the spreadsheet were presented in the previous chapter. The intent here is to reinforce the earlier material, with emphasis on the use of *relative* and ***absolute references*** in the various cell formulas.

The calculation of an individual's gross pay depends on the employment practices of the organization. The formula used in the worksheet is simply an algebraic statement of how employees are paid, in this example, straight time for regular hours, and time-and-a-half for each hour of overtime. The first employee, Adams, earns $400 for 40 regular hours (40 hours at $10/hour) plus $60 for overtime (4 overtime hours × $10/hour × 1.5 for overtime). The formula to compute Adams' gross pay is entered into cell E2 as follows:

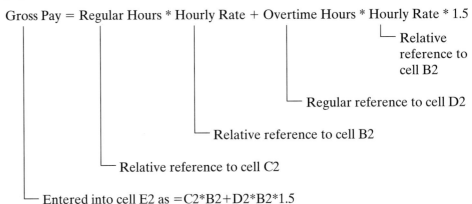

Gross Pay = Regular Hours * Hourly Rate + Overtime Hours * Hourly Rate * 1.5

Relative reference to cell B2

Regular reference to cell D2

Relative reference to cell B2

Relative reference to cell C2

Entered into cell E2 as =C2*B2+D2*B2*1.5

The cell references in the formula are relative references, which means that they will change when copied to another cell. Thus, you can copy the formula in cell E2 to the other rows in column E to compute the gross pay for the other employees. The formula in cell E3, for example, becomes C3*B3+D3*B3*1.5, as can be seen from the displayed formulas in Figure 2.1b.

The withholding tax is computed by multiplying an individual's gross pay by the withholding tax rate. (This is an approximate calculation because the true withholding tax rate is implemented on a sliding scale; that is, the more an individual earns, the higher the tax rate. We use a uniform rate, however, to simplify the example.) The formula in cell F2 to compute the withholding tax uses a combination of relative and absolute references as follows:

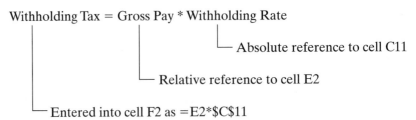

Withholding Tax = Gross Pay * Withholding Rate

Absolute reference to cell C11

Relative reference to cell E2

Entered into cell F2 as =E2*$C$11

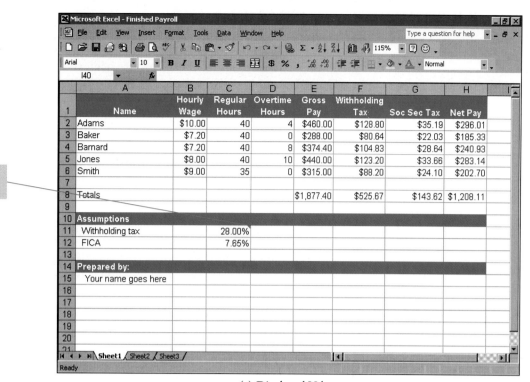

Red triangle indicates a comment

(a) Displayed Values

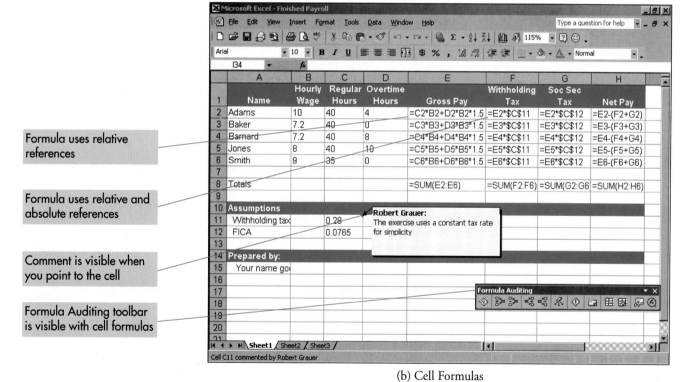

Formula uses relative references

Formula uses relative and absolute references

Comment is visible when you point to the cell

Formula Auditing toolbar is visible with cell formulas

(b) Cell Formulas

FIGURE 2.1   *Payroll*

It is important to emphasize that the formula to compute the withholding tax contains an absolute reference to the tax rate (cell C11), as opposed to the actual constant (.28 in this example). The distinction may seem trivial, but most assuredly it is not, as two important objectives are achieved. First, the user sees those factors that affect the results of the spreadsheet in a separate assumption area (e.g., the withholding rate). Second, the user can change the value in one place, cell C11, then have the change automatically reflected in the calculations for all of the employees. The calculation of the employee's Social Security tax in cell G2 is performed in similar fashion and includes an absolute reference to cell C12.

The remaining formulas in the worksheet are also straightforward. An employee's net pay is computed by subtracting the deductions (the withholding tax and the Social Security tax) from the gross pay. Thus the net pay for the first employee is entered in cell H2 using the formula =E2−(F2+G2). The cell references are relative, which enables us to copy the formula to the remaining rows in column H, and thus calculate the net pay for the other employees.

The employee totals for gross pay, withholding tax, social security tax, and net pay are computed using the SUM function in the appropriate cells in row 8. The formula to compute the gross pay, =SUM(E2:E6), is entered into cell E8, after which it is copied to the remaining cells in row 8.

Pointing

Any cell reference can be entered into a formula by typing the address explicitly into a cell. Entering addresses in this way is not recommended, however, because it is all too easy to make a mistake, such as typing A40 when you really mean A41. *Pointing* to the cell is a more accurate method, since you use the mouse (or arrow keys) to select the cell directly when you build the formula. In essence you 1) Click in the cell that will contain the formula, 2) Type an equal sign to begin entering the formula, and 3) Click in the cell you want to reference. You then type any arithmetic operator, then continue pointing to additional cells using the steps we just described. And finally, you press the enter key to complete the formula. It's easier than it sounds and you get to practice in our next exercise.

The Fill Handle

There are several ways to copy the contents of a cell. You can use the Copy and Paste buttons on the Standard toolbar, the associated keyboard shortcuts, and/or the corresponding commands in the Edit menu. You can also use the *fill handle*, a tiny black square that appears in the lower-right corner of a selected cell. All you do is 1) Select the cell or cells to be copied, 2) Point to the fill handle for the selected cell(s), which changes the mouse pointer to a thin crosshair, 3) Click and drag the fill handle over the destination range, and 4) Release the mouse to complete the operation. (The fill handle can be used to copy only to adjacent cells.) Again, it's easier than it sounds, and as you may have guessed, it's time for our next hands-on exercise in which you build the payroll worksheet in Figure 2.1.

Comments

The *Insert Comment command* creates the equivalent of a screen tip that displays information about the worksheet. Cell C11 in Figure 2.1a contains a tiny red triangle to indicate the presence of a comment, which appears as a screen tip when you point to the cell, as shown in Figure 2.1b. (An option can be set to display the comment permanently, but most people opt for just the triangle.) Comments may be subsequently edited, or deleted altogether if they are no longer appropriate.

Objective Develop a spreadsheet for a simplified payroll to illustrate relative and absolute references. Use pointing to enter formulas and the fill handle to copy formulas. Use Figure 2.2 as a guide in the exercise.

Step 1: **Compute the Gross Pay**

➤ Start Excel. Open the **Payroll workbook** in the **Exploring Excel folder** to display the worksheet in Figure 2.2a.
➤ Save the workbook as **Finished Payroll** so that you may return to the original workbook if necessary.
➤ Click in cell **E2**, the cell that contains the gross pay for the first employee. Press the **equal sign** on the keyboard to begin pointing, click in cell **C2** (which produces a moving border around the cell), press the **asterisk key**, then click in cell **B2**. You have entered the first part of the formula to compute an employee's gross pay.
➤ Press the **plus sign**, click in cell **D2**, press the **asterisk**, click in cell **B2**, press the **asterisk**, type **1.5**, then press **enter**. You should see 460 as the displayed value for cell E2.
➤ Click in cell **E2**, then check to be sure that the formula you entered matches the formula in the formula bar in Figure 2.2a. If necessary, click in the formula bar and make the appropriate changes so that you have the correct formula in cell E2.
➤ Save the workbook.

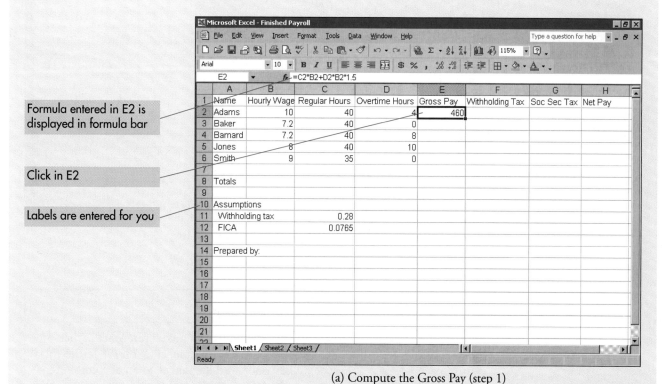

(a) Compute the Gross Pay (step 1)

FIGURE 2.2 *Hands-on Exercise 1*

Step 2: **Complete the Calculations**

➤ Click in cell **F2**, the cell that contains the withholding tax for the first employee. Press the **equal sign** on the keyboard to begin pointing, then click in cell **E2**, the cell that contains the employee's gross pay.

➤ Press the **asterisk key**, then click in cell **C11**, the cell that contains the withholding tax. Cell F2 should now contain the formula, =E2*C11, but this is not quite correct.

➤ Check that the insertion point (the flashing vertical line) is within (or immediately behind) the reference to cell C11, then press the **F4 key** to change the cell reference to $C$11 as shown in Figure 2.2b.

➤ Press **enter**. The displayed value in cell F2 should be 128.8, corresponding to the withholding tax for this employee.

➤ Use pointing to enter the remaining formulas for the first employee. Click in cell **G2**, then enter the formula **=E2*$C$12**. The displayed value is 35.19, corresponding to the Social Security Tax.

➤ Click in cell **H2**, and enter the formula **=E2−(F2+G2)**. The displayed value is 296.01, corresponding to the net pay for this individual.

➤ Save the workbook.

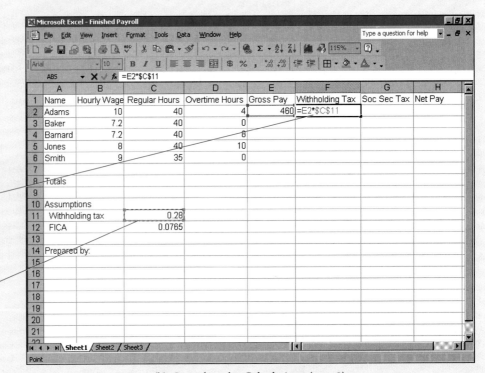

Enter formula in F2 that references E2 and C11

Moving border indicates cell selected during pointing operation

(b) Complete the Calculations (step 2)

FIGURE 2.2 *Hands-on Exercise 1 (continued)*

THE F4 KEY

The F4 key cycles through relative, absolute, and mixed references. Click on any reference within the formula bar; for example, click on A1 in the formula =A1+A2. Press the F4 key once, and it changes to an absolute reference. Press the F4 key a second time, and it becomes a mixed reference, A$1; press it again, and it is a different mixed reference, $A1. Press the F4 key a fourth time, and return to the original relative reference, A1.

Step 3: **Copy the Formulas**

➤ Click in cell **E2**, then click and drag to select cells **E2:H2**, as shown in Figure 2.2c. Point to the **fill handle** in the lower-right corner of cell H2. The mouse pointer changes to a thin crosshair.

➤ Drag the **fill handle** to cell H6 (the lower-right cell in the range of employee calculations). A dim border appears as you drag the fill handle as shown in Figure 2.2c.

➤ Release the mouse to complete the copy operation. The formulas for the first employee have been copied to the corresponding rows for the other employees.

➤ Click in cell **E3**, the cell containing the gross pay for the second employee. You should see the formula =C3*B3+D3*B3*1.5. Now click in cell **F3**, the cell containing the withholding tax for the second employee.

➤ You should see the formula =E3*$C$11, which contains a relative reference (cell E3) that is adjusted from one row to the next, and an absolute reference (cell $C$11) that remains constant from one employee to the next.

➤ Save the workbook.

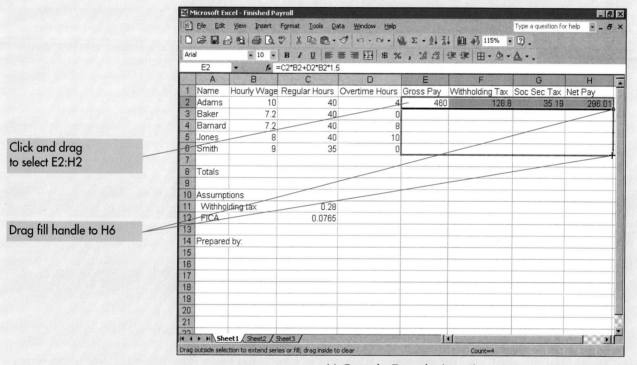

Click and drag to select E2:H2

Drag fill handle to H6

(c) Copy the Formulas (step 3)

FIGURE 2.2 *Hands-on Exercise 1 (continued)*

IT'S ONLY ALGEBRA

There are several ways to enter the formula to compute an employee's gross pay. You could, for example, factor out the hourly rate and enter the formula as =B3*(C3+D3*1.5). It doesn't matter how you enter the formula as long as the results are algebraically correct. What is important is the combination of relative and absolute references, so that the formula is copied correctly from one row to the next.

Step 4: **Compute the Totals**

➤ Click in cell **E8**, the cell that is to contain the total gross pay for all employees. Type the **=sign**, type **SUM(**, then click and drag over cells **E2** through **E6**.

➤ Type a **closing parenthesis**, and then press **enter** to complete the formula. Cell E8 should display the value 1877.4. Now click in cell **E8** and you should see the function, =SUM(E2:E6).

➤ Click and drag the **fill handle** in cell E8 to the remaining cells in this row (cells F8 through H8). Release the mouse to complete the copy operation.

➤ You should see 1208.1069 in cell H8, corresponding to the total net pay for all employees. Click in cell **H8** to view the formula, =SUM(H2:H6), which results from the copy operation.

➤ Save the workbook.

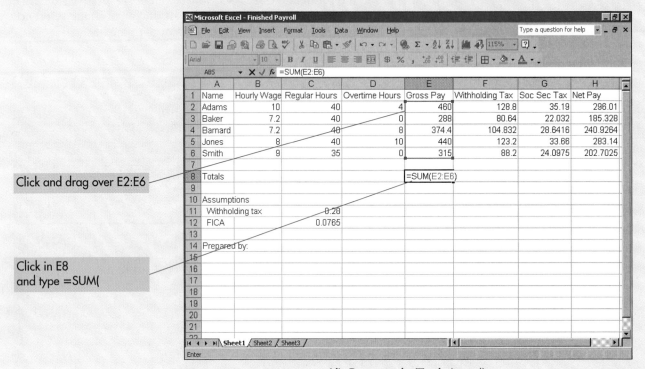

(d) Compute the Totals (step 4)

FIGURE 2.2 *Hands-on Exercise 1 (continued)*

FORMULAS VERSUS FUNCTIONS

There are in essence two ways to compute the total gross pay for all employees, using the SUM function, or the equivalent formula (e.g., =E2+E3+E4+E5+E6). The function is preferable for two reasons. First, it's easier to enter, and therefore less prone to error. Second, the function adjusts automatically to include any additional employees that will be entered within the cell range. Try inserting a new employee between the existing employees in rows 3 and 4, then observe how the values for this employee will be included automatically in the computed totals. The function also adjusts for deleted rows, whereas the formula does not.

Step 5: **Format the Spreadsheet**

➤ Click in cell **B2**, then click and drag to select cells **B2 through B6**. Press and hold the **Ctrl key** as you click and drag to select cells **E2 through H8** (in addition to the previously selected cells).

➤ Pull down the **Format menu** and click the **Cells command** to display the Format Cells dialog box in Figure 2.2e. Click the **Number tab** and choose **Currency** from the Category list box. Specify **2** as the number of decimal places.

➤ If necessary, choose the **$ sign** as the currency symbol. (Note, too, that you can select a variety of alternative symbols such as the British Pound or the Euro symbol for the European Community.) Click **OK** to accept the settings and close the dialog box.

➤ Click and drag to select cells **C11 and C12**, then click the **Percent Style button** on the Formatting toolbar. Click the **Increase/Decrease Decimals buttons** to format each number to two decimal places.

➤ Save the workbook.

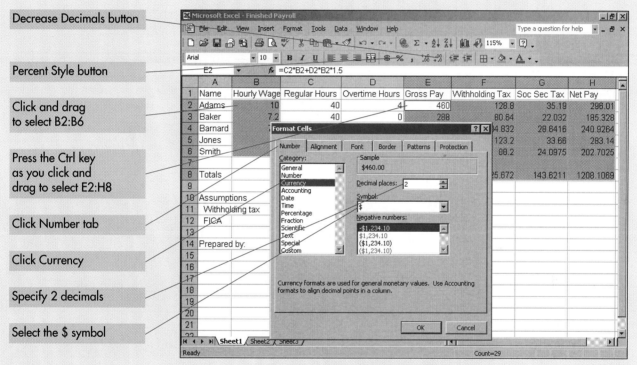

(e) Format the Spreadsheet (step 5)

FIGURE 2.2 *Hands-on Exercise 1 (continued)*

THE FORMAT STYLE COMMAND

A style is a collection of formats such as the font, alignment, and number of decimal places. Common styles, such as percent or currency, are represented by buttons on the Formatting toolbar and are most easily applied by clicking the appropriate tool. You can also apply the style by pulling down the Format menu, clicking the Style command, and selecting the style from the Style Name list box. The latter allows you to modify the definition of existing styles and/or to create a new style.

Step 6: **Complete the Formatting**

> ➤ Click and drag to select cells **A1 though H1**. Press and hold the **Ctrl key**, then click and drag to select **cells A10 through H10** in addition to the cells in row one. Continue to press and hold the **Ctrl key**, then click and drag to select cells **A14 through II14**.
>
> ➤ Click the **Fill Color arrow** on the Formatting toolbar, then select **blue** as the fill color. Click the **Font Color arrow** on the Formatting toolbar, then select **white** as the color for the text. Click the **Bold button** so that the text stands out from the fill color.
>
> ➤ Click and drag to select cells **A1 through H1** (which also deselects the cells in rows 10 and 14). Click the **Right mouse button** to display a context-sensitive menu, then click the **Format Cells command** to display the dialog box in Figure 2.2f.
>
> ➤ Click the **Alignment tab**, then check the box to **Wrap text** in a cell. Click **OK** to accept the settings and close the dialog box.
>
> ➤ Click the **Center button** to center the text as well. Reduce the width of columns C and D. Save the workbook.

Bold button

Click and drag
to select A1:H1

Fill Color button

Font Color button

Press the Ctrl key
as you click and drag
to select A10:H10
and then A14:H14

Wrap text check box

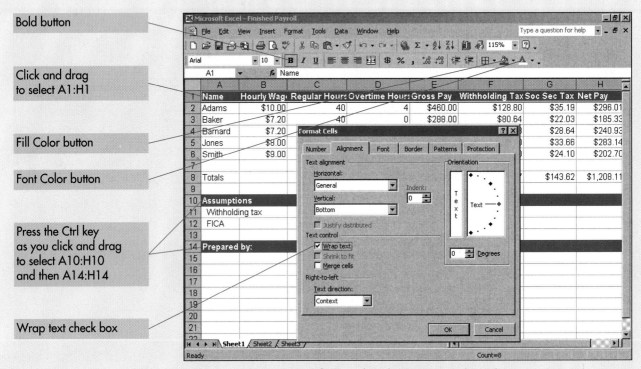

(f) Complete the Formatting (step 6)

FIGURE 2.2   *Hands-on Exercise 1 (continued)*

SORT THE EMPLOYEE LIST

The employees are listed on the worksheet in alphabetical order, but you can rearrange the list according to any other field, such as the net pay. Click a cell containing employee data in the column on which you want to sort, then click the Sort Ascending or Sort Descending button on the Standard toolbar. Click the Undo button if the result is different from what you intended.

Step 7: **The Completed Workbook**

➤ Click in cell **C11**. Pull down the **Insert menu** and click **Comment**, then insert the text of the comment as shown in Figure 2.2g. (The name that appears in the comment box will be different on your system.)

➤ Click in any other cell when you have finished inserting the comment. The text of the comment is no longer visible, but you should still see the tiny triangle. Now point to cell C11 and you see the text of the comment.

➤ Pull down the **File menu** and click the **Page Setup command** to display the Page Setup dialog box. Click the **Page tab**. Click the **Landscape** option **button**. Click the option to **Fit to 1 page**.

➤ Click the **Margins tab**. Check the box to center the worksheet horizontally. Click the **Sheet tab**. Check the boxes to print **Row and Column Headings** and **Gridlines**. Click **OK**. Print the worksheet.

➤ Press **Ctrl+~** to show the cell formulas rather than the displayed values. Adjust the column widths as necessary, then print the worksheet a second time.

➤ Save the workbook. Close the workbook. Exit Excel.

Print Preview button

Triangle appears to indicate a comment

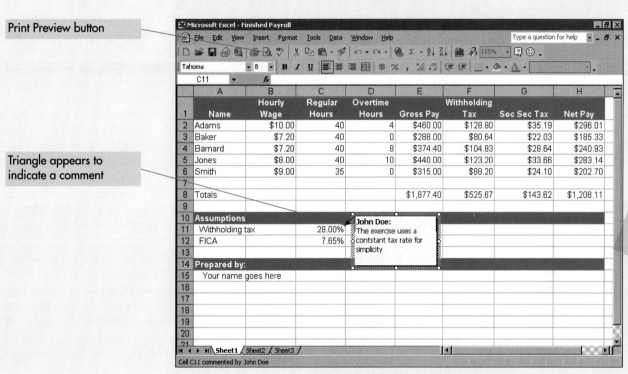

(g) The Completed Workbook (step 7)

FIGURE 2.2 *Hands-on Exercise 1 (continued)*

EDIT AND DELETE COMMENTS

Point to any cell that contains a comment, then click the right mouse button to display a context sensitive menu with commands to edit or delete a comment. (The menu also contains the option to show or hide the comment.) The name that appears within the comment box corresponds to the user name set during installation. Pull down the Tools menu, click the Option command, click the General tab, then go to the User Name area to modify this information.

The ***Internet*** is closely tied to Microsoft Excel 2002 through three basic capabilities. First, you can insert a ***hyperlink*** (a reference to another document) into any Excel worksheet, then view the associated document by clicking the link without having to start your Web browser manually. Second, you can save any Excel workbook as a ***Web page*** (or ***HTML document***), which in turn can be displayed through a Web browser. And finally, you can download information from a Web server directly into an Excel workbook through a ***Web query*** (a capability that we illustrate later in the chapter).

Consider, for example, Figure 2.3a, which contains an Excel worksheet that displays a consolidated statement of earnings for a hypothetical company. The information in this worksheet is typical of what companies publish in their annual report, a document that summarizes the financial performance of a corporation. Every public corporation is required by law to publish this type of information so that investors may evaluate the strength of the company. The annual report is mailed to the shareholders and it is typically available online as well.

The worksheet in Figure 2.3a is easy to create, and you do not have to be a business major to understand the information. Indeed, if you have any intention of investing in the stock market, you should be able to analyze the data in the worksheet, which conveys basic information about the financial strength of a company to potential investors. In essence, the worksheet shows the sales for the company in the current year, subtracts the expenses to obtain the earnings before taxes, displays the income taxes that were paid, then arrives at the net earnings after taxes.

The worksheet also contains a calculation that divides the net earnings for the company by the number of shares to determine the earnings per share (a number that is viewed closely by investors). There is also comparable information for the previous year in order to show the increase or decrease for each item. And finally, the worksheet contains a hyperlink or reference to a specific Web site, such as the home page for the corporation. You can click the link from within Excel, and provided you have an Internet connection, your Web browser will display the associated page. Once you click the link, its color will change, just as it would if you were viewing the page in Netscape Navigator or Internet Explorer.

The Web page in Figure 2.3b is, for all intents and purposes, identical to the worksheet in Figure 2.3a. Look closely, however, and you will see that the Web page in Figure 2.3b is displayed in Internet Explorer, whereas the worksheet in Figure 2.3a is displayed in Microsoft Excel. Excel contains the ***Save as Web Page command***, whereby a worksheet is converted to a Web page (or HTML document). The page can be uploaded to the Internet, but it can also be viewed from a PC or local area network, as was done in Figure 2.3b. Use the ***Web Page Preview command*** in the File menu to view the page, or open the page directly in your browser.

Our next exercise has you create the worksheet in Figure 2.3a, after which you create the HTML document in Figure 2.3b. All applications in Office XP incorporate a concept known as ***round trip HTML***, which means that you can subsequently edit the Web page in the application that created it originally. In other words, you start with an Excel worksheet, save it as a Web page, then you can open the Web page and return to Excel in order to edit the document.

WHAT IS HTML?

Most Web documents are written in HTML (HyperText Markup Language), a universal standard that is recognized by both Internet Explorer and Netscape Navigator. The Address bar of a Web browser displays the document name and extension. The latter may appear as either html or htm, depending on how the Web document was created initially. The distinction is immaterial.

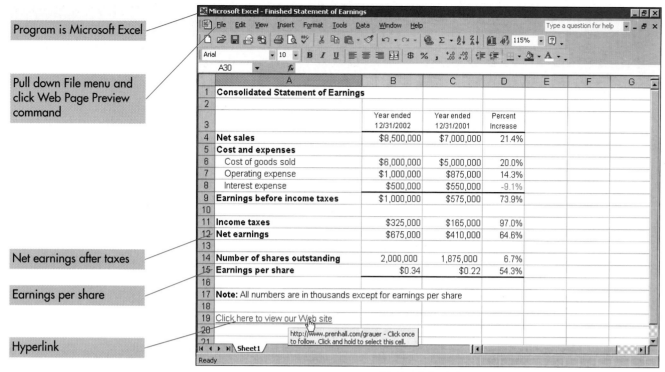

Program is Microsoft Excel

Pull down File menu and click Web Page Preview command

Net earnings after taxes

Earnings per share

Hyperlink

(a) Excel Worksheet

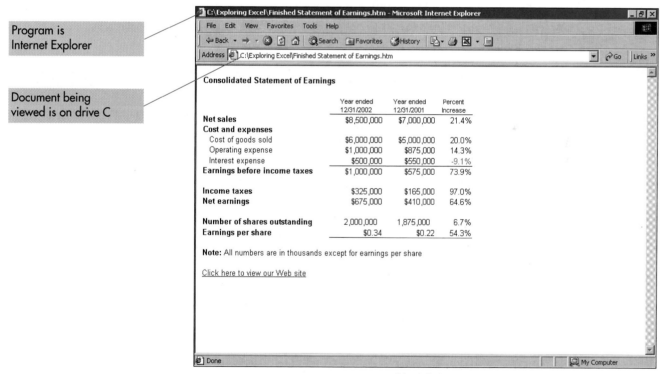

Program is Internet Explorer

Document being viewed is on drive C

(b) Web Page

FIGURE 2.3   *Consolidated Statement of Earnings*

CREATING A WEB PAGE

Objective   To insert a hyperlink into an Excel workbook; to save a workbook as an HTML document, then subsequently edit the Web page. Use Figure 2.4 as a guide in the exercise.

Step 1:   **Compute the Net Earnings**

> ➤ Open the **Statement of Earnings workbook** in the **Exploring Excel** folder. Save the workbook as **Finished Statement of Earnings** so that you can always go back to the original workbook if necessary.
> ➤ We have entered the labels and data for you, but you have to create the formulas. Click in cell **B9**. Type an **equal sign**, then click in cell **B4** to begin the pointing operation.
> ➤ Type a **minus sign**, type **SUM(**, then click and drag to select cells **B6 through B8** as shown in Figure 2.4a.
> ➤ Type a **closing parenthesis**, then press the **enter key** to complete the formula. You should see 1000000 as the displayed value in cell B4.
> ➤ Click in cell **B12**, then use pointing to enter the formula for net earnings, **=B9−B11**.
> ➤ Click in cell **B15**, then use pointing to enter the formula for earnings per share, **=B12/B14**.
> ➤ Copy the formulas in cells B9, B12, and B15 to the corresponding cells in column C. You have to copy the formulas one at a time.
> ➤ Save the workbook.

Click in B4 to enter that address in formula; then type −SUM(

Click and drag to select B6:B8

Click in B9 and type =

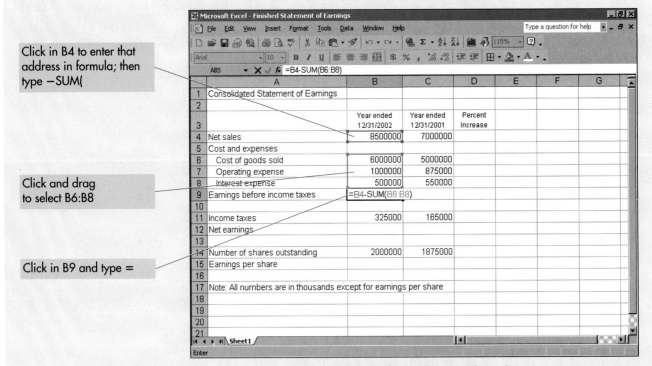

(a) Compute the Net Earnings (step 1)

FIGURE 2.4   *Hands-on Exercise 2*

Step 2: **Compute the Percent Increases**

➤ Click in cell **D4**, then enter the formula to compute the percent increase from the previous year. Use pointing to enter the formula, **=(B4-C4)/C4**.

➤ You should see .214288 as the displayed value in cell D4 as shown in Figure 2.4b. Do not worry about formatting at this time.

➤ Click in cell **D4**. Click the **Copy button** on the Standard toolbar (or use the **Ctrl+C** keyboard shortcut) to copy the contents of this cell to the clipboard. You should see a moving border around cell D4.

➤ Press and hold the **Ctrl key** to select cells **D6 through D9**, **D11 and D12**, and **D14 and D15** as shown in Figure 2.4b. (We have selected a noncontiguous range of cells, because we do not want to copy the formula to cells D10 or D13.)

➤ Click the **Paste button** on the Standard toolbar (or use the **Ctrl+V** keyboard shortcut) to paste the contents of cell D4 into these cells. Ignore the Paste Options button if it appears.

➤ Press the **Esc key** to remove the moving border around cell D4.

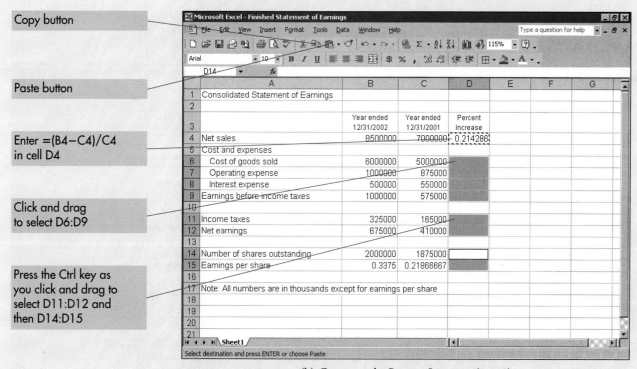

(b) Compute the Percent Increases (step 2)

FIGURE 2.4   *Hands-on Exercise 2 (continued)*

USE POINTING TO ENTER CELL FORMULAS

A cell reference can be typed directly into a formula, or it can be entered more easily through pointing. The latter is also more accurate as you use the mouse or arrow keys to reference cells directly. To use pointing, select (click) the cell to contain the formula, type an equal sign to begin entering the formula, click (or move to) the cell containing the reference, then press the F4 key as necessary to change from relative to absolute references. Type any arithmetic operator to place the cell reference in the formula, then continue pointing to additional cells. Press the enter key to complete the formula.

Step 3: **Format the Worksheet**

➤ Format the worksheet as shown in Figure 2.4c. Click in cell **A1**, then press and hold the **Ctrl key** to select cells **A4, A5, A9, A11, A12, A14, and A15**. Click the **Bold button** on the Formatting toolbar (or use the **Ctrl+B** keyboard shortcut).

➤ Double click in cell **A17**, then click and drag **Note:** within the cell to select this portion of the label. Press **Ctrl+B** to boldface the selected text.

➤ Remember that boldfacing the contents of a cell functions as a toggle switch; that is, click the Boldface button and the text is bold. Click the button a second time and the boldface is removed.

➤ Select cells **B3 through D3, B8 through D8,** and **B15 through D15** as shown in Figure 2.4c. Click the **down arrow** on the Borders button on the Formatting toolbar to display the available borders. Click the bottom border icon to implement this formatting in the selected cells.

➤ Complete the formatting in the remainder of the worksheet by using currency, comma, and percent formats as appropriate. Save the workbook.

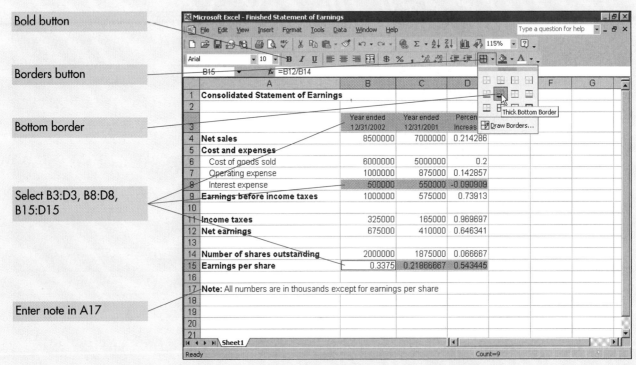

(c) Format the Worksheet (step 3)

FIGURE 2.4   *Hands-on Exercise 2 (continued)*

THE FORMAT PAINTER

The Format Painter copies the formatting of the selected cell to other cells in the worksheet. Click the cell whose formatting you want to copy, then double click the Format Painter button on the Standard toolbar. The mouse pointer changes to a paintbrush to indicate that you can copy the current formatting; just click and drag the paintbrush over the cells that you want to assume the formatting of the original cell. Repeat the painting process as often as necessary, then click the Format Painter button a second time to return to normal editing.

Step 4: **Conditional Formatting**

➤ Click and drag to select cells **D4 through D15**, the cells that contain the percentage increase from the previous year. Pull down the **Format menu** and click the **Conditional Formatting command** to display the Conditional Formatting dialog box.
➤ Check that the Condition 1 list box displays Cell Value Is. Click the **down arrow** in the relationship list box and choose **less than**. Press **Tab** to move to the next list box and enter a **zero** as shown in Figure 2.4d.
➤ Click the **Format button** to display the Format Cells dialog box. Click the **Font tab**, click the **down arrow** on the Color list box and choose **Red**. Click **OK** to close the Format Cells dialog box.
➤ Click **OK** to close the Conditional Formatting dialog box. The decrease in the interest expense should be displayed in red as −9.1%.
➤ Save the workbook.

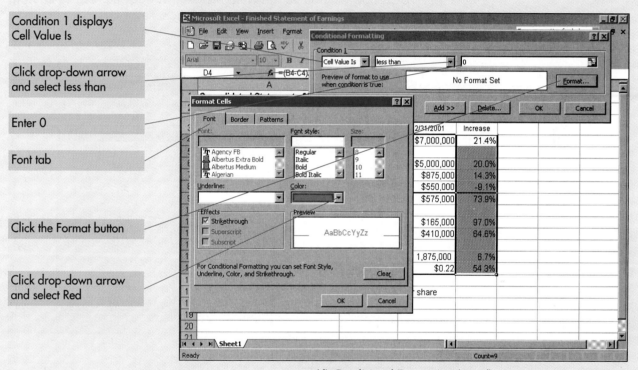

(d) Conditional Formatting (step 4)

FIGURE 2.4   *Hands-on Exercise 2 (continued)*

ADDING MULTIPLE CONDITIONS

Use the Conditional Formatting command to impose additional conditions with alternative formats depending on the value within a cell. You can, for example, display negative values in red (as was done in this example) and positive values (above a certain number) in blue. Pull down the Format menu and click the Conditional Formatting command, then click the Add button within the dialog box to add the additional conditions. Conditional formatting is a lesser-known feature that adds significantly to the appearance of a worksheet.

Step 5: **Insert the Hyperlink**

➤ Click in cell **A19**. Pull down the **Insert menu** and click the **Hyperlink command** (or click the **Insert Hyperlink button** on the Standard toolbar) to display the Insert Hyperlink dialog box in Figure 2.4e. Click in the **Text to display** text box and enter **Click here to view our Web site**.

➤ Click **Existing File or Web Page**, then click the button for **Browsed Pages**, then click in the Address text box (toward the bottom of the dialog box) and enter the Web address such as **www.prenhall.com/grauer** (the http:// is assumed). Click **OK** to accept the settings and close the dialog box.

➤ The hyperlink should appear as an underlined entry in the worksheet. Point to the hyperlink (the Web address should appear as a ScreenTip), then click the link to start your browser and view the Web page. You need an Internet connection to see the actual page.

➤ You are now running two applications, Excel and the Web browser, each of which has its own button on the Windows taskbar. Click the **Excel button** to continue working (and correct the hyperlink if necessary).

➤ Save the workbook.

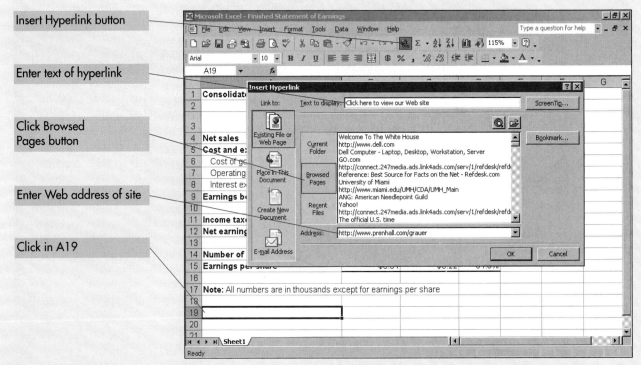

(e) Insert the Hyperlink (step 5)

FIGURE 2.4 *Hands-on Exercise 2 (continued)*

SELECTING (EDITING) A HYPERLINK

In an ideal world, you will enter all the information for a hyperlink correctly on the first attempt. But what if you make a mistake and need to edit the information? You cannot select a hyperlink by clicking it, because that displays the associated Web page. You can, however, right click the cell containing the hyperlink to display a context-sensitive menu, then click the Edit Hyperlink command to display the associated dialog box in which to make the necessary changes.

Step 6: **Save the Web Page**

➤ Pull down the **File menu** and click the **Save as Web Page command** to display the Save As dialog box in Figure 2.4f. Note the following:
  • The Exploring Excel folder is entered automatically as the default folder, since that is the location of the original workbook.
  • Finished Statement of Earnings is entered automatically as the name of the Web page, corresponding to the name of the workbook, Finished Statement of Earnings.
  • It does not matter whether you save the entire workbook or a single sheet, since the workbook contains only a single sheet. However, you need to specify a single sheet if and when you want to add interactivity (i.e., Excel functionality) when the page is opened through a Web browser.
➤ Click the **Save button**. There are now two versions of the workbook on disk, both with the same name (Finished Statement of Earnings), but with different extensions, html and xls, corresponding to a Web page and Excel workbook, respectively.
➤ Close Microsoft Excel. (We will restart the application later in the exercise.)

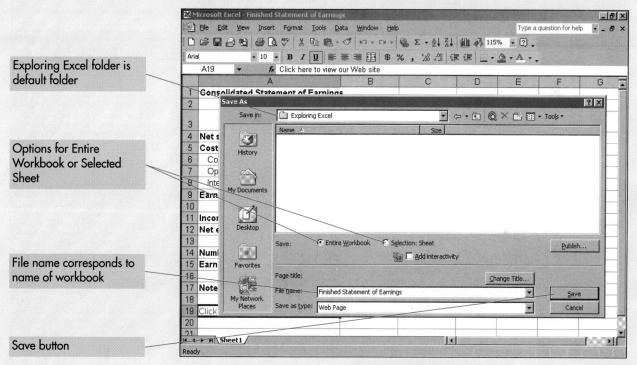

Exploring Excel folder is default folder

Options for Entire Workbook or Selected Sheet

File name corresponds to name of workbook

Save button

(f) Save the Web Page (step 6)

FIGURE 2.4   *Hands-on Exercise 2 (continued)*

CHANGE THE DEFAULT FILE LOCATION

The default file location is the folder Excel uses to open and save a workbook unless it is otherwise instructed. To change the default location, pull down the Tools menu, click Options, and click the General tab. Enter the name of the new folder (e.g., C:\Exploring Excel) in the Default File Location text box, then click OK. The next time you access the Open or Save command from the File menu, the Look In text box will reflect the change.

Step 7:   **Start Windows Explorer**

> ➤ Click the **Start button**, start **Windows Explorer**, then change to the Exploring Excel folder. The location of this folder depends on whether you have your own computer.
>   • If you are working from a floppy disk, select drive A in the left pane.
>   • If you are working on your own computer, select drive C in the left pane, then scroll until you can select the Exploring Excel folder.
> ➤ Either way, you should see the contents of the Exploring Excel folder in the right pane as shown in Figure 2.4g. As indicated, there are two versions of the Finished Statement of Earnings, with different icons and file types.
> ➤ Right click the file with the Excel icon and file type to display a shortcut menu, then click the **Delete command** to delete this file. You do not need the Excel workbook any longer because you can edit the workbook from the Web page through the concept of round trip HTML.
> ➤ Double click the Web page version of the earnings statement to view the document in your default browser.

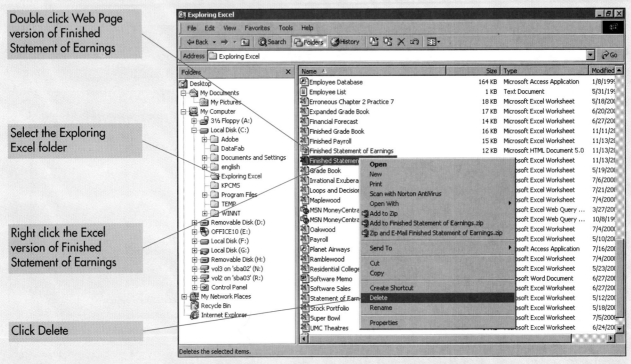

(g) Start Windows Explorer (step 7)

FIGURE 2.4   *Hands-on Exercise 2 (continued)*

ROUND TRIP HTML

Each application in Microsoft Office XP lets you open an HTML document in both Internet Explorer and the application that created the Web page initially. In other words, you can start with an Excel worksheet and use the Save as Web Page command to convert the document to a Web page, then view that page in a Web browser. You can then reopen the Web page in Excel (the application that created it initially) with full access to all Excel commands in order to edit the document.

Step 8: **View the Web Page**

➤ You should see the Finished Statement of Earnings displayed within Internet Explorer (or Netscape Navigator) as shown in Figure 2.4h. The Web page looks identical to the worksheet that was displayed earlier in Excel.

➤ Click the hyperlink to view the Web site that was inserted through the Insert Hyperlink command. You should see our Web site (**www.prenhall.com/grauer**) if that was the address you used earlier.

➤ Click the **Back button** on the Standard Buttons toolbar to return to the Finished Earnings Web page. Look carefully at the Address bar and note that unlike other Web documents, this page is displayed from your local system (drive C or drive A), depending on the location of the file.

➤ Click the **Edit with Microsoft Excel button** on the Standard Buttons toolbar to start Excel in order to modify the Web page.

➤ Both applications, Internet Explorer and Microsoft Excel, are open as can be seen by the taskbar, which contains buttons for both.

Program is
Internet Explorer

Back button

Address bar indicates
page is on local hard drive

Edit with
Microsoft Excel button

Click hyperlink

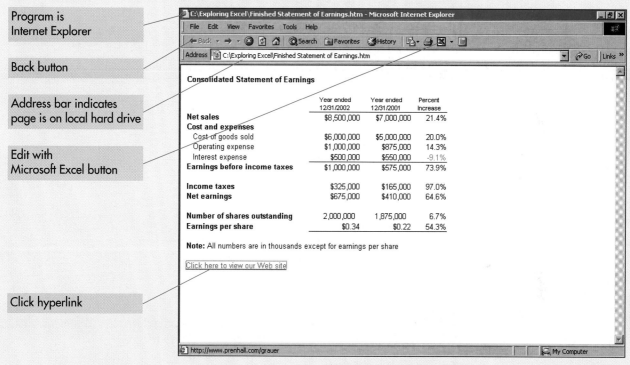

(h) View the Web Page (step 8)

FIGURE 2.4   *Hands-on Exercise 2 (continued)*

MULTITASKING

Multitasking, the ability to run multiple applications at the same time, is one of the primary advantages of the Windows environment. Minimizing an application is different from closing it, and you want to minimize, rather than close, an application to take advantage of multitasking. Closing an application removes it from memory so that you have to restart the application if you want to return to it later in the session. Minimizing, however, leaves the application open in memory, but shrinks its window to a button on the Windows taskbar.

Step 9: **Edit the Web Page**

> ➤ You should be back in Microsoft Excel as shown in Figure 2.4i. Click in cell **A21** and enter the label, **Prepared by**, followed by your name.
> ➤ Save the worksheet.
> ➤ Click the **Internet Explorer button** on the toolbar to return to your browser. The change you made (the addition of your name) is not yet visible because the browser displays the previous version of the page.
> ➤ Click the **Refresh button** on the Standard Buttons toolbar to bring in the most current version of the worksheet. Your changes should now be visible.
> ➤ Pull down the **File menu** (within Internet Explorer) and click the **Print command**, then click the **Print command button** to print the Web page for your instructor.
> ➤ Close Internet Explorer. Exit Excel if you do not wish to continue with the next exercise at this time.

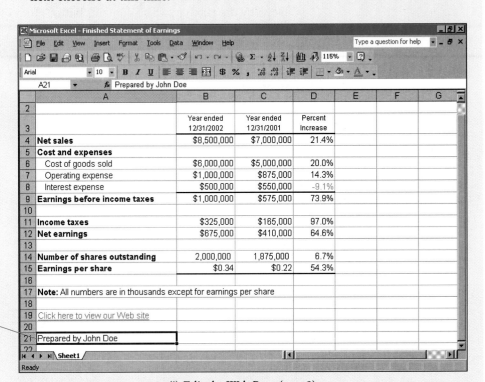

(i) Edit the Web Page (step 9)

FIGURE 2.4 *Hands-on Exercise 2 (continued)*

USE A TEMPLATE

A template is a partially completed workbook that is used to create other workbooks. It typically contains formulas and formatting but no specific data. Thus you open a template and enter the information that is specific to your application, then you save the template as an ordinary workbook. Excel provides several business templates. See practice exercise 11 at the end of the chapter.

Our next example is a worksheet to maintain a stock portfolio and compute the gain or loss associated with investment. The worksheet in Figure 2.5 lists several stocks, each with its recognized symbol, and records the purchase price, number of shares, and date of purchase of each investment. This information is "fixed" for each stock at the time of purchase. The worksheet then uses the current (today's) price to determine the gain or loss. It also uses today's date to compute the length of time the investment was held. The interesting thing about the worksheet is that the current price is entered into the worksheet via a Web query, a capability that enables Excel to go to a specific site on the Web to retrieve the information.

The top half of the worksheet is typical of the worksheets we have studied thus far. The bottom portion (from row 14 down) represents the result of the Web query, which is entered into the worksheet via the *Import External Data command*. Execution of this command prompts you for the location of the result (e.g., cell A14 in Figure 2.5) and the location of the parameters (or stock symbols), for which you want to determine the price (cells A5 through A10 in this example). Excel does the rest and places the results of the query into the worksheet. The results of the query can be continually updated through the *Refresh command*, which is represented by the exclamation point button on the *External Data toolbar*.

The worksheet in Figure 2.5 also illustrates the use of *date arithmetic* to determine the length of time an investment is held. (This is an important consideration for investors who can reduce their tax liability through a capital gains tax break on investments held for more than one year.) Date arithmetic is made possible through a simple concept by which Excel stores all dates as integers (serial numbers) beginning with January 1, 1900. Thus, January 1, 1900 is stored as the number 1, January 2, 1900 as the number 2, and so on. December 27, 1999 (the purchase date of DIS) is stored as 36521 as can be seen by comparing the contents of cell B5 in Figures 2.5a and 2.5b, respectively.

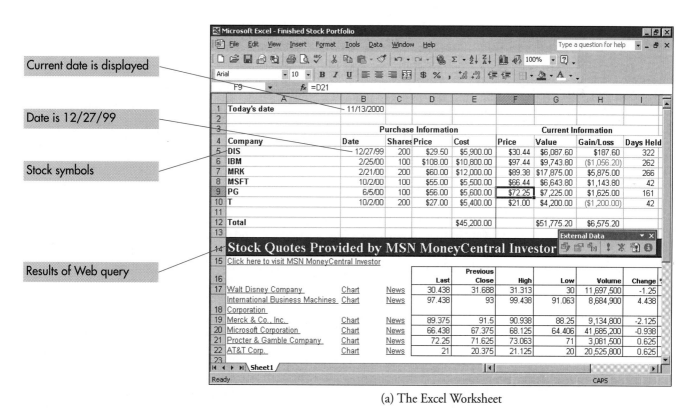

(a) The Excel Worksheet

FIGURE 2.5 *Web Queries*

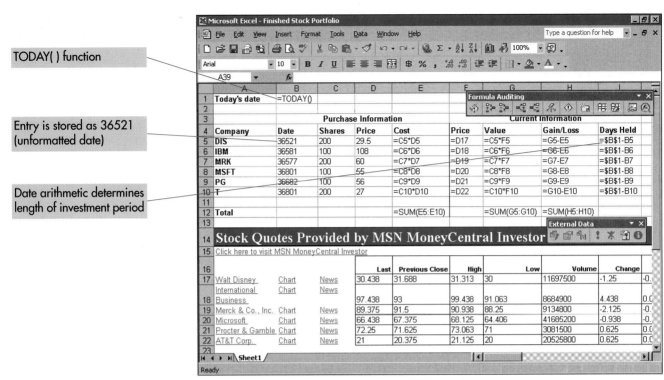

TODAY( ) function

Entry is stored as 36521 (unformatted date)

Date arithmetic determines length of investment period

(b) Cell Formulas

FIGURE 2.5 *Web Queries (continued)*

The **Today( ) function** returns the current date (i.e., the date on which the spreadsheet is opened). If, for example, you entered the Today( ) function into a spreadsheet that was created on May 14, and you opened the spreadsheet a month later, the value of the function would be automatically updated to June 14. The fact that dates are stored as integers enables you to add or subtract two different dates and/or to use a date in any type of arithmetic computation. A person's age can be computed by subtracting the date of birth from today's date, and dividing the result by 365.

In similar fashion, you can subtract the purchase date of an investment from today's date to determine the number of days the investment was held. Look now at the formula in cell I5 of Figure 2.5b, which subtracts the date of purchase (cell B5) from an absolute reference to today's date (cell B1) to compute the length of the investment. The formula in cell I5 (=$B$1 − B5) can then be copied to the remaining rows in column I to determine the length of each investment.

A date is entered in different ways, most easily by typing the date in conventional fashion such as 12/31/99 or 12/31/1999. If you specify a two-digit year, then any year from 00 to 29, is assumed to be in the 21st century; for example, 1/21/00, will be stored as January 21, 2000. (The number 29 is arbitrary and you will have to ask Microsoft why it was chosen.) Any year between 30 and 99 is stored as a date in the 20th century. Thus, 3/23/48 would be stored as March 23, 1948. To avoid confusion, you should enter all four digits of the year—for example, 10/31/2001 for October 31, 2001.

YOU MUST UNDERSTAND THE PROBLEM

The formulas to compute the cost of an investment, its current value, the associated gain or loss, and the number of days the investment was held have nothing to do with Excel per se. Neither did the formulas to compute the gross pay, net pay, and so on in the payroll example. In other words, Excel is a means to an end, rather than an end unto itself, and you must understand the underlying problem if you are to use Excel successfully.

WEB QUERIES

Objective Include a Web query into a worksheet to retrieve current stock prices from the Internet. (The exercise requires an Internet connection.) Use the Today( ) function to illustrate the use of date arithmetic. Use Figure 2.6 as a guide in the exercise.

Step 1: **Open the Stock Portfolio**

> ➤ Open the **Stock Portfolio workbook** in the **Exploring Excel folder** to display the worksheet in Figure 2.6a.
> ➤ Save the workbook as **Finished Stock Portfolio** so that you can return to the original workbook if necessary.
> ➤ Cell **B1** displays today's date 11/13/2000 in our figure, but a different date on your machine. If necessary, click in cell **B1**, and note that it contains the function, **=Today( )**. Thus the displayed value in cell B1 will always reflect the current date.
> ➤ Click in cell **B5**, the cell containing the date on which the shares in DIS were purchased. The contents of cell B5 are 12/27/1999 (there is no equal sign). This is a "fixed" date and its value will not change from one day to the next.
> ➤ Pull down the **Data menu**, click **the Import External Data command**, then choose **Import Data command** to display the Select Data Source dialog box in Figure 2.6a.
> ➤ Choose the **MSN MoneyCentral Investor Stock Quotes** query, then click the **Open button**.

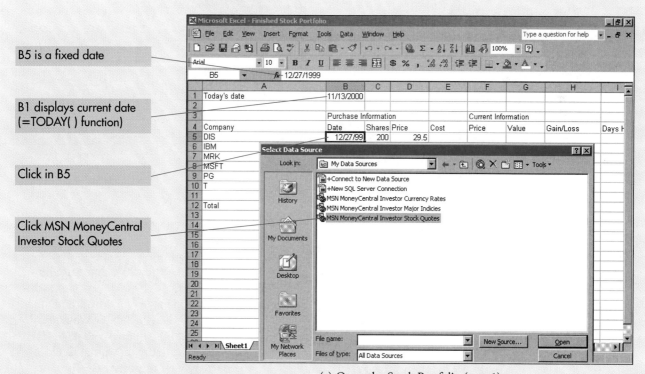

B5 is a fixed date

B1 displays current date (=TODAY( ) function)

Click in B5

Click MSN MoneyCentral Investor Stock Quotes

(a) Open the Stock Portfolio (step 1)

FIGURE 2.6 *Hands-on Exercise 3*

Step 2:   **Complete the Web Query**

> ➤ The Import Data dialog box opens and prompts you for information about the Web query. Click the option button to put the data into the existing worksheet, then click in cell **A14** to indicate the location within the current worksheet. Click **OK**.
> ➤ Click and drag to select cells A5 through A10, as the cells containing the stock symbols as shown in Figure 2.6b. Check the box to use this value reference for future refreshes. Click **OK**.
> ➤ Your system will pause as Excel goes to the Web to retrieve the information, provided you have an Internet connection. You should then see the stock quotes provided by MSN Money Central Investor.
> ➤ Do not be concerned if the column widths change as a result of the query. (You can widen them later.)
> ➤ Save the workbook.

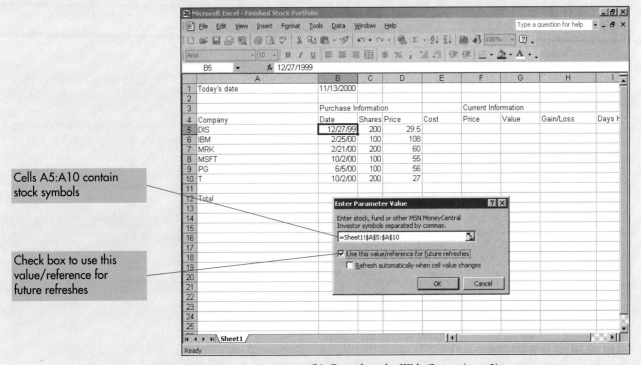

Cells A5:A10 contain stock symbols

Check box to use this value/reference for future refreshes

(b) Complete the Web Query (step 2)

FIGURE 2.6   *Hands-on Exercise 3 (continued)*

CREATE A NEW WEB QUERY

Web queries were available in both Office 97 and Office 2000, but were limited in that you had to use existing queries. Office XP, however, makes it easy to create new queries from virtually any Web page. Pull down the Data menu, click the Import External Data command, then click New Web query to display the associated dialog box. Enter the address of any Web page (try your favorite professional sport) that contains the data you want, then look for the yellow arrows that indicate the data may be imported. See practice exercise 10 at the end of the chapter.

Step 3:   **Compute the Gain/Loss**

➤ You should see the information that was obtained via the Web query as shown in Figure 2.6c. Use pointing to enter the cell references to complete the formulas for the first investment.
  • Click in cell **E5** (the cell that contains the cost of the investment) and enter the formula, **=C5*D5**.
  • Click in cell **F5** (the cell that contains today's price), and enter the formula **=D17**, which references the cell that contains the current price of DIS.
  • Click in cell **G5** (the cell that contains today's value of the investment) and enter the formula, **=C5*F5**.
  • Click in cell **H5** (the cell that contains the gain or loss) and enter the formula, **=G5−E5**, corresponding to today's value minus the cost.
  • Click in cell **I5** (the cell that contains the days held) and enter the formula, **=$B$1−B5**.
➤ If necessary, change the format in cell I5 to reflect a number, rather than a date. Click in cell **I5**, pull down the **Format menu**, click the **Cells command**, click the **Number tab**, choose **Number** as the category, and specify **zero decimal places**.
➤ Save the workbook.

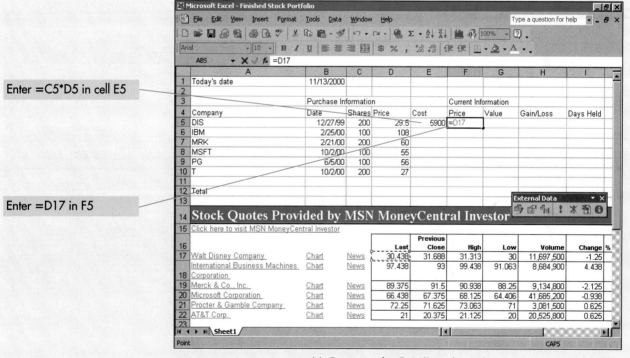

Enter =C5*D5 in cell E5

Enter =D17 in F5

(c) Compute the Gain/Loss (step 3)

FIGURE 2.6   *Hands-on Exercise 3 (continued)*

NUMBERS, DATES, AND FORMATS

Any cell that contains a numeric value may be formatted in a variety of styles such as date, number, percentage, currency, and so on. Excel does not know which format to use, and thus it is up to the user to select the cell, pull down the Format menu, click the Cells command to display the Format cells dialog box, click the Number tab, then choose the appropriate category.

Step 4: **Copy the Formulas**

➤ Click and drag to select cells **E5 through I5**, the cells containing the formulas associated with the first investment, as shown in Figure 2.6d.

➤ Point to the fill handle in the lower-right corner of cell I5, then click and drag the fill handle to copy the formulas in row 5 to rows 6 through 10. Release the mouse to complete the copy operation.

➤ Click in cell **E12**, the cell that contains the total cost of your investments. Type **=SUM(** then click and drag to select cells **E5:E10**.

➤ Type a **closing parenthesis**, then press the **enter key**. Cell E12 should contain the formula **=SUM(E5:E10)**.

➤ Copy the formula in cell **E12** to cells **G12 and H12**. The displayed value in cell E12 should be 45200. The displayed values in cells G12 and H12 depend on the current stock prices.

➤ Save the workbook.

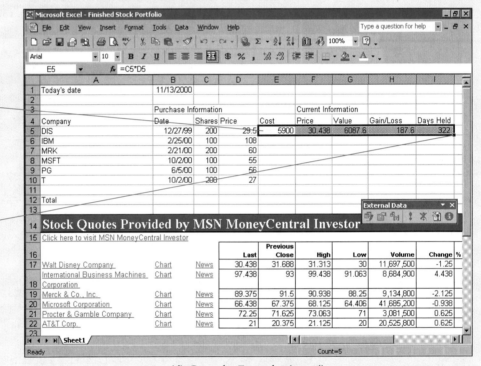

Click and drag to select E5:I5

Click and drag the fill handle to I10

(d) Copy the Formulas (step 4)

FIGURE 2.6 *Hands-on Exercise 3 (continued)*

EDITING A CELL FORMULA

The fastest way to change the contents of a cell is to double click in the cell (or press the F2 key), then make the changes directly in the cell rather than to change the entries on the formula bar. Note, too, that if the cell contains a formula (as opposed to a literal entry), Excel will display each cell reference in the formula in a different color, which corresponds to border colors of the referenced cells elsewhere in the worksheet. This makes it easy to see which cell or cell range is referenced by the formula.

Step 5: **Format the Worksheet**

➤ Click and drag to select cells **D5 through H12**, the cells that contain dollar amounts. Pull down the **Format menu**, click the **Cells command** to display the Format Cells dialog box, then click the **Number tab**. Format these cells in **Currency format**, with **two decimal places**. Display negative values in **red** and enclosed in **parentheses**. Click **OK**.

➤ Select all of the cells that contain a label (cell **A1**, cells **A3 through I4**, **A4 through A10**, and cell **A12**). Click the **Bold button** to boldface this information.

➤ Click and drag to select cells **B3 through E3**, then click the **Merge and Center button**. Merge cells **F3 through I3** in similar fashion.

➤ Click and drag to select cells E3 through E12. Click the **down arrow** on the Borders button on the Formatting toolbar, then click the **right border icon** as shown in Figure 2.6e. Click cell A1 (to deselect these cells). You should see a vertical line separating the purchase information from the current values.

➤ Adjust the column widths if necessary. Save the workbook.

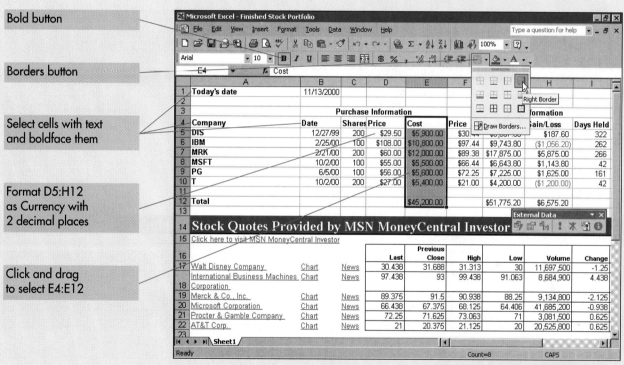

(e) Format the Worksheet (step 5)

FIGURE 2.6 *Hands-on Exercise 3 (continued)*

CAPITAL GAINS AND CONDITIONAL FORMATTING

The Internal Revenue Service offers a significant tax break on stock transactions that are considered a "long term" capital gain (more than one year under today's tax code). Click and drag to select cells I5 through I11, the cells that show how long a stock has been held. Pull down the Format menu, click the Conditional Formatting command, then enter the condition as cell value is > 365. Click the Format button, click the Font tab, then choose a different color (e.g., blue) to highlight those investments that qualify for this consideration.

Step 6: **Refresh the Query**

➤ Right click anywhere within the Web query (i.e., within cells A14 to I22) to display the context-sensitive menu in Figure 2.6f. Click the **Refresh Data command** to retrieve the current prices from the Web.

➤ The numbers in your worksheet will change provided you have an Internet connection and the stock market is open. The column widths may also change since the Web query automatically adjusts the width of its columns (see boxed tip). Adjust the column widths if necessary.

➤ Save the workbook a final time. Print the workbook twice, once to show the displayed values, and once to show the cell contents.

➤ Now that you have completed this exercise, you can experiment further with the various links within the Web query. Scroll to the bottom of the query, for example, then click the link for Symbol Lookup to find the symbol for your favorite stock or index.

➤ Good luck with your stock portfolio, and congratulations on a job well done.

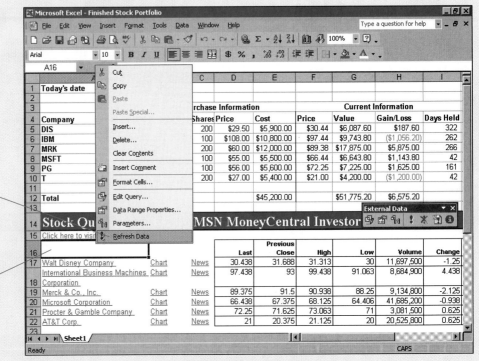

(f) Refresh the Query (step 6)

FIGURE 2.6 *Hands-on Exercise 3 (continued)*

DATA RANGE PROPERTIES

The Web query associated with MSN Stock quotes will, by default, change the column widths in the entire worksheet each time the query is refreshed. You can prevent this from happening by right clicking in the query area, then clicking the Data Range Properties command to display the associated dialog box. Clear the check box to adjust column width, then click OK to accept the settings and close the dialog box. The next time you refresh the query, the column widths will not change.

The distinction between relative, absolute, and mixed references, coupled with the importance of isolating the assumptions on which a worksheet is based, is a basic concept in spreadsheet design. A relative reference (such as A1) changes both the row and column, when the cell containing the reference is copied to other cells in the worksheet. An absolute reference (such as $A$1) remains constant throughout the copy operation. A mixed reference, either $A1 or A$1, modifies the row or column, respectively. Most spreadsheets can be built through combinations of relative and absolute addresses. Mixed references are required for more advanced spreadsheets.

The initial conditions and/or assumptions on which a spreadsheet is based should be isolated so that their values can be easily changed. The formulas in the main body of the spreadsheet typically contain absolute references to these assumptions. The placement of the assumptions and initial conditions is not a requirement of Excel per se, but is crucial to the development of accurate and flexible worksheets. The Insert Comment command creates the equivalent of a screen tip that displays information about the worksheet.

Pointing and the fill handle are two techniques that facilitate the development of a spreadsheet. Although any cell reference can be entered into a formula by typing the reference directly, it is easier and more accurate to enter the reference through pointing. In essence you click in the cell that contains the formula, type an equal sign to begin the formula, then use the mouse (or arrow keys) to enter the various cell references as you build the formula. The fill handle, a tiny black square in the lower-right corner of the selected cell(s), is the easiest way to copy a cell formula to adjacent cells. Just select the cell or cells to be copied, point to the fill handle for the selected cell(s), click and drag the fill handle over the destination range, and release the mouse.

The Internet is built into Microsoft Excel through three basic capabilities. First, a hyperlink can be inserted into any Excel worksheet, then the associated page viewed by clicking the link, without having to start the Web browser manually. Second, any worksheet or workbook can be saved as a Web page (or HTML document), which in turn can be stored on a Web server and displayed through a Web browser. And finally, information from the Web can be downloaded and inserted directly into an Excel workbook through a Web query.

Dates are entered into a worksheet by typing the date in conventional fashion such as 11/24/2000 or December 24, 2000. Either way all dates are stored as integers, beginning with January 1, 1900; that is January 1, 1900 is stored as the number 1. This simple concept enables date arithmetic, whereby calculations can be made between two dates to determine the number of days that have elapsed. The Today( ) function always returns the current date and is used in conjunction with date arithmetic.

KEY TERMS

Absolute reference (p. 66)
Conditional formatting (p. 81)
Date arithmetic (p. 87)
External Data toolbar (p. 87)
Fill handle (p. 68)
HTML document (p. 76)
Hyperlink (p. 76)

Import External Data command (p. 87)
Insert Comment command (p. 68)
Insert Hyperlink command (p. 82)
Internet (p. 76)
Pointing (p. 68)
Refresh command (p. 87)

Relative reference (p. 66)
Round trip HTML (p. 76)
Save as Web Page command (p. 76)
Template (p. 86)
Today( ) function (p. 88)
Web page (p. 76)
Web query (p. 76)

1. The formula to compute the gross pay of an employee in the payroll example that was developed in this chapter uses:
   (a) Absolute references for hourly wage, regular hours, and overtime hours
   (b) Relative references for hourly wage, regular hours, and overtime hours
   (c) Mixed references for hourly wage, regular hours, and overtime hours
   (d) Impossible to determine

2. Which of the following best describes the formula to compute the withholding tax of an employee in the payroll example that was developed in this chapter?
   (a) It contains a relative reference to the gross pay and an absolute reference to the withholding tax rate
   (b) It contains an absolute reference to the gross pay and a relative reference to the withholding tax rate
   (c) It contains absolute references to both the gross pay and withholding tax
   (d) It contains relative references to both the gross pay and withholding tax

3. Cell D12 contains the formula, =SUM (A12:C12). What will the contents of cell D13 be, if the formula in cell D12 is copied to cell D13?
   (a) =SUM (A12:C12)
   (b) =SUM (A13:C13)
   (c) =SUM (A12:C13)
   (d) =SUM (A13:C12)

4. A formula containing the entry =$B$3 is copied to a cell one column over and two rows down. How will the entry appear in its new location?
   (a) =$C$5
   (b) =$B$3
   (c) =B3
   (d) =C5

5. How do you insert a hyperlink into an Excel workbook?
   (a) Pull down the Insert menu and click the Hyperlink command
   (b) Click the Insert Hyperlink button on the Standard toolbar
   (c) Right click a cell and click the Hyperlink command
   (d) Any of the above

6. A Web browser such as Internet Explorer can display a page from:
   (a) A local drive such as drive A or drive C
   (b) A drive on a local area network
   (c) The World Wide Web
   (d) All of the above

7. What is the best way to enter the current price of a stock into an Excel worksheet?
   (a) Copy the price directly from today's copy of *The Wall Street Journal*
   (b) Save the worksheet as a Web page or HTML document
   (c) Create a Web query, then refresh the query to obtain the current price
   (d) Use Internet Explorer to locate a Web page that contains the current price

8. The estimated sales for the first year of a financial forecast are contained in cell B3. The sales for year two are assumed to be 10% higher than the first year, with the rate of increase (10%) stored in cell C23 at the bottom of the spreadsheet. Which of the following is the best way to enter the sales for year two?
   (a) =B3+B3*.10
   (b) =B3+B3*C23
   (c) =B3+B3*$C$23
   (d) All of the above are equivalent entries

9. Which of the following requires an Internet connection?
   (a) Using Internet Explorer to view a Web page that is stored locally
   (b) Updating the values that are obtained through a Web query
   (c) Clicking a hyperlink that references a document that is stored on drive C
   (d) All of the above

10. Which of the following best describes a formula to compute the sales in the second year, given that the second year is dependent on the sales of the first year, and that the rate of increase from one year to the next is a fixed percentage?
   (a) It contains a relative reference to the assumed rate of increase and an absolute reference to the sales from the previous year
   (b) It contains an absolute reference to the assumed rate of increase and a relative reference to the sales from the previous year
   (c) It contains absolute references to both the assumed rate of increase and the sales from the previous year
   (d) It contains relative references to both the assumed rate of increase and the sales from the previous year

11. What will be stored in a cell if 2/5 is entered in it?
   (a) 2/5
   (b) .4
   (c) The date value February 5 of the current year
   (d) 2/5 or .4 depending on the format in effect

12. You type 11/24/00 into a cell, press the enter key, and expect to see Nov 24, 2000. Instead you see the value 36854. Which of the following is a likely explanation?
   (a) Something is radically wrong with the date functions
   (b) The cell is formatted to display a numeric value rather than a date
   (c) You should have used an equal sign to enter the date
   (d) None of the above makes any sense at all

13. Which of the following formulas can be used to compute an individual's age, given that the individual's birth date is stored in cell A4?
   (a) =(Today( )−A4)/365
   (b) =(Today−A4)/365
   (c) =(A4−Today)/365
   (d) =(A4−Today( ))/365

14. Microsoft Excel and Internet Explorer are both open and display the "same" worksheet. You make a change in the Excel file that is not reflected in the Web page. What is the most likely explanation?
   (a) The two files are not linked to one another
   (b) The files are stored locally as opposed to a Web server
   (c) You did not refresh the Web page in Microsoft Excel
   (d) You did not refresh the Web page in Internet Explorer

15. You notice that the values in a specific column are displayed in three different colors, red for values less than zero, blue for values greater than $100,000, and black otherwise. How is this possible?
   (a) The colored formatting is automatically built into every Excel worksheet
   (b) A Web query was used to implement the red and blue formatting
   (c) Conditional formatting was applied to the column
   (d) It is not possible; that is, the question is in error

ANSWERS

1. b	**5.** d	**9.** b	**13.** a
2. a	**6.** d	**10.** b	**14.** d
3. b	**7.** c	**11.** c	**15.** c
4. b	**8.** c	**12.** b	

BUILDS ON

HANDS-ON EXERCISE 1 PAGES 69–75

1. Alternate Payroll: Figure 2.7 contains an alternate version of the payroll that was created in the first hands-on exercise in the chapter. The revised spreadsheet includes the number of dependents for each employee and a fixed deduction per dependent, which combine to reduce an individual's taxable income. The revised spreadsheet also isolates the overtime rate, making it possible to change the overtime rate in a single place should that become necessary.
   a. Open the *Chapter 2 Practice 1* workbook, then complete the spreadsheet `so that it matches ours. Substitute your name for the employee named "Grauer," then sort the worksheet so that the employees appear in alphabetical order. (Click anywhere within column A and click the Sort Ascending button on the Standard toolbar. There must be a blank row above the total row, or else it will be sorted with the other rows.) Highlight the row containing your name.
   b. Print the completed worksheet twice, once with displayed values, and once to show the cell formulas. Use the Page Setup command for the cell formulas to switch to landscape printing and force the output onto one page. Print gridlines and row and column headings. Change the column headings as appropriate. Add a cover sheet, then submit all three pages (cover sheet, displayed values, and cell formulas) to your instructor as proof you did this exercise.

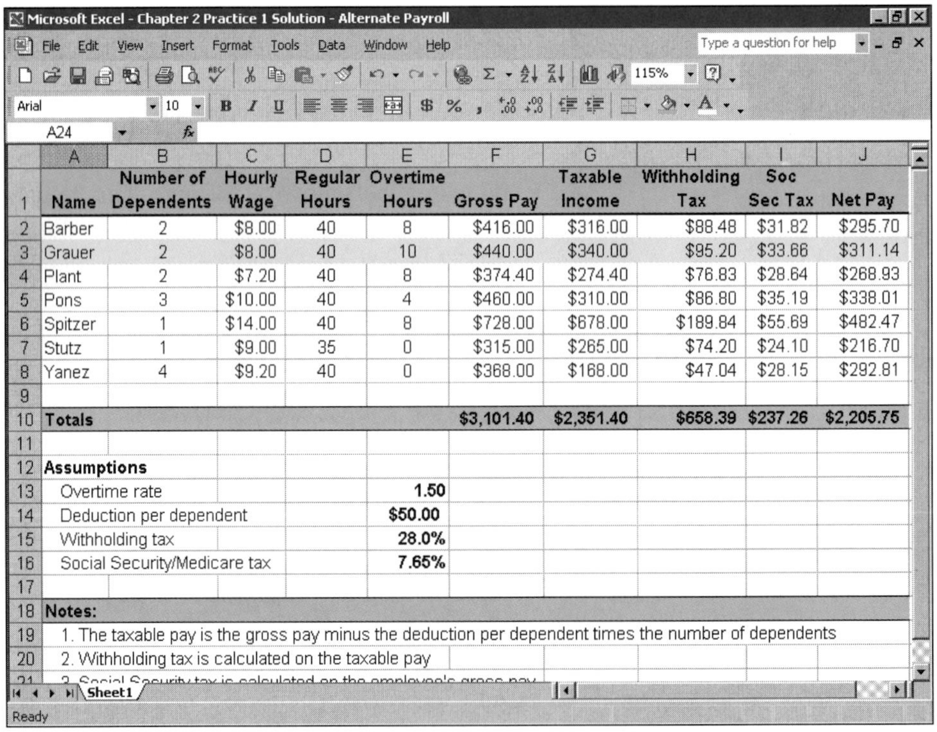

	A	B	C	D	E	F	G	H	I	J
1	Name	Number of Dependents	Hourly Wage	Regular Hours	Overtime Hours	Gross Pay	Taxable Income	Withholding Tax	Soc Sec Tax	Net Pay
2	Barber	2	$8.00	40	8	$416.00	$316.00	$88.48	$31.82	$295.70
3	Grauer	2	$8.00	40	10	$440.00	$340.00	$95.20	$33.66	$311.14
4	Plant	2	$7.20	40	8	$374.40	$274.40	$76.83	$28.64	$268.93
5	Pons	3	$10.00	40	4	$460.00	$310.00	$86.80	$35.19	$338.01
6	Spitzer	1	$14.00	40	8	$728.00	$678.00	$189.84	$55.69	$482.47
7	Stutz	1	$9.00	35	0	$315.00	$265.00	$74.20	$24.10	$216.70
8	Yanez	4	$9.20	40	0	$368.00	$168.00	$47.04	$28.15	$292.81
9										
10	Totals					$3,101.40	$2,351.40	$658.39	$237.26	$2,205.75
11										
12	Assumptions									
13	Overtime rate				1.50					
14	Deduction per dependent				$50.00					
15	Withholding tax				28.0%					
16	Social Security/Medicare tax				7.65%					
17										
18	Notes:									
19	1. The taxable pay is the gross pay minus the deduction per dependent times the number of dependents									
20	2. Withholding tax is calculated on the taxable pay									

FIGURE 2.7 *Alternate Payroll (Exercise 1)*

2. The Sports Statistician: Figure 2.8 illustrates how Excel can be used to tabulate statistics for a hypothetical softball league. Open the worksheet in the *Chapter 2 Practice 2* workbook, then complete the worksheet as follows:
   a. An individual batting average is computed by dividing the number of hits by the number of at bats (e.g., 30/80 or .375 for Maryann Barber). The batting average should be formatted to three decimal places. (Create the Custom format .000 to eliminate the 0 before the batting average to display .375, rather than the default numerical format of 0.000.)

b. The total bases for an individual is computed by multiplying the number of singles by one, the number of doubles by two, the number of triples by three, and the number of home runs by four, then adding the results.

c. The slugging percentage is computed by dividing the total bases by the number of at bats (e.g., 48/80 or .600 for Maryann Barber). The slugging average should be formatted to three decimal places.

d. The team totals for all columns except batting average and slugging percentage are determined by summing the appropriate values. The team batting average and slugging percentage are computed by dividing the number of hits and total bases, respectively, by the number of at bats.

e. Substitute your name for Jessica Grauer (our league is coed), sort the players in alphabetical order.

f. Format the worksheet so that it matches Figure 2.8. Be sure that your name is highlighted, rather than Jessica's.

g. Add an appropriate clip art image somewhere in the worksheet using the same technique as in any other Office application. Pull down the Insert menu, click (or point to) Picture, then click Clip Art. The task pane opens and displays the Insert Clip Art pane. Click in the Search text box. Enter "baseball" to search for any clip art image that is described with this key word and click the Go button. The images are displayed in the Results box.

h. Select (click) an image to display a drop-down arrow to its right. Click the arrow to display a context menu. Click Insert to insert the image into the document. Close the task pane. Click and drag a sizing handle to make the image smaller, then click and drag to move the image as necessary.

i. Print the completed worksheet twice, once with displayed values, and once to show the cell formulas. Use the Page Setup command for the cell formulas to switch to landscape printing and force the output onto one page. Print gridlines and row and column headings.

j. Add a cover sheet, then submit all three pages (cover sheet, displayed values, and cell formulas) to your instructor.

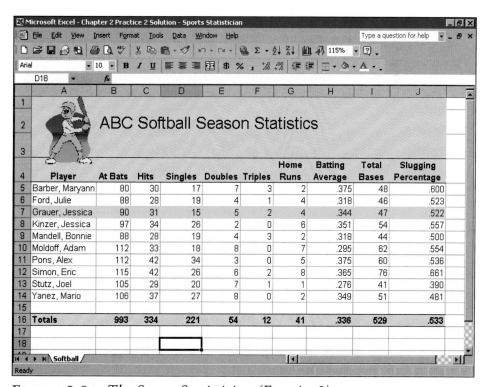

FIGURE 2.8 *The Sports Statistician (Exercise 2)*

3. Web Pages and Hyperlinks: Open the *Chapter 2 Practice 3* workbook as the basis for the Web page in Figure 2.9. Complete the worksheet as follows:

    a. Compute the total points for each player by multiplying the number of free throws, 2-point field goals, and 3-point field goals by 1, 2, and 3, respectively.

    b. Compute the points per game for each player by dividing the total points by the number of games. Display the result to one decimal point. Compute the rebounds per game in similar fashion.

    c. Add clip art as you see fit. We used the same image twice to bracket the title of the worksheet. Format your page to match ours.

    d. Add your name at the bottom of the worksheet. Instead of merely typing your name, however, add your name as a hyperlink that points to your home page if you have one. If you do not have a home page, use any Web address, such as www.nba.com for the National Basketball Association.

    e. Save the workbook as a Web page, then open the workbook in Internet Explorer or Netscape Navigator. Print the Web page from your Web browser.

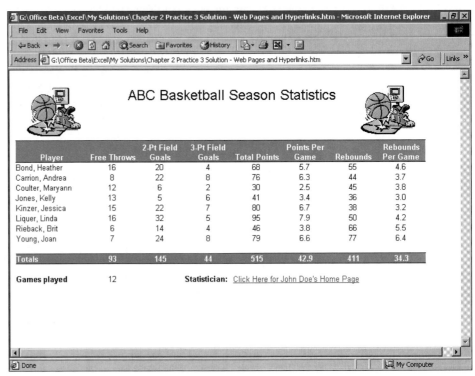

FIGURE 2.9   *Web Pages and Hyperlinks (Exercise 3)*

4. Wishful Thinking CD Portfolio: It must be nice to have a portfolio of CDs (Certificates of Deposit) where all you do is collect the interest as shown in Figure 2.10. Open the partially completed worksheet, which is found in the *Chapter 2 Practice 4* workbook, then complete the worksheet as follows.

    a. The maturity date is computed by adding the term (converted to days) to the purchase date.

    b. The days until maturity is determined by subtracting today's date from the maturity date.

    c. The annual income is determined by multiplying the amount of the CD times its interest rate.

    d. The estimated tax is found by multiplying the annual income by the tax rate.

    e. The net income is the annual income minus the estimated tax.

    f. Format the completed worksheet to match Figure 2.10.

    g. Add your name in cell A19. Print the worksheet twice, once with displayed values, and once to show the cell formulas.

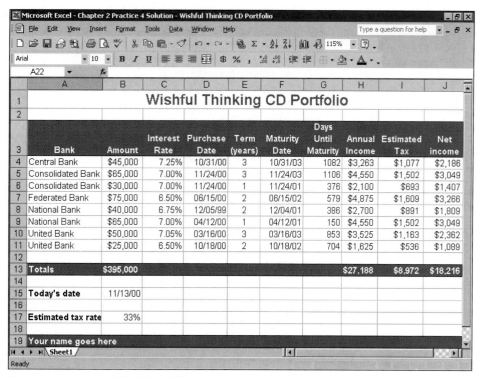

						Days			
		Interest	Purchase	Term	Maturity	Until	Annual	Estimated	Net
Bank	Amount	Rate	Date	(years)	Date	Maturity	Income	Tax	income
Central Bank	$45,000	7.25%	10/31/00	3	10/31/03	1082	$3,263	$1,077	$2,186
Consolidated Bank	$65,000	7.00%	11/24/00	3	11/24/03	1106	$4,550	$1,502	$3,049
Consolidated Bank	$30,000	7.00%	11/24/00	1	11/24/01	376	$2,100	$693	$1,407
Federated Bank	$75,000	6.50%	06/15/00	2	06/15/02	579	$4,875	$1,609	$3,266
National Bank	$40,000	6.75%	12/05/99	2	12/04/01	386	$2,700	$891	$1,809
National Bank	$65,000	7.00%	04/12/00	1	04/12/01	150	$4,550	$1,502	$3,049
United Bank	$50,000	7.05%	03/16/00	3	03/16/03	853	$3,525	$1,163	$2,362
United Bank	$25,000	6.50%	10/18/00	2	10/18/02	704	$1,625	$536	$1,089
Totals	$395,000						$27,188	$8,972	$18,216
Today's date	11/13/00								
Estimated tax rate	33%								
Your name goes here									

FIGURE 2.10 *Wishful Thinking CD Portfolio (Exercise 4)*

5. Web Queries for Currency Conversion: Excel includes a Web query to determine the exchange rates for popular currencies as can be seen in Figure 2.11. The worksheet contains formulas for two parallel sets of conversions, from British pounds to dollars, and from dollars to British pounds. Open the partially completed workbook in *Chapter 2 Practice 5,* then proceed as follows:

a. Use the Import External Data command to enter the Web query (MS MoneyCentral Investor Currency Rates) into the worksheet. Click in cell B11 and enter the appropriate cell reference within the query (cell B24 in our example, which is not visible in Figure 2.11) to obtain the current value of the conversion factor. Use the value in cell B11 to convert the amounts in British pounds to the equivalent dollar amounts. Note that Microsoft is continually changing the format of its queries to include different currencies, so you may have to enter a different cell.

b. Click in cell E11 and enter the conversion factor to convert dollars to pounds. (This is the reciprocal of the value in cell B11.) Complete the entries in column E, which convert dollars to the equivalent amount in British pounds.

c. Format the worksheet to match Figure 2.11. Be sure to use the appropriate currency symbols for dollars and pounds. Add your name and today's date as shown.

d. Click the tab for the Euro (European Currency) worksheet and enter the formulas for the appropriate conversion from Euros to dollars and vice versa. You do not have to enter the query on this worksheet, because you can reference the values in the existing query. The entry in cell B11 of the Euro worksheet is Pounds!B34 on our worksheet. (Remember, the query changes continually, so you may have to adjust the cell reference.) Click in cell B11 of the Euro worksheet, type an equal sign to begin pointing, click the Pounds worksheet, and click in the cell containing the appropriate conversion, then click enter to finish the formula.

e. Format the Euro worksheet to include the European Currency Symbol as appropriate. Print both worksheets for your instructor.

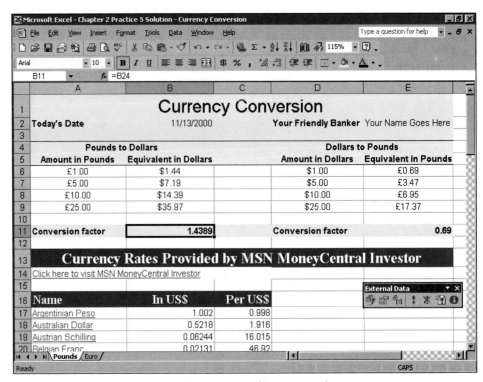

FIGURE 2.11 *Currency Conversion (Exercise 5)*

6. Accounting 101: The worksheet in Figure 2.12 computes the depreciation of an asset, an important accounting concept. You don't have to be an accounting major to create the spreadsheet, but you do have to understand the concept of depreciation. In essence, a business buys an asset, then uses that asset over a period of years. Each year the asset loses value (i.e., it depreciates) and is worth less than the year before.
   a. The amount of value that the asset loses each year is the depreciation expense for that year. The straight method assumes that the asset loses value uniformly over its projected life. To determine the depreciation amount for each year, take the cost of the asset, subtract its residual (salvage) value, then divide the result by the number of years the asset will be used.
   b. Your assignment is to open the *Chapter 2 Practice 6* workbook and enter the necessary formulas so that your worksheet matches ours. Add your name, today's date and the appropriate formatting, then print the worksheet twice, once with displayed values, and once to show the cell formulas.

7. Financial Forecast: Financial planning and budgeting is a common business application of spreadsheets. Figure 2.13 depicts one such illustration, in which the income and expenses of Get Rich Quick Enterprises are projected over a six-year period.
   a. The projected income in 2000, for example, is $225,000 based on sales of 75,000 units at a price of $3.00 per unit. The overhead (fixed costs) consists of the production facility at $50,000 and administrative expenses of $25,000. The variable costs for the same year are broken down into manufacturing and sales of $75,000 (75,000 units at $1.00 per unit) and $15,000 (75,000 units at $.20 per unit). Subtracting the total expenses from the estimated income yields a net income before taxes of $75,000. The income tax is subtracted from this amount, leaving net earnings of $38,400 in the first year. The estimated income and expenses for each succeeding year are based on an assumed percentage increase over the previous year. The projected rates of increase as well as the initial conditions are shown at the bottom of the worksheet. Specifications continue on page 104.

FIGURE 2.12 *Accounting 101 (Exercise 6)*

FIGURE 2.13 *Financial Forecast (Exercise 7)*

b. Your assignment is to open the partially completed worksheet in *Chapter 2 Practice 7,* then complete the spreadsheet so that it matches Figure 2.13. We suggest you use pointing throughout the exercise, as that is the most efficient way to enter cell formulas into a worksheet.

c. Develop the formulas for the first year of the forecast based on the initial conditions at the bottom of the spreadsheet.

d. Develop the formulas for the second year based on the values in year one and the assumed rates of change.

e. Copy the formulas for year two to the remaining years of the forecast.

f. Format the spreadsheet, then print the completed forecast. Add your name somewhere in the worksheet, then submit the completed assignment.

8. **Mixed References:** The majority of spreadsheets can be developed using a combination of relative and absolute references. Occasionally, however, you will need to incorporate mixed references as in the multiplication table of Figure 2.14. Creating the row and column headings is easy in that you can enter the numbers manually. (You can also use the AutoFill feature. Simply enter 1 and 2 in the first two cells for the row headings, select both of these cells, then drag the fill handle to continue the series in the remaining cells. Repeat the process to enter the column headings.)

a. The interesting part of this problem is creating the formulas in the body of the worksheet (we don't want you to enter the results manually). The trick is to use mixed references for the formula in cell B4, then copy that formula to the remainder of the table. The formula in cell B4 is a product of two numbers. To develop the proper mixed reference, you need to think about what will vary and what will remain constant. (One of the numbers in the product will always reference a value from column A, but the row will vary. The other number will always use a value from row three, but the column will vary.)

b. Add your name to the worksheet. Print the cell formulas as well so that you can see how the mixed reference changes throughout the worksheet. Submit the complete assignment to your instructor.

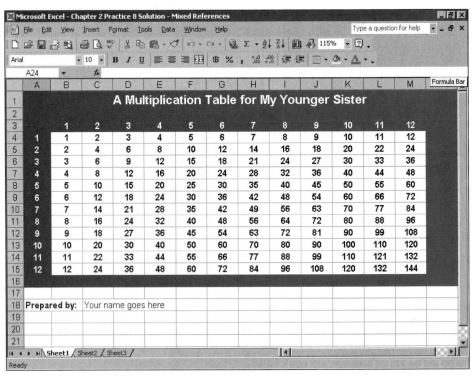

FIGURE 2.14 *Mixed References (Exercise 8)*

9. The Birthday Problem: How much would you bet *against* two people in your class having the same birthday? Don't be too hasty, for the odds of two classmates sharing the same birthday (month and day) are much higher than you would expect; e.g., there is a fifty percent chance (.5063) in a class of 23 students that two people will have been born on the same day. The probability jumps to seventy percent (.7053) in a class of thirty, and to ninety percent (.9025) in a class of forty-one. Ask the question in your own class to see if the probabilities hold.
   a. Your assignment is to create the worksheet in Figure 2.15 that displays the set of probabilities. Enter your name and birthdate in cells B3 and B4, respectively, then use either the Now( ) or the Today( ) function to compute your age in cell B5. Change the default alignment and number of decimal places in cell B5 so that your worksheet matches ours.
   b. You need a basic knowledge of probability to create the remainder of the worksheet. In essence you calculate the probability of individuals not having the same birthday, then subtract this number from one to obtain the probability of the event coming true. In a group of two people, for example, the probability of not being born on the same day is 365/366; that is, the second person can be born on any of 365 days and still have a different birthday. The probability of two people having the same birthday becomes 1 − 365/366.
   c. The probability for different birthdays in a group of three is (365/366) * (364/366). The probability of not having different birthdays—that is, of two people having the same birthday—is one minus this number. This logic continues for the remaining rows in the spreadsheet, where each row is calculated from the previous row. It's not as hard as it looks and the results are quite interesting.
   d. Print the worksheet two ways, once to show displayed values and once to show cell formulas. Add a cover sheet. Submit all three pages to your instructor.

	A	B	C
1		The Birthday Problem	
2			
3	My name:	Jessica Grauer	
4	My birthdate:	3/16/1977	
5	My Age:	23.7	
6			
7	Number of People	Probability of Different Birthdays	Probability of the Same Birthday
8	2	99.73%	0.27%
9	3	99.18%	0.82%
10	4	98.37%	1.63%
11	5	97.29%	2.71%
12	6	95.96%	4.04%
13	7	94.39%	5.61%
14	8	92.59%	7.41%
15	9	90.56%	9.44%
16	10	88.34%	11.66%
17	11	85.92%	14.08%
18	12	83.34%	16.66%
19	13	80.61%	19.39%
20	14	77.74%	22.26%
21	15	74.77%	25.23%

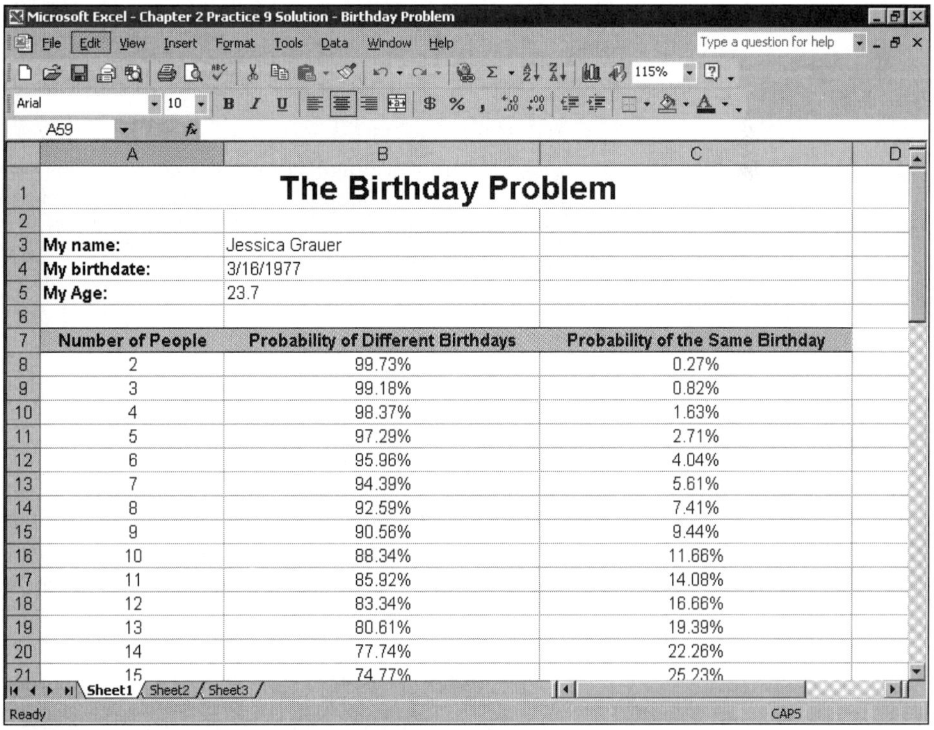

FIGURE 2.15 *The Birthday Problem (Exercise 9)*

10. Create a New Web Query: You can create a Web query to obtain data from virtually any site, then use that data as the basis of calculations within an Excel workbook. Start a new workbook, pull down the Data menu, click the Import External Data command, then click New Web Query to display the associated dialog box. Enter the address of any Web page as shown in Figure 2.16. We used the Microsoft Investor site (investor.msn.com), but you may want to try the home page of your favorite sport. The key is that the page contains one or more yellow arrows that indicate the data may be imported.

Click a yellow arrow to select the table, click the Import button in the New Query dialog box, then follow the regular steps to create a Web query. Continue to develop the worksheet using formulas that reference the data that was imported by the query. Save the workbook, then open it the next day. Right click in the query and click the Refresh data command to update the data. Print the workbook at two different times to show your instructor that the data is updated from the Web.

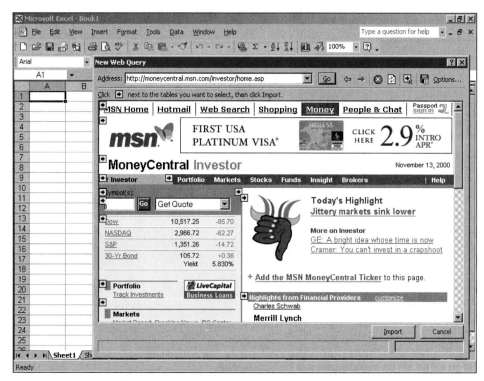

FIGURE 2.16 *Create a New Web Query (Exercise 10)*

11. Excel Templates: Figure 2.17a displays a worksheet that was created from the Balance Sheet template that is built into Office XP. Pull down the View menu and open the task pane. Click the General Templates command to open the Templates dialog box from where you can click the Spreadsheets Solutions tab to open the Balance Sheet template.

a. Enter an appropriate description and initial balance, then enter data for at least three transactions of each type. Print the completed worksheet for your instructor.

b. What is contained on the Balance over time worksheet within this workbook? Print this worksheet for your instructor as well.

c. What happens if you attempt to add more transactions than the template provides initially? Does this limit the utility of the template? Summarize your results in a brief note to your instructor.

d. Use the Sales Invoice template to create a worksheet similar to Figure 2.17b. Print the worksheet for your instructor.

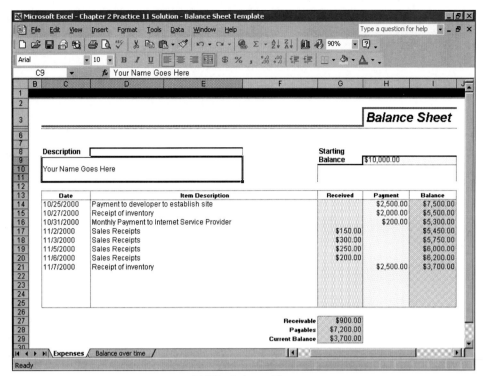

(a) The Balance Sheet

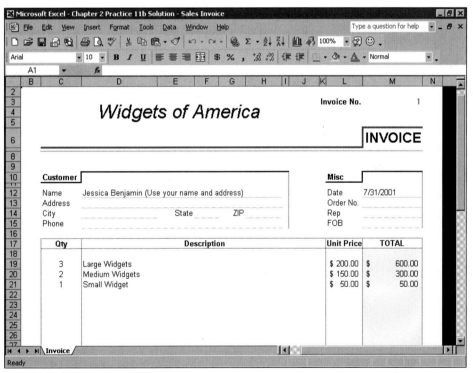

(b) The Sales Invoice

FIGURE 2.17 *Excel Templates (Exercise 11)*

The Checkbook

A spreadsheet can be created as an aid in balancing your checkbook. Each row in the spreadsheet will contain the data for a specific transaction, such as a check, deposit, or ATM withdrawal. Each row should also include the date of the transaction and the current balance. The spreadsheet is easy to create, but you need to think carefully about its design. We suggest you start with the *Checkbook* workbook that is found in the Exploring Excel folder. Open the workbook, develop the necessary formulas, then submit the completed workbook to your instructor. If you find this to be a useful exercise, then you can modify our workbook to reflect your own data.

The Spreadsheet Audit

The spreadsheet is an invaluable tool in decision making, but what if the spreadsheet contains an error? Unfortunately, it is all too easy to get caught up in the appearance of an attractively formatted spreadsheet without paying attention to its underlying accuracy. The *Erroneous Chapter 2 Practice 7* is based on problem 7, but it contains one or more errors within the body of the spreadsheet. This worksheet also contains a different set of assumptions and initial conditions, but these values are not to be considered in error; that is, the mistakes in the spreadsheet stem from formulas that are in error. Examine the spreadsheet carefully, correct the formulas that are in error (but leave the assumptions and initial conditions as is), then print the corrected worksheet. Submit the revised forecast based on the new assumptions to your instructor.

Publishing to the Web

It's easy to create a Web page (HTML document) from an Excel worksheet. The document can be stored locally, where you are the only one who can view it. It's more interesting, however, to place the page on a Web server, where it becomes part of the World Wide Web.

In order to place a page on the Web, you will need Internet access, and further, you will need storage space on a Web server. Check with your instructor to see if these resources are available to you, and if so, find out the steps necessary to upload your page to the server. Choose any worksheet that you have completed in this chapter, save the worksheet as an HTML document, then upload the document. Send a note to your instructor that contains the Web address where he or she may view your Web page.

Break-even Analysis

Widgets of America has developed the perfect product and is ready to go into production pending a review of a five-year break-even analysis. The manufacturing cost in the first year is $1.00 per unit and is estimated to increase at 5% annually. The projected selling price is $2.00 per unit and can increase at 10% annually. Overhead expenses are fixed at $100,000 per year over the life of the project. The advertising budget is $50,000 in the first year but will decrease 15% a year as the product gains acceptance. How many units have to be sold each year for the company to break even, given the current cost estimates and projected rates of increase?

Your worksheet should be completely flexible and capable of accommodating a change in any of the initial conditions or projected rates of increase. Be sure to isolate all of the assumptions (i.e., the initial conditions and rates of increase) in one area of the worksheet, and then reference these cells as absolute references when building the formulas.

Spreadsheets in Decision Making: What If?

OVERVIEW

Excel is a truly fascinating program, but it is only a means to an end. A spreadsheet is first and foremost a tool for decision making, and the objective of this chapter is to show you just how valuable that tool can be. Decisions typically involve money, and so we begin by introducing two financial functions, PMT and FV, either of which is entered directly into a worksheet.

The PMT (Payment) function calculates the periodic payment on a loan, such as one you might incur with the purchase of an automobile. The FV (Future Value) function determines the future value of a series of periodic payments, such as annual contributions to a retirement account. Either function can be used in conjunction with the Goal Seek command that lets you enter the desired end result (such as the monthly payment on a car loan) and from that, determines the input (e.g., the price of the car) to produce that result.

The second half of the chapter presents an expanded version of the professor's grade book that uses several commands associated with large spreadsheets. We describe scrolling and explain how its effects are modified by freezing and/or hiding rows and columns in a worksheet. We describe various statistical functions such as MAX, MIN, COUNT, and COUNTA as well as the IF and VLOOKUP functions that provide decision making within a worksheet. We also review the important concepts of relative and absolute cell references, as well as the need to isolate the assumptions and initial conditions in a worksheet.

ANALYSIS OF A CAR LOAN

Figure 3.1 shows how a worksheet might be applied to the purchase of a car. In essence you need to know the monthly payment, which depends on the price of the car, the down payment, and the terms of the loan. In other words:

- Can you afford the monthly payment on the car of your choice?
- What if you settle for a less expensive car and receive a manufacturer's rebate?
- What if you work next summer to earn money for a down payment?
- What if you extend the life of the loan and receive a more favorable interest rate?

The answers to these and other questions determine whether you can afford a car, and if so, which car, and how you will pay for it. The decision is made easier by developing the worksheet in Figure 3.1, and then by changing the various parameters as indicated.

Figure 3.1a contains the *template*, or "empty" worksheet, in which the text entries and formulas have already been entered, the formatting has already been applied, but no specific data has been input. The template requires that you enter the price of the car, the manufacturer's rebate, the down payment, the interest rate, and the length of the loan. The worksheet uses these parameters to compute the monthly payment. (Implicit in this discussion is the existence of a PMT function within the worksheet program, which is explained in the next section.)

The availability of the worksheet lets you consider several alternatives, and therein lies its true value. You quickly realize that the purchase of a $14,999 car as shown in Figure 3.1b is prohibitive because the monthly payment is almost $500. Settling for a less expensive car, coming up with a substantial down payment, and obtaining a manufacturer's rebate in Figure 3.1c help considerably, but the $317 monthly payment is still too steep. Extending the loan to a fourth year at a lower interest rate in Figure 3.1d reduces the monthly payment to (a more affordable) $244.

CAR SHOPPING ON THE WEB

Why guess about the price of a car or its features if you can obtain exact information from the Web? You can go to the site of a specific manufacturer, usually by entering an address of the form www.company.com (e.g., www. ford.com). You can also go to a site that provides information about multiple vendors. Our favorite is carpoint.msn.com, which provides detailed information about specifications and current prices. See practice exercise 8 at the end of the chapter.

No specific data has been input

	A	B
1	Price of car	
2	Manufacturer's rebate	
3	Down payment	
4	Amount to finance	=B1-(B2+B3)
5	Interest rate	
6	Term (in years)	
7	Monthly payment	=PMT(B5/12,B6*12,-B4)

(a) The Template

Data entered

	A	B
1	Price of car	$14,999
2	Manufacturer's rebate	
3	Down payment	
4	Amount to finance	$14,999
5	Interest rate	9%
6	Term (in years)	3
7	Monthly payment	$476.96

(b) Initial Parameters

Less expensive car

Rebate

Down payment made

	A	B
1	Price of car	$13,999
2	Manufacturer's rebate	$1,000
3	Down payment	$3,000
4	Amount to finance	$9,999
5	Interest rate	9%
6	Term (in years)	3
7	Monthly payment	$317.97

(c) Less Expensive Car with Down Payment and Rebate

Lower interest rate

Longer term

	A	B
1	Price of car	$13,999
2	Manufacturer's rebate	$1,000
3	Down payment	$3,000
4	Amount to finance	$9,999
5	Interest rate	8%
6	Term (in years)	4
7	Monthly payment	$244.10

(d) Longer Term and Better Interest Rate

FIGURE 3.1 *Spreadsheets in Decision Making*

PMT Function

A *function* is a predefined formula that accepts one or more **arguments** as input, performs the indicated calculation, then returns another value as output. Excel has more than 100 different functions in various categories. Financial functions, such as the PMT function we are about to study, are especially important in business.

The **PMT function** requires three arguments (the interest rate per period, the number of periods, and the amount of the loan), from which it computes the associated payment on a loan. The arguments are placed in parentheses and are separated by commas. Consider the PMT function as it might apply to Figure 3.1b:

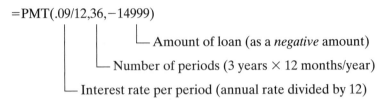

=PMT(.09/12,36,−14999)

└─ Amount of loan (as a *negative* amount)

└─ Number of periods (3 years × 12 months/year)

└─ Interest rate per period (annual rate divided by 12)

Instead of using specific values, however, the arguments in the PMT function are supplied as cell references, so that the computed payment can be based on values supplied by the user elsewhere in the worksheet. Thus, the PMT function is entered as =PMT(B5/12,B6*12,−B4) to reflect the terms of a specific loan whose arguments are in cells B4, B5, and B6. (The principal is entered as a negative amount because the money is lent to you and represents an outflow of cash from the bank.)

FV Function

The **FV function** returns the future value of an investment based on constant periodic payments and a constant interest rate. It can be used to determine the future value of a retirement plan such as an IRA (Individual Retirement Account) or 401K, two plans that are very popular in today's workplace. Under either plan, an individual saves for his or her retirement by making a fixed contribution each year. The money is allowed to accumulate tax-free until retirement and it is an excellent way to save for the future.

Assume, for example, that you plan to contribute $2,000 a year to an IRA, that you expect to earn 8% annually, and that you will be contributing for 40 years (i.e., you began contributing at age 25 and will continue to contribute until age 65). The future value of that investment—that is, the amount you will have at age 65—would be $518,113! All told, you would have contributed $80,000 ($2,000 a year for 40 years). The difference, more than $400,000, results from compound interest over the life of your investment.

The FV function is entered into a worksheet in similar fashion to the PMT function. There are three arguments—the interest rate (also called the rate of return), the number of periods, and the periodic investment. The FV function corresponding to our earlier example would be:

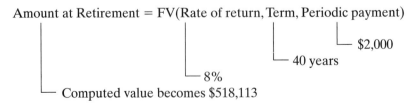

Amount at Retirement = FV(Rate of return, Term, Periodic payment)

└─ $2,000

└─ 40 years

└─ 8%

└─ Computed value becomes $518,113

It's more practical, however, to enter the values into a worksheet, then use cell references within the FV function. If, for example, cells A1, A2, and A3 contained the rate of return, term, and annual contribution, respectively, the resulting FV function would be =FV(A1, A2, −A3). The periodic payment is preceded by a minus sign, just as the principal in the PMT function.

Inserting a Function

The ***Insert Function command*** places a function into a worksheet. You can select a function from within a category as was done in Figure 3.2a, or you can enter a brief description of the function you are searching for to see which functions are suggested. The Function Arguments dialog box in Figure 3.2b appears after you choose the function. This is where you enter the various arguments in order to compute the value of the function. (Only the first three arguments are required for the Future Value function.) Excel displays the calculated value of each argument as well as the value of the function within the dialog box.

Enter a description of function

Click drop-down arrow to select a category

Select function

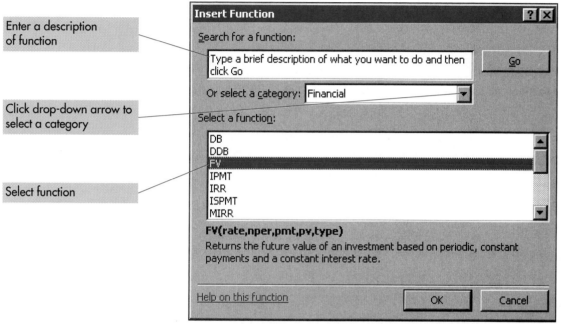

(a) Select the Function

Arguments

Calculated value

Computed value for function

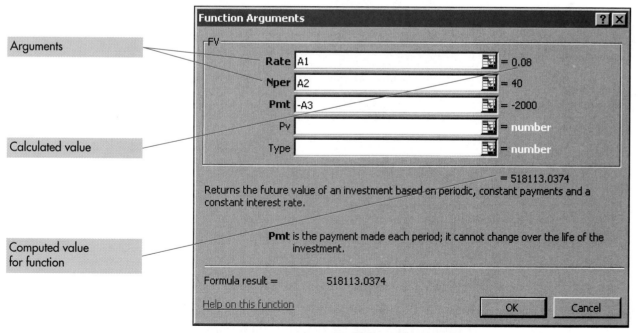

(b) Enter the Arguments

FIGURE 3.2   *Inserting a Function*

The Goal Seek Command

The analysis in Figure 3.1 enabled us to reduce the projected monthly payment from $476 to a more affordable $244. What if, however, you can afford a payment of only $200, and you want to know the maximum you can borrow in order to keep the payment to the specified amount? The **Goal Seek command** is designed to solve this type of problem, as it enables you to set an end result (such as the monthly payment) in order to determine the input (the price of the car) to produce that result. Only one input (the price of the car, the interest rate, or the term) can be varied at a time.

Figure 3.3 extends our earlier analysis to illustrate the Goal Seek command. You create the spreadsheet as usual, then you pull down the Tools menu, and select the Goal Seek command to display the dialog box in Figure 3.3a. Enter the address of the cell containing the dependent formula (the monthly payment in cell B7) and the desired value of this cell ($200). Indicate the cell whose contents should be varied (the price of the car in cell B1), then click OK to execute the command. The Goal Seek command then varies the price of the car until the monthly payment returns the desired value of $200. (Not every problem has a solution, in which case Excel returns a message indicating that a solution cannot be found.)

In this example, the Goal Seek command is able to find a solution and returns a purchase price of $12,192 as shown in Figure 3.3b. You now have all the information you need. Find a car that sells for $12,192 (or less), hold the other parameters to the values shown in the figure, and your monthly payment will be (at most) $200.

The analysis in Figure 3.3 illustrates how a worksheet is used in the decision-making process. An individual defines a problem, then develops a worksheet that includes all of the associated parameters. He or she can then plug in specific numbers, changing one or more of the variables until a decision can be reached. Excel is invaluable in arriving at the solution.

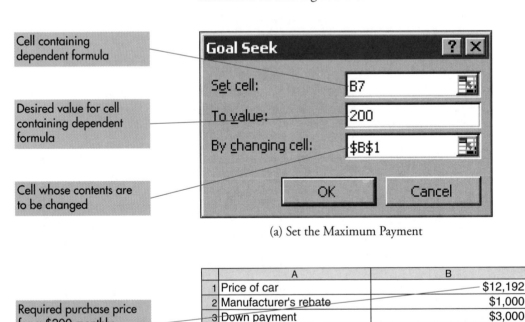

Cell containing dependent formula

Desired value for cell containing dependent formula

Cell whose contents are to be changed

(a) Set the Maximum Payment

Required purchase price for a $200 monthly payment

	A	B
1	Price of car	$12,192
2	Manufacturer's rebate	$1,000
3	Down payment	$3,000
4	Amount to finance	$8,192
5	Interest rate	8%
6	Term (in years)	4
7	Monthly payment	$200.00

(b) Solution

FIGURE 3.3   *The Goal Seek Command*

BASIC FINANCIAL FUNCTIONS

Objective To illustrate the PMT and FV functions; to illustrate the Goal Seek command. Use Figure 3.4 as a guide in the exercise.

Step 1: **Enter the Descriptive Labels**

> ➤ Start Excel. If necessary, click the **New button** on the Standard toolbar to open a new workbook or click **Blank Workbook** in the task pane.
> ➤ Click in cell **A1**, type the label **Basic Financial Functions**, then press the **enter key** to complete the entry. Enter the remaining labels for column A as shown in Figure 3.4a.
> ➤ Click and drag the column border between columns A and B to increase the column width of column A to accommodate the widest entry in column A (other than cell A3).
> ➤ Click in cell **B4** and type **$14,999** corresponding to the price of the automobile you hope to purchase. Be sure to include the dollar sign as you enter the data to format the cell automatically.
> ➤ Enter **$1,000** and **$3,000** in cells B5 and B6, respectively, corresponding to the manufacturer's rebate and down payment, respectively.
> ➤ Click in cell **B7**. Use pointing to enter the formula **=B4−(B5+B6)**, which calculates the amount to finance (i.e., the principal of the loan).
> ➤ Enter **9%** and **3** in cells **B8** and **B9**. (If necessary, click in cell **B9**, pull down the **Edit menu**, select the **Clear command**, and choose the **Format command** to remove the dollar sign.)
> ➤ All of the loan parameters have been entered.

New button

Click and drag border to widen column A

Enter =B4−(B5+B6)

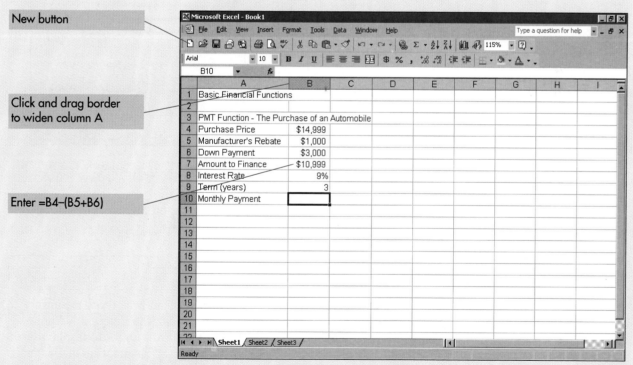

(a) Enter the Descriptive Labels (step 1)

FIGURE 3.4 *Hands-on Exercise 1*

Step 2: **Insert a Function**

➤ Click in cell **B10**. Pull down the **Insert menu** and click the **Function command** (or click the **Insert Function button** on the formula bar) to display the Insert Function dialog box.

➤ Click the **down arrow** in the Select a category list box and select **Financial**, select the **PMT function** and click **OK** to display the Function Arguments dialog box in Figure 3.4b.

➤ Click the **Rate text box** and use pointing to enter the rate. Click in cell **B8** of the worksheet, then type **/12**, so that the text box contains the entry B8/12.

➤ Click the **Nper text box** and use pointing to enter the number of periods. Click in cell **B9**, then type *12, so that the formula bar contains the entry B9*12.

➤ Click the **Pv text box**. Type a − sign, then click in cell **B7**. You should see $349.7652595 as the value for the PMT function. Click **OK** to close the Function Arguments dialog box.

➤ Pull down the **File menu** and click the **Save command** (or click the **Save button** on the Standard toolbar) to display the Save As dialog box, then save the workbook as **Basic Financial Functions** in the **Exploring Excel** folder.

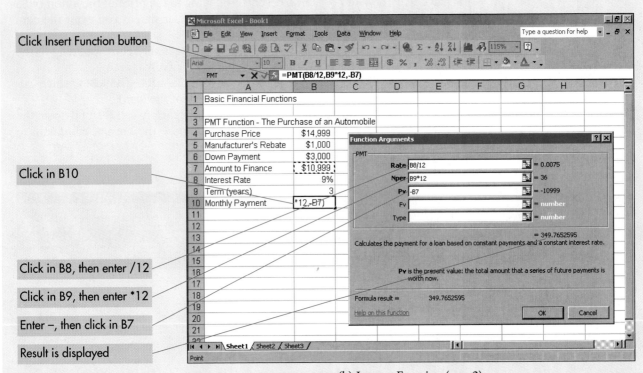

(b) Insert a Function (step 2)

FIGURE 3.4 *Hands-on Exercise 1 (continued)*

SEARCH FOR THE FUNCTION

It's easy to select a function if you know its name, but what if you are unsure of the name or don't know the category in which the function is found? Click the Insert Function button on the Standard toolbar to display the Insert Function dialog box, type a keyword such as "payment" in the search text box, then click the Go button. Excel returns four functions in this example, one of which is the PMT function that you are looking for.

Step 3: **The Goal Seek Command**

➤ You can reduce the monthly payment in various ways. Click in cell **B4** and change the price of the car to **$13,999**. The monthly payment drops to $317.97.

➤ Change the interest rate to **8%** and the term of the loan to **4** years. The payment drops to $244.10.

➤ You can reduce the payment still further by using the Goal Seek command to fix the payment at a specified level. Click in cell **B10**, the cell containing the formula for the monthly payment.

➤ Pull down the **Tools menu**. Click **Goal Seek** to display the dialog box in Figure 3.4c. Click in the **To value** text box. Type **200** (the desired payment).

➤ Click in the **By changing cell** text box. Type **B4**, the cell containing the price of the car. This is the cell whose value will be determined. Click **OK**.

➤ The Goal Seek command returns a successful solution consisting of $12,192 and $200 in cells B4 and B10, respectively. Click **OK** to accept the solution and close the Goal Seek dialog box.

➤ Save the workbook.

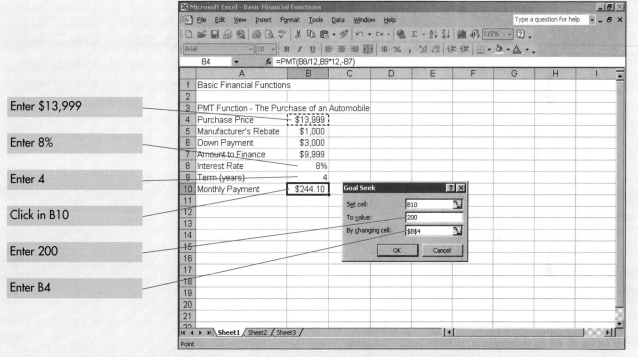

(c) The Goal Seek Command (step 3)

FIGURE 3.4   *Hands-on Exercise 1 (continued)*

THE FORMATTING IS IN THE CELL

Once a number format has been assigned to a cell, either by including the format as you entered a number, or through execution of a formatting command, the formatting remains in the cell. Thus, to change the contents in a formatted cell, all you need to do is enter the new number without the formatting. Entering 5000, for example, in a cell that was previously formatted as currency will display the number as $5,000. To remove the formatting, pull down the Edit menu, select the Clear command, then choose Format.

Step 4: **The Future Value Function**

> ➤ Check your work to be sure that your worksheet matches the top half of Figure 3.4d. Make corrections as necessary.
> ➤ Enter the labels in cells **A13 through A17** as shown in the figure. Click in cell **B14** and type **$2,000** corresponding to the annual contribution. Be sure to include the dollar sign.
> ➤ Enter **8%** (type the percent sign) and **40**, in cells **B15 and B16**, respectively.
> ➤ Click in cell **B17**, type **=FV(** . You will see a ScreenTip that shows the arguments in the FV function. There are five arguments, but only the first three (rate, nper, and pv) are required. (The last two arguments are enclosed in square brackets to indicate they are optional.)
> ➤ Use pointing to complete the function, which is **=FV(B15,B16,−B14)**. Press **enter** when you have finished.
> ➤ You should see $518,113.04 in cell B17. This is the amount you will have at retirement, given that you save $2,000 a year for 40 years and earn 8% interest over the life of your investment.
> ➤ Save the workbook.

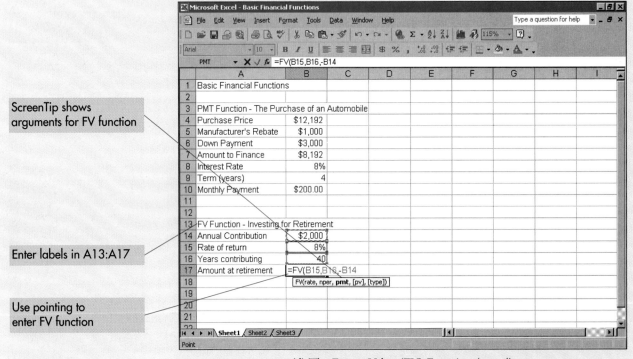

ScreenTip shows arguments for FV function

Enter labels in A13:A17

Use pointing to enter FV function

(d) The Future Value (FV) Function (step 4)

FIGURE 3.4   *Hands-on Exercise 1 (continued)*

IT'S COLOR CODED

Double click in the cell that contains the FV function, then look closely at the arguments within the function to see that each argument is a different color. Each color corresponds to the border color of the referenced cell. You can change any reference in the function (e.g., from B15 to C15) by dragging the color-coded border surrounding cell B15 (the reference you want to change) to cell C15 (the new reference).

Step 5: **Format the Worksheet**

➤ Your workbook should match Figure 3.4e except for the formatting. Click and drag cells **A1 and B1**, then click the **Merge and Center button**.

➤ Click the **down arrow** on the Font Size list box to change the font size to **12**. Click the **Bold button** to boldface the title.

➤ Click cell **A3**. Press and hold the **Ctrl key** as you click cells **A10:B10, A13**, and **A17:B17** to select all of these cells. Click the **Bold button** to boldface the contents of these cells.

➤ Click and drag to select cells **A4 through A9**. Press and hold the **Ctrl key** as you click and drag to select cells **A14 through A16** (in addition to cells A4 through A9).

➤ Click the **Increase Indent button** on the Formatting toolbar to indent the labels as shown in Figure 3.4e.

➤ Click in cell **A19** and enter your name, then click the **Bold button** to boldface the type.

➤ Save the workbook.

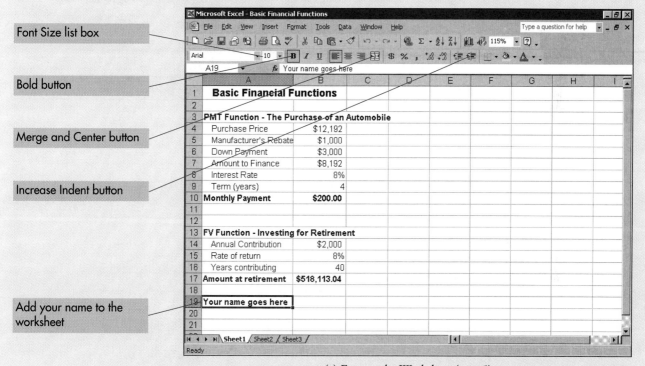

Font Size list box

Bold button

Merge and Center button

Increase Indent button

Add your name to the worksheet

(e) Format the Worksheet (step 5)

FIGURE 3.4 *Hands-on Exercise 1 (continued)*

SELECTING NONCONTIGUOUS RANGES

You can apply the same formatting to noncontiguous (nonadjacent) cells within a worksheet by using the Ctrl key to select the cells. Click and drag to select the first cell range, then press and hold the Ctrl key as you select a second range. Continue to press the Ctrl key to select additional ranges, then format all of the selected cells with a single command. Click anywhere in the worksheet to deselect the cells.

Step 6: **Print the Cell Formulas**

➤ Pull down the **File menu** and click the **Page Setup command** to display the Page Setup dialog box. Click the **Sheet tab**, then check the boxes to print gridlines and row and column headings.

➤ Click the **Margins tab** and check the box to center the worksheet horizontally. Click **OK** to accept the settings and close the dialog box.

➤ Save the workbook. Click the **Print Preview button** on the Standard toolbar to be sure you are satisfied with the appearance of the workbook. Click the **Print button**, then click **OK** to print the worksheet.

➤ Press **Ctrl+~** to display the cell contents as opposed to the displayed values. Preview the worksheet in this format, then print it when you are satisfied with its appearance. Press **Ctrl+~** to return the worksheet to displayed values.

➤ Submit printouts—the displayed values and the cell formulas—to your instructor as proof that you did this exercise.

➤ Exit Excel if you do not want to continue with the next exercise at this time.

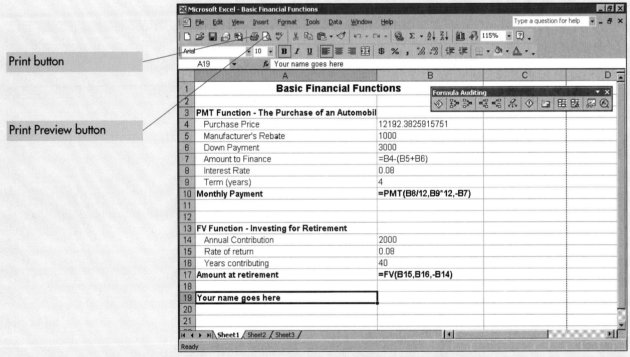

(f) Print the Cell Formulas (step 6)

FIGURE 3.4   *Hands-on Exercise 1 (continued)*

ARE THE PAYMENTS MONTHLY OR ANNUAL?

The FV function in this example computes the future value of a series of annual payments, with the term and interest rate specified as annual values, and thus there is no need to multiply or divide these values by 12. The car payment in the previous example, however, was on a monthly basis. Thus the annual interest rate was divided by 12 (to obtain the monthly rate), while the term of the loan was multiplied by 12, in order to put the numbers on a monthly basis.

The PMT function is used in our next example in conjunction with the purchase of a home. The example also reviews the concept of relative and absolute addresses from Chapter 2. In addition, it introduces several other techniques to make you more proficient in Excel.

The spreadsheets in Figure 3.5 illustrate a variable rate mortgage, which will be developed over the next several pages. The user enters the amount he or she wishes to borrow and a starting interest rate, and the spreadsheet displays the associated monthly payment. The spreadsheet in Figure 3.5a enables the user to see the monthly payment at varying interest rates, and to contrast the amount of the payment for a 15- and a 30-year mortgage.

Most first-time buyers opt for the longer term, but they would do well to consider a 15-year mortgage. Note, for example, that the difference in monthly payments for a $100,000 mortgage at 7.5% is only $227.80 (the difference between $927.01 for a 15-year mortgage versus $699.21 for the 30-year mortgage). This is a significant amount of money, but when viewed as a percentage of the total cost of a home (property taxes and maintenance), it becomes less important, especially when you consider the substantial saving in interest over the life of the mortgage.

Figure 3.5b expands the spreadsheet to show the total interest over the life of the loan for both the 15- and the 30-year mortgage. The total interest on a $100,000 loan at 7.5% is $151,717 for a 30-year mortgage, but only $66,862 for a 15-year mortgage. In other words, you will pay back the $100,000 in principal plus another $151,717 in interest if you select the longer term.

Difference in monthly payment between a 30-year and a 15-year mortgage at 7.5%

	A	B	C	D
1	Amount Borrowed		$100,000	
2	Starting Interest		7.50%	
3				
4		Monthly Payment		
5	Interest	30 Years	15 Years	Difference
6	7.50%	$699.21	$927.01	$227.80
7	8.50%	$768.91	$984.74	$215.83
8	9.50%	$840.85	$1,044.22	$203.37
9	10.50%	$914.74	$1,105.40	$190.66
10	11.50%	$990.29	$1,168.19	$177.90
11	12.50%	$1,067.26	$1,232.52	$165.26

(a) Difference in Monthly Payment

Less interest is paid on a 15-year loan ($66,862 vs $151,717 on a 30-year loan)

	A	B	C	D	E
1	Amount Borrowed			$100,000	
2	Starting Interest			7.50%	
3					
4		30 Years		15 Years	
5	Interest	Monthly Payment	Total Interest	Monthly Payment	Total Interest
6	7.50%	$699.21	$151,717	$927.01	$66,862
7	8.50%	$768.91	$176,809	$984.74	$77,253
8	9.50%	$840.85	$202,708	$1,044.22	$87,960
9	10.50%	$914.74	$229,306	$1,105.40	$98,972
10	11.50%	$990.29	$256,505	$1,168.19	$110,274
11	12.50%	$1,067.26	$284,213	$1,232.52	$121,854

(b) Total Interest

FIGURE 3.5   *15- versus 30-Year Mortgage*

Relative versus Absolute Addresses

Figure 3.6 displays the cell formulas for the mortgage analysis. All of the formulas are based on the amount borrowed and the starting interest, in cells C1 and C2, respectively. You can vary either or both of these parameters, and the worksheet will automatically recalculate the monthly payments.

The similarity in the formulas from one row to the next implies that the copy operation will be essential to the development of the worksheet. You must, however, remember the distinction between a ***relative*** and an ***absolute reference***—that is, a cell reference that changes during a copy operation (relative) versus one that does not (absolute). Consider the PMT function as it appears in cell B6:

$$=PMT(A6/12, 30*12, -\$C\$1)$$

└── The amount of the loan, $-\$C\$1$, is an absolute reference that remains constant

└── Number of periods (30 years*12 months/year)

└── The interest rate, A6/12, is a relative reference that changes

The entry A6/12 (which is the first argument in the formula in cell B6) is interpreted to mean "divide the contents of the cell one column to the left by 12." Thus, when the PMT function in cell B6 is copied to cell B7, it (the copied formula) is adjusted to maintain this relationship and will contain the entry A7/12. The Copy command does not duplicate a relative address exactly, but adjusts it from row to row (or column to column) to maintain the relative relationship. The cell reference for the amount of the loan should not change when the formula is copied, and hence it is specified as an absolute address.

Relative reference (adjusts during copy operation)

Absolute reference (doesn't adjust during copy operation)

	A	B	C	D
1	Amount Borrowed		$100,000	
2	Starting Interest		7.50%	
3				
4	Monthly Payment			
5	Interest	30 Years	15 Years	Difference
6	=C2	=PMT(A6/12,30*12,-$C$1)	=PMT(A6/12,15*12,-$C$1)	=C6-B6
7	=A6+0.01	=PMT(A7/12,30*12,-$C$1)	=PMT(A7/12,15*12,-$C$1)	=C7-B7
8	=A7+0.01	=PMT(A8/12,30*12,-$C$1)	=PMT(A8/12,15*12,-$C$1)	=C8-B8
9	=A8+0.01	=PMT(A9/12,30*12,-$C$1)	=PMT(A9/12,15*12,-$C$1)	=C9-B9
10	=A9+0.01	=PMT(A10/12,30*12,-$C$1)	=PMT(A10/12,15*12,-$C$1)	=C10-B10
11	=A10+0.01	=PMT(A11/12,30*12,-$C$1)	=PMT(A11/12,15*12,-$C$1)	=C11-B11

FIGURE 3.6 *Cell Formulas*

ISOLATE ASSUMPTIONS

The formulas in a worksheet should be based on cell references rather than specific values—for example, C1 or $C$1 rather than $100,000. The cells containing these values should be clearly labeled and set apart from the rest of the worksheet. You can then vary the inputs (***assumptions***) to the worksheet and immediately see the effect. The chance for error is also minimized because you are changing the contents of a single cell, rather than changing multiple formulas.

Mixed References

Figure 3.7 displays a new worksheet that uses the FV function to calculate the value of an *IRA (Individual Retirement Account)* under various combinations of interest rates and years for investing. The annual contribution is $2,000 in all instances (the maximum that is allowed under current law). The interest rates appear in row 5, while the years for investing are shown in column B. The intersection of a row and column contains the future value of a series of $2,000 investments for the specific interest rate and year combination. Cell F21, for example, shows that $2,000 a year, invested over 40 years at 8%, will compound to $518,113.

The key to the worksheet is to realize that the Future Value function requires *mixed references* for both the interest rate and number of years. The interest rate will always come from row 5, but the column will vary. In similar fashion, the number of years will always come from column B, but the row will vary. Using this information we can enter the appropriate formula in cell C6, then copy that formula to the remaining cells in row 6, and finally copy row 6 to the remaining rows in the worksheet. The key to the worksheet is the formula in cell C6. Consider:

Future Value = FV(C$5, $B6, –$D$3)

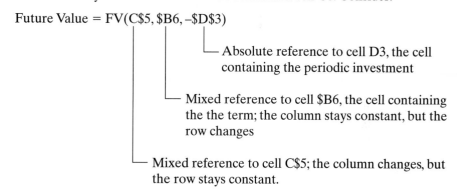

Absolute reference to cell D3, the cell containing the periodic investment

Mixed reference to cell $B6, the cell containing the the term; the column stays constant, but the row changes

Mixed reference to cell C$5; the column changes, but the row stays constant.

The majority of spreadsheets can be developed using a combination of relative and absolute references. Occasionally, however, you will need to incorporate mixed references as you will see in our next exercise.

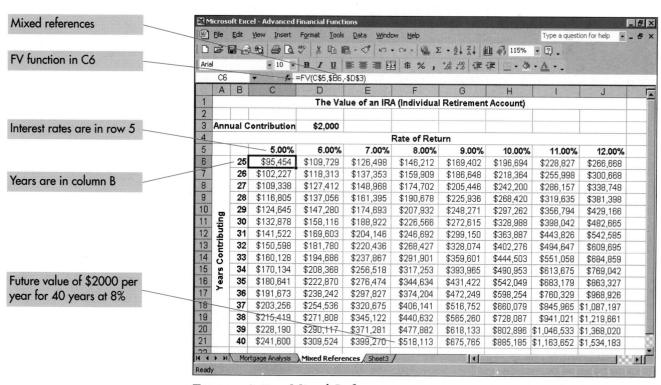

FIGURE 3.7 *Mixed References*

ADVANCED FINANCIAL FUNCTIONS

Objective   To use relative, absolute, and mixed references in conjunction with the PMT and FV functions; to practice various formatting commands. Use Figure 3.8 as a guide in the exercise.

Step 1:   **The Spell Check**

> ➤ Start Excel. Close the task pane if it is open. Click in cell **A1**. Type **Amount Borrowed**. Do not be concerned that the text is longer than the cell width, as cell B1 is empty and thus the text will be displayed in its entirety. Press the **enter key** or **down arrow** to complete the entry.
> ➤ Type **Starting Interest** in cell **A2**. Click in cell **A4**. Type **Monthly Payment**. Enter the remaining labels in cells **A5 through D5**, as shown in Figure 3.8a without concern for the column width.
> ➤ We suggest that you deliberately misspell one or more words in order to try the spell check. Click in cell **A1** to begin the spell check at the beginning of the worksheet.
> ➤ Click the **Spelling button** on the Standard toolbar to initiate the spell check as shown in Figure 3.8a. Make corrections, as necessary, just as you would in Microsoft Word.
> ➤ Click in cell **C1**. Type **$100,000** (include the dollar sign). Press the **enter key** or **down arrow** to complete the entry and move to cell **C2**. Type **7.5%** (include the percent sign). Press **enter**.
> ➤ Save the workbook as **Advanced Financial Functions** in the **Exploring Excel** folder on the appropriate drive.

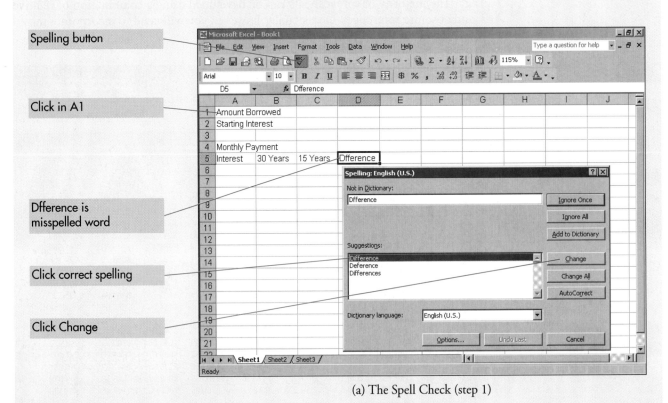

(a) The Spell Check (step 1)

FIGURE 3.8   *Hands-on Exercise 2*

Step 2: **The Fill Handle**

➤ Click in cell **A6**. Use pointing to enter the formula **=C2** to reference the starting interest rate in cell C2.

➤ Click in cell **A7**. Use pointing to enter the formula **=A6+.01** to compute the interest rate in this cell, which is one percent more than the interest rate in row six. Press **enter**.

➤ Click in cell **A7**. Point to the **fill handle** in the lower corner of cell A7. The mouse pointer changes to a thin crosshair.

➤ Drag the **fill handle** over cells **A8 through A11**. A border appears to indicate the destination range as in Figure 3.8b. Release the mouse to complete the copy operation. The formula and associated percentage format in cell A7 have been copied to cells A8 through A11.

➤ Click in Cell **C2**. Type **5%**. The entries in cells A6 through A11 change automatically. Click the **Undo button** on the Standard toolbar to return to the 7.5% interest rate.

➤ Save the workbook.

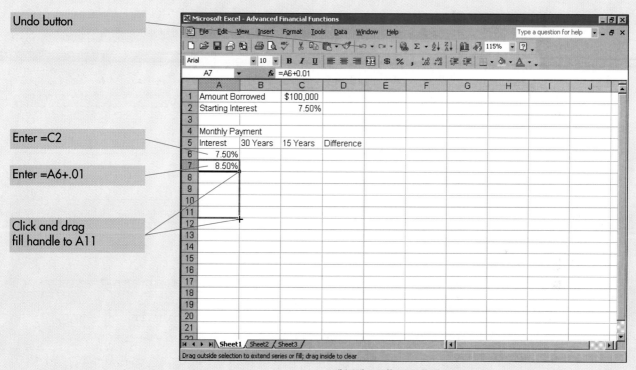

(b) The Fill Handle (step 2)

FIGURE 3.8   *Hands-on Exercise 2 (continued)*

FIND AND REPLACE

Anyone familiar with a word processor takes the Find and Replace commands for granted, but did you know the same capabilities exist in Excel? Pull down the Edit menu and choose either command. You have the same options as in the parallel command in Word, such as a case-sensitive (or insensitive) search. Use the command in the current worksheet to change "Interest" to "Interest Rate".

Step 3: **Determine the 30-year Payments**

➤ Click in cell **B6** and enter the formula **=PMT(A6/12,30*12,−$C$1)** as shown in Figure 3.8c. Note the ScreenTip that appears as you enter the function to indicate the order of the arguments. Note, too, that you can enter the references directly or you can use pointing (click the **F4 key** as necessary to change from relative to absolute addresses).

➤ Click in cell **B6**, which should display the value $699.21, as shown in Figure 3.8c. Click and drag the **fill handle** in the bottom right corner of cell B6 over cells B7 through B11. Release the mouse to complete the copy operation.

➤ The PMT function in cell B6 has been copied to cells B7 through B11. The payment amounts are visible in cells B7 through B10, but cell B11 displays a series of number signs, meaning that the cell (column) is too narrow to display the computed results in the selected format.

➤ Check that cells B6:B11 are still selected. Pull down the **Format menu**, click **Column**, then click **AutoFit Selection** from the cascaded menu. Cell B11 should display $1,067.26.

➤ Save the workbook.

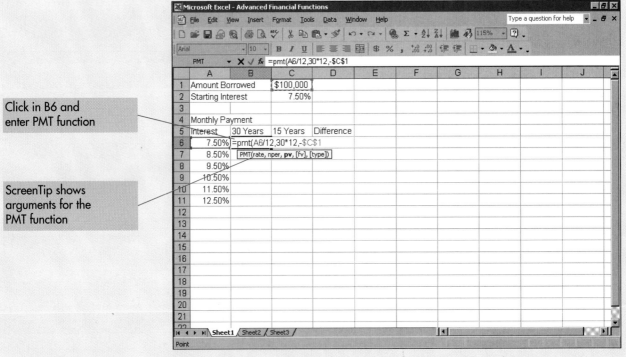

Click in B6 and enter PMT function

ScreenTip shows arguments for the PMT function

(c) Determine the 30-year Payments (step 3)

FIGURE 3.8 *Hands-on Exercise 2 (continued)*

POUND SIGNS AND COLUMN WIDTH

The appearance of pound signs within a cell indicates that the cell width (column width) is insufficient to display the computed results in the selected format. Double click the right border of the column heading to change the column width to accommodate the widest entry in that column. For example, to increase the width of column B, double click the border between the column headings for columns B and C.

Step 4:   **Determine the 15-year Payments**

> ➤ Click in cell **C6** and enter the formula **=PMT(A6/12,15*12,−$C$1)** as shown in Figure 3.8d. Note the ScreenTip that appears as you enter the function to indicate the order of the arguments. You can enter the references directly, or you can use pointing (click the **F4 key** as necessary to change from relative to absolute addresses).
> ➤ Press **enter** to complete the formula. Check that cell C6 displays the value $927.01. Make corrections as necessary.
> ➤ Use the **fill handle** to copy the contents of cell **C6** to cells **C7 through C11**. If necessary, increase the width of column C. Cell C11 should display $1,232.52 if you have done this step correctly.
> ➤ Click in cell **D6** and enter the formula **=C6−B6**, then copy this formula to the remaining cells in this column. Cell D11 should display $165.26.
> ➤ Save the workbook.

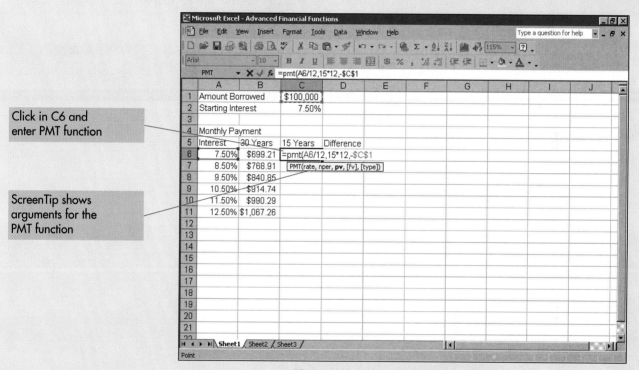

Click in C6 and enter PMT function

ScreenTip shows arguments for the PMT function

(d) Determine the 15-year Payments (step 4)

FIGURE 3.8   *Hands-on Exercise 2 (continued)*

KEYBOARD SHORTCUTS—CUT, COPY, AND PASTE

Ctrl+X (the X is supposed to remind you of a pair of scissors), Ctrl+C, and Ctrl+V are keyboard shortcuts to cut, copy, and paste, respectively, and apply to Excel as well as to Windows applications in general. The keystrokes are easier to remember when you realize that the operative letters X, C, and V are next to each other at the bottom left side of the keyboard. There is no need to memorize the keyboard shortcuts, but as you gain proficiency they will become second nature.

Step 5: **Format the Worksheet**

➤ Click in cell **A13** and enter the label **Financial Consultant**. Enter **your name** in cell A14. Add formatting as necessary using Figure 3.8e as a guide.

➤ Click cell **A4**. Drag the mouse over cells **A4 through D4**. Click the **Merge and Center button** on the Formatting toolbar to center the entry.

➤ Center the column headings in row 5. Add boldface and/or italics to the text and/or numbers as you see fit. Widen columns as necessary.

➤ Pull down the **File menu** and click the **Page Setup command** to display the Page Setup dialog box.

➤ Click the **Margins tab**. Check the box to center the worksheet horizontally. Click the **Sheet tab**. Check the boxes to include row and column headings and gridlines. Click **OK** to exit the Page Setup dialog box.

➤ Save the workbook. Pull down the **File menu**, click the **Print command** to display the Print dialog box, then click **OK** to print the worksheet. Press **Ctrl+~** to display the cell formulas. Widen the columns as necessary, then print.

➤ Press **Ctrl+~** to return to displayed values.

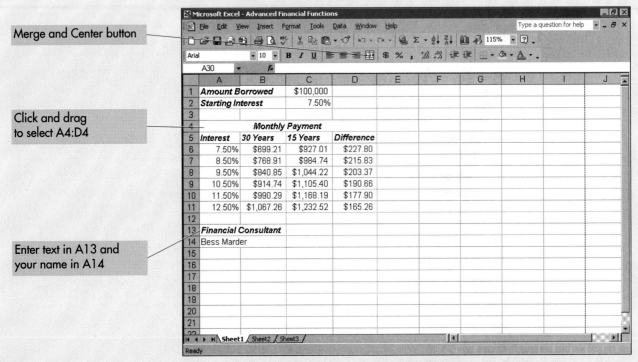

(e) Format the Worksheet (step 5)

FIGURE 3.8   *Hands-on Exercise 2 (continued)*

THE PPMT AND IPMT FUNCTIONS

The PMT function determines the periodic payment for a loan, which in turn is comprised of two components, interest and principal. The amount of the payment that goes toward interest decreases each period, and conversely, the amount for the principle increases. These values can be computed through the IPMT and PPMT functions, respectively, which are used to compute the amortization schedule (payoff) for the loan. See practice exercise 7 at the end of the chapter.

Step 6: **Merge and Center Text**

➤ Click the **Sheet2 tab** to change to this worksheet. Click in cell **A1** and enter the title of the worksheet, **The Value of an IRA (Individual Retirement Account)**.
➤ Enter the indicated labels in cells **A3 and C4** as shown in Figure 3.8f. Click in cell **A6** and type the label **Years Contributing**.
➤ Click and drag to select cells **A6 through A21**, then click the **Merge and Center button** on the Standard toolbar to merge the cells. Right click within the merged cell, then click the **Format Cells command** to display the Format cells dialog box. Click the **Alignment tab**.
➤ Enter **90** in the **Degrees list box** to change to 90 degrees. Click the **down arrow** on the Vertical list box and choose **Center**. Click **OK**. Click the **Undo button** if the results are different from what you intended.
➤ Click and drag to select cells **A1 through J1**, then click the **Merge and Center button** to center the title. Merge and center cells **C4 through J4** in similar fashion.
➤ Click and drag the border between columns A and B to make the column narrower, as appropriate. Save the workbook.

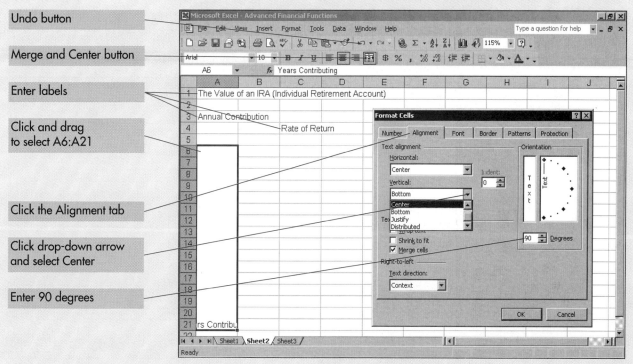

(f) Merge and Center Text (step 6)

FIGURE 3.8 *Hands-on Exercise 2 (continued)*

THE MERGE AND CENTER COMMAND

The Merge and Center command combines multiple cells into a single cell and is best used in conjunction with the headings in a worksheet. Cells can be merged horizontally or vertically, then the text in the merged cells can be aligned in a variety of styles. Text can also be rotated to provide interest in the worksheet. If necessary, you can restore the individual cells and remove the associated formatting using the Edit Clear command. Click in the merged cell, pull down the Edit menu, and click the Clear command. Click Formats to restore the individual cells to the default format.

Step 7: Enter the Row and Column Headings

> Check that the labels in your worksheet match those in Figure 3.8g. Click in cell **D3** and enter **$2,000**. Click in cell **C5** and type **5.00%**. Be sure to include the decimal point, zeros, and percent sign.

> Click in cell **D5** and enter the formula **=C5+.01**, then click and drag the **fill handle** to copy this formula to cells **E5 through J5**.

> Click in cell **B6** and type the number **25**. Click in cell **B7** and enter the formula **=B6+1**, then click and drag the **fill handle** to copy this formula to cells **B8 through B21**.

> Double click the **Sheet2 tab** to select the worksheet name, then type **Mixed References** as the name of this worksheet. Double click the **Sheet1 tab** to select the worksheet name, then type **Mortgage Analysis** as the name of this worksheet.

> Click the newly named **Mixed References worksheet** tab to return to this worksheet and continue working.

> Save the workbook.

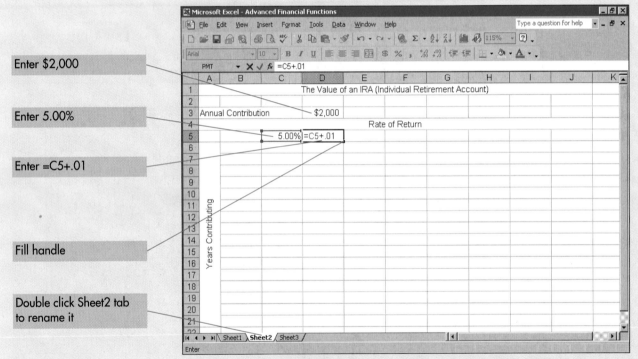

(g) Enter the Row and Column Headings (step 7)

FIGURE 3.8 *Hands-on Exercise 2 (continued)*

AUTOMATIC FORMATTING

Excel converts any number entered with a beginning dollar sign to currency format, and any number entered with an ending percent sign to percentage format. The automatic formatting enables you to save a step by typing $100,000 or 7.5% directly into a cell, rather than entering 100000 or .075 and having to format the number. The formatting is applied to the cell and affects any subsequent numbers in that cell. (Use the Clear command in the Edit menu to remove the formatting.)

Step 8:   **Create the Mixed References**

➤ Click in cell **C6**. Pull down the **Insert menu** and click **Function** (or click the **Insert Function button** on the formula bar) to display the Insert Function dialog box.

➤ Click the **drop-down arrow**, then click **Financial** in the Function Category list box. Click **FV** in the Function Name list box. Click **OK**.

➤ Click and drag the **Formula Palette** so that you can see the underlying cells as shown in Figure 3.8h.

➤ Click the text box for rate, click in cell **C5**, then press the **F4 key** until you see **C$5** within the dialog box.

➤ Press **Tab** to move to (or click in) the **Nper text box**, click in cell **B6**, then press the **F4 key** until you see $B6 within the dialog box.

➤ Press **Tab** to move to (or click in) the **Pmt text box**, type a **minus sign**, click in cell **D3**, then press the **F4 key** until you see **−$D$3** in the dialog box.

➤ Check that the entries on your screen match those in Figure 3.8h, then click **OK**. Cell C6 should display the value $95,454.20.

➤ Save the workbook.

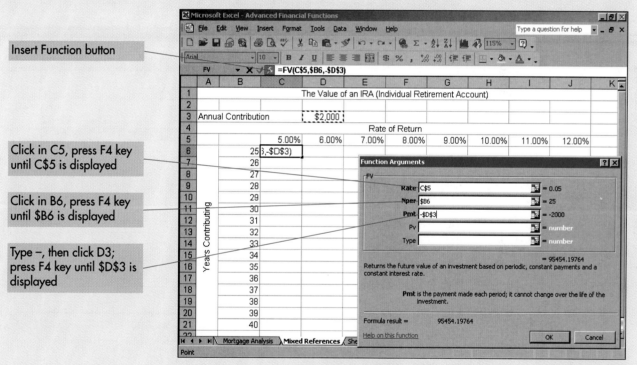

Insert Function button

Click in C5, press F4 key until C$5 is displayed

Click in B6, press F4 key until $B6 is displayed

Type −, then click D3; press F4 key until $D$3 is displayed

(h) Create the Mixed References (step 8)

FIGURE 3.8 *Hands-on Exercise 2 (continued)*

MIXED REFERENCES ARE NOT DIFFICULT

Mixed references are not difficult, provided you think clearly about what is required. In our example, the interest rate will always come from row 5, but the column will change. Hence you enter C$5 for this parameter within the FV function. In similar fashion, the term of the investment will always come from column B, but the row will change. Thus you enter $B6 for this parameter. It's easy and it's powerful.

Step 9: **Copy the Formula**

➤ If necessary, click in cell **C6**, the cell that contains the formula you just created. Click and drag the **fill handle** in cell **C6** to cells **D6 through J6**.

➤ Change the formatting to **zero decimal places**, then change column widths as necessary. Cell J6 should display the value $266,668.

➤ If necessary, select cells **C6 through D6** as shown in Figure 3.8i. Click and drag the fill handle in cell **J6** to cell **J21** to copy the entire row to the remaining rows in the worksheet.

➤ Release the mouse. Cell J21 should display the value $1,534,183, corresponding to the future value of a $2,000 investment for 40 years at 12 percent. Change column widths as necessary.

➤ Click in cell **C6**, then press the **right arrow** to move from one cell to the next in this row to see how the cell formulas change to reflect the mixed references. Return to cell C6, then press the **down arrow** to view the cell formulas for the other cells in this column.

➤ Save the workbook.

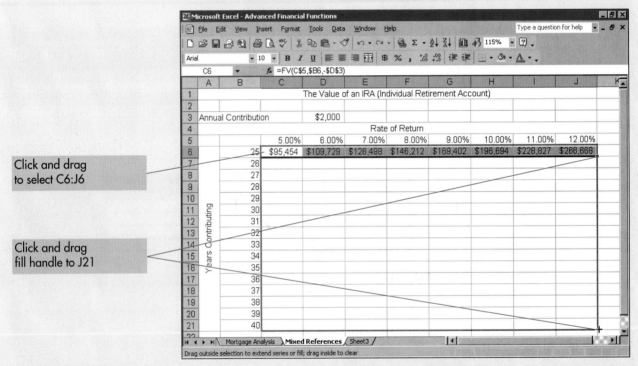

Click and drag to select C6:J6

Click and drag fill handle to J21

(i) Copy the Formula (step 9)

FIGURE 3.8 *Hands-on Exercise 2 (continued)*

THE ROTH IRA

Anyone can start a Roth IRA provided his or her annual earnings are less than $95,000 (under current law). The Roth IRA is different from a traditional IRA in that the annual contribution is not tax-deductible, but all future earnings are. If, for example, you contribute $2,000 a year for 40 years and earn 8%, you will accumulate more than $500,000 at retirement. Once you retire, you can withdraw as much as you like each year, and any money that you withdraw is tax-free. The remaining funds continue to compound on a tax-free basis.

Step 10: **The Finishing Touches**

➤ Check that the numbers in your worksheet match those in Figure 3.8j. Make corrections as necessary, then format the worksheet as shown.

➤ Print the worksheet two ways, once with the displayed values and once with the cell contents.

➤ Use the **Page Setup command** to include gridlines and row and column headings. Use landscape formatting if necessary.

➤ Add a cover sheet, then submit all five pages (the cover sheet, the displayed values and cell formulas for the mortgage analysis from step 5, and the displayed values and cell formulas from this step) to your instructor as proof that you completed this exercise.

➤ Exit Excel if you do not want to continue with the next exercise at this time.

Formula bar shows mixed references

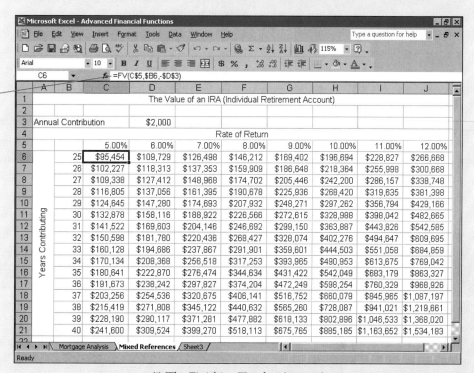

(j) The Finishing Touches (step 10)

FIGURE 3.8   *Hands-on Exercise 2 (continued)*

START SAVING EARLY

The longer you invest, the more time that compound interest has to work its magic. Investing $2,000 for 40 years at 8%, for example, yields a future value of $518,113. Delay for five years, that is invest for 35 years rather than 40, and the amount goes down to $344,634. Put another way—Start your IRA at age 25 and 40 years later you will have accumulated more than half a million dollars. Wait until age 30 and you wind up with significantly less. The out of pocket difference is only $10,000 ($2,000 a year for five years), but the end result at retirement is more than $170,000. Too many people try to time the stock market, which is impossible. It is the time *in* the market that matters.

Financial functions are only one of several categories of functions that are included in Excel. Our next example presents an expanded version of the professor's grade book. It introduces several new functions and shows how those functions can aid in the professor's determination of a student's grade. The expanded grade book is shown in Figure 3.9. Consider:

Statistical functions: The AVERAGE, MAX, and MIN functions are used to compute the statistics on each test for the class as a whole. The range on each test is computed by subtracting the minimum value from the maximum value.

IF function: The IF function conditionally adds a homework bonus of three points to the semester average, prior to determining the letter grade. The bonus is awarded to those students whose homework is "OK." Students whose homework is not "OK" do not receive the bonus.

VLOOKUP function: The expanded grade book converts a student's semester average to a letter grade, in accordance with the table shown in the lower-right portion of the worksheet. A student with an average of 60 to 69 will receive a D, 70 to 79 a C, 80 to 89 a B, and 90 or higher an A. Any student with an average less than 60 receives an F.

The Sort command: The rows within a spreadsheet can be displayed in any sequence by clicking on the appropriate column within the list of students, then clicking the Ascending or Descending sort button on the Standard toolbar. The students in Figure 3.9 are listed alphabetically, but could just as easily have been listed by social security number.

	A	B	C	D	E	F	G	H	I	J
1	Professor's Grade Book - Final Semester Averages									
2										
3	Name	Soc Sec Num	Test 1	Test 2	Test 3	Test 4	Test Average	Homework	Semester Average	Grade
4	Adams, John	111-22-3333	80	71	70	84	77.8	Poor	77.8	C
5	Barber, Maryann	444-55-6666	96	98	97	90	94.2	OK	97.2	A
6	Boone, Dan	777-88-9999	78	81	70	78	77.0	OK	80.0	B
7	Borow, Jeff	123-45-6789	65	65	65	60	63.0	OK	66.0	D
8	Brown, James	999-99-9999	92	95	79	80	85.2	OK	88.2	B
9	Carson, Kit	888-88-8888	90	90	90	70	82.0	OK	85.0	B
10	Coulter, Sara	100-00-0000	60	50	40	79	61.6	OK	64.6	D
11	Fegin, Richard	222-22-2222	75	70	65	95	80.0	OK	83.0	B
12	Ford, Judd	200-00-0000	90	90	80	90	88.0	Poor	88.0	B
13	Glassman, Kris	444-44-4444	82	78	62	77	75.2	OK	78.2	C
14	Goodman, Neil	555-55-5555	92	88	65	78	80.2	OK	83.2	B
15	Milgrom, Marion	666-66-6666	94	92	86	84	88.0	OK	91.0	A
16	Moldof, Adam	300-00-0000	92	78	65	84	80.6	OK	83.6	B
17	Smith, Adam	777-77-7777	60	50	65	80	67.0	Poor	67.0	D
18										
19	Average		81.9	78.3	71.4	80.6	HW Bonus	3	Grading Criteria	
20	Highest Grade		96.0	98.0	97.0	95.0			0	F
21	Lowest Grade		60.0	50.0	40.0	60.0			60	D
22	Range		36.0	48.0	57.0	35.0			70	C
23									80	B
24	Exam Weights		20%	20%	20%	40%			90	A

Statistical functions   IF Function   VLOOKUP Function

FIGURE 3.9   *The Expanded Grade Book*

Statistical Functions

The **MAX**, **MIN**, and **AVERAGE functions** return the highest, lowest, and average values, respectively, from an argument list. The list may include individual cell references, ranges, numeric values, functions, or mathematical expressions (formulas). The **statistical functions** are illustrated in the worksheet of Figure 3.10.

The first example, =AVERAGE(A1:A3), computes the average for cells A1 through A3 by adding the values in the indicated range (70, 80, and 90), then dividing the result by three, to obtain an average of 80. Additional arguments in the form of values and/or cell addresses can be specified within the parentheses; for example, the function =AVERAGE(A1:A3,200), computes the average of cells A1, A2, and A3, and the number 200.

Cells that are empty or cells that contain text values are *not* included in the computation. Thus, since cell A4 is empty, the function =AVERAGE(A1:A4) also returns an average of 80 (240/3). In similar fashion, the function =AVERAGE(A1:A3,A5) includes only three values in its computation (cells A1, A2, and A3), because the text entry in cell A5 is excluded. The results of the MIN and MAX functions are obtained in a comparable way, as indicated in Figure 3.10. Empty cells and text entries are not included in the computation.

The COUNT and COUNTA functions each tally the number of entries in the argument list and are subtly different. The **COUNT function** returns the number of cells containing a numeric entry, including formulas that evaluate to numeric results. The **COUNTA function** includes cells with text as well as numeric values. The functions =COUNT(A1:A3) and =COUNTA(A1:A3) both return a value of 3 as do the two functions =COUNT(A1:A4) and =COUNTA(A1:A4). (Cell A4 is empty and is excluded from the latter computations.) The function =COUNT(A1:A3,A5) also returns a value of 3 because it does not include the text entry in cell A5. However, the function =COUNTA(A1:A3,A5) returns a value of 4 because it includes the text entry in cell A5.

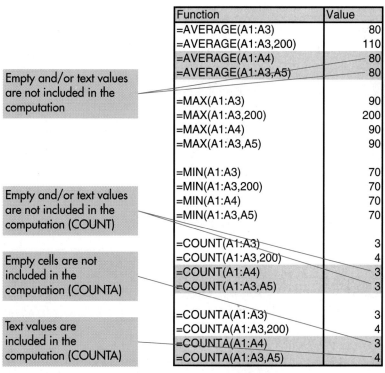

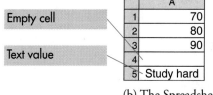

Empty and/or text values are not included in the computation

Empty and/or text values are not included in the computation (COUNT)

Empty cells are not included in the computation (COUNTA)

Text values are included in the computation (COUNTA)

Function	Value
=AVERAGE(A1:A3)	80
=AVERAGE(A1:A3,200)	110
=AVERAGE(A1:A4)	80
=AVERAGE(A1:A3,A5)	80
=MAX(A1:A3)	90
=MAX(A1:A3,200)	200
=MAX(A1:A4)	90
=MAX(A1:A3,A5)	90
=MIN(A1:A3)	70
=MIN(A1:A3,200)	70
=MIN(A1:A4)	70
=MIN(A1:A3,A5)	70
=COUNT(A1:A3)	3
=COUNT(A1:A3,200)	4
=COUNT(A1:A4)	3
=COUNT(A1:A3,A5)	3
=COUNTA(A1:A3)	3
=COUNTA(A1:A3,200)	4
=COUNTA(A1:A4)	3
=COUNTA(A1:A3,A5)	4

(a) Illustrative Functions

Empty cell

Text value

	A
1	70
2	80
3	90
4	
5	Study hard

(b) The Spreadsheet

FIGURE 3.10 *Statistical Functions with a Text Entry*

Arithmetic Expressions versus Functions

Many worksheet calculations, such as an average or a sum, can be performed in two ways. You can enter a formula such as =(A1+A2+A3)/3, or you can use the equivalent function =AVERAGE(A1:A3). *The use of functions is generally preferable* as shown in Figure 3.11.

The two worksheets in Figure 3.11a may appear equivalent, but the SUM function is superior to the arithmetic expression. This is true despite the fact that the entries in cell A5 of both worksheets return a value of 100.

Consider what happens if a new row is inserted between existing rows 2 and 3, with the entry in the new cell equal to 25 as shown in Figure 3.11b. The SUM function adjusts automatically to include the new value (returning a sum of 125) because the SUM function was defined originally for the cell range *A1 through A4*. The new row is inserted within these cells, moving the entry in cell A4 to cell A5, and changing the range to include cell A5.

No such accommodation is made in the arithmetic expression, which was defined to include four *specific* cells rather than a range of cells. The addition of the new row modifies the cell references (since the values in cells A3 and A4 have been moved to cells A4 and A5), and does not include the new row in the adjusted expression.

Similar reasoning holds for deleting a row. Figure 3.11c deletes row two from the *original* worksheets, which moves the entry in cell A4 to cell A3. The SUM function adjusts automatically to =SUM(A1:A3) and returns the value 80. The formula, however, returns an error (to indicate an illegal cell reference) because it is still attempting to add the entries in four cells, one of which no longer exists. In summary, a function expands and contracts to adjust for insertions or deletions, and should be used wherever possible.

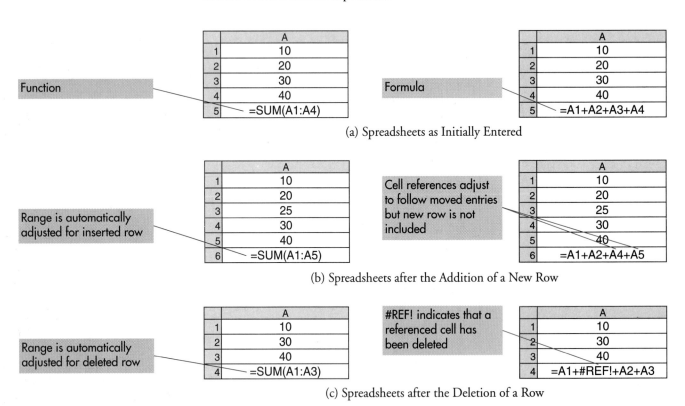

(a) Spreadsheets as Initially Entered

(b) Spreadsheets after the Addition of a New Row

(c) Spreadsheets after the Deletion of a Row

FIGURE 3.11 *Arithmetic Expressions versus Functions*

IF Function

The ***IF function*** enables decision making to be implemented within a worksheet. It has three arguments: a condition that is either true or false, the value if the condition is true, and the value if the condition is false. Consider:

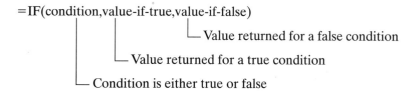

$$=IF(condition, value\text{-}if\text{-}true, value\text{-}if\text{-}false)$$

Value returned for a false condition

Value returned for a true condition

Condition is either true or false

The IF function returns either the second or third argument, depending on the result of the condition; that is, if the condition is true, the function returns the second argument. If the condition is false, the function returns the third argument.

The condition includes one of the six ***relational operators*** in Figure 3.12a. The IF function is illustrated in the worksheet in Figure 3.12b, which is used to create the examples in Figure 3.12c. The arguments may be numeric (1000 or 2000), a cell reference to display the contents of the specific cell (B1 or B2), a formula (=B1+10 or =B1−10), a function (MAX(B1:B2) or MIN(B1:B2)), or a text entry enclosed in quotation marks ("Go" or "Hold").

Operator	Description
=	Equal to
<>	Not equal to
<	Less than
>	Greater than
<=	Less than or equal to
>=	Greater than or equal to

(a) Relational Operators

	A	B	C
1	10	15	April
2	10	30	May

(b) The Spreadsheet

IF Function	Evaluation	Result
=IF(A1=A2,1000,2000)	10 is equal to 10: TRUE	1000
=IF(A1<>A2,1000,2000)	10 is not equal to 10: FALSE	2000
=IF(A1<>A2,B1,B2)	10 is not equal to 10:FALSE	30
=IF(A1<B2,MAX(B1:B2),MIN(B1:B2))	10 is less than 30: TRUE	30
=IF(A1<A2,B1+10,B1-10)	10 is less than 10:FALSE	5
=IF(A1=A2,C1,C2)	10 is equal to 10: TRUE	April
=IF(SUM(A1:A2)>20,"Go","Hold")	10+10 is greater than 20:FALSE	Hold

(c) Examples

FIGURE 3.12 *The IF Function*

The IF function is used in the grade book of Figure 3.9 to award a bonus for homework. Students whose homework is "OK" receive the bonus, whereas other students do not. The IF function to implement this logic for the first student is entered in cell H4 as follows:

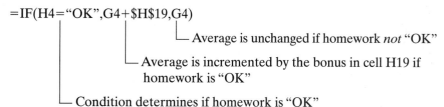

$$=IF(H4="OK", G4+\$H\$19, G4)$$

Average is unchanged if homework *not* "OK"

Average is incremented by the bonus in cell H19 if homework is "OK"

Condition determines if homework is "OK"

The IF function compares the value in cell H4 (the homework grade) to the literal "OK." If the condition is true (the homework is "OK"), the bonus in cell H19 is added to the student's test average in cell G4. If, however, the condition is false (the homework is not "OK"), the average is unchanged.

VLOOKUP Function

Consider, for a moment, how the professor assigns letter grades to students at the end of the semester. He or she computes a test average for each student and conditionally awards the bonus for homework. The professor then determines a letter grade according to a predetermined scale; for example, 90 or above is an A, 80 to 89 is a B, and so on.

The **VLOOKUP** (vertical lookup) *function* duplicates this process within a worksheet by assigning an entry to a cell based on a numeric value contained in another cell. The **HLOOKUP** (horizontal lookup) *function* is similar in concept except that the table is arranged horizontally. In other words, just as the professor knows where on the grading scale a student's numerical average will fall, the VLOOKUP function determines where within a specified table (the grading criteria) a numeric value (a student's average) is found, and retrieves the corresponding entry (the letter grade).

The VLOOKUP function requires three arguments: the value to look up, the range of cells containing the table in which the value is to be looked up, and the column-number within the table that contains the result. These concepts are illustrated in Figure 3.13, which was taken from the expanded grade book in Figure 3.9. The table in Figure 3.13 extends over two columns (I and J), and five rows (20 through 24); that is, the table is located in the range I20:J24. The **breakpoints** or matching values (the lowest numeric value for each grade) are contained in column I (the first column in the table) and are in ascending order. The corresponding letter grades are found in column J.

The VLOOKUP function in cell J4 determines the letter grade (for John Adams) based on the computed average in cell I4. Consider:

=VLOOKUP(I4,$I$20:$J$24,2)

└─ The column number containing the grade

└─ The range of the table

└─ Value to look up (the student's average)

The first argument is the value to look up, which in this example is Adams's computed average, found in cell I4. A relative reference is used so that the address will adjust when the formula is copied to the other rows in the worksheet.

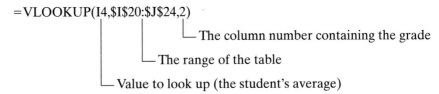

	A	. . .	G	H	I	J
1	Professor's Grade Book - Final Semester Averages					
2						
3	Name		Test Average	Homework	Semester Average	Grade
4	Adams, John		77.8	Poor		
.		.	.	.	.	.
.	.		.	.	.	.
.	.	.	.	.	.	.
19	Average		HW Bonus	3	Grading Criteria	
20	Highest Grade				0	F
21	Lowest Grade				60	D
22	Range				70	C
23					80	B
24	Exam Weights				90	A

=VLOOKUP(I4,$I$20:$J$24,2)   Breakpoints (in ascending order)   Grades are in column 2 of table

FIGURE 3.13 *Table Lookup Function*

A large worksheet, such as the extended grade book, can seldom be seen on the monitor in its entirety. It's necessary, therefore, to learn how to view the distant parts of a worksheet, to keep certain parts of the worksheet in constant view, and/or to hide selected rows and columns. These concepts are illustrated in Figure 3.14. Figure 3.14a displays the initial worksheet, with cell A1 selected as the active cell, so that you see the upper-left portion of the worksheet, rows 1 through 20 inclusive, and columns A through I inclusive. You cannot see the semester grades in column J, nor can you see the class averages and other statistics that begin in row 21.

Clicking the right arrow on the horizontal scroll bar (or pressing the right arrow key when the active cell is already in the rightmost column of the screen) causes the entire screen to move one column to the right. In similar fashion, clicking the down arrow in the vertical scroll bar (or pressing the down arrow key when the active cell is in the bottom row of the screen) causes the entire screen to move down one row. This is known as *scrolling* and it comes about automatically as the active cell is changed as you work with the worksheet.

Freezing Panes

Scrolling brings the distant portions of a worksheet into view, but it also moves the headings for existing rows and/or columns off the screen. You can, however, retain the headings by freezing panes as shown in Figure 3.14b. The letter grades and the grading criteria are visible as in the previous figure, but so too are the names at the left of the worksheet and the column headings at the top of the worksheet.

Look closely at Figure 3.14b and you will see column B (containing the Social Security numbers) is missing, as are rows 4 through 7 (the first four students). You will also notice a horizontal line under row three and a vertical line after column A, to indicate that these rows and columns have been frozen. This is accomplished through the *Freeze Panes command* that always displays the desired row or column headings (column A and rows 1, 2 and 3 in this example) regardless of the scrolling in effect. The rows and/or columns that are frozen are the ones above and to the left of the active cell when the command is issued. The *Unfreeze Panes command* returns to normal scrolling.

Hiding Rows and Columns

Figure 3.14c illustrates the ability to hide rows and/or columns in a worksheet. We have hidden columns C through F (inclusive) that contain the results of the individual tests, and rows 19 through 24 that contain the summary statistics. The "missing" rows and columns remain in the workbook but are hidden from view. The cells are not visible in the monitor, nor do they appear when the worksheet is printed. To hide a row or column, click the row or column heading to select the entire row or column, then execute the Hide command from within the Format menu. *Unhiding cells* is trickier because you need to select the adjacent rows or columns prior to executing the Unhide command.

Printing a Large Worksheet

The *Page Break Preview command* (in the View menu) lets you see and/or modify the page breaks that will occur when the worksheet is printed as shown in Figure 3.14d. The dashed blue line between columns H and I indicate that the worksheet will print on two pages, with columns A to H on page 1 and columns I and J on page 2. The dialog box shows that you adjust (eliminate) the page break by dragging the dashed line to the right.

The *Page Setup command* also contains various options that are used in conjunction with printing a large worksheet. You might, for example change from Portrait (8½ × 11) orientation to Landscape (11 × 8½), use scaling to force the entire worksheet on one page, and/or reduce the margins. You can also select an option to repeat the row and/or column headings on every page of a multiple-page printout.

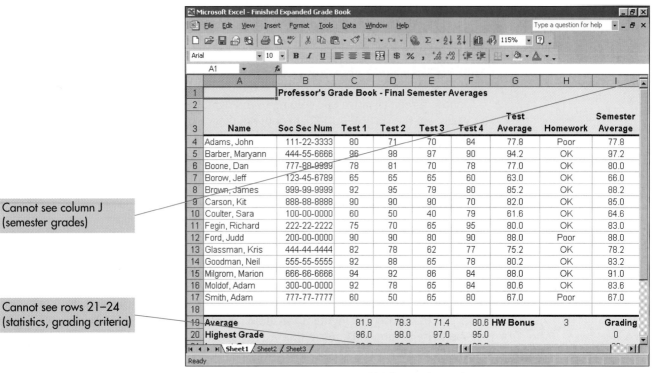

Cannot see column J (semester grades)

Cannot see rows 21–24 (statistics, grading criteria)

(a) The Grade Book

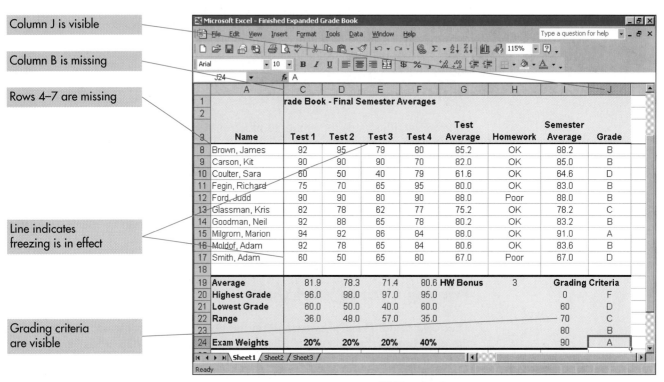

Column J is visible

Column B is missing

Rows 4–7 are missing

Line indicates freezing is in effect

Grading criteria are visible

(b) Freezing Panes

FIGURE 3.14   *Working with Large Spreadsheets*

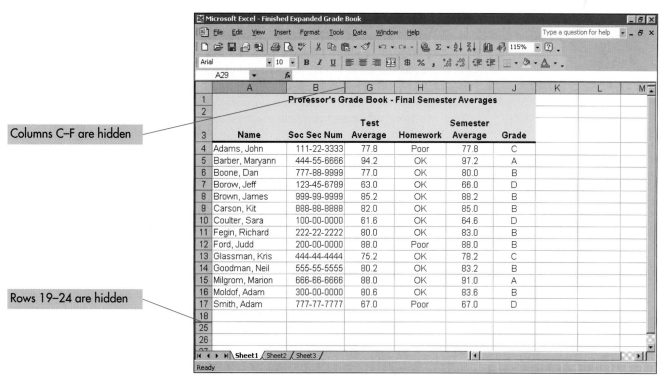

Columns C–F are hidden

Rows 19–24 are hidden

(c) Hiding Rows and Columns

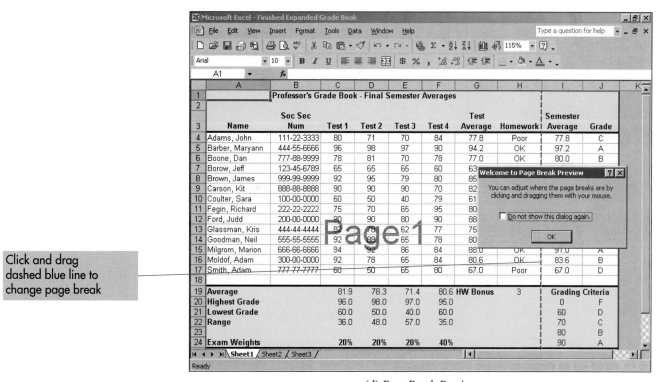

Click and drag dashed blue line to change page break

(d) Page Break Preview

FIGURE 3.14   *Working with Large Spreadsheets (continued)*

AutoFilter Command

The *AutoFilter command* lets you display a selected set of students (rows) within a worksheet as shown in Figure 3.15. The hidden rows are *not* deleted, but are simply not displayed. We begin with Figure 3.15a, which shows the list of all students (with selected columns hidden from view). Look closely at the column headings in row three and note the presence of drop-down arrows that appear in response to the AutoFilter command.

Clicking a drop-down arrow produces a list of the unique values for that column, enabling you to establish the criteria-selected records. To display the students with poor homework, for example, click the drop-down arrow for Homework, then click Poor from the resulting list. Figure 3.15b shows three students in rows 4, 12, and 17 that satisfy the filter. The remaining students are still in the worksheet but are not shown because of the selection criterion.

A filter condition can be imposed on multiple columns as shown in Figure 3.15c. As indicated, the worksheet in Figure 3.15b displays the only students with poor homework. Clicking the arrow next to Grade, then clicking "B", will filter the list further to display the students who received a "B" *and* who have poor homework. Only one student meets both conditions, as shown in Figure 3.15c. The drop-down arrows next to Homework and Grade are displayed in blue to indicate that a filter is in effect for these columns.

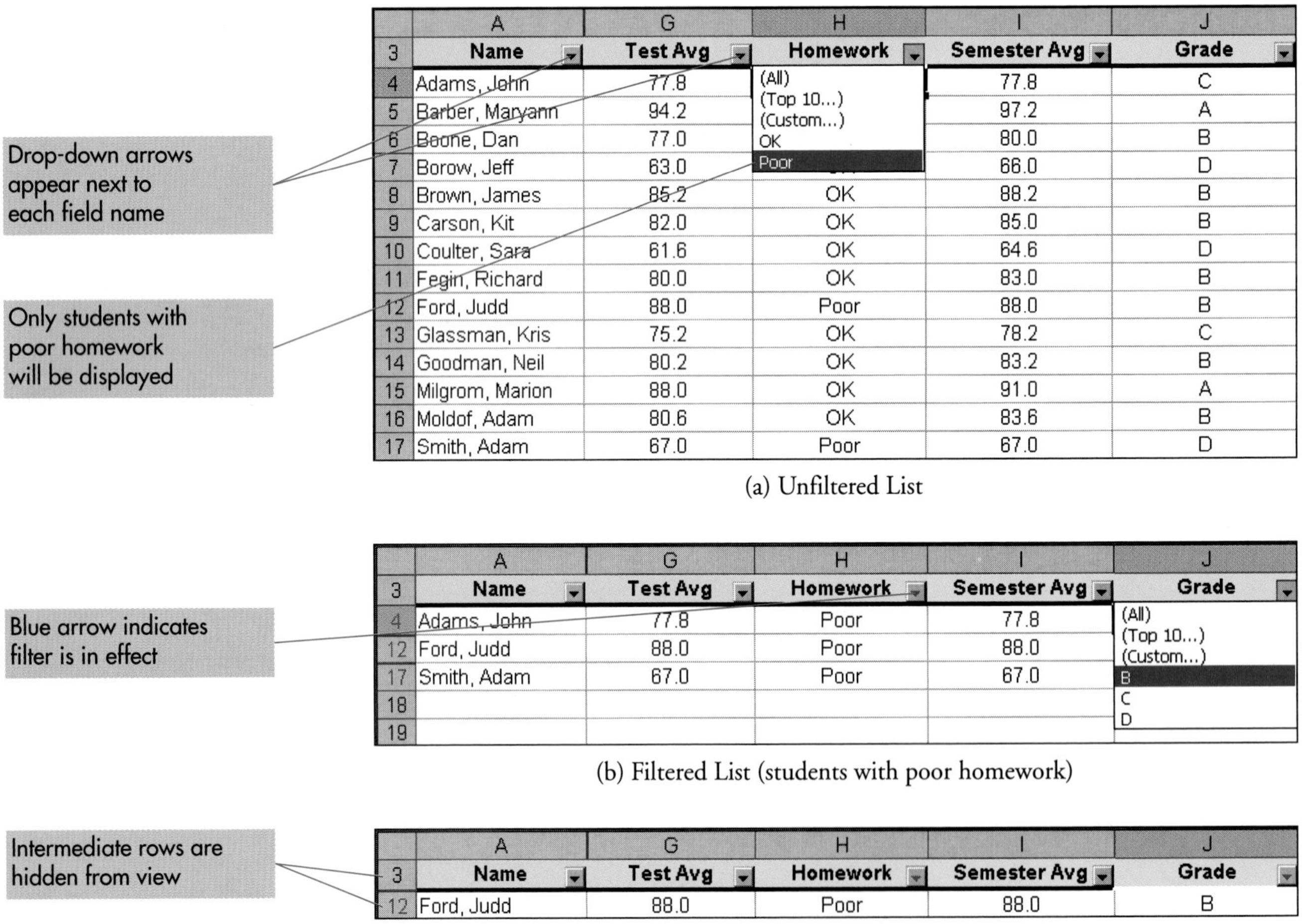

Drop-down arrows appear next to each field name

Only students with poor homework will be displayed

	A	G	H	I	J
3	Name	Test Avg	Homework	Semester Avg	Grade
4	Adams, John	77.8	(All)	77.8	C
5	Barber, Maryann	94.2	(Top 10...)	97.2	A
6	Boone, Dan	77.0	(Custom...)	80.0	B
7	Borow, Jeff	63.0	OK / Poor	66.0	D
8	Brown, James	85.2	OK	88.2	B
9	Carson, Kit	82.0	OK	85.0	B
10	Coulter, Sara	61.6	OK	64.6	D
11	Fegin, Richard	80.0	OK	83.0	B
12	Ford, Judd	88.0	Poor	88.0	B
13	Glassman, Kris	75.2	OK	78.2	C
14	Goodman, Neil	80.2	OK	83.2	B
15	Milgrom, Marion	88.0	OK	91.0	A
16	Moldof, Adam	80.6	OK	83.6	B
17	Smith, Adam	67.0	Poor	67.0	D

(a) Unfiltered List

Blue arrow indicates filter is in effect

	A	G	H	I	J
3	Name	Test Avg	Homework	Semester Avg	Grade
4	Adams, John	77.8	Poor	77.8	(All)
12	Ford, Judd	88.0	Poor	88.0	(Top 10...)
17	Smith, Adam	67.0	Poor	67.0	(Custom...)
18					B
19					C
					D

(b) Filtered List (students with poor homework)

Intermediate rows are hidden from view

	A	G	H	I	J
3	Name	Test Avg	Homework	Semester Avg	Grade
12	Ford, Judd	88.0	Poor	88.0	B

(c) Imposing a Second Condition

FIGURE 3.15   *The AutoFilter Command*

THE EXPANDED GRADE BOOK

Objective To develop the expanded grade book; to use statistical (AVERAGE, MAX, and MIN) and logical (IF and VLOOKUP) functions; to demonstrate scrolling and the Freeze Panes command. Use Figure 3.16 as a guide.

Step 1: **The Fill Handle**

➤ Open the **Expanded Grade Book** in the Exploring Excel folder. Click in cell **C3**, the cell containing the label Test 1 as shown in Figure 3.16a.

➤ Click and drag the **fill handle** over cells **D3, E3, and F3** (a ScreenTip shows the projected result in cell F3), then release the mouse. Cells D3, E3, and F3 contain the labels Test 2, Test 3, and Test 4, respectively.

➤ Save the workbook as **Finished Expanded Grade Book** so that you can always return to the original workbook if necessary.

Click and drag fill handle to F3

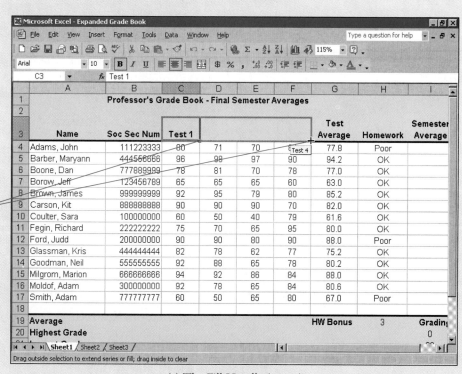

(a) The Fill Handle (step 1)

FIGURE 3.16 *Hands-on Exercise 3*

THE AUTOFILL CAPABILITY

The AutoFill capability is the fastest way to enter certain series into contiguous cells. Enter the starting value(s) in a series, then drag the fill handle to the adjacent cells. Excel completes the series based on the initial value. Type January (or Jan), Monday (or Mon), then drag the fill handle in the direction you want to fill. Excel will enter the appropriate months or days of the week, respectively. You can also type text followed by a number, such as Product 1 or Quarter 1, then use the fill handle to extend the series.

Step 2:   **Format the Social Security Numbers**

➤ Click and drag to select cells **B4 through B17**, the cells containing the unformatted Social Security numbers.

➤ Point to the selected cells and click the **right mouse button** to display a shortcut (context-sensitive) menu.

➤ Click the **Format Cells command**, click the **Number tab**, then click **Special** in the Category list box as shown in Figure 3.16b.

➤ Click **Social Security Number** in the Type box, then click **OK** to accept the formatting and close the Format Cells dialog box. The Social Security numbers are displayed with hyphens.

➤ Save the workbook.

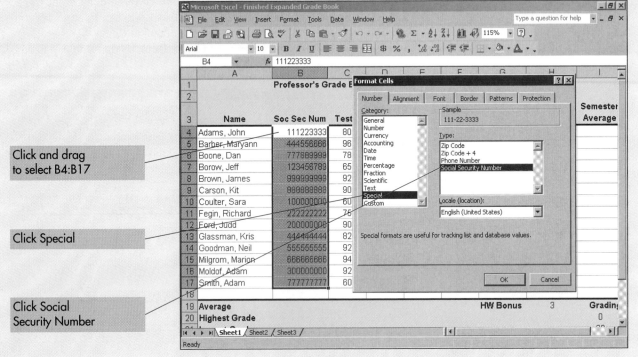

Click and drag to select B4:B17

Click Special

Click Social Security Number

(b) Format the Social Security Numbers (step 2)

FIGURE 3.16   *Hands-on Exercise 3 (continued)*

THE LEFT AND RIGHT FUNCTIONS

A professor may want to post grades, but cannot do so by student name or Social Security Number. One can, however, create an "ID number" consisting of the left- or rightmost digits in the Social Security number. Insert a new column into the worksheet, then go to the cell for the first student in this column (e.g., cell C4 if you insert a new column C). Enter the function =LEFT(B4,4) to display the first four digits from cell B4, corresponding to the first four (leftmost) digits in Adams's Social Security Number. You could also enter the function =RIGHT(B4,4) to display the last four (rightmost) digits. Hide the columns containing the names and Social Security numbers, then post the grades. See practice exercise 9 at the end of the chapter.

Step 3: **The Freeze Panes Command**

➤ Press **Ctrl+Home** to move to cell A1. Click the **right arrow** on the horizontal scroll bar until column A scrolls off the screen. Cell A1 is still the active cell, because scrolling with the mouse does not change the active cell.

➤ Press **Ctrl+Home**. Press the **right arrow key** until column A scrolls off the screen. The active cell changes as you scroll with the keyboard.

➤ Press **Ctrl+Home** again, then click in cell **B4**. Pull down the **Window menu**. Click **Freeze Panes** as shown in Figure 3.16c. You will see a line to the right of column A and below row 3.

➤ Click the **right arrow** on the horizontal scroll bar (or press the **right arrow key**) repeatedly until column J is visible. Note that column A is visible (frozen), but that one or more columns are not shown.

➤ Click the **down arrow** on the vertical scroll bar (or press the **down arrow key**) repeatedly until row 25 is visible. Note that rows one through three are visible (frozen), but that one or more rows are not shown.

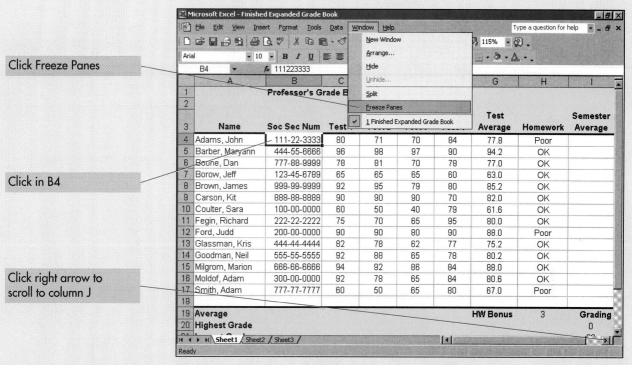

(c) The Freeze Panes Command (step 3)

FIGURE 3.16 *Hands-on Exercise 3 (continued)*

GO TO A SPECIFIC CELL

Ctrl+Home and Ctrl+End will take you to the upper-left and bottom-right cells within a worksheet, but how do you get to a specific cell? One way is to click in the Name box (to the left of the formula bar), enter the cell reference (e.g., K250), and press the enter key. You can also pull down the Edit menu and click the Go To command (or press the F5 key) to display the Go To dialog box, enter the name of the cell in the Reference text box, then press enter to go directly to the cell.

Step 4: **The IF Function**

➤ Scroll until Column I is visible on the screen. Click in cell **I4**.
➤ Click the **Insert Function button** on the formula bar. Click the **down arrow** and click **Logical** in the category list box. Click **IF** in the Function name list box, then click **OK** to display the Function Arguments dialog box in Figure 3.16d.
➤ You can enter the arguments directly, or you can use pointing as follows:
  • Click the **Logical_test** text box. Click cell **H4** in the worksheet. (You may need to click and drag the top border of the Formula Palette of the dialog box to move it out of the way.) Type ="**OK**" to complete the logical test.
  • Click the **Value_if_true** text box. Click cell **G4** in the worksheet, type a **plus sign**, click cell **H19** in the worksheet (scrolling if necessary), and finally press the **F4 key** (see boxed tip) to convert the reference to cell H19 to an absolute reference ($H$19).
  • Click the **Value_if_false** text box. Click cell **G4** in the worksheet.
➤ Check that the dialog box on your worksheet matches the one in Figure 3.16d. Click **OK** to insert the function into your worksheet.
➤ Save the workbook.

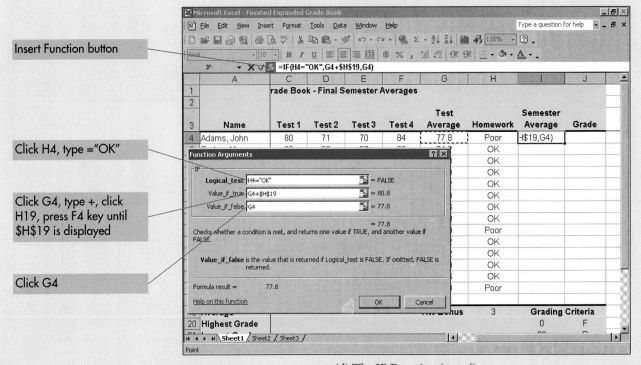

(d) The IF Function (step 4)

FIGURE 3.16 *Hands-on Exercise 3 (continued)*

THE F4 KEY

The F4 key cycles through relative, absolute, and mixed addresses. Click on any reference within the formula bar; for example, click on A1 in the formula =A1+A2. Press the F4 key once, and it changes to an absolute reference. Press the F4 key a second time, and it becomes a mixed reference, A$1; press it again, and it is a different mixed reference, $A1. Press the F4 key a fourth time, and return to the original relative address, A1.

Step 5: **The VLOOKUP Function**

➤ Click in cell **J4**. Click the **Insert Function button** on the formula bar. Click **Lookup & Reference** in the category list box. Scroll in the Function name list box until you can select **VLOOKUP**. Click **OK** to display the Function Arguments dialog box in Figure 3.16e.

➤ Enter the arguments for the VLOOKUP function as shown in the figure. You can enter the arguments directly, or you can use pointing as follows:
  • Click the **Lookup_value** text box. Click cell **I4** in the worksheet.
  • Click the **Table_array** text box. Click cell **I20** and drag to cell **J24** (scrolling if necessary). Press the **F4 key** to convert to an absolute reference.
  • Click the **Col_index_num** text box. Type **2**.

➤ Check that the dialog box on your worksheet matches the one in Figure 3.16e. Make corrections as necessary. Click **OK** to insert the completed function into your worksheet.

➤ Save the workbook.

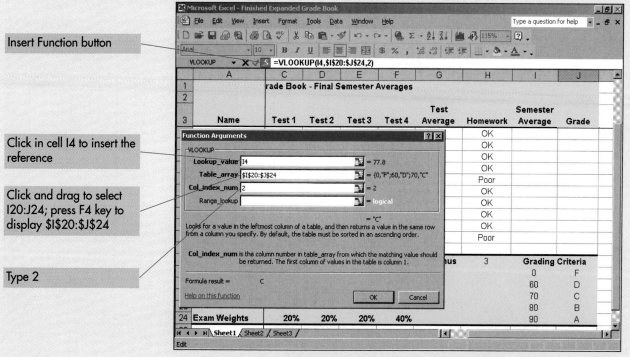

(e) The VLOOKUP Function (step 5)

FIGURE 3.16 *Hands-on Exercise 3 (continued)*

THE COLLAPSE DIALOG BUTTON

You can enter a cell reference in one of two ways: you can type it directly in the Function Arguments dialog box, or click the cell in the worksheet. The Function Arguments dialog box typically hides the necessary cell, however, in which case you can click the Collapse Dialog button (which appears to the right of any parameter within the dialog box). This collapses (hides) the Function Arguments dialog box so that you can click the underlying cell, which is now visible. Click the Collapse Dialog button a second time to display the entire dialog box.

Step 6: **Copy the IF and VLOOKUP Functions**

➤ If necessary, scroll to the top of the worksheet. Select cells **I4** and **J4** as in Figure 3.16f.

➤ Point to the **fill handle** in the lower-right corner of the selected range. The mouse pointer changes to a thin crosshair.

➤ Drag the **fill handle** over cells **I5 through J17**. A border appears, indicating the destination range as shown in Figure 3.16f. Release the mouse to complete the copy operation.

➤ If you have done everything correctly, Adam Smith should have a grade of D based on a semester average of 67.

➤ Format the semester averages in column I to one decimal place.

➤ Save the workbook.

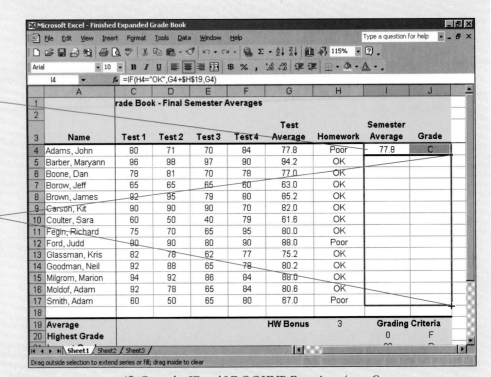

Click and drag to select I4:J4

Click and drag fill handle to J17

(f) Copy the IF and VLOOKUP Functions (step 6)

FIGURE 3.16 *Hands-on Exercise 3 (continued)*

USE NESTED IFS FOR MORE COMPLEX DECISION MAKING

A "nested IF" (or "IF within an IF") is a common logic structure in every programming language. It could be used in the expanded grade book to implement more complicated logic such as a variable homework bonus (of −2, 3, and 5), depending on the grade (for "poor", OK, and good, respectively). The IF function in Excel has three arguments—a condition, a value if the condition is true, and a value if the condition is false. A nested IF simply replaces the true and/or false value with another IF statement. See practice exercise 9 at the end of the chapter.

Step 7:   **Create the Summary Statistics**

> Scroll until you can click in cell **C19**. Type **=AVERAGE(C4:C17)**. Press **enter**. Cell C19 should display 81.9 as shown in Figure 3.16g.
> Click in cell **C20** and enter the formula **=MAX(C4:C17)**. Click in cell **C21** and enter the formula **=MIN(C4:C17)**.
> Click in cell **C22** and enter the formula **=C20–C21**. Check that the displayed values match those in Figure 3.16g.
> Click and drag to select cells C19 through C22, then click and drag the **fill handle** to cell F22. Release the mouse. Click outside the selection to deselect the cells.
> Save the workbook.

Enter summary statistics in C19:C22

Click and drag fill handle to F22

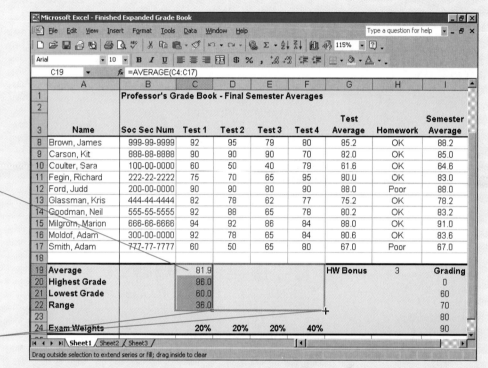

(g) Create the Summary Statistics (step 7)

FIGURE 3.16   *Hands-on Exercise 3 (continued)*

RANK IN CLASS

Use the Rank function to determine a student's rank in class. (Excel also has functions for quartiles and percentiles.) Add a new column to the worksheet, column K in this example, then click in the cell for the first student in the list (cell K4). Enter the function =RANK(I4,$I$4:$I$17), where I4 contains the value you want to look up (the individual student's semester average) and $I$4:$I$17 references the set of numbers on which to base the rank. The latter is entered as an absolute reference so that the cell formula may be copied to the remaining cells in column K. See practice exercise 9 at the end of the chapter.

Step 8:   **The Page Break Preview Command**

> ➤ Pull down the **View menu** and click the **Page Break Preview command** to see the potential page breaks as shown in Figure 3.16h. Click **OK** if you see the welcome message.
> ➤ Click and drag the dashed blue line to the right to eliminate the page break. (You can also drag the solid blue line that appears on the right border to the left to create a page break.)
> ➤ Pull down the **View menu** and click **Normal** to return to the Normal view.
> ➤ Pull down the **File menu**. Click **Page Setup** to display the Page Setup dialog box. Click the **Margins tab**. Check the box to center the worksheet horizontally on the page.
> ➤ Click the **Sheet tab**. Check the boxes for **Row and Column Headings** and for **Gridlines**.
> ➤ Click the **Print Preview button** to display the completed spreadsheet. Click the **Print button** and click **OK** to print the workbook.
> ➤ Print the worksheet with the cell formulas.

Print Preview button

Blue dashed line indicates page break

Click and drag dashed line to right

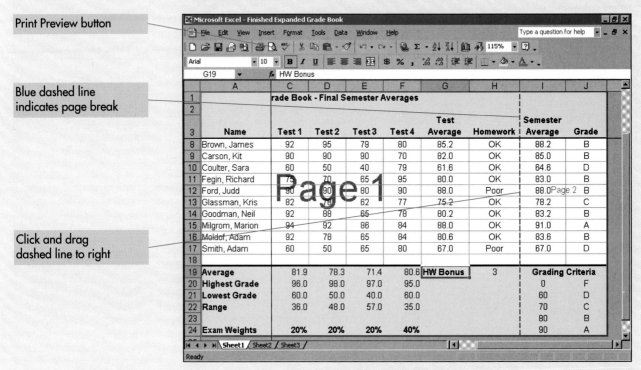

(h) The Page Break Preview Command (step 8)

FIGURE 3.16   *Hands-on Exercise 3 (continued)*

SET PRINT AREA(S)

Press and hold the Ctrl key as you click and drag to select one or more areas in the worksheet, then pull down the File menu, select the Print Area command and click Set Print Area. The print area is enclosed in dashed lines. The next time you execute the Print command, you will print just the print area(s), with each print area appearing on a separate page. Use the Print Area command in the File menu to clear the print area.

Step 9: **Hide the Rows and Columns**

➤ Click and drag the column headings for columns **C through F** to select these columns, point to the selected columns then click the **right mouse button** to display the context-sensitive menu in Figure 3.16h. Click **Hide** to hide these columns.

➤ Click and drag the row headings for rows **19 through 24** to select these rows, point to the selected rows, click the **right mouse button**, and click the **Hide command**. Print the worksheet.

➤ Now reverse the process and unhide the rows, but leave the columns hidden. Click and drag to select the row headings for rows **18 and 25** (which are contiguous), right click to display a context-sensitive menu, then click the **Unhide command**.

➤ You should see all of the rows in the entire worksheet (within the limitations of scrolling). Save the workbook.

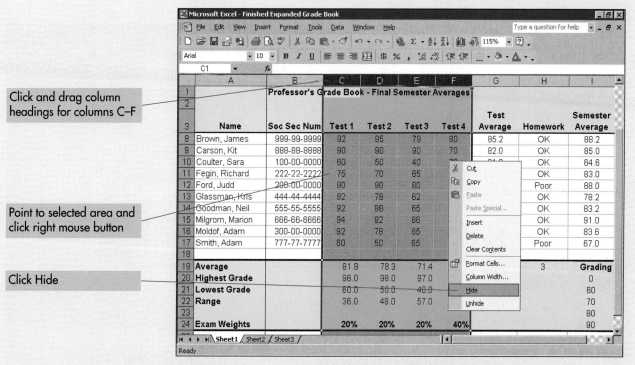

(i) Hide the Rows and Columns (step 9)

FIGURE 3.16 *Hands-on Exercise 3 (continued)*

UNHIDING ROWS AND COLUMNS

Hiding a row or column is easy; you just select the row or column(s) you want to hide, click the right mouse button, then select the Hide command from the shortcut menu. Unhiding a row or column is trickier, because you cannot see the target cells. To unhide a column, for example, you need to select the columns on either side; for example, select columns A and C if you are trying to unhide column B. To unhide column A, however, click in the Name box and enter A1. Pull down the Format menu, click Column, then click the Unhide command.

Step 10: **The AutoFilter Command**

➤ Click anywhere within the list of students. Pull down the **Data menu**, click the **Filter command**, then click **AutoFilter**. The worksheet is essentially unchanged except that each column heading is followed by a drop-down arrow.

➤ Click the **drop-down arrow** in cell H3 (the column containing the students' homework grades). Click **Poor**. The list of students changes to show only those students who received this grade on their homework as shown in Figure 3.16j.

➤ Click the **drop-down arrow** in cell J3, then select **B** from the drop-down list of grade values. The list changes to show the one student who managed to receive a "B" despite having poor homework.

➤ Add your name and title (**Grading Assistant**) in cells G26 and G27. Save the workbook, then print it for your instructor.

➤ Pull down the **Data menu** and click the **AutoFilter command** to remove the filter and display all of the students.

➤ Exit Excel.

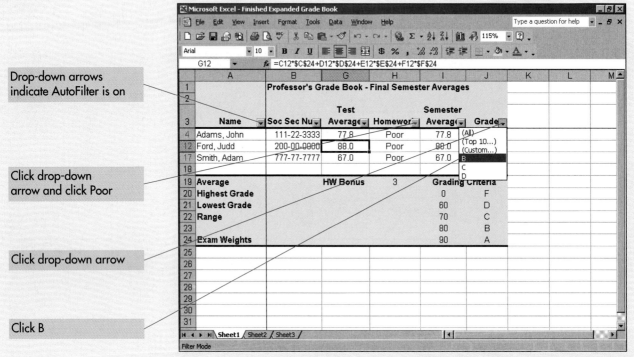

Drop-down arrows indicate AutoFilter is on

Click drop-down arrow and click Poor

Click drop-down arrow

Click B

(j) The AutoFilter Command (step 10)

FIGURE 3.16 *Hands-on Exercise 3 (continued)*

USE COMMENTS WITH COLLEAGUES

It's helpful to insert comments into a workbook to send suggestions to colleagues who will be using the same workbook. Click in the cell where you want the comment to go, pull down the Insert menu to enter the comment, then click elsewhere in the worksheet when you are finished. Point to the cell (which should have a tiny red triangle) and you will see the comment you just entered. Right click in the cell after the comment has been entered to edit and/or delete the comment if necessary. See practice exercise 2 at the end of the chapter.

Excel contains several categories of built-in functions. The PMT function computes the periodic payment for a loan based on three arguments (the interest rate per period, the number of periods, and the amount of the loan). The IPMT and PPMT functions determine the amount of each payment that goes toward interest and principal, respectively. The FV function returns the future value of an investment based on constant periodic payments and a constant interest rate.

Statistical functions were also discussed. The AVERAGE, MAX, and MIN functions return the average, highest, and lowest values in the argument list. The COUNT function returns the number of cells with numeric entries. The COUNTA function displays the number of cells with numeric and/or text entries.

The IF, VLOOKUP, and HLOOKUP functions implement decision making within a worksheet. The IF function has three arguments: a condition, which is evaluated as true or false; a value if the test is true; and a value if the test is false. The VLOOKUP and HLOOKUP functions also have three arguments: the value to look up, the range of cells containing the table, and the column or row number within the table that contains the result.

The hands-on exercises introduced several techniques to make you more proficient. The fill handle is used to copy a cell or group of cells to a range of adjacent cells. Pointing is a more accurate way to enter a cell reference into a formula as it uses the mouse or arrow keys to select the cell as you build the formula. The AutoFill capability creates a series based on the initial value(s) you supply.

Scrolling enables you to view any portion of a large worksheet but moves the labels for existing rows and/or columns off the screen. The Freeze Panes command keeps the row and/or column headings on the screen while scrolling within a large worksheet.

A spreadsheet is first and foremost a tool for decision making, and thus Excel includes several commands to aid in that process. The Goal Seek command lets you enter the desired end result of a spreadsheet model (such as the monthly payment on a car loan) and determines the input (the price of the car) necessary to produce that result.

The assumptions and initial conditions in a spreadsheet should be clearly labeled and set apart from the rest of the worksheet. This facilitates change and reduces the chance for error.

KEY TERMS

Absolute reference (p. 122)
Arguments (p. 112)
Assumptions (p. 122)
AutoFill capability (p. 143)
AutoFilter command (p. 142)
AVERAGE function (p. 135)
Breakpoint (p. 138)
COUNT function (p. 135)
COUNTA function (p. 135)
Freeze Panes command (p. 139)
Function (p. 112)
FV function (p. 112)
Goal Seek command (p. 114)

HLOOKUP function (p. 138)
IF function (p. 137)
Insert Function command (p. 113)
IRA (Individual Retirement Account) (p. 123)
MAX function (p. 135)
MIN function (p. 135)
Mixed reference (p. 123)
Nested IF (p. 148)
Page Break Preview command (p. 139)
Page Setup command (p. 140)
PMT function (p. 112)

Relational operator (p. 137)
Relative reference (p. 122)
Scrolling (p. 139)
Sort command (p. 134)
Spell check (p. 124)
Statistical functions (p. 135)
SUM function (p. 136)
Template (p. 110)
Unfreeze Panes command (p. 139)
Unhiding cells (p. 139)
VLOOKUP function (p. 138)

1. Which of the following options may be used to print a large worksheet?
   (a) Landscape orientation
   (b) Scaling
   (c) Reduced margins
   (d) All of the above

2. If the results of a formula contain more characters than can be displayed according to the present format and cell width,
   (a) The extra characters will be truncated under all circumstances
   (b) All of the characters will be displayed if the cell to the right is empty
   (c) A series of asterisks will be displayed
   (d) A series of pound signs will be displayed

3. Which cell—A1, A2, or A3—will contain the amount of the loan, given the function =PMT(A1,A2,A3)?
   (a) A1
   (b) A2
   (c) A3
   (d) Impossible to determine

4. Which of the following will compute the average of the values in cells D2, D3, and D4?
   (a) The function =AVERAGE(D2:D4)
   (b) The function =AVERAGE(D2,D4)
   (c) Both (a) and (b)
   (d) Neither (a) nor (b)

5. The function =IF(A1>A2,A1+A2,A1*A2) returns
   (a) The product of cells A1 and A2 if cell A1 is greater than A2
   (b) The sum of cells A1 and A2 if cell A1 is less than A2
   (c) Both (a) and (b)
   (d) Neither (a) nor (b)

6. Which of the following is the preferred way to sum the values contained in cells A1 to A4?
   (a) =SUM(A1:A4)
   (b) =A1+A2+A3+A4
   (c) Either (a) or (b) is equally good
   (d) Neither (a) nor (b) is correct

7. Which of the following will return the highest and lowest arguments from a list of arguments?
   (a) HIGH/LOW
   (b) LARGEST/SMALLEST
   (c) MAX/MIN
   (d) All of the above

8. Which of the following is a *required* technique to develop the worksheet for the mortgage analysis?
   (a) Pointing
   (b) Copying with the fill handle
   (c) Both (a) and (b)
   (d) Neither (a) nor (b)

9. Given that cells B6, C6, and D6 contain the numbers 10, 20, and 30, respectively, what value will be returned by the function =IF(B6>10,C6*2,D6*3)?
   (a) 10
   (b) 40
   (c) 60
   (d) 90

10. Which of the following is not an input to the Goal Seek command?
    (a) The cell containing the end result
    (b) The desired value of the end result
    (c) The cell whose value will change to reach the end result
    (d) The value of the input cell that is required to reach the end result

11. What is the correct order of the arguments for the FV function?
    (a) Interest Rate, Term, Principal
    (b) Term, Interest Rate, Principal
    (c) Interest Rate, Term, Annual Amount
    (d) Term, Interest Rate, Annual Amount

12. Which function will return the number of nonempty cells in the range A2 through A6, including in the result cells that contain text as well as numeric entries?
    (a) =COUNT(A2:A6)
    (b) =COUNTA(A2:A6)
    (c) =COUNT(A2,A6)
    (d) =COUNTA(A2,A6)

13. The annual interest rate, term in years, and principal of a loan are stored in cells A1, A2, and A3, respectively. Which of the following is the correct PMT function given monthly payments?
    (a) =PMT(A1, A2, −A3)
    (b) =PMT(A1/12, A2*12, −A3)
    (c) =PMT(A1*12, A2/12, −A3)
    (d) =PMT(A1, A2, A3)

14. The worksheet displayed in the monitor shows columns A and B, skips columns D, E, and F, then displays columns G, H, I, J, and K. What is the most likely explanation for the missing columns?
    (a) The columns were previously deleted
    (b) The columns are empty and thus are automatically hidden from view
    (c) Either (a) or (b) is a satisfactory explanation
    (d) Neither (a) nor (b) is a likely reason

15. Given the function =VLOOKUP(C6,D12:F18,3)
    (a) The entries in cells D12 through D18 are in ascending order
    (b) The entries in cells D12 through D18 are in descending order
    (c) The entries in cells F12 through F18 are in ascending order
    (d) The entries in cells F12 through F18 are in descending order

ANSWERS

1. d	**6.** a	**11.** c
2. d	**7.** c	**12.** b
3. c	**8.** d	**13.** b
4. a	**9.** d	**14.** d
5. d	**10.** d	**15.** a

1. **Calculating Your Retirement:** Retirement is years away, but it is never too soon to start planning. Most corporations include some type of retirement contribution in their benefits package, and/or you can supplement that money through an individual retirement account (IRA). In any event, the Future Value function enables you to calculate the amount of money you will have at retirement, based on a series of uniform contributions during your working years. Once you reach retirement, however, you do not withdraw all of the money immediately, but withdraw it periodically as a monthly pension.

a. Create a new worksheet similar to the one in Figure 3.17. The "accrual phase" uses the FV function to determine the amount of money you will accumulate. The total contribution in cell B7 is a formula based on a percentage of your annual salary, plus a matching contribution from your employer. The 6.2% in our figure corresponds to the percentages that are currently in effect for Social Security. (In actuality, the government currently deducts 7.65% from your paycheck, and allocates 6.2% for Social Security and the remaining 1.45% for Medicare.)

b. The pension phase takes the amount of money you have accumulated and uses the PMT function to determine the payments you will receive in retirement. The formula in cell E4 is a simple reference to the amount accumulated in cell B10, whereas the formula in cell E7 uses the PMT function to compute your monthly pension. Note that we used a lower interest rate during retirement than during your working years on the assumption that you will want to be more conservative with your investments. Note, too, that the accrual phase uses an annual contribution in its calculations, whereas the pension phase determines a monthly pension.

c. Add a hyperlink to the page that goes to the Social Security Administration (www.ssa.gov), then compare your calculation to the benefits provided by the government. Add your name to the worksheet, print the worksheet both ways to show displayed values and cell formulas.

Microsoft Excel - Chapter 3 Practice 1 Solution - Calculating Your Retirement

Type a question for help

Arial — 10 —

A31

Calculating Your Retirement

	A	B	C	D	E	
1						
2						
3	**Accrual Phase**			**Pension Phase**		
4	Annual Salary	$35,000		The size of your "nest egg"	$1,124,305	
5	Employee contribution	6.20%		Interest rate	6%	
6	Employer contribution	6.20%		Years in retirement	25	
7	Total contribution	$4,340		**Monthly Pension**	$7,244	
8	Interest Rate	8%				
9	Years contributing	40				
10	**Future Value**	$1,124,305		**Your Name Goes Here**		
11						
12	Click here to compare to Social Security Projection					
13						
14						
15						
16						
17						
18						
19						
20						
21						

Sheet1 / Sheet2 / Sheet3 /

Ready

FIGURE 3.17 *Calculating Your Retirement (Exercise 1)*

BUILDS ON

HANDS-ON EXERCISE 3 PAGES 143–152

2. Alternate Grade Book: Figure 3.18 displays an alternate version of the grade book from the third hands-on exercise. The student names have changed as has the professor's grading scheme. Open the partially completed version of this worksheet in the *Chapter 3 Practice 2* workbook, then complete the workbook as follows:
   a. Click in cell F4 to compute the test average for the first student. The test average is computed by dropping the student's lowest grade, then giving equal weight to the three remaining tests. Steve Weinstein's test average, for example, is computed by dropping the 70 on test 1, then taking the average of 80, 90, and 100, his grades for tests 2, 3, and 4. You will need to use the SUM and MIN functions to implement this requirement.
   b. Students are required to complete a designated number of homework assignments (12 in Figure 3.18), then receive a bonus or penalty for every additional or deficient home assignment. Andrea Carrion completed 9 homeworks, rather than 12, and thus has a 6-point penalty (2 points per each missing assignment). The bonus or penalty is added to the test average to determine the semester average. Enter the formulas for the first student in cells H4 and I4.
   c. The grade for the course is based on the semester average and table of grading criteria according to an HLOOKUP function within the worksheet. Enter the formula in cell I4.
   d. Copy the formulas in row 4 to the remaining rows in the worksheet.
   e. Format the worksheet as shown. Use conditional formatting to display all failing grades and homework penalties in red. Add your name to the worksheet, then print the worksheet twice, once with displayed values and once with cell formulas.
   f. Print the worksheet a second time to reflect Maryann's comment. Submit both copies of the worksheet together to your instructor.

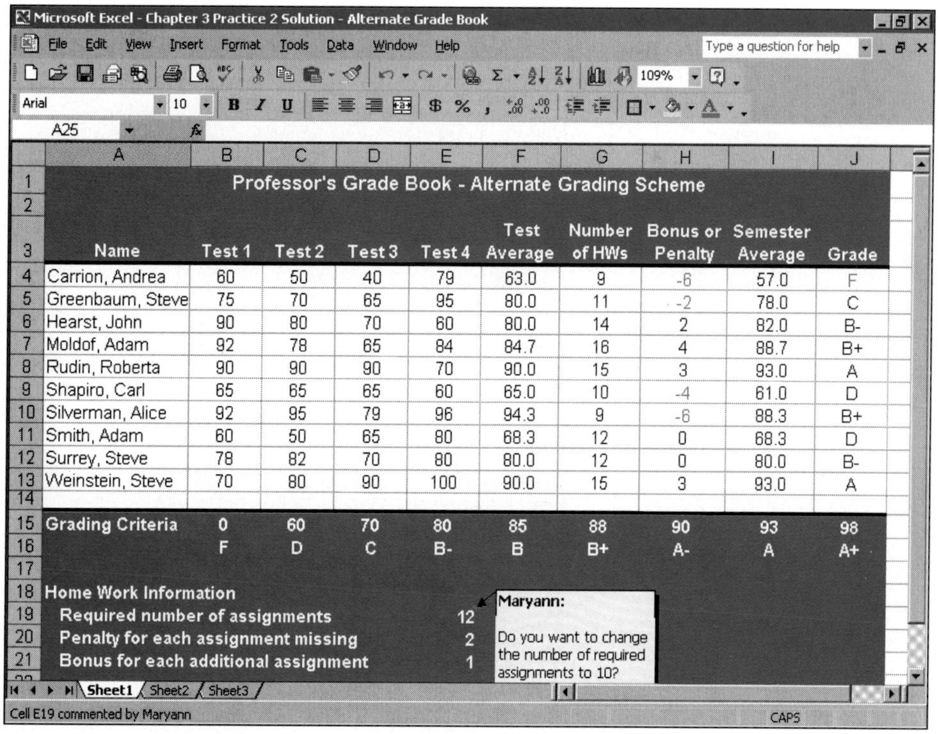

Name	Test 1	Test 2	Test 3	Test 4	Test Average	Number of HWs	Bonus or Penalty	Semester Average	Grade
Carrion, Andrea	60	50	40	79	63.0	9	-6	57.0	F
Greenbaum, Steve	75	70	65	95	80.0	11	-2	78.0	C
Hearst, John	90	80	70	60	80.0	14	2	82.0	B-
Moldof, Adam	92	78	65	84	84.7	16	4	88.7	B+
Rudin, Roberta	90	90	90	70	90.0	15	3	93.0	A
Shapiro, Carl	65	65	65	60	65.0	10	-4	61.0	D
Silverman, Alice	92	95	79	96	94.3	9	-6	88.3	B+
Smith, Adam	60	50	65	80	68.3	12	0	68.3	D
Surrey, Steve	78	82	70	80	80.0	12	0	80.0	B-
Weinstein, Steve	70	80	90	100	90.0	15	3	93.0	A
Grading Criteria	0	60	70	80	85	88	90	93	98
	F	D	C	B-	B	B+	A-	A	A+

Home Work Information	
Required number of assignments	12
Penalty for each assignment missing	2
Bonus for each additional assignment	1

FIGURE 3.18 *Alternate Grade Book (Exercise 2)*

BUILDS ON

CHAPTER 2
PRACTICE
EXERCISE 1
PAGE 98

3. Expanded Payroll: Figure 3.19 displays an expanded version of the payroll example that was used earlier in the text. The assumptions used to determine an individual's net pay are listed at the bottom of the worksheet and repeated below. Proceed as follows:

a. Open the partially completed worksheet, which is found in the *Chapter 3 Practice 3* workbook. Enter the formulas for the first employee in row 2, then copy those formulas to the remaining rows in the worksheet.

b. An employee's regular pay is computed by multiplying the number of regular hours by the hourly wage. The number of regular hours does not appear explicitly in the worksheet and is calculated from the hours worked and the overtime threshold (which is entered in the assumption area). Barber, for example, works a total of 48 hours, 40 regular, and 8 (every hour over the threshold) of overtime.

c. Overtime pay is earned for all hours above the overtime threshold, which is shown as 40 hours. The employee receives the overtime rate (1.5 in this worksheet) times the regular wage for every hour over the threshold.

d. An individual's taxable pay is determined by subtracting the deduction per dependent times the number of dependents.

e. The withholding tax is based on the taxable pay and the tax table. The Social Security/Medicare tax is a fixed percentage of gross pay.

f. Compute the indicated totals in row 10.

g. Format the worksheet as shown in Figure 3.19.

h. Add your name to the worksheet, then print the worksheet to show both displayed values and cell formulas. Be sure to use the appropriate combination of relative and absolute addresses so that your worksheet will reflect changes in any value within the assumption area.

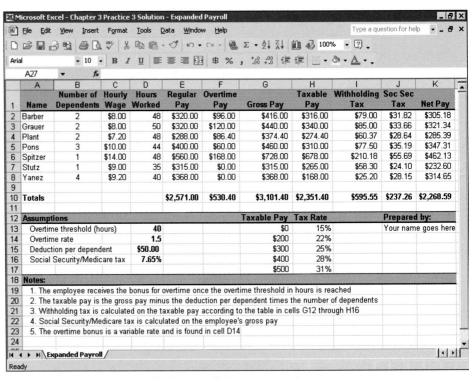

FIGURE 3.19   *Expanded Payroll (Exercise 3)*

4. Fuel Estimates: Figure 3.20 displays a worksheet an airline uses to calculate the fuel requirements and associated cost for available flights. Open the partially completed worksheet in the *Chapter 3 Practice 4* workbook, then complete the worksheet to match our figure. Note the following:
   a. Enter the formulas for the first flight in row 4, then copy those formulas to the remainder of the worksheet.
   b. The fuel required for each flight is dependent on the type of aircraft and the number of flying hours. Use a VLOOKUP function in the formula to determine the amount of fuel for each flight. (The associated table extends over three columns.)
   c. Use the fuel required from part (b) to compute the additional requirements for reserve fuel and holding fuel, which must then be added to the initial fuel requirements to get the total fuel needed for a trip. These parameters are shown at the bottom of the worksheet and are susceptible to change.
   d. The estimated fuel cost for each flight is the number of gallons times the price per gallon. There is a price break, however, if the fuel required reaches or exceeds a threshold number of gallons. The Boeing-727 flight from Miami to Los Angeles, for example, requires 71,500 gallons, which exceeds the threshold, and therefore qualifies for the reduced price of fuel.
   e. Compute the total, average, and maximum values in rows 11, 12, and 13.
   f. Format the worksheet as you see fit. (You need not match our formatting exactly.)
   g. Your worksheet should be completely flexible and amenable to change; that is, the hourly fuel requirements, price per gallon, price threshold, and holding and reserve percentages are all subject to change.
   h. Add your name to the worksheet, then print the worksheet to show both displayed values and cell formulas.

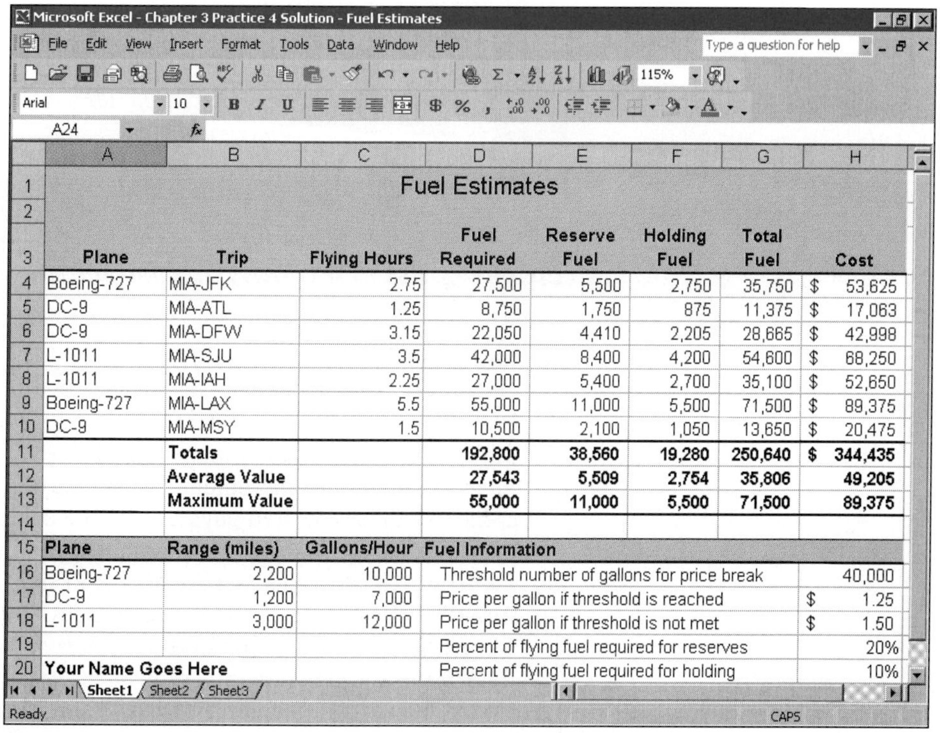

	A	B	C	D	E	F	G	H
1				Fuel Estimates				
2								
3	Plane	Trip	Flying Hours	Fuel Required	Reserve Fuel	Holding Fuel	Total Fuel	Cost
4	Boeing-727	MIA-JFK	2.75	27,500	5,500	2,750	35,750	$ 53,625
5	DC-9	MIA-ATL	1.25	8,750	1,750	875	11,375	$ 17,063
6	DC-9	MIA-DFW	3.15	22,050	4,410	2,205	28,665	$ 42,998
7	L-1011	MIA-SJU	3.5	42,000	8,400	4,200	54,600	$ 68,250
8	L-1011	MIA-IAH	2.25	27,000	5,400	2,700	35,100	$ 52,650
9	Boeing-727	MIA-LAX	5.5	55,000	11,000	5,500	71,500	$ 89,375
10	DC-9	MIA-MSY	1.5	10,500	2,100	1,050	13,650	$ 20,475
11		Totals		192,800	38,560	19,280	250,640	$ 344,435
12		Average Value		27,543	5,509	2,754	35,806	49,205
13		Maximum Value		55,000	11,000	5,500	71,500	89,375
14								
15	Plane	Range (miles)	Gallons/Hour	Fuel Information				
16	Boeing-727	2,200	10,000	Threshold number of gallons for price break				40,000
17	DC-9	1,200	7,000	Price per gallon if threshold is reached				$ 1.25
18	L-1011	3,000	12,000	Price per gallon if threshold is not met				$ 1.50
19				Percent of flying fuel required for reserves				20%
20	Your Name Goes Here			Percent of flying fuel required for holding				10%

FIGURE 3.20 *Fuel Estimates (Exercise 4)*

5. Flexibility and Formatting: The worksheet in Figure 3.21 is an improved version of the worksheet developed in the chapter because of its flexibility. (The nicer formatting is secondary.) The spreadsheet is designed so that the user can change the starting interest rate and associated increment—6% and .5%, respectively, in the figure—then have those values reflected in the body of the spreadsheet. The user can also change the number of years for the investment and the associated increment, as well as the annual contribution.

Your assignment is to create the worksheet in Figure 3.21 using mixed references in appropriate fashion. The worksheet is similar to the one in the chapter, except that we have reversed the row and column headings. You can duplicate the formatting in our figure or choose your own design. Print the worksheet two ways, once with displayed values, and once with the cell formulas.

The Value of an IRA

Years Contributing

Rate of Return	10	15	20	25	30	35	40	45
6.00%	$26,362	$46,552	$73,571	$109,729	$158,116	$222,870	$309,524	$425,487
6.50%	$26,989	$48,364	$77,651	$117,775	$172,750	$248,069	$351,264	$492,649
7.00%	$27,633	$50,258	$81,991	$126,498	$188,922	$276,474	$399,270	$571,499
7.50%	$28,294	$52,237	$86,609	$135,956	$206,799	$308,503	$454,513	$664,129
8.00%	$28,973	$54,304	$91,524	$146,212	$226,566	$344,634	$518,113	$773,011
8.50%	$29,670	$56,465	$96,754	$157,336	$248,429	$385,403	$591,365	$901,061
9.00%	$30,386	$58,722	$102,320	$169,402	$272,615	$431,422	$675,765	$1,051,717
9.50%	$31,121	$61,080	$108,244	$182,492	$299,375	$483,377	$773,040	$1,229,039
10.00%	$31,875	$63,545	$114,550	$196,694	$328,988	$542,049	$885,185	$1,437,810
10.50%	$32,649	$66,120	$121,262	$212,104	$361,763	$608,318	$1,014,503	$1,683,672

Starting Interest Rate	6%	Annual Contribution	$2,000
Increment	0.50%		
Number of Years	10	Your Name Goes Here	
Increment	5		

FIGURE 3.21 *Flexibility and Formatting (Exercise 5)*

6. Mortgage Calculator: Figure 3.22 provides another example of mixed references, this time to vary the principal and interest rate in conjunction with the PMT function. The worksheet also provides flexibility in that the user inputs the initial principal and increment (e.g., $150,000 and $5,000) as well as the initial interest rate and its increment (7% and .5%, respectively). The worksheet then computes the associated payment for the different combinations of interest and principal, based on the term of the associated mortgage.

The "trick" to this assignment, as in the previous example, is to develop a formula with the correct mixed references. Click in cell B9 and start to enter the PMT function. You know that the interest rate is in cell B8, but you have to determine the appropriate reference. Ask yourself if the interest rate will always come from column B. (No.) Will it always come from row 8? (Yes.) The answers tell you how to enter the mixed reference within the PMT function. Use similar logic to enter the principal. Once you have the formula for cell B9, you can copy it to the remaining cells in the body of the worksheet.

Your assignment is to create the worksheet in Figure 3.22. You can duplicate the formatting in our figure or choose your own design. Print the worksheet two ways, once with displayed values, and once with the cell formulas.

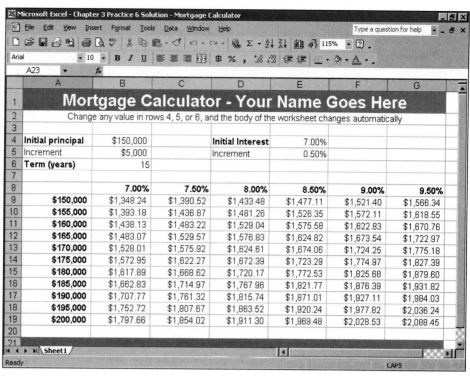

FIGURE 3.22 *Mortgage Calculator (Exercise 6)*

BUILDS ON

HANDS-ON
EXERCISE 2
PAGES 124–133

7. Amortization Schedule: Figure 3.23 displays the Print Preview view of a worksheet to compute the amortization (payoff) schedule for a loan. The user enters the principal, interest rate, and length of the loan, and these values are used to determine the monthly payment, which remains constant throughout the life of the loan. Be sure to enter a formula in cell F4, so that your worksheet will adjust automatically if the user changes any of the loan parameters.

The monthly payment in turn is divided into interest and principal. The amount that goes toward interest decreases each month, while the amount that goes toward principal increases. Two functions, IPMT and PPMT, are used to calculate these amounts for each period. Your assignment is to calculate the amortization schedule as shown in Figure 3.23. There are a total of 180 payments (12 payments a year for 15 years). Note, however, that various rows are hidden within the worksheet so that only selected payments are visible. Thus the worksheet shows the first six payments (in rows 8–13), payment number 12 at the end of the first year, payment number 24 at the end of the second year, and so on. The balance after the last payment is zero, indicating that the loan has been paid off.

Create the worksheet in Figure 3.23, then print the worksheet two ways, once with displayed values, and once with the cell formulas. Use our formatting or choose your own. Add your name to the worksheet, then submit the assignment to your professor.

8. Information from the Web: The compound document in Figure 3.24 contains a spreadsheet to compute a car payment together with a description and picture of the associated car. The latter two were taken from the Web site, carpoint.msn.com. Choose any car you like, then go to the indicated Web site to obtain the retail price of that car so you can create the spreadsheet. Download a picture and description of the car in order to complete the document. *Be sure to credit the source in your document.* Add your name and submit the assignment to your instructor.

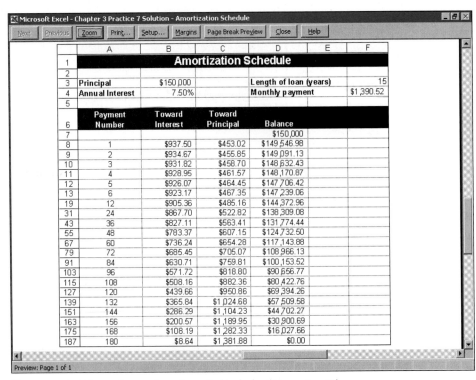

FIGURE 3.23 *Amortization Schedule (Exercise 7)*

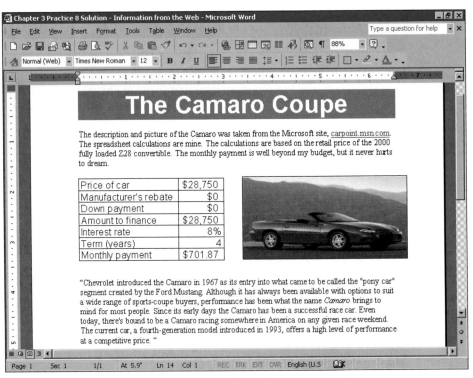

FIGURE 3.24 *Information from the Web (Exercise 8)*

9. Nested IFs and Other Functions: Figure 3.25 displays a modified version of the expanded grade book, with two additional columns, the Student ID in column C and the Rank in column L. (The Student ID was added since the instructor intends to post this worksheet to the Web and does not want to show the complete Social Security number.) The grading criteria have also been modified with respect to the homework bonus as explained below. Complete the third hands-on exercise in the chapter, then continue with the steps below to create the workbook in Figure 3.25:

a. Insert a new column, Student ID, after column B that contains the students' Social Security numbers. Use the LEFT function in column C to display the first four digits of each student's Social Security number.

b. Sort the worksheet according to the first four digits of the newly created Student ID. Be sure that your results correspond to our figure.

c. Modify the contents of cells H19 through J22 as shown in Figure 3.25. Students are now penalized two points for poor homework, and are rewarded three and five points, for satisfactory (OK) and good homework, respectively. Modify the formula in cell J4 to include a nested IF statement that takes the homework bonus or penalty into account. Change the homework grade for the last three students (after sorting the worksheet) to good, so that you can test the modified formula.

d. Use the Rank function to determine each student's rank in class according to the computed value of his or her semester average. Use the Help menu if necessary to learn more about this function.

e. Add your name to the worksheet as the grading assistant.

f. Hide the first two rows and the first two columns, then print the worksheet from within Excel.

e. Use the Save As Web Page command to save the worksheet as a Web page, open the newly created page using your browser, then print the Web page from your browser. Submit both printouts to your instructor.

Microsoft Excel - Chapter 3 Practice 9 Solution - Nested If and Other Functions

	Student ID	Test 1	Test 2	Test 3	Test 4	Average	Homework	Average	Grade	Rank
4	1000	60	50	40	79	61.6	OK	64.6	D	14
5	1112	80	71	70	84	77.8	Poor	75.8	C	11
6	1234	65	65	65	60	63.0	OK	66.0	D	12
7	2000	90	90	80	90	88.0	Poor	86.0	B	5
8	2222	75	70	65	95	80.0	OK	83.0	B	8
9	3000	92	78	65	84	80.6	OK	83.6	B	6
10	4444	82	78	62	77	75.2	OK	78.2	C	10
11	4445	96	98	97	90	94.2	OK	97.2	A	1
12	5555	92	88	65	78	80.2	OK	83.2	B	7
13	6666	94	92	86	84	88.0	OK	91.0	A	2
14	7777	60	50	65	80	67.0	Poor	65.0	D	13
15	7778	78	81	70	78	77.0	Good	82.0	B	9
16	8888	90	90	90	70	82.0	Good	87.0	B	4
17	9999	92	95	79	80	85.2	Good	90.2	A	3
18										
19	Average	81.9	78.3	71.4	80.6	**HW Bonus/Penalty**		**Grading Criteria**		
20	Maximum	96.0	98.0	97.0	95.0	Poor	-2	0	F	
21	Minimum	60.0	50.0	40.0	60.0	OK	3	60	D	
22	Range	36.0	48.0	57.0	35.0	Good	5	70	C	

FIGURE 3.25 *Nested IFs and Other Functions (Exercise 9)*

10. Election 2000: Election 2000 has come and gone, but it will always be remembered as the closest election in our history. You will find a partially completed version of Figure 3.26 in the file, *Chapter 3 Practice 10*. Open the partially completed workbook and proceed as follows:

a. Enter an appropriate IF function in cells D9 and F9 to determine the electoral votes for each candidate. The electoral votes are awarded on an all-or-nothing basis—that is, the candidate with the larger popular vote wins all of that state's electoral votes.

b. Copy the entries in cells D9 and F9 to the remaining rows in the respective columns. Format these columns to display red and blue values, for Bush and Gore, respectively.

c. Enter a function of formula in cell G9 to determine the difference in the popular vote between the two candidates. The result should always appear as a positive number. You can do this in one of two ways, by using either an absolute value function or an appropriate IF function. Copy this formula to the remaining rows in the column.

d. Click in cell H9 and determine the percentage differential in the popular vote. This is the difference in the number of votes divided by the total number of votes.

e. Enter the appropriate SUM functions in cells B4 to C5 to determine the electoral and popular totals for each candidate.

f. Add your name somewhere in the worksheet, then print the completed sheet for your instructor. Be sure your worksheet fits on one page. Print the worksheet a second time to show the cell formulas.

g. Use the Sort function to display the states in a different sequence, such as the smallest (or largest) vote differential. Print the worksheet with the alternate sequence.

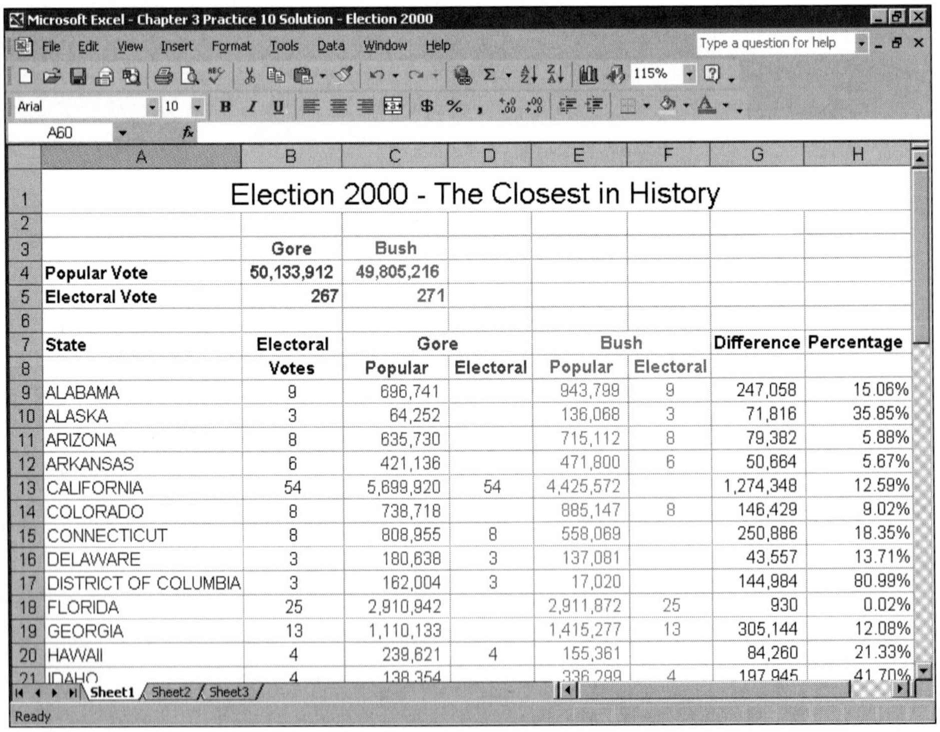

	A	B	C	D	E	F	G	H
1	Election 2000 - The Closest in History							
2								
3		Gore	Bush					
4	**Popular Vote**	50,133,912	49,805,216					
5	**Electoral Vote**	267	271					
6								
7	**State**	**Electoral**	**Gore**		**Bush**		**Difference**	**Percentage**
8		**Votes**	**Popular**	**Electoral**	**Popular**	**Electoral**		
9	ALABAMA	9	696,741		943,799	9	247,058	15.06%
10	ALASKA	3	64,252		136,068	3	71,816	35.85%
11	ARIZONA	8	635,730		715,112	8	79,382	5.88%
12	ARKANSAS	6	421,136		471,800	6	50,664	5.67%
13	CALIFORNIA	54	5,699,920	54	4,425,572		1,274,348	12.59%
14	COLORADO	8	738,718		885,147	8	146,429	9.02%
15	CONNECTICUT	8	808,955	8	558,069		250,886	18.35%
16	DELAWARE	3	180,638	3	137,081		43,557	13.71%
17	DISTRICT OF COLUMBIA	3	162,004	3	17,020		144,984	80.99%
18	FLORIDA	25	2,910,942		2,911,872	25	930	0.02%
19	GEORGIA	13	1,110,133		1,415,277	13	305,144	12.08%
20	HAWAII	4	239,621	4	155,361		84,260	21.33%
21	IDAHO	4	138,354		336,299	4	197,945	41.70%

FIGURE 3.26 *Election 2000 (Exercise 10)*

The Financial Consultant

A friend of yours is in the process of buying a home and has asked you to compare the payments and total interest on a 15- and a 30-year loan. You want to do as professional a job as possible and have decided to analyze the loans in Excel, then incorporate the results into a memo written in Microsoft Word. As of now, the principal is $150,000, but it is very likely that your friend will change his mind several times, and so you want to use the OLE capability within Windows to dynamically link the worksheet to the word processing document. Your memo should include a letterhead that takes advantage of the formatting capabilities within Word; a graphic logo would be a nice touch.

The Rule of 72

Delaying your IRA for one year can cost you as much as $64,000 at retirement, depending on when you begin. That may be hard to believe, but you can check the numbers without a calculator, using the "Rule of 72." This financial rule of thumb states that to find out how long it takes money to double, divide the number 72 by the interest rate; e.g., money earning 8% annually will double in approximately 9 years (72 divided by 8). The money doubles again in 18 years, again in 27 years, and so on. Now assume that you start your IRA at age 21, rather than 20, effectively losing 45 years of compound interest for the initial contribution. Use the rule of 72 to determine approximately how much you will lose, assuming an 8% rate of return. Check your calculation by creating a worksheet to determine the exact amount.

Individual Retirement Accounts

There are two types of individual retirement accounts, a Roth IRA and a traditional IRA. The Roth IRA is newer and has been called "the deal of the century." Search the Web to learn the benefits and limitations of each type of account. Which one is better for you? Summarize your findings in a brief note to your instructor.

The Automobile Dealership

The purchase of a car usually entails extensive bargaining between the dealer and the consumer. The dealer has an asking price but typically settles for less. The commission paid to a salesperson depends on how close the selling price is to the asking price. Exotic Motors has the following compensation policy for its sales staff:

- A 5% commission on the actual selling price for cars sold at 98% or more of the asking price
- A 3% commission on the actual selling price for cars sold at 95% or more (but less than 98%) of the asking price.
- A 2% commission on the actual selling price for cars sold at 90% or more (but less than 95%) of the asking price
- A 1% commission on the actual selling price for cars sold at less than 90% of the asking price. The dealer will not go below 85% of his asking price.

The dealer's asking price is based on the dealer's cost plus a 20% markup; for example, the asking price on a car that cost the dealer $20,000 would be $24,000. Develop a worksheet to be used by the dealer that shows his profit (the selling price minus the cost of the car minus the salesperson's commission) on every sale. The worksheet should be completely flexible and allow the dealer to vary the markup or commission percentages without having to edit or recopy any of the formulas. Use the data in the *Automobile Dealership* workbook to test your worksheet.

The Lottery

Many states raise money through lotteries that advertise prizes of several million dollars. In reality, however, the actual value of the prize is considerably less than the advertised value, although the winners almost certainly do not care. One state, for example, recently offered a twenty million dollar prize that was to be distributed in twenty annual payments of one million dollars each. How much was the prize actually worth, assuming a long-term interest rate of seven percent?

A Penny a Day

What if you had a rich uncle who offered to pay you "a penny a day," then double your salary each day for the next month? It does not sound very generous, but you will be surprised at how quickly the amount grows. Create a simple worksheet that enables you to use the Goal Seek command to answer the following questions. On what day of the month (if any) will your uncle pay you more than one million dollars? How much money will your uncle pay you on the 31st day?

CHAPTER 4

Graphs and Charts: Delivering a Message

OBJECTIVES

AFTER READING THIS CHAPTER YOU WILL BE ABLE TO:

1. Distinguish between the different types of charts, stating the advantages and disadvantages of each.
2. Distinguish between a chart embedded in a worksheet and one in a separate chart sheet; explain how many charts can be associated with the same worksheet.
3. Use the Chart Wizard to create and/or modify a chart.
4. Use the Drawing toolbar to enhance a chart by creating lines, objects, and 3-D shapes.
5. Differentiate between data series specified in rows and data series specified in columns.
6. Create a compound document consisting of a word processing memo, a worksheet, and a chart.

OVERVIEW

Business has always known that the graphic representation of data is an attractive, easy-to-understand way to convey information. Indeed, business graphics has become one of the most exciting Windows applications, whereby charts (graphs) are easily created from a worksheet, with just a few simple keystrokes or mouse clicks.

The chapter begins by emphasizing the importance of determining the message to be conveyed by a chart. It describes the different types of charts available within Excel and how to choose among them. It explains how to create a chart using the Chart Wizard, how to embed a chart within a worksheet, and how to create a chart in a separate chart sheet. It also describes how to use the Drawing toolbar to enhance a chart by creating lines, objects, and 3-D shapes.

The second half of the chapter explains how one chart can plot multiple sets of data, and how several charts can be based on the same worksheet. It also describes how to create a compound document, in which a chart and its associated worksheet are dynamically linked to a memo created by a word processor. All told, we think you will find this to be one of the most enjoyable chapters in the text.

CHART TYPES

A *chart* is a graphic representation of data in a worksheet. The chart is based on descriptive entries called *category labels*, and on numeric values called *data points*. The data points are grouped into one or more *data series* that appear in row(s) or column(s) on the worksheet. In every chart there is exactly one data point in each data series for each value of the category label.

The worksheet in Figure 4.1 will be used throughout the chapter as the basis for the charts we will create. Your manager believes that the sales data can be understood more easily from charts than from the strict numerical presentation of a worksheet. You have been given the assignment of analyzing the data in the worksheet and are developing a series of charts to convey that information.

The sales data in the worksheet can be presented several ways—for example, by city, by product, or by a combination of the two. Ask yourself which type of chart is best suited to answer the following questions:

- What percentage of total revenue comes from each city? from each product?
- What is the dollar revenue produced by each city? by each product?
- What is the rank of each city with respect to sales?
- How much revenue does each product contribute in each city?

In every instance, realize that a chart exists only to deliver a message, and that *you cannot create an effective chart unless you are sure of what that message is*. The next several pages discuss various types of business charts, each of which is best suited to a particular type of message.

	A	B	C	D	E	F
1	Superior Software Sales					
2						
3		Miami	Denver	New York	Boston	Total
4	Word Processing	$50,000	$67,500	$9,500	$141,000	$268,000
5	Spreadsheets	$44,000	$18,000	$11,500	$105,000	$178,500
6	Database	$12,000	$7,500	$6,000	$30,000	$55,500
7	Total	$106,000	$93,000	$27,000	$276,000	$502,000

FIGURE 4.1   *Superior Software*

KEEP IT SIMPLE

Keep it simple. This rule applies to both your message and the means of conveying that message. Excel makes it almost too easy to change fonts, styles, type sizes, and colors, but such changes will often detract from, rather than enhance, a chart. More is not necessarily better, and you do not have to use the features just because they are there. Remember that a chart must ultimately succeed on the basis of content, and content alone.

Pie Charts

A **pie chart** is the most effective way to display proportional relationships. It is the type of chart to select whenever words like *percentage* or *market share* appear in the message to be delivered. The pie, or complete circle, denotes the total amount. Each slice of the pie corresponds to its respective percentage of the total.

The pie chart in Figure 4.2a divides the pie representing total sales into four slices, one for each city. The size of each slice is proportional to the percentage of total sales in that city. The chart depicts a single data series, which appears in cells B7 through E7 on the associated worksheet. The data series has four data points corresponding to the total sales in each city.

To create the pie chart, Excel computes the total sales ($502,000 in our example), calculates the percentage contributed by each city, and draws each slice of the pie in proportion to its computed percentage. Boston's sales of $276,000 account for 55 percent of the total, and so this slice of the pie is allotted 55 percent of the area of the circle.

An **exploded pie chart**, as shown in Figure 4.2b, separates one or more slices of the pie for emphasis. Another way to achieve emphasis in a chart is to choose a title that reflects the message you are trying to deliver. The title in Figure 4.2a, for example, *Revenue by Geographic Area*, is neutral and leaves the reader to develop his or her own conclusion about the relative contribution of each area. By contrast, the title in Figure 4.2b, *New York Accounts for Only 5% of Revenue,* is more suggestive and emphasizes the problems in this office. Alternatively, the title could be changed to *Boston Exceeds 50% of Total Revenue* if the intent were to emphasize the contribution of Boston.

Three-dimensional pie charts may be created in exploded or nonexploded format as shown in Figures 4.2c and 4.2d, respectively. Excel also enables you to add arrows and text for emphasis.

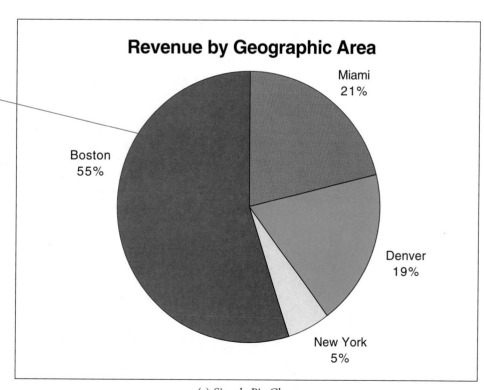

Size of slice is proportional to percentage of total sales from Boston

(a) Simple Pie Chart

FIGURE 4.2 *Pie Charts*

Title emphasizes
problems in New York

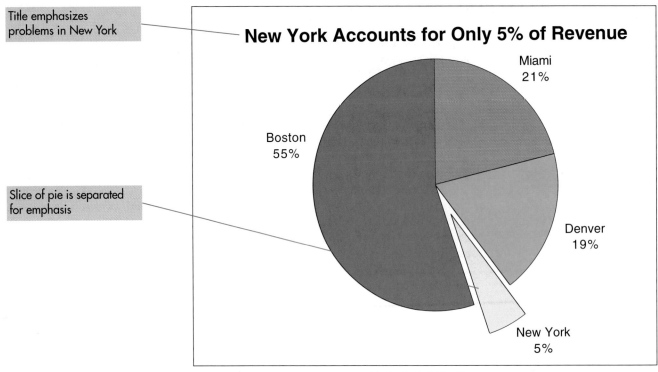

Slice of pie is separated
for emphasis

(b) Exploded Pie Chart

Title emphasizes
Boston's contribution

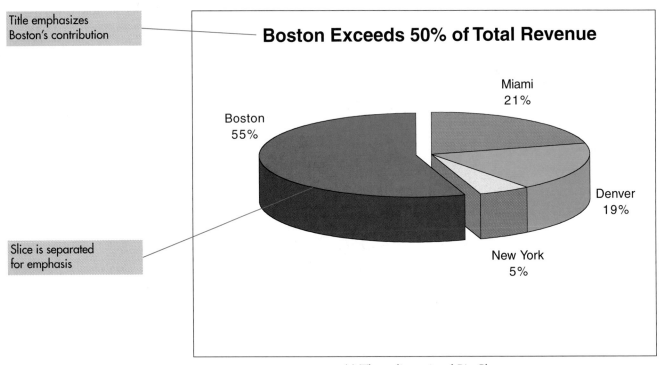

Slice is separated
for emphasis

(c) Three-dimensional Pie Chart

FIGURE 4.2   *Pie Charts (continued)*

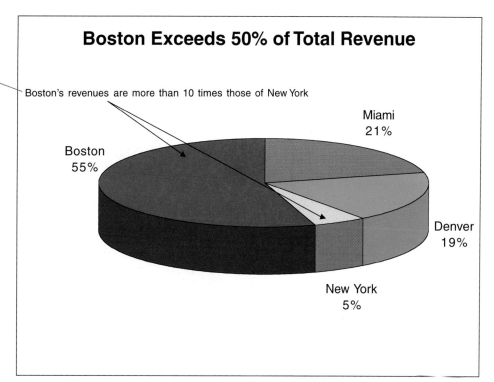

Arrows and text added for emphasis

Boston Exceeds 50% of Total Revenue

Boston's revenues are more than 10 times those of New York

Miami
21%

Boston
55%

Denver
19%

New York
5%

(d) Enhanced Pie Chart

FIGURE 4.2   *Pie Charts (continued)*

A pie chart is easiest to read when the number of slices is limited (i.e., not more than six or seven), and when small categories (percentages less than five) are grouped into a single category called "Other."

EXPLODED PIE CHARTS

Click and drag wedges out of a pie chart to convert an ordinary pie chart to an exploded pie chart. For best results pull the wedge out only slightly from the main body of the pie.

Column and Bar Charts

A *column chart* is used when there is a need to show actual numbers rather than percentages. The column chart in Figure 4.3a plots the same data series as the earlier pie chart, but displays it differently. The category labels (Miami, Denver, New York, and Boston) are shown along the *X* (horizontal) *axis*. The data points (monthly sales) are plotted along the *Y* (vertical) *axis*, with the height of each column reflecting the value of the data point.

A column chart can be given a horizontal orientation and converted to a *bar chart* as in Figure 4.3b. Some individuals prefer the bar chart over the corresponding column chart because the longer horizontal bars accentuate the difference between the items. Bar charts are also preferable when the descriptive labels are long, to eliminate the crowding that can occur along the horizontal axis of a column chart. As with the pie chart, a title can lead the reader and further emphasize the message, as with *Boston Leads All Cities* in Figure 4.3b.

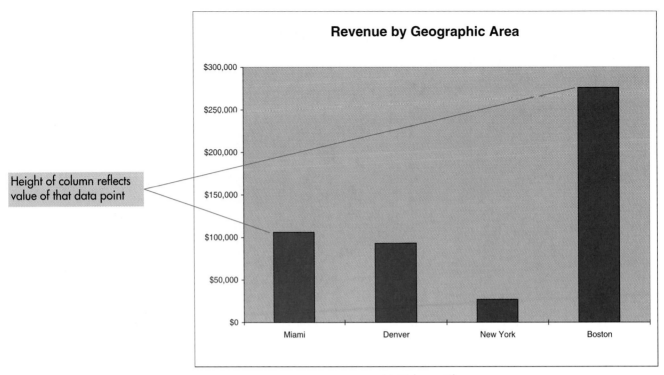

(a) Column Chart

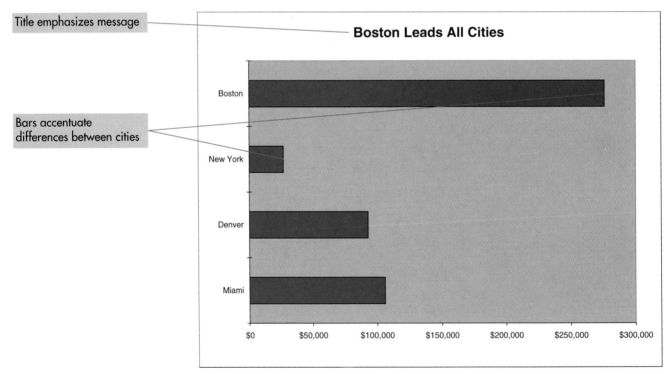

(b) Horizontal Bar Chart

FIGURE 4.3   *Column/Bar Charts*

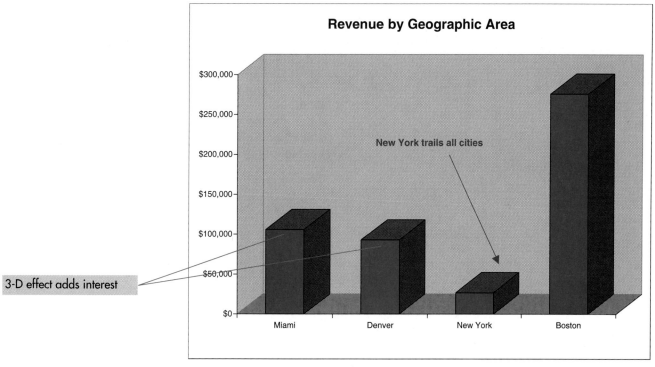

(c) Three-dimensional Column Chart

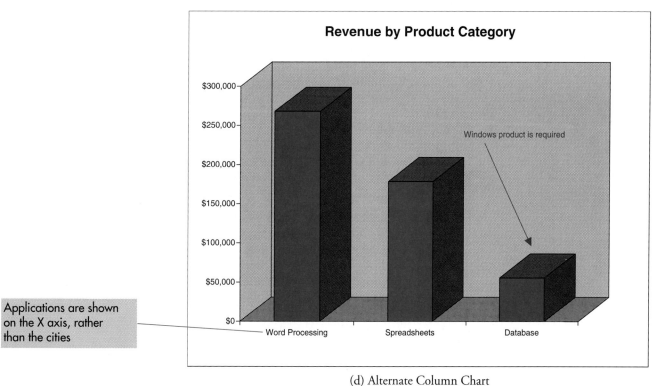

(d) Alternate Column Chart

FIGURE 4.3   *Column/Bar Charts (continued)*

A three-dimensional effect can produce added interest as shown in Figures 4.3c and 4.3d. Figure 4.3d plots a different set of numbers than we have seen so far (the sales for each product, rather than the sales for each city). The choice between the charts in Figures 4.3c and 4.3d depends on the message you want to convey—whether you want to emphasize the contribution of each city or each product. The title can be used to emphasize the message. Arrows, text, and 3-D shapes can be added to either chart to enhance the message.

As with a pie chart, column and bar charts are easiest to read when the number of categories is relatively small (seven or fewer). Otherwise, the columns (bars) are plotted so close together that labeling becomes impossible.

CREATING A CHART

There are two ways to create a chart in Excel. You can *embed* the chart in a worksheet, or you can create the chart in a separate *chart sheet*. Figure 4.4a displays an embedded column chart. Figure 4.4b shows a pie chart in its own chart sheet. Both techniques are valid. The choice between the two depends on your personal preference.

Regardless of where it is kept (embedded in a worksheet or in its own chart sheet), a chart is linked to the worksheet on which it is based. The charts in Figure 4.4 plot the same data series (the total sales for each city). Change any of these data points on the worksheet, and both charts will be updated automatically to reflect the new data.

Both charts are part of the same workbook (Software Sales) as indicated in the title bar of each figure. The tabs within the workbook have been renamed to indicate the contents of the associated sheet. Additional charts may be created and embedded in the worksheet and/or placed on their own chart sheets. And, as previously stated, if you change the worksheet, the chart (or charts) based upon it will also change.

Study the column chart in Figure 4.4a to see how it corresponds to the worksheet on which it is based. The descriptive names on the X axis are known as category labels and match the entries in cells B3 through E3. The quantitative values (data points) are plotted on the Y axis and match the total sales in cells B7 through E7. Even the numeric format matches; that is, the currency format used in the worksheet appears automatically on the scale of the Y axis.

The *sizing handles* on the *embedded chart* indicate it is currently selected and can be sized, moved, or deleted the same way as any other Windows object:

- To size the selected chart, point to a sizing handle (the mouse pointer changes to a double arrow), then drag the handle in the desired direction.
- To move the selected chart, point to the chart (the mouse pointer is a single arrow), then drag the chart to its new location.
- To copy the selected chart, click the Copy button to copy the chart to the clipboard, click in the workbook where you want the copied chart to go, then click the Paste button to paste the chart at that location.
- To delete the selected chart, press the Del key.

The same operations apply to any of the objects within the chart (such as its title), as will be discussed in the next section on enhancing a chart. Note, too, that both figures contain the chart toolbar that enables you to modify a chart after it has been created.

Workbook name

Chart toolbar

Sizing handles

Data points (match entries in B7:E7)

Category labels (match entries in B3:E3)

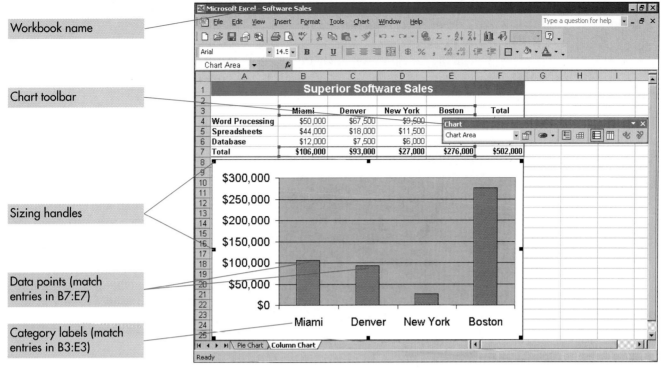

(a) Embedded Chart

Workbook name

Chart toolbar

Chart sheet is selected

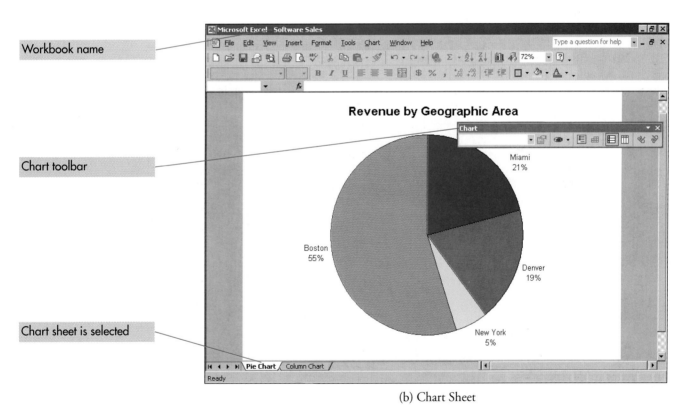

(b) Chart Sheet

FIGURE 4.4   Creating a Chart

The Chart Wizard

The **Chart Wizard** is the easiest way to create a chart. Just select the cells that contain the data as shown in Figure 4.5a, click the Chart Wizard button on the Standard toolbar, and let the Wizard do the rest. The process is illustrated in Figure 4.5, which shows how the Wizard creates a column chart to plot total sales by geographic area (city).

The steps in Figure 4.5 appear automatically as you click the Next command button to move from one step to the next. You can retrace your steps at any time by pressing the Back command button, access the Office Assistant for help with the Chart Wizard, or abort the process with the Cancel command button.

Step 1 in the Chart Wizard (Figure 4.5b) asks you to choose one of the available **chart types**. Step 2 (Figure 4.5c) shows you a preview of the chart and enables you to confirm (and, if necessary, change) the category names and data series specified earlier. (Only one data series is plotted in this example. Multiple data series are illustrated later in the chapter.) Step 3 (Figure 4.5d) asks you to complete the chart by entering its title and specifying additional options (such as the position of a legend and gridlines). And finally, step 4 (Figure 4.5e) has you choose whether the chart is to be created as an embedded chart (an object) within a specific worksheet, or whether it is to be created in its own chart sheet. The entire process takes but a few minutes.

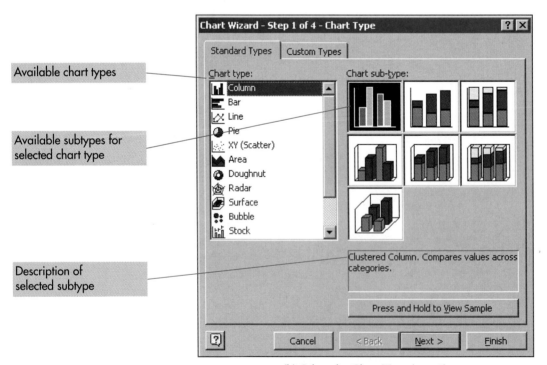

	A	B	C	D	E	F
1	Superior Software Sales					
2						
3		Miami	Denver	New York	Boston	Total
4	Word Processing	$50,000	$67,500	$9,500	$141,000	$268,000
5	Spreadsheets	$44,000	$18,000	$11,500	$105,000	$178,500
6	Database	$12,000	$7,500	$6,000	$30,000	$55,500
7	Total	$106,000	$93,000	$27,000	$276,000	$502,000

Selected cells (B3:E3 and B7:E7)

(a) The Worksheet

Available chart types

Available subtypes for selected chart type

Description of selected subtype

(b) Select the Chart Type (step 1)

FIGURE 4.5 *The Chart Wizard*

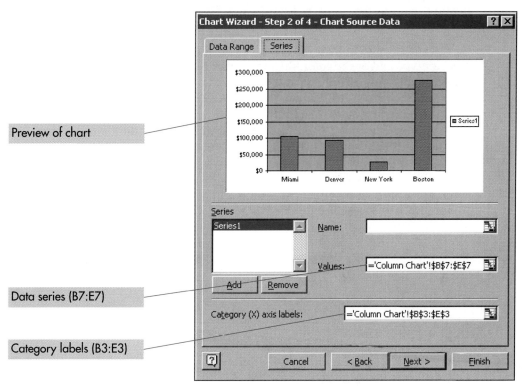

Preview of chart

Data series (B7:E7)

Category labels (B3:E3)

(c) Check the Data Series (step 2)

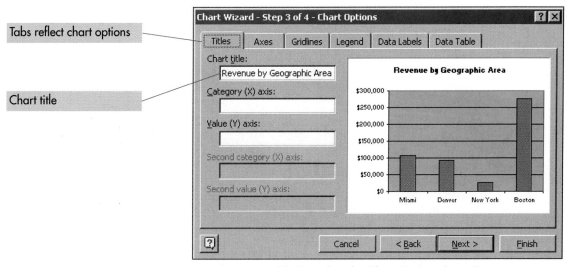

Tabs reflect chart options

Chart title

(d) Complete the Chart Options (step 3)

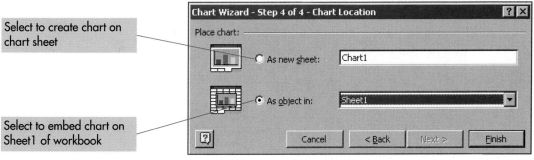

Select to create chart on chart sheet

Select to embed chart on Sheet1 of workbook

(e) Choose the Location (step 4)

FIGURE 4.5   *The Chart Wizard (continued)*

Modifying a Chart

A chart can be modified in several ways after it has been created. You can change the chart type and/or the color, shape, or pattern of the data series. You can add (or remove) gridlines and/or a legend. You can add labels to the data series. You can also change the font, size, color, and style of existing text anywhere in the chart by selecting the text, then changing its format. All of these features are implemented from the Chart menu or by using the appropriate button on the **Chart toolbar**.

You can also use the **Drawing toolbar** to add text boxes, arrows, and other objects for added emphasis. Figure 4.6, for example, contains a three-dimensional arrow with a text box within the arrow to call attention to the word processing sales. It also contains a second text box with a thin arrow in reference to the database product. Each of these objects is created separately using the appropriate tool from the Drawing toolbar. It's easy, as you will see in our next exercise.

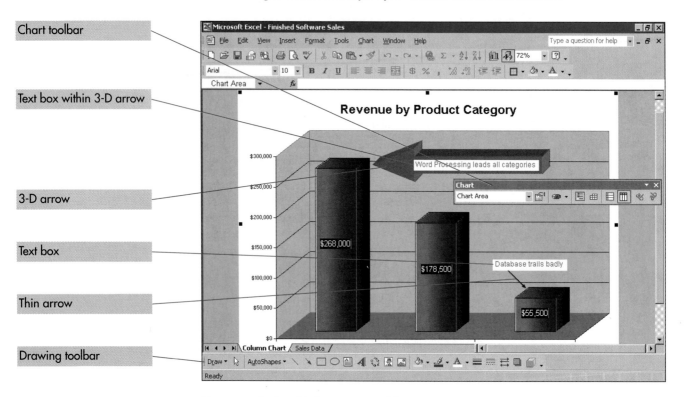

FIGURE 4.6 *Enhancing a Chart*

SET A TIME LIMIT

Excel enables you to customize virtually every aspect of every object within a chart. That is the good news. It's also the bad news, because you can spend inordinate amounts of time for little or no gain. It's fun to experiment, but set a time limit and stop when you reach the allocated time. The default settings are often adequate to convey your message, and further experimentation might prove counterproductive.

THE CHART WIZARD

Objective To create and modify a chart by using the Chart Wizard; to embed a chart within a worksheet; to enhance a chart to include arrows and text. Use Figure 4.7 as a guide in the exercise.

Step 1: **The AutoSum Command**

> ➤ Start Excel. Open the Software Sales workbook in the Exploring Excel folder. Save the workbook as **Finished Software Sales**.
> ➤ Click and drag to select cells **B7 through E7** (the cells that will contain the total sales for each location). Click the **AutoSum button** on the Standard toolbar to compute the total for each city.
> ➤ The totals are computed automatically as shown in Figure 4.7a. The formula bar shows that Cell B7 contains the Sum function to total all of the numeric entries immediately above the cell.
> ➤ Click and drag to select cells **F4 through F7**, then click the **AutoSum button**. The Sum function is entered automatically into these cells to total the entries to the left of the selected cells.
> ➤ Click and drag to select cells **B4 through F7** to format these cells with the currency symbol and no decimal places.
> ➤ Boldface the row and column headings and the totals. Add a red border and center the headings.
> ➤ Save the workbook.

AutoSum button

Sum function automatically entered by AutoSum button

Click and drag to select B7:E7

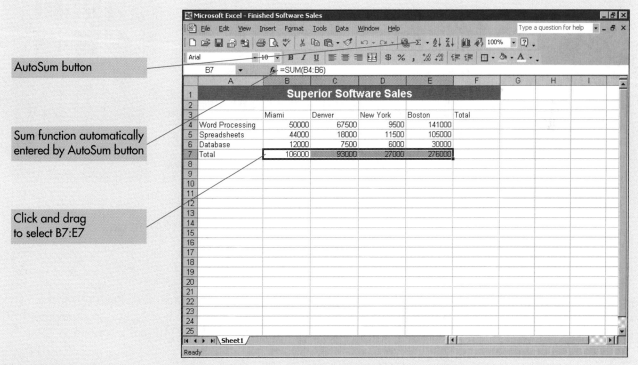

(a) The AutoSum Command (step 1)

FIGURE 4.7 *Hands-on Exercise 1*

Step 2:   **Start the Chart Wizard**

➤ Separate the toolbars if they occupy the same row. Pull down the **Tools menu**, click the **Customize command**, click the **Options tab**, then check the box that displays the toolbars on two rows.

➤ Drag the mouse over cells **B3 through E3** to select the category labels (the names of the cities). Press and hold the **Ctrl key** as you drag the mouse over cells **B7 through E7** to select the data series (the cells containing the total sales for the individual cities).

➤ Check that cells B3 through E3 and B7 through E7 are selected. Click the **Chart Wizard button** on the Standard toolbar to start the wizard. If you don't see the button, pull down the **Insert menu** and click the **Chart command**.

➤ You should see the dialog box for step 1 of the Chart Wizard as shown in Figure 4.7b. The **Column** chart type and **Clustered column** subtype are selected.

➤ Click (and hold) the button to see a sample chart. Click **Next**.

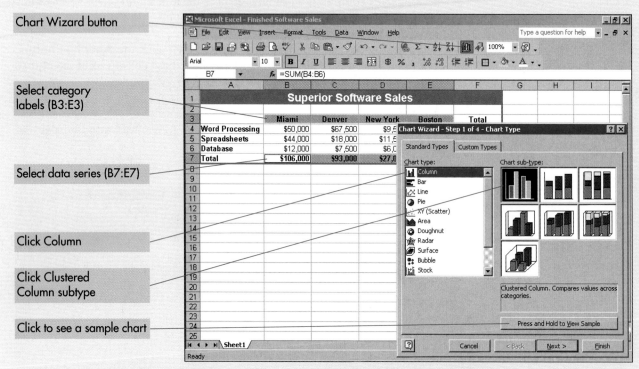

(b) Start the Chart Wizard (step 2)

FIGURE 4.7   *Hands-on Exercise 1 (continued)*

RETRACE YOUR STEPS

The Chart Wizard guides you every step of the way, but what if you make a mistake or change your mind? Click the Back command button at any time to return to a previous screen in order to enter different information, then continue working with the Wizard.

Step 3: **The Chart Wizard (continued)**

➤ You should see step 2 of the Chart Wizard. Click the **Series tab** in the dialog box so that your screen matches Figure 4.7c. Note that the values (the data being plotted) are in cells B7 through E7, and that the Category labels for the X axis are in cells B3 through E3. Click **Next** to continue.

➤ You should see step 3 of the Chart Wizard. If necessary, click the **Titles tab**, then click in the text box for the Chart title.

➤ Type **Revenue by Geographic Area**. Click the **Legend tab** and clear the box to show a legend. Click **Next**.

➤ You should see step 4 of the Chart Wizard. If necessary, click the option button to place the chart **As object** in Sheet1 (the name of the worksheet in which you are working).

➤ Click **Finish**.

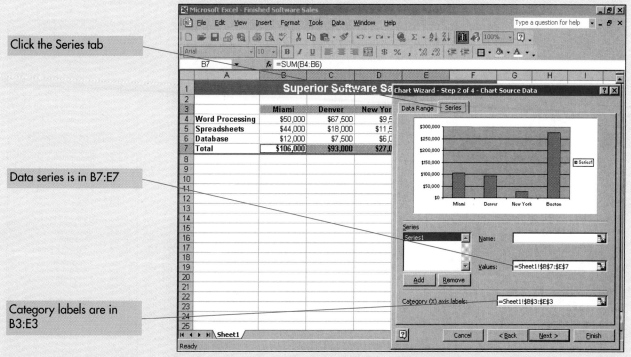

(c) The Chart Wizard (step 3)

FIGURE 4.7 *Hands-on Exercise 1 (continued)*

THE F11 KEY

The F11 key is the fastest way to create a chart in its own sheet. Select the data, including the legends and category labels, then press the F11 key to create the chart according to the default format built into the Excel column chart. After the chart has been created, you can use the menu bar, Chart toolbar, or shortcut menus to choose a different chart type and/or customize the formatting.

Step 4:   **Move and Size the Chart**

➤ You should see the completed chart as shown in Figure 4.7d. The sizing handles indicate that the chart is selected and will be affected by subsequent commands. The Chart toolbar is displayed automatically whenever a chart is selected.

➤ Move and/or size the chart just as you would any other Windows object:
  • To move the chart, click the chart (background) area to select the chart (a ScreenTip, "Chart Area," is displayed), then click and drag (the mouse pointer changes to a four-sided arrow) to move the chart.
  • To size the chart, drag a corner handle (the mouse pointer changes to a double arrow) to change the length and width of the chart simultaneously, keeping the chart in proportion as it is resized.

➤ Click outside the chart to deselect it. The sizing handles disappear and the Chart toolbar is no longer visible.

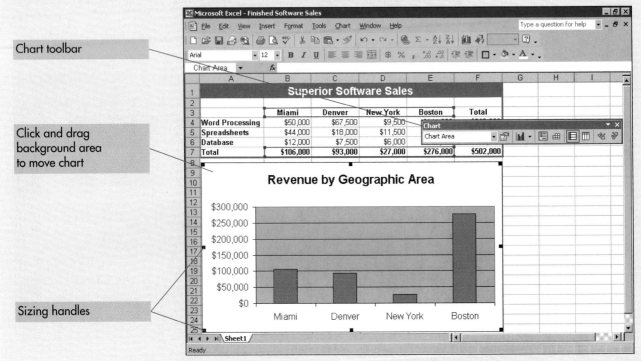

(d) Move and Size the Chart (step 4)

FIGURE 4.7   *Hands-on Exercise 1 (continued)*

EMBEDDED CHARTS

An embedded chart is treated as an object that can be moved, sized, copied, or deleted just as any other Windows object. To move an embedded chart, click the background of the chart to select the chart, then drag it to a new location in the worksheet. To size the chart, select it, then drag any of the eight sizing handles in the desired direction. To delete the chart, select it, then press the Del key. To copy the chart, select it, click the Copy button on the Standard toolbar to copy the chart to the clipboard, click elsewhere in the workbook where you want the copied chart to go, then click the Paste button.

Step 5: **Change the Worksheet**

➤ Any changes in a worksheet are automatically reflected in the associated chart. Click in cell **B4**, change the entry to **$400,000**, and press the **enter key**.

➤ The total sales for Miami in cell B7 change automatically to reflect the increased sales for word processing, as shown in Figure 4.7e. The column for Miami also changes in the chart and is now larger than the column for Boston.

➤ Click in cell **B3**. Change the entry to **Chicago**. Press **enter**. The category label on the X axis changes automatically.

➤ Click the **Undo button** to change the city back to Miami. Click the **Undo button** a second time to return to the initial value of $50,000. The worksheet and chart are restored to their earlier values.

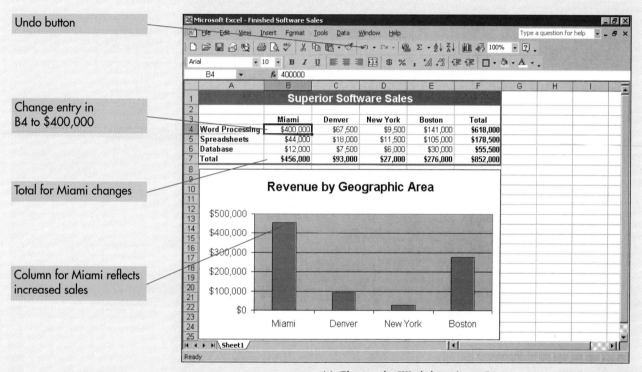

Undo button

Change entry in B4 to $400,000

Total for Miami changes

Column for Miami reflects increased sales

(e) Change the Worksheet (step 5)

FIGURE 4.7 *Hands-on Exercise 1 (continued)*

THE AUTOFORMAT COMMAND

The AutoFormat command does not do anything that could not be done through individual formatting commands, but it does provide inspiration by suggesting several attractive designs. Select the cells you want to format, pull down the Format menu, and click the AutoFormat command to display the AutoFormat dialog box. Select (click) a design, then click the Options button to determine the formats to apply (font, column width, patterns, and so on). Click OK to close the dialog box and apply the formatting. Click the Undo button if you do not like the result. See practice exercise 1 at the end of the chapter.

Step 6: **Change the Chart Type**

➤ Click the chart (background) area to select the chart, click the **drop-down arrow** on the Chart type button on the Chart toolbar, then click the **3-D Pie Chart icon**. The chart changes to a three-dimensional pie chart.

➤ Point to the chart area, click the **right mouse button** to display a shortcut menu, then click the **Chart Options command** to display the Chart Options dialog box shown in Figure 4.7f.

➤ Click the **Data Labels tab**, then click the check boxes for Category name and Percentage. Click **OK** to accept the settings and close the dialog box.

➤ The pie chart changes to reflect the options you just specified. Modify each component as necessary:

• Select (click) the (gray) **Plot area**. Click and drag the sizing handles to increase the size of the plot area within the embedded chart.

• Point to any of the labels, click the **right mouse button** to display a shortcut menu, and click **Format Data Labels** to display a dialog box. Click the **Font tab**, and select a smaller point size. It may also be necessary to click and drag each label away from the plot area.

➤ Make other changes as necessary. Save the workbook.

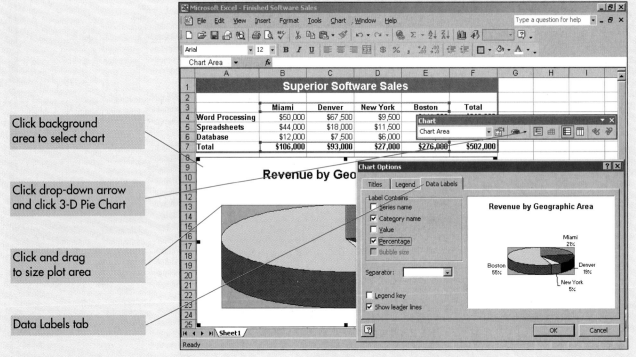

(f) Change the Chart Type (step 6)

FIGURE 4.7 *Hands-on Exercise 1 (continued)*

ADDITIONAL CHART TYPES

Excel offers a total of 14 standard chart types, each with several formats. Line charts are best to display time-related information such as a five-year trend of sales or profit data. A combination chart uses two or more chart types to display different kinds of data or when different scales are required for multiple data series. See practice exercise 6 at the end of the chapter.

Step 7: **Create a Second Chart**

➤ Click and drag to select cells **A4 through A6** in the worksheet. Press and hold the **Ctrl key** as you drag the mouse to select cells **F4 through F6**.

➤ Click the **Chart Wizard button** on the Standard toolbar to start the Chart Wizard and display the dialog box for step 1 as shown in Figure 4.7g. The Column Chart type is already selected. Click the **Clustered column with a 3-D visual effect subtype**. Press and hold the indicated button to preview the chart with your data. Click **Next**.

➤ Click the **Series tab** in the dialog box for step 2 to confirm that you selected the correct data points. The values for series1 should consist of cells F4 through F6. The Category labels for the X axis should be cells A4 through A6. Click **Next**.

➤ You should see step 3 of the Chart Wizard. Click the **Titles tab**, then click in the text box for the Chart title. Type **Revenue by Product Category**. Click the **Legend tab** and clear the box to show a legend. Click **Next**.

➤ You should see step 4 of the Chart Wizard. Select the option button to create the chart **As new sheet** (Chart1). Click **Finish**.

➤ The 3-D column chart has been created in the chart sheet labeled Chart1.

Chart Wizard button

Click and drag to select A4:A6

Click Column

Click Clustered column with a 3-D visual effect

Press Ctrl key and click and drag to select F4:F6

Click to preview chart

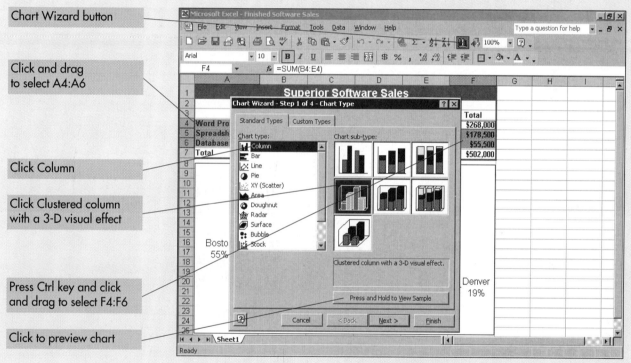

(g) Create a Second Chart (step 7)

FIGURE 4.7 *Hands-on Exercise 1 (continued)*

ANATOMY OF A CHART

A chart is composed of multiple components (objects), each of which can be selected and changed separately. Point to any part of a chart to display a ScreenTip indicating the name of the component, then click the mouse to select that component and display the sizing handles. You can then click and drag the object within the chart and/or click the right mouse button to display a shortcut menu with commands pertaining to the selected object.

Step 8: **Add a Text Box**

➤ Point to any visible toolbar, click the **right mouse button** to display a shortcut menu listing the available toolbars, then click **Drawing** to display the Drawing toolbar as shown in Figure 4.7h.

➤ Click the **Text Box button** on the Drawing toolbar. Click in the chart (the mouse pointer changes to a thin crosshair), then click and drag to create a text box. Release the mouse, then enter the text, **Word Processing leads all categories**.

➤ Point to the thatched border around the text box, then right click the border to display a context-sensitive menu. Click **Format Text Box** to display the Format Text dialog box. Click the **Font tab** and change the font to **12 point bold**. Choose **Red** as the font color.

➤ Click the **Colors and Lines tab** and select **white** as the fill color. Click **OK**. You should see red text on a white background. If necessary, size the text box so that the text fits on one line. Do not worry about the position of text box.

➤ Click the title of the chart. You will see sizing handles around the title to indicate it has been selected. Click the **drop-down arrow** in the Font Size box on the Formatting toolbar. Click **22** to increase the size of the title. Save the workbook.

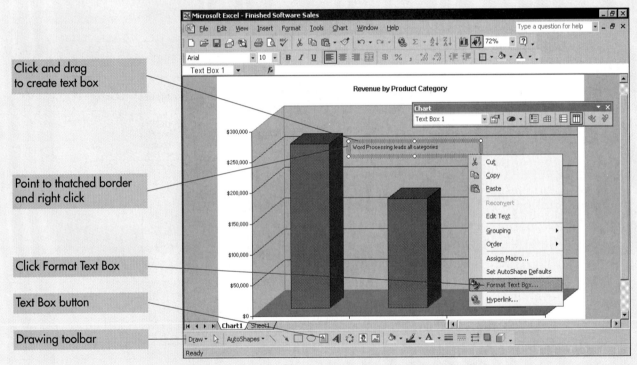

(h) Add a Text Box (step 8)

FIGURE 4.7 *Hands-on Exercise 1 (continued)*

FLOATING TOOLBARS

Any toolbar can be docked along the edge of the application window, or it can be displayed as a floating toolbar within the application window. To move a docked toolbar, drag the move handle. To move a floating toolbar, drag its title bar. To size a floating toolbar, drag any border in the direction you want to go. Double click the title bar of any floating toolbar to dock it. A floating toolbar will dim and disappear if it is not used.

Step 9:   **Create a 3-D Shape**

➤ Click on the **AutoShapes button** and, if necessary, click the double arrow to display additional commands. Click **Block Arrows**. Select an arrow style.

➤ Click in the chart (the mouse pointer changes to a thin crosshair), then click and drag to create an arrow. Release the mouse.

➤ Click the **3-D button** on the drawing toolbar and click **3-D Style 1** as shown in Figure 4.7i. Right click the arrow and click the **Format AutoShape** command to display the Format AutoShape dialog box. Click the **Colors and Lines tab**. Choose **Red** as the fill color. Click **OK**, then size the arrow.

➤ Select (click) the text box you created in the previous step, then click and drag the text box out of the way. Select (click) the 3-D arrow and position it next to the word processing column.

➤ Click and drag the text box on top of the arrow. If you do not see the text, right click the arrow, click the **Order command**, and click **Send to Back**.

➤ Save the workbook, but do not print it at this time. Exit Excel if you do not want to continue with the next exercise at this time.

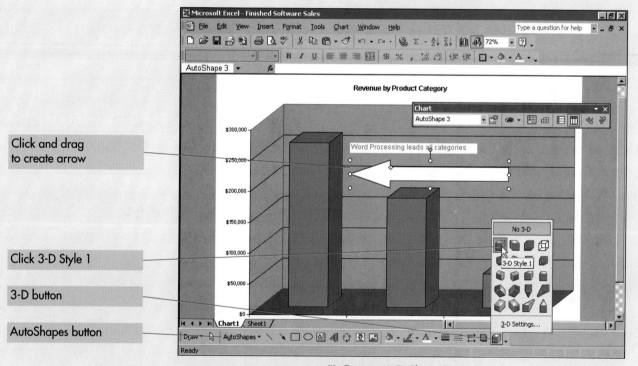

Click and drag to create arrow

Click 3-D Style 1

3-D button

AutoShapes button

(i) Create a 3-D Shape (step 9)

FIGURE 4.7   *Hands-on Exercise 1 (continued)*

FORMAT THE DATA SERIES

Use the Format Data Series command to change the color, shape, or pattern of the columns within the chart. Right click any column to select the data series (be sure that all three columns are selected), then click Format Data Series to display the Format Data Series dialog box. Experiment with the various options, especially those on the Shapes and Patterns tabs within the dialog box. Click OK when you are satisfied with the changes.

The charts presented so far displayed only a single data series such as the total sales by location or the total sales by product category. Although such charts are useful, it is often more informative to view **multiple data series** on the same chart. Figure 4.8a displays the worksheet we have been using throughout the chapter. Figure 4.8b displays a side-by-side column chart that plots multiple data series that exist as rows (B4:E4, B5:E5, and B6:E6) within the worksheet. Figure 4.8c displays a chart based on the same data when the series are in columns (B4:B6, C4:C6, D4:D6, and E4:E6).

Both charts plot a total of twelve data points (three product categories for each of four locations), but they group the data differently. Figure 4.8b displays the data by city in which the sales of three product categories are shown for each of four cities. Figure 4.8c is the reverse and groups the data by product category. This time the sales in the four cities are shown for each of three product categories. The choice between the two charts depends on your message and whether you want to emphasize revenue by city or by product category. It sounds complicated, but it's not; Excel will create either chart for you according to your specifications.

A3:E6 is selected

	A	B	C	D	E	F
1			Superior Software Sales			
2						
3		Miami	Denver	New York	Boston	Total
4	Word Processing	$50,000	$67,500	$9,500	$141,000	$268,000
5	Spreadsheets	$44,000	$18,000	$11,500	$105,000	$178,500
6	Database	$12,000	$7,500	$6,000	$30,000	$55,500
7	Total	$106,000	$93,000	$27,000	$276,000	$502,000

(a) Worksheet Data

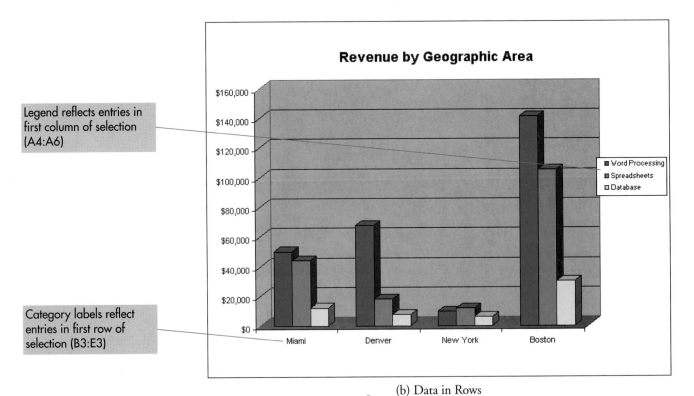

Legend reflects entries in first column of selection (A4:A6)

Category labels reflect entries in first row of selection (B3:E3)

(b) Data in Rows

FIGURE 4.8 *Side-by-Side Column Charts*

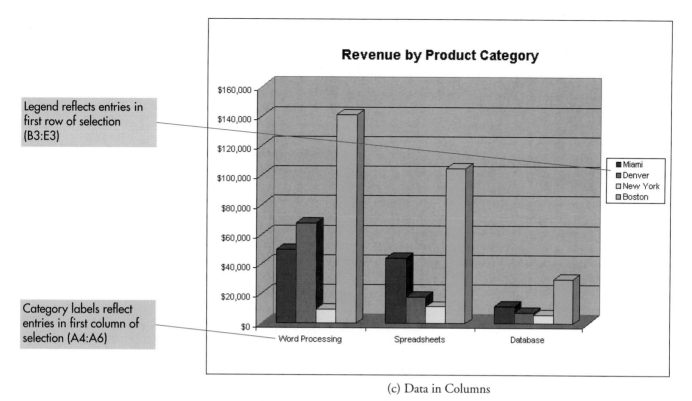

Legend reflects entries in first row of selection (B3:E3)

Category labels reflect entries in first column of selection (A4:A6)

(c) Data in Columns

FIGURE 4.8 *Side-by-Side Column Charts (continued)*

- If you specify that the data series are in rows (Figure 4.8b), the Wizard will:
  - Use the first row (cells B3 through E3) for the category labels
  - Use the remaining rows (rows four, five, and six) for the data series
  - Use the first column (cells A4 through A6) for the legend text

- If you specify the data series are in columns (Figure 4.8c), the Wizard will:
  - Use the first column (cells A4 through A6) for the category labels
  - Use the remaining columns (columns B, C, D, and E) for the data series
  - Use the first row (cells B3 through E3) for the legend text

Stacked Column Charts

The next decision associated with charts that contain multiple data series is the choice between ***side-by-side column charts*** versus ***stacked column charts*** such as those shown in Figure 4.9. Stacked column charts also group data in one of two ways, in rows or in columns. Thus Figure 4.9a is a stacked column chart with the data in rows. Figure 4.9b is also a stacked column chart, but the data is in columns.

The choice of side-by-side versus stacked column charts depends on the intended message. If you want the audience to see the individual sales in each city or product category, then the side-by-side columns in Figure 4.8 are more appropriate. If, on the other hand, you want to emphasize the total sales for each city or product category, the stacked columns in Figure 4.9 are preferable. The advantage of the stacked column is that the totals are clearly shown and can be easily compared. The disadvantage is that the segments within each column do not start at the same point, making it difficult to determine the actual sales for the individual categories.

Note, too, that the scale on the y axis in charts is different for charts with side-by-side columns versus charts with stacked columns. The side-by-side columns in Figure 4.8 show the sales of each product category and so the Y axis goes only to $160,000. The stacked columns in Figure 4.9, however, reflect the total sales for all products in each city and thus the scale goes to $300,000. Realize too, that for a stacked column chart to make sense, its numbers must be additive. It would not make sense, for example, to convert a column chart that plots units and dollar sales side by side, to a stacked column chart, because units and dollars should not be added together.

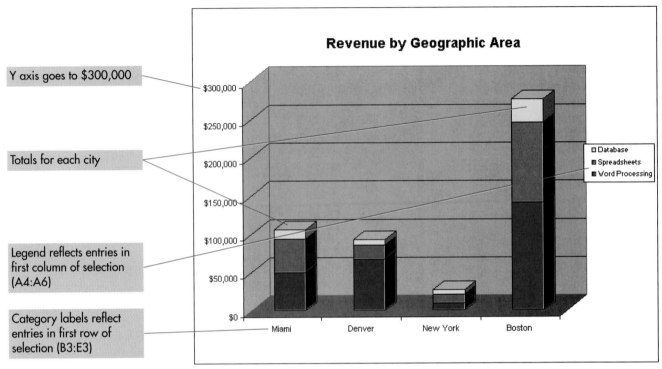

Y axis goes to $300,000

Totals for each city

Legend reflects entries in first column of selection (A4:A6)

Category labels reflect entries in first row of selection (B3:E3)

(a) Data in Rows

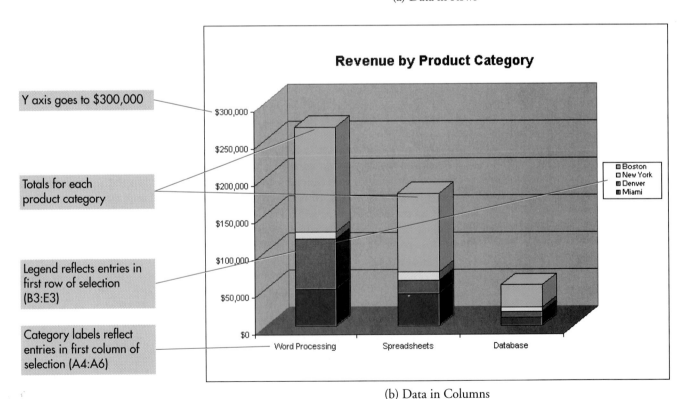

Y axis goes to $300,000

Totals for each product category

Legend reflects entries in first row of selection (B3:E3)

Category labels reflect entries in first column of selection (A4:A6)

(b) Data in Columns

FIGURE 4.9   *Stacked Column Charts*

MULTIPLE DATA SERIES

Objective   To plot multiple data series in the same chart; to differentiate between data series in rows and columns; to create and save multiple charts that are associated with the same worksheet. Use Figure 4.10 as a guide in the exercise.

Step 1:   **Rename the Worksheets**

> ➤ Open the **Finished Software Sales** workbook from the previous exercise as shown in Figure 4.10a. The workbook contains an embedded chart and a separate chart sheet.
> ➤ Point to the workbook tab labeled **Sheet1**, click the **right mouse button** to display a shortcut menu, then click the **Rename** command. The name of the worksheet (Sheet1) is selected.
> ➤ Type **Sales Data** to change the name of the worksheet to the more descriptive name. Press the **enter key**.
> ➤ Point to the tab labeled **Chart1** (which contains the three-dimensional column chart created in the previous exercise). Click the **right mouse button** to display a shortcut menu.
> ➤ Click **Rename**. Enter **Column Chart** as the name of the chart sheet. Press the **enter key**.
> ➤ Save the workbook.

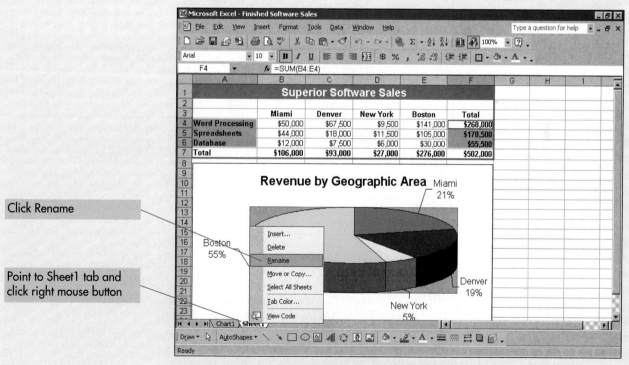

Click Rename

Point to Sheet1 tab and click right mouse button

(a) Rename the Worksheets (step 1)

FIGURE 4.10   *Hands-on Exercise 2*

Step 2:   **The Office Assistant**

➤ Click the **Sales Data tab**, then click and drag to select cells **A3 through E6**. Click the **Chart Wizard button** on the Standard toolbar to start the Wizard and display the dialog box shown in Figure 4.10b.

➤ If necessary, click the **Office Assistant button** in the Chart Wizard dialog box to display the Office Assistant and the initial help screen. Click the option button for **Help with this feature**.

➤ The display for the Assistant changes to offer help about the various chart types available. (It's up to you whether you want to explore the advice at this time. You can close the Assistant, or leave it open and drag the title bar out of the way.)

➤ Select **Column** as the chart type and **Clustered column with a 3-D visual effect** as the subtype. Click **Next** to continue with the Chart Wizard.

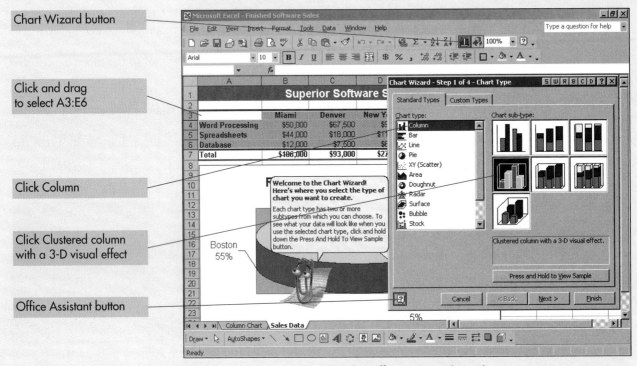

(b) The Office Assistant (step 2)

FIGURE 4.10   *Hands-on Exercise 2 (continued)*

THE OFFICE ASSISTANT

The Office Assistant button is common to all Office applications and is an invaluable source of online help. You can activate the Assistant at any time by clicking its button on the Standard toolbar or from within a specialized dialog box. You can ask the Assistant a specific question and/or you can have the Assistant monitor your work and suggest tips as appropriate. You can tell that the Assistant has a suggestion when you see a lightbulb appear adjacent to the character.

Step 3: **View the Data Series**

➤ You should see step 2 of the Chart Wizard as shown in Figure 4.10c. The help supplied by the Office Assistant changes automatically with the steps in the Chart Wizard.

➤ The data range should be specified as **Sales Data!$A$3:$E$6** as shown in Figure 4.10c. The option button for **Series in Rows** should be selected. Click the **Series tab**:

- The series list box shows three data series (Word Processing, Spreadsheets, and Database) corresponding to the legends for the chart.
- The **Word Processing** series is selected by default. The legend in the sample chart shows that the data points in the series are plotted in blue. The values are taken from cells B4 through E4 in the Sales Data Worksheet.
- Click **Spreadsheets** in the series list box. The legend shows that the series is plotted in red. The values are taken from cells B5 through E5 in the Sales Data worksheet.
- Click **Database** in the series list box. The legend shows that the series is plotted in yellow. The values are taken from cells B6 through E6 in the Sales Data worksheet.

➤ Click **Next** to continue creating the chart. You should see step 3 of the Chart Wizard. Click the **Titles tab**. Click the text box for Chart title. Type **Revenue by City**. Click **Next**.

➤ You should see step 4 of the Chart Wizard. Click the option button for **As new sheet**. Type **Revenue by City** in the associated text box to give the chart sheet a meaningful name. Click **Finish**.

➤ Excel creates the new chart in its own sheet named Revenue by City. Click **No** to tell the Assistant that you don't need further help. Right click the Assistant. Click **Hide**. Save the workbook.

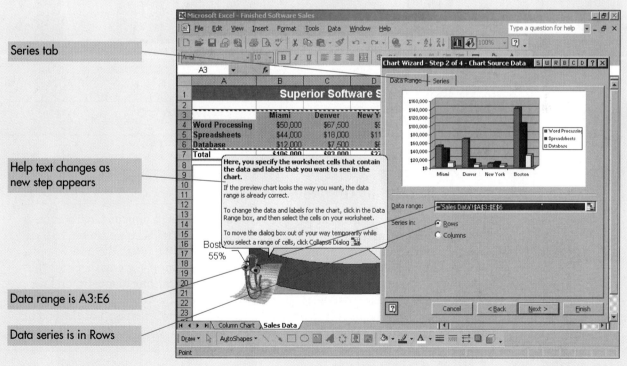

Series tab

Help text changes as new step appears

Data range is A3:E6

Data series is in Rows

(c) View the Data Series (step 3)

FIGURE 4.10   *Hands-on Exercise 2 (continued)*

Step 4:   **Copy the Chart**

➤ Point to the tab named **Revenue by City**. Click the **right mouse button**. Click **Move or Copy** to display the dialog box in Figure 4.10d.

➤ Click **Sales Data** in the Before Sheet list box. Check the box to **Create a Copy**. Click **OK**.

➤ A duplicate worksheet called Revenue by City(2) is created and appears before (to the left of) the Sales Data worksheet. (You can also press and hold the Ctrl key as you drag the worksheet tab to create a copy of the worksheet.)

➤ Double click the newly created worksheet tab to select the name. Enter **Revenue by Product** as the new name.

➤ Save the workbook.

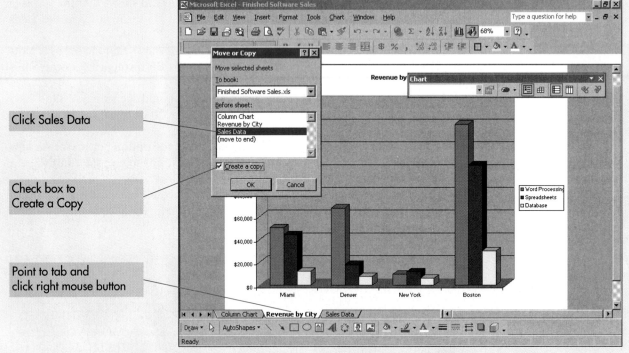

Click Sales Data

Check box to Create a Copy

Point to tab and click right mouse button

(d) Copy the Chart (step 4)

FIGURE 4.10   *Hands-on Exercise 2 (continued)*

MOVING AND COPYING A WORKSHEET

The fastest way to move or copy a chart sheet is to drag its tab. To move a sheet, point to its tab, then click and drag the tab to its new position. To copy a sheet, press and hold the Ctrl key as you drag the tab to the desired position for the second sheet. Rename the copied sheet (or any sheet for that matter) by double clicking its tab to select the existing name. Enter a new name for the worksheet, then press the enter key. You can also right click the worksheet tab to change its color. See practice exercise 1 at the end of the chapter.

Step 5: **Change the Source Data**

➤ Click the **Revenue by Product tab** to make it the active sheet. Click anywhere in the title of the chart, drag the mouse over the word **City** to select the text, then type **Product Category** to replace the selected text. Click outside the title to deselect it.

➤ Pull down the **Chart menu**. If necessary, click the double arrow to see more commands, click **Source Data** (you will see the Sales Data worksheet), then click the **Columns option button** so that your screen matches Figure 4.10e.

➤ Click the **Series tab** and note the following:
  • The current chart plots the data in rows. There are three data series (one series for each product).
  • The new chart (shown in the dialog box) plots the data in columns. There are four data series (one for each city as indicated in the Series list box).

➤ Click **OK** to close the Source Data dialog box.
➤ Save the workbook.

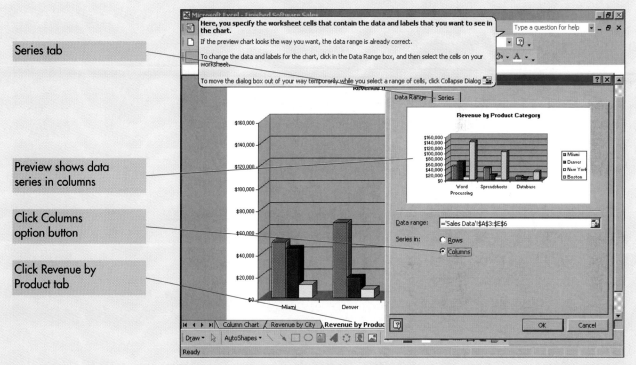

(e) Change the Source Data (step 5)

FIGURE 4.10   *Hands-on Exercise 2 (continued)*

THE HORIZONTAL SCROLL BAR

The horizontal scroll bar contains four scrolling buttons to scroll through the sheet tabs in a workbook. Click ◄ or ► to scroll one tab to the left or right. Click ◄ or ► to scroll to the first or last tab in the workbook. Once the desired tab is visible, click the tab to select it. Change the color of any tab by right clicking the tab and selecting Tab Color from the context-sensitive menu. See practice exercise 1 at the end of the chapter.

Step 6: **Change the Chart Type**

➤ Point to the chart area, click the **right mouse button** to display a shortcut menu, then click the **Chart Type command** to display the Chart Type dialog box. (You can also access the command from the Chart menu.)

➤ Select the **Stacked Column with a 3-D visual effect chart** (the middle entry in the second row). Click **OK**. The chart changes to a stacked column chart as shown in Figure 4.10f.

➤ Save the workbook.

➤ Pull down the **File menu**, click the **Print command**, then click the option button to print the **Entire Workbook**. Click **OK**.

➤ Submit the workbook to your instructor as proof that you completed the exercise. Close the workbook. Exit Excel if you do not want to continue with the next exercise at this time.

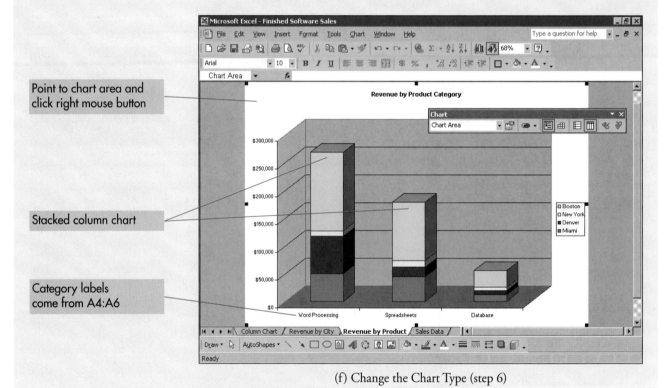

(f) Change the Chart Type (step 6)

FIGURE 4.10 *Hands-on Exercise 2 (continued)*

THE RIGHT MOUSE BUTTON

Point to a cell (or group of selected cells), a chart or worksheet tab, a toolbar, or chart (or a selected object on the chart), then click the right mouse button to display a shortcut menu. All shortcut menus are context-sensitive and display commands appropriate for the selected item. Right clicking a toolbar, for example, enables you to display (hide) additional toolbars. Right clicking a sheet tab enables you to rename, move, copy, or delete the sheet.

The applications within Microsoft Office enable you to create a document in one application that contains data (objects) from another application. The memo in Figure 4.11, for example, was created in Microsoft Word and it contains *objects* (a worksheet and a chart) that were developed in Microsoft Excel. The Excel objects are *linked* to the Word document, so that any changes to the Excel workbook are automatically reflected in the Word document.

The following exercise uses *object linking and embedding (OLE)* to create a Word document containing an Excel worksheet and chart. As you do the exercise, both applications (Word and Excel) will be open, and it will be necessary to switch back and forth between them. This in turn demonstrates the *multitasking* capability within Windows and the use of the *taskbar* to switch between the open applications.

Superior Software

Miami, Florida

To: Mr. White
        Chairman, Superior Software

From: Heather Bond
          Vice President, Marketing

Subject: May Sales Data

The May sales data clearly indicate that Boston is outperforming our other geographic areas. It is my feeling that Ms. Brown, the office supervisor, is directly responsible for its success and that she should be rewarded accordingly. In addition, we may want to think about transferring her to New York, as they are in desperate need of new ideas and direction. I will be awaiting your response after you have time to digest the information presented.

Superior Software Sales					
	Miami	**Denver**	**New York**	**Boston**	**Total**
Word Processing	$50,000	$67,500	$200,000	$141,000	**$458,500**
Spreadsheets	$44,000	$18,000	$11,500	$105,000	**$178,500**
Database	$12,000	$7,500	$6,000	$30,000	**$55,500**
Total	**$106,000**	**$93,000**	**$217,500**	**$276,000**	**$692,500**

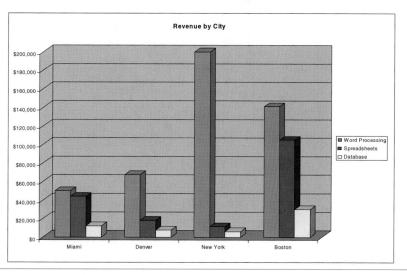

FIGURE 4.11   *Object Linking and Embedding*

OBJECT LINKING AND EMBEDDING

Objective To create a compound document consisting of a memo, worksheet, and chart. Use Figure 4.12 as a guide in the exercise.

Step 1: **Open the Software Sales Document**

➤ Click the **Start button** on the taskbar to display the Start menu. Click (or point to) the **Programs menu**, then click **Microsoft Word 2002** to start the program. Hide the Office Assistant if it appears.

➤ If necessary, click the **Maximize button** in the application window so that Word takes the entire desktop as shown in Figure 4.12a. (The Open dialog box is not yet visible.)

➤ Pull down the **File menu** and click **Open** (or click the **Open button** on the Standard toolbar).
  • Click the **drop-down arrow** in the Look In list box. Click the appropriate drive, drive C or drive A, depending on the location of your data.
  • Double click the **Exploring Excel folder** (we placed the Word memo in the Exploring Excel folder) to open the folder. Double click the **Software Memo** to open the document.
  • Save the document as **Finished Software Memo**.

➤ Pull down the **View menu**. Click **Print Layout** to change to the Print Layout view. Pull down the **View menu**. Click **Zoom**. Click **Page Width**.

➤ The software memo is open on your desktop.

Open button

Click drop-down arrow to select drive/folder

Double click to open Software Memo

Start button

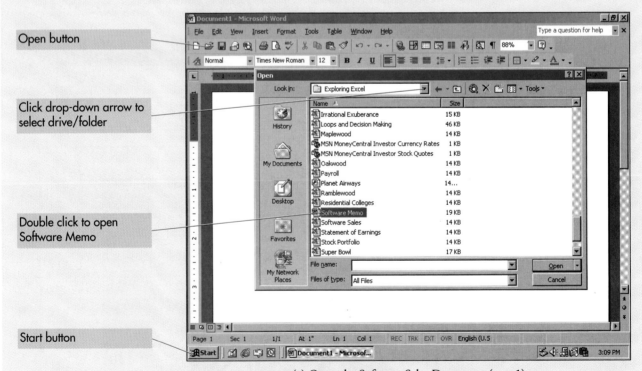

(a) Open the Software Sales Document (step 1)

FIGURE 4.12 *Hands-on Exercise 3*

Step 2:   **Copy the Worksheet**

➤ Open the **Finished Software Sales workbook** from the previous exercise.
  • If you did not close Microsoft Excel at the end of the previous exercise, you
    will see its button on the taskbar. Click the **Microsoft Excel button** to return
    to the Finished Software Sales workbook.
  • If you closed Microsoft Excel, click the **Start button** to start Excel, then open
    the Finished Software Sales workbook.
➤ The taskbar should now contain a button for both Microsoft Word and
  Microsoft Excel. Click either button to move back and forth between the open
  applications. End by clicking the **Microsoft Excel button**.
➤ Click the tab for **Sales Data**. Click and drag to select **A1 through F7** to select
  the entire worksheet as shown in Figure 4.12b.
➤ Point to the selected area and click the **right mouse button** to display the short-
  cut menu. Click **Copy**.
➤ A moving border appears around the entire worksheet, indicating that it has
  been copied to the clipboard.

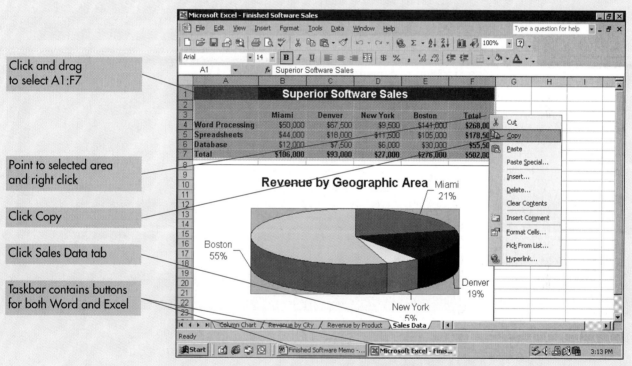

Click and drag
to select A1:F7

Point to selected area
and right click

Click Copy

Click Sales Data tab

Taskbar contains buttons
for both Word and Excel

(b) Copy the Worksheet (step 2)

FIGURE 4.12   *Hands-on Exercise 3 (continued)*

THE WINDOWS TASKBAR

Multitasking, the ability to run multiple applications at the same time, is one
of the primary advantages of the Windows environment. Each button on
the taskbar appears automatically when its application or folder is opened,
and disappears upon closing. (The buttons are resized automatically
according to the number of open windows.) The taskbar can be moved to
the left or right edge of the desktop, or to the top of the desktop, by dragging a blank area of the taskbar to the desired position.

Step 3: **Create the Link**

➤ Click the **Microsoft Word button** on the taskbar to return to the memo as shown in Figure 4.12c. Press **Ctrl+End** to move to the end of the memo, which is where you will insert the Excel worksheet.

➤ Pull down the **Edit menu**. If necessary, click the **double arrow** to see more commands, then click **Paste Special** to display the dialog box in Figure 4.12c.

➤ Click **Microsoft Excel Worksheet Object** in the As list. Click the **Paste Link** option **button**. Click **OK** to insert the worksheet into the document.

➤ Right click the worksheet to display a context-sensitive menu, click **Format Object** to display the associated dialog box, and click the **Layout tab**.

➤ Choose **Square** in the Wrapping Style area, then click the option button to **Center** the object. Click **OK** to accept the settings and close the dialog box.

➤ Save the memo.

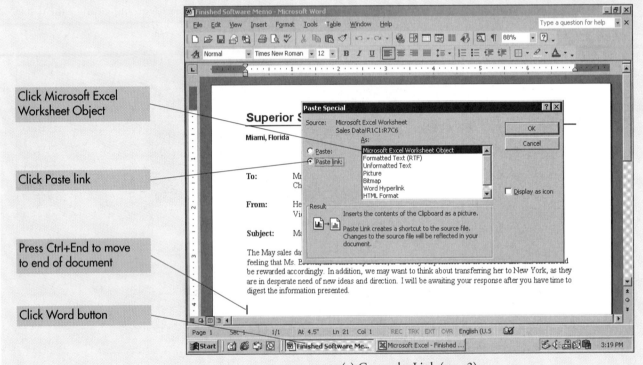

Click Microsoft Excel Worksheet Object

Click Paste link

Press Ctrl+End to move to end of document

Click Word button

(c) Create the Link (step 3)

FIGURE 4.12 *Hands-on Exercise 3 (continued)*

THE COMMON USER INTERFACE

The common user interface provides a sense of familiarity from one Office application to the next. The applications share a common menu structure with consistent ways to execute commands from those menus. The Standard and Formatting toolbars are present in both applications. Many keyboard shortcuts are also common, such as Ctrl+Home and Ctrl+End to move to the beginning and end of a document, respectively.

Step 4: **Copy the Chart**

➤ Click the **Microsoft Excel button** on the taskbar to return to the worksheet. Click outside the selected area (cells A1 through F7) to deselect the cells. Press **Esc** to remove the moving border.

➤ Click the **Revenue by City tab** to select the chart sheet. Point to the chart area, then click the left mouse button to select the chart.

➤ Be sure you have selected the entire chart and that you see the same sizing handles as in Figure 4.12d.

➤ Pull down the **Edit menu** and click **Copy** (or click the **Copy button** on the Standard toolbar). A moving border appears around the entire chart, indicating that the chart has been copied to the clipboard.

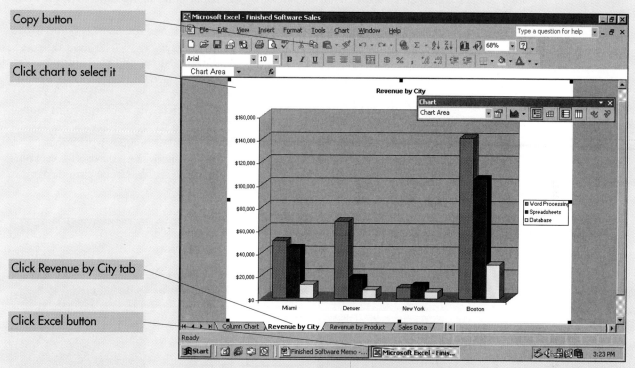

Copy button

Click chart to select it

Click Revenue by City tab

Click Excel button

(d) Copy the Chart (step 4)

FIGURE 4.12 *Hands-on Exercise 3 (continued)*

ALT+TAB STILL WORKS

Alt+Tab was a treasured shortcut in Windows 3.1 that enabled users to switch back and forth between open applications. The shortcut also works in all subsequent versions of Windows. Press and hold the Alt key while you press and release the Tab key repeatedly to cycle through the open applications, whose icons are displayed in a small rectangular window in the middle of the screen. Release the Alt key when you have selected the icon for the application you want.

Step 5: **Add the Chart**

➤ Click the **Microsoft Word button** on the taskbar to return to the memo. If necessary, press **Ctrl+End** to move to the end of the Word document. Press the **enter key** to add a blank line.

➤ Pull down the **Edit menu**. Click **Paste Special**. Click the **Paste link option button**. If necessary, click **Microsoft Excel Chart Object**. Click **OK** to insert the chart into the document.

➤ Right click the chart to display a context-sensitive menu, click **Format Object**, click the **Layout tab**, and choose **Square** in the Wrapping Style area.

➤ Zoom to **Whole Page** to facilitate moving and sizing the chart. You need to reduce its size so that it fits on the same page as the memo. Thus, scroll to the chart and click the chart to select it. This displays the sizing handles as shown in Figure 4.12e.

➤ Click and drag a corner sizing handle inward to make the chart smaller. Move the chart to the first page and center it on the page.

➤ Zoom to **Page Width**. Look carefully at the worksheet and chart in the document. The sales for Word Processing in New York are currently $9,500, and the chart reflects this amount. Save the memo.

➤ Point to the **Microsoft Excel button** on the taskbar and click the **right mouse button** to display a shortcut menu. Click **Close** to close Excel. Click **Yes** if prompted to save the changes to the Finished Software Sales workbook.

➤ Pull down the **File menu** and click the **Exit command**. The Microsoft Excel button disappears from the taskbar, indicating that Excel has been closed. Word is now the only open application.

Zoom button

Sizing handles

Click chart to select it

Right click on Excel button

Click Word button

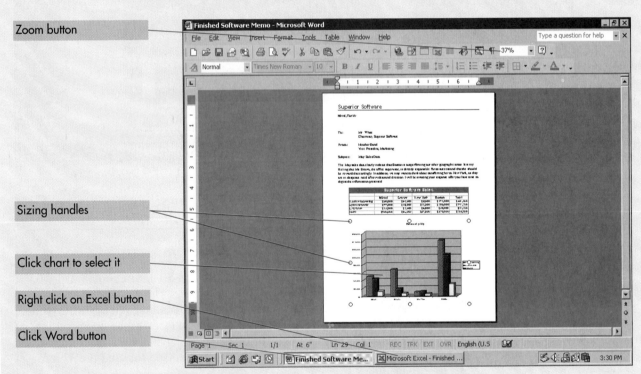

(e) Add the Chart (step 5)

FIGURE 4.12 *Hands-on Exercise 3 (continued)*

Step 6: **Modify the Worksheet**

➤ Click anywhere in the worksheet to select the worksheet and display the sizing handles as shown in Figure 4.12f.

➤ The status bar indicates that you can double click to edit the worksheet. Double click anywhere within the worksheet to reopen Excel in order to change the data.

➤ The system pauses as it loads Excel and reopens the Finished Software Sales workbook. If necessary, click the **Maximize button** to maximize the Excel window. Hide the Office Assistant if it appears.

➤ If necessary, click the **Sales Data tab** within the workbook. Click in **cell D4**. Type **$200,000**. Press **enter**.

➤ Click the |◀ **button** to scroll to the first tab. Click the **Revenue by City tab** to select the chart sheet. The chart has been modified automatically and reflects the increased sales for New York.

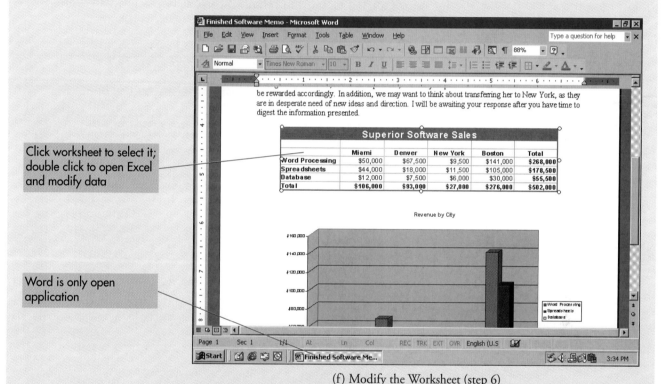

Click worksheet to select it; double click to open Excel and modify data

Word is only open application

(f) Modify the Worksheet (step 6)

FIGURE 4.12 *Hands-on Exercise 3 (continued)*

LINKING VERSUS EMBEDDING

A linked object maintains its connection to the source file. An embedded object does not. Thus, a linked object can be placed in any number of destination files, each of which maintains a pointer (link) to the same source file. Any change to the object in the source file is reflected automatically in every destination file containing that object.

Step 7:   **Update the Links**

➤ Click the **Microsoft Word button** on the taskbar to return to the Software memo. The worksheet and chart should be updated automatically. If not:
  • Pull down the **Edit menu**. Click **Links to** display the Links dialog box in Figure 4.12g.
  • Select the link(s) to update. (You can press and hold the **Ctrl key** to select multiple links simultaneously.)
  • Click the **Update Now button** to update the selected links.
  • Close the Links dialog box.
➤ The worksheet and chart should both reflect $200,000 for word processing sales in New York.
➤ Zoom to the **Whole Page** to view the completed document. Click and drag the worksheet and/or the chart within the memo to make any last-minute changes. Save the memo a final time.
➤ Print the completed memo and submit it to your instructor. Exit Word. Exit Excel. Save the changes to the Finished Software Sales workbook.

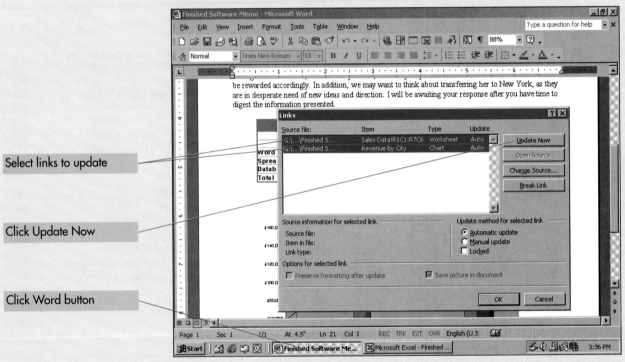

Select links to update

Click Update Now

Click Word button

(g) Update the Links (step 7)

FIGURE 4.12   *Hands-on Exercise 3 (continued)*

LINKING WORKSHEETS

A Word document can be linked to an Excel chart and/or worksheet; that is, change the chart in Excel, and the Word document changes automatically. The chart itself is linked to the underlying worksheet; change the worksheet, and the chart changes. Worksheets can also be linked to one another; for example, a summary worksheet for the corporation as a whole can reflect data from detail worksheets for individual cities. See practice exercise 5 at the end of the chapter.

A chart is a graphic representation of data in a worksheet. The type of chart chosen depends on the message to be conveyed. A pie chart is best for proportional relationships. A column or bar chart is used to show actual numbers rather than percentages. A line chart is preferable for time-related data. A combination chart uses two or more chart types when different scales are required for different data series. The title of a chart can help to convey the message.

The Chart Wizard is an easy way to create a chart. Once created, a chart can be enhanced with arrows and text boxes found on the Drawing toolbar. These objects can be moved or sized and/or modified with respect to their color and other properties. The chart itself can also be modified using various commands from the Chart menu or tools on the Chart toolbar.

A chart may be embedded in a worksheet or created in a separate chart sheet. An embedded chart may be moved within a worksheet by selecting it and dragging it to its new location. An embedded chart may be sized by selecting it and dragging any of the sizing handles in the desired direction.

Multiple data series may be specified in either rows or columns. If the data is in rows, the first row is assumed to contain the category labels, and the first column is assumed to contain the legend. Conversely, if the data is in columns, the first column is assumed to contain the category labels, and the first row the legend. The Chart Wizard makes it easy to switch from rows to columns and vice versa.

Object Linking and Embedding enables the creation of a compound document containing data (objects) from multiple applications. The essential difference between linking and embedding is whether the object is stored within the compound document (embedding) or in its own file (linking). An embedded object is stored in the compound document, which in turn becomes the only user (client) of that object. A linked object is stored in its own file, and the compound document is one of many potential clients of that object. The same chart can be linked to a Word document and a PowerPoint presentation.

It is important that charts are created accurately and that they do not mislead the reader. Stacked column charts should not add dissimilar quantities such as units and dollars.

KEY TERMS

Bar chart (p. 171)
Category label (p. 168)
Chart (p. 168)
Chart sheet (p. 174)
Chart toolbar (p. 178)
Chart type (p. 176)
Chart Wizard (p. 176)
Column chart (p. 171)
Combination chart (p. 184)
Common user interface (p. 200)
Data point (p. 168)
Data series (p. 168)
Docked toolbar (p. 186)

Drawing toolbar (p. 178)
Embedded chart (p. 174)
Embedded object (p. 203)
Exploded pie chart (p. 169)
Floating toolbar (p. 186)
Line chart (p. 184)
Linked object (p. 203)
Linking (p. 197)
Multiple data series (p. 188)
Multitasking (p. 197)
Object (p. 197)
Object Linking and Embedding
  (OLE) (p. 197)

Pie chart (p. 169)
Side-by-side column charts (p. 189)
Sizing handles (p. 174)
Stacked column charts (p. 189)
Taskbar (p. 197)
Three-dimensional column chart
  (p. 173)
Three-dimensional pie chart
  (p. 169)
X axis (p. 171)
Y axis (p. 171)

1. Which type of chart is best to portray proportion or market share?
   (a) Pie chart
   (b) Line
   (c) Column chart
   (d) Combination chart

2. Which of the following is a true statement about the Chart Wizard?
   (a) It is accessed via a button on the Standard toolbar
   (b) It enables you to choose the type of chart you want as well as specify the location for that chart
   (c) It enables you to retrace your steps via the Back command button
   (d) All of the above

3. Which of the following chart types is *not* suitable to display multiple data series?
   (a) Pie chart
   (b) Horizontal bar chart
   (c) Column chart
   (d) All of the above are equally suitable

4. Which of the following is best to display additive information from multiple data series?
   (a) A column chart with the data series stacked one on top of another
   (b) A column chart with the data series side by side
   (c) Both (a) and (b) are equally appropriate
   (d) Neither (a) nor (b) is appropriate

5. A workbook must contain:
   (a) A separate chart sheet for every worksheet
   (b) A separate worksheet for every chart sheet
   (c) Both (a) and (b)
   (d) Neither (a) nor (b)

6. Which of the following is true regarding an embedded chart?
   (a) It can be moved elsewhere within the worksheet
   (b) It can be made larger or smaller
   (c) Both (a) and (b)
   (d) Neither (a) nor (b)

7. Which of the following will produce a shortcut menu?
   (a) Pointing to a workbook tab and clicking the right mouse button
   (b) Pointing to an embedded chart and clicking the right mouse button
   (c) Pointing to a selected cell range and clicking the right mouse button
   (d) All of the above

8. Which of the following is done *prior* to invoking the Chart Wizard?
   (a) The data series are selected
   (b) The location of the embedded chart within the worksheet is specified
   (c) Both (a) and (b)
   (d) Neither (a) nor (b)

9. Which of the following will display sizing handles when selected?
   (a) An embedded chart
   (b) The title of a chart
   (c) A text box or arrow
   (d) All of the above

10. How do you switch between open applications?
    (a) Click the appropriate button on the taskbar
    (b) Use Alt+Tab to cycle through the applications
    (c) Both (a) and (b)
    (d) Neither (a) nor (b)

11. You want to create a Word document that is linked to an Excel worksheet and associated chart. Which of the following best describes the way the documents are stored on disk?
    (a) There is a single file that contains the Word document, the Excel worksheet, and the associated chart
    (b) There are two files—one for the Word document and one for the Excel workbook, which contains both the worksheet and associated chart
    (c) There are three files—one for the Word document, one for the Excel worksheet, and one for the Excel chart
    (d) None of the above

12. In order to represent multiple data series on the same chart:
    (a) The data series must be in rows and the rows must be adjacent to one another on the worksheet
    (b) The data series must be in columns and the columns must be adjacent to one another on the worksheet
    (c) The data series may be in rows or columns so long as they are adjacent to one another
    (d) The data series may be in rows or columns with no requirement to be next to one another

13. If multiple data series are selected and rows are specified:
    (a) The first row will be used for the category (X axis) labels
    (b) The first column will be used for the legend
    (c) Both (a) and (b)
    (d) Neither (a) nor (b)

14. If multiple data series are selected and columns are specified:
    (a) The first column will be used for the category (X axis) labels
    (b) The first row will be used for the legend
    (c) Both (a) and (b)
    (d) Neither (a) nor (b)

15. Which of the following is true about the scale on the Y axis in a column chart that plots multiple data series side-by-side versus one that stacks the values one on top of another?
    (a) The scale for the stacked columns will contain larger values than if the columns are plotted side-by-side
    (b) The scale for the side-by-side columns will contain larger values than if the columns are stacked
    (c) The values on the scale will be the same regardless of whether the columns are stacked or side-by-side
    (d) The values on the scale will be different but it is not possible to tell which chart will contain the higher values

ANSWERS

1. a	**6.** c	**11.** b
2. d	**7.** d	**12.** d
3. a	**8.** a	**13.** c
4. a	**9.** d	**14.** c
5. d	**10.** c	**15.** a

1. **Theme Park Admissions:** A partially completed version of the worksheet in Figure 4.13 is available in the Exploring Excel folder as *Chapter 4 Practice 1*. Follow the directions in steps (a) and (b) to compute the totals and format the worksheet, then create each of the charts listed below.

   a. Use the AutoSum command to enter the formulas to compute the total number of admissions for each region and each quarter.

   b. Select the entire worksheet (cells A1 through F8), then use the AutoFormat command to format the worksheet. You do not have to accept the entire design nor do you have to use the design we selected. You can also modify the design after it has been applied to the worksheet by changing the font size of selected cells and/or changing boldface and italics.

   c. A column chart showing the total number of admissions in each quarter as shown in Figure 4.13. Add the graphic shown in the figure for emphasis.

   d. A pie chart showing the percentage of the total number of admissions in each region. Create this chart in its own chart sheet with an appropriate name.

   e. A stacked column chart showing the total number of admissions for each region and the contribution of each quarter within each region. Create this chart in its own chart sheet with an appropriate name.

   f. A stacked column chart showing the total number of admissions for each quarter and the contribution of each region within each quarter. Create this chart in its own chart sheet with an appropriate name.

   g. Change the color of each of the worksheet tabs.

   h. Print the entire workbook, consisting of the worksheet in Figure 4.13 plus the three additional sheets that you create. Submit the completed assignment to your instructor.

   i. This workbook is also the basis for a PowerPoint presentation in practice exercise 9.

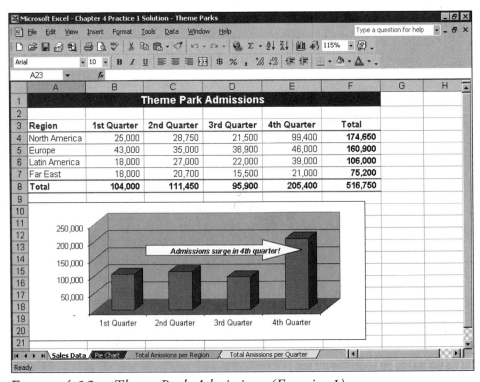

FIGURE 4.13 *Theme Park Admissions (Exercise 1)*

2. Rows versus Columns: Figure 4.14 displays the Page Preview view of a worksheet with two similar charts, one that plots data by rows and the other by columns. The distinction depends on the message you want to deliver. Both charts are correct. Your assignment is to open the partially completed worksheet in the *Chapter 4 Practice 2* workbook and do the following:
   a. Complete the worksheet by computing the total number of visits for each pet category and each quarter, then format the worksheet attractively. (You need not follow our formatting.)
   b. Create each of the charts in Figure 4.14. You can embed the charts in the same worksheet as the data, or you can place the charts on separate worksheets.
   c. Add your name to the worksheet, then print the entire workbook for your instructor. Use the Page Setup command to add a header or footer that contains the name of your course and instructor.

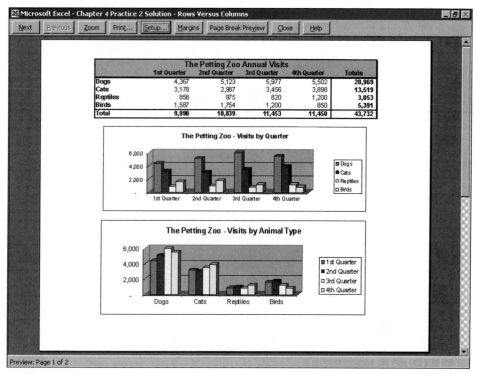

FIGURE 4.14   *Rows versus Columns (Exercise 2)*

3. Exploded Pie Charts: Tom Liquer Men's Wear is a privately owned chain of four stores in various cities. Your assignment is to open the partially completed workbook in *Chapter 4 Practice 3* workbook in order to create the worksheet and associated chart in Figure 4.15.
   a. Use the AutoSum and AutoFormat commands to compute the totals and format the worksheet appropriately. You do not have to match our formatting exactly and are free to modify the suggested designs as you see fit.
   b. Create the exploded pie chart in the figure that shows the percentage of total sales that is attributed to each city. Use the Help command as necessary to learn about pulling one slice out of the pie.
   c. Create a second three-dimensional pie chart in its own sheet that shows the percentage of sales that is attributed to each product line.
   d. Add your name to the worksheet, then print the entire workbook for your instructor. Use the Page Setup command to add an appropriate header or footer to each worksheet.

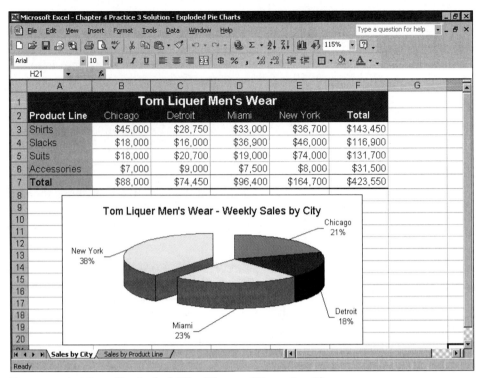

FIGURE 4.15 *Exploded Pie Charts (Exercise 3)*

4. Page Break Preview: Open the partially completed workbook in *Chapter 4 Practice 4* and create the four charts shown in Figure 4.16. Use the AutoSum and AutoFormat commands to complete the worksheet. Select cells A2 through E6 as the basis for each of the four charts in the figure. The charts should all appear as embedded objects on the worksheet, but do not worry about the placement of the charts until you have completed all four.

   a. The first chart is a side-by-side column chart that emphasizes the sales in each city (the data is in rows).

   b. The second chart is a stacked column version of the chart in part (a).

   c. The third chart (that begins in column H of the worksheet) is a side-by-side column chart that emphasizes the sale of each product line (the data is in columns).

   d. The last chart is a stacked column version of the chart in part c.

   e. Pull down the View command, then change to the Page Break Preview view as shown in Figure 4.16. You will see one or more dashed lines that show where the page breaks will occur. You will also see the message in Figure 4.16 indicating that you can change the location of the page breaks. Click OK after you have read the message.

   f. You can change the position of a page break and/or remove the break entirely by clicking and dragging the line that indicates the break. You can insert horizontal or vertical page breaks by clicking the appropriate cell, pulling down the Insert menu, and selecting Page Break. Pull down the View menu and click Normal view to return to the normal view.

   g. Add your name to the completed worksheet, then print the worksheet and four embedded charts on one page. If necessary, change to landscape printing for a more attractive layout.

   h. Write a short note to your instructor that describes the differences between the charts. Suggest a different title for one or more charts that helps to convey a specific message.

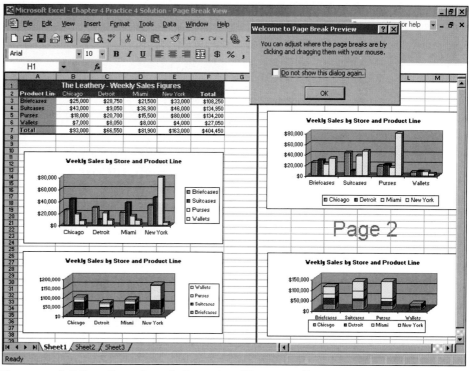

FIGURE 4.16 *Page Break Preview (Exercise 4)*

5. Linking Worksheets: This chapter described how a chart is linked to the data in an underlying worksheet. It is also possible to link the data from one worksheet to another as can be seen in Figure 4.16. The figure contains a table, which at first glance is similar to the example that was used throughout the chapter. Look closely, however, and you will see that the workbook contains individual worksheets for each city, in addition to a worksheet for the corporation as a whole.

The numbers in the corporate worksheet are linked to the numbers in the worksheets for the individual cities. The entry in cell B4 of the Corporate worksheet contains the formula =Phoenix!F2 to indicate that the entry comes from cell F2 in the Phoenix worksheet. Other cells in the table reference other cells in the Phoenix worksheet as well as cells in the other worksheets.

a. Open the *Chapter 4 Practice 5* workbook. Check that you are in the Corporate worksheet, then click in cell B4 of this worksheet. Type an = sign, click the Phoenix worksheet tab, click in cell F2 of this worksheet, and press the enter key. Click in cell C4, type an = sign, click the Minneapolis tab, click in cell F2 of that worksheet, and press enter.

b. Repeat the process to enter the sales for San Francisco and Los Angeles. Do you see how the worksheet name is reflected in the cell formula?

c. Click and drag cells B4 through E4, then drag the fill handle to row 6 to copy the formulas for the other product lines. The copy operation works because the worksheet references are absolute, but the cell references are relative.

d. Use the AutoSum button to compute the totals for the corporation as a whole.

e. Use the completed worksheet in Figure 4.17 as the basis for a side-by-side column chart with the data plotted in rows.

f. Plot a second side-by-side chart with the data in columns. Put each chart in a separate chart sheet.

g. Print the entire workbook for your instructor.

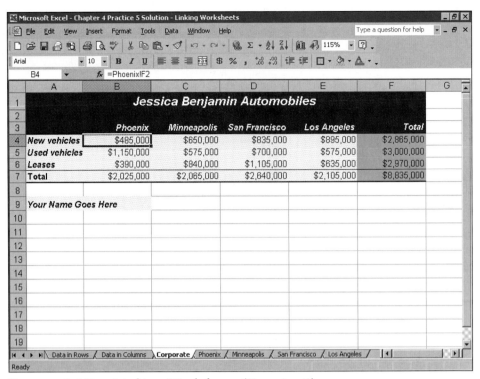

FIGURE 4.17 *Linking Worksheets (Exercise 5)*

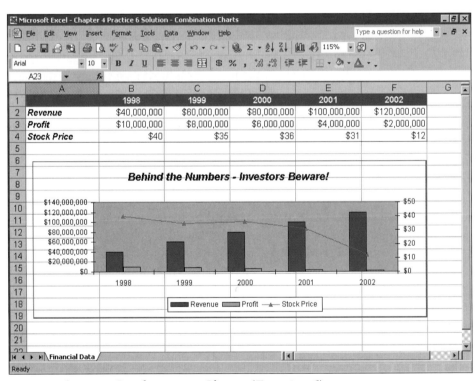

FIGURE 4.18 *Combination Charts (Exercise 6)*

6. Combination Charts: Figure 4.18 on the previous page contains a combination chart, which uses two or more chart types to display different kinds of information and/or different scales for multiple data series. A stacked column chart type is specified for both the revenue and profits, while a line chart is used for the stock price. Two different scales are necessary.

   a. Open the partially completed workbook in *Chapter 4 Practice 6* and format the worksheet appropriately.

   b. Select the entire worksheet (cells A1 through F4), then invoke the Chart Wizard. Click the Custom Types tab in step 1 of the Chart Wizard, choose Line-Column on 2 Axis as the chart type, then in step 2 specify the data in rows. The Chart Wizard will do the rest.

   c. Modify the completed chart so that its appearance is similar to our figure. We made the chart wider and moved the legend to the bottom. (Right click the legend, click the Format Legend command, click the Placement tab, then click the bottom option button.) To place a border around the chart, right click the completed chart, choose the Format Chart Area command, click the Patterns tab, then choose the style, thickness, and color of the border.

   d. Add your name to the worksheet, then submit the completed worksheet.

7. Object Linking and Embedding: The document in Figure 4.19 is based on the partially completed worksheet in the *Chapter 4 Practice 7* workbook. Your assignment is to open the partially completed workbook, compute the sales totals for each individual salesperson as well as the totals for each quarter, then format the resulting worksheet in an attractive fashion. You can use our formatting or develop your own. In addition, you are to create a stacked column chart comparing quarterly sales for each salesperson. Save the workbook.

   a. You will find the text of the document in the Exploring Excel folder in the file *Chapter 4 Practice 7 Memo*.

   b. Use object linking and embedding to link the Excel worksheet to the Word document as described in the chapter. Repeat the process to link the Excel chart to the word document.

   c. Save the Word document, then print the completed document.

BUILDS ON

CHAPTER 3
HANDS-ON
EXERCISE 2
PAGES 130–133

8. Investment Strategies: An IRA (Individual Retirement Account) is a wise investment for your future. In essence, you save a fixed amount each year (up to $2,000 in today's environment) and can invest that money in any way you choose. The money grows over time and the amount at retirement may surprise you. For example, $2000 a year, invested for 40 years and earning 8% a year, will grow to more than $518,000 as shown in Figure 4.20. If you are able to save for 45 years rather than 40 (i.e., you began saving at age 20 rather than 25), the amount at retirement exceeds $750,000.

   a. Open the partially completed workbook in *Chapter 4 Practice 8,* which contains the table shown in Figure 4.20. We have supplied the formula to obtain the future value for an investment earning 6% for 10 years. All you need to do is copy that formula to the remaining rows and columns in the worksheet, then format the worksheet appropriately. We highlighted the row showing the return at 8% since that is the historical rate of return in the stock market.

   b. Create a line chart that shows the growth of your investment over time as an embedded object in the same worksheet. Save the worksheet.

   c. You will find the text of the memo in a Word document, *Chapter 4 Practice 8 memo*, in the Exploring Excel folder. Open the Word document, then use object linking and embedding to link the worksheet and the line chart to the Word document.

   d. Add your name to the memo after the salutation, "To the New Graduate", then print the completed memo and submit it to your instructor. Compound interest has been called the eighth wonder of the world. Use it to your advantage!

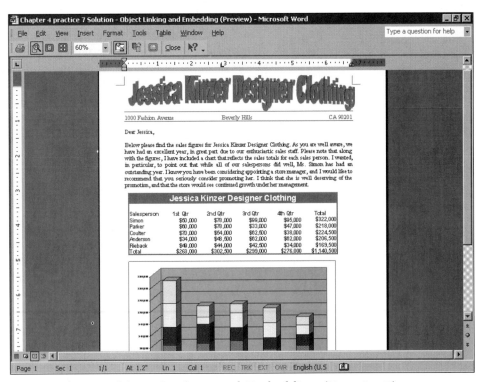

FIGURE 4.19   *Object Linking and Embedding (Exercise 7)*

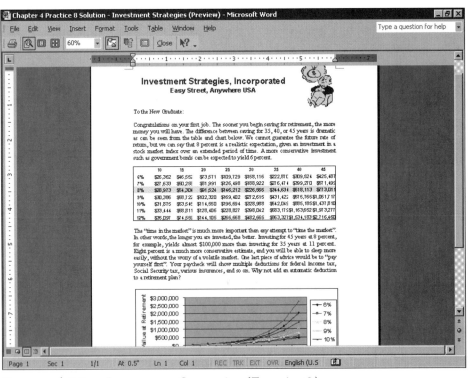

FIGURE 4.20   *Investment Strategies (Exercise 8)*

9. PowerPoint Presentations: The third hands-on exercise in the chapter showed you how to create a Word document containing an Excel chart and/or worksheet. You can use the same technique to create a PowerPoint presentation similar to those in Figure 4.21. The objective of this exercise is to show you how you can link an object such as an Excel chart or worksheet to other Office documents.

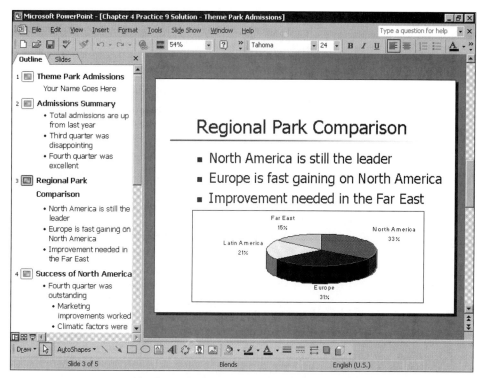

BUILDS ON

PRACTICE
EXERCISE 1
PAGE 208

(a) Theme Park Admissions (from exercise 1)

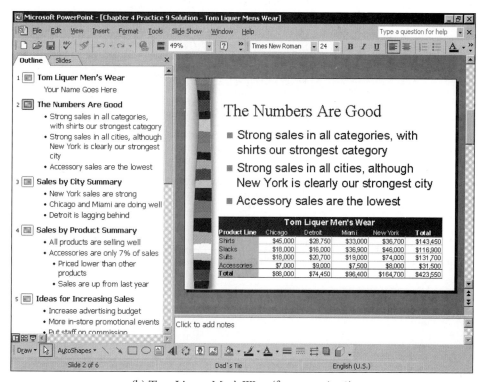

BUILDS ON

PRACTICE
EXERCISE 3
PAGE 209

(b) Tom Liquer Men's Wear (from exercise 3)

FIGURE 4.21 *PowerPoint Presentations (Exercise 9)*

The Census Bureau

Use your favorite search engine to locate the home page of the United States Census Bureau, then download one or more series of population statistics of interest to you. Use the data to plot one or more charts that describe the population growth of the United States. There is an abundance of information available, and you are free to choose any statistics you deem relevant.

UMC Theatres

You are currently working for UMC Theatres, a local chain of movie theatres. Your current assignment is to create a series of charts that show how the ticket sales in the various theatres compare to one another. The assignment is open ended in that you can create any chart you like based on the data in the *UMC Theatres Workbook*. Open the partially completed workbook, format the worksheet attractively, and then create at least two charts based on the data.

The Convention Planner

Your first task as a convention planner is to evaluate the hotel capacity for the host city in order to make recommendations as to where to host the convention. The data can be found in the *Convention Planner* workbook, which contains a single worksheet showing the number of rooms in each hotel, divided into standard and deluxe categories, together with the associated room rates. Open the workbook and format the worksheet in attractive fashion. Create a stacked column chart that shows the total capacity for each hotel, then create a second chart that shows the percentage of total capacity for each hotel. Store each chart in its own worksheet, then print the entire workbook for your instructor.

Irrational Exuberance

Your brother-in-law has called you with a stock tip based on sales and profit data found in the file *Irrational Exuberance*. Open the file, examine the data and associated chart that your brother-in-law has created, and then respond with a short note on what you think of the investment. Be sure to comment on the chart that accompanies the data.

CHAPTER 5

Consolidating Data: 3-D Workbooks and File Linking

OBJECTIVES

AFTER READING THIS CHAPTER YOU WILL BE ABLE TO:

1. Distinguish between a cell reference, a worksheet reference, and a 3-D reference; use appropriate references to consolidate data from multiple worksheets within a workbook.
2. Select and group multiple worksheets to enter common formulas and/or formats.
3. Use the AutoFormat command to format a worksheet.
4. Explain the advantage of using a function rather than a formula when consolidating data from multiple worksheets.
5. Explain the importance of properly organizing and documenting a workbook.
6. Use the Copy and Paste commands to copy selected data to a second workbook; copy an entire worksheet by dragging its tab from one workbook to another.
7. Distinguish between a source workbook and a dependent workbook; create external references to link workbooks.

OVERVIEW

This chapter considers the problem of combining data from different sources into a summary report. Assume, for example, that you are the marketing manager for a national corporation with offices in several cities. Each branch manager reports to you on a quarterly basis, providing information about each product sold in his or her office. Your job is to consolidate the data into a single report.

The situation is depicted graphically in Figure 5.1. Figures 5.1a, 5.1b, and 5.1c show reports for the Atlanta, Boston, and Chicago offices, respectively. Figure 5.1d shows the summary report for the corporation.

217

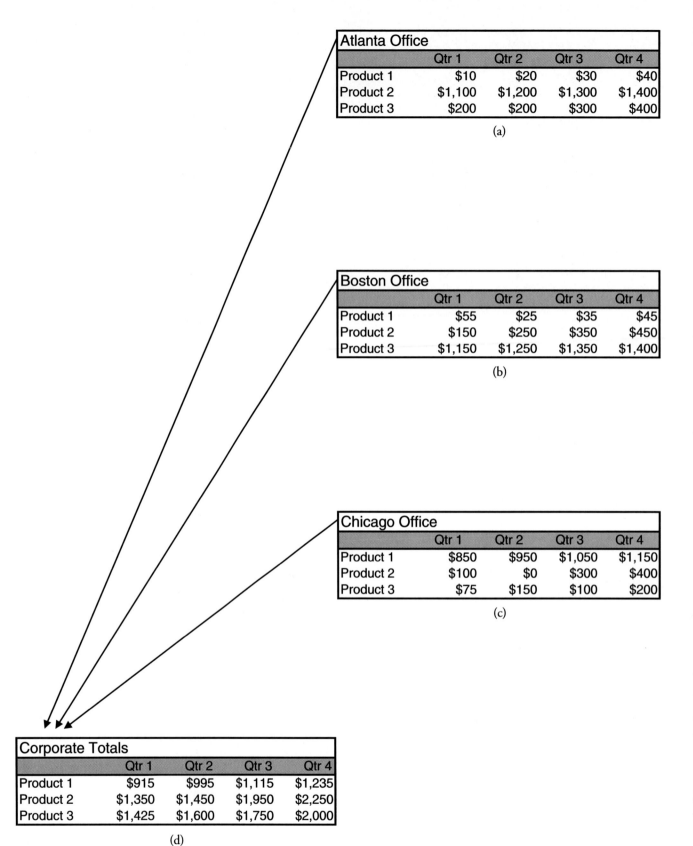

Atlanta Office

	Qtr 1	Qtr 2	Qtr 3	Qtr 4
Product 1	$10	$20	$30	$40
Product 2	$1,100	$1,200	$1,300	$1,400
Product 3	$200	$200	$300	$400

(a)

Boston Office

	Qtr 1	Qtr 2	Qtr 3	Qtr 4
Product 1	$55	$25	$35	$45
Product 2	$150	$250	$350	$450
Product 3	$1,150	$1,250	$1,350	$1,400

(b)

Chicago Office

	Qtr 1	Qtr 2	Qtr 3	Qtr 4
Product 1	$850	$950	$1,050	$1,150
Product 2	$100	$0	$300	$400
Product 3	$75	$150	$100	$200

(c)

Corporate Totals

	Qtr 1	Qtr 2	Qtr 3	Qtr 4
Product 1	$915	$995	$1,115	$1,235
Product 2	$1,350	$1,450	$1,950	$2,250
Product 3	$1,425	$1,600	$1,750	$2,000

(d)

FIGURE 5.1   *Consolidating Data*

You should be able to reconcile the corporate totals for each product in each quarter with the detail amounts in the individual offices. Consider, for example, the sales of Product 1 in the first quarter. The Atlanta office has sold $10, the Boston office $55, and the Chicago office $850; thus, the corporation as a whole has sold $915 ($10+$55+$850). In similar fashion, the Atlanta, Boston, and Chicago offices have sold $1,100, $150, and $100, respectively, of Product 2 in the first quarter, for a corporate total of $1,350.

The chapter presents two approaches to computing the corporate totals in Figure 5.1. One approach is to use the three-dimensional capability within Excel, in which one workbook contains multiple worksheets. The workbook contains a separate worksheet for each of the three branch offices, and a fourth worksheet to hold the corporate data. An alternate technique is to keep the data for each branch office in its own workbook, then create a summary workbook that uses file linking to reference cells in the other workbooks.

There are advantages and disadvantages to each technique, as will be discussed in the chapter. As always, the hands-on exercises are essential to mastering the conceptual material.

THE THREE-DIMENSIONAL WORKBOOK

An Excel workbook is the electronic equivalent of the three-ring binder. It contains one or more worksheets, each of which is identified by a tab at the bottom of the document window. The workbook in Figure 5.2, for example, contains four worksheets. The title bar displays the name of the workbook (Corporate Sales). The tabs at the bottom of the workbook window display the names of the individual worksheets (Summary, Atlanta, Boston, and Chicago). The highlighted tab indicates the name of the active worksheet (Summary). To display a different worksheet, click on a different tab; for example, click the Atlanta tab to display the Atlanta worksheet.

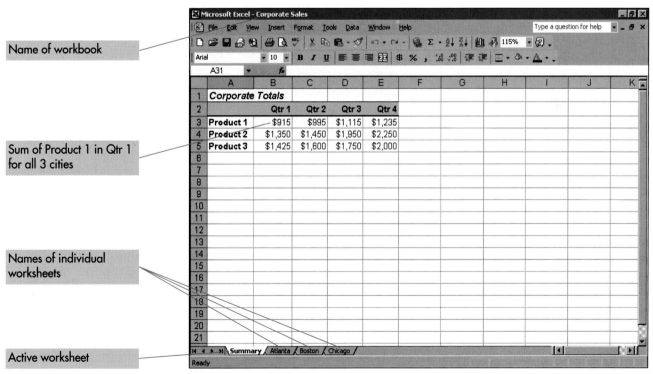

FIGURE 5.2 *A Three-dimensional Workbook*

The Summary worksheet shows the total amount for each product in each quarter. The data in the worksheet reflects the amounts shown earlier in Figure 5.1; that is, each entry in the Summary worksheet represents the sum of the corresponding entries in the worksheets for the individual cities. The amounts in the individual cities, however, are not visible in Figure 5.2. It is convenient, therefore, to open multiple windows in order to view the individual city worksheets at the same time you view the summary sheet.

Figure 5.3 displays the four worksheets in the Corporate Sales workbook, with a different sheet displayed in each window. The individual windows are smaller than the single view in Figure 5.2, but you can see at a glance how the Summary worksheet consolidates the data from the individual worksheets. The **New Window command** (in the Window menu) is used to open each additional window. Once the windows have been opened, the **Arrange command** (in the Window menu) is used to tile or cascade the open windows.

Only one window can be active at a time, and all commands apply to just the active window. In Figure 5.3, for example, the window in the upper left is active, as can be seen by the highlighted title bar. (To activate a different window, just click in that window.)

Copying Worksheets

The workbook in Figure 5.3 summarizes the data in the individual worksheets, but how was the data placed in the workbook? You could, of course, manually type in the entries, but there is an easier way, given that each branch manager sends you a workbook with the data for his or her office. All you have to do is copy the data from the individual workbooks into the appropriate worksheets in a new corporate workbook. (The specifics for how this is done are explained in detail in a hands-on exercise.)

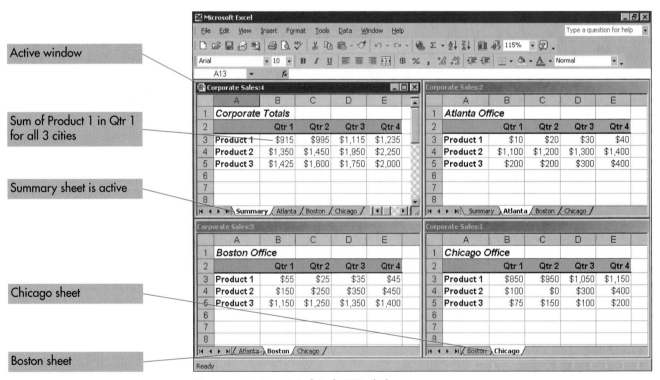

FIGURE 5.3 *Multiple Worksheets*

Consider now Figure 5.4, which at first glance appears almost identical to Figure 5.3. The two figures are very different, however. Figure 5.3 displayed four different worksheets from the same workbook. Figure 5.4, on the other hand, displays four different workbooks. There is one workbook for each city (Atlanta, Boston, and Chicago) and each of these workbooks contains only a single worksheet. The fourth workbook, Corporate Sales, contains four worksheets (Atlanta, Boston, Chicago, and Summary) and is the workbook displayed in Figure 5.3.

There are advantages and disadvantages to each technique. The single workbook in Figure 5.3 is easier for the manager in that he or she has all of the data in one file. The disadvantage is that the worksheets have to be maintained by multiple people (the manager in each city), and this can lead to confusion in that several individuals require access to the same workbook. The multiple workbooks of Figure 5.4 facilitate the maintenance of the data, but four separate files are required to produce the summary information. The choice is up to you.

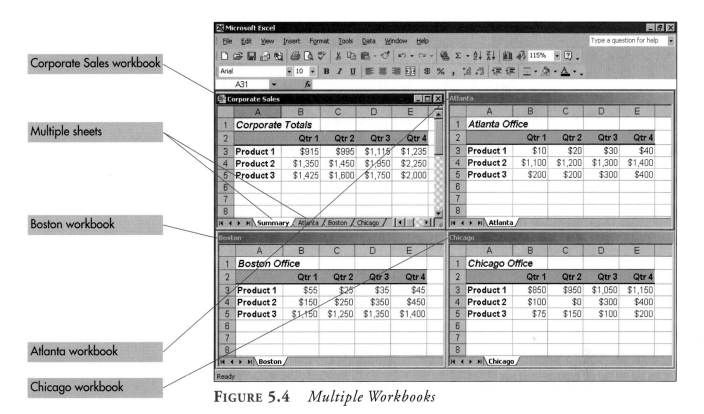

FIGURE 5.4 *Multiple Workbooks*

THE HORIZONTAL SCROLL BAR

The horizontal scroll bar contains four scrolling buttons to scroll through the worksheet tabs in a workbook. (The default workbook has three worksheets.) Click ◄ or ► to scroll one tab to the left or right. Click |◄ or ►| to scroll to the first or last tab in the workbook. Once the desired tab is visible, click the tab to select it. The number of tabs that are visible simultaneously depends on the setting of the horizontal scroll bar; that is, you can drag the *tab split bar* to change the number of tabs that can be seen at one time.

COPYING WORKSHEETS

Objective To open multiple workbooks; to use the Windows Arrange command to tile the open workbooks; to copy a worksheet from one workbook to another. Use Figure 5.5 as a guide in the exercise.

Step 1: **Open a New Workbook**

➤ Start Excel. Close the task pane if it is open. If necessary, click the **New button** on the Standard toolbar to open a new workbook as shown in Figure 5.5a.
➤ Delete all worksheets except for Sheet1:
 • Click the tab for **Sheet2**. Press the **Shift key** as you click the tab for **Sheet3**.
 • Point to the tab for **Sheet3** and click the **right mouse button** to display a shortcut menu. Click **Delete**.
➤ The workbook should contain only Sheet1 as shown in Figure 5.5a. Save the workbook as **Corporate Sales** in the **Exploring Excel folder**.

New button

Click Delete

Click tab for Sheet2; press Shift and click tab for Sheet3 to select both sheets

Point to Sheet3 and click right mouse button

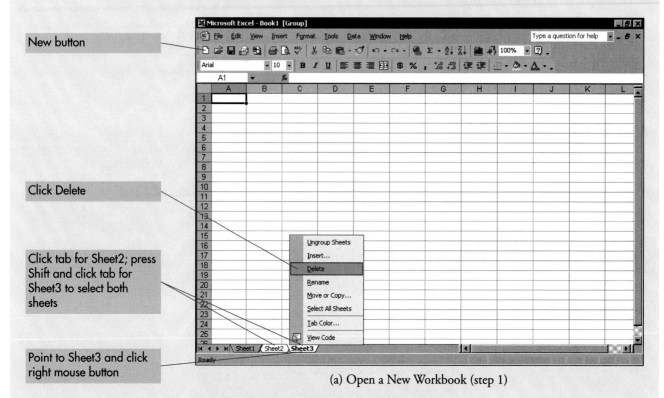

(a) Open a New Workbook (step 1)

FIGURE 5.5 *Hands-on Exercise 1*

THE RIGHT MOUSE BUTTON

Point to any object, then click the right mouse button to display a context-sensitive menu with commands appropriate to the item you are pointing to. Right clicking a cell, for example, displays a menu with selected commands from the Edit, Insert, and Format menus. Right clicking a toolbar displays a menu that lets you display (hide) additional toolbars. Right clicking a worksheet tab enables you to rename, move, copy, or delete a worksheet.

Step 2: **Open the Individual Workbooks**

➤ Pull down the **File menu**. Click **Open** to display the Open dialog box. (If necessary, open the Exploring Excel folder.)

➤ Click the **Atlanta workbook**, then press and hold the **Ctrl key** as you click the **Boston** and **Chicago workbooks** to select all three workbooks at the same time.

➤ Click **Open** to open the selected workbooks. The workbooks will be opened one after another with a brief message appearing on the status bar as each workbook is opened.

➤ Pull down the **Window menu**, which should indicate the four open workbooks at the bottom of the menu. Only the Chicago workbook is visible at this time.

➤ Click **Arrange** to display the Arrange Windows dialog box. If necessary, select the **Tiled option**, then click **OK**. You should see four open workbooks as shown in Figure 5.5b. (Do not be concerned if your workbooks are arranged differently from ours.)

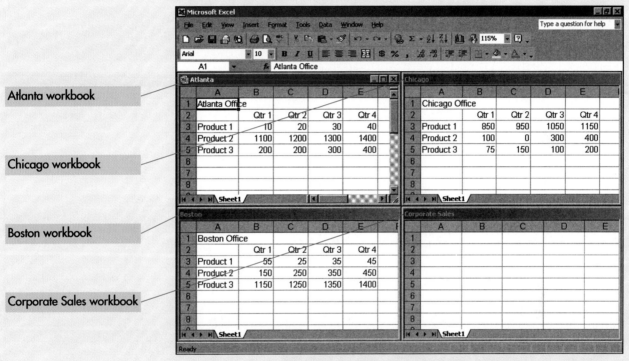

(b) Open the Individual Workbooks (step 2)

FIGURE 5.5 *Hands-on Exercise 1 (continued)*

THE DEFAULT WORKBOOK

A new workbook contains three worksheets, but you can change the default value to any number. Pull down the Tools menu, click Options, then click the General tab. Click the up (down) arrow in the Sheets in New Workbook text box to enter a new default value, then click OK to exit the Options dialog box and continue working. The next time you open a new workbook, it will contain the new number of worksheets.

Step 3: **Copy the Atlanta Data**

➤ Click in the **Atlanta workbook** to make it the active workbook. Reduce the column widths (if necessary) so that you can see the entire worksheet.
➤ Click and drag to select **cells A1** through **E5** as shown in Figure 5.5c. Pull down the **Edit menu** and click **Copy** (or click the **Copy button**).
➤ Click in cell A1 of the **Corporate Sales** workbook.
➤ Click the **Paste button** on the Standard toolbar to copy the Atlanta data into this workbook. Press **Esc** to remove the moving border from the copy range.
➤ Point to the **Sheet1 tab** at the bottom of the Corporate Sales worksheet window, then click the **right mouse button** to produce a shortcut menu. Click **Rename**, which selects the worksheet name.
➤ Type **Atlanta** to replace the existing name and press **enter**. The worksheet tab has been changed from Sheet1 to Atlanta.
➤ Click the **Save button** to save the active workbook (Corporate Sales).

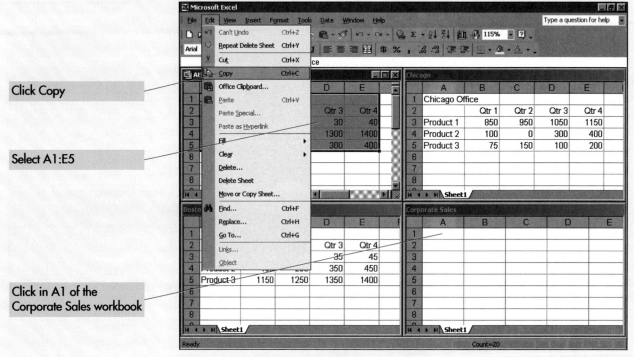

(c) Copy the Atlanta Data (step 3)

FIGURE 5.5   *Hands-on Exercise 1 (continued)*

CHANGE THE ZOOM SETTING

You can increase or decrease the size of a worksheet as it appears on the monitor by clicking the down arrow on the zoom box and selecting an appropriate percentage. If you are working with a large spreadsheet and cannot see it at one time on the screen, choose a number less than 100%. Conversely, if you find yourself squinting because the numbers are too small, select a percentage larger than 100%. Changing the magnification on the screen does not affect printing; that is, worksheets are printed at 100% unless you change the scaling within the Page Setup command.

Step 4: **Copy the Boston and Chicago Data**

➤ Click in the **Boston workbook** to make it the active workbook as shown in Figure 5.5d.

➤ Click the **Sheet1 tab**, then press and hold the **Ctrl key** as you drag the tab to the right of the Atlanta tab in the Corporate Sales workbook. You will see a tiny spreadsheet with a plus sign as you drag the tab. The plus sign indicates that the worksheet is being copied; the ▼ symbol indicates where the worksheet will be placed.

➤ Release the mouse, then release the Ctrl key. The worksheet from the Boston workbook should have been copied to the Corporate Sales workbook and appears as Sheet1 in that workbook.

➤ The Boston workbook should still be open; if it isn't, it means that you did not press the Ctrl key as you were dragging the tab to copy the worksheet. If this is the case, pull down the **File menu**, reopen the Boston workbook, and if necessary, tile the open windows.

➤ Double click the **Sheet1 tab** in the Corporate Sales workbook to rename the tab. Type **Boston** as the new name, then press the **enter key**.

➤ The Boston worksheet should appear to the right of the Atlanta worksheet; if the worksheet appears to the left of Atlanta, click and drag the tab to its desired position. (The ▼ symbol indicates where the worksheet will be placed.)

➤ Repeat the previous steps to copy the Chicago data to the Corporate Sales workbook, placing the new sheet to the right of the Boston sheet. Rename the copied worksheet **Chicago**. Remember, you must click in the window containing the Chicago workbook to activate the window before you can copy the worksheet.

➤ Save the Corporate Sales workbook. (The Summary worksheet will be built in the next exercise.)

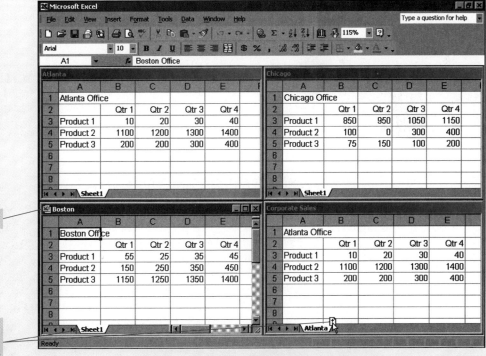

Boston workbook is active

Click Sheet1 tab, press Ctrl key and drag to Corporate Sales workbook

(d) Copy the Boston and Chicago Data (step 4)

FIGURE 5.5   *Hands-on Exercise 1 (continued)*

Step 5:   **The Corporate Sales Workbook**

➤ Check that the Corporate Sales workbook is the active workbook. Click the **Maximize button** so that this workbook takes the entire screen.

➤ The Corporate Sales workbook contains three worksheets, one for each city, as can be seen in Figure 5.5e.

➤ Click the **Atlanta tab** to display the worksheet for Atlanta.

➤ Click the **Boston tab** to display the worksheet for Boston.

➤ Click the **Chicago tab** to display the worksheet for Chicago.

➤ Close all of the open workbooks, saving changes if requested to do so.

➤ Exit Excel if you do not want to continue with the next hands-on exercise at this time.

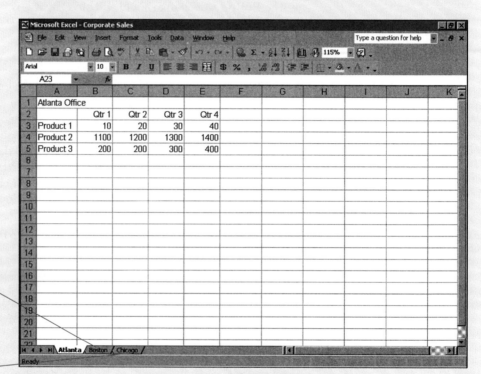

Click tab to display Boston worksheet

Click tab to display Chicago worksheet

(e) The Corporate Sales Workbook (step 5)

FIGURE 5.5   *Hands-on Exercise 1 (continued)*

MOVING AND COPYING WORKSHEETS

You can move or copy a worksheet within a workbook by dragging its tab. To move a worksheet, click its tab, then drag the tab to the new location (a black triangle shows where the new sheet will go). To copy a worksheet, click its tab, then press and hold the Ctrl key as you drag the tab to its new location. The copied worksheet will have the same name as the original worksheet, followed by a number in parentheses indicating the copy number. Add color to your workbook by changing the color of a worksheet tab. Right click the worksheet tab, click the View color command, select a new color, and click OK.

The presence of multiple worksheets in a workbook creates an additional requirement for cell references. You continue to use the same row and column convention when you reference a cell on the current worksheet; that is, cell A1 is still A1. What if, however, you want to reference a cell on another worksheet within the same workbook? It is no longer sufficient to refer to cell A1 because every worksheet has its own cell A1.

To reference a cell (or cell range) in a worksheet other than the current (active) worksheet, you need to preface the cell address with a ***worksheet reference***; for example, Atlanta!A1 references cell A1 in the Atlanta worksheet. A worksheet reference may also be used in conjunction with a cell range—for example, Summary!B2:E5 to reference cells B2 through E5 on the Summary worksheet. Omission of the worksheet reference in either example defaults to the cell reference in the active worksheet.

An exclamation point separates the worksheet reference from the cell reference. The worksheet reference is always an absolute reference. The cell reference can be either relative (e.g., Atlanta!A1 or Summary!B2:E5) or absolute (e.g., Atlanta!$A$1 or Summary!$B$2:$E$5).

Consider how worksheet references are used in the Summary worksheet in Figure 5.6. Each entry in the Summary worksheet computes the sum of the corresponding cells in the Atlanta, Boston, and Chicago worksheets. The cell formula in cell B3, for example, would be entered as follows:

=Atlanta!B3+Boston!B3+Chicago!B3

                             └─ Chicago is the worksheet reference

                └─ Boston is the worksheet reference

   └─ Atlanta is the worksheet reference

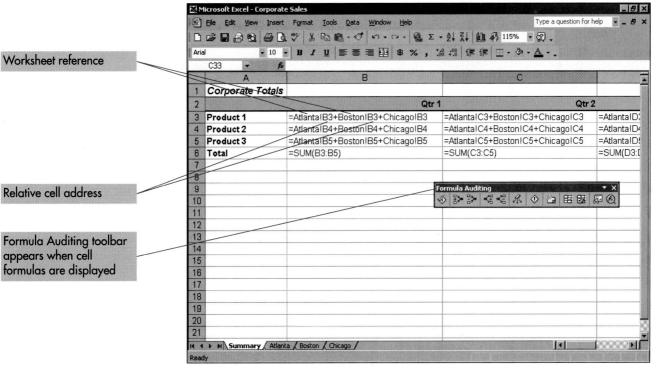

FIGURE 5.6 *Worksheet References*

The combination of relative cell references and constant worksheet references enables you to enter the formula once (in cell B3), then copy it to the remaining cells in the worksheet. In other words, you enter the formula in cell B3 to compute the total sales for Product 1 in Quarter 1, then you copy that formula to the other cells in row 3 (C3 through E3) to obtain the totals for Product 1 in Quarters 2, 3, and 4. You then copy the entire row (B3 through E3) to rows 4 and 5 (cells B4 through E5) to obtain the totals for Products 2 and 3 in all four quarters.

The proper use of relative and absolute references in the original formula in cell B3 is what makes it possible to copy the cell formulas. Consider, for example, the formula in cell C3 (which was copied from cell B3):

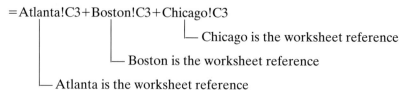

=Atlanta!C3+Boston!C3+Chicago!C3
— Chicago is the worksheet reference
— Boston is the worksheet reference
— Atlanta is the worksheet reference

The worksheet references remain absolute (e.g., Atlanta!) while the cell references adjust for the new location of the formula (cell C3). Similar adjustments are made in all of the other copied formulas.

3-D Reference

A *3-D reference* is a range that spans two or more worksheets in a workbook—for example, =SUM(Atlanta:Chicago!B3) to sum cell B3 in the Atlanta, Boston, and Chicago worksheets. The sheet range is specified with a colon between the beginning and ending sheets. An exclamation point follows the ending sheet, followed by the cell reference. The worksheet references are constant and will not change if the formula is copied. The cell reference may be relative or absolute.

Three-dimensional references can be used in the Summary worksheet as an alternative way to compute the corporate total for each product–quarter combination. To compute the corporate sales for Product 1 in Quarter 1 (which appears in cell B3 of the Summary worksheet), you would use the following function:

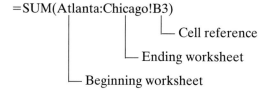

=SUM(Atlanta:Chicago!B3)
— Cell reference
— Ending worksheet
— Beginning worksheet

The 3-D reference includes all worksheets between the Atlanta and Chicago worksheets. (Only one additional worksheet, Boston, is present in the example, but the reference would automatically include any additional worksheets that were inserted between Atlanta and Chicago. In similar fashion, it would also adjust for the deletion of worksheets between Atlanta and Chicago.) Note, too, that the cell reference is relative and thus the formula can be copied from cell B3 in the Summary worksheet to the remaining cells in row 3 (C3 through E3). Those formulas can then be copied to the appropriate cells in rows 4 and 5.

A 3-D reference can be typed directly into a cell formula, but it is easier to enter the reference by pointing. Click in the cell that is to contain the 3-D reference, then enter an equal sign to begin the formula. To reference a cell in another worksheet, click the tab for the worksheet you want to reference, then click the cell or cell range you want to include in the formula. To reference a range from multiple worksheets, click in the cell in the first worksheet, press the Shift key as you click the tab for the last worksheet in the range, then click in the cell in the last worksheet.

Grouping Worksheets

The worksheets in a workbook are often similar to one another in terms of content and/or formatting. In Figure 5.3, for example, the formatting is identical in all four worksheets of the workbook. You can format the worksheets individually or more easily through grouping.

Excel provides the capability for **grouping worksheets** to enter or format data in multiple worksheets at the same time. Once the worksheets are grouped, anything you do in one of the worksheets is automatically done to the other sheets in the group. You could, for example, group all of the worksheets together when you enter row and column labels, when you format data, or when you enter formulas to compute row and column totals. You must, however, ungroup the worksheets when you enter data in a specific worksheet. Grouping and ungrouping is illustrated in the following hands-on exercise.

The AutoFormat Command

The formatting commands within Excel can be applied individually (as you have done throughout the text), or automatically and collectively by choosing a predefined set of formatting specifications. Excel provides several such designs as shown in Figure 5.7. You can apply any of these designs to your worksheet by selecting the range to be formatted, then executing the **AutoFormat command** from within the Format menu. The AutoFormat command does not do anything that could not be done through the individual commands, but it does provide inspiration by suggesting several attractive designs. You can enter additional formatting commands after the AutoFormat has been executed, as you will see in our next exercise.

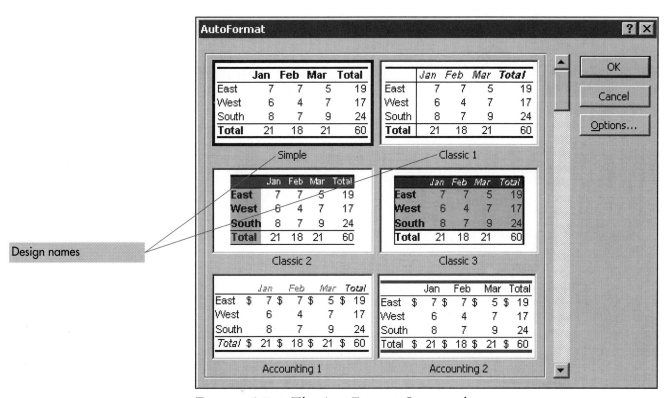

FIGURE 5.7   *The AutoFormat Command*

Objective To use 3-D references to summarize data from multiple worksheets within a workbook; to group worksheets to enter common formatting and formulas; to open multiple windows to view several worksheets at the same time. Use Figure 5.8 as a guide in the exercise.

Step 1: **Insert a Worksheet**

> ➤ Start Excel. Open the **Corporate Sales workbook** created in the previous exercise. The workbook contains three worksheets.
> ➤ Click the **Atlanta tab** to select this worksheet. Pull down the **Insert menu**, and click the **Worksheet command**. You should see a new worksheet, Sheet1.
> ➤ Double click the **tab** of the newly inserted worksheet to select the name. Type **Summary** and press **enter**. The name of the new worksheet has been changed.
> ➤ Click in **cell A1** of the Summary worksheet. Type **Corporate Totals** as shown in Figure 5.8a.
> ➤ Click in **cell B2**. Enter **Qtr 1**. Click in **cell B2**, then point to the fill handle in cell B2. The mouse pointer changes to a thin crosshair.
> ➤ Click and drag the fill handle over **cells C2**, **D2**, and **E2**. A border appears to indicate the destination range. Release the mouse. Cells C2 through E2 contain the labels Qtr 2, Qtr 3, and Qtr 4, respectively. Right align the column labels.
> ➤ Click in **cell A3**. Enter **Product 1**. Use the AutoFill capability to enter the labels **Product 2** and **Product 3** in cells A4 and A5.

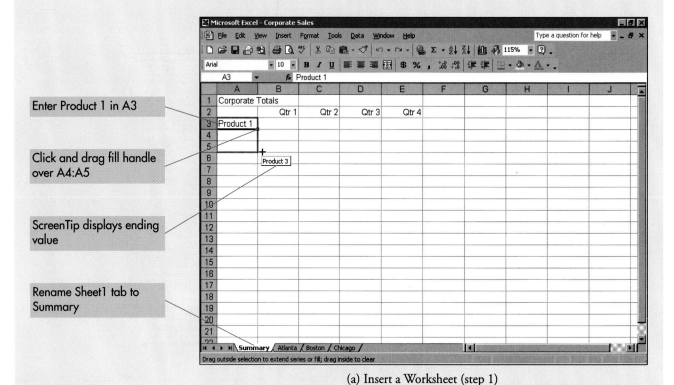

Enter Product 1 in A3

Click and drag fill handle over A4:A5

ScreenTip displays ending value

Rename Sheet1 tab to Summary

(a) Insert a Worksheet (step 1)

FIGURE 5.8 *Hands-on Exercise 2*

Step 2: **Sum the Worksheets**

➤ Click in **cell B3** of the Summary worksheet as shown in Figure 5.8b. Enter **=SUM(Atlanta:Chicago!B3)**, then press the **enter key**. You should see 915 as the sum of the sales for Product 1 in Quarter 1 for the three cities (Atlanta, Boston, and Chicago).

➤ Click the **Undo button** on the Standard toolbar to erase the function so that you can re-enter the function by using pointing.

➤ Check that you are in cell B3 of the Summary worksheet. Enter **=SUM(**.
  • Click the **Atlanta tab** to begin the pointing operation.
  • Press and hold the **Shift key**, click the **Chicago tab** (scrolling if necessary), then release the Shift key and click **cell B3**. The formula bar should now contain =SUM(Atlanta:Chicago!B3.
  • Press the **enter key** to complete the function (which automatically enters the closing right parenthesis) and return to the Summary worksheet.

➤ You should see once again the displayed value of 915 in cell B3 of the Summary worksheet.

➤ If necessary, click in **cell B3**, then drag the fill handle over **cells C3** through **E3** to copy this formula and obtain the total sales for Product 1 in quarters.

➤ Be sure that cells B3 through E3 are still selected, then drag the fill handle to **cell E5**. You should see the total sales for all products in all quarters.

➤ Click **cell E5** to examine the formula in this cell and note that the worksheet references are constant (i.e., they remained the same), whereas the cell references are relative (they were adjusted). Click in other cells to review their formulas in similar fashion. Save the workbook.

Undo button

Sum function is entered in B3

Drag fill handle over C3:E3

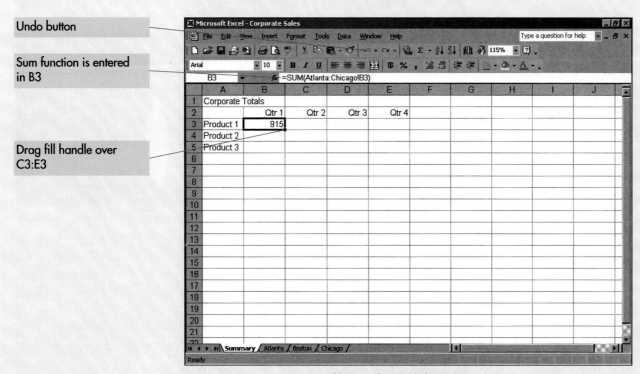

(b) Sum the Worksheets (step 2)

FIGURE 5.8 *Hands-on Exercise 2 (continued)*

Step 3: **The Arrange Windows Command**

➤ Pull down the **Window menu**, which displays the names of the open windows.
➤ The Corporate Sales workbook should be the only open workbook. Close any other open workbooks, including Book1.
➤ Click **New Window** to open a second window. Note, however, that your display will not change at this time.
➤ Pull down the **Window menu** a second time. Click **New Window** to open a third window. Open a fourth window in similar fashion.
➤ Pull down the **Window menu** once again. You should see the names of the four open windows as shown in Figure 5.8c.
➤ Click **Arrange** to display the Arrange Windows dialog box. If necessary, select the **Tile option**, then click **OK**. You should see four tiled windows.
➤ If necessary, change the column widths in the Summary worksheet so that they are approximately the same as in the other windows.

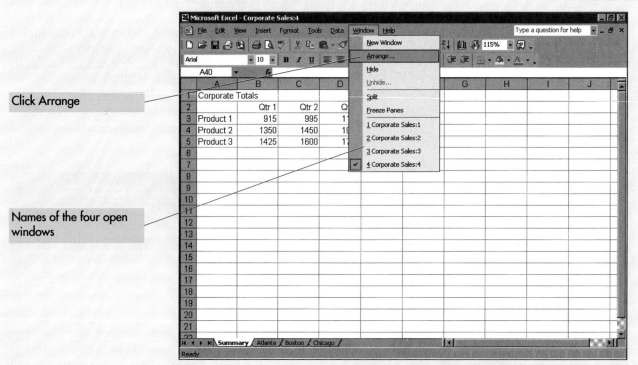

(c) The Arrange Windows Command (step 3)

FIGURE 5.8   *Hands-on Exercise 2 (continued)*

POINTING TO CELLS IN OTHER WORKSHEETS

A worksheet reference can be typed directly into a cell formula, but it is easier to enter the reference by pointing. Click in the cell that is to contain the reference, then enter an equal sign to begin the formula. To reference a cell in another worksheet, click the tab for the worksheet you want to reference, then click the cell or cell range you want to include in the formula. Complete the formula as usual, continuing to first click the tab whenever you want to reference a cell in another worksheet.

Step 4:   **Changing Data**

➤ Click in the **upper-right window** in Figure 5.8d. Click the **Atlanta tab** to display the Atlanta worksheet in this window.

➤ Click the **lower-left window**. Click the **Boston tab** to display the Boston worksheet in this window.

➤ Click in the **lower-right window**. Click the **Tab scrolling button** until you can see the Chicago tab, then click the **Chicago tab**.

➤ Note that cell B3 in the Summary worksheet displays the value 915, which reflects the total sales for Product 1 in Quarter 1 for Atlanta, Boston, and Chicago (10, 55, and 850, respectively).

➤ Click in **cell B3** of the Chicago worksheet. Enter **250**. Press **enter**. The value of cell B3 in the Summary worksheet changes to 315 to reflect the decreased sales in Chicago.

➤ Click the **Undo button** on the Standard toolbar. The sales for Chicago revert to 850 and the Corporate total is again 915.

Undo button

Click in window, click Atlanta tab

Formula recalculates and reflects decreased sales in Chicago

Enter 250 in B3

Click in window, click Boston tab

Click in window, click Chicago tab

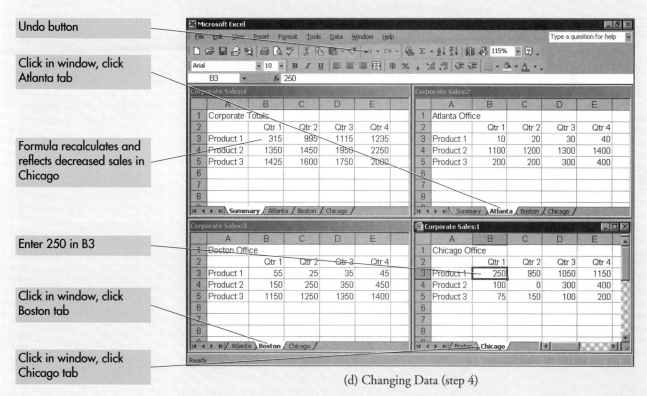

(d) Changing Data (step 4)

FIGURE 5.8   *Hands-on Exercise 2 (continued)*

CONTEXT-SENSITIVE MENUS

A context-sensitive menu provides an alternate (and generally faster) way to execute common commands. Point to a tab, then click the right mouse button to display a menu with commands to insert, delete, rename, move, copy, change color, or select all worksheets. Point to the desired command, then click the left mouse button to execute the command from the shortcut menu. Press the Esc key or click outside the menu to close the menu.

Step 5: **Group Editing**

➤ Click in the window where the Summary worksheet is active. Point to the split box separating the tab scrolling buttons from the horizontal scroll bar. (The pointer becomes a two-headed arrow.) Click and drag to the right until you can see all four tabs at the same time.

➤ If necessary, click the **Summary tab**. Press and hold the **Shift key** as you click the tab for the **Chicago worksheet**. All four tabs should be selected (and thus displayed in white) as shown in Figure 5.8e. You should also see [Group] in the title bar.

➤ Enter **Total** in **cell A6**. The text is centered in cell A6 of all four worksheets.

➤ Click in cell **B6** and enter the function **=SUM(B3:B5)**. Note that the formula is entered in all four sheets simultaneously because of group editing. Copy this formula to **cells C6** through **E6**.

➤ Stay in the Summary worksheet and scroll until you can see column F. Enter **Total** in **cell F2**. Click in **cell F3** and enter the function **=SUM(B3:E3)**. Copy this formula to **cells F4** through **F6**. Save the workbook.

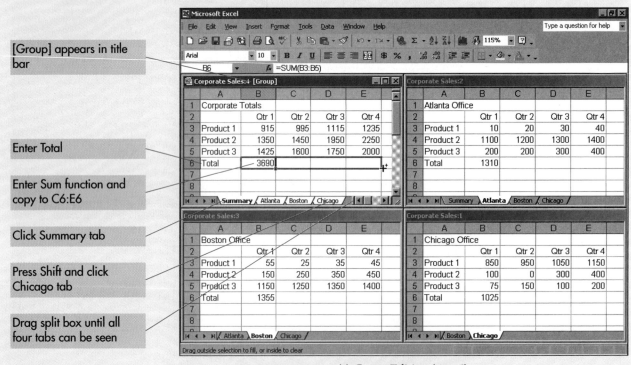

(e) Group Editing (step 5)

FIGURE 5.8 *Hands-on Exercise 2 (continued)*

THE AUTOSUM BUTTON

The AutoSum button on the Standard toolbar invokes the Sum function over a range of cells. To sum a single row or column, click in the blank cell at the end of the row or column, click the AutoSum button to see the suggested function, then click the button a second time to enter the function into the worksheet. To enter a sum function for multiple rows or columns, select the cell range prior to clicking the AutoSum button.

Step 6: **The AutoFormat Command**

➤ Be sure that all four tabs are still selected so that group editing is still in effect. Click and drag to select **cells A1** through **F6** as shown in Figure 5.8f. (You may need to scroll in the worksheet to select all of the cells.)

➤ Pull down the **Format menu** and click the **AutoFormat command** to display the AutoFormat dialog box. Choose a format that appeals to you, then click the **Options button** to determine which parts of the format you want to apply.

➤ Experiment freely by selecting different designs and/or checking and unchecking the various check boxes within a design. Set a time limit, then make a decision. We chose the **Colorful 2** format and left all of the boxes checked. Click **OK**.

➤ The format is applied to all four selected sheets. You cannot see the effects in the summary worksheet, however, until you click elsewhere in the worksheet to deselect the cells. Save the workbook.

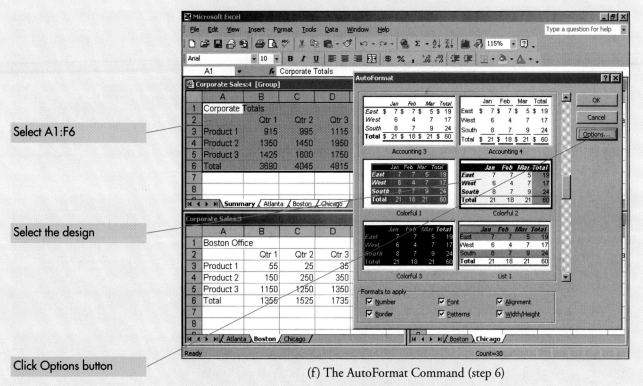

Select A1:F6

Select the design

Click Options button

(f) The AutoFormat Command (step 6)

FIGURE 5.8 *Hands-on Exercise 2 (continued)*

SELECT MULTIPLE SHEETS

You can group multiple worksheets simultaneously, then perform the same operation on the selected sheets at one time. To select adjacent worksheets, click the first sheet in the group, then press and hold the Shift key as you click the last sheet in the group. If the worksheets are not adjacent to one another, click the first tab, then press and hold the Ctrl key as you click the tab of each additional sheet. Excel indicates that grouping is in effect by appending [Group] to the workbook name in the title bar. Click any tab (other than the active sheet) to deselect the group.

Step 7: **The Finishing Touches**

➤ Click and drag to select **cells B3** through **F6**, then pull down the **Format menu** and click the **Cells command** to display the Format Cells dialog box in Figure 5.8g. (You can also right click the selected cells, then select the **Format Cells command** from the context-sensitive menu.)

➤ Click the **Number tab**, click **Currency**, and set the number of decimal places to **zero**. Click **OK**.

➤ Change the width of columns B through F as necessary to accommodate the additional formatting. It's easiest to select all of the columns at the same time, then click and drag the border of the right-most column to change the width of all selected columns.

➤ Save the workbook. Close all four windows. Exit Excel if you do not want to continue with the next exercise at this time.

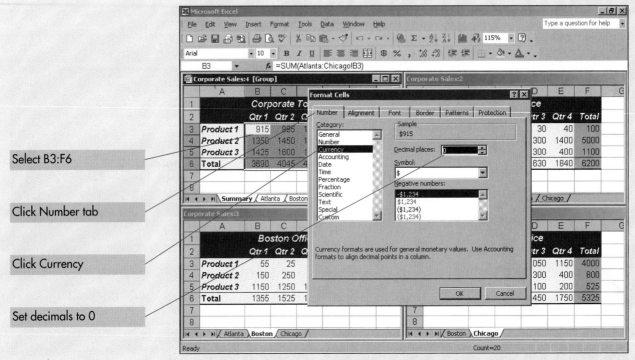

(g) The Finishing Touches (step 7)

FIGURE 5.8 *Hands-on Exercise 2 (continued)*

THE OPTIMAL (AUTOFIT) COLUMN WIDTH

The appearance of pound signs within a cell indicates that the cell width (column width) is insufficient to display the computed results in the selected format. Double click the right border of the column heading to change the column width to accommodate the widest entry in that column. For example, to increase the width of column B, double click the border between the column headings for columns B and C.

Throughout the text we have emphasized the importance of properly designing a worksheet and of isolating the assumptions and initial conditions on which the worksheet is based. A workbook can contain up to 255 worksheets, and it, too, should be well designed so that the purpose of every worksheet is evident. Documenting a workbook, and the various worksheets within it, is important because spreadsheets are frequently used by individuals other than the author. You are familiar with every aspect of your workbook because you created it. Your colleague down the hall (or across the country) is not, however, and that person needs to know at a glance the purpose of the workbook and its underlying structure. Even if you don't share your worksheet with others, you will appreciate the documentation six months from now, when you have forgotten some of the nuances you once knew so well.

One way of documenting a workbook is through the creation of a ***documentation worksheet*** that describes the contents of each worksheet within the workbook as shown in Figure 5.9. The worksheet in Figure 5.9 has been added to the Corporate Sales workbook that was created in the first two exercises. (The Insert menu contains the command to add a worksheet.)

The documentation worksheet shows the author and date the spreadsheet was last modified. It contains a description of the overall workbook, a list of all the sheets within the workbook, and the contents of each. The information in the documentation worksheet may seem obvious to you, but it will be greatly appreciated by someone seeing the workbook for the first time.

The documentation worksheet is attractively formatted and takes advantage of the ability to wrap text within a cell. The description in cell B6, for example, wraps over several lines (just as in a word processor). The worksheet also takes advantage of color and larger fonts to call attention to the title of the worksheet. The grid lines have been suppressed through the View tab in the Options command of the Tools menu. The documentation worksheet is an important addition to any workbook.

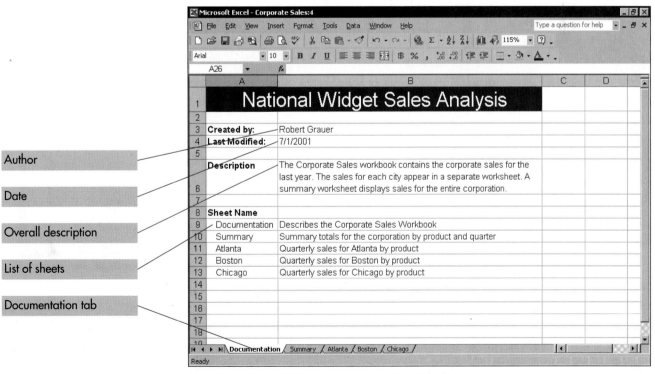

FIGURE 5.9 *The Documentation Worksheet*

THE DOCUMENTATION WORKSHEET

Objective To improve the design of a workbook through the inclusion of a documentation worksheet; to illustrate sophisticated formatting. Use Figure 5.10 as a guide in the exercise.

Step 1: **Add the Documentation Worksheet**

> ➤ Open the **Corporate Sales workbook** that was created in the previous exercise. Maximize the window. If necessary, click the **Atlanta** tab to turn off the group-editing feature. Click the **Summary tab** to select this worksheet.
> ➤ Pull down the **Insert menu** and click the **Worksheet command** to insert a new worksheet to the left of the Summary worksheet. Double click the **tab** of the newly inserted worksheet. Enter **Documentation** as the new name and press **enter**.
> ➤ Enter the descriptive entries in column A as shown in Figure 5.10a. Use bold-face and indentation as appropriate. Double click the column border between columns A and B to increase the width of column A to accommodate the widest entry in the column.
> ➤ Enter your name in **cell B3**. Enter **=Today( )** in cell B4. Press **enter**. Click the **Left Align button** to align the date as shown in the figure.
> ➤ Save the workbook.

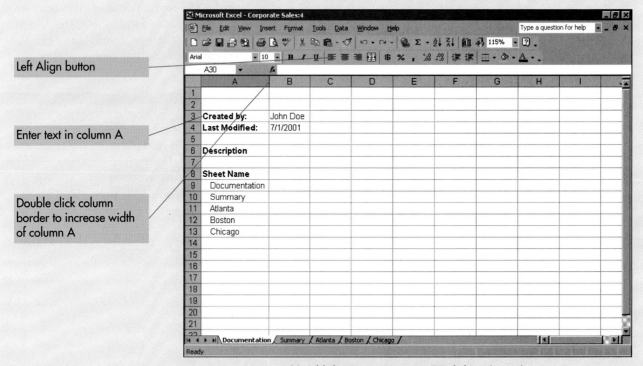

(a) Add the Documentation Worksheet (step 1)

FIGURE 5.10 *Hands-on Exercise 3*

Step 2:   **The Wrap Text Command**

➤ Increase the width of column B as shown in Figure 5.10b, then click in **cell B6** and enter the descriptive entry shown in the formula bar.

➤ Do not press the enter key until you have completed the entire entry. Do not be concerned if the text in cell B6 appears to spill into the other cells in row six. Press the **enter key** when you have completed the entry.

➤ Click in **cell B6**, then pull down the **Format menu** and click **Cells** (or right click **cell B6** and click the **Format Cells command**) to display the dialog box in Figure 5.10b.

➤ Click the **Alignment tab**, click the box to **Wrap Text** as shown in the figure, then click **OK**. The text in cell B6 wraps to the width of column B.

➤ Point to **cell A6**, then click the **right mouse button** to display a shortcut menu. Click **Format Cells** to display the Format Cells dialog box. If necessary, click the **Alignment tab**, click the **drop-down arrow** in the Vertical list box, and select **Top**. Click **OK**. Save the workbook.

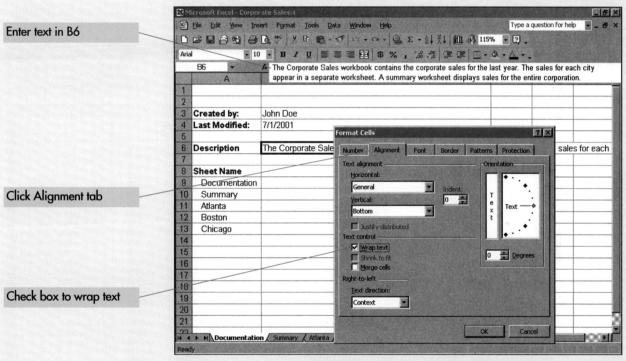

(b) The Wrap Text Command (step 2)

FIGURE 5.10   *Hands-on Exercise 3 (continued)*

EDIT WITHIN A CELL

Double click in the cell whose contents you want to change, then make the changes directly in the cell itself rather than on the formula bar. Use the mouse or arrow keys to position the insertion point at the point of correction. Press the Ins key to toggle between the insertion and overtype modes and/or use the Del key to delete a character. Press the Home and End keys to move to the first and last characters, respectively.

Step 3:   **Add the Worksheet Title**

> ➤ Click in **cell A1**. Enter **National Widgets Sales Analysis**. Change the font size to **22**.
> ➤ Click and drag to select **cells A1** and **B1**. Click the **Merge and Center button** to center the title across cells A1 and B1.
> ➤ Check that cells A1 and B1 are still selected. Pull down the **Format menu**. Click **Cells** to display the Format Cells dialog box as shown in Figure 5.10c.
> - Click the **Patterns tab**. Click the **Burgundy** color (to match the color used in the Colorful 2 AutoFormat that was applied in the previous exercise).
> - Click the **Font tab**. Click the drop-down arrow in the **Color list box**. Click the **White** color.
> - Click **OK** to accept the settings and close the Format Cells dialog box.
> ➤ Click outside the selected cells to see the effects of the formatting change. You should see white letters on a burgundy background.
> ➤ Complete the text entries in **cells B9** through **B13**. Add any additional documentation and formatting that you think is appropriate.
> ➤ Click in **cell A1**. Click the **Spelling button** to check the worksheet for spelling.

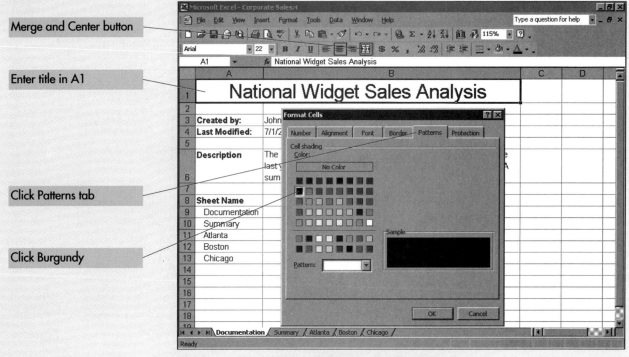

Merge and Center button

Enter title in A1

Click Patterns tab

Click Burgundy

(c) Add the Worksheet Title (step 3)

FIGURE 5.10   *Hands-on Exercise 3 (continued)*

THE SPELL CHECK

Anyone familiar with a word processor takes the spell check for granted, but did you know the same capability exists within Excel? Click the Spelling button on the Standard toolbar to initiate the spell check, then implement corrections just as you do in Microsoft Word.

Step 4:   **The Page Setup Command**

➤ If necessary, click the **Documentation tab** at the bottom of the window, then press and hold the **Shift key** as you click the tab for the **Chicago worksheet**. All five worksheet tabs should be selected, as shown in Figure 5.10d.

➤ Pull down the **File menu** and click the **Page Setup command** to display the Page Setup dialog box.

• Click the **Header/Footer tab**. Click the **down arrow** on the Header list box and choose **Documentation** (the name of the worksheet). Click the **down arrow** on the Footer list box and choose **Corporate Sales** (the name of the workbook).

• Click the **Margins tab**, then click the check box to center the worksheet horizontally. Change the top margin to **2 inches**.

• Click the **Sheet tab**. Check the boxes to include row and column headings and gridlines. Click **OK** to exit the Page Setup dialog box.

➤ Save the workbook. Pull down the **File menu**. Click **Print** to display the Print dialog box. Click the option button to print the **Entire Workbook**. Click **OK**.

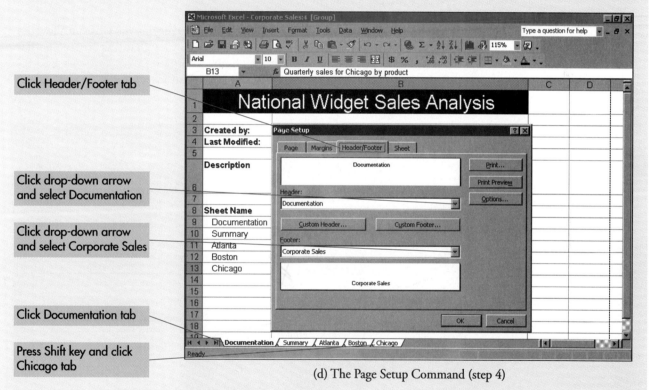

Click Header/Footer tab

Click drop-down arrow and select Documentation

Click drop-down arrow and select Corporate Sales

Click Documentation tab

Press Shift key and click Chicago tab

(d) The Page Setup Command (step 4)

FIGURE 5.10   *Hands-on Exercise 3 (continued)*

THE PRINT PREVIEW COMMAND

Use the Print Preview command to check the appearance of a worksheet to save time as well as paper. You can execute the command by clicking the Print Preview button on the Standard toolbar or from the Print Preview command button within the Page Setup or Print dialog box.

Step 5:   **Print the Cell Formulas**

➤ Right click the **Summary tab** to display a context-sensitive menu, then click the **Ungroup Sheets command** to remove the group editing.

➤ Pull down the **View menu**, click **Custom Views** to display the Custom Views dialog box. Click the **Add button** to display the Add View dialog box.

➤ Enter **Displayed Values** as the name of the view (this is different from Figure 5.10e). Be sure that the Print Settings box is checked, and click **OK**.

➤ Press **Ctrl+`** to display the cell formulas. Double click the column borders between adjacent columns to increase the width of each column so that the cell formulas are completely visible.

➤ Pull down the **File menu** and click the **Page Setup command**. Click the **Page tab** and change to **Landscape orientation**. Click the option button to **Fit to 1 page**. Click **OK** to accept these settings and close the Page Setup dialog box. Click the **Print button** to print the summary worksheet.

➤ Pull down the **View menu**, click **Custom Views** to display the Custom View dialog box, then click the **Add button** to display the Add View dialog box. Enter **Cell Formulas** as shown in Figure 5.10f, verify that the Print Settings box is checked, and click **OK**.

➤ Pull down the **View menu**, click **Custom Views** to display the Custom View dialog box, then double click the **Displayed Values** view that was created earlier. You can switch back and forth at any time.

➤ Save the workbook. Close all open windows. Exit Excel if you do not want to continue with the next exercise at this time.

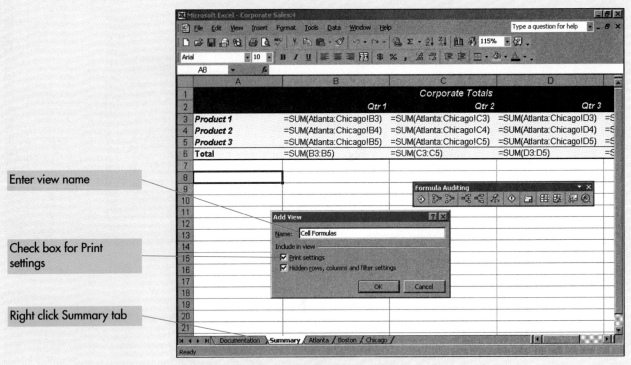

Enter view name

Check box for Print settings

Right click Summary tab

(e) Print the Cell Formulas (step 5)

FIGURE 5.10   *Hands-on Exercise 3 (continued)*

There are two approaches to combining data from multiple sources. You can store all of the data on separate sheets in a single workbook, then create a summary worksheet within that workbook that references values in the other worksheets. Alternatively, you can retain the source data in separate workbooks, and create a summary workbook that references (links to) those workbooks.

Linking is established through the creation of *external references* that specify a cell (or range of cells) in another workbook. The *dependent workbook* (the Corporate Links workbook in our next example) contains the external references and thus reflects (is dependent on) data in the source workbook(s). The *source workbooks* (the Atlanta, Boston, and Chicago workbooks in our example) contain the data referenced by the dependent workbook.

Figure 5.11 illustrates the use of linking within the context of the example we have been using. Four different workbooks are open, each with one worksheet. The Corporate Links workbook is the dependent workbook and contains external references to obtain the summary totals. The Atlanta, Boston, and Chicago workbooks are the source workbooks.

Cell B3 is the active cell, and its contents are displayed in the formula bar. The corporate sales for Product 1 in the first quarter are calculated by summing the corresponding values in the source workbooks. Note how the workbook names are enclosed in square brackets to indicate the external references to the Atlanta, Boston, and Chicago workbooks.

The formulas to compute the corporate totals for Product 1 in the second, third, and fourth quarters contain external references similar to those shown in the formula bar. The *workbook references* and sheet references are absolute, whereas the cell reference may be relative (as in this example) or absolute. Once the formula has been entered into cell B3, it may be copied to the remaining cells in this row to compute the totals for Product 1 in the remaining quarters.

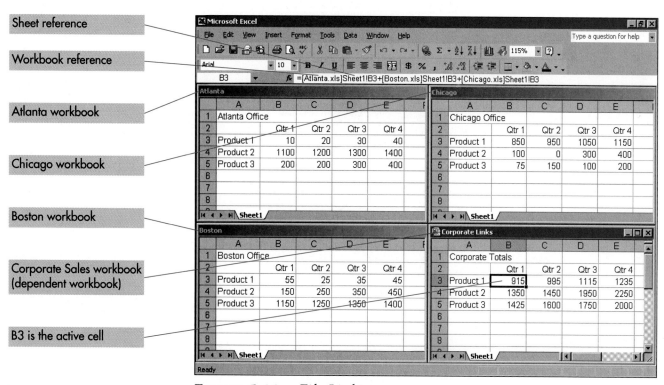

FIGURE 5.11   *File Linking*

LINKING WORKBOOKS

>
> *Objective*   To create a dependent workbook with external references to multiple source workbooks; to use pointing to create the external reference rather than entering the formula explicitly. Use Figure 5.12 as a guide in doing the exercise.

Step 1:   **Open the Workbooks**

> ➤ Start Excel. If necessary, click the **New Workbook button** on the Standard toolbar to open a new workbook.
>
> ➤ Delete all worksheets except for Sheet1. Save the workbook as **Corporate Links** in the **Exploring Excel folder**.
>
> ➤ Pull down the **File menu**. Click **Open** to display the Open dialog box. Click the **Atlanta workbook**. Press and hold the **Ctrl key** as you click the **Boston** and **Chicago workbooks** to select all three workbooks at the same time as shown in Figure 5.12a.
>
> ➤ Click **Open** to open the selected workbooks. The workbooks will be opened one after another, with a brief message appearing on the status bar as each workbook is opened.
>
> ➤ Pull down the **Window menu**, which should indicate four open workbooks at the bottom of the menu. Click **Arrange** to display the Arrange Windows dialog box. If necessary, select the **Tiled option**, then click **OK**.

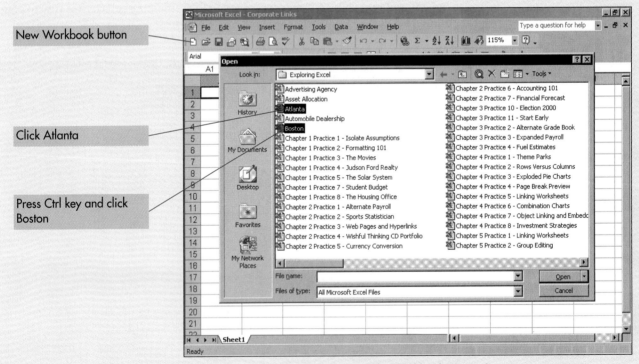

New Workbook button

Click Atlanta

Press Ctrl key and click Boston

(a) Open the Workbooks (step 1)

FIGURE 5.12   *Hands-on Exercise 4*

Step 2:   **The AutoFill Command**

> You should see four open workbooks as shown in Figure 5.12b, although the row and column labels have not yet been entered in the Corporate Links workbook. (Do not be concerned if your workbooks are arranged differently.)
> Click in **cell A1** in the **Corporate Links workbook** to make this the active cell in the active workbook. Enter **Corporate Totals**.
> Click **cell B2**. Enter **Qtr 1**. Click in **cell B2**, then point to the fill handle in the lower-right corner. The mouse pointer changes to a thin crosshair.
> Drag the fill handle over **cells C2**, **D2**, and **E2**. A border appears, to indicate the destination range. Release the mouse. Cells C2 through E2 contain the labels Qtr 2, Qtr 3, and Qtr 4, respectively.
> Right-align the entries in **cells B2** through **E2**, then reduce the column widths so that you can see the entire worksheet in the window.
> Click **cell A3**. Enter **Product 1**. Use the AutoFill capability to enter the labels **Product 2** and **Product 3** in cells A4 and A5.

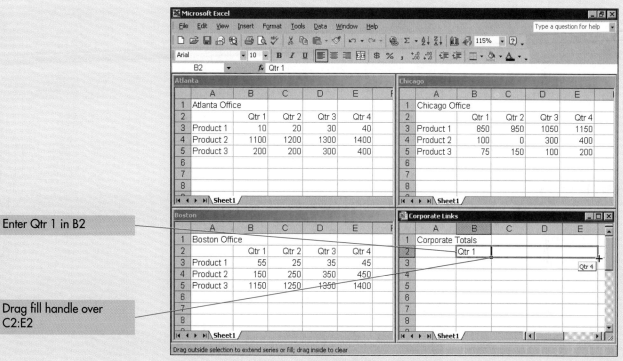

Enter Qtr 1 in B2

Drag fill handle over C2:E2

(b) The AutoFill Command (step 2)

FIGURE 5.12   *Hands-on Exercise 4 (continued)*

CREATE A CUSTOM SERIES

The AutoFill command is the fastest way to enter a series into adjacent cells. Type the first entry in the series (such as January, Monday, or Quarter 1), then click and drag the fill handle to adjacent cells to complete the series. You can also create your own series. Pull down the Tools menu, click Options, click the Custom Lists tab, and select New List. Enter the items in your series separated by commas (e.g., Tom, Dick, and Harry), click Add, and click OK. The next time you type Tom, Dick, or Harry in a cell you can use the fill handle to complete the series.

Step 3: **File Linking**

➤ Click **cell B3** of the **Corporate Links workbook**. Enter an **equal sign** so that you can create the formula by pointing:

- Click in the window for the **Atlanta workbook**. Click **cell B3**. The formula bar should display =[ATLANTA.XLS]Sheet1!$B$3. Press the **F4 key** continually until the cell reference changes to B3.
- Enter a **plus sign**. Click in the window for the **Boston workbook**. Click **cell B3**. The formula expands to include +[BOSTON.XLS]Sheet1!$B$3. Press the **F4 key** continually until the cell reference changes to B3.
- Enter a **plus sign**. Click in the window for the **Chicago workbook**. Click **cell B3**. The formula expands to include +[CHICAGO.XLS]Sheet1!$B$3. Press the **F4 key** continually until the cell reference changes to B3.
- Press **enter**. The formula is complete, and you should see 915 in cell B3 of the Corporate Links workbook. Click in **cell B3**. The entry on the formula bar should match the entry in Figure 5.12c. Save the workbook.

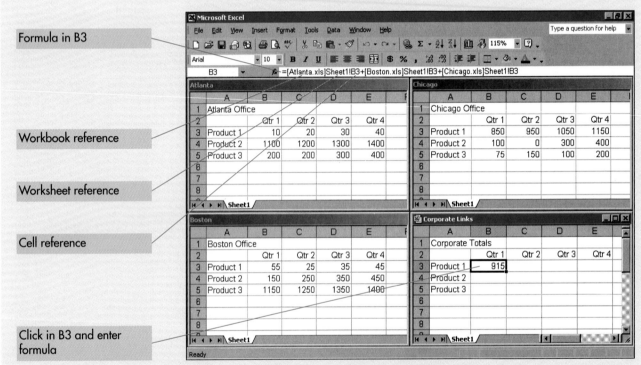

(c) File Linking (step 3)

FIGURE 5.12   *Hands-on Exercise 4 (continued)*

THE F4 KEY

The F4 key cycles through relative, absolute, and mixed addresses. Click on any reference within the formula bar; for example, click on A1 in the formula =A1+A2. Press the F4 key once, and it changes to an absolute reference, $A$1. Press the F4 key a second time, and it becomes a mixed reference, A$1; press it again, and it is a different mixed reference, $A1. Press the F4 key a fourth time, and it returns to the original relative address, A1.

Step 4: **Copy the Cell Formulas**

> ➤ If necessary, click **cell B3** in the **Corporate Links workbook**, then drag the fill handle over **cells C3** through **E3** to copy this formula to the remaining cells in row 3.
> ➤ Be sure that cells B3 through E3 are still selected, then drag the fill handle to **cell E5**. You should see the total sales for all products in all quarters as shown in Figure 5.12d.
> ➤ Click **cell E5** to view the copied formula as shown in the figure. Note that the workbook and sheet references are the same but that the cell references have adjusted.
> ➤ Save the workbook.

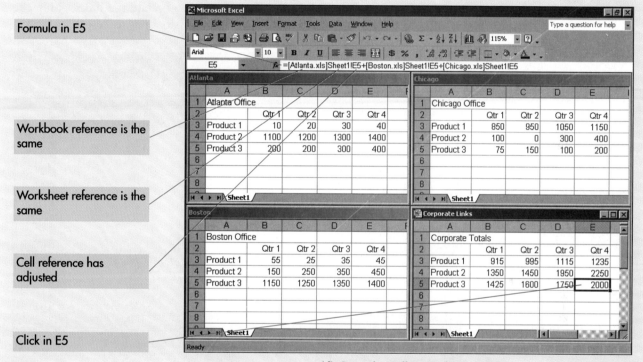

Formula in E5

Workbook reference is the same

Worksheet reference is the same

Cell reference has adjusted

Click in E5

(d) Copy the Cell Formulas (step 4)

FIGURE 5.12 *Hands-on Exercise 4 (continued)*

DRIVE AND FOLDER REFERENCE

An external reference is updated regardless of whether or not the source workbook is open. The reference is displayed differently, depending on whether or not the source workbook is open. The references include the path (the drive and folder) if the source workbook is closed; the path is not shown if the source workbook is open. The external workbooks must be available to update the summary workbook. If the location of the workbooks changes (as may happen if you copy the workbooks to a different folder), pull down the Edit menu and click the Links command, then change the source of the external data.

Step 5: **Create a Workspace**

➤ Pull down the **File menu** and click the **Save Workspace command** to display the Save Workspace dialog box in Figure 5.12e.

➤ If necessary, click the **down arrow** in the Save in list box to select the **Exploring Excel folder**. Enter **Linked workbooks** as the file name. Click the **Save button** in the dialog box to save the workspace. Click **Yes** if asked whether to save the changes to the Corporate Links workbook.

➤ The workspace is saved and you can continue to work as usual. The advantage of the workspace is that you can open all four workbooks with a single command.

➤ Click the **Close button** in each window to close all four workbooks. Pull down the **File menu**, click the **Open command**, then open the **Linked workbooks** workspace that you just created.

➤ Click **Update** when asked whether you want to update the links within the Corporate Links workbook. All four workbooks are open as before.

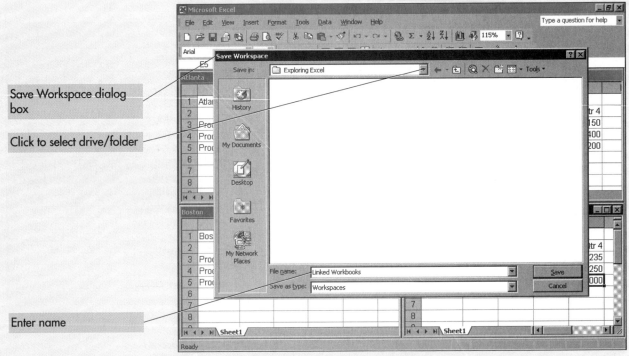

(e) Create a Workspace (step 5)

FIGURE 5.12 *Hands-on Exercise 4 (continued)*

THE WORKSPACE

A workspace enables you to open multiple workbooks in a single step, and further, will retain the arrangement of those workbooks within the Excel window. The workspace file does not contain the workbooks themselves, however, and thus you must continue to save changes you make to the individual workbooks.

Step 6: **Change the Data**

➤ Click **cell B3** to make it the active cell. Note that the value displayed in the cell is 915.

➤ Pull down the **File menu**. Click **Close**. Answer **Yes** if asked whether to save the changes.

➤ Click in the window containing the **Chicago workbook**, click **cell B3**, enter **250**, and press **enter**. Pull down the **File menu**. Click **Close**. Answer **Yes** if asked whether to save the changes. Only two workbooks, Atlanta and Boston, are now open.

➤ Pull down the **File menu** and open the **Corporate Links workbook**. You should see the dialog box in Figure 5.12f, asking whether to update the links. (Note that cell B3 still displays 915). Click **Update** to update the links.

➤ The value in cell B3 of the Corporate Links workbook changes to 315 to reflect the change in the Chicago workbook, even though the latter is closed.

➤ If necessary, click in **cell B3**. The formula bar displays the contents of this cell, which include the drive and folder reference for the Chicago workbook, because the workbook is closed.

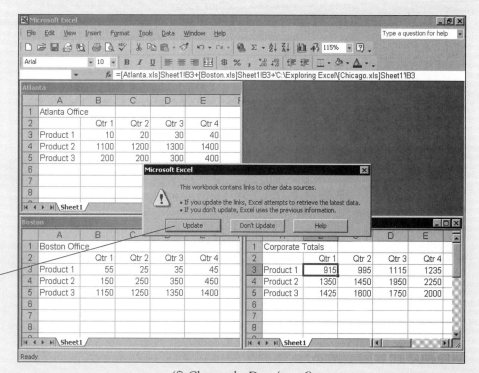

(f) Change the Data (step 6)

FIGURE 5.12 *Hands-on Exercise 4 (continued)*

Step 7: **Close the Workbooks**

➤ Close the Atlanta and Boston workbooks. Close the Corporate Links workbook. Click **Yes** if asked whether to save the changes.

➤ Saving the source workbook(s) before the dependent workbook ensures that the formulas in the source workbooks are calculated, and that all external references in the dependent workbook reflect current values.

➤ Exit Excel.

The chapter showed how to combine data from different sources into a summary report. The example is quite common and applicable to any business scenario requiring both detail and summary reports. One approach is to store all of the data in separate sheets of a single workbook, then summarize the data in a summary worksheet within that workbook. Alternatively, the source data can be kept in separate workbooks and consolidated through linking to a summary workbook. Both approaches are equally valid, and the choice depends on where you want to keep the source data.

An Excel workbook may contain up to 255 worksheets, each of which is identified by a tab at the bottom of the window. Worksheets may be added, deleted, moved, copied, or renamed through a shortcut menu. The highlighted tab indicates the active worksheet.

A worksheet reference is required to indicate a cell in another worksheet of the same workbook. An exclamation point separates the worksheet reference from the cell reference. The worksheet reference is absolute and remains the same when the formula is copied. The cell reference may be relative or absolute. A 3-D reference refers to a cell or range in another worksheet.

The best way to enter a reference to a cell in a different worksheet (or in a different workbook) is by pointing. Click in the cell that is to contain the formula, type an equal sign, click the worksheet tab that contains the external reference, then click in the appropriate cell. Use the F4 key to switch between relative, absolute, and mixed cell references.

Multiple worksheets may be selected (grouped) to execute the same commands on all of the selected worksheets simultaneously. An AutoFormat is a predefined set of formats that includes font size, color, boldface, alignment, and other attributes that can be applied automatically to a selected range.

A workbook should be clearly organized so that the purpose of every worksheet is evident. One way of documenting a workbook is through the creation of a documentation worksheet that describes the purpose of each worksheet within the workbook.

A workbook may also be linked to cells in other workbooks through an external reference that specifies a cell (or range of cells) in a source workbook. The dependent workbook contains the external references and uses (is dependent on) the data in the source workbook(s). The external workbooks must be available to update the summary workbook. If the location of the workbooks changes (as may happen if you copy the workbooks to a different folder), pull down the Edit menu and click the Links command, then change the source of the external data.

3-D reference (p. 228)
Arrange command (p. 220)
AutoFormat command (p. 229)
AutoSum (p. 234)
Custom view (p. 242)
Dependent workbook (p. 243)

Documentation worksheet (p. 237)
External reference (p. 243)
Grouping worksheets (p. 229)
Linking (p. 243)
New Window command (p. 220)
Source workbook (p. 243)

Tab split bar (p. 221)
Workbook reference (p. 243)
Worksheet reference (p. 227)
Workspace (p. 248)

1. Which of the following is true regarding workbooks and worksheets?
   (a) A workbook contains one or more worksheets
   (b) Only one worksheet can be selected at a time within a workbook
   (c) Every workbook contains the same number of worksheets
   (d) All of the above

2. Assume that a workbook contains three worksheets. How many cells are included in the function =SUM(Sheet1:Sheet3!A1)?
   (a) Three
   (b) Four
   (c) Twelve
   (d) Twenty-four

3. Assume that a workbook contains three worksheets. How many cells are included in the function =SUM(Sheet1:Sheet3!A1:B4)?
   (a) Three
   (b) Four
   (c) Twelve
   (d) Twenty-four

4. Which of the following is the preferred way to sum the value of cell A1 from three different worksheets?
   (a) =Sheet1!A1+Sheet2!A1+Sheet3!A1
   (b) =SUM(Sheet1:Sheet3!A1)
   (c) Both (a) and (b) are equally good
   (d) Neither (a) nor (b)

5. The reference CIS120!$A$2:
   (a) Is an absolute reference to cell A2 in the CIS120 workbook
   (b) Is a relative reference to cell A2 in the CIS120 workbook
   (c) Is an absolute reference to cell A2 in the CIS120 worksheet
   (d) Is a relative reference to cell A2 in the CIS120 worksheet

6. Assume that Sheet1 is the active worksheet and that cells A2 through A4 are currently selected. What happens if you press and hold the Shift key as you click the tab for Sheet3, then press the Del key?
   (a) Only Sheet1 will be deleted from the workbook
   (b) Only Sheet3 will be deleted from the workbook
   (c) Sheet1, Sheet2, and Sheet3 will be deleted from the workbook
   (d) The contents of cells A2 through A4 will be erased from Sheet1, Sheet2, and Sheet3

7. Which of the following is true about the reference Sheet1:Sheet3!A1:B2?
   (a) The worksheet reference is relative, the cell reference is absolute
   (b) The worksheet reference is absolute, the cell reference is relative
   (c) The worksheet and cell references are both absolute
   (d) The worksheet and cell references are both relative

8. You are in the Ready mode and are positioned in cell B2 of Sheet1. You enter an equal sign, click the worksheet tab for Sheet2, click cell B1, and press enter.
   (a) The content of cell B2 in Sheet1 is =Sheet2!B1
   (b) The content of cell B1 in Sheet2 is = Sheet1!B2
   (c) Both (a) and (b)
   (d) Neither (a) nor (b)

9. You are in the Ready mode and are positioned in cell A10 of Sheet1. You enter an equal sign, click the worksheet tab for the worksheet called This Year, and click cell C10. You then enter a minus sign, click the worksheet tab for the worksheet called Last Year, click cell C10, and press enter. What are the contents of cell A10?
   (a) =ThisYear:LastYear!C10
   (b) =(ThisYear−LastYear)!C10
   (c) =ThisYear!C10-LastYear!C10
   (d) =ThisYear:C10-LastYear:C10

10. Which of the following can be accessed from a shortcut menu?
    (a) Inserting or deleting a worksheet
    (b) Moving or copying a worksheet
    (c) Renaming a worksheet
    (d) All of the above

11. You are in the Ready mode and are positioned in cell A1 of Sheet1 of Book1. You enter an equal sign, click in the open window for Book2, click the tab for Sheet1, click cell A1, then press the F4 key continually until you have a relative cell reference. What reference appears in the formula bar?
    (a) =[BOOK1.XLS]Sheet1!$A$1
    (b) =[BOOK1.XLS]Sheet1!A1
    (c) =[BOOK2.XLS]Sheet1!$A$1
    (d) =[BOOK2.XLS]Sheet1!A1

12. The Arrange Windows command can display:
    (a) Multiple worksheets from one workbook
    (b) One worksheet from multiple workbooks
    (c) Both (a) and (b)
    (d) Neither (a) nor (b)

13. Pointing can be used to reference a cell in:
    (a) A different worksheet
    (b) A different workbook
    (c) Both (a) and (b)
    (d) Neither (a) nor (b)

14. The appearance of [Group] within the title bar indicates that:
    (a) Multiple workbooks are open and are all active
    (b) Multiple worksheets are selected within the same workbook
    (c) Both (a) and (b)
    (d) Neither (a) nor (b)

15. Which of the following is true regarding the example on file linking that was developed in the chapter?
    (a) The Atlanta, Boston, and Chicago workbooks were dependent workbooks
    (b) The Linked workbook was a source workbook
    (c) Both (a) and (b)
    (d) Neither (a) nor (b)

ANSWERS

1. a	6. d	11. d
2. a	7. b	12. c
3. d	8. a	13. c
4. b	9. c	14. b
5. c	10. d	15. d

1. Linking Worksheets: A partially completed version of the workbook in Figure 5.13 can be found on the data disk as *Chapter 5 Practice 1*. This workbook contains worksheets for the individual sections but does not contain the summary worksheet.
   a. Retrieve the *Chapter 5 Practice 1* workbook from the data disk.
   b. Group the worksheets, then add the appropriate formulas (functions) to compute the class average on each test.
   c. Ungroup the worksheets, then add a summary worksheet that includes the test averages from each of the sections as shown in the figure.
   d. Add a documentation worksheet that includes your name as the grading assistant, the date of modification, and lists of all the worksheets in the workbook.
   e. Print the entire workbook and submit it to your instructor.

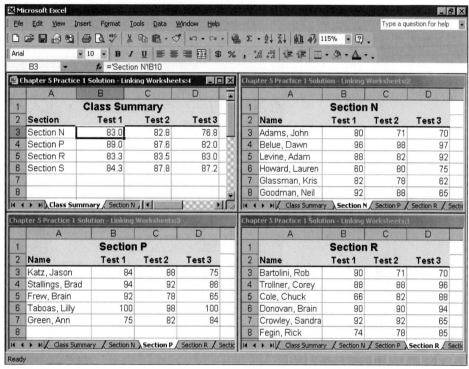

FIGURE 5.13   *Linking Worksheets (Exercise 1)*

2. A partially completed version of the workbook in Figure 5.14 can be found on the data disk as *Chapter 5 Practice 2*. The workbook contains a separate worksheet for each month of the year as well as a summary worksheet for the entire year. Thus far, only the months of January, February, and March are complete. Each monthly worksheet tallies the expenses for five divisions in each of four categories to compute a monthly total for each division. The summary worksheet displays the total expense for each division.
   a. Retrieve the *Chapter 5 Practice 2* workbook from the data disk, then open multiple windows so that the display on your monitor matches Figure 5.14.
   b. Use the Group Editing feature to select the worksheets for January, February, and March simultaneously. Enter the formula to compute the monthly total for each division and each expense category in each month.
   c. Use the Group Editing feature to format the worksheets.

d. Enter the appropriate formulas in the summary worksheet to compute the year-to-date totals for each division.

e. Add an additional worksheet for the month of April. Assume that Division 1 spends $100 in each category, Division 2 spends $200 in each category, and so on. Update the summary worksheet to include the expenses for April.

f. Add a documentation worksheet that includes your name, the date of modification, plus a description of each worksheet within the workbook.

g. Print the entire workbook (all six worksheets), then print the cell formulas for the summary worksheet only. Use an appropriate header or footer for each printout. Add a title page, then submit the assignment to your instructor.

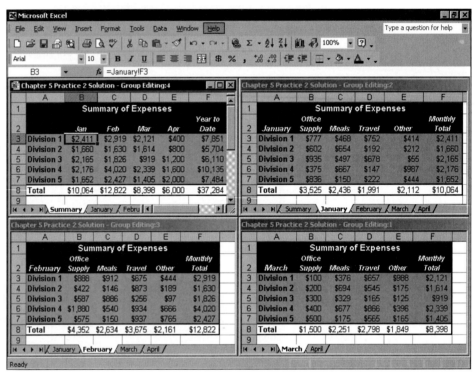

FIGURE 5.14   *Group Editing (Exercise 2)*

HANDS-ON
EXERCISE 3
PAGES 238–242

3. Object Linking and Embedding: Create the compound document in Figure 5.15, which consists of a memo, summary worksheet, and three-dimensional chart. The chart is to be created in its own chart sheet within the Corporate Sales workbook and then incorporated into the memo. Address the memo to your instructor, sign your name, then print the memo as it appears in Figure 5.15.

Prove to yourself that Object Linking and Embedding really works by returning to the Atlanta worksheet *after* you have created the document in Figure 5.15. Change the sales for Product 1 in Quarter 4 to $3,000. Switch back to the Word memo, and the chart should reflect the dramatic increase in the sales for Product 1. Add a postscript to the memo indicating that the corrected chart reflects the last-minute sale of Product 1 in Atlanta, and that you no longer want to discontinue the product. Print the revised memo and submit it to your instructor with the earlier version.

National Widgets, Inc.

Atlanta   ◆   Boston   ◆   Chicago

To: John Graves, President
         National Widgets, Inc.

From: Susan Powers
         Vice President, Marketing

Subject: Sales Analysis Data

Our overall fourth quarter sales have improved considerably over those in the first quarter. Please note, however, that Product 1, despite a growth in sales, is still trailing the other products, and discontinuing its production should be considered. I will await your reply on this matter.

Corporate Totals					
	Qtr 1	Qtr 2	Qtr 3	Qtr 4	Total
Product 1	$915	$995	$1,115	$1,235	$4,260
Product 2	$1,350	$1,450	$1,950	$2,250	$7,000
Product 3	$1,425	$1,600	$1,750	$2,000	$6,775
Total	$3,690	$4,045	$4,815	$5,485	$18,035

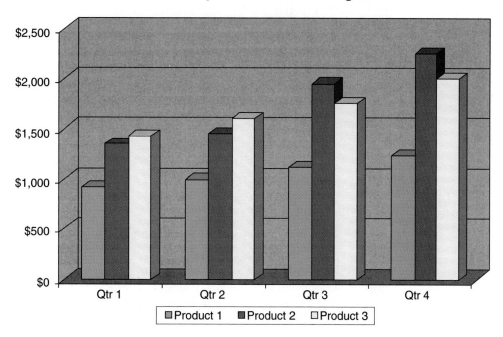

I look forward to hearing from you.

Susan

FIGURE 5.15   *Object Linking and Embedding (Exercise 3)*

4. National Computers: You will find a partially completed version of the workbook in Figure 5.16 in the *Chapter 5 Practice 4* workbook in the Exploring Excel folder. That workbook has four partially completed worksheets, one for each city. Your assignment is to complete the workbook so that it parallels the Corporate Sales workbook that was used in the first three hands-on exercises in this chapter. Proceed as follows:

a. Complete the individual worksheets by adding the appropriate formulas to compute the necessary row and column totals, then format these worksheets in attractive fashion. You can apply your own formatting, or you can use the AutoFormat command. You will find it easier, however, to use the Group editing feature as you add the totals and apply the formatting, since all of the worksheets contain parallel data. Be sure to ungroup the worksheets after you have applied the formatting.

b. Add a summary worksheet that provides corporate totals by product line and quarter. Apply the formatting from the individual worksheets to the summary worksheet.

c. Create two side-by-side column charts, each in its own chart sheet, which display the summary information in graphical fashion. One chart should compare the sales revenue for each office by product, the other should compare the revenue for each office by quarter.

d. Add a documentation worksheet similar to the sheet in Figure 5.16, then print the entire workbook for your instructor.

e. Print the cell formulas for the corporate worksheet. Add a cover sheet and submit the entire assignment to your instructor.

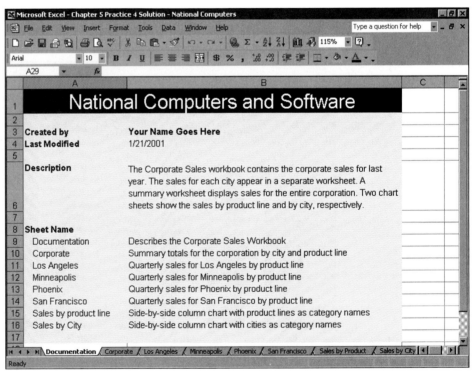

FIGURE 5.16 *National Computers (Exercise 4)*

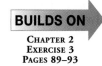

BUILDS ON

CHAPTER 2
EXERCISE 3
PAGES 89–93

5. The Stock Portfolio: The workbook in Figure 5.17 uses Web queries (discussed in Chapter 2) to obtain current stock quotations from the Web, then uses those prices within an Excel workbook. The workbook contains five worksheets in all—a worksheet for each of three clients, Tom, Dick, and Harry; a worksheet containing stock prices as retrieved by the Web query; and a summary worksheet that shows the gain or loss for each client. Your assignment is to open the partially completed workbook in *Chapter 5 Practice 5*, and complete the workbook as follows.

a. Complete the individual worksheets for Tom, Dick, and Harry by entering the appropriate formulas to obtain the current price of each company in the client's portfolio, then determining the value of that investment by multiplying the price times the number of shares. Tom, for example, has AOL in his portfolio, the current price of which is found in cell D11 of the Stock Prices worksheet. Compute the gain or loss for each investment based on the difference between today's price and the purchase price.

b. Update the current price of each client's portfolio by right clicking anywhere within the table of prices in the Stock Prices worksheet, then clicking the Refresh Data command. (The stock symbols that appear at the top of the Stock Prices worksheet were entered manually from the investments in the individual worksheets and are the basis of the Web query.)

c. Enter the summary data for each client in the Summary worksheet using appropriate worksheet references. The total cost of Tom's portfolio, for example, is $33,000 and is found in cell D7 of Tom's worksheet. Thus the corresponding entry in the summary worksheet would be =Tom!E7, indicating that the number is to come from this cell in Tom's worksheet.

d. Add your name in row 9 of the summary worksheet as the investment adviser. Print the entire workbook for your instructor.

e. Print the cell formulas for the summary worksheet. Add a cover sheet and submit the entire assignment to your instructor.

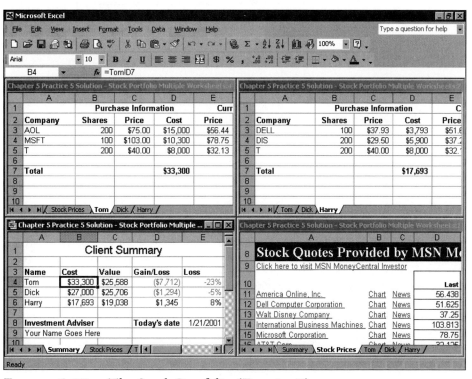

FIGURE 5.17   *The Stock Portfolio (Exercise 5)*

BUILDS ON

HANDS-ON
EXERCISE 3
PAGES 238–242

6. **Creating a Web Page:** Complete the first three hands-on exercises in the chapter, then pull down the File menu and click the Save as Web Page command to convert the completed workbook to its HTML equivalent. Save the file to a separate folder or desktop, then close Excel. Be sure you remember where you save the Web page.

a. Start Windows Explorer, go the folder that contains the Web page, then double click the HTML document that you just created, to start your Web browser and display the document. You should see the corporate sales workbook displayed as a Web page within your browser, either Internet Explorer or Netscape Navigator, as shown in Figure 5.18. The address bar indicates that you are viewing the page locally (from a folder on drive C), as opposed to a Web server.

b. Look carefully at the bottom of the page to note the various tabs corresponding to the different worksheets within the workbook. Click any tab to view the associated page. If you have trouble viewing the tabs, it is because you have an older version of the browser that does not support this feature. Pull down the Help menu within the browser, then click the About command to display the version of the browser you are currently using.

c. Summarize the procedure to convert an Excel workbook to its HTML equivalent in a short note to your instructor. Describe how you would upload the Web page(s) to a server so that the workbook can be viewed by anyone with an Internet connection.

d. Are you able to view the Web page in both Internet Explorer and Netscape Navigator? What differences, if any, do you see? Summarize these findings in a brief note to your instructor.

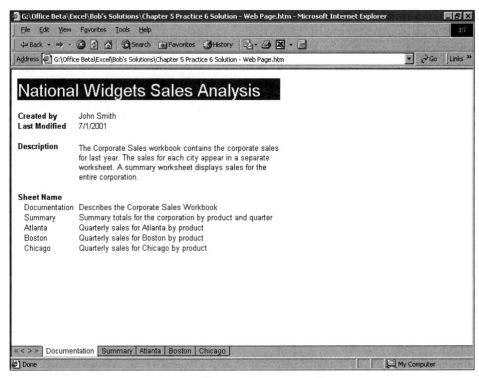

FIGURE 5.18 *Creating a Web Page (Exercise 6)*

BUILDS ON

HANDS-ON EXERCISE 3
PAGES 238–242

7. Pivot Tables: A pivot table is an extremely flexible tool that enables you to manipulate the data in multiple worksheets to produce new reports as shown in Figure 5.19. (Pivot tables are covered in more detail in Chapter 7.) Complete the first three hands-on exercises, then follow the instructions below:
   a. Open the Corporate Sales workbook that was completed at the end of the third hands-on exercise. Pull down the Data menu and click the Pivot Table and PivotChart Report command. Click the option buttons to select Multiple Consolidation Ranges and to specify Pivot Table. Click Next.
   b. Click the option button that says I will create the page fields. Click Next.
   c. Specify the range in step 2b of the PivotTable Wizard through pointing. Click the Sheet tab for Atlanta, select cells A2 through E5, then click the Add command button. You should see Atlanta!A$2:$E$5 in the All Ranges list box. Repeat this step for the other two cities.
   d. Remain in step 2b of the PivotTable Wizard. Click the option button for 1 page field. Select (click) the Atlanta range within the All Ranges list box, then click in the Field One list box and type Atlanta. Do not press the enter key. Select (click) the Boston range within the All ranges list box, then click in the Field One list box and type Boston. Repeat this step for Chicago.
   e. Click Next. Click the option button to create the pivot table on a New Worksheet. Click Finish.
   f. You have a pivot table, but it does not match our figure. Click in cell B3 (the entry in the cell is Column), then click the formula bar and type Quarter (which replaces the previous Column entry). Change the entry in cell A4 from Row to Product. Change the entry in cell A1 from Page1 to City.
   g. Pivot the table to match the figure. Drag Quarter to the row position (cell A4), Product to the column position (cell C3), and City to the row position below Quarter (cell A5). Release the mouse, and the Quarter and City labels will move to the positions shown in the figure.
   h. Format the pivot table so that it matches Figure 5.19. Modify the description on the Documentation worksheet to include the pivot table, then print the pivot table (or the entire workbook if you haven't done so previously).

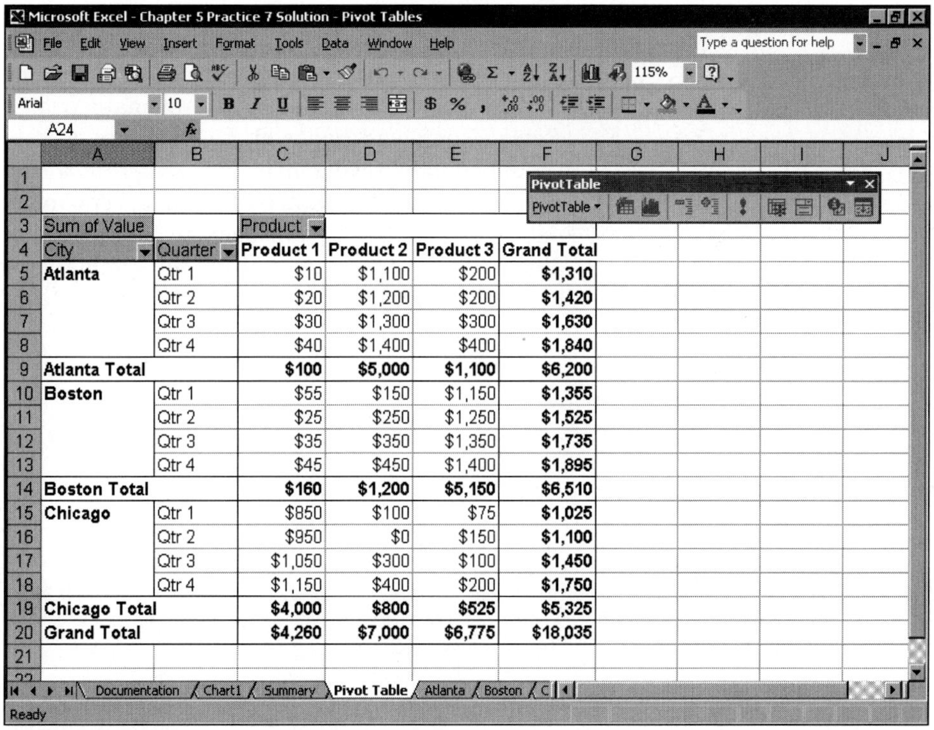

Sum of Value		Product			
City	Quarter	Product 1	Product 2	Product 3	Grand Total
Atlanta	Qtr 1	$10	$1,100	$200	**$1,310**
	Qtr 2	$20	$1,200	$200	**$1,420**
	Qtr 3	$30	$1,300	$300	**$1,630**
	Qtr 4	$40	$1,400	$400	**$1,840**
Atlanta Total		**$100**	**$5,000**	**$1,100**	**$6,200**
Boston	Qtr 1	$55	$150	$1,150	**$1,355**
	Qtr 2	$25	$250	$1,250	**$1,525**
	Qtr 3	$35	$350	$1,350	**$1,735**
	Qtr 4	$45	$450	$1,400	**$1,895**
Boston Total		**$160**	**$1,200**	**$5,150**	**$6,510**
Chicago	Qtr 1	$850	$100	$75	**$1,025**
	Qtr 2	$950	$0	$150	**$1,100**
	Qtr 3	$1,050	$300	$100	**$1,450**
	Qtr 4	$1,150	$400	$200	**$1,750**
Chicago Total		**$4,000**	**$800**	**$525**	**$5,325**
Grand Total		**$4,260**	**$7,000**	**$6,775**	**$18,035**

FIGURE 5.19 *Pivot Tables (Exercise 7)*

Designs by Jessica

The *Designs by Jessica* workbook on the data disk is only partially complete as it contains worksheets for individual stores, but does not yet have a summary worksheet. Your job is to retrieve the workbook and create a summary worksheet, then use the summary worksheet as the basis of a three-dimensional column chart reflecting the sales for the past year. Add a documentation worksheet containing your name as financial analyst, then print the entire workbook and submit it to your instructor.

External References

As marketing manager you are responsible for consolidating the sales information for all of the branch offices within the corporation. Each branch manager creates an identically formatted workbook with the sales information for his or her branch office. Your job is to consolidate the information into a single table, then graph the results appropriately. The branch data is to remain in the individual workbooks; that is, the formulas in your workbook are to contain external references to the *Eastern, Western,* and *Foreign workbooks* on the data disk. Your workbook is to be developed in such a way that any change in the individual workbooks should be automatically reflected in the consolidated workbook.

Pivot Tables

What advantages, if any, does a pivot table have over a conventional worksheet with respect to analyzing and consolidating data from multiple sources? What are the disadvantages? Does the underlying data have to be entered in the form of a list, or can it be taken directly from a worksheet? Use what you learn to extend the analysis of the Atlanta, Boston, and Chicago data that appeared throughout the chapter. (See practice exercise 7 for one example of a pivot table.)

Babyland

Create a new workbook based on data from the *Maplewood, Oakwood,* and *Ramblewood workbooks* in the Exploring Excel folder. The completed workbook should contain a worksheet for each store, a summary worksheet, an appropriate chart reflecting the summary data, and a documentation worksheet with your name, date, and a list of all worksheets in the workbook. Print the completed workbook, along with the cell formulas from the summary worksheet, then submit the printout to your instructor as proof you did this exercise.

CHAPTER 6

A Financial Forecast: Workgroups, Auditing, and Templates

OBJECTIVES

AFTER READING THIS CHAPTER YOU WILL BE ABLE TO:

1. Develop a spreadsheet model for a financial forecast; explain the importance of isolating the assumptions and initial conditions within a worksheet.
2. Explain how the Scenario Manager facilitates the decision-making process; create individual scenarios and a scenario summary.
3. Differentiate between precedent and dependent cells; use the Formula Auditing toolbar to detect errors that may exist within a spreadsheet.
4. Track the editing changes that are made to a spreadsheet; display, create, and edit cell comments.
5. Explain how workgroup functions enable several individuals to work on the same spreadsheet; resolve conflicts among different users.
6. Describe the use of data validation within a spreadsheet; use conditional formatting to display the value of a cell in different formats according to its value.
7. Explain how a template facilitates the creation of a new spreadsheet; create a template based on an existing worksheet.

OVERVIEW

Financial planning and budgeting are two of the most common business applications of a spreadsheet. We thought it appropriate, therefore, to use a financial forecast as the vehicle with which to illustrate several additional capabilities in Excel. We begin by developing the forecast itself, with emphasis on the importance of isolating the assumptions on which the spreadsheet is based. We introduce the Scenario Manager, which enables you to specify multiple sets of assumptions and input conditions (scenarios), then see the results at a glance.

It's important to remember, however, that a spreadsheet is first and foremost a tool for decision-making, and thus its accuracy is critical. Accordingly, we introduce the Formula Auditing toolbar and explain how its various tools can help ensure the accuracy of a spreadsheet. We describe how to share a workbook among multiple users, how to trace the editing changes that are made, and how to resolve conflicts if they occur. The last section in the chapter describes how to create a template on which to base future spreadsheets that use the same financial model. As always, the hands-on exercises help you to apply the conceptual material at the computer.

A FINANCIAL FORECAST

Figure 6.1 displays a financial forecast for Get Rich Quick Enterprises, which contains the projected income and expenses for the company over a five-year period. The spreadsheet enables management to vary any of the *assumptions* at the bottom of the spreadsheet to see the effects on the projected earnings. You don't have to be a business major to follow our forecast. All you have to realize is that the profit for any given year is determined by subtracting expenses from income.

The income is equal to the number of units sold times the unit price. The projected revenue in 2001, for example, is $300,000 based on selling 100,000 units at a price of $3.00 per unit. The variable costs for the same year are estimated at $150,000 (100,000 units times $1.50 per unit). The production facility costs $50,000 and administrative expenses add another $25,000. Subtracting the total expenses from the estimated income yields a net income before taxes of $75,000.

The income and expenses for each succeeding year are based on estimated percentage increases over the previous year, as shown at the bottom of the worksheet. It is absolutely critical to isolate the initial values and assumed rates of increase in this manner, and further, that all entries in the body of the spreadsheet are developed as formulas that reference these cells. The entry in cell C4, for example, is *not* the constant 100,000, but rather a reference to cell C18, which contains the value 100,000.

The distinction may seem trivial, but most assuredly it is not, as two important objectives are achieved. The user sees at a glance which factors affect the results of the spreadsheet (i.e., the cost and earnings projections) and, further, the user can easily change any of those values to see their effect on the overall forecast. Assume, for example, that the first-year forecast changes to 80,000 units sold and that this number will increase at 8 percent a year (rather than 10). The only changes in the worksheet are to the entries in cells C18 and E18, because the projected gross revenue is calculated using the values in these cells.

Once you appreciate the necessity of isolating the assumptions and *initial conditions*, you can design the actual spreadsheet. Ask yourself why you are building the spreadsheet in the first place and what you hope to accomplish. (The financial forecast in this example is intended to answer questions regarding projected rates of growth, and more importantly, how changes in the assumptions and initial conditions will affect the income, expenses, and earnings in later years.) By clarifying what you hope to accomplish, you facilitate the creation of the spreadsheet, which is done in five general stages:

1. Enter the row and column headings, and the values for the initial conditions and the assumed rates of change.
2. Develop the formulas for the first year of the forecast based on the initial conditions at the bottom of the spreadsheet.
3. Develop the formulas for the second year based on the values in year one and the assumed rates of change.
4. Copy the formulas for year two to the remaining years of the forecast.
5. Format the spreadsheet, then print the completed forecast.

Projected revenues

Conditional formatting

Net income

Initial values

Projected percent increases

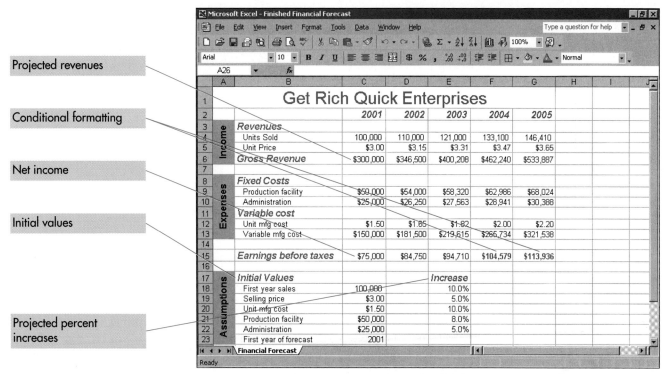

(a) Displayed Values

Rotated text

Indented text

Relative reference

Absolute reference

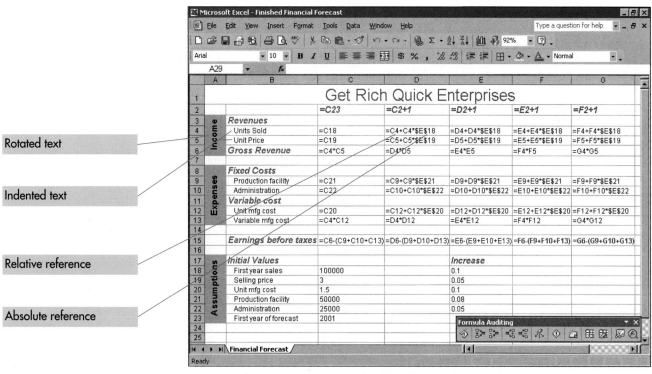

(b) Cell Formulas

FIGURE 6.1 *A Financial Forecast*

Perhaps the most critical step is the development of the formulas for the second year (2002 in Figure 6.1), which are based on the results for 2001 and the assumption about how these results will change for the next year. The units sold in 2002, for example, are equal to the sales in 2001 (cell C4) plus the estimated increase in unit sales (C4*$E$18); that is,

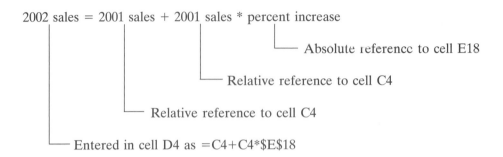

2002 sales = 2001 sales + 2001 sales * percent increase

— Absolute reference to cell E18

— Relative reference to cell C4

— Relative reference to cell C4

— Entered in cell D4 as =C4+C4*$E$18

The formula to compute the sales for the year 2002 uses both absolute and relative references, which ensures that it will be copied properly to the other columns for the remaining years in the forecast. An absolute reference ($E$18) is used for the cell containing the percent increase in unit sales, because this reference should remain the same when the formula is copied. A relative reference (C4) is used for the sales from the previous year, because this reference should change when the formula is copied. Many of the other formulas in column D are also based on percentage increases from column C, and are developed in similar fashion, as shown in Figure 6.1b.

Advanced Formatting

The spreadsheet in Figure 6.1 incorporates many of the formatting commands that have been used throughout the text. The spreadsheet also illustrates additional capabilities that will be implemented in the hands-on exercise that follows shortly. Some of these features are obvious, such as the ability to *rotate text* as seen in column A or the ability to *indent text* as was done in column B.

Other capabilities, such as *conditional formatting*, are more subtle. Look at the projected earnings, for example, and note that amounts over $100,000 are displayed in blue, whereas values under $100,000 are not. One could simply select the two cells and change the font color to blue, but as the earnings change, the cells would have to be reformatted. Accordingly, we implemented the color by selecting the entire row of projected earnings and specifying a conditional format to display the value in blue if it exceeds $100,000, display it in red if it is negative, and default to black otherwise. The use of conditional formatting lets you vary any of the assumptions or initial conditions, which in turn change the projected earnings, yet automatically display the projected earnings in the appropriate color.

The last formatting feature in Figure 6.1 is the imposition of a user-defined style (Main Heading) for various cells in the spreadsheet. A *style* (or *custom format*) is a set of formatting characteristics that is stored under a specific name. You've already used styles throughout the text that were predefined by Excel. Clicking the Comma, Currency, or Percent button on the Formatting toolbar, for example, automatically applies these styles to the selected cells. You can also define your own styles (e.g., Main Heading), as will be done in the hands-on exercise. The advantage of storing the formatting characteristics within a style, as opposed to applying the commands individually, is that you can change the definition of the style, which automatically changes the appearance of all cells defined by that style.

The **Scenario Manager** enables you to specify multiple sets of assumptions (**scenarios**), then see at a glance the results of any given scenario. Each scenario represents a different set of what-if conditions that you want to consider in assessing the outcome of a spreadsheet model. You could, for example, look at optimistic, pessimistic, and most likely (consensus) assumptions, as shown in Figure 6.2.

Figure 6.2a displays the Scenario Manager dialog box that contains the various scenarios that have been created. Each scenario is stored under its own name and is comprised of a set of cells whose values vary from scenario to scenario. Figure 6.2b, for example, shows the value of the **changing cells** for the consensus scenario. Figure 6.2c shows the values for the optimistic scenario. (The cells in the dialog box are identified by name, rather than cell reference through the **Define Name command** as will be shown in the next hands-on exercise. First_Year_Sales, for example, refers to cell C18 in the financial forecast. The use of a mnemonic name, as opposed to a cell reference, makes it much easier to understand precisely which values change from one scenario to the next.)

The **scenario summary** in Figure 6.2d compares the effects of the different scenarios to one another by showing the value of one or more **result cells**. We see, for example, that the consensus scenario yields earnings of $113,936 in the fifth year (the same value shown earlier) compared to significantly higher or lower values for the other two scenarios.

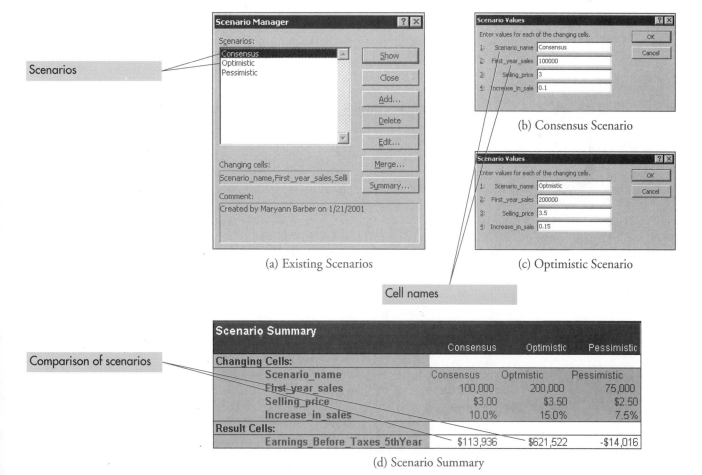

(a) Existing Scenarios   (b) Consensus Scenario   (c) Optimistic Scenario   (d) Scenario Summary

FIGURE 6.2 *Scenario Manager*

A FINANCIAL FORECAST

Objective To develop a spreadsheet for a financial forecast that isolates the assumptions and initial values; to use conditional formatting, styles, indentation, and rotated text to format the spreadsheet. Use Figure 6.3 as a guide in the exercise.

Step 1: **Enter the Formulas for Year One**

➤ Start Excel. Open the **Financial Forecast** workbook in the **Exploring Excel folder** to display the worksheet in Figure 6.3a. (Cells C4 through C15 are currently empty.)

➤ Click in **cell C2**. Type **=C23** and press **enter**. Note that you are not entering the year explicitly, but rather a reference to the cell that contains the year, which is located in the assumptions area of the worksheet.

➤ Enter the remaining formulas for year one of the forecast:
  • Click in **cell C4**. Type **=C18**. Click in **cell C5**. Type **=C19**.
  • Click in **cell C6**. Type **=C4*C5**. Click in **cell C9**. Type **=C21**.
  • Click in **cell C10**. Type **=C22**. Click in **cell C12**. Type **=C20**.
  • Click in **cell C13**. Type **=C4*C12**.
  • Click in **cell C15**. Type **=C6-(C9+C10+C13)**.

➤ The cell contents for year one (2001 in this example) are complete. The displayed values in this column should match the numbers shown in Figure 6.3a.

➤ Save the workbook as **Finished Financial Forecast** in the **Exploring Excel Folder** you have used throughout the text.

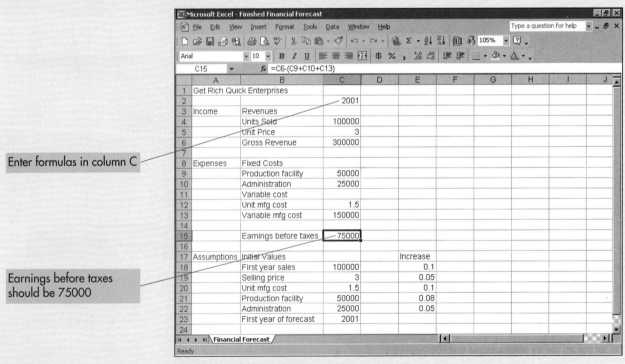

(a) Enter the Formulas for Year One (step 1)

FIGURE 6.3 *Hands-on Exercise 1*

Step 2: **Enter the Formulas for Year Two**

➤ Click in **cell D2**. Type **=C2+1** to determine the second year of the forecast.
➤ Click in **cell D4**. Type **=C4+C4*$E$18**. This formula computes the sales for year two as a function of the sales in year one and the rate of increase.
➤ Enter the remaining formulas for year two:
  • Click in **cell D5**. Type **=C5+C5*$E$19**. Copy the formula in cell C6 to D6.
  • Click in **cell D9**. Type **=C9+C9*$E$21**.
  • Click in **cell D10**. Type **=C10+C10*$E$22**.
  • Click in **cell D12**. Type **=C12+C12*$E$20**.
  • Copy the formulas in cells C13 and C15 to cells D13 and D15.
➤ The cell contents for the second year (2002) are complete. The displayed values should match the numbers shown in Figure 6.3b.
➤ Save the workbook.

Enter formulas in column D

Earnings before taxes should be 84750

(b) Enter the Formulas for Year Two (step 2)

FIGURE 6.3 *Hands-on Exercise 1 (continued)*

USE POINTING TO ENTER CELL FORMULAS

A cell reference can be typed directly into a formula, or it can be entered more easily through pointing. The latter is also more accurate as you use the mouse or arrow keys to reference cells directly. To use pointing, select (click) the cell to contain the formula, type an equal sign to begin entering the formula, click (or move to) the cell containing the reference, then press the F4 key as necessary to change from relative to absolute references. Type any arithmetic operator to place the cell reference in the formula, then continue pointing to additional cells. Press the enter key to complete the formula.

Step 3: **Copy the Formulas to the Remaining Years**

➤ Click and drag to select **cells D2** through **D15** (the cells containing the formulas for year two). Click the **Copy button** on the Standard toolbar (or use the **Ctrl+C** keyboard shortcut).

➤ A moving border will surround these cells to indicate that their contents have been copied to the clipboard.

➤ Click and drag to select **cells E2** through **G15** (the cells that will contain the formulas for years three to five). Point to the selection and click the **right mouse button** to display the context-sensitive menu in Figure 6.3c.

➤ Click **Paste** to paste the contents of the clipboard into the selected cells. The displayed values for the last three years of the forecast should be visible in the worksheet.

➤ You should see earnings before taxes of 113936 for the last year in the forecast. Press **Esc** to remove the moving border.

➤ Save the workbook.

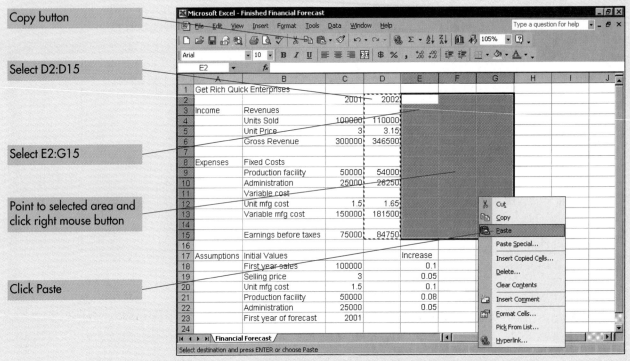

Copy button

Select D2:D15

Select E2:G15

Point to selected area and click right mouse button

Click Paste

(c) Copy the Formulas to the Remaining Years (step 3)

FIGURE **6.3** *Hands-on Exercise 1 (continued)*

THE FILL HANDLE

Use the fill handle (the tiny black square) that appears in the lower-right corner of the selected cells to copy a cell (or range of cells) to an adjacent range. Select the cell (cells) to be copied, then click and drag the fill handle over the destination range. Release the mouse to complete the operation.

Step 4: **Create a Style**

➤ Point to any toolbar, click the **right mouse button** to display a context-sensitive menu, then click the **Customize command** to display the Customize dialog box. Click the **Commands tab**, then select (click) the **Format category**.

➤ Click and drag the **Style List box** from within the command section to the right of the font color button on the Formatting toolbar. (You must drag the tool inside the toolbar and will see a large I-beam as you do so.)

➤ Release the mouse when you position the tool where you want. Click **Close** to close the Custom dialog box.

➤ The Style list box now appears on the Formatting toolbar as shown in Figure 6.3d. (The Style dialog box is not yet visible.) Click in **cell C2** and note that the Style list box indicates the Normal style (the default style for all cells in a worksheet).

➤ Change the font in cell C2 to **12 point Arial bold italic**. Click the **down arrow** on the Font Color tool and click **blue**. Pull down the **Format menu** and click the **Style command** to display the Style dialog box.

➤ The Normal style is already selected. Type **Main Heading** to define a new style according to the characteristics of the selected cell. Click **OK** to create the style and close the dialog box.

➤ Click and drag to select **cells D2** through **G2**. Click the down arrow on the Style list box and select the **Main Heading style** you just created to apply this style to the selected cells.

➤ Select **cell B3**. Press and hold the **Ctrl key** as you select **cells B6**, **B8**, **B11**, **B15**, **B17**, and **E17**, then apply the **Main Heading style** to these cells as well.

➤ Increase the width of column B so that you can see the text in cell B15.

➤ Save the workbook.

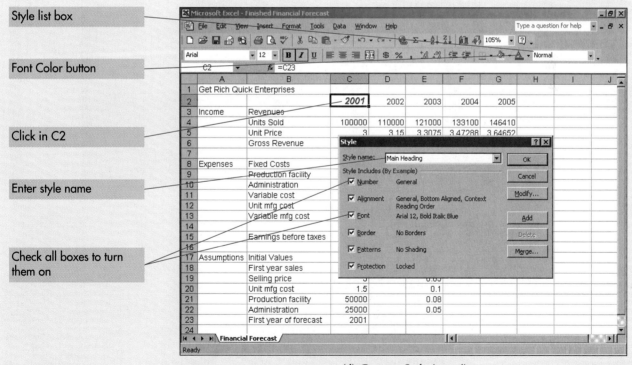

(d) Create a Style (step 4)

FIGURE 6.3 *Hands-on Exercise 1 (continued)*

Step 5:   **Rotate and Indent Text**

> ➤ Click and drag to select **cells A3** through **A6**, as shown in Figure 6.3e. Pull down the **Format menu** and click the **Cells command** to display the Format Cells dialog box shown in the figure.
>   • Click the **Alignment tab** and specify **center alignment** in both the horizontal and vertical list boxes. Check the box to **Merge cells**. Click in the **Degrees text box** and enter **90**.
>   • Click the **Font tab**, then change the font to **12 point Arial bold**. Change the font color to **blue**.
>   • Click the **Patterns tab** and choose **gray shading**.
>   • Click **OK** to accept these changes and close the Format Cells dialog box.
> ➤ Apply the same formatting to **cells A8** through **A13** and **A17** through **A23**. Select **cells A8** through **A13** and click the **Merge and Center button** on the Formatting toolbar. Select **cells A17** through **A23** and merge these cells as well.
> ➤ Click and drag to select the labels in **cells B4** and **B5**. Click the **Increase Indent button** on the Formatting toolbar to indent these labels.
> ➤ Press and hold the **Ctrl key** as you select **cells B9** and **B10**, **B12** and **B13**, and **B18** through **B23**. Click the **Increase Indent button** to indent these labels.

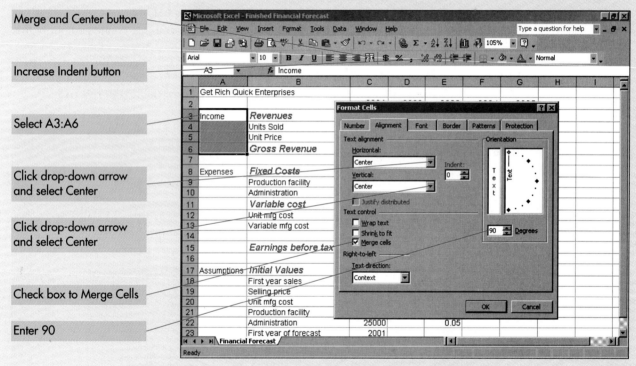

(e) Rotate and Indent Text (step 5)

FIGURE 6.3   *Hands-on Exercise 1 (continued)*

TOGGLE MERGE CELLS ON AND OFF

Click and drag to select multiple cells, then click the Merge and Center button on the Formatting toolbar to merge the cells into a single cell. Click in the merged cell, then click the Merge and Center button a second time and the cell is split. (This is different from Office 2000, where the only way to split cells was to clear the Merge cells check box within the Format Cells dialog box.)

Step 6:   **Conditional Formatting**

➤ Click and drag to select **cells C15** through **G15**. Pull down the **Format menu** and click the **Conditional Formatting** command to display the Conditional Formatting dialog box in Figure 6.3f.

➤ Set the relationships for condition 1. Click the **Format button** to display the Format Cells dialog box and click the **Font tab**. Change the font style to **bold** and the font color to **blue**. Click **OK**.

➤ Click the **Add button** and enter the parameters for condition 2. Click the **Format button**. Change the Font style to **bold** and the color to **red**. Click **OK**.

➤ Click **OK** to close the Conditional Formatting dialog box. Click any cell to de-select cells C15 to G15. The earnings before taxes for the last two years of the forecast are displayed in bold and in blue, since they exceed $100,000.

➤ Click in **cell C19**, change the selling price to **2.00**, and press the **enter key**. The earnings before taxes are displayed in red since they are negative for every year. Click the **Undo button** to return the initial sales price to 3.00.

➤ Save the workbook.

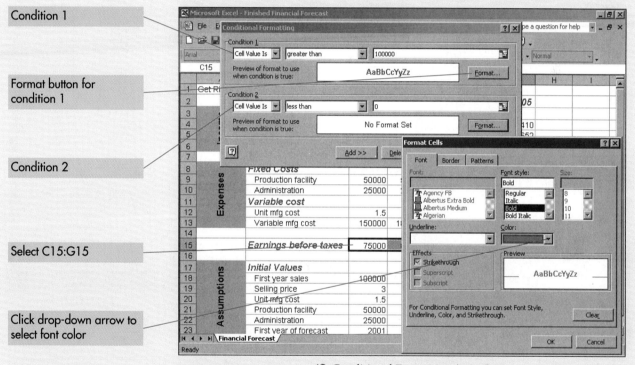

(f) Conditional Formatting (step 6)

FIGURE 6.3   *Hands-on Exercise 1 (continued)*

THE RIGHT MOUSE BUTTON

Point to a cell (or cell range), a worksheet tab, or a toolbar, then click the right mouse button to display a context-sensitive menu. Right clicking a cell, for example, displays a menu with selected commands from the Edit, Insert, and Format menus. Right clicking a toolbar displays a menu that lets you display or hide additional toolbars. Right clicking a worksheet tab enables you to rename, move, copy, or delete the worksheet.

Step 7: **Complete the Formatting**

➤ Click in **cell A1**. Change the font color to **blue**, and the font size to **22 points**. Click and drag to select **cells A1** through **G1** as shown in Figure 6.3g, then click the **Merge and Center button** to center the entry.

➤ Use Figure 6.3g as a guide to implement the appropriate formatting for the remaining entries in the worksheet. Remember to press and hold the **Ctrl key** if you want to select noncontiguous cells prior to executing a command.

➤ Add your name in **cell A2**. Save the workbook.

➤ Print the spreadsheet twice, once to show the displayed values and once to show the cell formulas. Press **Ctrl+~** to toggle between cell formulas and displayed values.

➤ Submit both printouts to your instructor.

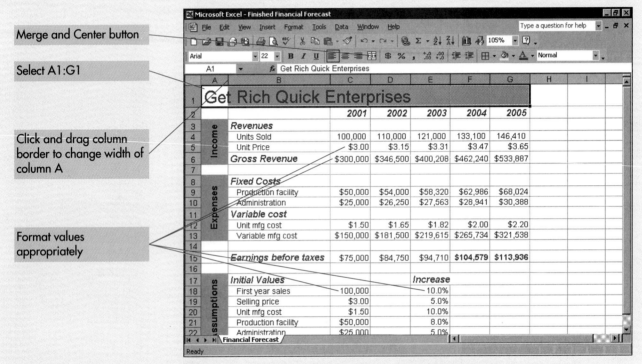

(g) Complete the Formatting (step 7)

FIGURE 6.3 *Hands-on Exercise 1 (continued)*

CREATE A CUSTOM VIEW

Format the spreadsheet to print the displayed values, then pull down the View menu and click Custom Views to display the Custom Views dialog box. Click the button to Add a view, enter the name (e.g., Displayed Values), and click OK. Press Ctrl+` to display the cell formulas, adjust the column widths as necessary, then pull down the View menu a second time to create a second custom view (e.g., Cell Formulas). You can switch to either view at any time by selecting the Custom Views command and selecting the appropriate view.

The Insert Name Command

> ➤ Click in **cell C18**, pull down the **Insert menu**, select the **Name command**, then click **Define** to display the Define Name dialog box in Figure 6.3h.
> ➤ **First_year_sales** is already entered as the default name (because this text appears as a label in the cell immediately to the left of the active cell. Underscores were added between the words, however, because blanks are not permitted in a cell name.) Click **OK** to accept this name.
> ➤ Name the other cells that will be used in the various scenarios in similar fashion. Use **Selling_price** as the name for **cell C19**, **Increase_in_sales** for **cell E18**, and **Scenario_name** for **cell E23**. (Do not be concerned that cell E23 is currently empty.)
> ➤ Save the workbook.

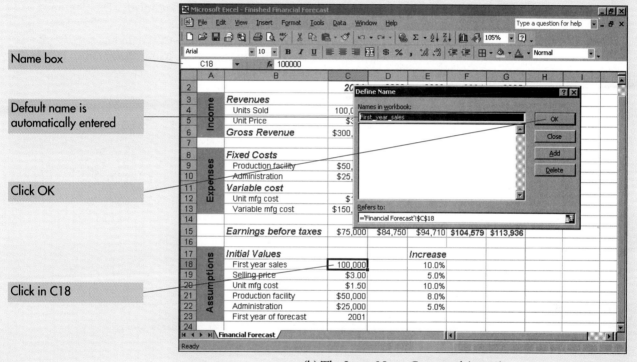

Name box

Default name is automatically entered

Click OK

Click in C18

(h) The Insert Name Command (step 8)

FIGURE 6.3   *Hands-on Exercise 1 (continued)*

THE NAME BOX

Use the Name box on the formula bar to define a named range, by first selecting the cell in the worksheet to which the name is to apply, clicking in the Name box to enter the range name, and then pressing the enter key. Once the name has been defined, you can use the Name box to select a named range by clicking in the box and then typing the appropriate cell reference or name or simply by clicking the drop-down arrow next to the Name box to select the cell from a drop-down list.

Step 9:   **Create the Scenarios**

➤ Click in **cell E23** and type the word **Consensus**. Click in **cell E17**, click the **Format Painter button** on the Formatting toolbar, then click in **cell E23** to copy the format from cell E17.

➤ Pull down the **Tools menu**. Click **Scenarios** to display the Scenario Manager dialog box. Click the **Add command button** to display the Add Scenario dialog box in Figure 6.3i. Type **Consensus** in the Scenario Name text box.

➤ Click in the **Changing Cells text box**. Cell E23 (the active cell) is already entered as the first cell in the scenario. Type a comma, then enter **C18**, **C19**, and **E18** as the remaining cells in the scenario. Click **OK**.

➤ You should see the Scenario Values dialog box with the values of this scenario already entered from the corresponding cells in the worksheet. Click **OK**.

➤ The Scenario Manager dialog box should still be open. Click the **Add command button** to add a second scenario called **Optimistic**. The changing cells are already entered and match the Consensus scenario. Click **OK**. Enter **Optimistic**, **200000**, **3.5**, and **.15**, as the values for the changing cells. Click **OK**.

➤ Enter a **Pessimistic scenario** in similar fashion, using **Pessimistic**, **75000**, **2.5**, and **.075**, for the changing cells. Click **OK**.

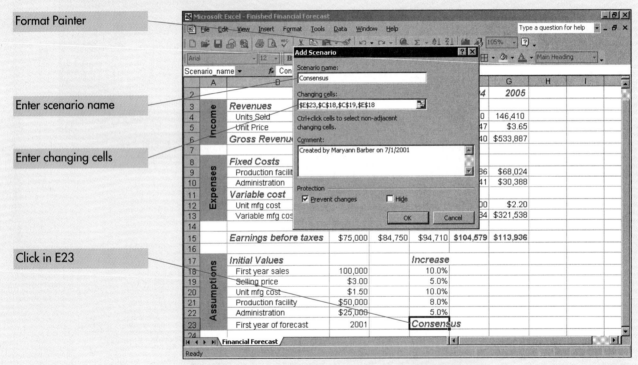

Format Painter

Enter scenario name

Enter changing cells

Click in E23

(i) Create the Scenarios (step 9)

FIGURE 6.3   *Hands-on Exercise 1 (continued)*

ISOLATE THE ASSUMPTIONS

The formulas in a worksheet should always be based on cell references that are clearly labeled, set apart from the rest of the worksheet. You can then vary the inputs (or assumptions) on which the worksheet is based to see the effect within the worksheet. You can change the values manually, or store sets of values within a specific scenario,

Step 10: **View the Scenarios**

➤ The Scenario Manager dialog box should still be open as shown in Figure 6.3j. If necessary, pull down the **Tools menu** and click the **Scenarios command** to reopen the Scenario Manager.

➤ There should be three scenarios listed—Consensus, Optimistic, and Pessimistic—corresponding to the scenarios that were just created.

➤ Select the **Optimistic scenario**, then click the **Show button** (or simply double click the scenario name) to display the financial forecast under the assumptions of this scenario.

➤ Double click the **Pessimistic scenario**, which changes the worksheet to show the forecast under these assumptions.

➤ Double click the **Consensus scenario** to return to this scenario. Do you see how easy it is to change multiple assumptions at one time by storing the values in a scenario?

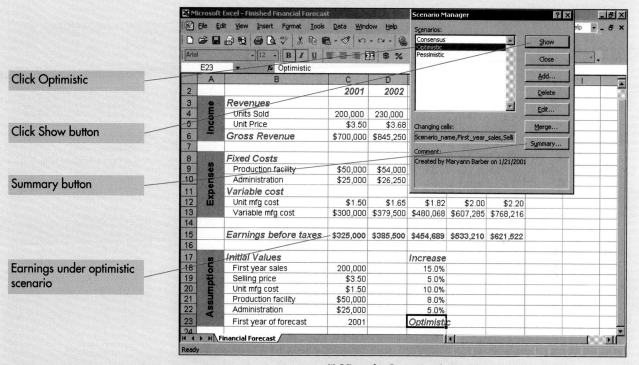

(j) View the Scenarios (step 10)

FIGURE 6.3 *Hands-on Exercise 1 (continued)*

THE SCENARIO MANAGER LIST BOX

The Scenario Manager List Box lets you select a scenario directly from a toolbar. Point to any toolbar, click the right mouse button to display a short-cut menu, then click Customize to display the Customize dialog box. Click the Commands tab, select Tools in the Categories list box, then click and drag the Scenario list box to an empty space on the toolbar. Click Close to close the dialog box and return to the workbook. Click the down arrow on the Scenario list box, which now appears on the toolbar, to choose from the scenarios that have been defined within the current workbook. See exercise 6 at the end of the chapter.

Step 11:   **The Scenario Summary**

➤ The Scenario Manager dialog box should still be open. Click the **Summary button** to display the Scenario Summary dialog box.

➤ If necessary, click the **Scenario Summary option button**. Click in the **Result Cells text box**, then click in **cell G15** (the cell that contains the earnings before taxes in the fifth year of the forecast). Click **OK**.

➤ You should see a Scenario Summary worksheet as shown in Figure 6.3k. Each scenario has its own column in the worksheet. The changing cells, identified by name rather than cell reference, are listed in column C.

➤ The Scenario Summary worksheet is an ordinary worksheet to the extent that it can be modified like any other worksheet. Right click the header for **row 6**, then press and hold the **Ctrl key** as you click and drag **rows 12** to **14**. Right click the selected cells, then click the **Delete command** from the context-sensitive menu.

➤ Delete Column D in similar fashion. Add your name to the worksheet. Save the workbook, then print the summary worksheet for your instructor.

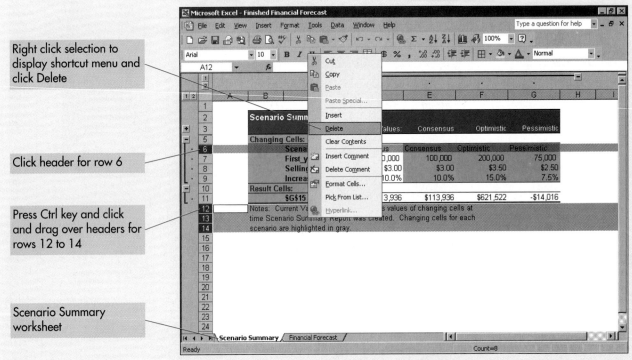

Right click selection to display shortcut menu and click Delete

Click header for row 6

Press Ctrl key and click and drag over headers for rows 12 to 14

Scenario Summary worksheet

(k) The Scenario Summary (step 11)

FIGURE 6.3   *Hands-on Exercise 1 (continued)*

THE SCENARIO SUMMARY WORKSHEET

You can return to the Scenario Manager to add or modify an individual scenario, after which you can create a new scenario summary. You must, however, modify the scenario from the original worksheet and not from the summary worksheet. Note, too, that each time you click the Summary button within the Scenario Manager, you will create another summary worksheet called Scenario Summary 2, Scenario Summary 3, and so on. You can delete the extraneous worksheets by right clicking the worksheet tab, then clicking the Delete command.

The spreadsheet containing the financial forecast is a tool that will be used by management as the basis for decision making. Executives in the company will vary the assumptions on which the spreadsheet is based to see the effects on profitability, then implement changes in policy based on the results of the spreadsheet. But what if the spreadsheet is in error? Think, for a moment, how business has become totally dependent on the spreadsheet, and what the consequences might be of basing corporate policy on an erroneous spreadsheet.

It's one thing if the assumptions about the expected increases turn out to be wrong, but the very nature of a forecast requires us to deal with uncertainty. It's inexcusable, however, if the formulas that use those numbers are invalid. Thus, it's common for several people to collaborate on the same spreadsheet to minimize the chance for error. One person creates the initial version, then distributes copies to the *workgroup* (the persons working on a project). Each person enters his or her changes, then the various workbooks can be merged into a single workbook. It's easier, however, to create a *shared workbook* and place it on a network drive to give all reviewers access to a common file.

Consider, for example, Figure 6.4, which displays an *invalid* version of the financial forecast. One of the first things you notice about Figure 6.4 is the comments by different people, Marion and Ben, who have reviewed the spreadsheet and suggested changes. Anyone with access to the shared workbook can change it using the tools on the *Reviewing toolbar* or through the *Track Changes command*. The changes made by different people to cell formulas are even displayed in different colors. You, as the developer, can then review the collective changes and resolve any conflicts that might occur.

How can you, or any of the reviewers, know when a spreadsheet displays invalid results? One way is to "eyeball" the spreadsheet and try to approximate its results.

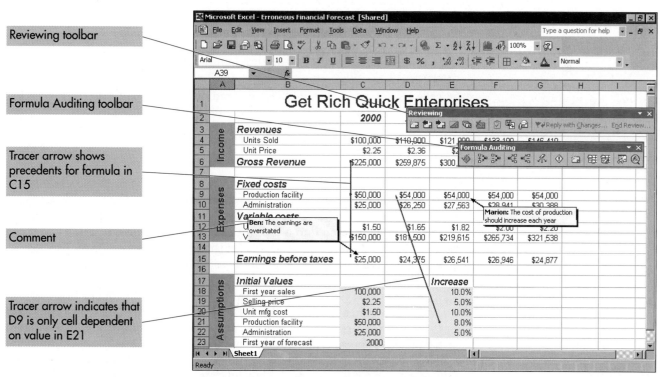

FIGURE 6.4   *Workgroups and Auditing*

Look for any calculations that are obviously incorrect. Look at the financial forecast, for example, and see whether all the values are growing at the projected rates of change. The number of units sold and the unit price increase every year as expected, but the cost of the production facility remains constant after 2001 (Marion's comment). This is an obvious error, because the production facility is supposed to increase at 8 percent annually, according to the assumptions at the bottom of the spreadsheet. The consequence of this error is that the production costs are too low and hence the projected earnings are too high. The error was easy to find, even without the use of a calculator.

A more subtle error occurs in the computation of the earnings before taxes. Look at the numbers for 2000. The gross revenue is $225,000. The total cost is also $225,000 ($50,000 for the production facility, $25,000 for administration, and $150,000 for the manufacturing cost). The projected earnings should be zero, but are shown incorrectly as $25,000 (Ben's comment), because the administration cost was not subtracted from the gross revenue in determining the profit.

You may be good enough to spot either of these errors just by looking at the spreadsheet. You can also use the *Formula Auditing toolbar* to display the relationships between the various cells in a worksheet. It enables you to trace the *precedents* for a formula and identify the cells in the worksheet that are referenced by that formula. It also enables you to trace the *dependents* of a cell and identify the formulas in the worksheet that reference that cell.

The identification of precedent and/or dependent cells is done graphically by displaying *tracers* on the worksheet. You simply click in the cell for which you want the information, then you click the appropriate button on the Formula Auditing toolbar. The blue lines (tracers) appear on the worksheet, and will remain on the worksheet until you click the appropriate removal button. The tracers always point forward, from the precedent cells to the dependent formula.

Look again at Figure 6.4 to see how the tracers are used. Cell C15 contains the formula to compute the earnings for the first year. There is a tracer (blue line) pointing to this cell and it indicates the precedents for the cell. In other words, we can see that cells C6, C9, and C13 are used to compute the value of cell C15. Cell C10 is not a precedent, however, and therein lies the error.

The analysis of the cost of the production facility is equally telling. There is a single tracer pointing away from cell E21, indicating that there is only one other cell (cell D9) in the worksheet that depends on the value of cell E21. In actuality, however, cells E9, F9, and G9 should also depend on the value of cell E21. Hence the cost of the production facility does not increase as it is supposed to.

Data Validation

The results of the financial forecast depend on the accuracy of the spreadsheet as well as the underlying assumptions. One way to stop such errors from occurring is through the *Data Validation command*, which enables the developer to restrict the values that can be entered into a cell. If the cell is to contain a text entry, you can limit the values to those that appear in a list such as Atlanta, Boston, or Chicago. In similar fashion, you can specify a quantitative relationship for numeric values such as > 0 or < 100.

Figure 6.5a displays the Settings tab in the Data Validation dialog box in which the developer requires the value in cell E18 (the annual sales increase) to be less than 15%. Figure 6.5b shows the type of error alert (a Warning) and the associated message that is to appear if the user does not enter a valid value. Figure 6.5c displays the dialog box the user sees if the criteria are violated, together with the indicated choice of actions. "Yes" accepts the invalid data into the cell despite the warning, "No" returns the user to the cell for further editing, and "Cancel" restores the previous value to the cell.

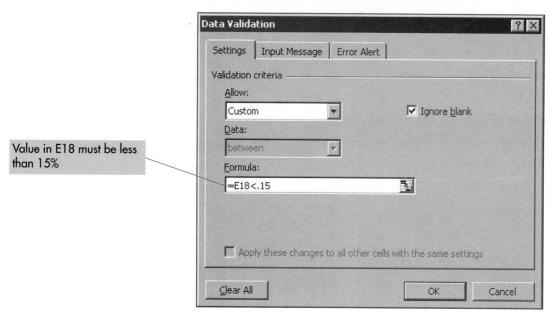

Value in E18 must be less than 15%

(a) Settings Tab

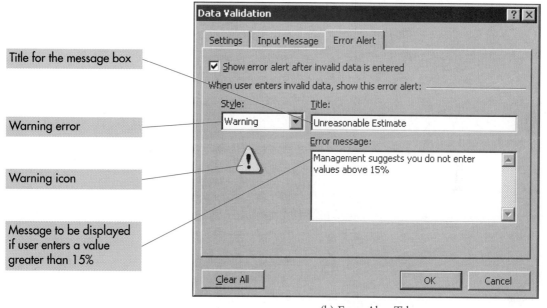

Title for the message box

Warning error

Warning icon

Message to be displayed if user enters a value greater than 15%

(b) Error Alert Tab

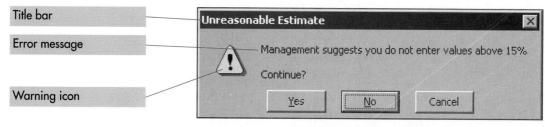

Title bar

Error message

Warning icon

(c) Displayed Error Message

FIGURE 6.5   *The Data Validation Command*

AUDITING AND WORKGROUPS

Objective To illustrate the tools on the Formula Auditing toolbar; to trace errors in spreadsheet formulas; to identify precedent and dependent cells; to insert and delete comments. Use Figure 6.6 as a guide in the exercise.

Step 1: **Display the Formula Auditing and Reviewing Toolbars**

> Open the **Erroneous Financial Forecast workbook** in the **Exploring Excel folder**. Save the workbook as **Finished Erroneous Financial Forecast**.
> Point to any toolbar, click the **right mouse button** to display a context-sensitive menu, then click **Customize** to display the Customize dialog box.
> Click the **Toolbars tab**, check the boxes for the **Reviewing** and **Formula Auditing toolbars**, then close the dialog box to display the toolbars, in Figure 6.6a.

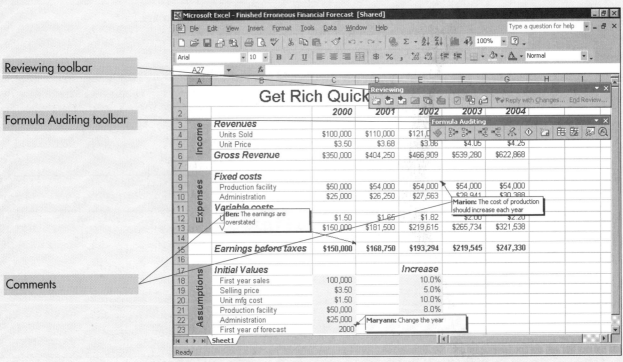

(a) Display the Formula Auditing and Reviewing Toolbars (step 1)

FIGURE 6.6 *Hands-on Exercise 2*

COMPARE AND MERGE WORKBOOKS

Send a copy of your workbook to one or more reviewers for comments, then merge the comments into the original workbook with a single command. Pull down the Tools menu and click the Share Workbook command, then check the box to allow changes by more than one user at a time. Send a copy of this shared workbook (with a unique file name) to each reviewer. Use the Merge and Compare workbooks command to combine the comments when they return the workbooks to you. See exercise 9 at the end of the chapter.

Step 2: **Highlight Changes**

➤ Pull down the **Tools menu**, click (or point to) the **Track Changes command**, then click **Highlight Changes** to display the Highlight Changes dialog box. Set the various options to match our selections in Figure 6.6b. Click **OK**.

➤ You should see a border around cell C19 to indicate that a change has been made to the contents of that cell. Point to the cell and you will see a ScreenTip indicating that Bob changed the contents from $2.25 to $3.50.

➤ Click in **cell C23**. Type **2001** to modify the year (as suggested by Maryann) and press **enter**. The years change automatically at the top of the forecast.

➤ Maryann's comment is now obsolete. Thus, right click in **cell C23** to display the context-sensitive menu, then click the **Delete Comment command**.

➤ The comment is removed from the cell and the red triangle disappears. The cell is still enclosed in a blue border to indicate that its value has changed.

➤ Click the **Hide All Comments button** on the Reviewing toolbar. The comments are still in the worksheet, but are no longer visible.

Track changes should be on

When should be set to A11

Highlight changes should be on

Show All/Hide All button

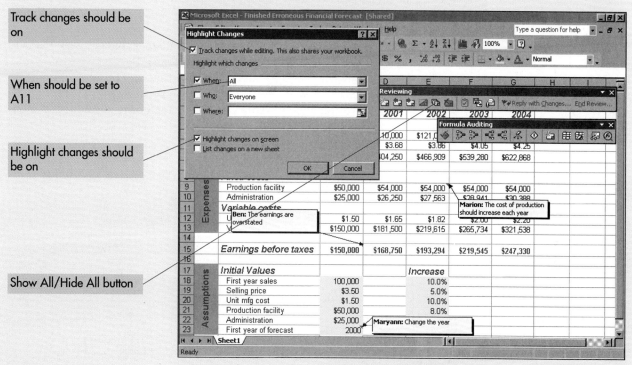

(b) Highlight Changes (step 2)

FIGURE 6.6 *Hands-on Exercise 2 (continued)*

CHANGE THE YEAR

A well-designed spreadsheet facilitates change by isolating the assumptions and initial conditions. 2000 has come and gone, but all you have to do to update the forecast is to click in cell C23, and enter 2001 as the initial year. The entries in cells C2 through G2 (containing years of the forecast) are changed automatically as they contain formulas (rather than specific values) that reference the value in cell C23.

Step 3: **Trace Dependents**

➤ Point to **cell E9** to display the comment, which indicates that the production costs do not increase after the second year. Click in **cell E21** (the cell containing the projected increase in the cost of the production facility).

➤ Click the **Trace Dependents button** on the Formula Auditing toolbar to display the dependent cells as shown in Figure 6.6c. Only one dependent cell (cell D9) is shown. This is clearly an error because cells E9 through G9 should also depend on cell E21.

➤ Click in **cell D9** to examine its formula. The production costs for the second year are based on the first-year costs (cell C9) and the rate of increase (cell E21). The latter, however, was entered as a relative rather than an absolute address.

➤ Change the formula in **cell D9** to include an absolute reference to cell E21 (i.e., the correct formula is =C9+C9*$E$21). The tracer arrow disappears due to the correction.

➤ Drag the fill handle in **cell D9** to copy the corrected formula to cells E9, F9, and G9. The displayed value for cell G9 should be $68,024. Delete Marion's comment in cell E9, which is no longer applicable.

➤ Cells D9 through G9 have a blue border to indicate that changes were made to these cells.

➤ Click in **cell E21**. Click the **Trace Dependents button**, and this time it points to the production costs for years two through five in the forecast.

➤ Click the **Remove Dependent Arrows button** on the Formula Auditing toolbar to remove the arrows.

➤ Save the workbook.

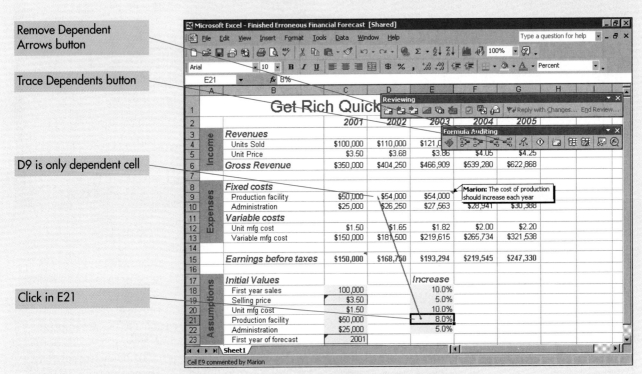

(c) Trace Dependents (step 3)

FIGURE 6.6 *Hands-on Exercise 2 (continued)*

Step 4: **Trace Precedents**

➤ Point to **cell C15** to display Ben's comment that questions the earnings before taxes. Now click the **Trace Precedents button** to display the precedent cells as shown in Figure 6.6d.

➤ There is an error in the formula because the earnings do not account for the administration expense (cell C10).

➤ Change the formula in cell C15 to **=C6-(C9+C10+C13)**. The earnings change to $125,000 after the correction.

➤ Drag the fill handle in **cell C15** to copy the corrected formula to cells D15 through G15. (The latter displays a value of $202,918 after the correction.)

➤ Delete Ben's comment in cell C15, which is no longer applicable.

➤ Save the workbook.

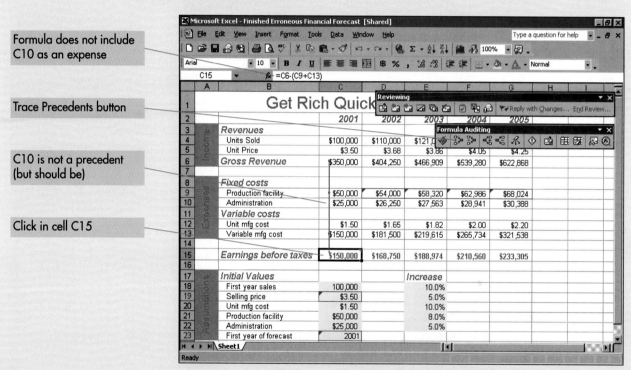

Formula does not include C10 as an expense

Trace Precedents button

C10 is not a precedent (but should be)

Click in cell C15

(d) Trace Precedents (step 4)

FIGURE 6.6 *Hands-on Exercise 2 (continued)*

THE FORMULAS ARE COLOR-CODED

The fastest way to change the contents of a cell is to double click in the cell, then make the changes directly in the cell rather than to change the entries on the formula bar. Note, too, that if the cell contains a formula (as opposed to a literal entry), Excel will display each cell reference in the formula in a different color, which corresponds to the border color of the referenced cells elsewhere in the worksheet. This makes it easy to see which cell or cell range is referenced by the formula. You can also click and drag the colored border to a different cell to change the cell formula.

Step 5: **Accept or Reject Changes (Resolve Conflicts)**

> ➤ Pull down the **Tools menu**, click the **Share Workbook command** to display the Share Workbook dialog box, then click the **Advanced tab**.
> ➤ Look for the Conflicting Changes Between Users section (toward the bottom of the dialog box), then if necessary, click the option button that says "Ask me which changes win". Click **OK**.
> ➤ Pull down the **Tools menu**, click (or point to) the **Track Changes command**, then click **Accept or Reject Changes**. You can accept the default selections in the Selection Changes dialog box. Click **OK**.
> ➤ You should see the Accept or Reject Changes dialog box in Figure 6.6e. Select (click) **$2.25**, the value that was entered by Caroline, then click the **Accept button**. (The contents of cell C19 change in the worksheet to $2.25, which in turn affects several other values throughout the spreadsheet.)
> ➤ Click **Accept** (or press **Ctrl+A**) to accept the next change, which was the change you made earlier in the first year of the forecast. Press the **Accept button** as you are presented with each additional change.

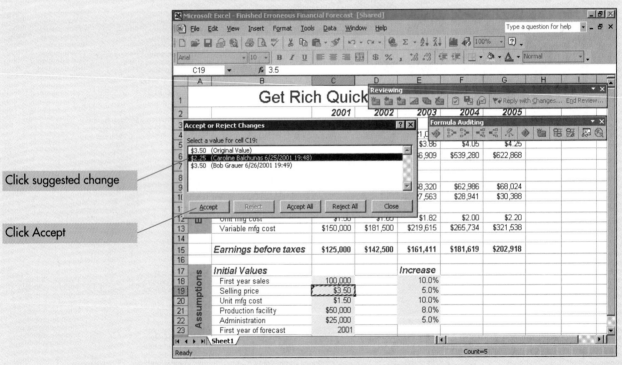

Click suggested change

Click Accept

(e) Accept or Reject Changes (Resolve Conflicts) (step 5)

FIGURE 6.6   *Hands-on Exercise 2 (continued)*

EDITING OR DELETING COMMENTS

The easiest way to edit or delete an existing comment is to point to the cell containing the comment, then click the right mouse button to display a context-sensitive menu, in which you select the appropriate command. You can use the right mouse button to insert a comment by right clicking in the cell, then choosing the Insert Comment command.

Step 6: **Insert a Comment**

➤ Click in **cell C19** (the cell containing the selling price for the first year). Pull down the **Insert menu** and click the **Comment command** (or click the **New Comment button** on the Reviewing toolbar).

➤ A comment box opens, as shown in Figure 6.6f. Enter the text of your comment as shown in the figure, then click outside the comment when you are finished.

➤ The comment box closes, but a tiny red triangle appears in the upper-right corner of cell C19. (If you do not see the triangle, pull down the **Tools menu**, click **Options**, click the **View tab**, then click the option button in the Comments area to show **Comment Indicator only**.)

➤ Point to **cell C19** and the text of your comment appears as part of the ScreenTip. Point to a different cell and the comment disappears.

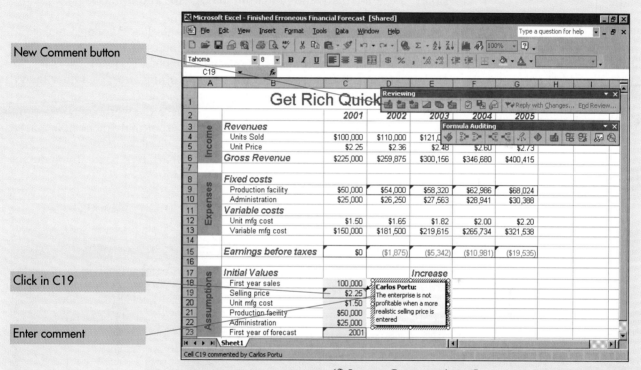

(f) Insert a Comment (step 6)

FIGURE 6.6 *Hands-on Exercise 2 (continued)*

LIMITATIONS OF SHARED WORKBOOKS

A shared workbook enables multiple people to view and/or modify a workbook simultaneously, but many of the more sophisticated features are disabled. You cannot, for example, delete worksheets, merge cells, apply conditional formats, or insert a hyperlink. Nor can you use subtotals, group or outline data, create a pivot table, or implement data validation. To use these features, you must remove the workbook from shared status as described in the next step.

Step 7: **Data Validation**

> ➤ Click in cell **E18**. Type **.18**. Excel displays the error message shown in Figure 6.6g. Press **Esc** to cancel and try another entry. No matter how many times you try, you will not be able to enter a value above .15 in cell E18 because the error type was specified as "Stop" rather than a warning.
> ➤ Pull down the **Data menu**. The Validation command is dim and not currently accessible because the workbook is currently a shared workbook.
> ➤ Pull down the **Tools menu**, click (or point to) the **Track Changes command**, then click **Highlight Changes** to display the Highlight Changes dialog box. Clear the box to track changes while editing. Click **OK**. Click **Yes** when prompted to remove the workbook from shared use.
> ➤ Pull down the **Data menu**. Click the **Validation command** (which is now accessible) to display the Data Validation dialog box, and if necessary, click the **Error Alert tab**.
> ➤ Click the **drop-down arrow** on the Style list box and click **Warning**. Change the text of the message to **Management frowns on values of 15% or higher**. Click **OK** to accept the new settings and close the dialog box.
> ➤ Reenter **.18** in **cell E18**. This time you see a Warning message, rather than a Stop message. Click **Yes** to accept the new value.
> ➤ Add your name somewhere in the workbook. Save the workbook, then print the completed workbook for your professor as proof that you completed the exercise.
> ➤ Close the Reviewing and Formula Auditing toolbars. Exit Excel if you do not want to continue with the next exercise at this time.

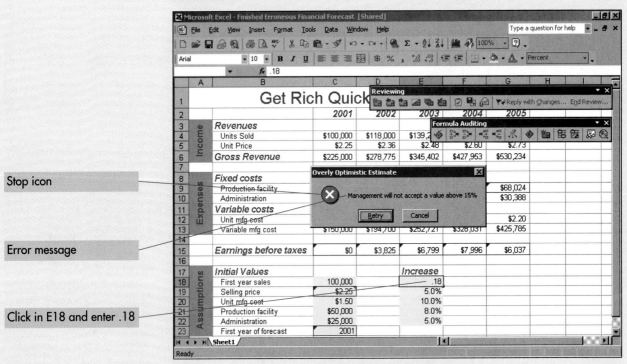

(g) Data Validation (step 7)

FIGURE 6.6 *Hands-on Exercise 2 (continued)*

The spreadsheet just completed is tailored to the needs of financial forecasting for Get Rich Quick Enterprises. It could also serve as the basis of a financial forecast for any organization, which leads in turn to the creation of a template. A *template* is a special type of workbook (it has its own file format) that is used as the basis for other workbooks. It contains text, formatting, formulas, and/or macros, but it does not contain data; the latter is entered by the end-user as he or she uses the template to create a workbook.

Figure 6.7a contains the template you will create in the next hands-on exercise. It resembles the completed forecast from earlier in the chapter, except that the assumption area has been cleared of all values except the initial year of the forecast. Even the name of the company in cell A1 has been erased. Look at the active cell (cell C15), however, and note that its contents are visible in the Formula bar. Thus, you can see that the template contains the formulas from the worksheet, but without any data. (The results of the calculations within the body of the spreadsheet are uniformly zero, but the zeros are suppressed through an option set through the Tools menu.)

The template in Figure 6.7a is used to create specific forecasts such as the one in Figure 6.7b. Look closely at the entry in the title bar for that forecast, noting that it appears as Get Rich Quick1; that is, the number 1 has been appended to the name of the template. This is done automatically by Excel, which will add the next sequential number to the name of each additional forecast during a session. To create a specific forecast, just enter the desired values in the assumption area, then as each value is entered, the formulas in the body of the spreadsheet will automatically calculate the results.

Most templates are based on *protected worksheets* that enable the user to modify only a limited number of cells within the worksheet. The template for financial forecast, for example, enables the user to change the contents of any cell in the assumption area, but precludes changes elsewhere in the worksheet. This is very important, especially when templates are used throughout an organization. The protection prevents an individual who is not familiar with Excel from accidentally (or otherwise) changing a cell formula. Any attempt to do so produces a protected-cell message on the screen.

To create a template, you start with a finished workbook and check it for accuracy. Then you clear the assumption area and protect the worksheet. The latter is a two-step process. First, you *unlock* all of the cells that are subject to change, then you protect the worksheet. Once this is done, the user will be able to change the value of any cell that was unlocked, but will be unable to change the contents of any other cell. Finally, you save the template under its own name, but as a template rather than an ordinary workbook. (Ideally, the template should be saved in a special *Templates folder* within the Microsoft Office folder so that it can be accessed automatically from the task pane. This is possible only if you have your own computer and/or if the network administrator puts the template in the folder for you.)

Once created, a template can be accessed three different ways—through the File Open command, from the task pane, or by double clicking its icon from within Windows Explorer or My Computer. The File Open command opens the actual template, enabling you to modify the template if and when that becomes necessary. The task pane provides a link to General Templates that combines the function of the File Open command with that of the Save As command. It opens a template and automatically saves it as a workbook, assigning a name to the workbook by appending a number to the name of the template (e.g., Get Rich Quick1). Double clicking a file from within My Computer or Windows Explorer has the same effect as accessing the template from the task pane.

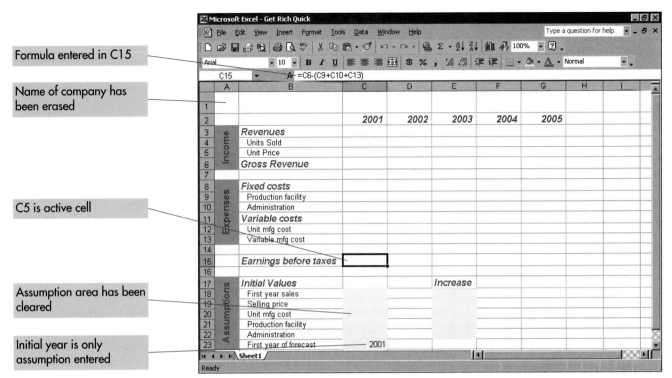

Formula entered in C15

Name of company has been erased

C5 is active cell

Assumption area has been cleared

Initial year is only assumption entered

(a) Template

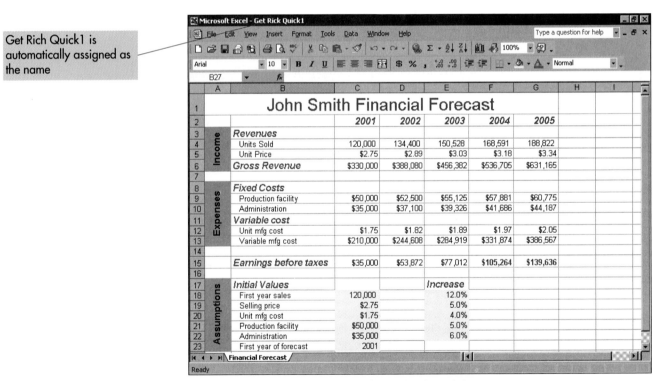

Get Rich Quick1 is automatically assigned as the name

(b) Completed Worksheet

FIGURE 6.7   *The Get Rich Quick Template*

CREATING A TEMPLATE

Objective To unlock cells in a worksheet, then protect the worksheet; to create a template and then create a workbook from that template. Use Figure 6.8.

Step 1: **Clear the Assumption Area**

> ➤ Open the **Finished Erroneous Financial Forecast** from the previous exercise. Click in **cell A1**, then press and hold the **Ctrl key** as you click and drag to select **cells C18** through **E23**.
> ➤ Pull down the **Edit menu**, click (or point to) the **Clear command**, then click **Contents** to delete the contents from the selected cells as shown in Figure 6.8a. The values in the body of the spreadsheet are all zero.
> ➤ Pull down the **Edit menu** a second time, click the **Clear command**, then click **Comments** to delete the comments from these cells as well.

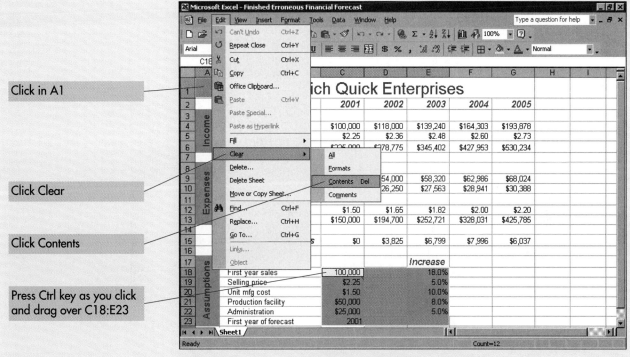

Click in A1

Click Clear

Click Contents

Press Ctrl key as you click and drag over C18:E23

(a) Clear the Assumption Area (step 1)

FIGURE 6.8 *Hands-on Exercise 3*

WORKBOOK PROPERTIES

Do you know the original author of the workbook or other Office document that is currently open? When was the file created, modified, and last accessed? This and other information are stored within the workbook and can be viewed (or changed) by pulling down the File menu and clicking the Properties command.

Step 2: **Protect the Worksheet**

➤ Protecting a worksheet is a two-step process. First you unlock the cells that you want to be able to change after the worksheet has been protected, then you protect the worksheet. Accordingly:
- If necessary, click in **cell A1**, then press and hold the **Ctrl key** as you click and drag to select **cells C18** through **E23**. Pull down the **Format menu**, click the **Cells command** to display the Format Cells dialog box. Click the **Protection tab**, then clear the **Locked check box**. Click **OK**.
- Pull down the **Tools menu**, click **Protection**, then click the **Protect Sheet command** to display the Protect Sheet dialog box in Figure 6.8b. Be sure that your settings match those in the figure, then click **OK**.

➤ Pull down the **Tools menu**, click the **Options command**, click the **View tab** and clear the box to show Zero values. Click **OK**. The zeros disappear.

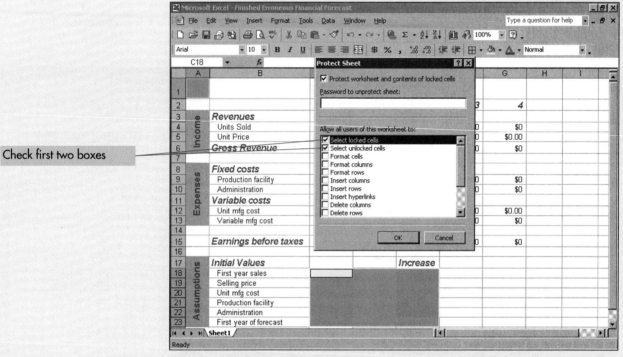

(b) Protect the Worksheet (step 2)

FIGURE 6.8 *Hands-on Exercise 3 (continued)*

THE OPTIONS MENU

Pull down the Tools menu and click the Options command to display the Options dialog box from where you can customize virtually every aspect of Excel. The General tab is especially useful as it enables you to change the default file location, the number of worksheets in a new workbook, and/or the number of recently opened files that appear on the File menu. There is no need to memorize anything, just spend a few minutes exploring the options on the various tabs, then think of the Options command the next time you want to change an Excel feature.

Step 3: **Test the Template**

➤ Test the assumption area to be sure that you can change the contents of these cells. Click in **cell A1** and enter your name followed by the words **Financial Forecast**. The text will be centered automatically across the top of the worksheet.

➤ Click in **cell C23**, type **2001**, and press the **enter key**. Excel should accept this value, and in addition, it should change the years as shown in Figure 6.8c. Enter the values **100000** and **.10** in **cells C18** and **E18**, respectively. Excel should accept these values and build the spreadsheet accordingly.

➤ If you are prevented from entering a value in the assumption area, you need to unprotect the worksheet and unlock the cells.

 • Pull down the **Tools menu**, click **Protection**, then click the **Unprotect Sheet command**.

 • Select the cells in the assumption area, pull down the **Format menu**, click the **Cells command**, click the **Protection tab**, and clear the Locked box.

 • Repeat the steps to protect the worksheet.

➤ Test the protection feature by clicking in any cell in the body of the worksheet (e.g., cell C5) and entering a value. You should see the dialog box in Figure 6.8c indicating that the cell is protected. Click **OK**. If you do not see this message, undo the entry and then repeat the commands to protect the worksheet.

➤ Clear the contents from **cells A1**, **C18**, **E18**, and **C23**. You're ready to save the template.

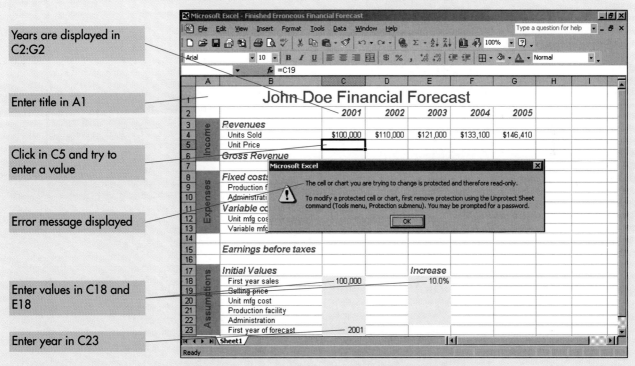

(c) Test the Template (step 3)

FIGURE 6.8 *Hands-on Exercise 3 (continued)*

Step 4:   **Save the Template**

➤ Pull down the **File menu**, click the **Save As command** to display the Save As dialog box in Figure 6.8d. Enter **Get Rich Quick** as the name of the template.
➤ Click the **down arrow** in the Save as Type list box and choose **Template**. The folder where you will save the template depends on whether you have your own machine.
  • If you are working on your own computer and have access to all of its folders, save the template in the **Templates folder** (the default folder that is displayed automatically).
  • If you are working at school or otherwise sharing a computer, save the template in the **Exploring Excel folder** that you have used throughout the text.
➤ Click the **Save button** to save the template.

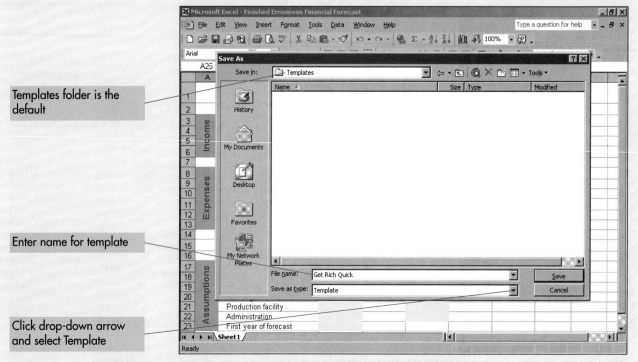

Templates folder is the default

Enter name for template

Click drop-down arrow and select Template

(d) Save the Template (step 4)

FIGURE 6.8   *Hands-on Exercise 3 (continued)*

PROTECT THE WORKBOOK

A template or workbook is not truly protected unless it is saved with a password, because a knowledgeable user can always pull down the Tools menu and access the Protect command to unprotect a worksheet. You can, however, use password protection to prevent this from happening. Pull down the File menu, click the Save As command to the Save As dialog box, then click the Tools button and click General Options to display the Save Options dialog box. You can enter one or two passwords, one to open the file, and one to modify it. Be careful, however, because once you save a workbook or template with a password, you cannot open it if you forget the password.

Step 5:   **Open the Template**

➤ Close Excel, then restart the program. The way in which you open the template depends on where you saved in the previous step.
  • If you are working on your own computer, open the task pane and click the link to **General Templates** to display the dialog box in Figure 6.8e. The Get Rich Quick template appears automatically because it was saved in the Templates folder. Double click the **Get Rich Quick template** to open it.
  • If you are working at school or otherwise sharing a computer, start Windows Explorer, change to the **Exploring Excel folder**, then double click the **Get Rich Quick template** to open it.
➤ You should see a blank workbook, named Get Rich Quick1. Excel automatically saves a copy of the template as a workbook and assigns it a name consisting of the template's name followed by a number.
➤ Complete and save the financial forecast. Print the completed workbook with displayed values and with the cell formulas. Exit Excel.

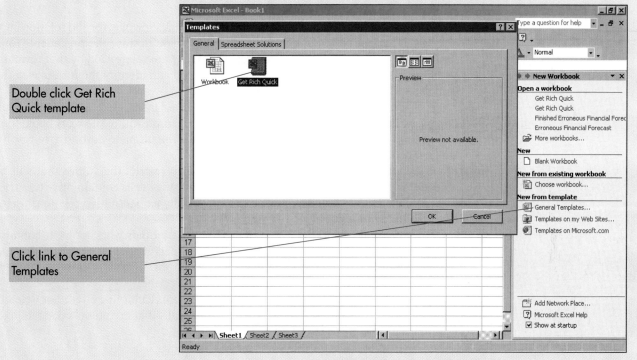

Double click Get Rich Quick template

Click link to General Templates

(e) Open the Template (step 5)

FIGURE 6.8   *Hands-on Exercise 3 (continued)*

CREATE A CHART AND ASSOCIATED TREND LINE

A chart adds impact to any type of numerical analysis. Use the template to create a financial forecast, then plot the earnings before taxes against the associated year. A simple column chart is best. Pull down the Chart menu after the chart has been drawn, then click the Add Trendline command to display the associated dialog box. Click Type tab and choose a linear (straight-line) trend. (You cannot add trendlines to data series in 3-D, stacked-column, or pie charts.) Click OK to accept the setting and close the dialog box. Print the chart for your instructor.

A spreadsheet is used frequently as a tool in decision making, and as such, is the subject of continual what-if speculation. Thus, the initial conditions and assumptions on which the spreadsheet is based should be clearly visible so that they can be easily varied. In addition, the formulas in the body of the spreadsheet should be dependent on these cells.

A style is a set of formatting instructions that has been saved under a distinct name. Styles provide a consistent appearance to similar elements throughout a workbook. Existing styles can be modified to change the formatting of all cells that are defined by that style.

The Scenario Manager lets you specify multiple sets of assumptions (scenarios), then see the results at a glance within the associated worksheet. The scenario summary compares the effects of the different scenarios to one another by showing the value of one or more result cells in a summary table.

Conditional formatting may be implemented to change the appearance of a cell based on its calculated value. The text in a cell may be rotated vertically to give the cell greater emphasis.

The Formula Auditing toolbar provides a graphical display for the relationships among the various cells in a worksheet. It enables you to trace the precedents for a formula and identify the cells in the worksheet that are referenced by that formula. It also enables you to trace the dependents of a cell and identify the formulas in the worksheet that reference that cell.

A shared workbook may be viewed and/or edited by multiple individuals simultaneously. The changes made by each user can be stored within the workbook, then subsequently reviewed by the developer, who has the ultimate authority to resolve any conflicts that might occur.

The Data Validation command enables you to restrict the values that will be accepted into a cell. You can limit the values to a list for cells containing text entries (e.g., Atlanta, Boston, or Chicago), or you can specify a quantitative relationship for cells that hold numeric values.

A template is a workbook that is used to create other workbooks. It contains text, formatting, formulas, and/or macros, but no specific data. A template that has been saved to the Templates or Spreadsheet Solutions folder is accessed automatically from the link to General Templates in the task pane.

A worksheet may be protected so that its contents cannot be altered or deleted. A protected worksheet may also contain various cells that are unlocked, enabling a user to vary the contents of these cells.

Assumptions (p. 262)
Changing cells (p. 265)
Conditional formatting (p. 264)
Custom format (p. 264)
Custom view (p. 272)
Data Validation command (p. 278)
Define Name command (p. 265)
Dependent cells (p. 278)
Formula Auditing toolbar (p. 278)
Indent text (p. 264)

Initial conditions (p. 262)
Insert Comment command (p. 285)
Insert Name command (p. 273)
Precedent cells (p. 278)
Protected worksheet (p. 287)
Result cells (p. 265)
Reviewing toolbar (p. 277)
Rotate text (p. 264)
Scenario (p. 265)
Scenario Manager (p. 265)

Scenario summary (p. 265)
Shared workbook (p. 277)
Style (p. 264)
Template (p. 287)
Templates folder (p. 287)
Tracers (p. 278)
Track Changes command (p. 277)
Unlock cells (p. 287)
Workgroup (p. 277)

1. Which of the following best describes the formula to compute the sales in the second year of the financial forecast?
   (a) It contains a relative reference to the assumed rate of increase and an absolute reference to the sales from the previous year
   (b) It contains an absolute reference to the assumed rate of increase and a relative reference to the sales from the previous year
   (c) It contains absolute references to both the assumed rate of increase and the sales from the previous year
   (d) It contains relative references to both the assumed rate of increase and the sales from the previous year

2. The estimated sales for the first year of a financial forecast are contained in cell B3. The sales for year two are assumed to be 10% higher than the first year, with the rate of increase (10%) stored in cell C23 at the bottom of the spreadsheet. Which of the following is the best way to enter the projected sales for year two, assuming that this formula is to be copied to the remaining years of the forecast?
   (a) =B3+B3*.10
   (b) =B3+B3*C23
   (c) =B3+B3*$C$23
   (d) All of the above are equivalent entries

3. Which of the following describes the placement of assumptions in a worksheet as required by Microsoft Excel?
   (a) The assumptions must appear in contiguous cells but can be placed anywhere within the worksheet
   (b) The assumptions must appear in contiguous cells and, further, must be placed below the main body of the worksheet
   (c) The assumptions are not required to appear in contiguous cells and, further, can be placed anywhere within the worksheet
   (d) None of the above

4. Given that cell D4 contains the formula =D1+D2:
   (a) Cells D1 and D2 are precedent cells for cell D4
   (b) Cell D4 is a dependent cell of cells D1 and D2
   (c) Both (a) and (b)
   (d) Neither (a) nor (b)

5. Which of the following is true, given that cell C23 is displayed with three blue tracers that point to cells E4, F4, and G4, respectively?
   (a) Cells E4, F4, and G4, and precedent cells for cell C23
   (b) Cell C23 is a precedent cell for cells E4, F4, and G4
   (c) Both (a) and (b)
   (d) Neither (a) nor (b)

6. How can you enter a comment into a cell?
   (a) Click the New Comment command on the Formula Auditing toolbar
   (b) Click the New Comment command on the Reviewing toolbar
   (c) Right click in the cell, then select the Insert Comment command
   (d) All of the above

7. Which of the following best describes how to protect a worksheet, but still enable the user to change the value of various cells within the worksheet?
   (a) Protect the entire worksheet, then unlock the cells that are to change
   (b) Protect the entire worksheet, then unprotect the cells that are to change
   (c) Unprotect the cells that are to change, then protect the entire worksheet
   (d) Unlock the cells that are to change, then protect the entire worksheet

8. Which of the following describes the protection associated with the financial forecast that was developed in the chapter?
   (a) The worksheet is protected and all cells are locked
   (b) The worksheet is protected and all cells are unlocked
   (c) The worksheet is protected and the assumption area is locked
   (d) The worksheet is protected and the assumption area is unlocked

9. Which of the following may be stored within a style?
   (a) The font, point size, and color
   (b) Borders and shading
   (c) Alignment and protection
   (d) All of the above

10. What is the easiest way to change the formatting of five cells that are scattered throughout a worksheet, each of which has the same style?
    (a) Select the cells individually, then click the appropriate buttons on the Formatting toolbar
    (b) Select the cells at the same time, then click the appropriate buttons on the Formatting toolbar
    (c) Change the format of the existing style
    (d) Reenter the data in each cell according to the new specifications

11. Each scenario in the Scenario Manager:
    (a) Is stored in a separate worksheet
    (b) Contains the value of a single assumption or input condition
    (c) Both (a) and (b)
    (d) Neither (a) nor (b)

12. The Formula Auditing and Reviewing toolbars are floating toolbars by default. Which of the following is (are) true about fixed (docked) and floating toolbars?
    (a) Floating toolbars can be changed to fixed toolbars, but the reverse is not true
    (b) Fixed toolbars can be changed into floating toolbars, but the reverse is not true
    (c) Fixed toolbars can be changed into floating toolbars and vice versa
    (d) Fixed toolbars can be displayed only at the top of the screen

13. You open a template called Expense Account but see Expense Account1 displayed on the title bar. What is the most likely explanation?
    (a) You are the first person to use this template
    (b) Some type of error must have occurred
    (c) All is in order since Excel has appended the number to differentiate the workbook from the template on which it is based
    (d) The situation is impossible

14. Two adjacent cells within the worksheet are enclosed in hairline borders of different colors. Each of these cells also contains a tiny shaded triangle in the upper-left part of the cell. Which of the following is the most likely explanation?
    (a) Conditional formatting is in effect for the cells in question
    (b) Data validation is in effect for the cells in question
    (c) A comment has been entered into each of the cells
    (d) The cells have been changed by different members of a workgroup

ANSWERS

1. b	**6.** d	**11.** d
2. c	**7.** d	**12.** c
3. c	**8.** d	**13.** c
4. c	**9.** d	**14.** d
5. a	**10.** c	

1. **Erroneous Payroll:** The worksheet in Figure 6.9 displays an *erroneous* version of a worksheet that computes the payroll for a fictitious company. The worksheet is nicely formatted, but several calculations are in error. You can find the worksheet shown in Figure 6.9 in the *Chapter 6 Practice 1* workbook within the Exploring Excel folder.

   Your assignment is to open the workbook, find the errors, and correct the worksheet. The *correct* specifications are shown below:

   a. The taxable income is the gross pay, minus the deduction per dependent, multiplied by the number of dependents.

   b. The withholding tax is based on the individual's taxable income. The Social Security tax is based on the individual's gross pay.

   c. The overtime bonus is entered as an assumption within the worksheet, making it possible to change the overtime rate in a single place should that become necessary.

   d. The net pay is the gross pay minus the withholding tax and the Social Security tax.

   e. You can "eyeball" the worksheet to find the mistakes and/or you can use the Formula Auditing toolbar. Figure 6.9, for example, displays the precedent cells for computing the withholding tax for the first employee and reveals the first error (i.e., that the withholding tax is incorrectly computed on the gross pay rather than on the taxable income).

   f. Print the corrected worksheet with both displayed values and cell formulas. Add a cover sheet and submit the assignment to your instructor. Do you see the importance of checking a worksheet for accuracy?

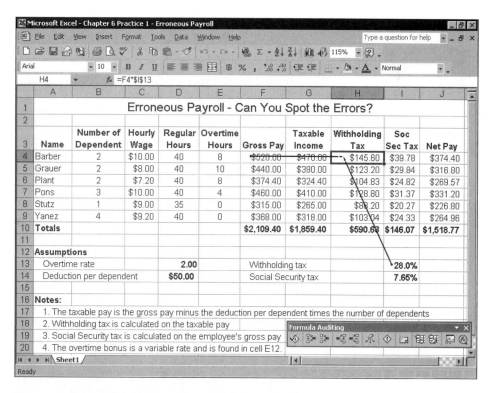

FIGURE 6.9 *Erroneous Payroll (Exercise 1)*

BUILDS ON

CHAPTER 3
PRACTICE
EXERCISE 1
PAGE 156

2. Protection and Validation: The worksheet in Figure 6.10 will calculate the value of your retirement based on a set of uniform annual contributions to a retirement account. In essence, you contribute a fixed amount of money each year ($2,000 in Figure 6.10) and the money accumulates at an estimated rate of return (9% in Figure 6.10). You indicate the age when you start to contribute, your projected retirement age, the number of years in retirement, and the rate of return you expect to earn on your money when you retire.

a. The worksheet determines the total amount you will have contributed, the amount of money you will have accumulated, and the value of your monthly pension. The numbers are impressive, and the sooner you begin to save, the better. The calculations use the Future Value (FV) and Payment (Pmt) functions, respectively. These functions are discussed in Chapter 3.

b. You will find the completed worksheet in the *Chapter 6 Practice 2* workbook in the Exploring Excel folder. Your assignment is to implement data validation and password protection to ensure that the user does not enter unrealistic numbers nor alter the formulas within the worksheet.

c. Three validity checks are required as indicated in the assumption area of the worksheet. The retirement age must be 59.5 or greater (as required by current law), the rate of return during the period you are investing money cannot exceed 8%, and the rate of return during retirement cannot exceed 7%. You are to display a warning message similar to that in Figure 6.10 if the user violates any of these conditions. The warning will allow the user to override the assumptions.

d. Unlock cells B2 through B8, where the user enters his or her name and assumptions. Protect the remainder of the worksheet. Use "password" as the password.

e. Enter your name and your assumptions in the completed worksheet, then print the worksheet twice to show both displayed values and cell formulas for your instructor.

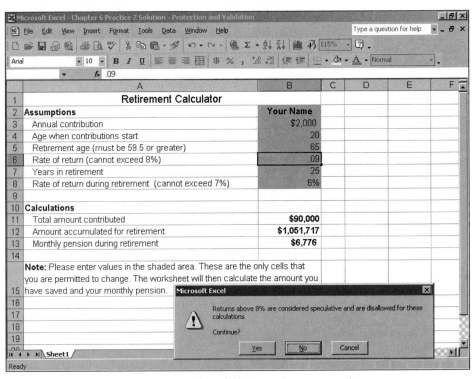

FIGURE 6.10   *Protection and Validation (Exercise 2)*

3. Retirement Scenarios: The worksheet in Figure 6.11 illustrates a retirement plan in which you and your employer each contribute a percentage of your salary toward your retirement. (The percentages are not necessarily equal, although Figure 6.11 shows the same percentage for both you and your employer.) The money accumulates for a specified number of years, at the specified rate of return. At that point, the "nest egg" or future value of the combined contributions will be used to fund your monthly pension in retirement.

a. The amount of money that you will have depends on a variety of factors, as can be seen in the scenario summary of Figure 6.11. Your assignment is to open the worksheet in *Chapter 6 Practice 3,* create four different scenarios, then combine those scenarios in a scenario summary. You can match ours or you can supply your own parameters.

b. Use the Define Name command to assign meaningful names to both the changing cells and the result cells, so that the scenario summary is easily understood.

c. Add your name to the worksheet that performs the retirement calculations, then print that worksheet with both the displayed values and cell formulas.

d. Print the scenario summary worksheet as well, then submit both worksheets to your instructor.

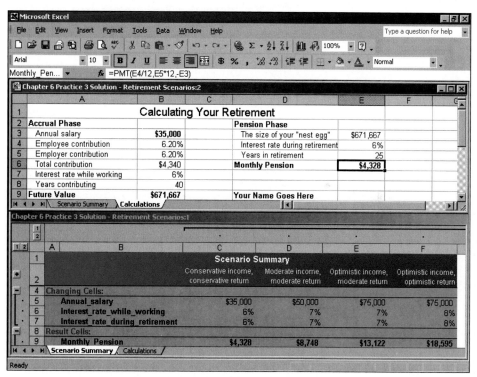

FIGURE 6.11   *Retirement Scenarios (Exercise 3)*

4. Erroneous Grade Book: The worksheet in Figure 6.12 is to compute class grades. The parameters (assumptions) on which the grades are based are shown in the lower portion of the worksheet. The worksheet is nicely formatted, but it contains some fundamental errors. Your assignment is to retrieve the workbook in the *Chapter 6 Practice 4* workbook and correct the errors.

a. "Eyeball" the worksheet and/or use the Formula Auditing toolbar to determine the formulas that are in error. Figure 6.12 shows the precedent cells to determine the semester average for Charles. The cell formula is shown in the formula bar.

b. What is the meaning of the green triangle that appears in cell H5 (the cell that contains the Quiz Average for Goodman)? What command, if any, was executed to display the triangle?

c. Implement conditional formatting for the final grade after you have corrected the worksheet. All As are to be displayed in blue. All Fs are to be displayed in red.

d. Add your name as the grading assistant. Print the worksheet with both displayed values and cell formulas for your professor. Add a cover sheet to complete the assignment.

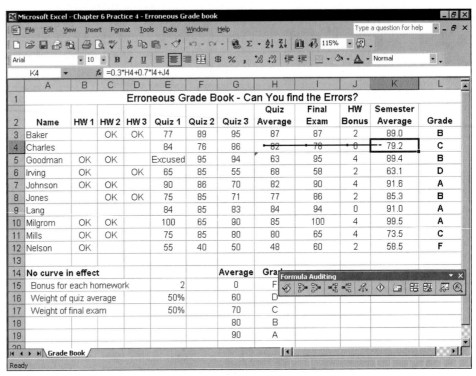

FIGURE 6.12 *Erroneous Grade Book (Exercise 4)*

PRACTICE
EXERCISE 4
PAGES 299–300

5. Grading on a Curve: Figure 6.13 displays a corrected version of the erroneous grade book from the previous problem. The formulas have been corrected, and in addition, the grading parameters have been changed to reflect a curve. The bonus for each homework assignment has been changed to three points, and the required average for each letter grade has been modified. The order of the students within the worksheet has also been changed so that students appear in descending order of the semester average.

a. Open the corrected workbook from the previous problem. Click anywhere within the semester average column, then click the Descending Sort button, so that students appear in order of descending semester average.

b. Create two scenarios, with and without a curve. The changing cells are the same for each scenario, and consist of the name of the scenario (cell A14), the homework bonus (cell E15), and the required average for each grade (cells G15 through G19). Use the parameters from the previous problem for the no curve scenario.

c. Print the displayed values for both scenarios for your professor. Add a cover sheet. Submit the completed assignment to your instructor.

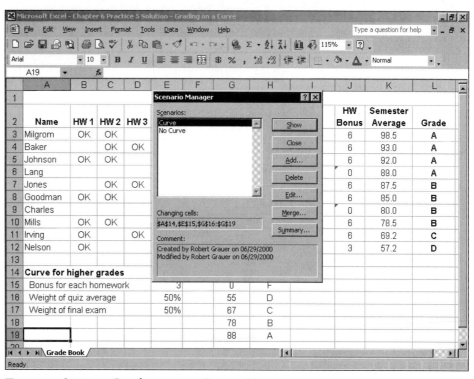

FIGURE 6.13 *Grading on a Curve (Exercise 5)*

6. **The Scenario List Box:** Look closely at Figure 6.14 and note the presence of a scenario list box on the Standard toolbar. This helpful list box lets you display a scenario (without going to the Tools menu) by clicking the down arrow and choosing the scenario from the displayed list.

a. Choose any workbook that contains one or more scenarios (we used the Finished Financial workbook at the end of the first hands-on exercise). To display the list box, point to any toolbar, click the right mouse button to display a shortcut menu, then click Customize to display the Customize dialog box. Click the Commands tab, select Tools in the Categories list box, then click and drag the Scenario list box to an empty space on any toolbar. Click Close to close the dialog box and return to the workbook. The Scenario list box should appear on the toolbar.

b. Prove to your instructor that you have added the list box to your toolbar by capturing the Excel screen, then pasting it into a Word document. All you have to do is press the Print Screen key within Excel (after you display the scenario list box) to copy the screen to the Windows clipboard. Start Word, then click the Paste button to add the contents of the clipboard to the Word document. Word will ask if you want to compress the picture. Click Yes.

c. You may find it useful to modify the position of the screen within the Word document. Thus right click the figure from within Word to display a shortcut menu, click the Format Picture command to display the Format Picture dialog box, click the Layout tab, select Square wrapping, and click OK. You can now click and drag the picture anywhere within the document. You can also click and drag a sizing handle just as you can with any other Windows object.

d. Complete the note in Figure 6.14, add your name somewhere in the document, then print the finished document for your instructor. Add a cover sheet to complete the assignment.

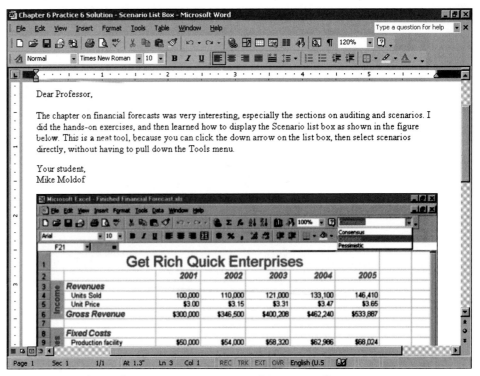

FIGURE 6.14 *The Scenario List Box (Exercise 6)*

7. The Expense Statement: Microsoft Excel includes several templates that are intended to help run a business or plan your personal finances. Pull down the View menu and open the task pane. Click the General Templates command to open the Templates dialog box, from where you can click the Spreadsheet Solutions tab to open the Expense Statement template shown in Figure 6.15. If necessary, click the command button to enable macros. Use the template to create a hypothetical business trip for yourself, then submit the completed worksheet to your instructor.

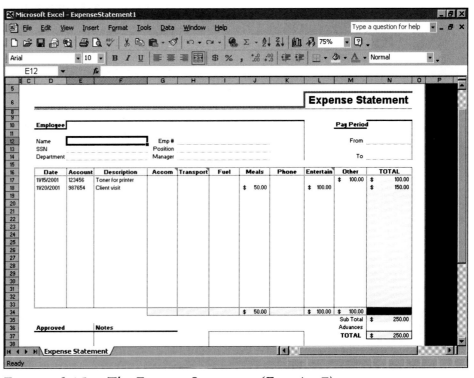

FIGURE 6.15 *The Expense Statement (Exercise 7)*

8. Excel Templates: The worksheet in Figure 6.16a was created from the loan amortization template in the Spreadsheet Solutions folder. Additional templates can be found on the Microsoft Web site. Pull down the File menu, click the New command to open the task pane, then select Templates on Microsoft.com to display the Template Gallery in Figure 6.16b. Choose at least one template, from either the Spreadsheet Solutions folder or the Template Gallery, and create a new spreadsheet based on that template.

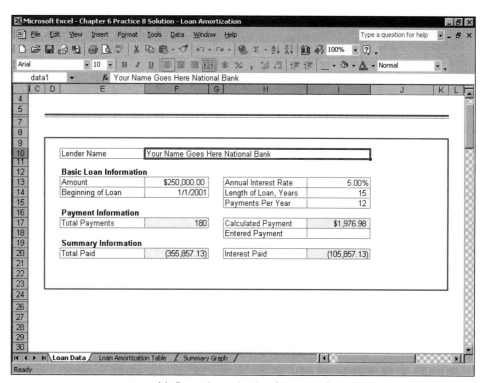

(a) Loan Amortization (Exercise 8)

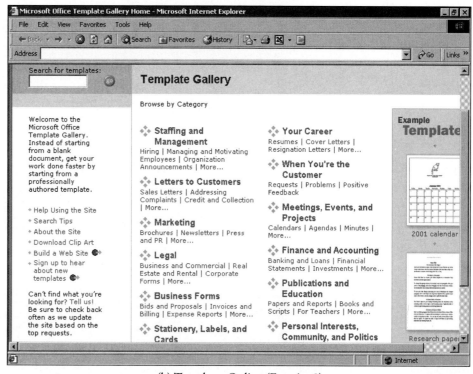

(b) Templates Online (Exercise 8)

FIGURE 6.16 *Excel Templates*

9. Compare and Merge Workbooks: The consensus workbook in Figure 6.17 is the result of merging three individual workbooks, provided by Tom, Dick, and Harry, each of whom added their comments to a shared workbook. Proceed as follows:

a. Open the workbook in *Chapter 6 Practice 9* that contains the original workbook sent out to each of the three reviewers.

b. Pull down the Tools menu, click the Compare and Merge Workbooks command to display the associated dialog box, select the individual workbooks for Tom's Forecast, Dick's Forecast, and Harry's Forecast, then click OK. The workbooks will be opened individually, and any changes will be automatically merged into the consensus workbook. If there are conflicting changes (e.g., two individuals make different changes to the same cell), the changes are entered in the order that the workbooks are opened.

c. Pull down the Tools menu and click the Highlight Changes command to display the Highlight Changes dialog box. Clear the Who, When, and Where check boxes so that you will see all of the changes made to the workbook. Check the box to list the changes on a new sheet. Click OK.

d. A History worksheet is created automatically that shows all of the changes made to the shared workbook. Pull down the Window menu, click New window, then pull down the Window menu a second time and tile the worksheets horizontally to match Figure 6.17.

e. Look closely at the History worksheet and note that Harry and Tom changed the value of cell E4 to $90,000 and $125,000, respectively. The value that is shown in the consensus workbook ($125,000 in our figure) depends on the order in which the workbooks were merged. Tom was last in our example, so his change dominates. You can, however, use the Track Changes command to go through all of the changes individually and accept (reject) the changes individually. If necessary, use this command to accept Tom's change ($125,000) rather than Harry's.

f. Print the completed workbook, with both worksheets, for your instructor.

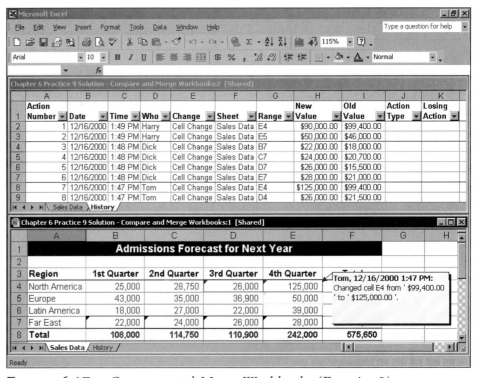

FIGURE 6.17 *Compare and Merge Workbooks (Exercise 9)*

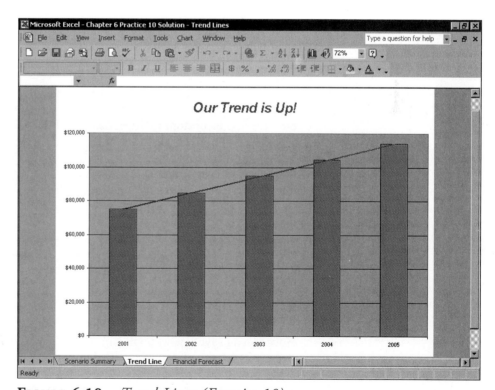

BUILDS ON

HANDS-ON
EXERCISE 1
PAGES 266–276

10. Trend Lines: Excel 2002 extends the charting capability within Excel to include trend lines as shown in Figure 6.18. You create a chart in the usual fashion, then you use the Trend Line command in the Chart menu to add an appropriate trend line by projecting the data in a linear or exponential fashion. Your assignment is to complete the first hands-on exercise for the financial forecast, then create the chart and associated trend line. Proceed as follows:

a. Click and drag to select cells C15 through G15 (the cells that contain the projected profits) in the worksheet, then click the Chart Wizard button on the Standard toolbar.

b. Choose the two-dimensional clustered column chart in step one of the Chart Wizard. (You cannot add a trend line to a three-dimensional chart.) Click Next. The option button to display data in rows is selected.

c. Remain in step two of the Wizard and click the Series tab in the Chart Wizard dialog box. Click in the Category X labels list box, then click and drag to select cells C2 through G2 in the worksheet (the cells that contain the years of the forecast). Click Next.

d. Enter the chart title, "Our trend is up!" Remain in step three of the Wizard, and click the Legend tab in the Chart Wizard dialog box. Clear the check box to display a legend. Click Next.

e. Click the option button to create the chart as a new sheet, then click Finish.

f. Pull down the Chart menu and click the Add Trend Line command to display the Add Trend Line dialog box. Choose a linear trend, then click OK to create the line. Right click the trend line after it is created to change its color and thickness.

g. Print the completed workbook for your instructor. Add a cover sheet to complete the assignment.

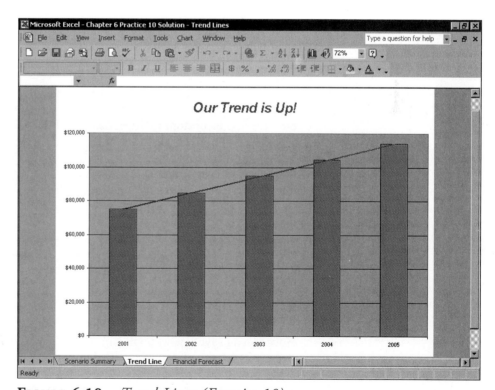

FIGURE 6.18 *Trend Lines (Exercise 10)*

The Entrepreneur

You have developed the perfect product and are seeking venture capital to go into immediate production. Your investors are asking for a projected income statement for the first four years of operation. The sales of your product are estimated at $250,000 the first year and are projected to grow at 15 percent annually. The cost of goods sold is 60 percent of the sales amount, and is expected to grow at 5% annually. You also have to pay a 10 percent sales commission, which is expected to remain constant.

Develop a financial forecast that will show the projected profits before and after taxes (assuming a tax rate of 36 percent). Your worksheet should be completely flexible and capable of accommodating a change in any of the initial conditions or projected rates of increase, *without* having to edit or recopy any of the formulas.

The worksheet should also be protected to the extent that the users can make any changes they like in the assumption area, but are prevented from making changes in the body of the worksheet. Use "password" (in lowercase) as the password.

Publishing to the Web

Use the completed financial forecast from the first hands-on exercise in the chapter as the basis for an HTML document. Complete the hands-on exercise, then use the Save as Web Page command to save the entire workbook as an HTML document. (You will see a message saying that scenarios will not be saved.) Post the document to your home page if you have one.

View the resulting page in Internet Explorer and/or Netscape Navigator. Are you able to see both worksheets in either browser? Are any Excel features lost in the conversion to HTML? Summarize this information in a brief note to your instructor.

Error Checking—Good News and Bad

Excel 2002 introduces automatic error checking, whereby a worksheet is checked for common errors. If, for example, you are adding a column of numbers and you omit the top or bottom number, Excel will flag the formula as a potential error. It will also flag an inconsistent formula within a row or column, and/or flag an unprotected cell if the cell contains a formula rather than a value. Potential errors are flagged with a green triangle, and the user is given the option to ignore or correct the error. Excel will even make the correction automatically.

This is a compelling feature, especially if you use Excel for financial calculations. Unfortunately, however, it falls short in one critical way. Your assignment is to open the workbook, *Error Checking—Good News and Bad*, and find the shortcoming. In addition, you are to use the Options command in the Tools menu to find the complete list of potential errors. Summarize your findings in a short note to your instructor.

Password Protection

How do you save a workbook with a password? Can you require one password to open a workbook and a different password to modify it? Can password protection be implemented for a shared workbook? What happens if you forget the password? Is the password case sensitive? Use the Help menu to learn about password protection in Excel, then summarize your findings in a short note to your instructor.

CHAPTER 7

List and Data Management: Converting Data to Information

OBJECTIVES

AFTER READING THIS CHAPTER YOU WILL BE ABLE TO:

1. Create a list within Excel; explain the importance of proper planning and design prior to creating the list.
2. Add, edit, and delete records in an existing list; explain the significance of data validation.
3. Use the Text Import Wizard to import data in character format.
4. Describe the TODAY( ) function and its use of date arithmetic.
5. Use the Sort command; distinguish between an ascending and a descending sort, and among primary, secondary, and tertiary keys.
6. Use DSUM, DAVERAGE, DMAX, DMIN, and DCOUNT functions.
7. Use the AutoFilter and Advanced Filter commands to display a subset of a list.
8. Use the Subtotals command to summarize data in a list; use the outline symbols to collapse and/or expand the summary information.
9. Create a pivot table and a corresponding pivot chart; save a pivot table as a Web page.

OVERVIEW

All businesses maintain data in the form of lists. Companies have lists of their employees. Magazines and newspapers keep lists of their subscribers. Political candidates monitor voter lists, and so on. This chapter presents the fundamentals of list management as it is implemented in Excel. We begin with the definition of basic terms, such as field and record, then cover the commands to create a list, to add a new record, and to modify or delete an existing record.

The second half of the chapter distinguishes between data and information and describes how one is converted to the other. We introduce the AutoFilter and Advanced Filter commands that display selected records in a list. We use the Sort command to rearrange the list. We discuss database functions and the associated criteria range. We also review date functions and date arithmetic. The chapter ends with a discussion of subtotals, pivot tables, and pivot charts—three powerful capabilities associated with lists.

Excel is the ideal application to analyze data, but other applications are better suited to collect and maintain the data. Thus, we include information on how to import data from other applications into an Excel workbook. The hands-on exercises enable you to implement the conceptual material at the computer.

LIST AND DATA MANAGEMENT

Imagine that you are the personnel director of a medium-sized company with offices in several cities, and that you manually maintain employee data for the company. Accordingly, you have recorded the specifics of every individual's employment (name, salary, location, title, and so on) in a manila folder, and you have stored the entire set of folders in a file cabinet. You have written the name of each employee on the label of his or her folder and have arranged the folders alphabetically in the filing cabinet.

The manual system just described illustrates the basics of data management terminology. The set of manila folders corresponds to a *file*. Each individual folder is known as a *record*. Each data item (fact) within a folder is called a *field*. The folders are arranged alphabetically in the file cabinet (according to the employee name on the label) to simplify the retrieval of any given folder. Likewise, the records in a computer-based system are also in sequence according to a specific field known as a *key*.

Excel maintains data in the form of a list. A *list* is an area in the worksheet that contains rows of similar data. A list can be used as a simple *database*, where the rows correspond to records and the columns correspond to fields. The first row contains the column labels or *field names*, which identify the data that will be entered in that column (field). Each additional row in the list contains a record. Each column represents a field. Each cell in the list area (other than the field names) contains a value for a specific field in a specific record. Every record (row) contains the same fields (columns) in the same order as every other record.

Figure 7.1 contains an employee list with 13 records. There are four fields in every record—name, location, title, and salary. The field names should be meaningful and must be unique. (A field name may contain up to 255 characters, but you should keep them as short as possible so that a column does not become too wide and thus difficult to work with.) The arrangement of the fields within a record is consistent from record to record. The employee name was chosen as the key, and thus the records are in alphabetical order.

Normal business operations require that you make repeated trips to the filing cabinet to maintain the accuracy of the data. You will have to add a folder whenever a new employee is hired. In similar fashion, you will have to remove the folder of any employee who leaves the company, or modify the data in the folder of any employee who receives a raise, changes location, and so on.

Changes of this nature (additions, deletions, and modifications) are known as file maintenance and constitute a critical activity within any system. Indeed, without adequate file maintenance, the data in a system quickly becomes obsolete and the information useless. Imagine the consequences of producing a payroll based on data that is six months old.

	A	B	C	D
1	Name	Location	Title	Salary
2	Adams	Atlanta	Trainee	$19,500
3	Adamson	Chicago	Manager	$52,000
4	Brown	Atlanta	Trainee	$18,500
5	Charles	Boston	Account Rep	$40,000
6	Coulter	Atlanta	Manager	$100,000
7	Frank	Miami	Manager	$75,000
8	James	Chicago	Account Rep	$42,500
9	Johnson	Chicag	Account Rep	$47,500
10	Manin	Boston	Accout Rep	$49,500
11	Marder	Chicago	Account Rep	$38,500
12	Milgrom	Boston	Manager	$57,500
13	Rubin	Boston	Account Rep	$45,000
14	Smith	Atlanta	Account Rep	$65,000

FIGURE 7.1   *The Employee List*

Nor is it sufficient simply to add (edit or delete) a record without adequate checks on the validity of the data. Look carefully at the entries in Figure 7.1 and ask yourself if a computer-generated report listing employees in the Chicago office will include Johnson. Will a report listing account reps include Manin? The answer to both questions is *no* because the data for these employees was entered incorrectly.

Chicago is misspelled in Johnson's record (the "o" was omitted). Account rep is misspelled in Manin's title. *You* know that Johnson works in Chicago, but the computer does not, because it searches for the correct spelling. It also will omit Manin from a listing of account reps because of the misspelled title. Remember, a computer does what you tell it to do, not necessarily what you want it to do. There is a difference.

GARBAGE IN, GARBAGE OUT (GIGO)

The information produced by a system is only as good as the data on which it is based. It is absolutely critical, therefore, that you validate the data that goes into a system, or else the associated information will not be correct. No system, no matter how sophisticated, can produce valid output from invalid input. In other words, garbage in—garbage out.

IMPLEMENTATION IN EXCEL

Creating a list is easy because there is little to do other than enter the data. You choose the area in the worksheet that will contain the list, then you enter the field names in the first row of the designated area. Each field name should be a unique text entry. The data for the individual records should be entered in the rows immediately below the row of field names.

Once a list has been created, you can edit any field, in any record, just as you would change the entries in an ordinary worksheet. The **Insert Rows command** lets you add new rows (records) to the list. The **Insert Columns command** lets you add additional columns (fields). The **Delete command** in the Edit menu enables you to delete a row or column. You can also use shortcut menus to execute commands more quickly. And finally, you can also format the entries within a list, just as you format the entries in any other worksheet.

Data Form Command

A *data form* provides an easy way to add, edit, and delete records in a list. The *Form command* in the Data menu displays a dialog box based on the fields in the list and contains the command buttons shown in Figure 7.2. Every record in the list contains the same fields in the same order (e.g., Name, Location, Title, and Salary in Figure 7.2), and the fields are displayed in this order within the dialog box. You do not have to enter a value for every field; that is, you may leave a field blank if the data is unknown.

Next to each field name is a text box into which data can be entered for a new record, or edited for an existing record. The scroll bar to the right of the data is used to scroll through the records in the list. The functions of the various command buttons are explained briefly:

New — Adds a record to the end of a list, then lets you enter data in that record. The formulas for computed fields, if any, are automatically copied to the new record.

Delete — Permanently removes the currently displayed record. The remaining records move up one row.

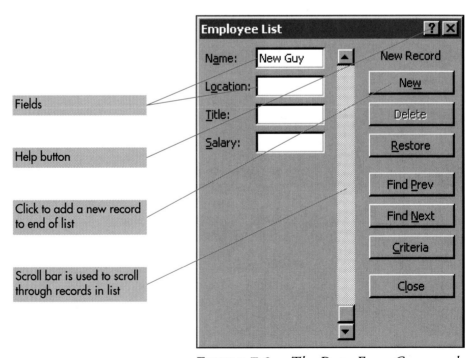

FIGURE 7.2   *The Data Form Command*

Restore — Cancels any changes made to the current record. (You must press the Restore button before pressing the enter key or scrolling to a new record.)

Find Prev — Displays the previous record (or the previous record that matches the existing criteria when criteria are defined).

Find Next — Displays the next record (or the next record that matches the existing criteria when criteria are defined).

Criteria — Displays a dialog box in which you specify the criteria for the Find Prev and/or Find Next command buttons to limit the displayed records to those that match the criteria.

Close — Closes the data form and returns to the worksheet.

The Help button (the question mark) on the title bar of the Data Form provides access to online help. Click the Help button, then click any of the command buttons for an explanation. As indicated, the Data Form command provides an easy way to add, edit, and delete records in a list. It is not required, however, and you can use the Insert and Delete commands within the Edit menu as an alternate means of data entry.

Sort Command

The *Sort command* arranges the records in a list according to the value of one or more fields within that list. You can sort the list in *ascending* (low-to-high) or *descending* (high-to-low) *sequence*. (Putting a list in alphabetical order is considered an ascending sort.) You can also sort on more than one field at a time—for example, by location and then alphabetically by last name within each location. The field(s) on which you sort the list is (are) known as the key(s).

The records in Figure 7.3a are listed alphabetically (in ascending sequence) according to employee name. Adams comes before Adamson, who comes before Brown, and so on. Figure 7.3b displays the identical records but in descending sequence by employee salary. The employee with the highest salary is listed first, and the employee with the lowest salary is last.

Figure 7.3c sorts the employees on two keys—by location, and by descending salary within location. Location is the more important, or primary key. Salary is the less important, or secondary key. The Sort command groups employees according to like values of the primary key (location) in ascending (alphabetical) sequence, then within the like values of the primary key arranges them in descending sequence (ascending could have been chosen just as easily) according to the secondary key (salary). Excel provides a maximum of three keys—primary, secondary, and tertiary.

CHOOSE A CUSTOM SORT SEQUENCE

Alphabetic fields are normally arranged in strict alphabetical order. You can, however, choose a custom sort sequence such as the days of the week or the months of the year. Pull down the Data menu, click Sort, click the Options command button, then click the arrow on the drop-down list box to choose a sequence other than the alphabetic. You can also create your own sequence. Pull down the Tools menu, click Options, click the Custom Lists tab, select NewList, then enter the items in desired sequence in the List Entries Box. Click Add to create the sequence, then close the dialog box.

Records are listed in ascending sequence by employee name

	A	B	C	D
1	Name	Location	Title	Salary
2	Adams	Atlanta	Trainee	$19,500
3	Adamson	Chicago	Manager	$52,000
4	Brown	Atlanta	Trainee	$18,500
5	Charles	Boston	Account Rep	$40,000
6	Coulter	Atlanta	Manager	$100,000
7	Frank	Miami	Manager	$75,000
8	James	Chicago	Account Rep	$42,500
9	Johnson	Chicago	Account Rep	$47,500
10	Manin	Boston	Account Rep	$49,500
11	Marder	Chicago	Account Rep	$38,500
12	Milgrom	Boston	Manager	$57,500
13	Rubin	Boston	Account Rep	$45,000
14	Smith	Atlanta	Account Rep	$65,000
15				

(a) Ascending Sequence (by name)

Records are listed in descending sequence by salary

	A	B	C	D
1	Name	Location	Title	Salary
2	Coulter	Atlanta	Manager	$100,000
3	Frank	Miami	Manager	$75,000
4	Smith	Atlanta	Account Rep	$65,000
5	Milgrom	Boston	Manager	$57,500
6	Adamson	Chicago	Manager	$52,000
7	Manin	Boston	Account Rep	$49,500
8	Johnson	Chicago	Account Rep	$47,500
9	Rubin	Boston	Account Rep	$45,000
10	James	Chicago	Account Rep	$42,500
11	Charles	Boston	Account Rep	$40,000
12	Marder	Chicago	Account Rep	$38,500
13	Adams	Atlanta	Trainee	$19,500
14	Brown	Atlanta	Trainee	$18,500
15				

(b) Descending Sequence (by salary)

Location is the primary key (ascending sequence)

Salary is the secondary key (descending sequence)

	A	B	C	D
1	Name	Location	Title	Salary
2	Coulter	Atlanta	Manager	$100,000
3	Smith	Atlanta	Account Rep	$65,000
4	Adams	Atlanta	Trainee	$19,500
5	Brown	Atlanta	Trainee	$18,500
6	Milgrom	Boston	Manager	$57,500
7	Manin	Boston	Account Rep	$49,500
8	Rubin	Boston	Account Rep	$45,000
9	Charles	Boston	Account Rep	$40,000
10	Adamson	Chicago	Manager	$52,000
11	Johnson	Chicago	Account Rep	$47,500
12	James	Chicago	Account Rep	$42,500
13	Marder	Chicago	Account Rep	$38,500
14	Frank	Miami	Manager	$75,000
15				

(c) Multiple Keys

FIGURE 7.3   *The Sort Command*

Microsoft Excel stores a date as the integer (serial number) equivalent to the elapsed number of days since January 1, 1900. Thus January 1, 1900 is stored as the number 1, January 2, 1900 as the number 2, and so on. March 16, 1981 corresponds to the number 29661 as can be seen in Figure 7.4.

The fact that dates are stored as numbers enables you to add and subtract two different dates and/or to use a date in any type of arithmetic computation. A person's age, for example, can be computed by subtracting the date of birth from today's date, and dividing the result by 365 (or more accurately by 365¼ to adjust for leap years). In similar fashion, you could add a constant (e.g., the number 30) to the date of purchase, to determine when payment is due (assuming, in this example, that payment is due 30 days after the item was purchased).

A date can be entered into a spreadsheet in various ways, most easily by typing the date in conventional fashion—for example, 1/21/97, to enter the date January 21, 1997. Any entry containing a year from 00 to 29 is assumed to be a date in the 21st century; for example, 1/21/00, will be stored as January 21, 2000. Any year between 30 and 99, however, is stored as a date in the 20th century. Thus, 3/23/48 would be stored as March 23, 1948. To avoid confusion and be sure of the date, you can enter all four digits of the year—for example, 10/31/2001 for October 31, 2001.

The **TODAY( ) function** is used in conjunction with date arithmetic and always returns the current date (i.e., the date on which the spreadsheet is opened). (The **Now( ) function** is similar in concept and includes the time of day as well as the date.) If, for example, you entered the Today() function into a spreadsheet created on March 21 and you opened the spreadsheet a month later, the value of the function would be automatically updated to April 21. The Today() function is illustrated in Figure 7.4 to calculate a person's age. Note, too, the IF function in Figure 7.4, which examines the computed age, then displays an appropriate message indicating whether the individual is of legal age or still under the age of 21.

Function displays current date

Enter 3/16/81 as a fixed date

Formula calculates person's age

	A	B	C	D
		Cell Formulas	Date Format	Number Format
1				
2	Today's Date	=TODAY()	7/29/01	37101
3	Birth Date	3/16/81	3/16/81	29661
4				
5	Elapsed Time (days)	=B2-B3		7440
6	Age (years)	=B5/365		20.4
7				
8		=IF(B6>=21,"You're Legal","Still a Minor")		Still a Minor

FIGURE 7.4   *Date Arithmetic*

BIRTH DATE VERSUS AGE

An individual's age and birth date provide equivalent information, as one is calculated from the other. It might seem easier, therefore, to enter the age directly into the list and avoid the calculation, but this would be a mistake. A person's age changes continually, whereas the birth date remains constant. Thus, the date, not the age, should be stored, so that the data in the list remains current. Similar reasoning applies to an employee's hire date and length of service.

It's easy to create a list in Excel and/or to modify data in that list. What if, however, the data already exists, but it is not in the form of a workbook? This is very common, especially in organizations that collect data on a mainframe, but analyze it on a PC. It can also occur when data is collected by one application, then analyzed in another. Excel provides a convenient solution in the form of the ***Text Import Wizard*** that converts a text (ASCII) file to an Excel workbook as shown in Figure 7.5. (Conversely, you can export an Excel workbook to another application by using the Save As command and specifying a text file.)

Figures 7.5a and 7.5b each contain the 13 records from the employee list shown, but in different formats. Both figures contain text files. The data in Figure 7.5a is in ***fixed width format***, where each field requires the same number of positions in an input record. The data in Figure 7.5b is in ***delimited format***, where the fields are separated from one another by a specific character.

You can access either file via the Open command in Excel, which in turn displays step 1 of the Text Import Wizard in Figure 7.5c. The Wizard prompts you for information about the external data, then it converts that data into an Excel workbook as shown in Figure 7.5d.

Name	Location	Title	Salary
Adams	Atlanta	Trainee	19500
Adamson	Chicago	Manager	52000
Brown	Atlanta	Trainee	18500
Charles	Boston	Account Rep	40000
Coulter	Atlanta	Manager	100000
Frank	Miami	Manager	75000
James	Chicago	Account Rep	42500
Johnson	Chicago	Account Rep	47500
Manin	Boston	Account Rep	49500
Marder	Chicago	Account Rep	38500
Milgrom	Boston	Manager	57500
Rubin	Boston	Account Rep	45000
Smith	Atlanta	Account Rep	65000

(a) Fixed Width

```
Name,Location,Title,Salary
Adams,Atlanta,Trainee,19500
Adamson,Chicago,Manager,52000
Brown,Atlanta,Trainee,18500
Charles,Boston,Account Rep,40000
Coulter,Atlanta,Manager,100000
Frank,Miami,Manager,75000
James,Chicago,Account Rep,42500
Johnson,Chicago,Account Rep,47500
Manin,Boston,Account Rep,49500
Marder,Chicago,Account Rep,38500
Milgrom,Boston,Manager,57500
Rubin,Boston,Account Rep,45000
Smith,Atlanta,Account Rep,65000
```

(b) Delimited

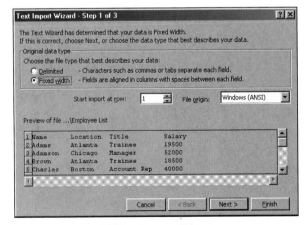

(c) Text Import Wizard

	A	B	C	D
1	Name	Location	Title	Salary
2	Adams	Atlanta	Trainee	19500
3	Adamson	Chicago	Manager	52000
4	Brown	Atlanta	Trainee	18500
5	Charles	Boston	Account Rep	40000
6	Coulter	Atlanta	Manager	100000
7	Frank	Miami	Manager	75000
8	James	Chicago	Account Rep	42500
9	Johnson	Chicago	Account Rep	47500
10	Manin	Boston	Account Rep	49500
11	Marder	Chicago	Account Rep	38500
12	Milgrom	Boston	Manager	57500
13	Rubin	Boston	Account Rep	45000
14	Smith	Atlanta	Account Rep	65000
15				

(d) Workbook

FIGURE 7.5 *Importing Data from Other Applications*

CREATING AND MAINTAINING A LIST

Objective   To use the Text Import Wizard; to add, edit, and delete records in an employee list. Use Figure 7.6 as a guide in the exercise.

Step 1:   **The Text Import Wizard**

> ➤ Start Excel. Pull down the **File menu** and click the **Open command** (or click the **Open button** on the Standard toolbar) to display the Open dialog box.
> ➤ Open the **Exploring Excel folder** that you have used throughout the text. Click the **drop-down arrow** on the Files of Type list box and specify **All Files**, then double click the **Employee List** text document.
> ➤ The Text Import Wizard opens automatically as shown in Figure 7.6a. The Wizard recognizes that the file is in Delimited format. Click **Next**.
> ➤ Clear the **Tab Delimiter** check box. Check the **Comma Delimiter** check box. Each field is now shown in a separate column. Click **Next**.
> ➤ There is no need to change the default format (general) of any of the fields. Click **Finish**. You see the Employee List within an Excel workbook.
> ➤ Click and drag to select **cells A1** through **D1**, then click the **Bold** and **Center buttons** to distinguish the field names from the data records. Click the **down arrow** for the **Fill Color button** and select **Pale Blue**. Adjust the column widths. Format the Salary field as Currency with zero decimals.
> ➤ Save the workbook as **Finished Employee List**. Click the **down arrow** in the Save as type list box and select **Microsoft Excel workbook**. Click **Save**.

Bold button

Center button

Fill Color button

Delimited format

Delimiter character is a comma

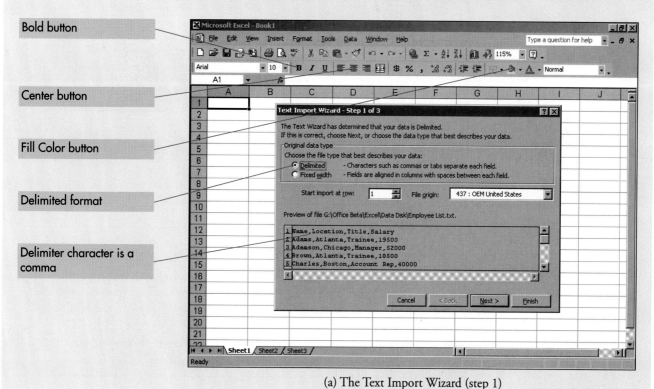

(a) The Text Import Wizard (step 1)

FIGURE 7.6   *Hands-on Exercise 1*

Step 2: **Add New Records**

➤ Click a single cell anywhere within the employee list (cells A1 through D14). Pull down the **Data menu**. Click **Form** to display a dialog box with data for the first record in the list (Adams).

➤ Click the **New command button** at the right of the dialog box to clear the text boxes and begin entering a new record.

➤ Enter the data for **Elofson** as shown in Figure 7.6b, using the **Tab key** to move from field to field within the data form.

➤ Click the **Close command button** after entering the salary. Elofson has been added to the list and appears in row 15.

➤ Add a second record for **Gillenson**, who works in **Miami** as an **Account Rep** with a salary of **$55,000**.

➤ Save the workbook.

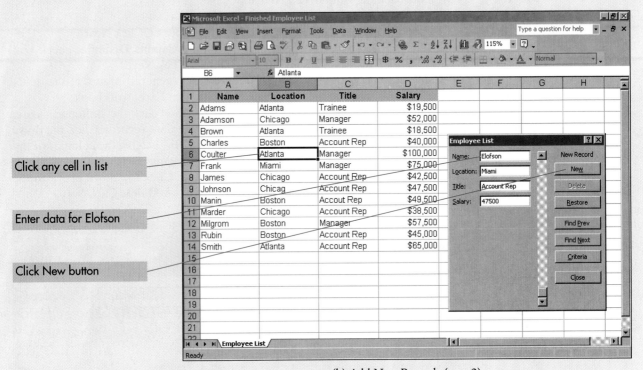

(b) Add New Records (step 2)

FIGURE 7.6   *Hands-on Exercise 1 (continued)*

EMPHASIZE THE COLUMN LABELS (FIELD NAMES)

Use a different font, alignment, style (boldface and/or italics), pattern, or border to distinguish the first row containing the field names from the remaining rows (records) in a list. This ensures that Excel will recognize the first row as a header row, enabling you to sort the list simply by selecting a cell in the list, then clicking the Ascending or Descending sort buttons on the Standard toolbar.

Step 3: **The Spell Check**

➤ Select **cells B2:C16** as in Figure 7.6c. Pull down the **Tools menu** and click **Spelling** (or click the **Spelling button** on the Standard toolbar).

➤ Chicago is misspelled in cell B9 and flagged accordingly. Click the **Change command button** to accept the suggested correction and continue checking the document.

➤ Account is misspelled in cell C10 and flagged accordingly. Click **Account** in the Suggestions list box, then click the **Change command button** to correct the misspelling.

➤ Excel will indicate that it has finished checking the selected cells. Click **OK** to return to the worksheet.

➤ Save the workbook.

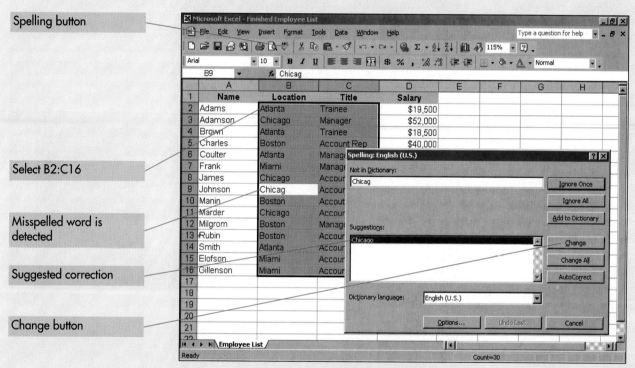

Spelling button

Select B2:C16

Misspelled word is detected

Suggested correction

Change button

(c) The Spell Check (step 3)

FIGURE 7.6   *Hands-on Exercise 1 (continued)*

CREATE YOUR OWN SHORTHAND

Use the AutoCorrect to create your own shorthand by having it expand abbreviations such as *cis* for *Computer Information Systems.* Pull down the Tools menu, click AutoCorrect, type the abbreviation in the Replace text box and the expanded entry in the With text box. Click the Add command button, then click OK to exit the dialog box and return to the document. The next time you type *cis* in a spreadsheet, it will automatically be expanded to *Computer Information Systems.*

Step 4: **Sort the Employee List**

➤ Click a single cell anywhere in the employee list (**cells A1** through **D16**). Pull down the **Data menu**. Click **Sort** to display the dialog box in Figure 7.6d.
  • Click the **drop-down arrow** in the Sort By list box. Select **Location**.
  • Click the **drop-down arrow** in the first Then By list box. Select **Name**.
  • Be sure the **Header Row option button** is selected (so that the field names are not mixed in with the records in the list).
  • Check that the **Ascending option button** is selected for both the primary and secondary keys. Click **OK**.
➤ The employees are listed by location and alphabetically within location.
➤ Save the workbook.

Click drop-down arrow and select Location

Click drop-down arrow and select Name

Header row should be selected

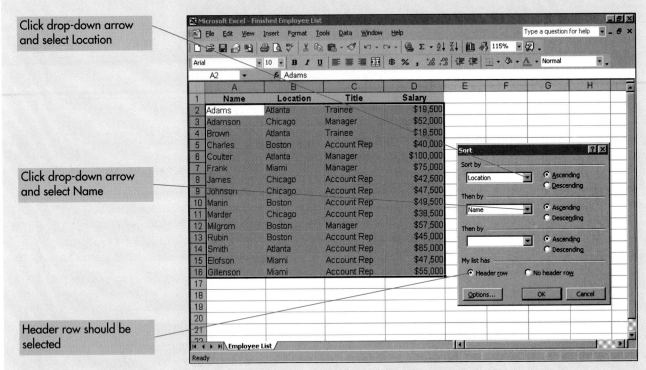

(d) Sort the Employee List (step 4)

FIGURE 7.6 *Hands-on Exercise 1 (continued)*

USE THE SORT BUTTONS

Use the Sort Ascending or Sort Descending button on the Standard toolbar to sort on one or more keys. To sort on a single key, click any cell in the column containing the key, then click the appropriate button, depending on whether you want an ascending or a descending sort. You can also sort on multiple keys, by clicking either button multiple times, but the trick is to do it in the right sequence. Sort on the least significant field first, then work your way up to the most significant. For example, to sort a list by location, and name within location, sort by name first (the secondary key), then sort by location (the primary key).

Step 5: **Delete a Record**

➤ A record may be deleted by using the Edit Delete command or the Data Form command. To delete a record by using the Edit Delete command:
   • Click the **row heading** in **row 15** (containing the record for Frank, which is slated for deletion).
   • Pull down the **Edit menu**. Click **Delete**. Frank has been deleted.
➤ Click the **Undo button** on the Standard toolbar. The record for Frank has been restored.
➤ To delete a record by using the Data Form command:
   • Click a single cell within the employee list. Pull down the **Data menu**. Click **Form** to display the data form. Click the **Criteria button**. Enter **Frank** in the Name text box, then click the **Find Next button** to locate Frank's record.
   • Click the **Delete command button**. Click **OK** in response to the warning message shown in Figure 7.6e. (The record cannot be undeleted as it could with the Edit Delete command.) Click **Close** to close the Data Form.
➤ Save the workbook.

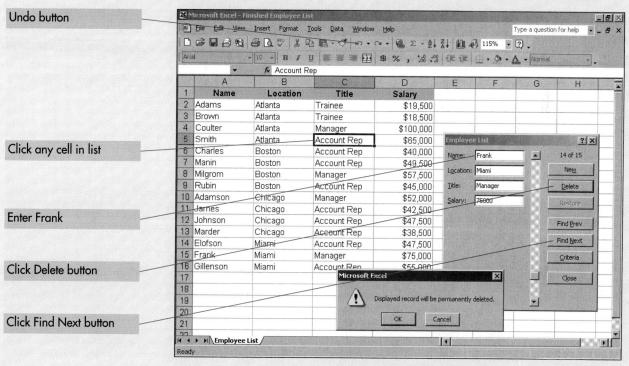

(e) Delete a Record (step 5)

FIGURE 7.6 *Hands-on Exercise 1 (continued)*

EDIT CLEAR VERSUS EDIT DELETE

The Edit Delete command deletes the selected cell, row, or column from the worksheet, and thus its execution will adjust cell references throughout the worksheet. It is very different from the Edit Clear command, which erases the contents (and/or formatting) of the selected cells, but does not delete the cells from the worksheet and hence has no effect on the cell references in other cells. Pressing the Del key erases the contents of a cell and thus corresponds to the Edit Clear command.

Step 6: **Enter the Hire Date**

➤ Click the **column heading** in column D. Point to the selection, then click the **right mouse button** to display a shortcut menu. Click **Insert**. The employee salaries have been moved to column E1, as shown in Figure 7.6f.

➤ Click **cell D1**. Type **Hire Date** and press **enter**. Adjust the column width if necessary. Dates may be entered in several different formats.
   • Type **11/24/93** in cell D2. Press the **down arrow key**.
   • Type **11/24/1993** in cell D3. Press the **down arrow key**.
   • Type **Nov 24, 1993** in cell D4. Type a **comma** after the day but do not type a period after the month. Press the **down arrow key** to move to cell D5.
   • Type **11-24-93** in cell D5. Press **enter**.

➤ For ease of data entry, assume that the next several employees were hired on the same day, 3/16/94. Click in **cell D6**. Type **3/16/94**. Press **enter**. Click in **cell D6**. Click the **Copy button** on the Standard toolbar.

➤ Drag the mouse over cells **D7** through **D10**. Click the **Paste button**. Press **Esc** to remove the moving border around cell D6.

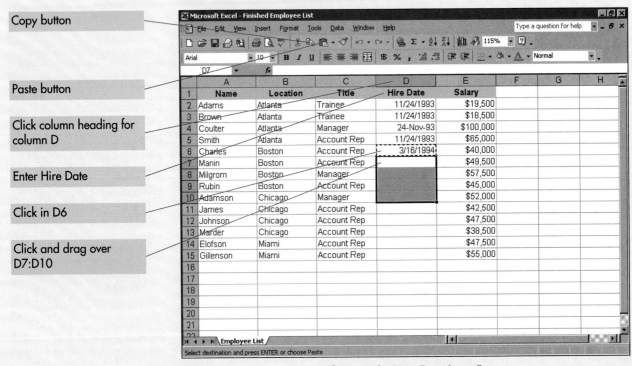

Copy button

Paste button

Click column heading for column D

Enter Hire Date

Click in D6

Click and drag over D7:D10

(f) Enter the Hire Date (step 6)

FIGURE 7.6   *Hands-on Exercise 1 (continued)*

TWO-DIGIT DATES AND THE YEAR 2000

Excel assumes that any two-digit year up to and including 29 is in the 21st century; that is, 12/31/29 will be stored as December 31, 2029. Any year after 29, however, is assumed to be in the 20th century; for example, 1/1/30 will be stored as January 1, 1930. When in doubt, however, enter a four-digit year to be sure.

Step 7: **Format the Hire Dates**

➤ The five employees were hired one year apart beginning October 31, 1994.
  • Click in cell **D11** and type **10/31/94**. Click in cell **D12** and type **10/31/95**.
  • Select cells **D11 and D12**.
  • Drag the **fill handle** at the bottom of cell D12 over cells **D13**, **D14**, and **D15**. Release the mouse to complete the AutoFill operation.
➤ Click in the column heading for **column D** to select the column of dates.
➤ Point to the selected cells and click the **right mouse button** to display a shortcut menu. Click **Format Cells**.
➤ Click the **Number tab** in the Format Cells dialog box. Click **Date** in the Category list box. Select (click) the date format shown in Figure 7.6g. Click **OK**.
➤ Click elsewhere in the workbook to deselect the dates. Reduce the width of column D as appropriate. Save the workbook.
➤ Exit Excel if you do not want to complete the next exercise at this time.

Click column heading for column D

Number tab

Click Date

Click desired format

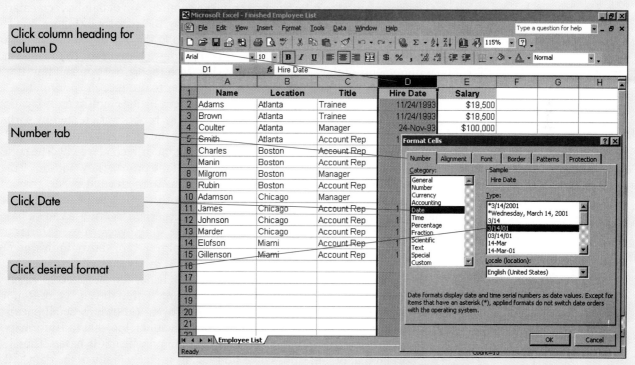

(g) Format the Hire Dates (step 7)

FIGURE 7.6   *Hands-on Exercise 1 (continued)*

DATES VERSUS FRACTIONS

A fraction is entered into a cell by preceding the fraction with an equal sign; for example, =1/4. The fraction is displayed as its decimal equivalent (.25) unless the cell is formatted to display fractions. Select the cell, pull down the Format menu, and click the Cells command. Click the Numbers tab, then choose Fraction from the Category list box. Omission of the equal sign treats the entry as a date; that is, typing 1/4 will store the entry as January 4th (of the current year).

Data and information are not synonymous. ***Data*** refers to a fact or facts about a specific record, such as an employee's name, title, or salary. ***Information,*** on the other hand, is data that has been rearranged into a form perceived as useful by the recipient. A list of employees earning more than $35,000 or a total of all employee salaries are examples of information produced from data about individual employees. Put another way, data is the raw material, and information is the finished product.

Decisions in an organization are based on information rather than raw data; for example, in assessing the effects of a proposed across-the-board salary increase, management needs to know the total payroll rather than individual salary amounts. In similar fashion, decisions about next year's hiring will be influenced, at least in part, by knowing how many individuals are currently employed in each job category.

Organizations maintain data to produce information. Data maintenance entails three basic operations—adding new records, modifying (editing or updating) existing records, and deleting existing records. The exercise just completed showed you how to maintain the data. This section focuses on using that data to create information.

Data is converted to information through a combination of database commands and functions whose capabilities are illustrated by the reports in Figure 7.7. The reports are based on the employee list as it existed at the end of the first hands-on exercise. Each report presents the data in a different way, according to the information requirements of the end-user. As you view each report, ask yourself how it was produced; that is, what was done to the data in order to produce the information?

Figure 7.7a contains a master list of all employees, listing employees by location, and alphabetically by last name within location. The report was created by sorting the list on two keys, location and name. Location is the more important field and is known as the primary key. Name is the less important or secondary key. The sorted report groups employees according to like values of the primary key (location), then within the primary key, groups the records according to the secondary key (name).

The report in Figure 7.7b displays a subset of the records in the list, which includes only those employees who meet specific criteria. The criteria can be based on any field or combination of fields—in this case, employees whose salaries are between $40,000 and $60,000 (inclusive). The employees are shown in descending order of salary so that the employee with the highest salary is listed first.

The report in Figure 7.7c displays summary statistics for the selected employees—in this example, the salaries for the account reps within the company. Reports of this nature omit the salaries of individual employees (known as detail lines), to present an aggregate view of the organization. Remember, too, that the information produced by any system is only as good as the data on which it is based. Thus, it is very important that organizations take steps to ensure the validity of the data as it is entered into a system.

CITY, STATE, AND ZIP CODE—ONE FIELD OR THREE?

The answer depends on whether the fields are referenced as a unit or individually. However, given the almost universal need to sort or select on zip code, it is almost invariably defined as a separate field. An individual's last name, first name, and middle initial are defined as individual fields for the same reason. The general rule, therefore, is to always enter data in its smallest parts.

Location Report

Name	Location	Title	Hire Date	Salary
Adams	Atlanta	Trainee	11/24/93	$19,500
Brown	Atlanta	Trainee	11/24/93	$18,500
Coulter	Atlanta	Manager	11/24/93	$100,000
Smith	Atlanta	Account Rep	11/24/93	$65,000
Charles	Boston	Account Rep	3/16/92	$40,000
Manin	Boston	Account Rep	3/16/92	$49,500
Milgrom	Boston	Manager	3/16/92	$57,500
Rubin	Boston	Account Rep	3/16/92	$45,000
Adamson	Chicago	Manager	3/16/92	$52,000
James	Chicago	Account Rep	10/31/89	$42,500
Johnson	Chicago	Account Rep	10/31/90	$47,500
Marder	Chicago	Account Rep	10/31/91	$38,500
Elofson	Miami	Account Rep	10/31/92	$47,500
Gillenson	Miami	Account Rep	10/31/93	$55,000

(a) Employees by Location and Name within Location

Employees Earning Between $40,000 and $60,000

Name	Location	Title	Hire Date	Salary
Milgrom	Boston	Manager	3/16/92	$57,500
Gillenson	Miami	Account Rep	10/31/93	$55,000
Adamson	Chicago	Manager	3/16/92	$52,000
Manin	Boston	Account Rep	3/16/92	$49,500
Johnson	Chicago	Account Rep	10/31/90	$47,500
Elofson	Miami	Account Rep	10/31/92	$47,500
Rubin	Boston	Account Rep	3/16/92	$45,000
James	Chicago	Account Rep	10/31/89	$42,500
Charles	Boston	Account Rep	3/16/92	$40,000

(b) Employees Earning between $40,000 and $60,000, inclusive

Summary Statistics

Total Salary for Account Reps:	$430,500
Average Salary for Account Reps:	$47,833
Maximum Salary for Account Reps:	$65,000
Minimum Salary for Account Reps:	$38,500
Number of Account Reps:	9

(c) Account Rep Summary Data

FIGURE 7.7   *Data versus Information*

AutoFilter Command

A *filtered list* displays a subset of records that meet a specific criterion or set of criteria. It is created by the **AutoFilter command** (or the Advanced Filter command discussed in the next section). Both commands temporarily hide those records (rows) that do not meet the criteria. The hidden records are *not* deleted; they are simply not displayed.

Figure 7.8a displays the employee list in alphabetical order. Figure 7.8b displays a filtered version of the list in which only the Atlanta employees (in rows 2, 4, 6, and 15) are visible. The remaining employees are still in the worksheet but are not shown as their rows are hidden.

Drop-down arrows appear next to each field name

Click to display only Atlanta employees

	A	B	C	D	E
1	Name	Location	Title	Hire Date	Salary
2	Adams	(All)	Trainee	11/24/93	$19,500
3	Adamson	(Top 10...)	Manager	3/16/94	$52,000
		(Custom...)			
4	Brown	Atlanta	Trainee	11/24/93	$18,500
5	Charles	Boston	Account Rep	3/16/94	$40,000
6	Coulter	Chicago	Manager	11/24/93	$100,000
		Miami			
7	Elofson	Miami	Account Rep	10/31/97	$47,500
8	Gillenson	Miami	Account Rep	10/31/98	$55,000
9	James	Chicago	Account Rep	10/31/94	$42,500
10	Johnson	Chicago	Account Rep	10/31/95	$47,500
11	Manin	Boston	Account Rep	3/16/94	$49,500
12	Marder	Chicago	Account Rep	10/31/96	$38,500
13	Milgrom	Boston	Manager	3/16/94	$57,500
14	Rubin	Boston	Account Rep	3/16/94	$45,000
15	Smith	Atlanta	Account Rep	11/24/93	$65,000

(a) Unfiltered List

Only Atlanta employees are displayed

	A	B	C	D	E
1	Name	Location	Title	Hire Date	Salary
2	Adams	Atlanta	Trainee	11/24/93	$19,500
4	Brown	Atlanta	Trainee	11/24/93	$18,500
6	Coulter	Atlanta	Manager	11/24/93	$100,000
15	Smith	Atlanta	Account Rep	11/24/93	$65,000

(b) Filtered List (Atlanta employees)

Click drop-down arrow to further filter list

	A	B	C	D	E
1	Name	Location	Title	Hire Date	Salary
2	Adams	Atlanta	(All)	11/24/93	$19,500
4	Brown	Atlanta	(Top 10...)	11/24/93	$18,500
6	Coulter	Atlanta	(Custom...)	11/24/93	$100,000
15	Smith	Atlanta	Account Rep	11/24/93	$65,000
16			Manager		
			Trainee		

(c) Imposing a Second Condition

Blue drop-down arrows indicate filter condition is in effect

	A	B	C	D	E
1	Name	Location	Title	Hire Date	Salary
6	Coulter	Atlanta	Manager	11/24/93	$100,000

(d) Filtered List (Atlanta managers)

FIGURE 7.8 *Filter Command*

Execution of the AutoFilter command places drop-down arrows next to each column label (field name). Clicking a drop-down arrow produces a list of the unique values for that field, enabling you to establish the criteria for the filtered list. Thus, to display the Atlanta employees, click the drop-down arrow for Location, then click Atlanta.

A filter condition can be imposed on multiple columns as shown in Figure 7.8c. The filtered list in Figure 7.8c contains just the Atlanta employees. Clicking the arrow next to Title, then clicking Manager, will filter the list further to display the employees who both work in Atlanta *and* have Manager as a title. Only one employee meets both conditions, as shown in Figure 7.8d. The drop-down arrows next to Location and Title are displayed in blue to indicate that a filter is in effect for these columns.

The AutoFilter command has additional options as can be seen from the drop-down list box in Figure 7.8c. (All) removes existing criteria in that column. (Custom . . .) enables you to use the relational operators (=, >, <, >=, <=, or <>) within a criterion. (Top 10 . . .) displays the records with the top (or bottom) values in the field, and makes most sense if you sort the list to see the entries in sequence.

Advanced Filter Command

The ***Advanced Filter command*** extends the capabilities of the AutoFilter command in two important ways. It enables you to develop more complex criteria than are possible with the AutoFilter Command. It also enables you to copy (extract) the selected records to a separate area in the worksheet. The Advanced Filter command is illustrated in detail in the hands-on exercise that follows shortly.

Criteria Range

A ***criteria range*** is used with both the Advanced Filter command and the database functions that are discussed in the next section. It is defined independently of the list on which it operates and exists as a separate area in the worksheet. A criteria range must be at least two rows deep and one column wide as illustrated in Figure 7.9.

The simplest criteria range consists of two rows and as many columns as there are fields in the list. The first row contains the field names as they appear in the list. The second row holds the value(s) you are looking for. The criteria range in Figure 7.9a selects the employees who work in Atlanta; that is, it selects those records where the value of the Location Field is equal to Atlanta.

Multiple values in the same row are connected by an AND and require that the selected records meet *all* of the specified criteria. The criteria range in Figure 7.9b identifies the account reps in Atlanta; that is, it selects any record in which the Location field is Atlanta *and* the Title field is Account Rep.

Values entered in multiple rows are connected by an OR in which the selected records satisfy *any* of the indicated criteria. The criteria range in Figure 7.9c will identify employees who work in Atlanta *or* whose title is Account Rep.

Relational operators may be used with date or numeric fields to return records within a designated range. The criteria range in Figure 7.9d selects the employees hired before January 1, 1993. The criteria range in Figure 7.9e returns employees whose salary is more than $40,000.

An upper and lower boundary may be established for the same field by repeating the field within the criteria range. This was done in Figure 7.9f, which returns all records in which the salary is more than $40,000 but less than $60,000.

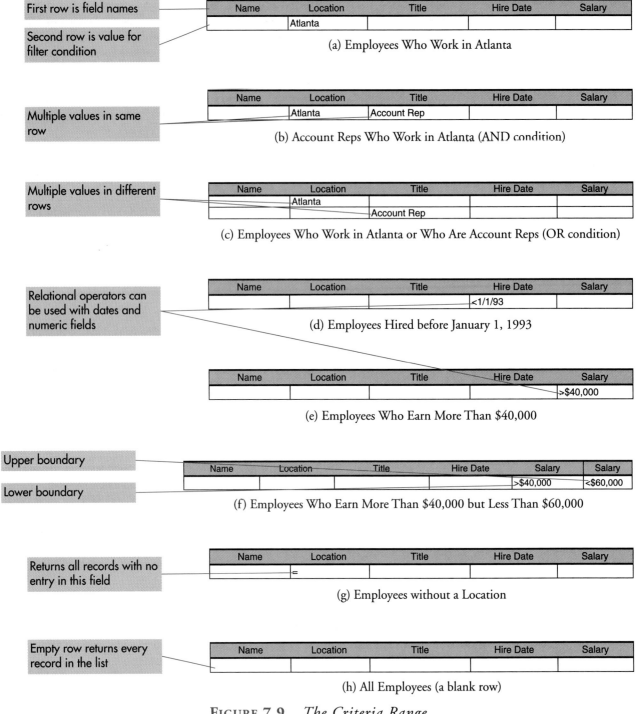

First row is field names

Second row is value for filter condition

Name	Location	Title	Hire Date	Salary
	Atlanta			

(a) Employees Who Work in Atlanta

Multiple values in same row

Name	Location	Title	Hire Date	Salary
	Atlanta	Account Rep		

(b) Account Reps Who Work in Atlanta (AND condition)

Multiple values in different rows

Name	Location	Title	Hire Date	Salary
	Atlanta			
		Account Rep		

(c) Employees Who Work in Atlanta or Who Are Account Reps (OR condition)

Relational operators can be used with dates and numeric fields

Name	Location	Title	Hire Date	Salary
			<1/1/93	

(d) Employees Hired before January 1, 1993

Name	Location	Title	Hire Date	Salary
				>$40,000

(e) Employees Who Earn More Than $40,000

Upper boundary

Lower boundary

Name	Location	Title	Hire Date	Salary	Salary
				>$40,000	<$60,000

(f) Employees Who Earn More Than $40,000 but Less Than $60,000

Returns all records with no entry in this field

Name	Location	Title	Hire Date	Salary
	=			

(g) Employees without a Location

Empty row returns every record in the list

Name	Location	Title	Hire Date	Salary

(h) All Employees (a blank row)

FIGURE 7.9   *The Criteria Range*

The equal and unequal signs select records with empty and nonempty fields, respectively. An equal sign with nothing after it will return all records without an entry in the designated field; for example, the criteria range in Figure 7.9g selects any record that is missing a value for the Location field. An unequal sign (<>) with nothing after it will select all records with an entry in the field.

An empty row in the criteria range returns *every* record in the list, as shown in Figure 7.9h. All criteria are *case-insensitive* and return records with any combination of upper- and lowercase letters that match the entry.

THE IMPLIED WILD CARD

Any text entry within a criteria range is treated as though it were followed by the asterisk *wild card*; that is, *New* is the same as *New**. Both entries will return New York and New Jersey. To match a text entry exactly, begin with an equal sign, enter a quotation mark followed by another equal sign, the entry you are looking for, and the closing quotation mark—for example, = "=New" to return only the entries that say New.

Database Functions

The *database functions* DSUM, DAVERAGE, DMAX, DMIN, and DCOUNT operate on *selected* records in a list. These functions parallel the statistical functions (SUM, AVERAGE, MAX, MIN, and COUNT) except that they affect only records that satisfy the established criteria.

The summary statistics in Figure 7.10 are based on the salaries of the managers in the list, rather than the salaries of all employees. Each database function includes the criteria range in cells A17:E18 as one of its arguments, and thus limits the employees that are included to managers. The *DAVERAGE function* returns the average salary for just the managers. The *DMAX* and *DMIN functions* display the maximum and minimum salaries for the managers. The *DSUM function* computes the total salary for all the managers. The *DCOUNT function* indicates the number of managers.

Each database function has three arguments: the range for the list on which it is to operate, the field to be processed, and the criteria range. Consider, for example, the DAVERAGE function as shown below:

=DAVERAGE(database,"field",criteria)

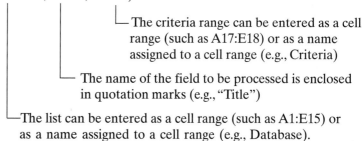

The criteria range can be entered as a cell range (such as A17:E18) or as a name assigned to a cell range (e.g., Criteria)

The name of the field to be processed is enclosed in quotation marks (e.g., "Title")

The list can be entered as a cell range (such as A1:E15) or as a name assigned to a cell range (e.g., Database).

The entries in the criteria range may be changed at any time, in which case the values of the database functions are automatically recalculated. The other database functions have arguments identical to those used in the DAVERAGE function. The functions will adjust automatically if rows or columns are inserted within the specified range.

	A	B	C	D	E
1	Name	Location	Title	Hire Date	Salary
2	Adams	Atlanta	Trainee	11/24/93	$19,500
3	Adamson	Chicago	Manager	3/16/92	$52,000
4	Brown	Atlanta	Trainee	11/24/93	$18,500
5	Charles	Boston	Account Rep	3/16/92	$40,000
6	Coulter	Atlanta	Manager	11/24/93	$100,000
7	Elofson	Miami	Account Rep	10/31/92	$47,500
8	Gillenson	Miami	Account Rep	10/31/93	$55,000
9	James	Chicago	Account Rep	10/31/89	$42,500
10	Johnson	Chicago	Account Rep	10/31/90	$47,500
11	Manin	Boston	Account Rep	3/16/92	$49,500
12	Marder	Chicago	Account Rep	10/31/91	$38,500
13	Milgrom	Boston	Manager	3/16/92	$57,500
14	Rubin	Boston	Account Rep	3/16/92	$45,000
15	Smith	Atlanta	Account Rep	11/24/93	$65,000
16					
17	Name	Location	Title	Hire Date	Salary
18			Manager		
19					
20					
21			Summary Statistics		
22	Average Salary:				$69,833
23	Maximum Salary:				$100,000
24	Minimum Salary:				$52,000
25	Total Salary:				$209,500
26	Number of Employees:				3

Criteria range is A17:E18 (filters list to Managers)

Summary statistics for Managers

FIGURE 7.10   *Database Functions*

Insert Name Command

The ***Name command*** in the Insert menu equates a mnemonic name such as *EmployeeList* to a cell or cell range such as *A1:E15,* then enables you to use that name to reference the cell(s) in all subsequent commands. A name can be up to 255 characters in length, but must begin with a letter or an underscore. It can include upper- or lowercase letters, numbers, periods, and underscore characters but no blank spaces.

Once defined, names adjust automatically for insertions and/or deletions within the range. If, in the previous example, you were to delete row 4, the definition of *EmployeeList* would change to A1:E14. And, in similar fashion, if you were to add a new column between columns B and C, the range would change to A1:F14.

A name can be used in any formula or function instead of a cell address; for example, =SALES−EXPENSES instead of =C1−C10, where Sales and Expenses have been defined as the names for cells C1 and C10, respectively. A name can also be entered into any dialog box where a cell range is required.

THE GO TO COMMAND

Names are frequently used in conjunction with the Go To command. Pull down the Edit menu and click Go To (or click the F5 key) to display a dialog box containing the names that have been defined within the workbook. Double click a name to move directly to the first cell in the associated range and simultaneously select the entire range.

The ***Subtotals command*** uses a summary function (such as SUM, AVERAGE, or COUNT) to compute subtotals for groups of records within a list. The records are grouped according to the value in a specific field, such as location, as shown in Figure 7.11. The Subtotals command inserts a subtotal row into the list whenever the value of the designated field (location in this example) changes from one record to the next.

The subtotal for the Atlanta employees is inserted into the list as we go from the last employee in Atlanta to the first employee in Boston. In similar fashion, the subtotal for Boston is inserted into the list as we go from the last employee in Boston to the first employee in Chicago. A grand total is displayed after the last record. The list must be in sequence, according to the field on which the subtotals will be grouped, prior to executing the Subtotals command.

The summary information can be displayed with different levels of detail. Figure 7.11a displays the salary data for each employee (known as the detail lines), the subtotals for each location, and the grand total. Figure 7.11b suppresses the detail lines but shows both the subtotals and grand total. Figure 7.11c shows only the grand total. The worksheet in all three figures is said to be in outline format, as seen by the ***outline symbols*** at the extreme left of the application window.

The records within the list are grouped to compute the summary information. A plus sign indicates that the group has been collapsed, and that the detail information is suppressed. A minus sign indicates the opposite, namely that the group has been expanded and that the detail information is visible. You can click any plus or minus sign to expand or collapse that portion of the outline. You can also click the symbols (1, 2, or 3) above the plus or minus signs to collapse or expand the rows within the worksheet. Level one shows the least amount of detail and displays only the grand total. Level two includes the subtotals as well as the grand total. Level three includes the detail records, the subtotals, and the grand total.

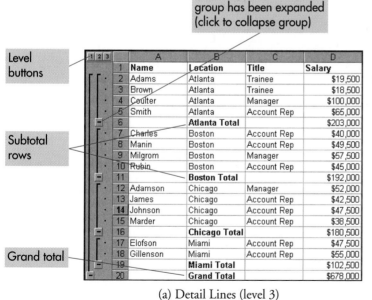

Minus sign indicates group has been expanded (click to collapse group)

Plus sign indicates group has been collapsed (click to expand group)

Level buttons

Subtotal rows

Grand total

(a) Detail Lines (level 3)

(b) Location Totals (level 2)

(c) Grand Total (level 1)

FIGURE 7.11   *Subtotals and Outlining*

DATA VERSUS INFORMATION

Objective To sort a list on multiple keys; to demonstrate the AutoFilter and Advanced Filter commands; to define a named range within a worksheet; to use the DSUM, DAVERAGE, DMAX, DMIN, and DCOUNT functions. Use Figure 7.12 as a guide in the exercise.

Step 1: **Calculate the Years of Service**

➤ Start Excel. Open the **Finished Employee List workbook** created in the previous exercise.

➤ Click the **column heading** in **column D**. Point to the selection and click the **right mouse button** to display a shortcut menu. Click **Insert**. The column of hire dates has been moved to column E. Click in **cell D1**. Type **Service** and press **enter**.

➤ Click in **cell D2** and enter the formula to compute the years of service **=(Today( )-E2)/365** as shown in Figure 7.12a. Press **enter**; the years of service for the first employee are displayed in cell D2.

➤ Click in **cell D2**, then click the **Decrease Decimal button** on the Formatting toolbar several times to display the length of service with only one decimal place. Reduce the column width as appropriate.

➤ Drag the **fill handle** in cell D2 to the remaining cells in that column (**cells D3** through **D15**) to compute the length of service for the remaining employees.

➤ Save the workbook.

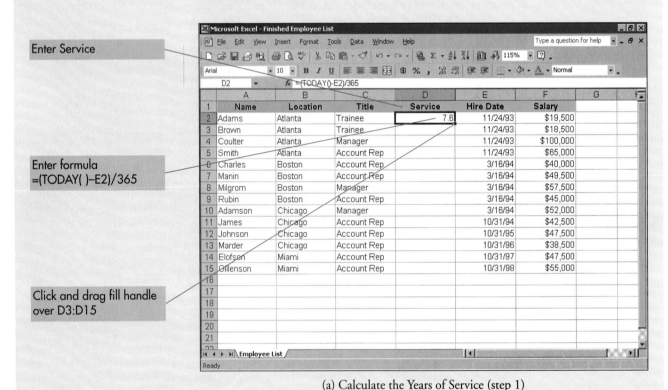

(a) Calculate the Years of Service (step 1)

FIGURE 7.12 *Hands-on Exercise 2*

Step 2: **The AutoFilter Command**

➤ Click a single cell anywhere within the list. Pull down the **Data menu**. Click the **Filter command**.

➤ Click **AutoFilter** from the resulting cascade menu to display the drop-down arrows to the right of each field name.

➤ Click the **drop-down arrow** next to **Title** to display the list of titles in Figure 7.12b. Click **Account Rep**.

➤ The display changes to show only those employees who meet the filter. The row numbers for the visible records are blue. The drop-down arrow for Title is also blue, indicating that it is part of the filter condition.

➤ Click the **drop-down arrow** next to **Location**. Click **Boston** to display only the employees in this city. The combination of the two filter conditions shows only the account reps in Boston.

➤ Click the **drop-down arrow** next to **Location** a second time. Click **(All)** to remove the filter condition on location. Only the account reps are displayed since the filter on Title is still in effect.

➤ Save the workbook.

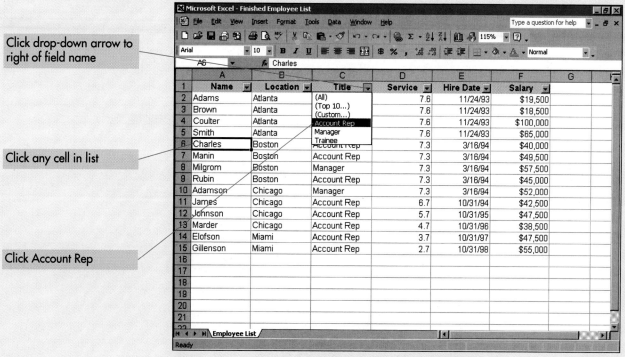

Click drop-down arrow to right of field name

Click any cell in list

Click Account Rep

(b) The AutoFilter Command (step 2)

FIGURE 7.12 *Hands-on Exercise 2 (continued)*

THE TOP 10 AUTOFILTER

Use the Top 10 AutoFilter option to see the top (or bottom) 10, or for that matter any number of records in a list. Just turn the AutoFilter condition on, click the down arrow in the designated field, then click Top 10 to display the associated dialog box, where you specify the records you want to view. See exercise 7 at the end of the chapter.

Step 3: **The Custom AutoFilter Command**

➤ Click the **drop-down arrow** next to **Salary** to display the list of salaries. Click **Custom** to display the dialog box in Figure 7.12c.
➤ Click the **arrow** in the leftmost drop-down list box for **Salary**, then click the **is greater than** as the relational operator.
➤ Click in the text box for the salary amount. Type **45000**. Click **OK**.
➤ The list changes to display only those employees whose title is account rep *and* who earn more than $45,000.
➤ Pull down the **Data menu**. Click **Filter**. Click **AutoFilter** to toggle the Auto-Filter command off, which removes the arrows next to the field names and cancels all filter conditions. All of the records in the list are visible.
➤ Save the workbook.

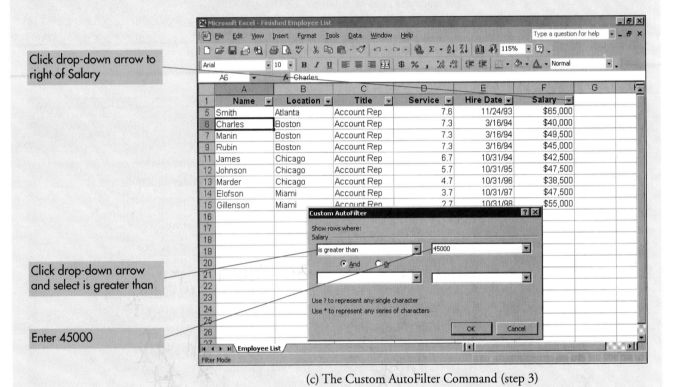

(c) The Custom AutoFilter Command (step 3)

FIGURE 7.12   *Hands-on Exercise 2 (continued)*

WILD CARDS

Excel recognizes the question mark and asterisk as wild cards in the specification of criteria. A question mark stands for a single character in the exact position; for example, B?ll returns Ball, Bill, Bell, and Bull. An asterisk stands for any number of characters; for example, *son will find Samson, Johnson, and Yohanson, among others.

Step 4: **The Advanced Filter Command**

➤ The field names in the criteria range must be spelled exactly the same way as in the associated list. The best way to ensure that the names are identical is to copy the entries from the list to the criteria range.

➤ Click and drag to select **cells A1** through **F1**. Click the **Copy button** on the Standard toolbar. A moving border appears around the selected cells. Click in **cell A17**. Click the **Paste button** on the Standard toolbar to complete the copy operation. Press **Esc** to cancel the moving border.

➤ Click in **cell C18**. Enter **Manager**. (Be sure you spell it correctly.)

➤ Click a single cell anywhere within the employee list. Pull down the **Data menu**. Click **Filter**. Click **Advanced Filter** from the resulting cascade menu to display the dialog box in Figure 7.12d. (The list range is already entered because you had selected a cell in the list prior to executing the command.)

➤ Click in the **Criteria Range** text box. Click in **cell A17** in the worksheet and drag the mouse to cell F18. Release the mouse. A moving border appears around these cells in the worksheet, and the corresponding cell reference is entered in the dialog box.

➤ Check that the **option button** to Filter the List in-place is selected. Click **OK**. The display changes to show just the managers; that is, only rows 4, 8, and 10 are visible.

➤ Click in **cell B18**. Type **Atlanta**. Press **enter**.

➤ Pull down the **Data menu**. Click **Filter**. Click **Advanced Filter**. The Advanced Filter dialog box already has the cell references for the list and criteria ranges (which were the last entries made).

➤ Click **OK**. The display changes to show just the manager in Atlanta; that is, only row 4 is visible.

➤ Pull down the **Data menu**. Click **Filter**. Click **Show All** to remove the filter condition. The entire list is visible.

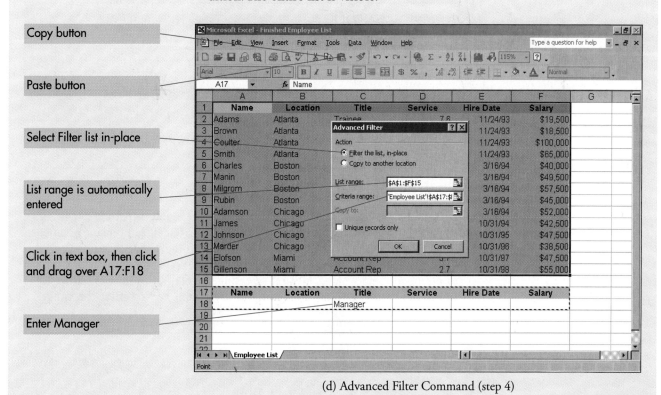

(d) Advanced Filter Command (step 4)

FIGURE 7.12 *Hands-on Exercise 2 (continued)*

Step 5: **The Insert Name Command**

> ➤ Click and drag to select **cells A1** through **F15** as shown in Figure 7.12e.
> ➤ Pull down the **Insert menu**. Click **Name**. Click **Define**. Type **Database** in the Define Name dialog box. Click **OK**.
> ➤ Pull down the **Edit menu** and click **Go To** (or press the **F5 key**) to display the Go To dialog box. There are two names in the box: Database, which you just defined, and Criteria, which was defined automatically when you specified the criteria range in step 4.
> ➤ Double click **Criteria** to select the criteria range (**cells A17** through **F18**). Click elsewhere in the worksheet to deselect the cells.
> ➤ Save the workbook.

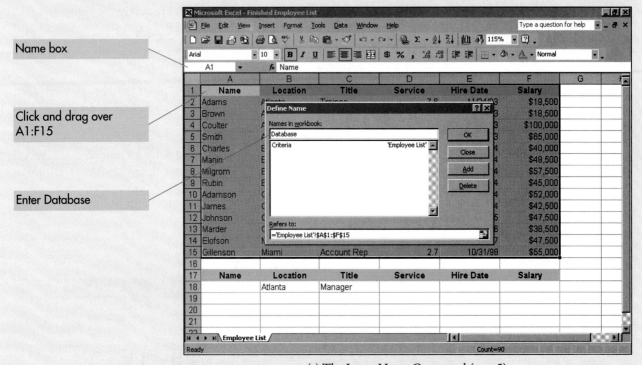

(e) The Insert Name Command (step 5)

FIGURE 7.12   *Hands-on Exercise 2 (continued)*

THE NAME BOX

Use the Name box on the formula bar to select a cell or named range by clicking in the box and then typing the appropriate cell reference or name. You can also click the drop-down arrow next to the Name box to select a named range from a drop-down list. And, finally, you can use the Name box to define a named range, by first selecting the cell(s) in the worksheet to which the name is to apply, clicking in the Name box to enter the range name, and then pressing the enter key.

Step 6: **Database Functions**

> ➤ Click in cell **A21**, type **Summary Statistics**, press the **enter key**, then click and drag to select cells **A21** through **F21**.
> ➤ Pull down the **Format menu**, click **Cells**, click the **Alignment tab**, then select **Center Across Selection** as the Horizontal alignment. Click **OK**.
> ➤ Enter the labels for **cells A22** through **A26** as shown in Figure 7.12f.
> ➤ Click in **cell B18**. Press the **Del key**. The criteria range is now set to select only managers.
> ➤ Click in **cell F22**. Click the **Insert Function button** on the formula bar to display the dialog box in Figure 7.12f.
> ➤ Select **Database** from the category list box, select **DAVERAGE** as the function name, then click **OK**.

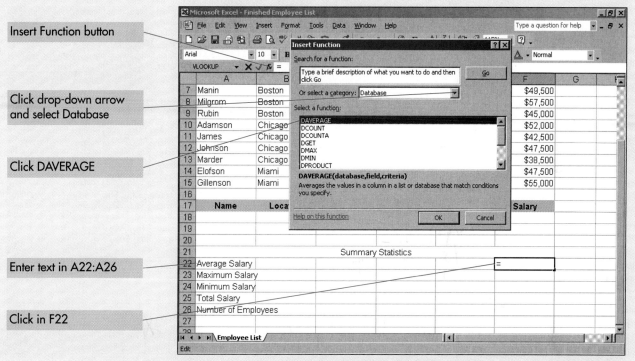

Insert Function button

Click drop-down arrow and select Database

Click DAVERAGE

Enter text in A22:A26

Click in F22

(f) Database Functions (step 6)

FIGURE 7.12 *Hands-on Exercise 2 (continued)*

HIDE A COLUMN

An individual's hire date and length of service convey essentially the same information, and thus there is no need to display both columns. Point to the column heading of the field you wish to hide, then click the right mouse button to select the column and display a shortcut menu. Click the Hide command, and the column is no longer visible (although it remains in the worksheet). To display (unhide) a column, click and drag the adjacent column headings on both sides, click the right mouse button to display a shortcut menu, then click the Unhide command.

Step 7: The DAVERAGE Function

➤ Click the **Database** text box in the dialog box as shown in Figure 7.12g. Type **Database** (the range name defined in step 5), which references the employee list.

➤ Click the **Field** text box. Type **"Salary"** (you must include the quotation marks), which is the name of the field (column name) within the list that you want to average.

➤ Click the **Criteria** text box. Type **Criteria** (the range name automatically assigned to the criteria range during the Advanced Filter operation). The dialog box displays the computed value of 69833.33333.

➤ Click **OK** to enter the DAVERAGE function into the worksheet.

➤ Save the workbook.

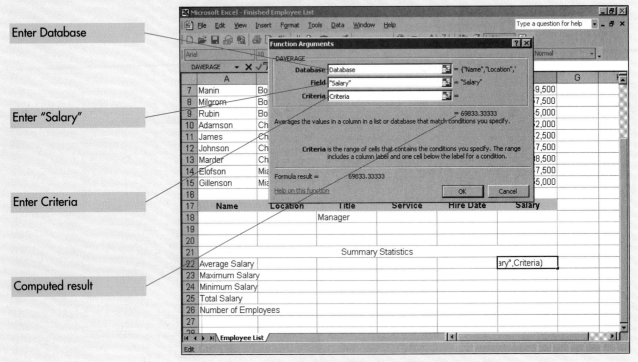

(g) The DAVERAGE Function (step 7)

FIGURE 7.12 *Hands-on Exercise 2 (continued)*

THE COLLAPSE DIALOG BUTTON

It's usually easier to enter a cell reference in the Formula Palette by clicking the underlying cell(s) within the worksheet, rather than explicitly typing the entry. The Formula Palette, however, often hides the cell(s). Should this occur, just click the Collapse Dialog button (which appears to the right of any parameter within the dialog box) to collapse (hide) the Formula Palette, enabling you to click the underlying cell(s), which is (are) now visible. Click the Collapse Dialog button a second time to display the entire dialog box.

Step 8: **The DMAX, DMIN, DSUM, and DCOUNT Functions**

➤ Enter the DMAX, DMIN, DSUM, and DCOUNT functions in cells F23 through F26, respectively. You can use the **Insert Function button** to enter each function individually, *or* you can copy the DAVERAGE function and edit appropriately:

• Click in **cell F22**. Drag the **fill handle** to **cells F23** through **F26** to copy the DAVERAGE function to these cells.

• Double click in **cell F23** to edit the contents of this cell, then click within the displayed formula to substitute **DMAX** for DAVERAGE. Press **enter**.

• Double click in the remaining cells and edit them appropriately.

➤ The computed values (except for the DCOUNT function, which has a computed value of 3) are shown in Figure 7.12h.

➤ Select **cells F22** through **F25**, then format these cells to currency with no decimals using the Formatting toolbar.

➤ Click and drag the border between columns F and G to widen column F as necessary. Save the workbook.

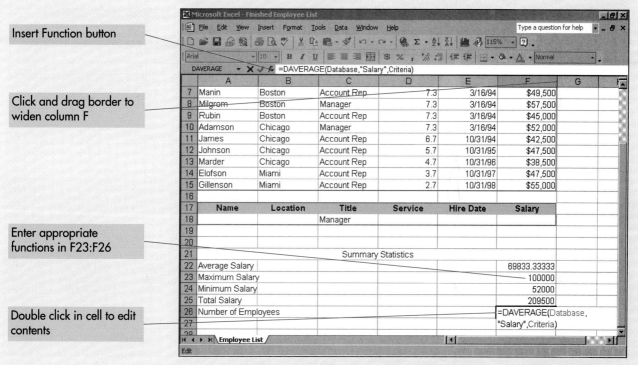

Insert Function button

Click and drag border to widen column F

Enter appropriate functions in F23:F26

Double click in cell to edit contents

(h) The DMAX, DMIN, DSUM, DCOUNT Functions (step 8)

FIGURE 7.12 *Hands-on Exercise 2 (continued)*

IMPORT DATA FROM ACCESS

The data in a worksheet can be imported from an Access database. Pull down the Data menu, click the Import External Data command, then click Import Data to display the Select Data Source dialog box. Use the Look in list box to locate the folder containing the database and choose Access Databases as the file type. Select the database, then click the Open command to bring the Access table(s) into an Excel workbook.

Step 9: **Change the Criteria**

➤ Click in the **Name box**. Type **B18** and press **enter** to make cell B18 the active cell. Type **Chicago** to change the criteria to Chicago managers. Press **enter**.

➤ The values displayed by the DAVERAGE, DMIN, DMAX, and DSUM functions change to $52,000, reflecting the one employee (Adamson) who meets the current criteria (a manager in Chicago). The value displayed by the DCOUNT function changes to 1 to indicate one employee as shown in Figure 7.12i.

➤ Click in **cell C18**. Press the **Del key**.

➤ The average salary changes to $45,125, reflecting all employees in Chicago.

➤ Click in **cell B18**. Press the **Del key**.

➤ The criteria range is now empty. The DAVERAGE function displays $48,429, which is the average salary of all employees in the database.

➤ Click in **cell C18**. Type **Manager** and press the **enter key**. The average salary is $69,833, the average salary for all managers.

➤ Save the workbook.

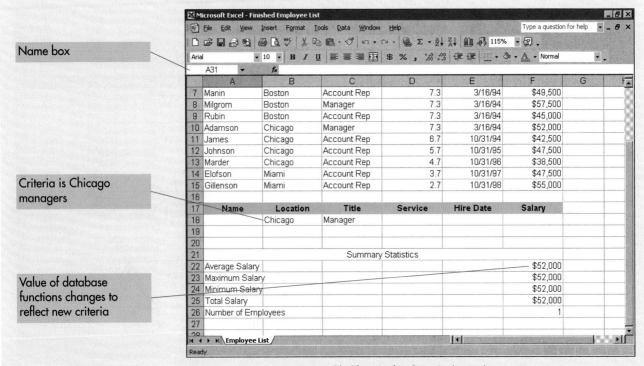

(i) Change the Criteria (step 9)

FIGURE 7.12 *Hands-on Exercise 2 (continued)*

FILTER THE LIST IN PLACE

Use the Advanced Filter command to filter the list in place and display the records that meet the current criteria. Click anywhere in the list, pull down the Data menu, click the Filter command, then choose Advanced Filter to display the Advanced Filter dialog box. Click the option button to filter the list in place, then click OK to display the selected records. You have to execute this command each time the criteria change.

Step 10:   **Create the Subtotals**

➤ A list must be in sequence prior to computing the subtotals. Click any cell in the list in **Column C**, the column containing the employee titles, then click the **Sort Ascending button** on the Standard toolbar. The employees should be sequenced according to title as shown in Figure 7.12j.

➤ Pull down the **Data menu** and click the **Subtotals command**. Click the **drop-down arrow** in the **At Each Change in** list box. Click **Title** to create a subtotal whenever there is a change in title. Set the other options to match the dialog box in Figure 7.12j. Click **OK** to create the subtotals.

➤ You should see the three subtotals, one for each title, followed by the grand total for the company. The total for the Account Reps should appear first and it is equal to $430,500.

➤ The total for managers is $209,500 and matches the value obtained by the DSUM command.

➤ Save the workbook.

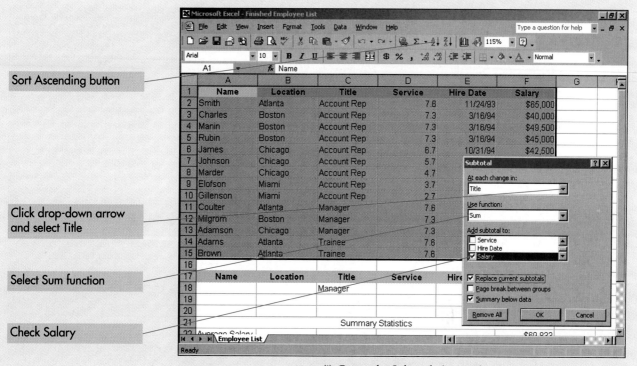

(j) Create the Subtotals (step 10)

FIGURE 7.12   *Hands-on Exercise 2 (continued)*

TWO SETS OF SUBTOTALS

You can obtain multiple sets of subtotals in the same list, provided you do the operations in the correct sequence. First sort the list according to the sequence you want, for example, by title within location. Click in the list, and compute the subtotals based on the primary key (location in this example). Click on the list a second time and compute the subtotals based on the secondary key (title in this example), but clear the check box to replace the current subtotals. You will see the subtotal for each title in the first location, followed by the subtotal for that location, and so on.

Step 11: **Collapse and Expand the Subtotals**

➤ The vertical lines at the left of the worksheet indicate how the data is aggregated within the list. Click the **minus sign** corresponding to the total for the Account Reps.

➤ The minus sign changes to a plus sign and the detail lines (the names of the Account Reps) disappear from the worksheet as shown in Figure 7.12k Click the **plus sign** next to the Account Rep total and you see the detailed information for each Account Rep.

➤ Click the **level 2 button** (under the Name box) to suppress the detail lines for all employees. The list collapses to display the subtotals and grand total.

➤ Click the **level 1 button** to suppress the subtotals. The list collapses further to display only the grand total. Click the **level 3 button** to restore the detail lines and subtotals.

➤ Click the **Print button** to print the list with the subtotals. Close the workbook. Exit Excel if you do not want to continue with the next exercise at this time.

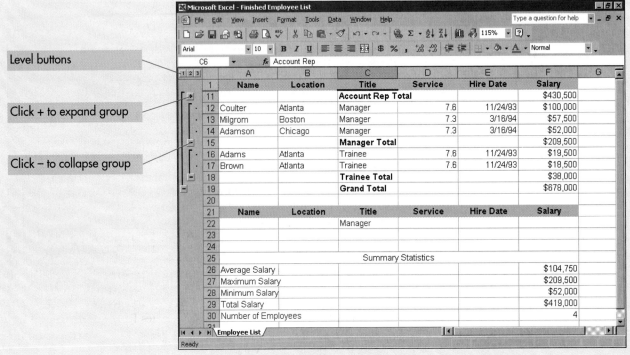

(k) Collapse and Expand the Subtotals (step 11)

FIGURE 7.12   *Hands-on Exercise 2 (continued)*

DETAIL LINES VERSUS SUMMARY TOTALS

The higher you go in an organization, the more aggregated the information. The CEO, for example, requires only summary information for the company as a whole. Division managers need additional information that shows the performance of their division. Branch managers require still more detail, and so on, down the line. Excel enables you to display the information that you need by expanding or compressing the detail lines within a subtotal list.

A *pivot table* provides the ultimate flexibility in data analysis. It divides the records in a list into categories, then computes summary statistics for those categories. Pivot tables are illustrated in conjunction with the data in Figure 7.13 that displays sales information for a hypothetical advertising agency. Each record in the list in Figure 7.13a displays the name of the sales representative, the quarter in which the sale was recorded, the type of media, and the amount of the sale.

The pivot table in Figure 7.13b shows the total sales for each Media–Sales Rep combination. Look closely and you will see four shaded buttons, each of which corresponds to a different area in the table. The Media and Sales Rep buttons are in the row and column areas, respectively. Thus, each row in the pivot table displays the data for a different media type (magazine, radio, or TV), whereas each column displays data for a different sales representative. The Quarter button in the page area provides a third dimension. The value in the drop-down list box indicates that all of the records in the underlying worksheet are used to compute the totals in the body of the table. You can, however, display different pages corresponding to the totals in the first, second, third, or fourth quarters. You can also click the arrows next to the other buttons to suppress selected values for the media type or sales representative.

The best feature about a pivot table is its flexibility because you can change the orientation to provide a different analysis of the associated data. Figure 7.13c, for example, displays an alternate version of the pivot table in which the fields have been rearranged to show the total for each combination of quarter and sales representative. You go from one pivot table to another simply by clicking and dragging the buttons corresponding to the field names to different positions.

You can also change the means of computation within the data area. Both of the pivot tables in Figure 7.13 use the Sum function, but you can choose other functions such as Average, Minimum, Maximum, or Count. You can also change the formatting of any element in the table. More importantly, pivot tables are dynamic in that they reflect changes to the underlying worksheet. Thus, you can add, edit, or delete records in the associated list and see the results in the pivot table, provided you execute the *Refresh command* to update the pivot table.

The *Pivot Table Wizard* is used to create the initial pivot table in conjunction with an optional pivot chart. The *pivot chart* in Figure 7.14, for example, corresponds to the pivot table in Figure 7.13b, and at first glance, it resembles any other Excel chart. Look closely, however, and you will see shaded buttons similar to those in the pivot table, enabling you to change the chart by dragging the buttons to different areas. Reverse the position of the Media and Sales Rep buttons, for example, and you have a completely different chart. Any changes to the chart are reflected in the underlying pivot table and vice versa.

Drop-down arrows next to each button on the pivot chart let you display selected values. Click either arrow to display a drop-down list in which you select the values you want to appear in the chart. You could, for example, click the drop-down arrow next to the Sales Rep field and clear the name of any sales rep to remove his/her data from the chart.

Pivot tables may also be saved as Web pages with full interactivity as shown in Figure 7.15. The Address bar indicates that you are viewing a Web document (note the htm extension), as opposed to an Excel workbook. As with an ordinary pivot table, you can pivot the table within the Web page by repositioning the buttons for the row, column, and page fields. The plus and minus next to the various categories enable you to show or hide the detailed information. (The interactivity extends to Netscape as well as Internet Explorer, provided that you install the Office Web components.)

Pivot tables are one of the best-kept secrets in Excel, even though they have been available in the last several releases of Excel. (Pivot charts were introduced in Excel 2000.) Be sure to share this capability with your friends and colleagues.

(a) Sales Data (Excel list)

	A	B	C	D
1	**Sales Rep**	**Quarter**	**Media**	**Amount**
2	Alice	1st quarter	TV	$15,000
3	Alice	1st quarter	Radio	$4,000
4	Alice	2nd quarter	Magazine	$2,000
5	Alice	2nd quarter	Radio	$4,000
6	Alice	3rd quarter	Radio	$2,000
7	Alice	4th quarter	Radio	$4,000
8	Alice	4th quarter	Radio	$1,000
9	Bob	1st quarter	Magazine	$2,000
10	Bob	1st quarter	Radio	$1,000
11	Bob	2nd quarter	Radio	$4,000
12	Bob	3rd quarter	TV	$10,000
13	Bob	4th quarter	Magazine	$10,000
14	Bob	4th quarter	Magazine	$12,000
15	Bob	4th quarter	Radio	$1,000
16	Bob	4th quarter	Magazine	$7,000

	A	B	C	D
17	Carol	1st quarter	Radio	$4,000
18	Carol	2nd quarter	Magazine	$2,000
19	Carol	2nd quarter	Magazine	$7,000
20	Carol	2nd quarter	TV	$10,000
21	Carol	3rd quarter	TV	$8,000
22	Carol	3rd quarter	TV	$18,000
23	Carol	4th quarter	TV	$13,000
24	Ted	1st quarter	Radio	$2,000
25	Ted	2nd quarter	TV	$6,000
26	Ted	2nd quarter	TV	$6,000
27	Ted	3rd quarter	TV	$20,000
28	Ted	3rd quarter	Magazine	$15,000
29	Ted	3rd quarter	Magazine	$2,000
30	Ted	4th quarter	TV	$13,000
31	Ted	4th quarter	TV	$15,000

(a) Sales Data (Excel list)

All records are used in calculations

Quarter is in page area

Computation is Sum of Amount

Media is in row area

Sales Rep is in column area

	A	B	C	D	E	F
1	Quarter	(All) ▼				
2						
3	Sum of Amount	Sales Rep ▼				
4	Media ▼	Alice	Bob	Carol	Ted	Grand Total
5	Magazine	$2,000	$31,000	$9,000	$17,000	$59,000
6	Radio	$15,000	$6,000	$4,000	$2,000	$27,000
7	TV	$15,000	$10,000	$49,000	$60,000	$134,000
8	Grand Total	$32,000	$47,000	$62,000	$79,000	$220,000

(b) Analysis by Media Type and Sales Representative

Media is in page area

Calculation is Sum of Amount

Sales Rep is in row area

Quarter is in column area

	A	B	C	D	E	F
1	Media	(All) ▼				
2						
3	Sum of Amount	Quarter ▼				
4	Sales Rep ▼	1st quarter	2nd quarter	3rd quarter	4th quarter	Grand Total
5	Alice	$19,000	$6,000	$2,000	$5,000	$32,000
6	Bob	$3,000	$4,000	$10,000	$30,000	$47,000
7	Carol	$4,000	$19,000	$26,000	$13,000	$62,000
8	Ted	$2,000	$12,000	$37,000	$28,000	$79,000
9	Grand Total	$28,000	$41,000	$75,000	$76,000	$220,000

(c) Analysis by Sales Representative and Quarter

FIGURE 7.13   *Pivot Tables*

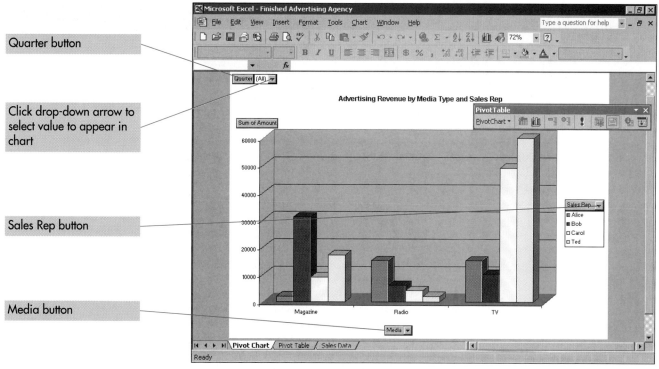

Quarter button

Click drop-down arrow to select value to appear in chart

Sales Rep button

Media button

FIGURE 7.14 *A Pivot Chart*

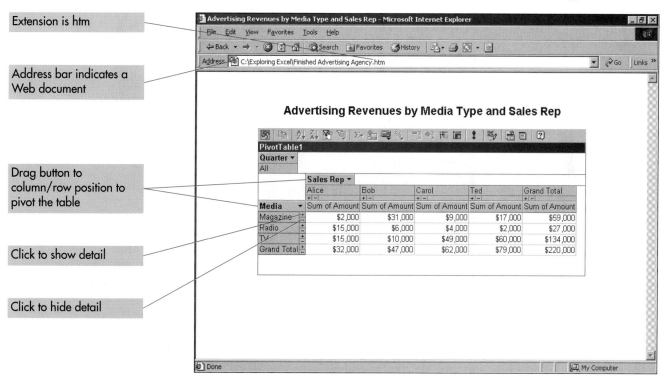

Extension is htm

Address bar indicates a Web document

Drag button to column/row position to pivot the table

Click to show detail

Click to hide detail

FIGURE 7.15 *Pivot Tables on the Web*

PIVOT TABLES AND PIVOT CHARTS

Objective   To create a pivot table and pivot chart; to create a Web page based on the pivot table. Use Figure 7.16 as a guide in the exercise.

Step 1:   **Start the Pivot Table Wizard**

➤ Start Excel. Open the **Advertising Agency workbook** in the **Exploring Excel folder**. Save the workbook as **Finished Advertising Agency** so that you will be able to return to the original workbook.

➤ The workbook contains a list of sales records for the advertising agency. Each record displays the name of the sales representative, the quarter in which the sale was recorded, the media type, and the amount of the sale.

➤ Click anywhere in the list of sales data. Pull down the **Data menu**. Click **PivotTable and PivotChart report** to start the Pivot Table Wizard as shown in Figure 7.16a. Close the Office Assistant, if necessary.

➤ Select the same options as in our figure. The pivot table will be created from data in a Microsoft Excel List or Database. In addition, you want to create a Pivot Chart report (that includes the Pivot Table). Click **Next**.

➤ Cells A1 through D31 have been selected automatically as the basis of the pivot table. Click **Next**.

➤ The option button to put the pivot table into a new worksheet is already selected. Click **Finish**. Two additional sheets have been added to the workbook, but the pivot table and chart area are not yet complete.

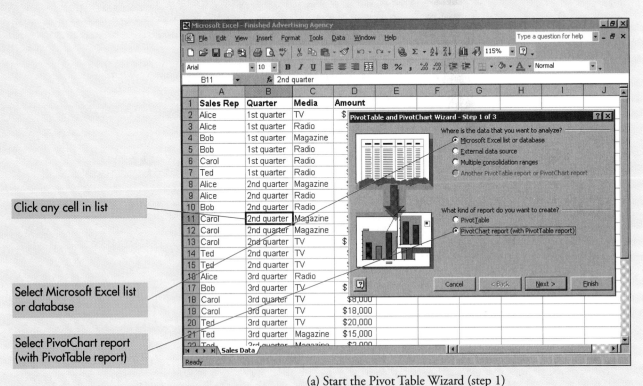

(a) Start the Pivot Table Wizard (step 1)

FIGURE 7.16   *Hands-on Exercise 3*

Step 2: **Complete the Pivot Table**

➤ Click the tab that takes you to the new worksheet (Sheet1 in our workbook). Your screen should be similar to Figure 7.16b. Complete the pivot table as follows:
  • Click the **Media field button** and drag it to the row area.
  • Click the **Sales Rep button** and drag it to the column area.
  • Click the **Quarter field button** and drag it to the page area.
  • Click the **Amount field button** and drag it to the data area.
➤ You should see the total sales for each sales representative for each type of media within a pivot table.
➤ Rename the worksheets so that they are more descriptive of their contents. Double click the **Sheet1 tab** (the worksheet that contains the pivot table) to select the name of the sheet. Type **Pivot Table** as the new name, and press **enter**.
➤ Double click the **Chart1** worksheet and change its name to **Pivot Chart** in similar fashion. Save the workbook.

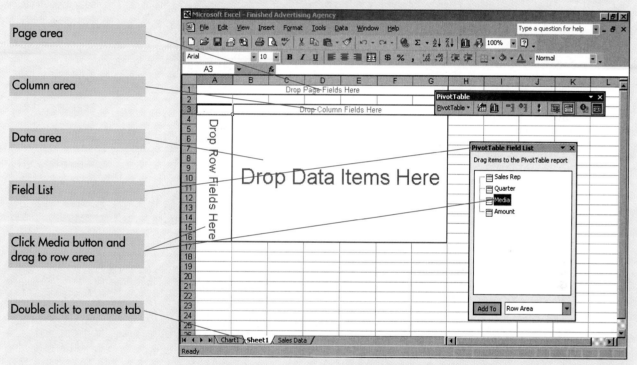

(b) Complete the Pivot Table (step 2)

FIGURE 7.16   *Hands-on Exercise 3 (continued)*

THE PAGE FIELD

A page field adds a third dimension to a pivot table. Unlike items in the row and column fields, however, the items in a page field are displayed one at a time. Creating a page field on Quarter, for example, lets you view the data for each quarter separately, by clicking the drop-down arrow on the page field list box, then clicking the appropriate quarter.

Step 3: **Modify the Sales Data**

➤ You will replace Bob's name within the list of transactions with your own name. Click the **Sales Data tab** to return to the underlying worksheet. Pull down the **Edit menu** and click the **Replace command** to display the Find and Replace dialog box.

➤ Enter **Bob** in the Find What dialog box, type **Your Name** (first and last) in the Replace With dialog box, then click the **Replace All button**. Click **OK** after the replacements have been made. Close the Find and Replace dialog box.

➤ Click the **Pivot Table tab** to return to the pivot table as shown in Figure 7.16c. The name change is not yet reflected in the pivot table because the table must be manually refreshed whenever the underlying data changes.

➤ Click anywhere in the pivot table, then click the **Refresh Data button** on the Pivot Table toolbar to update the pivot table. (You must click the Refresh button to update the pivot table whenever the underlying data changes.) You should see your name as one of the sales representatives.

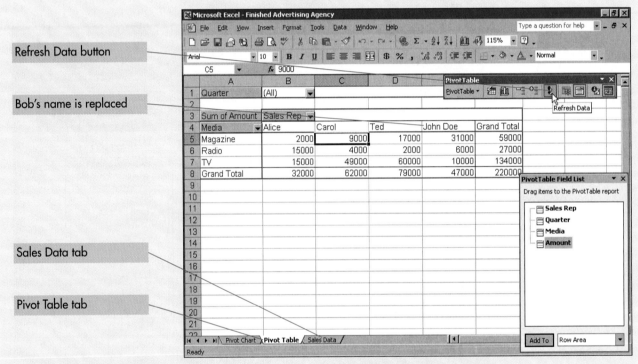

(c) Modify the Sales Data (step 3)

FIGURE 7.16   *Hands-on Exercise 3 (continued)*

THE FORMAT REPORT BUTTON

Why settle for a traditional report in black and white or shades of gray when you can choose from preformatted reports in a variety of styles and colors? Click the Format Report button on the Pivot Table toolbar to display the AutoFormat dialog box, where you select the style of your report. (To return to the default formatting, scroll to the end of the AutoFormat dialog box and select PivotTable Classic.)

Step 4: **Pivot the Table**

> ➤ You can change the contents of a pivot table simply by dragging fields from one area to another. Click and drag the **Quarter field** to the row area. The page field is now empty and you can see the breakdown of sales by quarter and media type.
> ➤ Click and drag the **Media field** to the column area, then drag the **Sales Rep field** to the page area. Your pivot table should match the one in Figure 7.16d.
> ➤ Click anywhere in the pivot table, then click the **Field Settings button** on the Pivot Table toolbar to display the PivotTable Field dialog box.
> ➤ Click the **Number button**, choose **Currency format** (with zero decimals). Click **OK** to close the Format Cells dialog box. Click **OK** a second time to close the Pivot Table Field dialog box.
> ➤ Save the workbook.

Field Settings button

Drag Sales Rep field to Page area

Drag Quarter field to row area

Drag Media field to column area

Number button

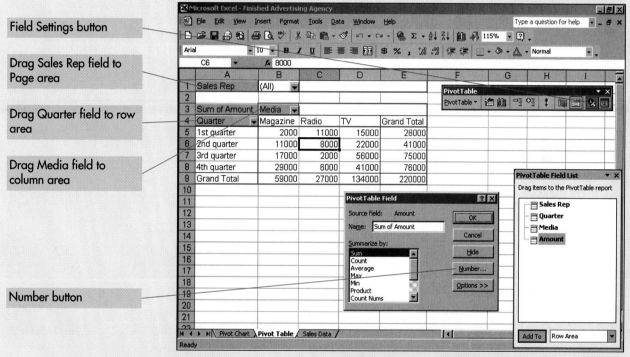

(d) Pivot the Table (step 4)

FIGURE 7.16 *Hands-on Exercise 3 (continued)*

CUSTOMIZE THE PIVOT TABLE

Right click anywhere within a pivot table to display a context-sensitive menu, then click the Table Options command to display the PivotTable Options dialog box. The default settings work well for most tables, but you can customize the table in a variety of ways. You can, for example, suppress the row or column totals or display a specific value in a blank cell. You can also change the formatting for any field within the table by right clicking the field and selecting the Format Cells button from the resulting menu.

Step 5: **Change the Chart Type**

➤ Click the **Pivot Chart tab** to view the default pivot chart as shown in Figure 7.16e. If necessary, close the field list to give yourself more room in which to work.

➤ Pull down the **Chart menu** and click the **Chart Type command** to display the dialog box in Figure 7.16e. Select the **Clustered column with a 3-D visual effect**. (Take a minute to appreciate the different types of charts that are available.)

➤ Check the box for **Default formatting**. This is a very important option, because without it, the chart is rotated in an awkward fashion. Click **OK**.

➤ The chart changes to display a three-dimensional column for each of the media in each data series.

➤ Save the workbook.

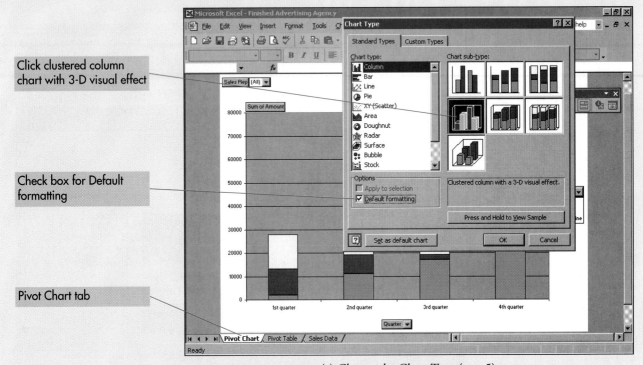

Click clustered column chart with 3-D visual effect

Check box for Default formatting

Pivot Chart tab

(e) Change the Chart Type (step 5)

FIGURE 7.16 *Hands-on Exercise 3 (continued)*

IT'S A PIVOT CHART

The shaded buttons for Sales Rep, Quarter, and Media that appear on the chart are similar in appearance and function to their counterparts in the underlying pivot table. Thus you can click and drag any of the buttons to a different position on the chart to change the underlying structure. You can also click and drag a field button from the PivotTable Field List to a new position on the chart. (Click the Show Field List button on the Pivot Table toolbar to show or hide the field list.)

Step 6: **Complete the Chart**

➤ Pull down the **Chart menu**, click **Chart Options** to display the Chart Options dialog box, then click the **Titles tab**. Enter **Advertising Revenue by Quarter and Media Type** as the chart title. Click **OK** to complete the chart as shown in Figure 7.16f.

➤ Click the **Sales Data tab** to select this worksheet. Press and hold the **Ctrl key** as you select the **Pivot Table tab** to select the worksheet containing the pivot table. Both worksheets are selected and hence both will be affected by the next command.

➤ Pull down the **File menu**, click the **Page Setup command**, and click the **Sheet tab**. Check the boxes to print **Gridlines** and **Row and Column headings**. Click the **Margins tab** and check the box to center the worksheet **horizontally**. Click **OK**. Save the workbook.

➤ Pull down the **File menu** and click the **Print command** to display the Print dialog box. Click the option button to print the entire workbook. Click **OK**.

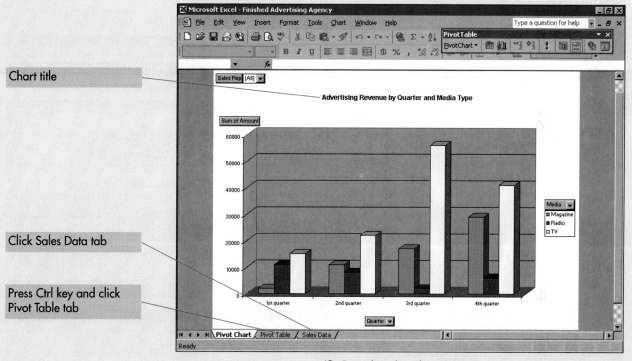

Chart title

Click Sales Data tab

Press Ctrl key and click Pivot Table tab

(f) Complete the Chart (step 6)

FIGURE 7.16 *Hands-on Exercise 3 (continued)*

FORMAT THE DATA SERIES

Why settle for a traditional bar chart when you can change the color, pattern, or shape of its components? Right click any column to select a data series to display a shortcut menu, then choose the Format Data Series command to display a dialog box in which you can customize the appearance of the vertical bars. We warn you that it is addictive, and that you can spend much more time than you intended initially. Set a time limit, and stop when you reach it.

Step 7:   **Save the Pivot Table as a Web Page**

➤ Click the **Pivot Chart tab** to deselect the two tabs, then click the **Pivot Table tab**. Click and drag to select the entire pivot table. (If you have difficulty selecting the table, click and drag from the bottom-right cell to the top-left cell.)

➤ Pull down the **File menu**, click the **Save As Web Page command** to display the Save As dialog box, then click the **Publish button** (within the Save As dialog box) to display the Publish as Web Page dialog box in Figure 7.16g. Click **No** if the Office Assistant offers help.

➤ The default file name is **Finished Advertising Agency** and it will be saved in the **Exploring Excel folder**. There is no need to change this information.

➤ Check the box to **Add interactivity** and select **Pivot Table functionality**. Check the boxes to **AutoRepublish every time this workbook is saved** and to **Open published web page in browser**.

➤ Click the **Change button** and enter an appropriate title that includes your name. Click **OK** to close the Set Title dialog box.

➤ Check that your settings match those in Figure 7.16g. Click the **Publish button** to publish the pivot table.

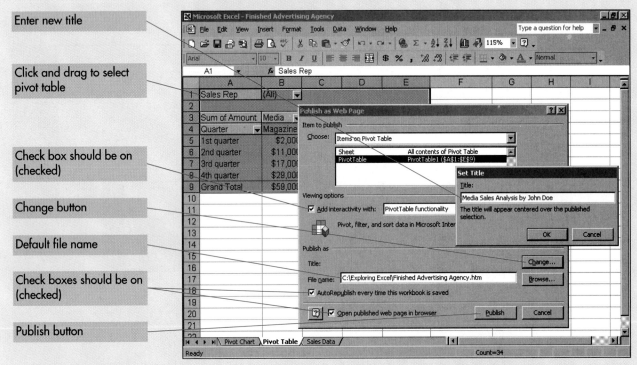

(g) Save the Pivot Table as a Web Page (step 7)

FIGURE 7.16   *Hands-on Exercise 3 (continued)*

AN EXTRA FOLDER

The Save As Web Page command creates an HTML document with the same name as the workbook on which it is based. The command also creates a folder with a similar name (the word "_files" is added to the end of the workbook name) that contains supporting Web pages to enable the interactivity. You must upload both the Web page and the folder if you intend to display the pivot table on a Web server.

Step 8: **Pivot the Web Page**

➤ The pivot table will open automatically in your browser because of the option you selected in the previous step. If Internet Explorer is your default browser, you will see the pivot table in Figure 7.16h.

➤ If Netscape Navigator is your default browser, you will be prompted to install the Microsoft Web components, after which you should see the pivot table.

➤ Pivot the table so that its appearance matches Figure 7.16h. Thus, you need to drag the **Sales Rep button** to the column area and the **Media button** to the row area. (You can click the **Fields List button** on the Pivot Table toolbar to display/hide the fields in the table, should you lose a field button.)

➤ Click the **Plus sign** next to each quarter to display the detailed information. Click the **Print button** on the Internet Explorer toolbar to print the pivot table for your instructor.

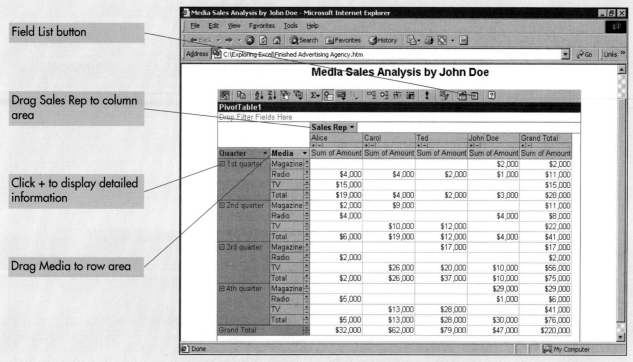

Field List button

Drag Sales Rep to column area

Click + to display detailed information

Drag Media to row area

(h) Pivot the Web Page (step 8)

FIGURE 7.16 *Hands-on Exercise 3 (continued)*

WHAT IS XML?

Extensible Markup Language (XML) takes structured data such as an Excel worksheet and converts it to a text file that can be read by a variety of applications. It enables the creator of an XML page to create his or her customized tags that enable the validation and transmission of data between applications. Formatting rules for XML are specified in style sheets. See practice exercise 10 at the end of the chapter.

Step 9: **Change the Underlying Data**

➤ Click the **Excel button** on the Windows taskbar to return to Excel. Click the **Sales Data worksheet** and change the data for John Doe's (your name) magazine sales in the first quarter from $2000 to $22000.

➤ Click the **worksheet tab** for the pivot table. Click anywhere in the pivot table and click the **refresh button** on the Pivot Table toolbar. The magazine sales in the 1st quarter increase to $22,000 and the grand total changes to $240,000.

➤ Click the **Save button** to save the changes to the worksheet. You will see the dialog box in Figure 7.16i. Click the option button to **Enable the Autopublish feature**. Click **OK**.

➤ Return to Internet Explorer. Click the **Refresh button** on the Pivot Table toolbar to update the Web page. The numbers within the Web pivot table change to reflect the change in magazine sales.

➤ Close Internet Explorer. Close Excel. Click **Yes** if prompted to save the changes.

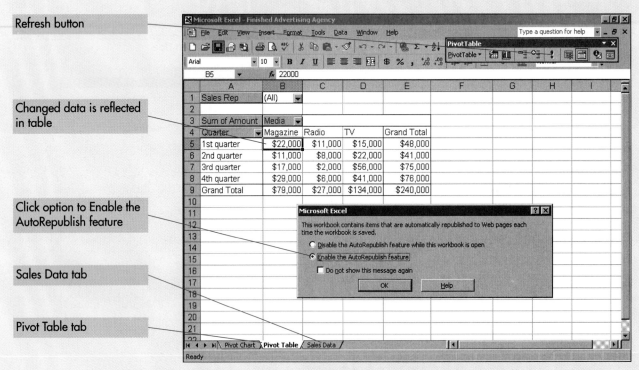

(i) Change the Underlying Data (step 9)

FIGURE 7.16   *Hands-on Exercise 3 (continued)*

THE NEED TO REFRESH

A pivot table and/or a Web page based on a pivot table do not automatically reflect changes in the underlying data. You must first refresh the pivot table as it exists within the workbook, by clicking in the pivot table, then clicking the refresh button on the Pivot Table toolbar. Next, you must save the workbook and enable the AutoPublish feature. Finally, you have to click in the Web page and click the Refresh button on the Web toolbar.

A list is an area in a worksheet that contains rows of similar data. The first row in the list contains the column labels (field names). Each additional row contains data for a specific record. A data form provides an easy way to add, edit, and delete records in a list.

A date is stored internally as an integer number corresponding to the number of days in this century. (January 1, 1900 is stored as the number 1.) The number of elapsed days between two dates can be determined by simple subtraction. The TODAY function always returns the current date (the date on which a worksheet is created or retrieved).

A filtered list displays only those records that meet specific criteria. Filtering is implemented through AutoFilter or the Advanced Filter command. The latter enables you to specify a criteria range and to copy the selected records elsewhere in the worksheet.

The Sort command arranges a list according to the value of one or more keys (known as the primary, secondary, and tertiary keys). Each key may be in ascending or descending sequence.

The database functions (DSUM, DAVERAGE, DMAX, DMIN, and DCOUNT) have three arguments: the associated list, the field name, and the criteria range. The simplest criteria range consists of two rows and as many fields as there are in the list.

The Text Import Wizard converts data in either fixed width or delimited format to an Excel workbook. The Wizard is displayed automatically if you attempt to open a text file. Data can also be imported into an Excel workbook from other applications such as Microsoft Access.

The Subtotals command uses a summary function (such as SUM, AVERAGE, or COUNT) to compute subtotals for data groups within a list. The data is displayed in outline view, where outline symbols can be used to suppress or expand the detail records.

A pivot table extends the capability of individual database functions by presenting the data in summary form. It divides the records in a list into categories, then computes summary statistics for those categories. Pivot tables provide the utmost flexibility in that you can vary the row or column categories and/or the way that the statistics are computed. A pivot chart extends the capability of a pivot table to a chart.

KEY TERMS

Advanced Filter command (p. 325)
Ascending sequence (p. 311)
AutoFilter command (p. 324)
Criteria range (p. 325)
Data (p. 322)
Data form (p. 310)
Database (p. 308)
Database functions (p. 327)
DAVERAGE function (p. 327)
DCOUNT function (p. 327)
Delete command (p. 309)
Delimited format (p. 314)
Descending sequence (p. 311)
DMAX function (p. 327)

DMIN function (p. 327)
DSUM function (p. 327)
Field (p. 308)
Field name (p. 308)
File (p. 308)
Filtered list (p. 324)
Fixed width format (p. 314)
Form command (p. 310)
Information (p. 322)
Insert Columns command (p. 309)
Insert Rows command (p. 309)
Key (p. 308)
List (p. 308)
Name command (p. 328)

Now ( ) function (p. 313)
Outline symbols (p. 329)
Pivot chart (p. 341)
Pivot table (p. 341)
Pivot Table Wizard (p. 341)
Record (p. 308)
Refresh command (p. 341)
Sort command (p. 311)
Subtotals command (p. 329)
Text Import Wizard (p. 314)
TODAY( ) function (p. 313)
Wild card (p. 327)

1. Which of the following best describes data management in Excel?
   (a) The rows in a list correspond to records in a file
   (b) The columns in a list correspond to fields in a record
   (c) Both (a) and (b)
   (d) Neither (a) nor (b)

2. How should a list be placed within a worksheet?
   (a) There should be at least one blank row between the list and the other entries in the worksheet
   (b) There should be at least one blank column between the list and the other entries in the worksheet
   (c) Both (a) and (b)
   (d) Neither (a) nor (b)

3. Which of the following is suggested for the placement of database functions within a worksheet?
   (a) Above or below the list with at least one blank row separating the database functions from the list to which they refer
   (b) To the left or right of the list with at least one blank column separating the database functions from the list to which they refer
   (c) Both (a) and (b)
   (d) Neither (a) nor (b)

4. Cells A21:B22 have been defined as the criteria range, cells A21 and B21 contain the field names City and Title, respectively, and cells A22 and B22 contain New York and Manager. The selected records will consist of:
   (a) All employees in New York, regardless of title
   (b) All managers, regardless of the city
   (c) Only the managers in New York
   (d) All employees in New York (regardless of title) or all managers

5. Cells A21:B23 have been defined as the criteria range, cells A21 and B21 contain the field names City and Title, respectively, and cells A22 and B23 contain New York and Manager, respectively. The selected records will consist of:
   (a) All employees in New York regardless of title
   (b) All managers regardless of the city
   (c) Only the managers in New York
   (d) All employees in New York or all managers

6. If employees are to be listed so that all employees in the same city appear together in alphabetical order by the employee's last name:
   (a) City and last name are both considered to be the primary key
   (b) City and last name are both considered to be the secondary key
   (c) City is the primary key and last name is the secondary key
   (d) Last name is the primary key and city is the secondary key

7. Which of the following can be used to delete a record from a database?
   (a) The Edit Delete command
   (b) The Data Form command
   (c) Both (a) and (b)
   (d) Neither (a) nor (b)

8. Which of the following is true about the DAVERAGE function?
   (a) It has a single argument
   (b) It can be entered into a worksheet using the Function Wizard
   (c) Both (a) and (b)
   (d) Neither (a) nor (b)

9. Which of the following can be converted to an Excel workbook?
   (a) A text file in delimited format
   (b) A text file in fixed width format
   (c) Both (a) and (b)
   (d) Neither (a) nor (b)

10. Which of the following is recommended to distinguish the first row in a list (the field names) from the remaining entries (the data)?
    (a) Insert a blank row between the first row and the remaining rows
    (b) Insert a row of dashes between the first row and the remaining rows
    (c) Either (a) or (b)
    (d) Neither (a) nor (b)

11. The AutoFilter command:
    (a) Permanently deletes records from the associated list
    (b) Requires the specification of a criteria range elsewhere in the worksheet
    (c) Either (a) or (b)
    (d) Neither (a) nor (b)

12. Which of the following is true of the Sort command?
    (a) The primary key must be in ascending sequence
    (b) The secondary key must be in descending sequence
    (c) Both (a) and (b)
    (d) Neither (a) nor (b)

13. What is the best way to enter January 21, 1996 into a worksheet, given that you create the worksheet on that date, and further, that you always want to display that specific date?
    (a) =TODAY()
    (b) 1/21/96
    (c) Both (b) and (b) are equally acceptable
    (d) Neither (a) nor (b)

14. Which of the following best describes the relationship between the Sort and Subtotals commands?
    (a) The Sort command should be executed before the Subtotals command
    (b) The Subtotals command should be executed before the Sort command
    (c) The commands can be executed in either sequence
    (d) There is no relationship because the commands have nothing to do with one another

15. Which of the following may be implemented in an existing pivot table?
    (a) A row field may be added or deleted
    (b) A column field may be added or deleted
    (c) Both (a) and (b)
    (d) Neither (a) nor (b)

ANSWERS

1. c	**6.** c	**11.** d
2. c	**7.** c	**12.** d
3. a	**8.** b	**13.** b
4. c	**9.** c	**14.** a
5. d	**10.** d	**15.** c

1. Election 2000: Election 2000 has been decided, but it will be remembered for its closeness and controversy. Open a partially completed version of the workbook in *Chapter 7 Practice 1*, then complete the workbook so that it matches Figure 7.17. Proceed as follows:

   a. Enter the appropriate IF function in cell C8 to determine the winner of the state's electoral votes. Use conditional formatting to display the indicated colors for Bush and Gore. Develop the formula in such a way that it can be copied to the remaining rows in this column.

   b. Enter the appropriate formulas in cells F8 and G8 to compute the difference in the number of votes and the associated percentages. (Use the absolute value function so that the difference in the number of votes is always shown as a positive number.) Copy the formulas to the remaining rows in the worksheet.

   c. Use an ordinary SUM function to determine the popular vote for each candidate as shown in cells B4 and C4. Use the DSUM function to determine the number of electoral votes for each candidate. (You will need to establish separate criteria ranges for each candidate.)

   d. Add your name somewhere in the worksheet, then print the completed worksheet to show both displayed values and cell formulas for your instructor. Be sure the worksheet fits on a single page.

   e. Print the worksheet in at least one other sequence—for example, by the smallest (or largest) vote differential.

   f. Add a cover sheet, then submit the complete assignment to your instructor.

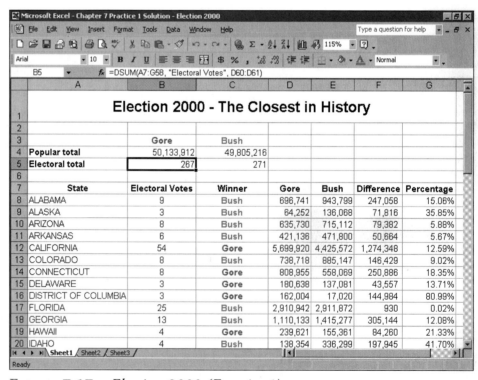

FIGURE 7.17   *Election 2000 (Exercise 1)*

2. The Dean's List: The *Chapter 7 Practice 2* workbook contains a partially completed version of the workbook in Figure 7.18. Open the workbook, then implement the following changes:

   a. Add a transfer student, Jeff Borow, majoring in Engineering. Jeff has completed 14 credits and has 45 quality points. (Jeff's record can be seen in Figure 7.18, but it is not in the workbook that you will retrieve from the Exploring Excel folder.) Do not, however, enter Jeff's GPA or year in school, as both will be computed from formulas in the next two steps.

   b. Enter the appropriate formula in F4 to compute the GPA for the first student (the quality points divided by the number of credits). Copy the formula to the other cells in this column.

   c. Enter the appropriate formula in cell G4 to determine the year in school for the first student. (Use the HLOOKUP function based on the table in cells B24 through E25. The entries in cells A24 and A25 contain labels and are not part of the table per se.) Copy the formula to the other cells in this column.

   d. Format the worksheet attractively. You can use our formatting or develop your own. Sort the list so that the students are listed alphabetically.

   e. Filter the list in place so that the only visible students are those on the Dean's list (with a GPA greater than 3.2) as shown in Figure 7.18.

   f. Add your name as the academic advisor in cell A28. Print the worksheet two ways, with displayed values and cell formulas, and submit both to your instructor. Use landscape printing and display gridlines and row and column headings. Be sure that each printout fits on a single sheet of paper.

   g. Remove the filter condition, then print the worksheet in a different sequence—for example, by ascending or descending GPA.

   h. Add a cover sheet, then submit the complete assignment to your instructor.

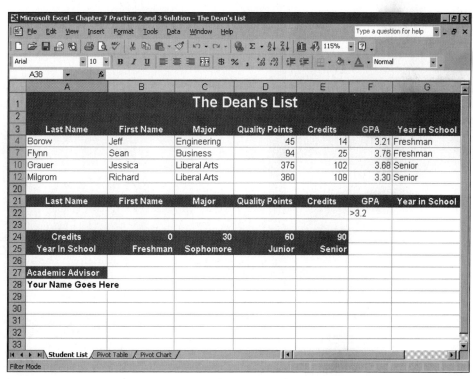

FIGURE 7.18   *The Dean's List (Exercise 2)*

BUILDS ON

PRACTICE
EXERCISE 2
PAGE 357

3. **The Pivot Chart:** Complete the previous exercise, then add a pivot table and pivot chart as shown in Figure 7.19. Start by creating the pivot table in its own worksheet, but be sure to select the option to create a pivot chart with the pivot table. Rename the resulting worksheets, Sheet1 and Chart1, to Pivot Table and Pivot Chart as shown in Figure 7.19.

a. Modify the pivot table so that major and year in school are the row and column fields, respectively. Use GPA as the data field, but be sure to specify the average GPA rather than the sum. Format the GPA to two decimal places.

b. Change the format of the pivot chart to a 3-D side-by-side column chart with default formatting. Right click any column within the chart, select the Format Data Series command, then select the Series Order tab. Change the order of the columns to Freshman, Sophomore, Junior, and Senior, as opposed to the default alphabetical order.

c. Pull down the Chart menu, click the Chart Options command to display the associated dialog box, then select the Data Table tab. Check the box to display the data table below the chart. Save the workbook.

d. Print the pivot table chart as shown in Figure 7.19. You do not need to print the pivot table since the equivalent information is shown in the data table that appears below the pivot chart.

e. Pivot tables are one of the best-kept secrets in Excel, even though they have been available in the last several releases of Excel. (Pivot charts, however, were first introduced in Excel 2000.) Write a short note to a colleague that describes how this feature facilitates data analysis.

f. Add a cover sheet, then submit the complete assignment to your instructor.

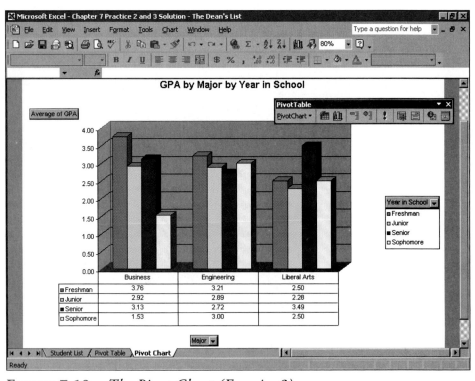

FIGURE 7.19   *The Pivot Chart (Exercise 3)*

4. Compensation Analysis: The workbook in Figure 7.20 is used to analyze employee compensation with respect to the dollar amount and percentage of their latest salary increase. Your assignment is to open the partially completed workbook in *Chapter 7 Practice 4* and complete the workbook to match our figure.

a. Open the workbook, then enter the formula to compute the dollar increase for the first employee in cell G3. Note, however, that not every employee has a previous salary, and thus the formula requires an If function to work correctly. Copy this formula to the remaining rows in column G.

b. Enter the formula to compute the percentage increase for the first employee in cell H3. The percentage increase is found by dividing the amount of the increase by the previous salary. Again, not every employee has a previous salary, and hence the formula requires an IF function to avoid dividing by zero. Copy this formula to the remaining rows in column H.

c. Enter the indicated database functions in rows 21 and 22 to reflect only those employees who have received a raise. Thus, be sure to include the greater than zero entry in the criteria row.

d. Format the worksheet in attractive fashion. You can copy our formatting or use your own design. Note, too, that you can suppress the display of zero values through the Options command. (If necessary, pull down the Tools menu, click the Options command, then click the View tab and clear the box to display zero values.)

e. Add your name as a financial analyst, then print the worksheet with both displayed values and cell formulas. Use landscape printing as necessary to be sure that the worksheet fits on a single sheet of paper.

f. Print the worksheet in at least one other sequence—for example, by the smallest (or largest) percentage increase.

g. Add a cover sheet, then submit the complete assignment to your instructor.

	A	B	C	D	E	F	G	H
1				Employee Compensation Analysis				
3	Name	Location	Title	Gender	Salary	Previous Salary	Increase	Percentage
4	Baker	Chicago	Analyst	F	$52,000	$45,000	$7,000	15.56%
5	Charles	Phoenix	Analyst	M	$40,000	$35,000	$5,000	14.29%
6	Goodman	New York	Senior Analyst	M	$100,000	$90,000	$10,000	11.11%
7	Irving	Miami	Analyst	F	$47,500	$45,000	$2,500	5.56%
8	Johnson	Miami	Analyst	M	$55,000			
9	Jones	Chicago	Analyst	F	$42,500	$41,000	$1,500	3.66%
10	Lang	Chicago	Analyst	M	$47,500	$42,000	$5,500	13.10%
11	Milgrom	Phoenix	Analyst	F	$49,500	$45,000	$4,500	10.00%
12	Mills	Chicago	Analyst	F	$38,500	$35,000	$3,500	10.00%
13	Nelson	Phoenix	Senior Analyst	M	$57,500	$55,000	$2,500	4.55%
14	Rubin	Phoenix	Analyst	F	$45,000	$40,000	$5,000	12.50%
15	Smith	New York	Analyst	M	$65,000	$61,000	$4,000	6.56%
16								
17	Name	Location	Title	Gender	Salary	Previous Salary	Increase	Percentage
18					>0			
19								
20	Evaluation of Salary Increase						Financial Analyst	
21	Average Increase		$4,636	9.71%			Your name goes here	
22	Minimum Increase		$1,500	3.66%				

FIGURE 7.20   *Compensation Analysis (Exercise 4)*

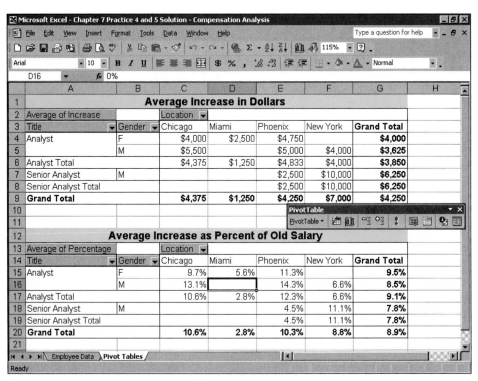

5. Pivot Tables: Continue the analysis from the previous exercise by creating the pivot tables shown in Figure 7.21. We have created two separate pivot tables, for the dollar and percentage increase, respectively, but you may find it more convenient to create a single table. (You can create two pivot tables on one worksheet by specifying that the second pivot table is to go on an existing worksheet, as opposed to a new worksheet.) Either solution is acceptable.

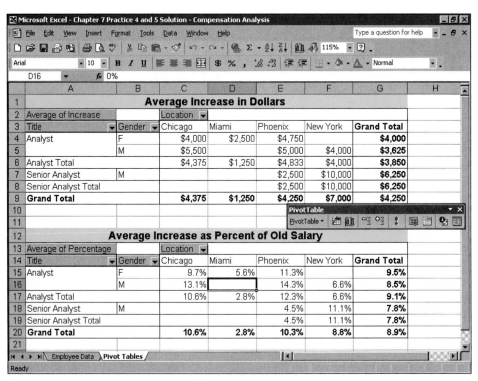

BUILDS ON

PRACTICE
EXERCISE 4
PAGE 359

a. You will, however, have to format your pivot table to include currency and percent symbols as appropriate, as well as a reasonable number of decimal places. Note, too, we use the average (as opposed to the default sum) function for both statistics.

b. Use the same style of formatting for the text in your pivot table as in the previous exercise, so that your workbook has a uniform look. Use the Options command as described in the previous exercise to suppress the display of zero values.

c. What is the meaning of the exclamation point that appears on the Pivot Table toolbar? When do you use this tool?

d. Combine the existing pivot tables into a single table that has two data fields—the amount of the increase and the percent of the increase. Do you prefer the combined table to the individual tables?

e. Pivot tables are one of the best-kept secrets in Excel, even though they have been available in the last several releases of Excel. (Pivot charts, however, were first introduced in Excel 2000.) Write a short note to a colleague that describes how this feature facilitates data analysis.

f. Add a cover sheet, then submit the complete assignment to your instructor.

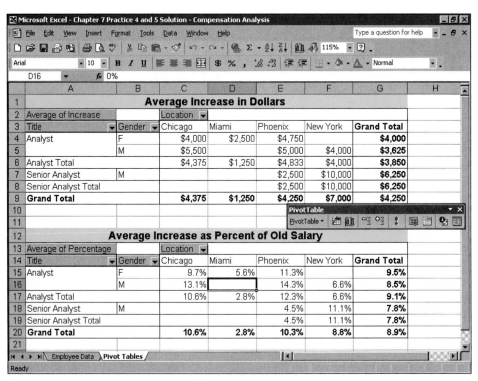

FIGURE 7.21 *Pivot Tables (Exercise 5)*

6. Consumer Loans: The worksheet in Figure 7.22 displays selected loans (those with a loan type of "A") from a comprehensive set of loan records. Your assignment is to open the partially completed *Chapter 7 Practice 6* workbook, to create the worksheet in our figure.

   a. Open the workbook, then go to cell H4, the cell containing the ending date for the first loan. Enter the formula to compute the ending date, based on the starting date and the term of the loan. For the sake of simplicity, you do not have to account for leap year. Thus, to compute the ending date, multiply the term of the loan by 365 and add that result to the starting date. Be sure to format the starting and ending dates to show a date format.

   b. Go to cell I4 and enter the PMT function to compute the monthly payment for the first loan. Copy the formulas in cells I4 and H4 to the remaining rows in the worksheet.

   c. Enter the indicated criteria in cell D31, then enter the indicated database functions toward the bottom of the worksheet.

   d. Filter the list in place to display only those loans that satisfy the indicated criteria.

   e. Format the list in attractive fashion. Add your name as the loan officer.

   f. Look closely at the bottom of Figure 7.22 and note the presence of a Pivot Table worksheet. You are to create a pivot table that has the loan type and branch location in the row and column fields, respectively. Your pivot table is to contain two data fields, the total amount of the loan type and the average interest rate.

   g. Print the entire workbook for your instructor. Print both the displayed values and cell formulas for the loans worksheet, but only the displayed values for the pivot table.

   h. Add a cover sheet, then submit the complete assignment to your instructor.

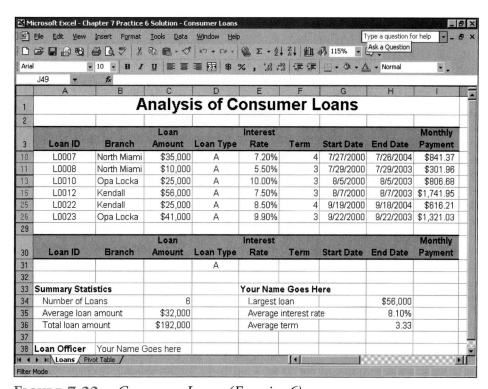

FIGURE 7.22 *Consumer Loans (Exercise 6)*

7. Top Ten Filter: Figure 7.23 displays a filtered list of the United States that displays the 10 states with the highest population density. You can duplicate the list and/or create several additional lists using the data in the *Chapter 7 Practice 7* workbook. Proceed as follows:

a. Open the workbook, and click in cell F5, the cell that contains the population density for the first state in the list, Alabama, since the states are in alphabetical order. Enter the formula to compute the density as population/area, then format the field to zero decimal places. Copy the formula to the remaining rows in the list.

b. Click anywhere in column F, the column that contains the newly created field. Pull down the Data menu, click the Filter command, and then click AutoFilter to toggle the feature on. You should see down arrows next to each of the field names in row four.

c. Click the down arrow next to the Density field, click Top 10 to display the Top 10 AutoFilter dialog box. Be sure that you have the appropriate entries in each of the three list boxes; i.e., Top rather than bottom, 10 for the number of entries, and items rather than percentages. Click OK to display the filtered list, which displays the records in the same order as in the original list. Click the Descending Sort button on the Standard toolbar to display the densities in descending sequence.

d. Format the worksheet appropriately, then add your name in cell A58 so that your instructor will know the assignment came from you.

e. Right click the worksheet tab, then select the command to Move or Copy the worksheet, check the box to create a copy, then rename the copied worksheet 13 Original States as shown in our figure.

f. Click the down arrow next to the Density field, then select the All command. Now click the down arrow next to the Year field, select the Top 10 command, then make the appropriate entries within the resulting dialog box to list the 13 original states. Sort these states in order of their admission to the Union.

g. Print the completed workbook for your instructor. Be sure to show grid lines, row and column headings, and an appropriate footer.

The United States of America
The Most Densely Populated States (People/Square Mile)

Name	Capital	Year Admitted	Population	Area	Population Density
New Jersey	Trenton	1787	7,730,188	7,836	986
Rhode Island	Providence	1790	1,003,464	1,214	827
Massachusetts	Boston	1788	6,016,425	8,257	729
Connecticut	Hartford	1788	3,287,116	5,009	656
Maryland	Annapolis	1788	4,781,468	10,577	452
New York	Albany	1788	17,990,455	49,576	363
Delaware	Dover	1787	666,168	2,057	324
Ohio	Columbus	1803	10,847,115	41,222	263
Pennsylvania	Harrisburg	1787	11,881,643	45,333	262
Florida	Tallahassee	1845	12,937,926	58,560	221

Your Name Goes Here

FIGURE 7.23 *Top Ten Filter (Exercise 7)*

PRACTICE
EXERCISES 4&5
PAGES 359–360

8. Compensation Report: The document in Figure 7.24 consists of a memo that was created in Microsoft Word that is linked to a pivot table from exercise 5. The document was created in such a way that any change in the pivot table within the Excel workbook will be automatically reflected in the memo.

a. Complete exercises 4 and 5 to create the pivot table that will be used in the memo. Start Word, create a simple letterhead (we used the Drop Cap command in the Format menu to create our letterhead), then enter the text of the memo in Figure 7.24. You can use our text, or modify the wording as you see fit. Be sure to include your name in the signature area.

b. Switch to Excel, copy either pivot table within the workbook to the clipboard, then use the Paste Link command within Word to bring the pivot table into the Word document.

c. Move and/or size the table as necessary. Note, too, that you may have to insert or delete hard returns within the memo to space it properly. *Print this version of the memo for your instructor.*

d. Prove to yourself that the linking really works by returning to Excel to modify the pivot table to show the total (as opposed to average) salary increase. Change the title of the pivot table as well.

e. Return to the Word memo, which should show an updated copy of the pivot table. If you did the exercise correctly, you should see $49,500 as the total amount for all salary increases. Modify the text of the memo to say "revised" salary analysis, as opposed to "preliminary," then print this version of the memo for your instructor.

f. Add a cover sheet, then submit the complete assignment to your instructor.

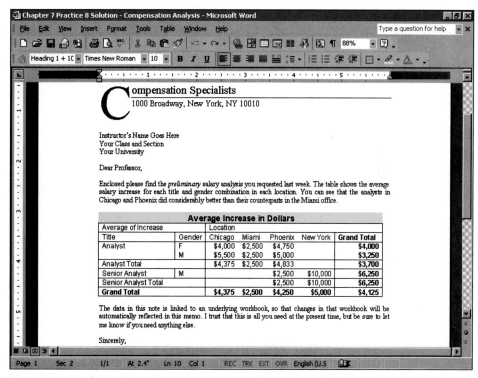

FIGURE 7.24 *Compensation Report (Exercise 8)*

BUILDS ON

PRACTICE
EXERCISE 2
PAGE 357

9. Subtotals: The document in Figure 7.25 consists of a memo that was created in Microsoft Word that is linked to an Excel worksheet from exercise 2. The document was created in such a way that any change in the worksheet will be automatically reflected in the memo.

a. Open the completed workbook from exercise 2 and, if necessary, remove the filter command that is in effect. Sort the students by major and by last name within major.

b. Click anywhere within the list, pull down the Data menu, and select the Subtotals command. Select subtotals for each change in major to display the statistics in Figure 7.25.

c. Start Word and create the text of the memo in Figure 7.25. Use the Paste Link command to link the memo to the worksheet. *Print this version of the memo for your instructor.*

d. Prove to yourself that linking really works by returning to Excel and substituting your name for Jeff Borow, but retain the other information (major, credits, and so on).

e. Use the Subtotals command in the Data menu to remove the subtotals, resort the list so that your name is in alphabetical order within the list of engineering students, then reexecute the Subtotals command.

f. Return to the Word memo, which should show an updated list of students with your name as an engineering student. Modify the text of the memo to say "revised" data as opposed to "preliminary," then print this version of the memo for your instructor.

g. Add a cover sheet, then submit the complete assignment to your instructor.

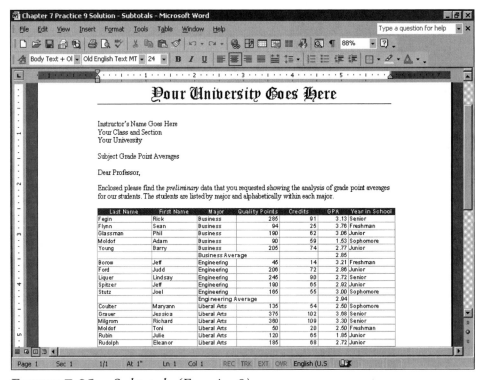

FIGURE 7.25   *Subtotals (Exercise 9)*

364   CHAPTER 7: LIST AND DATA MANAGEMENT

10. Web Pages and XML. Figure 7.26 displays the completed Election 2000 worksheet as a Web page and as an XML spreadsheet. Open the completed workbook from practice exercise 1 and proceed as follows.

a. Pull down the File menu and click the Save As Web Page command to display the Save As dialog box. The Web Page (HTML) file format is selected by default. Click the Save button.

b. Pull down the File menu and click the Save As Web Page command a second time to display the Save As dialog box. This time, however, select XML Spreadsheet as the file type. Click the Save button. Close the workbook. Exit Excel.

c. Start Windows Explorer and locate the newly created Web page document. Double click the icon for the Election Web page, which in turn will display the Web page within Internet Explorer as shown in Figure 7.26.

d. Click the Windows Explorer button a second time and locate the XML document. Double click its icon, which will display the XML page in Figure 7.26.

e. Minimize all open applications, then click the Internet Explorer button on the taskbar for both the Web page and the XML page. Right click the taskbar to display a context-sensitive menu, then click the Tile Vertically command to display the pages side by side.

f. Compare the appearance of the HTML page with that of XML. What is the advantage of the latter format?

g. Add a cover sheet, then submit the complete assignment to your instructor.

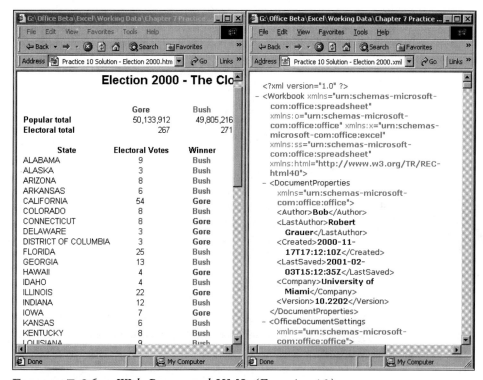

FIGURE 7.26 *Web Pages and XML (Exercise 10)*

The Super Bowl

How many times has the National Football Conference (NFC) won the Super Bowl? When was the last time the American Football Conference (AFC) won? What was the largest margin of victory? What was the closest game? What is the most points scored by two teams in one game? How many times have the Miami Dolphins appeared? How many times did they win? Use the data in the *Super Bowl workbook* to prepare a trivia sheet on the Super Bowl, then incorporate your analysis into a letter addressed to your instructor. Our workbook is almost complete, except you will have to determine the winner for each game based on the scores for the NFC and AFC teams. You can do it manually, but it's much easier if you use the IF function to determine the appropriate formula. Go to the NFL home page (www.nfl.com) to update our workbook to reflect the most recent game.

Data Validation

The best way to ensure that a workbook contains only valid data is to check the data as it is entered and reject any inappropriate values. Use the Excel Help menu to search for data validation to determine what (if any) capability is built into Excel. Is it possible, for example, to prevent a user from entering an invalid location or title in the Employee workbook that was used throughout the chapter? Summarize your findings in a brief note to your instructor. Better yet, take the final version of the Employee workbook (as it existed at the end of the last hands-on exercise) and incorporate any data validation you deem appropriate.

Asset Allocation

It's several years in the future and you find yourself happily married and financially prosperous. You and your spouse have accumulated substantial assets in a variety of accounts. Some of the money is in a regular account for use today, whereas other funds are in retirement accounts for later use. Much of the money, both regular and retirement, is invested in equities (i.e., the stock market), but a portion of your funds is also in nonequity funds such as money-market checking accounts and bank certificates of deposit. Your accounts are also in different places such as banks and brokerage houses. A summary of your accounts can be found in the *Asset Allocation workbook*. Your assignment is to open the workbook and develop a pivot table that will enable you and your spouse to keep track of your investments.

Planet Airways

Planet Airways is an independent airline offering charters and special tours. The airline has several independent agents, each of whom books trips for the airline. The data for all trips is maintained in the *Planet Airlines Access database* that is stored in the Exploring Excel folder. Your assignment is to start a new Excel workbook, then import the data from the Access database into the Excel workbook to create a pivot table for data analysis. Your pivot table should show the business by marketing representative and contract status (whether the trip is still in the proposal stage or whether it has already been signed). The data field should be the amount of the contract. The table should also have the flexibility to show which trips require passage through customs.

You may also want to explore the Access database for additional capabilities not found in Excel. In particular, look at the form and report that are contained within the database. What is the purpose of each of these objects?

CHAPTER 8

Automating Repetitive Tasks: Macros and Visual Basic for Applications

OBJECTIVES

AFTER READING THIS CHAPTER YOU WILL BE ABLE TO:

1. Define a macro; describe the relationship between macros and VBA.
2. Record and run a macro; view and edit the statements in a simple macro.
3. Use the InputBox function to obtain input for a macro as it is running; use the MsgBox statement to display a message.
4. Use a keyboard shortcut and/or a customized toolbar to run a macro; create a custom button to execute a macro.
5. Describe the function of the Personal Macro workbook.
6. Use the Step Into command to execute a macro one statement at a time.
7. Use the Copy and Paste commands to duplicate an existing macro; modify the copied macro to create an entirely new macro.
8. Use the Visual Basic If and Do statements to implement decision making and looping within an Excel macro.

OVERVIEW

Have you ever pulled down the same menus and clicked the same sequence of commands over and over? Easy as the commands may be to execute, it is still burdensome to have to continually repeat the same mouse clicks or keystrokes. If you can think of any task that you do repeatedly, whether in one workbook or in a series of workbooks, you are a perfect candidate to use macros.

A *macro* is a set of instructions that tells Excel which commands to execute. It is in essence a program, and its instructions are written in Visual Basic, a programming language. Fortunately, however, you don't have to be a programmer to write macros. Instead, you use the macro recorder within Excel to record your commands, and let Excel write the macros for you.

367

This chapter introduces you to the power of Excel macros. We begin by creating a simple macro to insert your name and class into a worksheet. We show you how to modify the macro once it has been created and how to execute the macro one statement at a time.

The second half of the chapter describes how to create more powerful macros that automate commands associated with list management, as presented in Chapter 7. We show you how to copy and edit a macro, and how to create customized buttons with which to execute a macro. We also show you how the power of an Excel macro can be extended through the inclusion of additional Visual Basic statements that implement loops and decision making.

INTRODUCTION TO MACROS

The **macro recorder** stores Excel commands, in the form of **Visual Basic** instructions, within a workbook. (***Visual Basic for Applications***, or **VBA**, is a subset of Visual Basic that is built into Microsoft Office.) To use the recorder, you pull down the Tools menu and click the Record New Macro command. From that point on (until you stop recording), every command you execute will be stored by the recorder. It doesn't matter whether you execute commands from pull-down menus via the mouse, or whether you use the toolbar or **keyboard shortcuts**. The macro recorder captures every action you take and stores the equivalent Visual Basic statements as a macro within the workbook.

Figure 8.1 illustrates a simple macro to enter your name and class in cells A1 and A2 of the active worksheet. The macro is displayed in the **Visual Basic Editor (VBE)**, which is used to create, edit, execute, and debug Excel macros. The Visual Basic Editor is a separate application (as can be determined from its button on the taskbar in Figure 8.1), and it is accessible from any application in Microsoft Office.

The left side of the VBE window in Figure 8.1 contains the **Project Explorer**, which is similar in concept and appearance to the Windows Explorer, except that it displays only open workbooks and/or other Visual Basic projects. The Visual Basic statements for the selected module (Module1 in Figure 8.1) appear in the **Code window** in the right pane. As you shall see, a Visual Basic module consists of one or more procedures, each of which corresponds to an Excel macro. Thus, in this example, Module1 contains the NameAndCourse procedure corresponding to the Excel macro of the same name. Module1 itself is stored in the My Macros.XLS workbook.

As indicated, a macro consists of Visual Basic statements that were created through the macro recorder. We don't expect you to be able to write the Visual Basic procedure yourself, and you don't have to. You just invoke the recorder and let it capture the Excel commands for you. We do think it is important, however, to understand the macro and so we proceed to explain its statements. As you read our discussion, do not be concerned with the precise syntax of every statement, but try to get an overall appreciation for what the statements do.

A macro always begins and ends with the Sub and End Sub statements, respectively. The **Sub statement** contains the name of the macro—for example, NameAndCourse in Figure 8.1. (Spaces are not allowed in a macro name.) The **End Sub statement** is physically the last statement and indicates the end of the macro. Sub and End Sub are Visual Basic key words and appear in blue.

The next several statements begin with an apostrophe, appear in green, and are known as **comments**. They provide information about the macro, but do not affect its execution. In other words, the results of a macro are the same, whether or not the comments are included. Comments are inserted automatically by the recorder to document the macro name, its author, and **shortcut key** (if any). You can add comments (a comment line must begin with an apostrophe), or delete or modify existing comments, as you see fit.

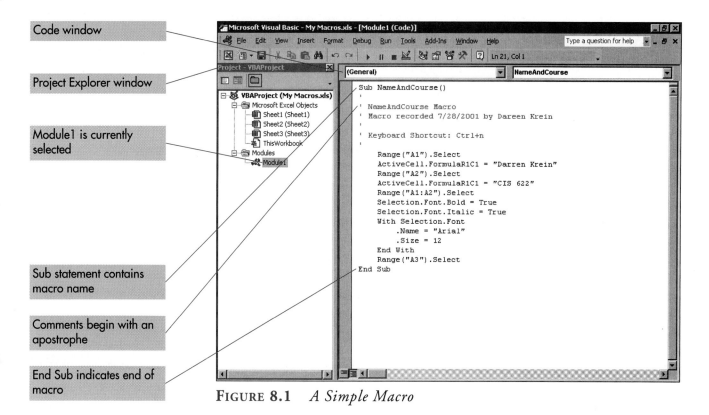

Code window

Project Explorer window

Module1 is currently selected

Sub statement contains macro name

Comments begin with an apostrophe

End Sub indicates end of macro

FIGURE 8.1   *A Simple Macro*

Every other statement is a Visual Basic instruction that was created as a result of an action taken in Excel. For example, the statements

Range ("A1").Select

and   ActiveCell.FormulaR1C1 = "Darren Krein"

select cell A1 as the active cell, then enter the text "Darren Krein" into the active cell. These statements are equivalent to clicking in cell A1 of a worksheet, typing the indicated entry into the active cell, then pressing the enter key (or an arrow key) to complete the entry. In similar fashion, the statements

Range ("A2").Select

and   ActiveCell.FormulaR1C1 = "CIS 622"

select cell A2 as the active cell, then enter the text entry "CIS 622" into that cell. The concept of select-then-do applies equally well to statements within a macro. Thus, the statements

Range ("A1:A2").Select
Selection.Font.Bold = True
Selection.Font.Italic = True

select cells A1 through A2, then change the font for the selected cells to bold italic. The ***With statement*** enables you to perform multiple actions on the same object. All commands between the With and corresponding ***End With statement*** are executed collectively; for example, the statements

With Selection.Font
    .Name = "Arial"
    .Size = 12
End With

change the formatting of the selected cells (A1:A2) to 12-point Arial. The last statement in the macro, Range ("A3").Select, selects cell A3, thus deselecting all other cells, a practice we use throughout the chapter.

INTRODUCTION TO MACROS

Objective To record, run, view, and edit a simple macro; to establish a keyboard shortcut to run a macro. Use Figure 8.2 as a guide in doing the exercise.

Step 1: **Create a Macro**

> ➤ Start Excel. Open a new workbook if one is not already open. Save the workbook as **My Macros** in the **Exploring Excel folder**.
> ➤ Pull down the **Tools menu**, click (or point to) the **Macro command**, then click **Record New Macro** to display the Record Macro dialog box in Figure 8.2a. (If you don't see the Macro comand, click the double arrow to see more commands.)
> ➤ Enter **NameAndCourse** as the name of the macro. (Spaces are not allowed in the macro name.)
> ➤ The description is entered automatically and contains today's date and the name of the person in whose name this copy of Excel is registered. If necessary, change the description to include your name.
> ➤ Click in the **Shortcut Key** check box and enter a **lowercase n**. Ctrl+n should appear as the shortcut as shown in Figure 8.2a. (If you see Ctrl+Shift+N it means you typed an uppercase N rather than a lowercase letter. Correct the entry to a lowercase n.)
> ➤ Check that the option to Store macro in **This Workbook** is selected. Click **OK** to record the macro, which displays the Stop Recording toolbar.

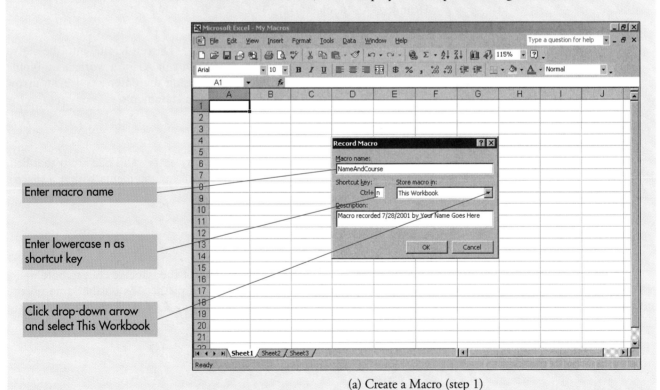

Enter macro name

Enter lowercase n as shortcut key

Click drop-down arrow and select This Workbook

(a) Create a Macro (step 1)

FIGURE 8.2 *Hands-on Exercise 1*

Step 2: **Record the Macro**

➤ Look carefully at the Relative References button on the Stop Recording button to be sure it is flush with the other buttons; that is, the button should *not* be pushed in. (See boxed tip on "Is the Button In or Out?")

➤ You should be in Sheet1, ready to record the macro, as shown in Figure 8.2b. The status bar indicates that you are in the Recording mode:
  - Click in **cell A1** even if it is already selected. Enter your name.
  - Click in **cell A2**. Enter the course you are taking.
  - Click and drag to select **cells A1** through **A2**.
  - Click the **Bold button**. Click the **Italic button**.
  - Click the arrow on the **Font Size list box**. Click **12** to change the point size.
  - Click in **cell A3** to deselect all other cells prior to ending the macro.

➤ Click the **Stop Recording button**.

➤ Save the workbook.

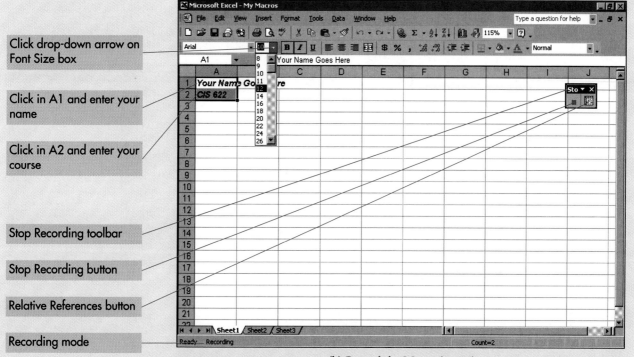

Click drop-down arrow on Font Size box

Click in A1 and enter your name

Click in A2 and enter your course

Stop Recording toolbar

Stop Recording button

Relative References button

Recording mode

(b) Record the Macro (step 2)

FIGURE 8.2   *Hands-on Exercise 1 (continued)*

IS THE BUTTON IN OR OUT?

The distinction between relative and absolute references within a macro is critical and is described in detail at the end of this exercise. The Relative References button on the Stop Recording toolbar toggles between the two—absolute references when the button is out, relative references when the button is in. The ScreenTip, however, displays Relative References regardless of whether the button is in or out. We wish that Microsoft had made it easier to tell which type of reference you are recording, but they didn't.

Step 3:   **Test the Macro**

> ➤ To run (test) the macro you have to remove the contents and formatting from cells A1 and A2. Click and drag to select **cells A1** through **A2.**
> ➤ Pull down the **Edit menu.** Click **Clear.** Click **All** from the cascaded menu to erase both the contents and formatting from the selected cells. Cells A1 through A2 are empty as shown in Figure 8.2c.
> ➤ Pull down the **Tools menu.** Click **Macro,** then click the **Macros . . . command** to display the dialog box in Figure 8.2c.
> ➤ Click **NameAndCourse,** which is the macro you just recorded. Click **Run.** Your name and class are entered in cells A1 and A2, then formatted according to the instructions in the macro.
> ➤ Clear the contents of cells A1 and A2. Press **Ctrl+n** (the keyboard shortcut) to rerun the NameAndCourse macro. Your name and class should reappear in cells A1 and A2.

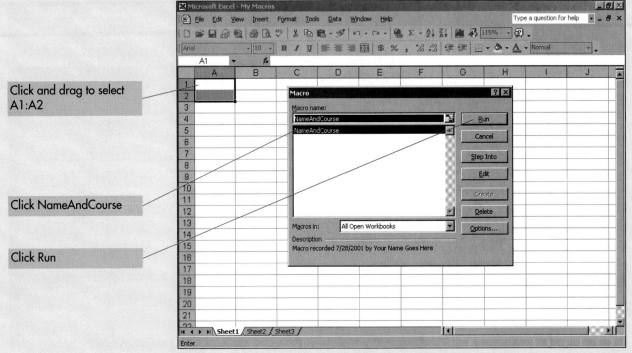

(c) Test the Macro (step 3)

FIGURE 8.2   *Hands-on Exercise 1 (continued)*

THE EDIT CLEAR COMMAND

The Edit Clear erases the contents of a cell, its formatting, and/or its comments. Select the cell or cells to erase, pull down the Edit menu, click the Clear command, then click All, Formats, Contents, or Comments from the cascaded menu. Pressing the Del key is equivalent to executing the Edit Clear Contents command as it clears the contents of a cell, but retains the formatting and comments.

Step 4: **Start the Visual Basic Editor**

➤ Pull down the **Tools menu**, click the **Macro command**, then click **Visual Basic Editor** (or press **Alt+F11**) to open the Visual Basic Editor. Maximize the VBE window.

➤ If necessary, pull down the **View menu**. Click **Project Explorer** to open the Project Explorer window in the left pane. There is currently one open VBA project, My Macros.xls, which is the name of the open workbook in Excel.

➤ If necessary, click the **plus sign** next to the Modules folder to expand that folder, click (select) **Module1**, pull down the **View menu**, and click **Code** to open the Code window in the right pane. Click the **Maximize button** in the Code window.

➤ Your screen should match the one in Figure 8.2d. The first statement below the comments should be *Range("A1").Select,* which indicates that the macro was correctly recorded with absolute references.

➤ If you see a very different statement, *ActiveCell.FormulaR1C1,* it means that you incorrectly recorded the macro with relative references. Right click **Module1** in the Project Explorer window, select the **Remove Module1 command**, then return to step 1 and rerecord the macro.

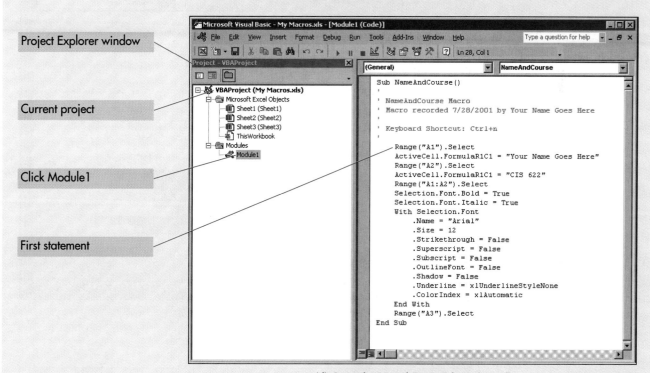

Project Explorer window

Current project

Click Module1

First statement

(d) Start the Visual Basic Editor (step 4)

FIGURE 8.2   *Hands-on Exercise 1 (continued)*

THE END RESULT

The macro recorder records only the result of the selection process, with no indication of how the selection was arrived at. It doesn't matter how you get to a particular cell. You can click in the cell directly, use the Go To command in the Edit menu, or use the mouse or arrow keys. The end result is the same and the macro indicates only the selected cell(s).

Step 5: **Edit the Macro**

➤ Edit the NameAndCourse macro by changing the font name and size to **"Times New Roman"** and **24**, respectively, as shown in Figure 8.2e.
➤ Click and drag to select the next seven statements as shown in Figure 8.2e.
➤ Press the **Del key** to delete these statements from the macro. (These statements contain default values and are unnecessary.) Delete any blank lines as well.
➤ Press **Alt+F11** to toggle back to the Excel workbook (or click the Excel button on the taskbar). Clear the entries and formatting in cells A1 and A2 as you did earlier, then rerun the NameAndCourse macro.
➤ Your name and class should once again be entered in cells A1 and A2 but in a different and larger font. (If the macro does not execute correctly, press **Alt+F11** to toggle back to the Visual Basic Editor to correct your macro.)
➤ Save the workbook.

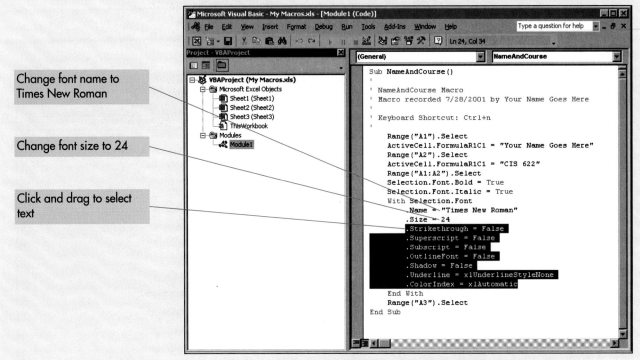

(e) Edit the Macro (step 5)

FIGURE 8.2 *Hands-on Exercise 1 (continued)*

SIMPLIFY THE MACRO

The macro recorder usually sets all possible options for an Excel command or dialog box even if you do not change those options. We suggest, therefore, that you make a macro easier to read by deleting the unnecessary statements. Take a minute, however, to review the statements prior to removing them, so that you can see the additional options. (You can click the Undo button to restore the deleted statements if you make a mistake.)

Step 6: **Create the Erase Macro**

➤ Pull down the **Tools menu**. Click the **Macro command**, then click **Record New Macro** from the cascaded menu. You will see the Record Macro dialog box.

➤ Enter **EraseNameAndCourse** as the name of the macro. Do not leave any spaces in the macro name. If necessary, change the description to include your name.

➤ Click in the **Shortcut Key** check box and enter a **lowercase e**. (Ctrl+e should appear as the shortcut.) Check that the option to Store macro in **This Workbook** is selected.

➤ Click **OK** to begin recording the macro, which displays the Stop Recording toolbar. Be sure you are recording absolute references (i.e., the Relative References button should be flush on the toolbar).

• Click and drag to select **cells A1** through **A2** as shown in Figure 8.2f, even if they are already selected.

• Pull down the **Edit menu**. Click **Clear**. Click **All** from the cascaded menu. Cells A1 through A2 should now be empty.

• Click in **cell A3** to deselect all other cells prior to ending the macro.

➤ Click the **Stop Recording button** to end the macro.

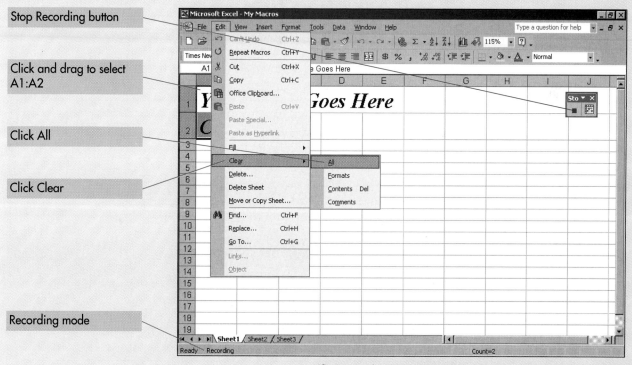

Stop Recording button

Click and drag to select A1:A2

Click All

Click Clear

Recording mode

(f) Create the Erase Macro (step 6)

FIGURE 8.2 *Hands-on Exercise 1 (continued)*

TO SELECT OR NOT SELECT

If you start recording, then select a cell(s) within the macro, the selection becomes part of the macro, and the macro will always operate on the same cell. If, however, you select the cell(s) prior to recording, the macro is more general and operates on the selected cells, which may differ every time the macro is executed. Both techniques are valid, and the decision depends on what you want the macro to do.

Step 7: **Shortcut Keys**

➤ Press **Ctrl+n** to execute the NameAndCourse macro. (You need to reenter your name and course in order to test the newly created EraseNameAndCourse macro.)

➤ Your name and course should again appear in cells A1 and A2 as shown in Figure 8.2g.

➤ Press **Ctrl+e** to execute the EraseNameAndCourse macro. Cells A1 and A2 should again be empty.

➤ You can press **Ctrl+n** and **Ctrl+e** repeatedly, to enter and then erase your name and course. End this step after having erased the data.

➤ Save the workbook.

Press Ctrl+n to run the NameAndCourse macro

	A	B	C	D	E	F	G	H	I	J
1	*Your Name Goes Here*									
2	*CIS 622*									

(g) Shortcut Keys (step 7)

FIGURE 8.2   *Hands-on Exercise 1 (continued)*

TROUBLESHOOTING

If the shortcut keys do not work, it is probably because they were not defined properly. Pull down the Tools menu, click Macro to display a cascaded menu, click the Macros . . . command, then select the desired macro in the Macro Name list box. Click the Options button, then check the entry in the Shortcut Key text box. A lowercase letter creates a shortcut with just the Ctrl key, whereas an uppercase letter uses Ctrl+Shift with the shortcut. Thus, "n" and "N" will establish shortcuts of Ctrl+n and Ctrl+Shift+N, respectively.

Step 8: **Step through the Macro**

➤ Press **Alt+F11** to switch back to the VBE window. Click the **Close button** to close the **Project window** within the Visual Basic Editor. The Code window expands to take the entire Visual Basic Editor window.

➤ Point to an empty area on the Windows taskbar, then click the **right mouse button** to display a shortcut menu. Click **Tile Vertically**.

➤ Your desktop should be similar to Figure 8.2h. It doesn't matter if the workbook is in the left or right window.

➤ Click in the **Visual Basic Editor window**, then click anywhere within the NameAndCourse macro. Pull down the **Debug menu** and click the **Step Into command** (or press the **F8 key**). The Sub statement is highlighted.

➤ Press the **F8 key** to move to the first executable statement (the comments are skipped). The statement is highlighted, but it has not yet been executed.

➤ Press the **F8 key** again to execute this statement (which selects cell A1 and moves to the next statement). Continue to press the **F8 key** to execute the statements one at a time. You see the effect of each statement in the Excel window.

View effects of statements as they are executed

Click anywhere within the NameAndCourse macro

Next executable statement

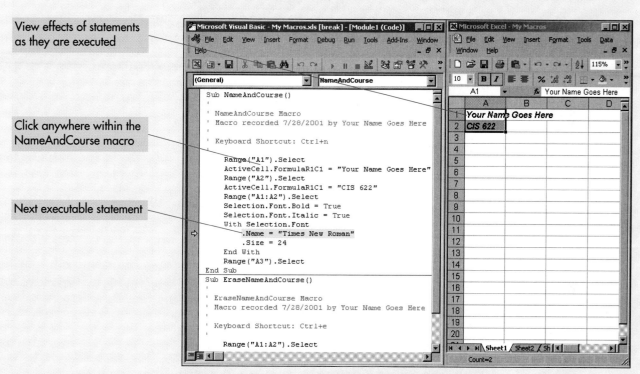

(h) Step through the Macro (step 8)

FIGURE 8.2 *Hands-on Exercise 1 (continued)*

THE STEP INTO COMMAND

The Step Into command is useful to slow down the execution of a macro in the event the macro does not perform as intended. In essence, you execute the macro one statement at a time, while viewing the results of each statement in the associated worksheet. If a statement does not do what you want it to do, just change the statement in the Visual Basic window, then continue to press the F8 key to step through the procedure.

Step 9: **Print the Module**

➤ Click in the **Visual Basic window**. Pull down the **File menu**. Click **Print** to display the Print VBA Project dialog box in Figure 8.2i.

➤ Click the option button to print the current module. Click **OK**. Submit the listing of the current module, which contains the procedures for both macros, to your instructor as proof you did this exercise.

➤ Close the My Macros workbook, which automatically closes the Visual Basic Project window (and Code window). Click **Yes** if asked to save the workbook. The macros are stored within the workbook.

➤ Exit Excel if you do not wish to continue with the next hands-on exercise at this time.

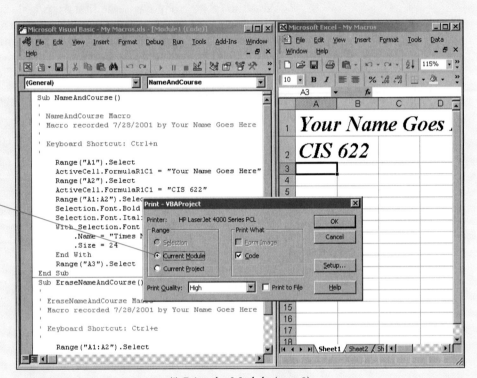

Click option button to print Current Module

(i) Print the Module (step 9)

FIGURE 8.2 *Hands-on Exercise 1 (continued)*

PROCEDURE VIEW VERSUS FULL MODULE VIEW

The procedures within a module can be displayed individually, or alternatively, multiple procedures can be viewed simultaneously. To go from one view to the other, click the Procedure View button at the bottom of the window to display just the procedure you are working on, or click the Full Module View button to display multiple procedures. You can press Ctrl+PgDn and Ctrl+PgUp to move between procedures in either view. Use the vertical scroll bar to move up and down within the VBA window.

One of the most important options to specify when recording a macro is whether the references are to be relative or absolute. A reference is a cell address. An *absolute reference* is a constant address that always refers to the same cell. A *relative reference* is variable in that the reference will change from one execution of the macro to the next, depending on the location of the active cell when the macro is executed.

To appreciate the difference, consider Figure 8.3, which displays two versions of the NameAndCourse macro from the previous exercise, one with absolute and one with relative references. Figure 8.3a uses absolute references to place your name, course, and date in cells A1, A2, and A3. The data will always be entered in these cells regardless of which cell is selected when you execute the macro.

Figure 8.3b enters the same data, but with relative references, so that the cells in which the data are entered depend on which cell is selected when the macro is executed. If cell A1 is selected, your name, course, and date will be entered in cells A1, A2, and A3. If, however, cell E4 is the active cell when you execute the macro, then your name, course, and date will be entered in cells E4, E5, and E6.

A relative reference is specified by an *offset* that indicates the number of rows and columns from the active cell. An offset of (1,0) indicates a cell one row below the active cell. An offset of (0,1) indicates a cell one column to the right of the active cell. In similar fashion, an offset of (1,1) indicates a cell one row below and one column to the right of the active cell. Negative offsets are used for cells above or to the left of the current selection.

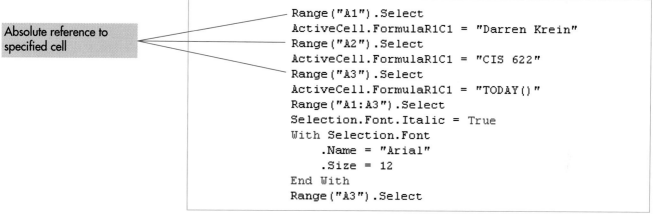

Absolute reference to specified cell

```
Range("A1").Select
ActiveCell.FormulaR1C1 = "Darren Krein"
Range("A2").Select
ActiveCell.FormulaR1C1 = "CIS 622"
Range("A3").Select
ActiveCell.FormulaR1C1 = "TODAY()"
Range("A1:A3").Select
Selection.Font.Italic = True
With Selection.Font
     .Name = "Arial"
     .Size = 12
End With
Range("A3").Select
```

(a) Absolute References

Relative reference to cell one row below active cell

Indicates a column of three cells, not cells A1 to A3

```
ActiveCell.FormulaR1C1 = "Darren Krein"
ActiveCell.Offset(1, 0).Range("A1").Select
ActiveCell.FormulaR1C1 = "CIS 622"
ActiveCell.Offset(1, 0).Range("A1").Select
ActiveCell.FormulaR1C1 = "=TODAY()"
ActiveCell.Offset(-2, 0).Range("A1:A3").Select
Selection.Font.Italic = True
With Selection.Font
     .Name = "Arial"
     .Size = 12
End With
ActiveCell.Offset(3, 0).Range("A1").Select
```

(b) Relative References

FIGURE 8.3 *Absolute versus Relative References*

Relative references may appear confusing at first, but they extend the power of a macro by making it more general. You will appreciate this capability as you learn more about macros. Let us begin by recognizing that the statement

ActiveCell.Offset (1,0).Range ("A1").Select

means select the cell one row below the active cell. It has nothing to do with cell A1, and you might wonder why the entry Range ("A1") is included. The answer is that the offset specifies the location of the new range (one row below the current cell), and the A1 indicates that the size of that range is a single cell (A1). In similar fashion, the statement

ActiveCell.Offset (−2,0).Range ("A1:A3").Select

selects a range, starting two rows above the current cell, that is one column by three rows in size. Again, it has nothing to do with cells A1 through A3. The offset specifies the location of a new range (two rows above the current cell) and the shape of that range (a column of three cells). If you are in cell D11 when the statement is executed, the selected range will be cells D9 through D11. The selection starts with the cell two rows above the active cell (cell D9), then it continues from that point to select a range consisting of one column by three rows (cells D9:D11).

RELATIVE VERSUS ABSOLUTE REFERENCES

Relative references appear confusing at first but they extend the power of a macro by making it more general. Macro statements that have been recorded with relative references include an offset to indicate the number of rows and columns the selection is to be from the active cell. An offset of (−1,0) indicates a cell one row above the active cell, whereas an offset of (0,−1) indicates a cell one column to the left of the active cell. Positive offsets are used for cells below or to the right of the current selection.

THE PERSONAL MACRO WORKBOOK

The hands-on exercise at the beginning of the chapter created the NameAndCourse macro in the My Macros workbook, where it is available to that workbook or to any other workbook that is in memory when the My Macros workbook is open. What if, however, you want the macro to be available at all times, not just when the My Macros workbook is open? This is easily accomplished by storing the macro in the Personal Macro workbook when it is first recorded.

The *Personal Macro workbook* opens automatically whenever Excel is loaded. This is because the Personal Macro workbook is stored in the XLStart folder, a folder that Excel checks each time it is loaded into memory. Once open, the macros in the Personal workbook are available to any other open workbook. The following hands-on exercise creates the NameAndCourse macro with relative references, then stores that macro in the Personal Macro workbook.

The exercise also expands the macro to enter the date of execution, and further generalizes the macro to accept the name of the course as input. The latter is accomplished through the Visual Basic *InputBox function* that prompts the user for a specific response, then stores that response within the macro. In other words, the Excel macro is enhanced through the inclusion of a VBA statement that adds functionality to the original macro. You start with the macro recorder to translate Excel commands into a VBA procedure, then you modify the procedure by adding the necessary VBA statements. (The InputBox function must be entered manually into the procedure since there is no corresponding Excel command, and hence the macro recorder would not work.)

THE PERSONAL MACRO WORKBOOK

Objective To create and store a macro in the Personal Macro workbook; to assign a toolbar button to a macro; to use the Visual Basic InputBox function. Use Figure 8.4 as a guide in the exercise.

Step 1: **The Personal Macro Workbook**

➤ Start Excel. Be sure to close the My Macros workbook from the previous exercise to avoid any conflict with an existing macro.

➤ Open a new workbook if one is not already open. Pull down the **Tools menu**, click (or point to) the **Macro command**, then click **Record New Macro** to display the Record Macro dialog box

➤ Enter **NameAndCourse** as the name of the macro. Do not leave any spaces in the macro name. Click in the **Shortcut Key** check box and enter a **lowercase n**. Ctrl+n should appear as the shortcut.

➤ Click the **drop-down arrow** in the Store macro in list box and select the Personal Macro workbook as shown in Figure 8.4a. (If you are working on a network as opposed to a standalone machine, you may not be able to access the **Personal Macro workbook**, in which case you can save the macro in this workbook.)

➤ Click **OK** to begin recording the macro, which displays the Stop Recording toolbar.

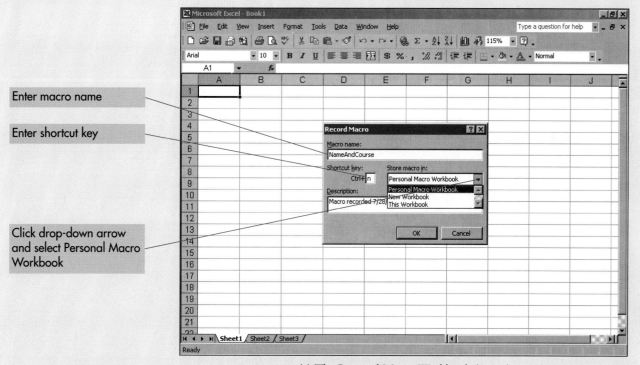

Enter macro name

Enter shortcut key

Click drop-down arrow and select Personal Macro Workbook

(a) The Personal Macro Workbook (step 1)

FIGURE 8.4   *Hands-on Exercise 2*

Step 2: **Record with Relative References**

➤ Click the **Relative References button** on the Stop Recording toolbar so that the button is pushed in as shown in Figure 8.4a.

➤ The Relative References button functions as a toggle switch—click it, and the button is pushed in to record relative references. Click it again, and you record absolute references. Be sure to record relative references.

➤ Enter your name in the active cell. Do *not* select the cell.

➤ Press the **down arrow key** to move to the cell immediately underneath the current cell. Enter the course you are taking.

➤ Press the **down arrow key** to move to the next cell. Enter **=TODAY()**.

➤ Click and drag to select the three cells containing the data values you just entered (cells A1 through A3 in Figure 8.4b).

  • Click the **Bold button**. Click the **Italic button**.

  • Click the arrow on the **Font Size list box**. Click **12** to change the point size.

  • If necessary, click and drag the border between the column headings for Columns A and B to increase the width of column A.

  • Click in **cell A4** to deselect all other cells prior to ending the macro.

➤ Click the **Stop Recording button** to end the macro.

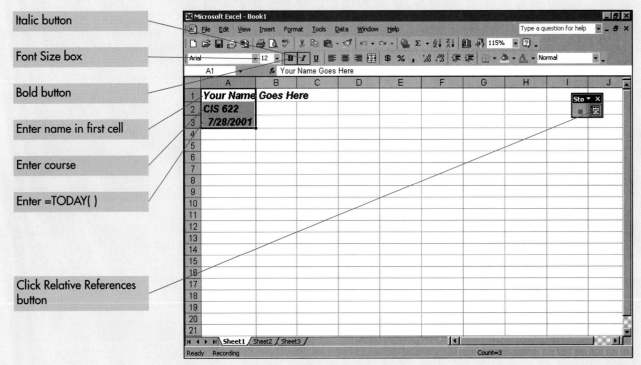

Italic button

Font Size box

Bold button

Enter name in first cell

Enter course

Enter =TODAY( )

Click Relative References button

(b) Record with Relative References (step 2)

FIGURE 8.4 *Hands-on Exercise 2 (continued)*

PLAN AHEAD

The macro recorder records everything you do, including entries that are made by mistake or commands that are executed incorrectly. Plan the macro in advance, before you begin recording. Write down what you intend to do, then try out the commands with the recorder off. Be sure you go all the way through the intended sequence of operations prior to turning the macro recorder on.

Step 3: **The Visual Basic Editor**

➤ Pull down the **Tools menu**, click the **Macro command**, then click **Visual Basic Editor** (or press **Alt+F11**) to open the Visual Basic Editor in Figure 8.4c.

➤ If necessary, pull down the **View menu**. Click **Project Explorer** to open the Project Explorer window in the left pane.

➤ There are currently two open VBA projects (Book1, the name of the open workbook, and Personal.XLS, the Personal Macro workbook).

➤ Click the **plus sign** to expand the Personal Workbook folder, then click the **plus sign** to expand the **Modules folder** within this project.

➤ Click (select) **Module1**, pull down the **View menu**, and click **Code** to open the Code window in the right pane. Maximize the Code window.

➤ Close any other open windows within the Visual Basic Editor. The first executable statement should begin with *ActiveCell.FormulaR1C1*.

➤ If you see a very different statement, *Range("A1").Select,* it means that you incorrectly recorded the macro with absolute references. Right click Module1 in the Project window, select the **Remove Module command**, then return to step 1 and rerecord the macro.

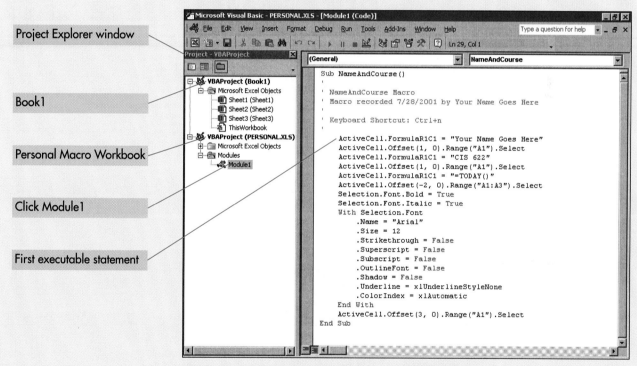

Project Explorer window

Book1

Personal Macro Workbook

Click Module1

First executable statement

(c) The Visual Basic Editor (step 3)

FIGURE 8.4 *Hands-on Exercise 2 (continued)*

WHAT DOES RANGE ("A1:A3") REALLY MEAN?

The statement ActiveCell.Offset(−2,0).Range ("A1:A3").Select has nothing to do with cells A1 through A3, so why is the entry Range ("A1:A3") included? The effect of the statement is to select three cells (one cell under the other) starting with the cell two rows above the current cell. The offset (−2,0) specifies the starting point of the selected range (two rows above the current cell). The range ("A1:A3") indicates the size and shape of the selected range (a vertical column of three cells) from the starting cell.

Step 4:   **Edit the Macro**

➤ Click and drag to select the name of the course, which is found in the third executable statement of the macro. Be sure to include the quotation marks (e.g., "CIS622" in our example) in your selection.

➤ Enter **InputBox("Enter the Course You Are Taking")** to replace the selected text. Note that as you enter the Visual Basic key word, *InputBox,* a prompt (containing the correct syntax for this statement) is displayed on the screen as shown in Figure 8.4d.

➤ Just ignore the prompt and keep typing to complete the entry. Press the **Home key** as you complete the entry to scroll back to the beginning of the line.

➤ Click immediately after the number **12**, then click and drag to select the next seven statements. Press the **Del key** to delete the highlighted statements from the macro.

➤ Delete the **Selection.Font.Bold = True** statement. Click the **Save button** to save the modified macro.

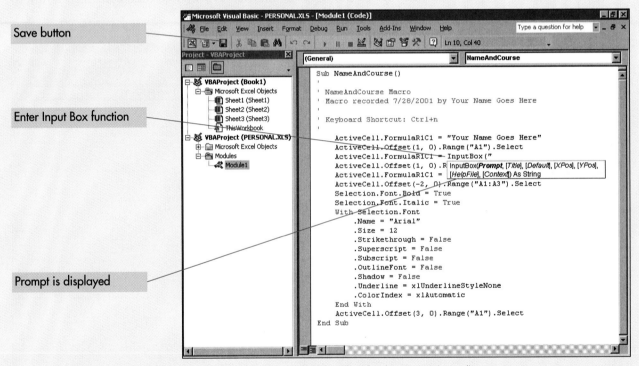

Save button

Enter Input Box function

Prompt is displayed

(d) Edit the Macro (step 4)

FIGURE 8.4   *Hands-on Exercise 2 (continued)*

THE INPUTBOX FUNCTION

The InputBox function adds flexibility to a macro by obtaining input from the user when the macro is executed. It is used in this example to generalize the NameAndCourse macro by asking the user for the name of the course, as opposed to storing the name within the macro. The InputBox function, coupled with storing the macro in the Personal Macro workbook, enables the user to personalize any workbook by executing the associated macro.

Step 5: **Test the Revised Macro**

➤ Press **Alt+F11** to view the Excel workbook. Click in any cell—for example, **cell C5** as shown in Figure 8.4e.

➤ Pull down the **Tools menu.** Click **Macro,** click the **Macros . . . command,** select **PERSONAL.XLS!NameAndCourse,** then click the **Run command button** to run the macro. (Alternatively you can use the **Ctrl+n** shortcut.)

➤ The macro enters your name in cell C5 (the active cell), then displays the input dialog box shown in Figure 8.4e.

➤ Enter any appropriate course and press the **enter key.** You should see the course you entered followed by the date. All three entries will be formatted according to the commands you specified in the macro.

➤ Click in a different cell, then press **Ctrl+n** to rerun the macro. The macro will enter your name, the course you specify, and the date in the selected location because it was recorded with relative references.

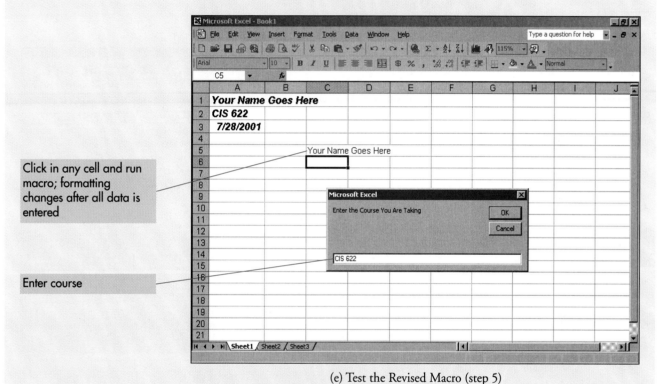

Click in any cell and run macro; formatting changes after all data is entered

Enter course

(e) Test the Revised Macro (step 5)

FIGURE 8.4 *Hands-on Exercise 2 (continued)*

RED, GREEN, AND BLUE

Visual Basic automatically assigns different colors to different types of statements (or a portion of those statements). Any statement containing a syntax error appears in red. Comments appear in green. Key words—such as Sub and End Sub, With and End With, and True and False—appear in blue.

Step 6: **Add a Custom Button**

➤ Point to any toolbar, then click the **right mouse button** to display a shortcut menu. Click **Customize** to display the Customize dialog box in Figure 8.4f.

➤ Click the **Commands tab**. Click the **down arrow** to scroll through the Categories list box until you can select the **Macros category**.

➤ Click and drag the **Custom (Happy Face) button** to an available space at the right of the Standard toolbar. Release the mouse. (You must drag the button *within* the toolbar.)

➤ Click the **Modify Selection button** within the Customize dialog box to display the cascaded menu in Figure 8.4f. Click and drag to select the name of the button (&Custom Button) and replace it with **NameAndCourse**, to create a ScreenTip for that button. Do not press the enter key.

➤ Click the **Assign Macro command** at the end of the cascaded menu to display the Assign Macro dialog box. Select **PERSONAL.XLS!NameAndCourse** and click **OK**.

➤ Click **Close** to exit the Custom dialog box.

Drag Custom button to toolbar

Enter macro name

Commands tab

Click Macro category

Click Assign Macro

Modify Selection button

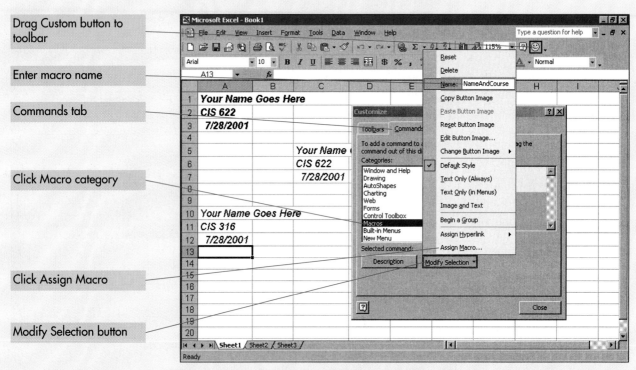

(f) Add a Custom Button (step 6)

FIGURE 8.4 *Hands-on Exercise 2 (continued)*

CUSTOMIZE THE TOOLBAR OR A MENU

You can customize any toolbar or menu to display additional buttons or commands as appropriate. Pull down the View menu, click Toolbars, click Customize to display the Customize dialog box, then click the Commands tab. Choose the category containing the button or command you want, then click and drag that object to an existing toolbar or menu.

Step 7: **Test the Custom Button**

➤ Click the **New button** on the Standard toolbar to open a new workbook (Book2 in Figure 8.4g; the book number is not important). Click **cell B2** as the active cell from which to execute the macro.

➤ Point to the **Happy Face button** to display the ScreenTip you just created. The ScreenTip will be useful in future sessions should you forget the function of this button.

➤ Click the **Happy Face button** to execute the NameAndCourse macro. Enter the name of a course you are taking. The macro inserts your name, course, and today's date in cells B2 through B4.

➤ Pull down the **File menu** and click the **Exit command** to exit the program. Click **Yes** if asked to save the changes to the Personal Workbook.

➤ Click **No** when prompted to save the changes to Book1 and/or Book2, the workbooks you created in this exercise.

Point to Custom button

New button

Click in B2

ScreenTip

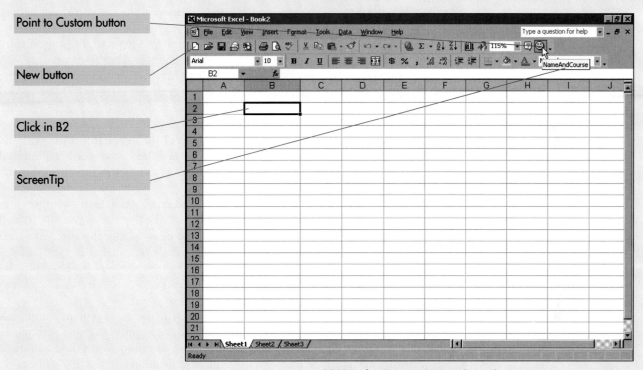

(g) Test the Custom Button (step 7)

FIGURE 8.4 *Hands-on Exercise 2 (continued)*

CHANGE THE CUSTOM BUTTON ICON

The Happy Face icon is automatically associated with the Custom Macro button. You can, however, change the image after the button has been added to a toolbar. Right click the button and click Customize to display the Customize dialog box, which must remain open to change the image. Right click the button a second time to display a different shortcut menu with commands pertaining to the specific button. Click the command to Change Button Image, select a new image, then close the Customize dialog box.

Thus far we have covered the basics of macros in the context of entering your name, course, and today's date in a worksheet. As you might expect, macros are capable of much more and can be used to automate any repetitive task. The next several pages illustrate the use of macros in conjunction with the list (data) management examples that were presented in an earlier chapter.

Data and information are not synonymous. Data is typically a fact (or facts) about a specific record (or set of records), such as an employee's name or title, or a list of all employees and their titles. Information is something more and refers to data that has been summarized, or otherwise rearranged, into a form perceived as useful by the recipient. A list of all the employees is considered raw data, whereas a subset of that list—such as the employees who worked in Chicago—could be thought of as information derived from that list. Information is also obtained by summarizing the data. Individual salaries are important to the employees who receive those salaries, whereas a manager is more interested in knowing the total of all salaries in order to make decisions. Macros can help in the conversion of data to information.

The worksheet in Figure 8.5a displays the employee list and associated summary statistics from the example in the previous chapter. The list is an area in a worksheet that contains rows of similar data. The first row in the list contains the column labels or field names. Each additional row contains a record. Every record contains the same fields in the same order. The list in Figure 8.5a has 14 records. Each record has six fields: name, location, title, service, hire date, and salary.

A criteria range has been established in cells A17 through F18 for use with the database functions in cells F22 through F26. Criteria values have not been entered in Figure 8.5a, and so the database functions reflect the values of the entire list (all 14 employees).

The worksheet in Figure 8.5b displays selected employees, those who work in Chicago. Look carefully at the worksheet and you will see that only rows 3, 9, 10, and 12 are visible. The other rows within the list have been hidden by the Advanced Filter command, which displays only those employees who satisfy the specified criteria. The summary statistics reflect only the Chicago employees; for example, the DCOUNT function in cell F26 shows four employees (as opposed to the 14 employees in Figure 8.5a).

The previous chapter described how to execute the list management commands to filter the list. The process is not difficult, but it does require multiple commands and keystrokes. Our purpose here is to review those commands and then automate the process through creation of a series of data management macros that will enable you to obtain the desired information with a single click. We begin by reviewing the commands that would be necessary to modify the worksheet in Figure 8.5b to show managers rather than the Chicago employees.

The first step is to clear the existing criterion (Chicago) in cell B18, then enter the new criterion (Manager) in cell C18. You would then execute the Advanced Filter command, which requires the specification of the list (cells A1 through F15), the location of the criteria range (cells A17 through F18), and the option to filter the list in place.

And what if you wanted to see the Chicago employees after you executed the commands to display the managers? You would have to repeat all of the previous commands to change the criterion back to what it was, then filter the list accordingly. Suffice it to say that the entire process can be simplified through creation of the appropriate macros.

The following exercise develops the macro to select the Chicago employees from the worksheet in Figure 8.5a. A subsequent exercise develops two additional macros, one to select the managers and another to select the managers who work in Chicago.

All of the macros use the concept of a ***named range*** to establish a mnemonic name (e.g., database) for a cell range (e.g., A1:F15). The advantage of using a named range in a macro over the associated cell reference is twofold. First, the macro is easier to read. Second, and perhaps more important, a named range adjusts automatically for insertions and/or deletions within the worksheet, whereas a cell reference remains constant. Thus, the use of a named range makes the macro immune to changes in the worksheet in that the macro references a flexible "database," as opposed to a fixed cell range. You can add or delete employee records within the list, and the macro will still work.

Field names

	A	B	C	D	E	F
1	**Name**	**Location**	**Title**	**Service**	**Hire Date**	**Salary**
2	Adams	Atlanta	Trainee	7.2	11/24/93	$19,500
3	Adamson	Chicago	Manager	6.9	3/16/94	$52,000
4	Brown	Atlanta	Trainee	7.2	11/24/93	$18,500
5	Charles	Boston	Account Rep	6.9	3/16/94	$40,000
6	Coulter	Atlanta	Manager	7.2	11/24/93	$100,000
7	Elofson	Miami	Account Rep	3.2	10/31/97	$47,500
8	Gillenson	Miami	Account Rep	2.2	10/31/98	$55,000
9	James	Chicago	Account Rep	6.2	10/31/94	$42,500
10	Johnson	Chicago	Account Rep	5.2	10/31/95	$47,500
11	Manin	Boston	Account Rep	6.9	3/16/94	$49,500
12	Marder	Chicago	Account Rep	4.2	10/31/96	$38,500
13	Milgrom	Boston	Manager	6.9	3/16/94	$57,500
14	Rubin	Boston	Account Rep	6.9	3/16/94	$45,000
15	Smith	Atlanta	Account Rep	7.2	11/24/93	$65,000
16						
17	**Name**	**Location**	**Title**	**Service**	**Hire Date**	**Salary**
18						
19						
20						
21			Summary Statistics			
22	Average Salary					$48,429
23	Maximum Salary					$100,000
24	Minimum Salary					$18,500
25	Total Salary					$678,000
26	Number of Employees					14

Criteria range (A17:F18)

Database functions (F22:F26)

(a) All Employees

Filtered list

	A	B	C	D	E	F
1	**Name**	**Location**	**Title**	**Service**	**Hire Date**	**Salary**
3	Adamson	Chicago	Manager	6.9	3/16/94	$52,000
9	James	Chicago	Account Rep	6.2	10/31/94	$42,500
10	Johnson	Chicago	Account Rep	5.2	10/31/95	$47,500
12	Marder	Chicago	Account Rep	4.2	10/31/96	$38,500
16						
17	**Name**	**Location**	**Title**	**Service**	**Hire Date**	**Salary**
18		Chicago				
19						
20						
21			Summary Statistics			
22	Average Salary					$45,125
23	Maximum Salary					$52,000
24	Minimum Salary					$38,500
25	Total Salary					$180,500
26	Number of Employees					4

Criterion

Database functions reflect current criteria

(b) Chicago Employees

FIGURE 8.5 *Data Management Macros*

DATA MANAGEMENT MACROS

Objective To create a data management macro in conjunction with an employee list; to create a custom button to execute a macro. Use Figure 8.6 as a guide in the exercise.

Step 1: **Data Management Functions**

➤ Start Excel. Open the **Finished Employee List workbook** that was created in the chapter on data management. Pull down the **Data Menu**, click **Subtotals**, and click the **Remove All button**.

➤ Click any cell between A2 and A15, then click the **Sort Ascending button** on the Standard toolbar. The employees should be listed in alphabetical order as shown in Figure 8.6a.

➤ Clear all entries in the range **A18** through **F18**.

➤ Click in **cell F22**, which contains the DAVERAGE function, to compute the average salary of all employees who satisfy the specified criteria. No criteria have been entered, however, so the displayed value of $48,429 represents the average salary of all 14 employees.

➤ Click **cell B18**. Enter **Chicago**. Press **enter**. The average salary changes to $45,125 to indicate the average salary of the four Chicago employees.

➤ Click **cell C18**. Enter **Manager**. Press **enter**. The average salary changes to $52,000 to indicate the average salary of the one Chicago manager.

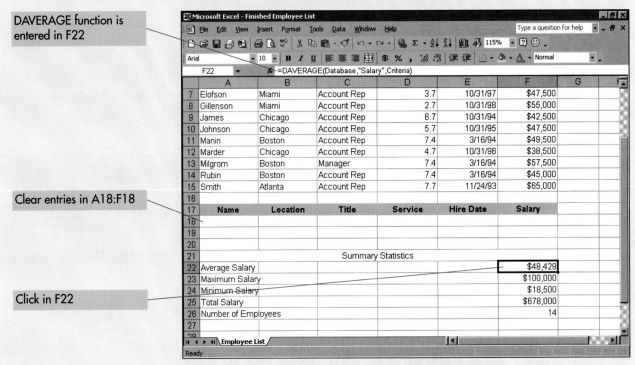

(a) Data Management Functions (step 1)

FIGURE 8.6 *Hands-on Exercise 3 (continued)*

Step 2: **The Create Name Command**

➤ Click and drag to select **cells A17** through **F18** as shown in Figure 8.6b. Pull down the **Insert menu**, click **Name**, then click **Create** to display the Create Names dialog box.

➤ The box to **Create Names in Top Row** is already checked. Click **OK**. This command assigns the text in each cell in row 17 to the corresponding cell in row 18; for example, cells B18 and C18 will be assigned the names Location and Title, respectively.

➤ Click and drag to select only **cells A18** through **F18**. (You need to assign a name to these seven cells collectively, as you will have to clear the criteria values in row 18 later in the chapter.)

➤ Pull down the **Insert menu**. Click **Name**. Click **Define**. Enter **Criteria Values** in the Define Name dialog box. Click **OK**.

➤ Save the workbook.

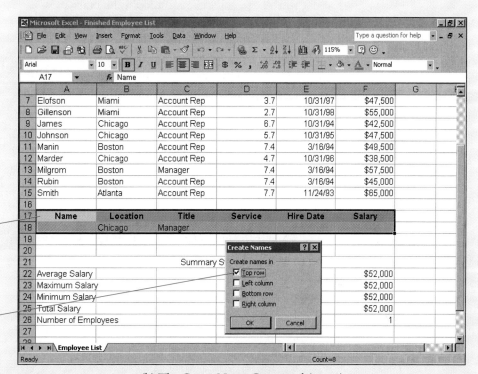

Click and drag to select
A17:A18

Click Top row

(b) The Create Name Command (step 2)

FIGURE 8.6   *Hands-on Exercise 3 (continued)*

CREATE SEVERAL NAMES AT ONCE

The Insert menu contains two different commands to create named ranges. The Insert Name Define command affects only one cell or range at a time, then has you enter the name in a dialog box. The Insert Name Create command requires you to select adjacent rows or columns, then assigns multiple names from the (adjacent row or column) in one command. Both commands are very useful.

Step 3: **The Go To Command**

➤ Pull down the **Edit menu**. Click **Go To** to produce the Go To dialog box in Figure 8.6c. If you do not see the command, click the double arrow to display more commands.

➤ You should see the names you defined (CriteriaValues, Hire_Date, Location, Name, Salary, Service, and Title) as well as the two names defined previously by the authors (Criteria and Database).

➤ Click **Database**. Click **OK**. Cells A1 through F15 should be selected, corresponding to cells assigned to the name *Database*.

➤ Press the **F5 key** (a shortcut for the Edit Go To command), which again produces the Go To dialog box. Click **Criteria**. Click **OK**. Cells A17 through F18 should be selected.

➤ Click the **drop-down arrow** next to the Name box. Click **Location**. Cell B18 should be selected.

➤ You are now ready to record the macro.

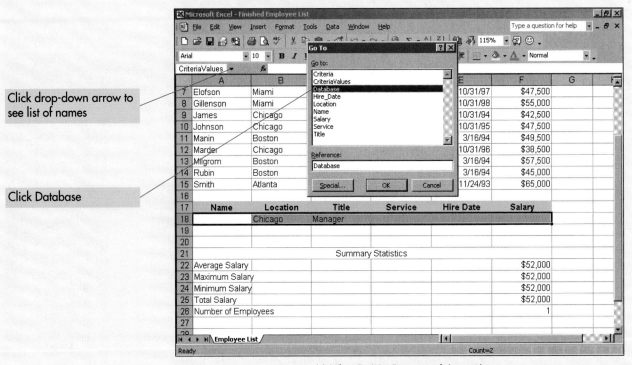

Click drop-down arrow to see list of names

Click Database

(c) The Go To Command (step 3)

FIGURE 8.6 *Hands-on Exercise 3 (continued)*

THE NAME BOX

Use the Name box (at the left of the Formula bar) to define a range by selecting the cell(s) in the worksheet to which the name is to apply, clicking the Name box, then entering the name. For example, to assign the name CriteriaValues to cells A18:F18, select the range, click in the Name box, type CriteriaValues, and press enter. The Name box can also be used to select a previously defined range by clicking the drop-down arrow next to the box and choosing the desired name from the drop-down list.

Step 4: **Record the Macro (Edit Clear Command)**

➤ Click the **Record Macro button** on the Visual Basic toolbar to display the Record Macro dialog box.

➤ Enter **Chicago** in the Macro Name text box. Verify that the macro will be stored in **This Workbook** and that the shortcut key check box is empty.

➤ Click **OK** to begin recording the macro. If necessary, click the **Relative References button** on the Stop Recording toolbar to record Absolute references (the button should be out).

➤ Pull down the **Edit menu**, click **Go To**, select **CriteriaValues** from the Go To dialog box, and click **OK**. Cells A18 through F18 should be selected as shown in Figure 8.6d. (Alternatively, you can also use the **F5 key** or the **Name box** to select CriteriaValues.)

➤ Pull down the **Edit menu**. Click **Clear**, then click **All** from the cascaded menu as shown in Figure 8.6d. Cells A18 through F18 (the criteria range) should be empty, and a new criterion can be entered into the macro.

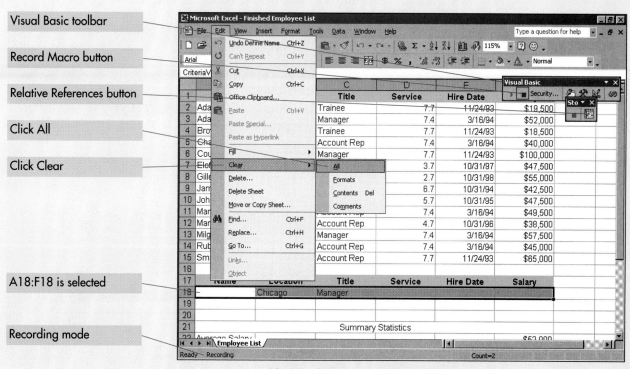

(d) Record the Macro (Edit Clear Command) (step 4)

FIGURE 8.6   *Hands-on Exercise 3 (continued)*

GOOD MACROS ARE FLEXIBLE MACROS

The macro to select Chicago employees has to be completely general and work under all circumstances, regardless of what may appear initially in the criteria row. Thus, you have to clear the entire criteria range prior to entering "Chicago" in the Location column. Note, too, the use of range names (e.g., CriteriaValues), as opposed to specific cells (e.g., A18:F18 in this example) to accommodate potential additions or deletions to the employee list.

Record the Macro (Advanced Filter Command)

> Pull down the **Edit menu**, click **Go To**, select **Location** from the Go To dialog box, and click **OK**.
> Cell B18 should be selected. Enter **Chicago** to establish the criterion for both the database functions and the Advanced Filter command.
> Click in **cell A2** to position the active cell within the employee list. Pull down the **Data menu**. Click **Filter**, then click **Advanced Filter** from the cascaded menu to display the dialog box in Figure 8.6e.
> Enter **Database** as the List Range. Press the **tab key**. Enter **Criteria** as the Criteria Range.
> Check that the option to **Filter the List in-place** is checked.
> Click **OK**. You should see only those employees who satisfy the current criteria (i.e., Adamson, James, Johnson, and Marder, who are the employees who work in Chicago).
> Click the **Stop Recording button** to stop recording.
> Click the **Save button** to save the workbook with the macro.

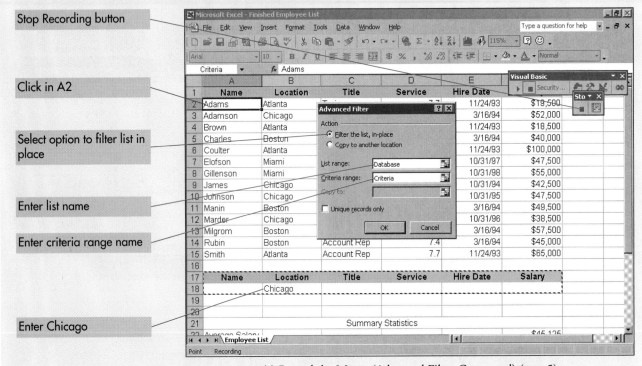

(e) Record the Macro (Advanced Filter Command) (step 5)

FIGURE 8.6 *Hands-on Exercise 3 (continued)*

THE FILTER VERSUS THE DATABASE FUNCTIONS

Change the criteria—for example, from Chicago to Chicago Managers—and the values displayed by the database functions (DAVERAGE, DSUM, and so on) change automatically. The filtered records do not change, however, until you re-execute the command to filter the records in place. The advantage of a macro becomes immediately apparent, because the macro is built to change the criteria and filter the records with a single click of the mouse.

Step 6: **View the Macro**

➤ Click the **Visual Basic Editor button** on the Visual Basic toolbar to open the editor as shown in Figure 8.6f. If necessary, pull down the **View menu**. Click **Project Explorer** to open the Project window in the left pane.

➤ If necessary, expand the **Modules folder**, under the VBA project for Finished Employee List. Click (select) **Module1**, pull down the **View menu**, and click **Code** to open the Code window in the right pane. Maximize the Code window.

➤ Close any other open windows within the Visual Basic Editor. Your screen should match the one in Figure 8.6f. If necessary, correct your macro so that it matches ours.

➤ If the correction is minor, it is easiest to edit the macro directly; otherwise delete the macro, then return to step 4 and rerecord the macro from the beginning. (To delete a macro, pull down the Tools menu, click Macros, select the macro you wish to delete, then click the Delete button.)

➤ Click the **View Microsoft Excel button** at the left of the toolbar or press **Alt+F11** to return to the Employee worksheet.

View Microsoft Excel button

Click Module1

Code for Chicago macro

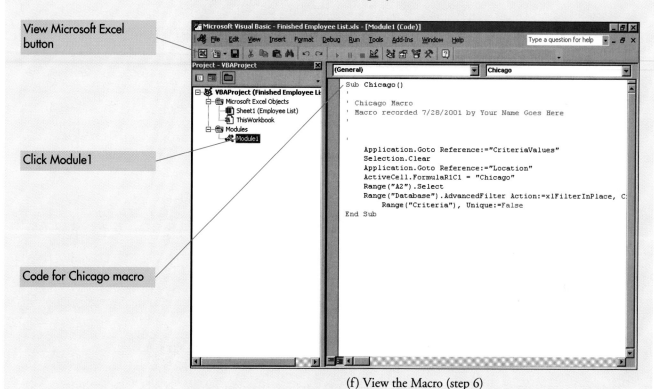

(f) View the Macro (step 6)

FIGURE 8.6   *Hands-on Exercise 3 (continued)*

THE VISUAL BASIC TOOLBAR

The Visual Basic Toolbar consists of seven buttons associated with macros and Visual Basic. You will find a button to run an existing macro, to record (or stop recording) a new macro, and to open (toggle to) the Visual Basic Editor. The toolbar can be displayed (or hidden) by right clicking any visible toolbar, then checking (or clearing) Visual Basic from the list of toolbars.

Step 7: **Assign the Macro**

> ➤ Pull down the **View menu**, click **Toolbars**, then click **Forms** to display the Forms toolbar as shown in Figure 8.6g.
> ➤ Click the **Button tool** (the mouse pointer changes to a tiny crosshair). Click and drag in the worksheet as shown in Figure 8.6g to draw a command button on the worksheet.
> ➤ Be sure to draw the button *below* the employee list, or the button may be hidden when a subsequent Data Filter command is executed.
> ➤ Release the mouse, and the Assign Macro dialog box will appear. Choose **Chicago** (the macro you just created) from the list of macro names. Click **OK**.
> ➤ The button should still be selected. Click and drag to select the name of the button, **Button 1**.
> ➤ Type **Chicago** as the new name. Do *not* press the enter key. Click outside the button to deselect it.
> ➤ Save the workbook.

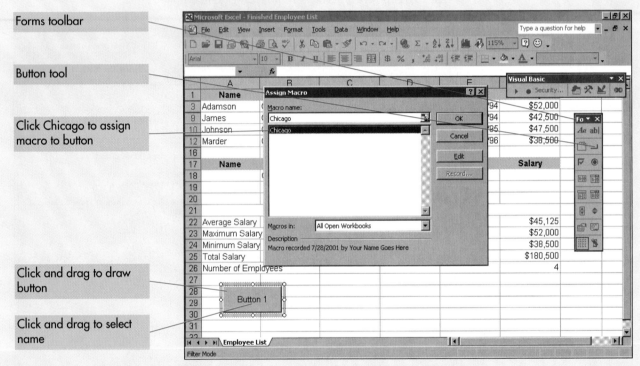

Forms toolbar

Button tool

Click Chicago to assign macro to button

Click and drag to draw button

Click and drag to select name

(g) Assign the Macro (step 7)

FIGURE 8.6 *Hands-on Exercise 3 (continued)*

SELECTING A BUTTON

You cannot select a Macro button by clicking it, because that executes the associated macro. Thus, to select a macro button, you must press and hold the Ctrl key as you click the mouse. (You can also select a button by clicking the right mouse button to produce a shortcut menu.) Once the button has been selected, you can edit its name, and/or move or size the button just as you can any other Windows object.

Step 8: **Test the Macro**

➤ Pull down the **Data menu**, click **Filter**, then click **Show All**.
➤ Click **cell B12**. Enter **Miami** to change the location for Marder. Press **enter**. The number of employees changes in the summary statistics area, as do the results of the other summary statistics.
➤ Click the **Chicago button** as shown in Figure 8.6h to execute the macro. Marder is *not* listed this time because she is no longer in Chicago.
➤ Pull down the **Data menu**. Click **Filter**. Click **Show All** to display the entire employee list.
➤ Click **cell B12**. Enter **Chicago** to change the location for this employee back to Chicago. Press **enter**. Click the **Chicago button** to execute the macro a second time. Marder is once again displayed with the Chicago employees.
➤ Pull down the **Data menu**. Click **Filter**. Click **Show All**.
➤ You do not have to print the workbook at this time, since we will print the entire workbook at the end of the next exercise.
➤ Save the workbook. Exit Excel if you do not want to continue with the next exercise at this time.

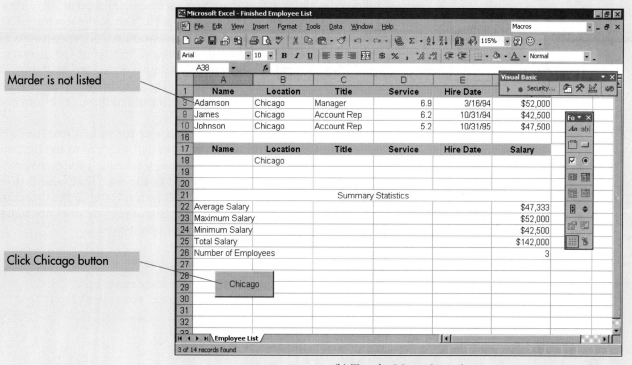

(h) Test the Macro (step 8)

FIGURE 8.6   *Hands-on Exercise 3 (continued)*

EXECUTING A MACRO

There are several different ways to execute a macro. The most basic way is to pull down the Tools menu, click Macro, click Macros to display the Macros dialog box, then double click the desired macro to run it. You can assign a macro to a button within a worksheet or to a custom button on a toolbar, then click the button to run the macro. The fastest way is to use a keyboard shortcut, provided that a shortcut has been defined.

Excel macros were originally nothing more than recorded keystrokes. Earlier versions of Excel had you turn on the macro recorder to capture the associated keystrokes, then "play back" those keystrokes when you ran the macro. Starting with Office 95, however, the recorded keystrokes were translated into Visual Basic commands, which made the macros potentially much more powerful because you could execute Visual Basic programs (known as procedures) from within Excel. (In actuality, Microsoft Office uses a subset of Visual Basic known as *Visual Basic for Applications (VBA)*, and we will use this terminology from now on.)

You can think of the macro recorder as a shortcut to generate the VBA code. Once you have that code, however, you can modify the various statements using techniques common to any programming language. You can move and/or copy statements within a procedure, search for one character string and replace it with another, and so on. And finally, you can insert additional VBA statements that are beyond the scope of ordinary Excel commands. You can, for example, display information to the user in the form of a message box any time during the execution of the macro. You can also accept information from the user into a dialog box for subsequent use in the macro.

Figure 8.7 illustrates the way that these tasks are accomplished in VBA. Figure 8.7a contains the VBA code, whereas Figures 8.7b and 8.7c show the resulting dialog boxes, as they would appear during execution of the associated VBA procedure. The *MsgBox statement* displays information to the user. The text of the message is entered in quotation marks, and the text appears within a dialog box as shown. The user clicks the OK command button to continue. (The MsgBox has other optional parameters that are not shown at this time, but are illustrated through various exercises at the end of the chapter.)

The InputBox function accepts input from the user for subsequent use in the procedure. Note the subtle change in terminology, in that we refer to the InputBox function, but the MsgBox statement. That is because a function returns a value, in this case the name of the location that was supplied by the user. That value is stored in the active cell within the worksheet, where it will be used later in the procedure. There is also a difference in syntax in that the MsgBox statement does not contain parentheses, whereas the InputBox function requires parentheses.

```
MsgBox "The MsgBox statement displays information"
ActiveCell.FormulaR1C1 = InputBox("Enter employee location")
```

(a) Visual Basic Statements

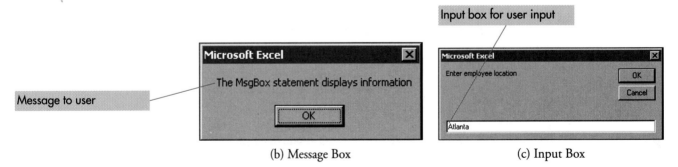

(b) Message Box   (c) Input Box

FIGURE 8.7   *VBA Statements*

CREATING ADDITIONAL MACROS

Objective   To duplicate an existing macro, then modify the copied macro to create an entirely new macro. Use Figure 8.8 as a guide.

Step 1:   **Enable Macros**

> ➤ Start Excel. Open the **Finished Employee List workbook** from the previous exercise. You should see the warning in Figure 8.8a.
> ➤ Click the **More Info button** to display the Help window to learn more about macro viruses. (Pull down the Tools menu, click Options, click the General tab, and check the Settings box for Micro Virus Protection if you do not see the warning message.)
> ➤ Click the **Close button** when you are finished reading the information.
> ➤ Click the **Enable Macros button** to open the Finished Employee List workbook.

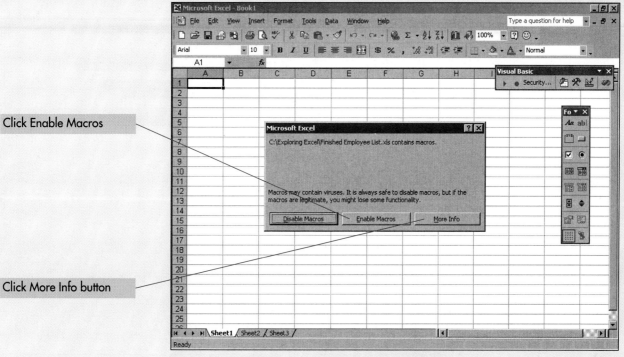

Click Enable Macros

Click More Info button

(a) Enable Macros (step 1)

FIGURE 8.8   *Hands-on Exercise 4*

MACRO VIRUSES

A computer virus is in actuality a program that can erase or delete the files on your computer. An Excel macro is also a program, and it too is capable of doing damage to your system. Thus, Excel will warn you that a workbook contains a macro, which in turn may carry a macro virus. If you are confident the workbook is safe, click the button to Enable macros; otherwise open the workbook with the macros disabled.

Step 2: **Copy the Chicago Macro**

➤ Pull down the **Tools menu**, click the **Macro command**, then click **Visual Basic Editor** (or press **Alt+F11**) to open the Visual Basic Editor.
➤ Click the **plus sign** on the Modules folder, select **Module1**, pull down the **View menu**, and click **Code**.
➤ Click and drag to select the entire Chicago macro as shown in Figure 8.8b.
➤ Pull down the **Edit menu** and click **Copy** (or click the **Copy button** on the Standard toolbar).
➤ Click below the End Sub statement to deselect the macro and simultaneously establish the position of the insertion point.
➤ Pull down the **Edit menu** and click **Paste** (or click the **Paste button** on the Standard toolbar). The Chicago macro has been copied and now appears twice in Module1.

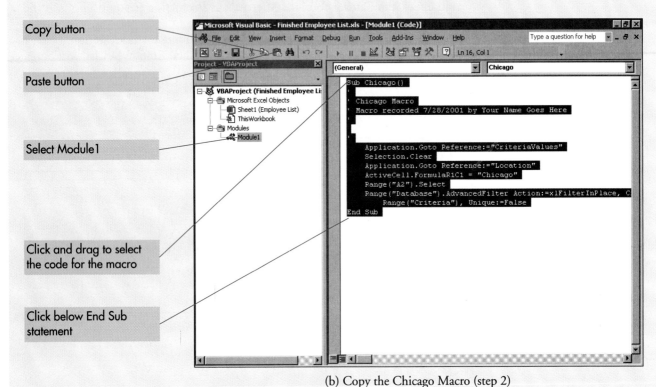

Copy button

Paste button

Select Module1

Click and drag to select the code for the macro

Click below End Sub statement

(b) Copy the Chicago Macro (step 2)

FIGURE 8.8 *Hands-on Exercise 4 (continued)*

THE SHIFT KEY

You can select text for editing (or replacement) with the mouse, or alternatively, you can select by using the cursor keys on the keyboard. Set the insertion point where you want the selection to begin, then press and hold the Shift key as you use the cursor keys to move the insertion point to the end of the selection.

Step 3: **Create the Manager Macro**

➤ Click in front of the second (i.e., the copied) Chicago macro to set the insertion point. Pull down the **Edit menu**. Click **Replace** to display the Replace dialog box as shown in Figure 8.8c.

➤ Enter **Chicago** in the Find What text box. Press the **tab key**. Enter **Manager** in the Replace With text box. Select the option button to search in the *current* procedure. Click the **Find Next command button**.

➤ Excel searches for the first occurrence of Chicago, which should be in the Sub statement of the copied macro. (If this is not the case, click the **Find Next command button** until your screen matches Figure 8.8c.)

➤ Click the **Replace command button**. Excel substitutes Manager for Chicago, then looks for the next occurrence of Chicago. Click **Replace**. Click **Replace** a third time to make another substitution. Close the Replace dialog box.

➤ Click and drag to select **Location** within the Application.Goto.Reference statement in the Manager macro. Enter **Title**. (The criteria within the macro have been changed to employees whose title is Manager.) Save the module.

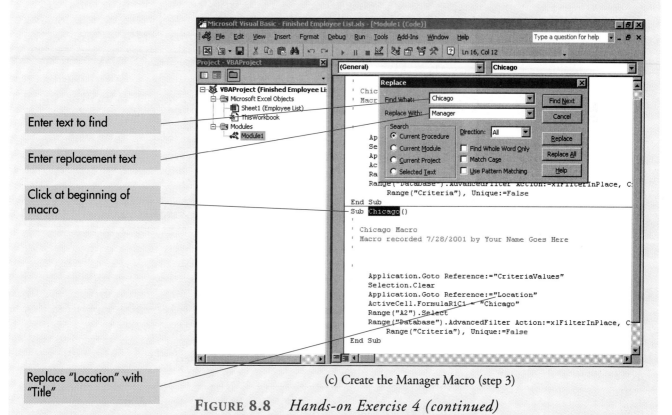

Enter text to find

Enter replacement text

Click at beginning of macro

Replace "Location" with "Title"

(c) Create the Manager Macro (step 3)

FIGURE 8.8   *Hands-on Exercise 4 (continued)*

THE FIND AND REPLACE COMMANDS

Anyone familiar with a word processor takes the Find and Replace commands for granted, but did you know the same capabilities exist in Excel as well as in the Visual Basic Editor? Pull down the Edit menu and choose either command. You have the same options as in the parallel command in Word, such as a case-sensitive (or insensitive) search or a limitation to a whole-word search.

Step 4: **Run the Manager Macro**

➤ Click the **Excel button** on the Windows taskbar or press **Alt+F11** to return to the Employee List worksheet.

➤ Pull down the **Tools menu**. Click **Macro**, then click the **Macros . . . command** to display the Macro dialog box as shown in Figure 8.8d.

➤ You should see two macros: Chicago, which was created in the previous exercise, and Manager, which you just created. (If the Manager macro does not appear, return to the Visual Basic Editor and correct the appropriate Sub statement to include Manager() as the name of the macro.)

➤ Select the **Manager macro**, then click **Run** to run the macro, after which you should see three employees (Adamson, Coulter, and Milgrom). If the macro does not execute correctly, return to the Visual Basic Editor to make the necessary corrections, then rerun the macro.

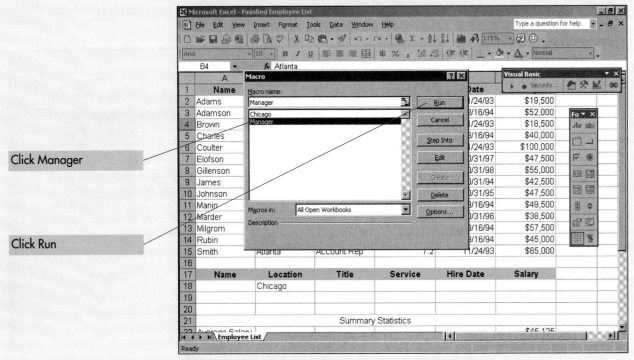

(d) Run the Manager Macro (step 4)

FIGURE 8.8 *Hands-on Exercise 4 (continued)*

THE STEP INTO COMMAND

The Step Into command helps to debug a macro, as it executes the statements one at a time. Pull down the Tools menu, click Macro, click Macros, select the macro to debug, then click the Step Into command button. Move and/or size the Visual Basic Editor window so that you can see both the worksheet and the macro. Pull down the Debug menu and click the Step Into command (or press the F8 function key) to execute the first statement in the macro and view its results. Continue to press the F8 function key to execute the statements one at a time until the macro has completed execution.

Step 5: **Assign a Button**

➤ Click the **Button tool** on the Forms toolbar (the mouse pointer changes to a tiny crosshair), then click and drag in the worksheet to draw a button on the worksheet. Release the mouse.

➤ Choose **Manager** (the macro you just created) from the list of macro names as shown in Figure 8.8e. Click **OK** to close the Assign Macro dialog box.

➤ The button should still be selected. Click and drag to select the name of the button, **Button 2**, then type **Manager** as the new name. Do *not* press the enter key. Click outside the button to deselect it.

➤ There should be two buttons on your worksheet, one each for the Chicago and Manager macros.

➤ Click the **Chicago button** to execute the Chicago macro. You should see four employees with an average salary of $45,125.

➤ Click the **Manager button** to execute the Manager macro. You should see three employees with an average salary of $69,833.

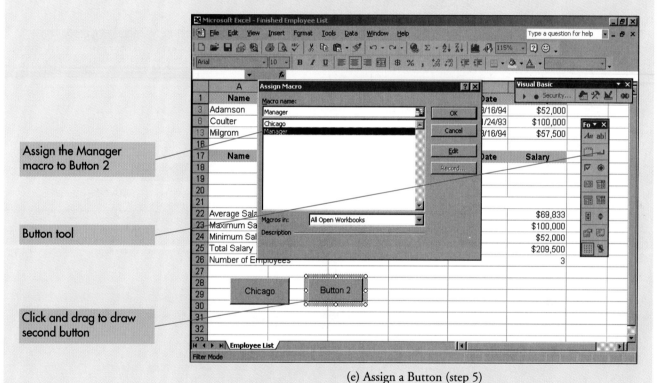

Assign the Manager macro to Button 2

Button tool

Click and drag to draw second button

(e) Assign a Button (step 5)

FIGURE 8.8 *Hands-on Exercise 4 (continued)*

CREATE UNIFORM BUTTONS

One way to create buttons of a uniform size is to create the first button, then copy that button to create the others. To copy a button, press the Ctrl key as you select (click) the button, then click the Copy button on the Standard toolbar. Click in the worksheet where you want the new button to appear, then click the Paste button. Click and drag over the name of the button and enter a new name. Right click the new button, then click Assign Macro from the shortcut menu. Select the name of the new macro, then click OK.

Step 6: **Create the Chicago Manager Macro**

➤ Return to the Visual Basic Editor. Press **Ctrl+Home** to move to the beginning of Module1. Click and drag to select the entire Chicago macro. Be sure to include the End Sub statement in your selection.

➤ Click the **Copy button** on the Standard toolbar to copy the Chicago macro to the clipboard. Press **Ctrl+End** to move to the end of the module sheet. Click the **Paste button** on the Standard toolbar to complete the copy operation.

➤ Change **Chicago** to **ChicagoManager** in both the comment statement and the Sub statement as shown in Figure 8.8f.

➤ Click and drag to select the two statements in the **Manager macro** as shown in Figure 8.8f. Click the **Copy button**.

➤ Scroll, if necessary, until you can click in the **ChicagoManager macro** at the end of the line, ActiveCell.FormulaR1C1 = "Chicago". Press **enter** to begin a new line. Click the **Paste button** to complete the copy operation.

➤ Delete any unnecessary blank lines or spaces that may remain.

➤ Save the module.

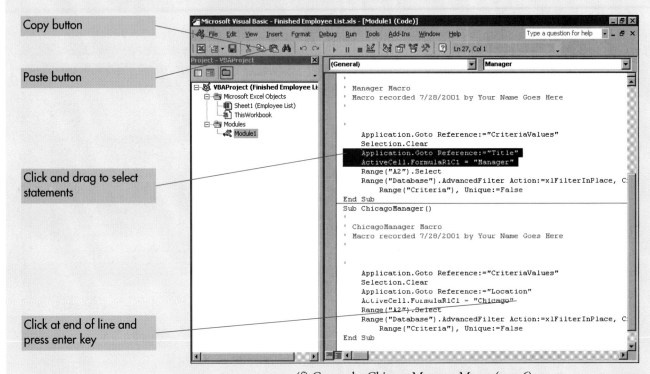

Copy button

Paste button

Click and drag to select statements

Click at end of line and press enter key

(f) Create the Chicago Manager Macro (step 6)

FIGURE 8.8 *Hands-on Exercise 4 (continued)*

ADD A SHORTCUT

You can add and/or modify the shortcut key associated with a macro at any time. Pull down the Tools menu, click the Macro command, then click Macros to display the Macro dialog box. Select the desired macro and click the Options button to display the Macro Options dialog box, where you assign a shortcut. Type a lowercase letter to create a shortcut with just the Ctrl key, such as Ctrl+m. Enter an uppercase letter to create a shortcut using the Ctrl and Shift keys, such as Ctrl+Shift+M.

Step 7: **The MsgBox Statement**

➤ Check that the statements in your ChicagoManager macro match those in Figure 8.8g. (The MsgBox statement has not yet been added.)

➤ Click immediately before the End Sub statement. Press **enter** to begin a new line, press the **up arrow** to move up one line, then press **Tab** to indent.

➤ Type the word **MsgBox** then press the **Space bar**. VBA responds with a Quick Info box that displays the complete syntax of the statement. You can ignore this information at the present time, since we are not entering any additional parameters.

➤ Enter the rest of the MsgBox statement exactly as it appears in Figure 8.8g. Be sure to include the underscore at the end of the first line, which indicates that the statement is continued to the next line.

➤ Save the module, then return to the Excel workbook.

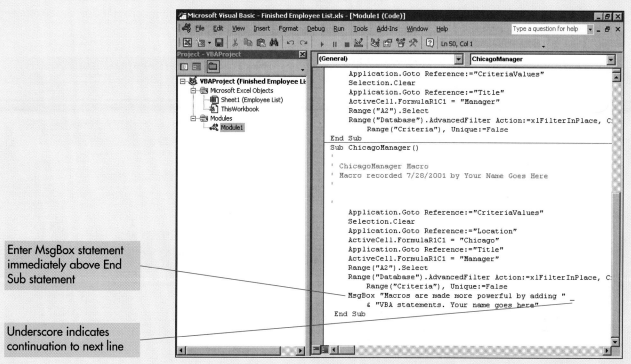

Enter MsgBox statement immediately above End Sub statement

Underscore indicates continuation to next line

(g) The MsgBox Statement (step 7)

FIGURE 8.8 *Hands-on Exercise 4 (continued)*

THE UNDERSCORE AND AMPERSAND

A VBA statement is continued from one line to the next by typing an underscore at the end of the line to be continued. You may not, however, break a line in the middle of a literal. Hence, the first line ends with a closing quotation mark, followed by a space and the underscore. The next line starts with an ampersand to indicated continuation of the previous literal, followed by the remainder of the literal in quotation marks.

Step 8: **Test the Chicago Manager Macro**

➤ You can assign a macro to a command button by copying an existing command button, then changing the name of the button and the associated macro. Right click either of the existing command buttons, click the **Copy command** from the shortcut menu, then click the **Paste button** on the Standard toolbar.

➤ Click and drag the copied button to the right of the two existing buttons. Click and drag the text of the copied button (which should still be selected) to select the text, then type **Chicago Manager** as the name of the button.

➤ Click anywhere in the worksheet to deselect the button, then **Right click** the new button, click the **Assign Macro command**, choose the newly created Chicago Manager, and click **OK**. Click anywhere in the workbook to deselect the button. Save the workbook.

➤ Click the **Chicago Manager button** to execute the macro. You should see the matching employees as shown in Figure 8.8h, followed by the message box.

➤ Click **OK**. Return to the VBA editor to correct the macro if it does not execute as intended.

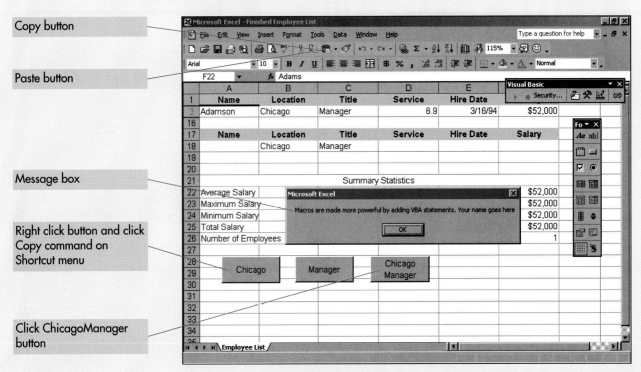

(h) Test the Chicago Manager Macro (step 8)

FIGURE 8.8 *Hands-on Exercise 4 (continued)*

CUSTOMIZE THE MESSAGE BOX

You can add a personal touch to the output of the MsgBox statement by including optional parameters to change the text of the title bar and/or include an icon within the message box. The statement, MsgBox "Hello World", vbinformation, "Your Name on Title Bar" uses both parameters. Try it.

Step 9:   **Create the Any City Any Title Macro**

> ➤ Press **Alt+F11** to return to the Visual Basic editor. Click and drag to select the entire ChicagoManager macro. Click the **Copy button**, click the blank line below the End Sub statement, then click the **Paste button** to duplicate the module.
>
> ➤ Click and drag the name of the copied macro. Type **AnyCityAnyTitle()** to change the name of the macro. Do not leave any spaces in the macro name. Delete or modify the comments as you see fit.
>
> ➤ Click and drag to select **"Chicago"** as shown in Figure 8.8i. You must include the quotation marks in your selection.
>
> ➤ Type **InputBox("Enter the location")** to replace the specific location with the InputBox function. Be sure to use left and right parentheses and to enclose the literal in quotation marks.
>
> ➤ Click and drag to select **"Manager"**. Type **InputBox("Enter the title")** to replace the specific title with the InputBox function.
>
> ➤ Save the module and return to the Excel workbook.

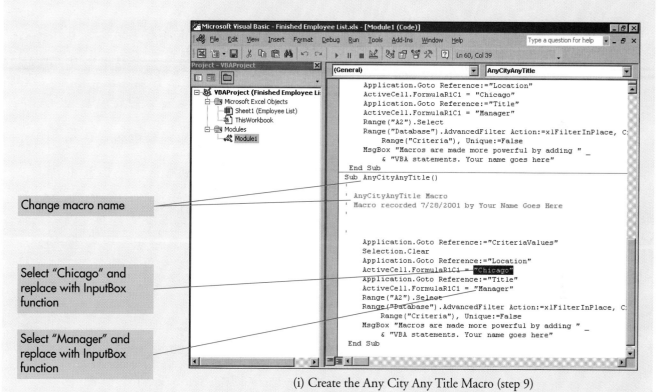

(i) Create the Any City Any Title Macro (step 9)

FIGURE 8.8   *Hands-on Exercise 4 (continued)*

USE WHAT YOU KNOW

Use the techniques acquired from other applications such as Microsoft Word to facilitate editing within the VBA window. Press the Ins key to toggle between the insert and overtype modes as you modify the statements within a procedure. You can also cut, copy, and paste statements (or parts of statements) within a procedure and from one procedure to another. The Find and Replace commands are also useful.

Step 10:   **Test the Any City Any Title Macro**

> ➤ Copy any of the existing command buttons to create a new button for the **Any City Any Title** macro as shown in Figure 8.8j. Be sure to assign the correct macro to this button.
> ➤ Click the **Any City Any Title command button** to run the macro. You will be prompted for the location. Type **Atlanta** and click **OK**. (A second input box will appear in which you will enter the title.)
> ➤ At this time Atlanta has been entered into the criteria area, and the summary statistics reflect the Atlanta employees. The filtered list will not change, however, until you have entered the title and completed the Advanced Filter command.
> ➤ Enter **Trainee** as the employee title as shown in Figure 8.8j. Click **OK**. The workbook changes to reflect the Atlanta trainees. Click **OK** in response to the message box.
> ➤ Return to the VBA editor if the macro does not execute as intended. Save the workbook.

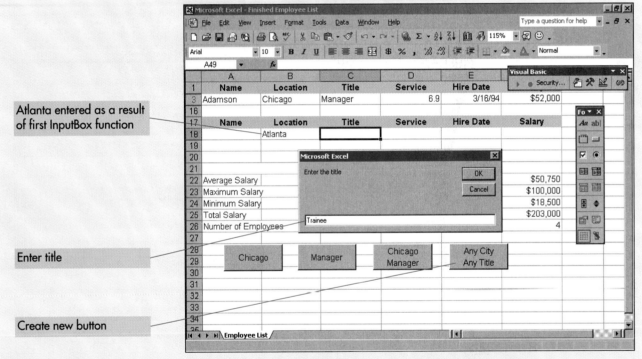

Atlanta entered as a result of first InputBox function

Enter title

Create new button

(j) Test the Any City Any Title Macro (step 10)

FIGURE 8.8   *Hands-on Exercise 4 (continued)*

ONE MACRO DOES IT ALL

The Any City Any Title macro is the equivalent of the more specific macros that were created earlier; that is, you would enter "Chicago" and "Manager" to replace the Chicago Manager macro. You can also enter "Chicago" as the city and leave the title field blank to select all Chicago employees, or alternatively, leave the city blank and enter "Manager" as the title to select all managers. And finally, you could omit both city and title to select all employees.

Step 11: **Change the Button Properties**

➤ Press and hold the **Shift** and **Ctrl keys**, then click each of the command buttons to select all four buttons as shown in Figure 8.8k.

➤ Pull down the **Format** menu and click the **Control command** to display the Format Control dialog box. Click the **Properties tab**, then check the box to **Print object** so that the command buttons will appear on the printed worksheet.

➤ Click the **Move but don't size with cells** option button. Click **OK** to exit the dialog box and return to the worksheet. Click anywhere in the worksheet to deselect the buttons.

➤ Click the **Print button** on the Standard toolbar to print the worksheet. Return to the Visual Basic Editor. Pull down the **File menu**, click the **Print command**, select **Current Module**, then click **OK**.

➤ Save the workbook a final time. Close the workbook. Exit Excel if you don't want to continue with the next exercise at this time.

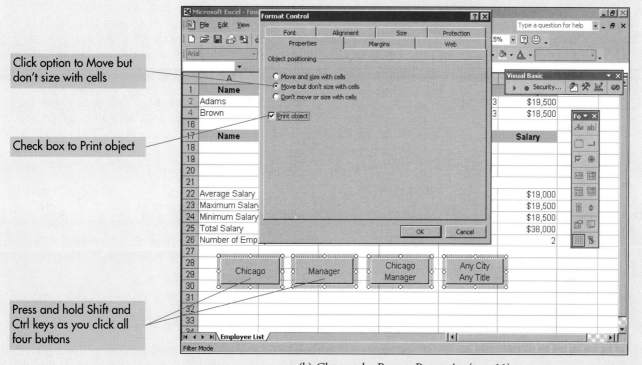

Click option to Move but don't size with cells

Check box to Print object

Press and hold Shift and Ctrl keys as you click all four buttons

(k) Change the Button Properties (step 11)

FIGURE 8.8 *Hands-on Exercise 4 (continued)*

THE SIZE PROPERTY

Use the Size property to obtain a consistent look for your command buttons. Press and hold the Shift and Ctrl keys as you select the individual buttons. Pull down the Format menu and click the Control command to display the Format Control dialog box. Click the Size tab, enter the width and height for the selected buttons, then click OK. The buttons will be a uniform size, but they may overlap. Click anywhere in the worksheet to deselect the buttons, then right click and drag to reposition a button.

Excel macros can be made significantly more powerful by incorporating additional Visual Basic statements that enable true programming. These include the If statement for decision making, and the Do statement to implement a *loop* (one or more commands that are executed repeatedly until a condition is met).

Consider, for example, the worksheet and associated macro in Figure 8.9. The worksheet is similar to those used in the preceding exercises, except that the font color of the data for managers is red. Think for a minute how you would do this manually. You would look at the first employee in the list, examine the employee's title to determine if that employee is a manager, and if so, change the font color for that employee. You would then repeat these steps for all of the other employees on the list. It sounds tedious, but that is exactly what you would do if asked to change the font color for the managers.

Now ask yourself whether you could implement the entire process with the macro recorder. You could use the recorder to capture the commands to select a specific row within the list and change the font color. You could not, however, use the recorder to determine whether or not to select a particular row (i.e., whether the employee is a manager) because you make that decision by comparing the cell contents to a specific criterion. Nor is there a way to tell the recorder to repeat the process for every employee. In other words, you need to go beyond merely capturing Excel commands. You need to include additional Visual Basic statements.

The HighlightManager macro in Figure 8.9 uses the If statement to implement a decision (to determine whether the selected employee is a manager) and the Do statement to implement a loop (to repeat the commands until all employees in the list have been processed). To understand how the macro works, you need to know the basic syntax of each statement.

If Statement

The *If statement* conditionally executes a statement (or group of statements), depending on the value of an expression (condition). The If statement determines whether an expression is true, and if so, executes the commands between the If and the *End If statement*. For example:

```
If ActiveCell.Offset(0, 2) = "Manager" Then
    Selection.Font.ColorIndex = 3
End If
```

This If statement determines whether the cell two columns to the right of the active cell (the offset indicates a relative reference) contains the text *Manager,* and if so, changes the font color of the (previously) selected text. The number three corresponds to the color red. No action is taken if the condition is false. Either way, execution continues with the command below the End If.

IF-THEN-ELSE

The If statement includes an optional Else clause whose statements are executed if the condition is false. Consider:

If condition Then statements [Else statements] End If

The condition is evaluated as either true or false. If the condition is true, the statements following Then are executed; otherwise the statements following Else are executed. Either way, execution continues with the statement following End If. Use the Help command for additional information and examples.

Do Statement

The ***Do statement*** repeats a block of statements until a condition becomes true. For example:

```
Do Until ActiveCell = ""
     ActiveCell.Range("A1:F1").Select
     If ActiveCell.Offset(0, 2) = "Manager" Then
          Selection.Font.ColorIndex = 3
     End If
     ActiveCell.Offset(1, 0).Select
Loop
```

The statements within the loop are executed repeatedly until the active cell is empty (i.e., ActiveCell = ""). The first statement in the loop selects the cells in columns A through F of the current row. Relative references are used, and you may want to refer to the earlier discussion that indicated that A1:F1 specifies the shape of a range rather than a specific cell address.

The If statement determines whether the current employee is a manager and, if so, changes the font color for the selected cells. (The offset (0, 2) refers to the entry two columns to the right of the active cell.) The last statement selects the cell one row below the active cell to process the next employee. (Omission of this statement would process the same row indefinitely, creating what is known as an infinite loop.)

The macro in Figure 8.9 is a nontrivial example that illustrates the potential of Visual Basic to enhance a macro. Try to gain a conceptual understanding of how the macro works, but do not be concerned if you are confused initially. Do the hands-on exercise, and you'll be pleased at how much clearer it will be when you have created the macro yourself.

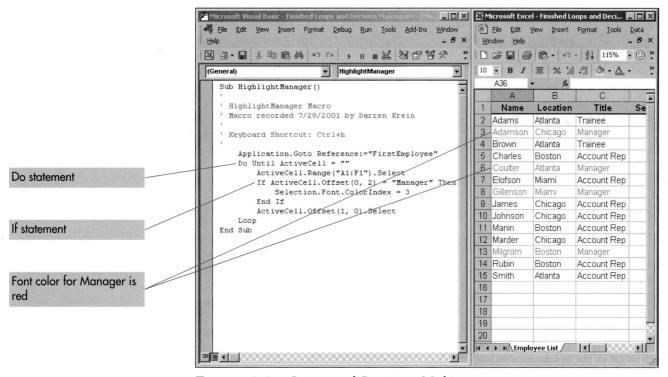

FIGURE 8.9 *Loops and Decision Making*

LOOPS AND DECISION MAKING

Objective   To implement loops and decision making in a macro through relative references and the Visual Basic Do Until and If statements. Use Figure 8.10 as a guide in doing the exercise.

Step 1:   **The ClearColor Macro**

➤ Open the **Loops and Decision Making workbook** in the **Exploring Excel folder**. Click the button to **Enable Macros**. Close the Forms and Visual Basic toolbars.

➤ Save the workbook as **Finished Loops and Decision Making workbook**. The data for the employees in rows 3, 6, 8, and 13 appears in red to indicate these employees are managers.

➤ Pull down the **Tools menu**. Click the **Macro command** and click **Macros** to display the dialog box in Figure 8.10a.

➤ Select **ClearColor**, then click **Run** to execute this macro and clear the red color from the managerial employees.

➤ It is important to know that the ClearColor macro works, as you will use it throughout the exercise.

➤ Save the workbook.

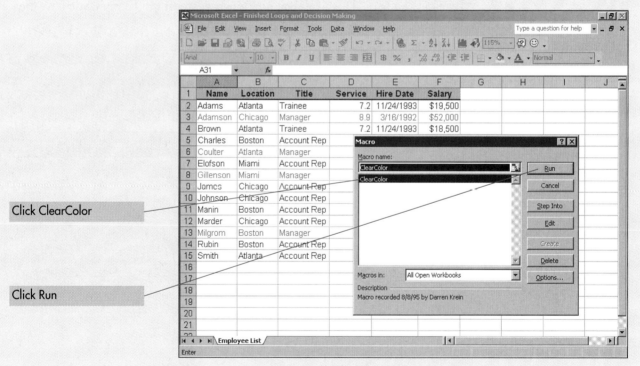

(a) The ClearColor Macro (step 1)

FIGURE 8.10   *Hands-on Exercise 5*

Step 2: **Record the HighlightManager Macro**

> ➤ You must choose the active cell before recording the macro. Click **cell A3**, the cell containing the name of the first manager.
> ➤ Pull down the **Tools menu**, click (or point to) the **Macro command**, then click **Record New Macro** (or click the **Record macro button** on the Visual Basic toolbar) to display the Record Macro dialog box.
> ➤ Enter **HighlightManager** as the name of the macro. Do not leave any spaces in the macro name. Click in the **Shortcut Key** check box and enter a **lowercase h**. Check that **This Workbook** is selected. Click **OK**.
> ➤ The Stop Recording toolbar appears and the status bar indicates that you are recording the macro as shown in Figure 8.10b. Click the **Relative References button** so that the button is pushed in.
> ➤ Click and drag to select **cells A3** through **F3** as shown in Figure 8.10b. Click the arrow in the **Font color list box**. Click **Red**. Click the **Stop Recording button**.
> ➤ Click anywhere in the worksheet to deselect cells A3 through F3 so you can see the effect of the macro; cells A3 through F3 should be displayed in red.
> ➤ Save the workbook.

Click drop-down arrow on Font Color list

Click and drag to select A3:F3

Click Red

Recording mode

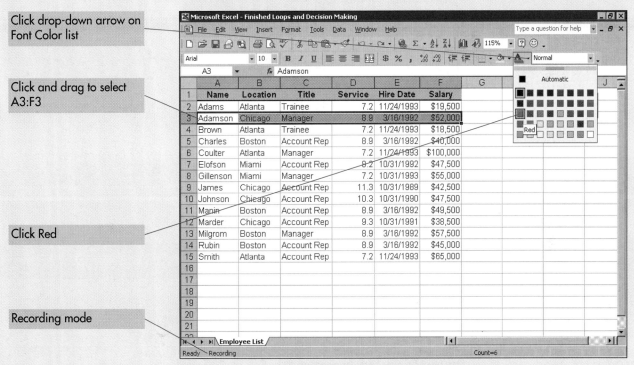

(b) Record the HighlightManager Macro (step 2)

FIGURE 8.10 *Hands-on Exercise 5 (continued)*

A SENSE OF FAMILIARITY

Visual Basic has the basic capabilities found in any other programming language. If you have programmed before, whether in Pascal, C, or even COBOL, you will find all of the familiar logic structures. These include the Do While and Do Until statements, the If-Then-Else statement for decision making, nested If statements, a Case statement, and/or calls to subprograms.

Step 3: **View the Macro**

➤ Press **Alt+F11** to open the Visual Basic Editor. If necessary, double click the **Modules folder** within the Project Explorer window to display the two modules within the workbook.

➤ Select (click) **Module2**. Pull down the **View menu** and click **Code** (or press the **F7 key**) to display the Visual Basic code for the HighlightManager macro you just created as shown in Figure 8.10c.

➤ Be sure that your code is identical to ours (except for the comments). If you see the absolute reference, Range("A3:F3"), rather than the relative reference in our figure, you need to correct your macro to match ours.

➤ Click the **close button** (the X on the Project Explorer title bar) to close the Project Explorer window. The Code window expands to occupy the entire Visual Basic Editor window.

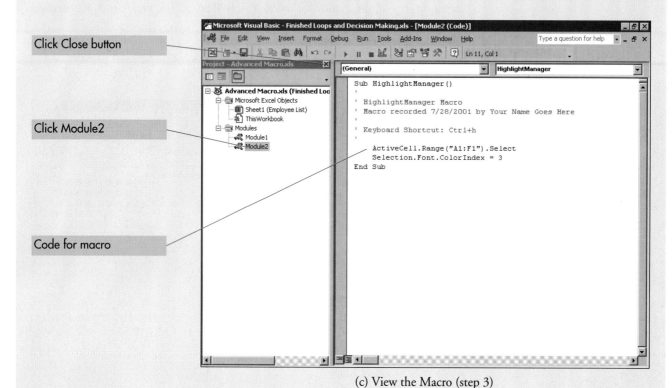

(c) View the Macro (step 3)

FIGURE 8.10 *Hands-on Exercise 5 (continued)*

WHY SO MANY MODULES?

Multiple macros that are recorded within the same Excel session are all stored in the same module. If you close the workbook, then subsequently reopen it, Excel will store subsequent macros in a new module. It really doesn't matter where (in which module) the macros are stored. You can, however, cut and paste macros from one module to another if you prefer to have all of the macros in a single module. Delete the additional (now superfluous) modules after you have copied the procedures.

Step 4: **Test the Macro**

➤ Point to an empty area on the Windows taskbar, then click the **right mouse button** to display a shortcut menu. Click **Tile Vertically** to tile the open windows (Excel and the Visual Basic Editor).

➤ Your desktop should be similar to Figure 8.10d except that the additional employees will not yet appear in red. It doesn't matter if the workbook is in the same window as ours. (If additional windows are open on the desktop, minimize each window, then repeat the previous step to tile the open windows.)

➤ Click the **Excel window**. Click **cell A6** (the cell containing the name of the next manager). Press **Ctrl+h** to execute the HighlightManager macro. The font in cells A6 to F6 changes to red.

➤ Click **cell A7**. Press **Ctrl+h** to execute the HighlightManager macro. The font for this employee is also in red, although the employee is not a manager.

➤ Save the workbook.

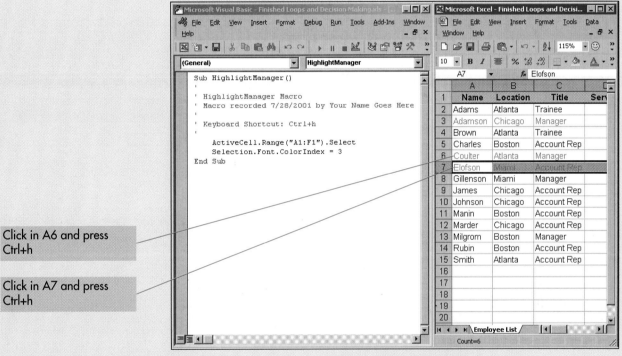

Click in A6 and press Ctrl+h

Click in A7 and press Ctrl+h

(d) Test the Macro (step 4)

FIGURE 8.10 *Hands-on Exercise 5 (continued)*

THE FIRST BUG

A bug is a mistake in a computer program; hence debugging refers to the process of correcting program errors. According to legend, the first bug was an unlucky moth crushed to death on one of the relays of the electromechanical Mark II computer, bringing the machine's operation to a halt. The cause of the failure was discovered by Grace Hopper, who promptly taped the moth to her logbook, noting, *"First actual case of bug being found."*

Step 5: **Add the If Statement**

➤ Press **Ctrl+c** to execute the ClearColor macro. The data for all employees is again displayed in black.

➤ Click in the window containing the **HighlightManager** macro. Add the **If** and **End If** statements exactly as they are shown in Figure 8.10e. Use the **Tab key** (or press the **space bar**) to indent the Selection statement within the If and End If statements.

➤ Click in the window containing the worksheet, then click **cell A3**. Press **Ctrl+h** to execute the modified HighlightManager macro. The text in cells A3 through F3 is red since this employee is a manager.

➤ Click **cell A4**. Press **Ctrl+h**. The row is selected, but the color of the font remains unchanged. The If statement prevents these cells from being highlighted because the employee is not a manager. Press **Ctrl+c** to remove all highlighting.

➤ Save the workbook.

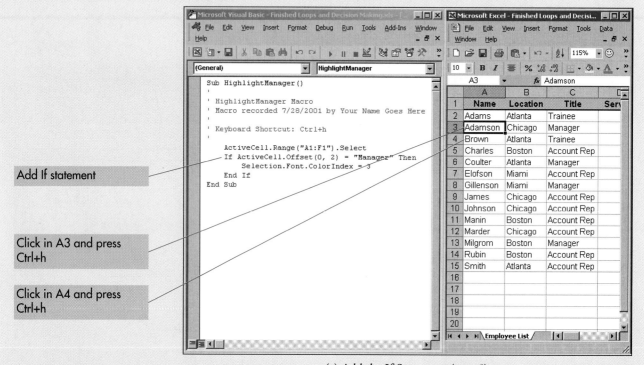

(e) Add the If Statement (step 5)

FIGURE 8.10   *Hands-on Exercise 5 (continued)*

INDENT

Indentation does not affect the execution of a macro. It, does, however, make the macro easier to read, and we suggest you follow common conventions in developing your macros. Indent the conditional statements associated with an If statement by a consistent amount. Place the End If statement on a line by itself, directly under the associated If.

Step 6: **An Endless Loop**

> ➤ Click in the window containing the **HighlightManager** macro. Add the **Do Until** and **Loop** statements exactly as they appear in Figure 8.10f. Indent the other statements as shown in the figure.
> ➤ Click **cell A3** of the worksheet. Press **Ctrl+h** to execute the macro. Cells A3 through F3 will be displayed in red, but the macro continues to execute indefinitely as it applies color to the same record over and over.
> ➤ Press **Ctrl+Break** to cease execution of the macro. You will see the dialog box in Figure 8.10f, indicating that an error has been encountered during the execution of the macro. Click the **End button**.
> ➤ Pull down the **Debug menu** and click the **Step Into command** (or press the **F8 key**) to enter the macro. The first statement is highlighted in yellow.
> ➤ Press the **F8 key** several times to execute the next several steps. You will see that the macro is stuck in a loop as the If statement is executed indefinitely.
> ➤ Click the **Reset button** in the Visual Basic window to end the debugging.

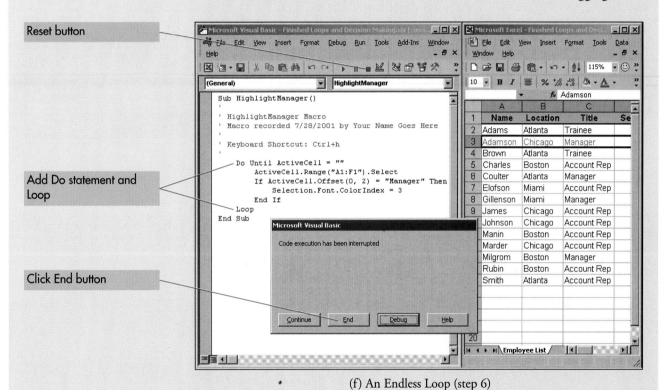

(f) An Endless Loop (step 6)

FIGURE 8.10 *Hands-on Exercise 5 (continued)*

AN ENDLESS LOOP

The glossary in the Programmer's Guide for a popular database contains the following definitions "Endless loop"—See loop, endless and "Loop, endless"—See endless loop.

We don't know whether these entries were deliberate or not, but the point is made either way. Endless loops are a common and frustrating bug. Press Ctrl+Break to halt execution, then click the Debug command button to step through the macro and locate the source of the error.

Step 7:   **The Completed Macro**

➤ Click in **cell A2** of the worksheet. Click in the **Name Box**. Enter **FirstEmployee** to name this cell. Press **enter**.

➤ Click in the window containing the macro. Click after the last comment and press **enter** to insert a blank line.

➤ Add the statement to select the cell named FirstEmployee as shown in Figure 8.10g. This ensures that the macro always begins in row two by selecting the cell named FirstEmployee.

➤ Click immediately after the End If statement. Press **enter**. Add the statement containing the offset (1,0) as shown in Figure 8.10g, which selects the cell one row below the current row.

➤ Click anywhere in the worksheet except cell A2. Press **Ctrl+c** to clear the color. Press **Ctrl+h** to execute the HighlightManager macro.

➤ The macro begins by selecting cell A2, then proceeds to highlight all managers in red. Save the workbook a final time.

➤ Print the workbook and its macro for your instructor. Exit Excel.

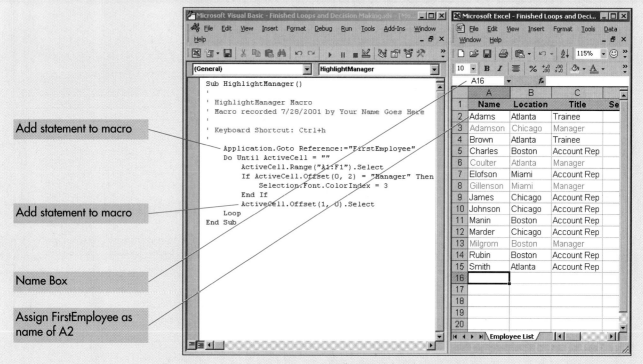

(g) The Completed Macro (step 7)

FIGURE 8.10   *Hands-on Exercise 5 (continued)*

HELP FOR VISUAL BASIC

Click within any Visual Basic key word, then press the F1 key for context-sensitive help. You will see a help screen containing a description of the statement, its syntax, key elements, and several examples. You can print the help screen by clicking the Options command button and selecting Print Topic. (If you do not see the help screens, ask your instructor to install Visual Basic Help.)

A macro is a set of instructions that automates a repetitive task. It is, in essence, a program, and its instructions are written in Visual Basic, a programming language. The macro recorder in Excel records your commands and writes the macro for you. Once a macro has been created, it can be edited by manually inserting, deleting, or changing its statements.

Macros are stored in one of two places, either in the current workbook or in a Personal Macro workbook. Macros that are specific to a particular workbook should be stored in that workbook. Generic macros that can be used with any workbook should be stored in the Personal Macro workbook.

A macro is run (executed) by pulling down the Tools menu and selecting the Run Macro command. A macro can also be executed through a keyboard shortcut, by placing a button on the worksheet, or by customizing a toolbar to include an additional button to run the macro.

A comment is a nonexecutable statement that begins with an apostrophe. Comments are inserted automatically at the beginning of a macro by the macro recorder to remind you of what the macro does. Comments may be added, deleted, or modified, just as any other statement.

A macro begins and ends with the Sub and End Sub statements, respectively. The Sub statement contains the name of the macro or VBA procedure.

The With statement enables you to perform multiple actions on the same object. All commands between the With and corresponding End With statements are executed collectively.

A macro contains either absolute or relative references. An absolute reference is constant; that is, Excel keeps track of the exact cell address and selects that specific cell. A relative reference depends on the previously selected cell, and is entered as an offset, or number of rows and columns from the current cell. The Relative Reference button on the Stop Recording toolbar toggles between the two.

An Excel macro can be made more powerful through inclusion of Visual Basic statements that enable true programming. These include the MsgBox statement to display information, the InputBox function to obtain user input, the If statement to implement decision making, and the Do statement to implement a loop. The macro recorder creates the initial macro by translating Excel commands to Visual Basic statements. The additional VBA statements are added to the resulting code using the Visual Basic Editor.

KEY TERMS

Absolute reference (p. 379)
Button tool (p. 396)
Code window (p. 368)
Comment (p. 368)
Debugging (p. 415)
Do statement (p. 411)
End If statement (p. 410)
End Sub statement (p. 368)
End With statement (p. 369)
If statement (p. 410)
InputBox function (p. 380)

Insert Name command (p. 391)
Keyboard shortcut (p. 368)
Loop (p. 410)
Macro (p. 367)
Macro recorder (p. 368)
MsgBox statement (p. 398)
Name box (p. 392)
Named range (p. 389)
Offset (p. 379)
Personal Macro workbook (p. 380)
Project Explorer (p. 368)

Relative reference (p. 379)
Shortcut key (p. 368)
Step Into command (p. 377)
Sub statement (p. 368)
Visual Basic (p. 368)
Visual Basic Editor (VBE) (p. 368)
Visual Basic for Applications (VBA) (p. 368)
With statement (p. 369)

1. Which of the following best describes recording and executing a macro?
   (a) A macro is recorded once and executed once
   (b) A macro is recorded once and executed many times
   (c) A macro is recorded many times and executed once
   (d) A macro is recorded many times and executed many times

2. Which of the following can be used to execute a macro?
   (a) A keyboard shortcut
   (b) A customized toolbar button
   (c) Both (a) and (b)
   (d) Neither (a) nor (b)

3. A macro can be stored:
   (a) In any Excel workbook
   (b) In the Personal Macro workbook
   (c) Both (a) and (b)
   (d) Neither (a) nor (b)

4. Which of the following is true regarding comments in Visual Basic?
   (a) A comment is executable; that is, its inclusion or omission affects the outcome of a macro
   (b) A comment begins with an apostrophe
   (c) Both (a) and (b)
   (d) Neither (a) nor (b)

5. Which statement must contain the name of the macro?
   (a) The Sub statement at the beginning of the macro
   (b) The first comment statement
   (c) Both (a) and (b)
   (d) Neither (a) nor (b)

6. Which of the following indicates an absolute reference within a macro?
   (a) ActiveCell.Offset(1,1).Range("A1")
   (b) $A$1
   (c) Range("A1")
   (d) All of the above

7. The statement Selection.Offset (1,0).Range ("A1").Select will select the cell:
   (a) In the same column as the active cell but one row below
   (b) In the same row as the active cell but one column to the right
   (c) In the same column as the active cell but one row above
   (d) In the same row as the active cell but one column to the left

8. The statement Selection.Offset (1,1).Range ("A1").Select will select the cell:
   (a) One cell below and one cell to the left of the active cell
   (b) One cell below and one cell to the right of the active cell
   (c) One cell above and one cell to the right of the active cell
   (d) One cell above and one cell to the left of the active cell

9. The statement Selection.Offset (1,1).Range ("A1:A2").Select will select:
   (a) Cell A1
   (b) Cell A2
   (c) Both (a) and (b)
   (d) Neither (a) nor (b)

10. Which commands are used to duplicate an existing macro so that it can become the basis of a new macro?
    (a) Copy command
    (b) Paste command
    (c) Both (a) and (b)
    (d) Neither (a) nor (b)

11. Which of the following is used to protect a macro from the subsequent insertion or deletion of rows or columns in the associated worksheet?
    (a) Range names
    (b) Absolute references
    (c) Both (a) and (b)
    (d) Neither (a) nor (b)

12. Which of the following is true regarding a customized button that has been inserted as an object onto a worksheet and assigned to an Excel macro?
    (a) Point to the customized button, then click the left mouse button to execute the associated macro
    (b) Point to the customized button, then click the right mouse button to select the macro button and simultaneously display a shortcut menu
    (c) Point to the customized button, then press and hold the Ctrl key as you click the left mouse to select the button
    (d) All of the above

13. The InputBox function:
    (a) Displays a message (prompt) requesting input from the user
    (b) Stores the user's response in a designated cell
    (c) Both (a) and (b)
    (d) Neither (a) nor (b)

14. You want to create a macro to enter your name into a specific cell. The best way to do this is to:
    (a) Select the cell for your name, turn on the macro recorder with absolute references, then type your name
    (b) Turn on the macro recorder with absolute references, select the cell for your name, then type your name
    (c) Either (a) or (b)
    (d) Neither (a) nor (b)

15. You want to create a macro to enter your name in the active cell (which will vary whenever the macro is used) and the course you are taking in the cell immediately below. The best way to do this is to:
    (a) Select the cell for your name, turn on the macro recorder with absolute references, type your name, press the down arrow, and type the course
    (b) Turn on the macro recorder with absolute references, select the cell for your name, type your name, press the down arrow, and type the course
    (c) Select the cell for your name, turn on the macro recorder with relative references, type your name, press the down arrow, and type the course
    (d) Turn on the macro recorder with relative references, select the cell for your name, type your name, press the down arrow, and type the course

ANSWERS

1.	b	6.	c	11.	a
2.	c	7.	a	12.	d
3.	c	8.	b	13.	c
4.	b	9.	d	14.	b
5.	a	10.	c	15.	c

BUILDS ON

HANDS-ON
EXERCISE 4
PAGES 399–409

1. Data Management Macros: Figure 8.11 displays an alternate version of the Finished Employee List workbook that was used in the third and fourth hands-on exercises. The existing macros have been deleted and replaced by the five macros represented by the command buttons in the figure. Your assignment is to create the indicated macros and assign the macros to the command buttons. The purpose of each macro should be apparent from the name of the command button.

   a. You can "cut and paste" macros from the Finished Employee workbook as it existed at the end of the fourth hands-on exercise, or you can create the macros from scratch using the *Chapter 8 Practice 1* workbook (which contains the equivalent workbook from the beginning of hands-on exercise 3). Choose whichever technique you think is easier. You will need to use the Insert Name Create command to assign names to various cells in the worksheet for use in your macros.

   b. The All Employees macro should clear the criteria row to display all employees within the list, as well as statistics for all employees toward the bottom of the worksheet. The other four macros prompt the user for the specific criteria. Note that the user can include relational operators for service or salary, such as >60000 to display employees with salaries greater than $60,000. All of the macros should include the same MsgBox statement to display the indicated message in Figure 8.11.

   c. Run the AnySalary macro, then print the workbook as it appears in Figure 8.11. Print the worksheet with row and column headings and be sure that it fits on a single sheet of paper. Be sure to change the properties of the command buttons so that the buttons appear on the printed worksheet.

   d. Change to the Visual Basic Editor, pull down the File menu, click the Print command, then print the current project to print all of the modules (macros) within your workbook.

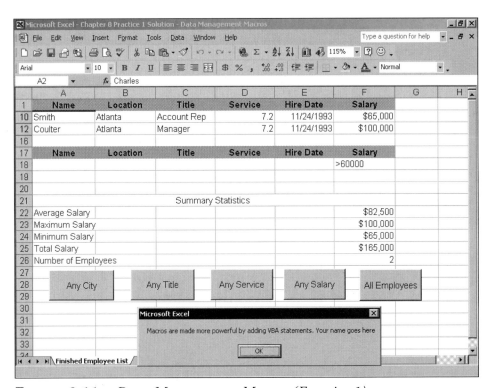

FIGURE 8.11 *Data Management Macros (Exercise 1)*

BUILDS ON

PRACTICE
EXERCISE 1
PAGE 422

2. **Employee Selection:** Figure 8.12 extends the previous problem to include one additional macro that prompts the user for city, title, service, and salary. The user enters all four parameters, then the macro displays the selected records within the list together with the summary statistics. Since you are specifying multiple criteria, however, it is quite possible that no employees will meet all the criteria, in which case the macro should display a message to that effect as shown in the figure. (This requires an If statement within the macro as explained in part d below.)

   a. Your assignment is to complete the previous problem, then add the additional macro to prompt for the multiple criteria. The macro will always ask the user for all four parameters, but you need not enter every parameter. If, for example, you do not specify a city, the macro will return matching employees regardless of the city. Leaving all four parameters blank is equivalent to creating a blank criteria row, which in turn will display all employees.

   b. You can include relational operators in the service and/or salary fields as shown in Figure 8.12. The figure is searching for Chicago Account reps, with less than eight years of service, earning more than $60,000.

   c. The DAVERAGE function displays a division by zero error message, if there are no employees that meet the specified criteria. You can suppress the error message, however, by using an If statement that tests whether the number of qualified employees (the entry in cell F26) is equal to zero.

   d. You need to include an If statement in your macro that tests whether the number of qualified employees is equal to zero, and if so, it should display the associated message box. It's easy to do. Use the Insert Name command within the Excel workbook to assign the name "QualifiedEmployees" to cell F26. Then insert a statement in the macro to go to this cell, which makes it the active cell. The If statement can then compare the value of the active cell to zero, and if it is zero, use the MsgBox statement to display the indicated message.

   e. Print the worksheet in Figure 8.12 for your instructor. (The dialog box will not appear on your printout.) Print the module containing the macro you just developed.

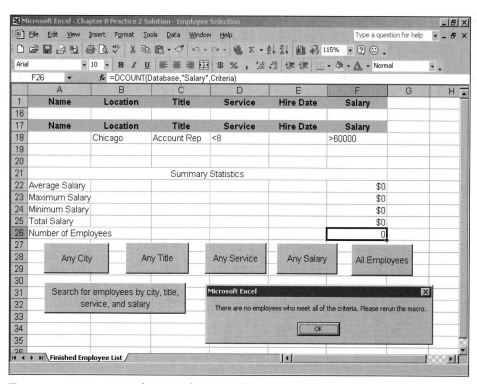

FIGURE 8.12 *Employee Selection (Exercise 2)*

BUILDS ON

HANDS-ON
EXERCISE 5
PAGES 412–418

3. Highlighting Employees: Figure 8.13 extends the Loops and Decision workbook from the fifth hands-on exercise to include command buttons and an additional macro. The new macro highlights the Atlanta and Chicago employees in red and blue, respectively.
   a. Open the Finished Loops and Decision Making workbook from the fifth hands-on exercise. Start the Visual Basic Editor, then copy the existing HighlightManager macro so that you can use it as the basis of the new macro to highlight the employees in two locations. (You will have to change the name of the copied macro.) You will have to change the offset in the If statement to (0, 1) to reference the location column within the list, and further to compare that value to "Atlanta," as opposed to "Manager."
   b. Switch to the Excel workbook, pull down the Tools menu, select the Macro command, click Macros, select the new macro, click Options, then assign a keyboard shortcut. (We used Ctrl+a). Press Ctrl+c to execute the ClearColor macro, then press Ctrl+a to test the newly created macro. The Atlanta employees should be highlighted in red.
   c. Return to the VBA editor and insert the ElseIf clause immediately above the existing EndIF clause. The ElseIf should compare the value of the active cell with the appropriate offset to "Chicago," and if that condition is true, assign the selection to the appropriate color. Test the new macro.
   d. Add command buttons to the worksheet as shown in Figure 8.13, then test the macros to be sure that they work properly. You should discover that the macros require one subtle adjustment; that is, if you run the Chicago and Atlanta macro, followed immediately by the Manager macro (or vice versa), employees from both macros will be highlighted. In other words, you need to run the Clear Color macro prior to running the other two. *You can make this happen automatically by including ClearColor (the name of the macro you want to run) as the first statement in the other two macros.*
   e. Print the completed worksheet for your instructor. Be sure to change the properties of the command buttons so that they print with the worksheet. Print the module containing the code for all three macros.

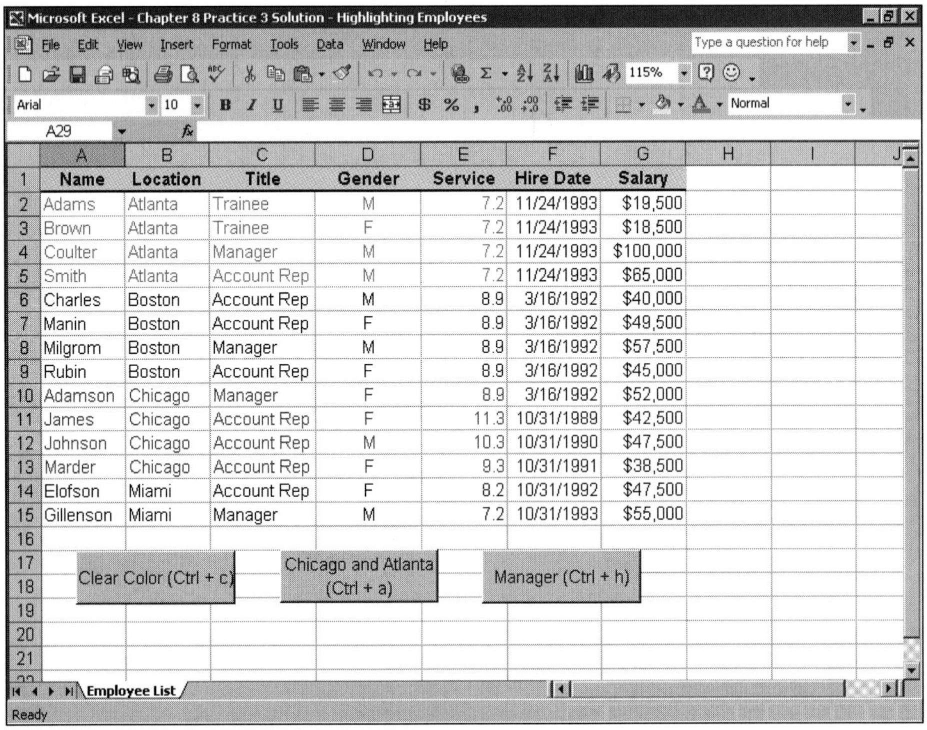

Name	Location	Title	Gender	Service	Hire Date	Salary
Adams	Atlanta	Trainee	M	7.2	11/24/1993	$19,500
Brown	Atlanta	Trainee	F	7.2	11/24/1993	$18,500
Coulter	Atlanta	Manager	M	7.2	11/24/1993	$100,000
Smith	Atlanta	Account Rep	M	7.2	11/24/1993	$65,000
Charles	Boston	Account Rep	M	8.9	3/16/1992	$40,000
Manin	Boston	Account Rep	F	8.9	3/16/1992	$49,500
Milgrom	Boston	Manager	M	8.9	3/16/1992	$57,500
Rubin	Boston	Account Rep	F	8.9	3/16/1992	$45,000
Adamson	Chicago	Manager	F	8.9	3/16/1992	$52,000
James	Chicago	Account Rep	F	11.3	10/31/1989	$42,500
Johnson	Chicago	Account Rep	M	10.3	10/31/1990	$47,500
Marder	Chicago	Account Rep	F	9.3	10/31/1991	$38,500
Elofson	Miami	Account Rep	F	8.2	10/31/1992	$47,500
Gillenson	Miami	Manager	M	7.2	10/31/1993	$55,000

FIGURE 8.13 *Highlighting Employees (Exercise 3)*

4. Student List: The worksheet in Figure 8.14 contains multiple macros that are created for the workbook, *Chapter 8 Practice 4,* in the Exploring Excel folder. Figure 8.14 displays the worksheet after execution of the macro, Any Major – Any Year, which prompts the user for these values (Engineering and Freshman in our figure), then displays the selected students and summary statistics. The function of the remaining macros should be apparent from the associated command buttons.

a. Open the *Chapter 8 Practice 4* workbook and create the indicated macros following the techniques that were discussed in the chapter. You will find it easiest to create the first macro, then copy that macro repeatedly to create the remaining macros. Every macro should end by displaying the message box in Figure 8.14.

b. Print the completed worksheet for at least two different sets of students—for example, engineering students who are freshmen1 and business students who are seniors. Be sure to change the properties of the command buttons so that they print with the worksheet.

c. Print the module containing all of the VBA procedures. Add a cover sheet to complete the assignment.

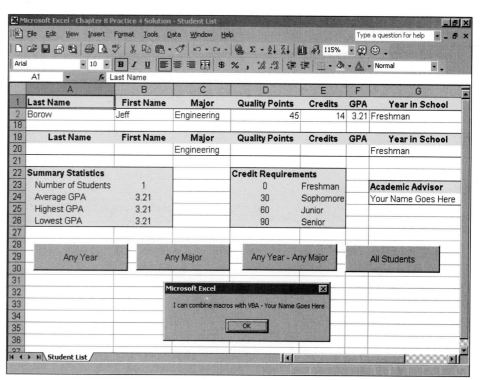

FIGURE 8.14   *Student List (Exercise 4)*

BUILDS ON

CHAPTER 7
PRACTICE
EXERCISE 1
PAGE 357

5. Election Macros: Election 2000 has come and gone, but it will be studied for years to come. Open the completed election workbook from the previous chapter (based on the workbook in *Chapter 7 Practice 1*) and add the macros shown in Figure 8.15. Each macro rearranges the states within the workbook according to the name on the corresponding button. The purpose of each macro should be evident from the name of its button.

a. Print the completed worksheet in at least two different sequences—for example, by the smallest and largest vote differential. Be sure to change the properties of the command buttons so that they print with the worksheet.

b. Print the VBA module containing all of the procedures. Add a cover sheet to complete the assignment.

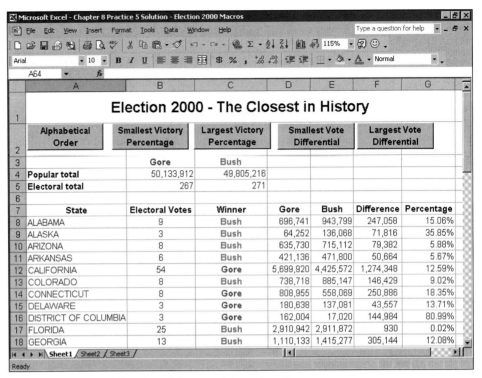

FIGURE 8.15 *Election Macros (Exercise 5)*

BUILDS ON

CHAPTER 5
PRACTICE
EXERCISE 5
PAGE 257

6. Stock Portfolio: Figure 8.16 displays a worksheet that uses macros in conjunction with Web queries to update a stock portfolio. You have seen this worksheet before, most recently in Chapter 5 when we studied worksheet references within a workbook. Now we complete the example through the introduction of macros.

a. Open the partially completed *Chapter 8 Practice 6* workbook and click the worksheet tab that contains your portfolio. The macros are already in the worksheet, and all you have to do is click the appropriate command buttons. The macro to enter your investments will prompt you for three investments for which you need to enter the company symbol, number of shares, and purchase price. This macro will also copy the stock symbols you have entered to the end of the stock symbol table in the Stock Prices worksheet.

b. Click the command button to Update Your Portfolio, which in turn will execute the Web query to retrieve the current price of your investments and automatically calculate the value of your portfolio. The worksheet is password protected to prevent you from accidentally changing any of the formulas that have been entered. (The password is "password", in lowercase letters so you can remove the protection if you like.)

c. After you have updated your portfolio, click the button to View Summary to take you to the summary worksheet. The macros for that worksheet have not been created, however, so it is up to you to create the macros and assign them to the indicated command buttons. The Update Prices macro refreshes the Web query in the Stock Prices worksheet. (It is similar to the Update Your Portfolio macro except that it returns to the Summary worksheet.) The Best Investors and Worst Investors list the portfolios in descending and ascending order according to the percentage gain or loss.

d. Print the Summary worksheet for your instructor as well as the worksheet that contains your portfolio. Print the module(s) containing all of the macros within the worksheet. Add a short note explaining the purpose of the various modules that were originally in the workbook.

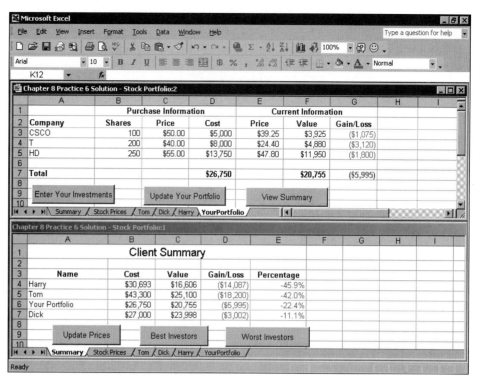

FIGURE 8.16   *Stock Portfolio (Exercise 6)*

7. Additional Practice: Figure 8.17 displays a worksheet containing hypothetical data for a series of consumer loans. The worksheet contains two macros, one to select loans by type and date, and a second macro to display all loans. The summary statistics beginning in row 31 reflect the loan records that appear in the filtered list. Your assignment is to open the workbook in *Chapter 8 Practice 7* to implement the indicated macros. You do not have to print the worksheet at this time if you continue with the next exercise.

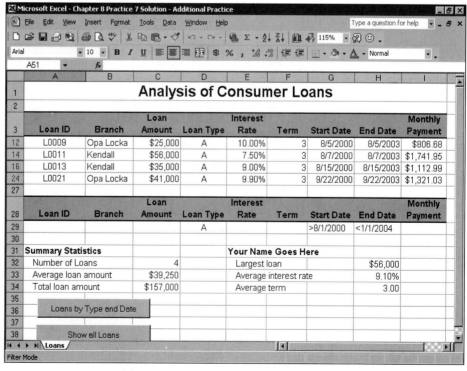

FIGURE 8.17   *Additional Practice (Exercise 7)*

8. Highlight Mortgages: Figure 8.18 expands the workbook from the previous exercise to contain two additional macros, one to highlight all mortgages and the second to clear the highlighted color. Note, too, that the macro to highlight the mortgages also changes the criteria so that the summary statistics will reflect the highlighted records.

a. Open the completed workbook from the previous exercise, then add the new macros, using the techniques from the fifth hands-on exercise in the chapter. Assign each macro to its own command button. Be sure that buttons are of uniform size and appearance.

b. The assignment is not difficult, but you will need to make the macros work in conjunction with one another. You will not be able to see the highlighted mortgage records, for example, unless the macro to show all loans is run prior to highlighting the mortgages. You can execute one macro from inside another macro simply by adding a statement with the name of the macro you want to execute. In other words, add ShowAllLoans at the beginning of the HighlightMortgages, where ShowAllLoans is the name of the macro to display all of the loan records. In similar fashion, the ShowAllLoans macro should execute the ClearColor macro.

c. Print the completed worksheet with gridlines and row and column headings. Be sure to change the properties of the command buttons so that they print with the worksheet.

d. Print the module(s) containing the four macros. Add a cover sheet, then submit all of your output to your instructor.

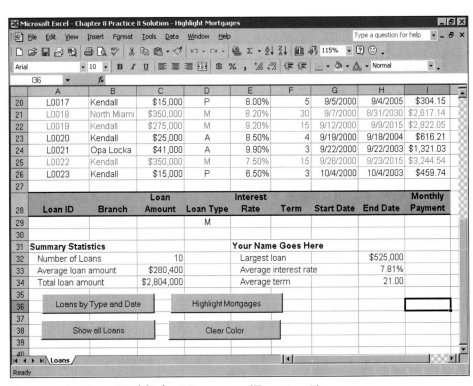

FIGURE 8.18 *Highlight Mortgages (Exercise 8)*

9. **A Look Ahead:** Figure 8.19 extends the previous exercise to include a procedure to highlight any loan, as opposed to highlighting only mortgages. The VBA code for that procedure is shown in the figure. Your job is to complete the previous hands-on exercise, delete the macro (and associated command button) for the HighlightMortgages macro, then substitute the new macro in its place. The VBA statements within the new procedure parallel those of its predecessor, but introduce some new material in Visual Basic. There are several comments within the macro to explain these statements, with additional explanation added below. Use the VBA primer that appears at the end of the Excel chapters in this text as a reference.

a. The most important concept is that of a variable to store information received from the user. The Dim statement near the beginning of the procedure assigns a name to the variable (strLoanType) and indicates that it will hold text (i.e., the variable is declared to be a character string). The subsequent Input Box statement prompts the user for the loan type, then stores that value in the strLoanType variable.

b. The If statement within the loop to highlight the selected records compares the loan type to the uppercase value of the strLoanType variable. This is important because if the user inadvertently enters a lowercase letter, the comparison would fail.

c. The MsgBox statement at the end of the procedure includes two additional parameters. The vbInformation variable indicates the type of icon that is supposed to appear within the message box. The underscore is there to show that the statement is continued to the next line, which in turn contains the text that will appear in the title bar of the message box.

d. Enter the procedure as it appears in Figure 8.19. Assign a command button to the macro within the worksheet, then test the macro.

e. Print the VBA module containing all of the procedures. Add a cover sheet to complete the assignment.

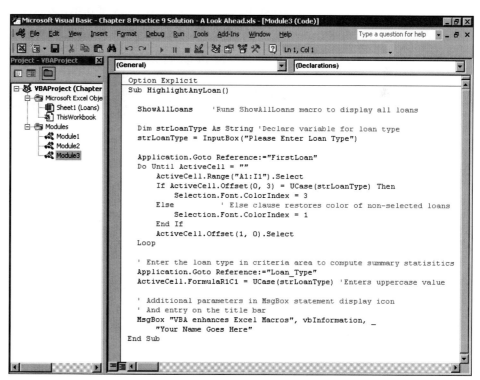

FIGURE 8.19 *A Look Ahead (Exercise 9)*

Microsoft Word

Do you use Microsoft Word on a regular basis? Are there certain tasks that you do repeatedly, whether in the same document or in a series of different documents? If so, you would do well to explore the macro capabilities within Microsoft Word. How are these capabilities similar to Excel's? How do they differ?

Starting Up

Your instructor is very impressed with the Excel workbook and associated macros that you have created. He would like you to take the automation process one step further and simplify the way in which Excel is started and the workbook is loaded. The problem is open ended, and there are many different approaches. You might, for example, create a shortcut on the desktop to open the workbook. You might also explore the use of the Startup folder in Microsoft Excel.

Antivirus Programs

What is an antivirus program and how do you get one? How do these programs supplement the macro virus protection that is built into Microsoft Excel? Use your favorite search engine to find two such programs, then summarize their capability and cost in a short note to your instructor. You can also visit the National Computer Security Association (www.ncsa.com) and the Computer Emergency Response Team (www.cert.org) to learn more about computer security.

Extending Excel Macros through VBA

You do not have to know VBA in order to create Excel macros, but knowledge of VBA will help you to create better macros. VBA is accessible from all major applications in Microsoft Office, so that anything you learn in one application is also applicable to other applications. The VBA syntax is identical. Locate the VBA primer that appears at the end of this text, study the basic statements it contains, and complete the associated hands-on exercises. Write a short note to your instructor that describes similarities and differences from one Office application to the next.

APPENDIX A

Toolbars

Microsoft Excel has 27 predefined toolbars that provide access to commonly used commands. The toolbars are displayed in Figure A.1 and are listed here for convenience. They are the Standard, Formatting, 3-D Settings, Borders, Chart, Circular Reference, Control Toolbox, Diagram, Drawing, Drawing Canvas, Exit Design Mode, External Data, Forms, Formula Auditing, Full Screen, Organization Chart, Picture, Pivot Table, Protection, Reviewing, Shadow Settings, Stop Recording, Text to Speech, Visual Basic, Watch Window, Web, and WordArt. The menu bar is also considered a toolbar.

The Standard and Formatting toolbars are displayed by default and appear on the same row immediately below the menu bar. The other predefined toolbars are displayed (hidden) at the discretion of the user, and in some cases are displayed automatically when their corresponding features are in use (e.g., the Chart toolbar and the Pivot Table toolbar).

The buttons on the toolbars are intended to indicate their functions. Clicking the Printer button (the fifth button from the left on the Standard toolbar), for example, executes the Print command. If you are unsure of any toolbar button, point to it, and a ScreenTip will appear that displays its name. You can display multiple toolbars, move them to new locations on the screen, customize their appearance, or suppress their display.

- To separate the Standard and Formatting toolbars and simultaneously display all of the buttons for each toolbar, pull down the Tools menu, click the Customize command, click the Options tab, then clear the check box that has the toolbars share one row. Alternatively, the toolbars appear on the same row, so that only a limited number of buttons are visible on each toolbar and hence you may need to click the double arrow (More Buttons) tool at the end of the toolbar to view additional buttons. Additional buttons will be added to either toolbar as you use the associated feature, and conversely, buttons will be removed from the toolbar if the feature is not used.
- To display or hide a toolbar, pull down the View menu and click the Toolbars command. Select (deselect) the toolbar(s) that you want to display (hide). The selected toolbar(s) will be displayed in the same position as when last

431

displayed. You may also point to any toolbar and click with the right mouse button to bring up a shortcut menu, after which you can select the toolbar to be displayed (hidden).

■ To change the size of the buttons or suppress the display of the ScreenTips, pull down the View menu, click Toolbars, and click Customize to display the Customize dialog box. If necessary, click the Options tab, then select (deselect) the appropriate check box. Alternatively, you can right click on any toolbar, click the Customize command from the context-sensitive menu, then select the appropriate check box from within the Options tab in the Customize dialog box.

■ Toolbars are either docked (along the edge of the window) or floating (in their own window). A toolbar moved to the edge of the window will dock along that edge. A toolbar moved anywhere else in the window will float in its own window. Docked toolbars are one tool wide (high), whereas floating toolbars can be resized by clicking and dragging a border or corner.

  • To move a docked toolbar, click anywhere in the gray background area and drag the toolbar to its new location. You can also click and drag the move handle (the vertical line) at the left of the toolbar.
  • To move a floating toolbar, drag its title bar to its new location.

■ To customize one or more toolbars, display the toolbar(s) on the screen. Then pull down the View menu, click Toolbars, and click Customize to display the Customize dialog box. Alternatively, you can click on any toolbar with the right mouse button and select Customize from the shortcut menu.

  • To move a button, drag the button to its new location on that toolbar or any other displayed toolbar.
  • To copy a button, press the Ctrl key as you drag the button to its new location on that toolbar or any other displayed toolbar.
  • To delete a button, drag the button off the toolbar and release the mouse.
  • To add a button, click the Commands tab in the Customize dialog box, select from the Categories list box the category that contains the button you want to add, then drag the button to the desired location on the toolbar. (To see a description of a tool's function prior to adding it to a toolbar, select the tool, then click the Description command button.)
  • To restore a predefined toolbar to its default appearance, click the Toolbars tab, select the desired toolbar, and click the Reset command button.

■ Buttons can also be moved, copied, or deleted without displaying the Customize dialog box.

  • To move a button, press the Alt key as you drag the button to the new location.
  • To copy a button, press the Alt and Ctrl keys as you drag the button.
  • To delete a button, press the Alt key as you drag the button off the toolbar.

■ To create your own toolbar, pull down the View menu, click Toolbars, click Customize, click the Toolbars tab, then click the New command button. Alternatively, you can click on any toolbar with the right mouse button, select Customize from the shortcut menu, click the Toolbars tab, and then click the New command button.

  • Enter a name for the toolbar in the dialog box that follows. The name can be any length and can contain spaces. Click OK.
  • The new toolbar will appear on the screen. Initially it will be big enough to hold only one button. Add, move, and delete buttons following the same procedures as outlined above. The toolbar will automatically size itself as new buttons are added and deleted.
  • To delete a custom toolbar, pull down the View menu, click Toolbars, click Customize, and click the Toolbars tab. *Verify that the custom toolbar to be deleted is the only one selected (highlighted).* Click the Delete command button. Click OK to confirm the deletion. (Note that a predefined toolbar cannot be deleted.)

Standard Toolbar

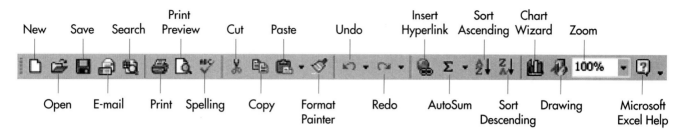

Formatting Toolbar

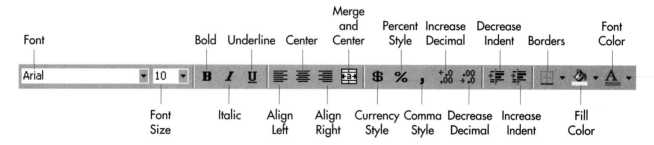

3-D Settings Toolbar

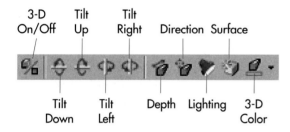

Borders Toolbar

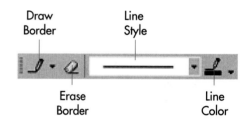

Chart Toolbar

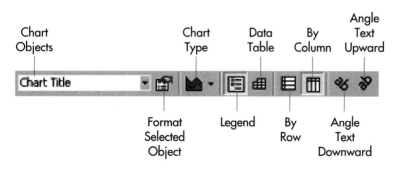

Circular Reference

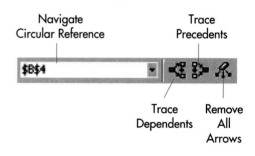

FIGURE A.1 *Toolbars*

Control Toolbox Toolbar

Design Mode   View Code   Text Box   Option Button   Combo Box   Spin Button   Label   More Controls

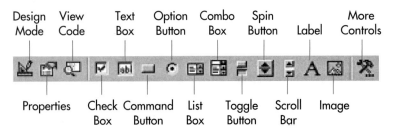

Properties   Check Box   Command Button   List Box   Toggle Button   Scroll Bar   Image

Full-Screen Toolbar

Toggle Full-Screen View

Diagram Toolbar

Insert Shape   Move Shape Forward   Layout   Change to

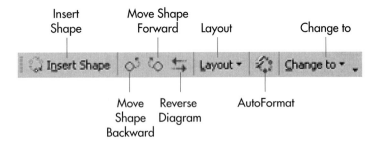

Move Shape Backward   Reverse Diagram   AutoFormat

External Data Toolbar

Edit Query   Query Parameters   Cancel Refresh   Refresh Status

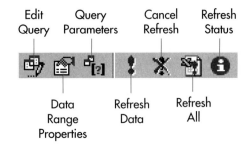

Data Range Properties   Refresh Data   Refresh All

Forms Toolbar

Label   Group Box   Check Box   List Box   Combination List-Edit   Scroll Bar   Control Properties   Toggle Grid

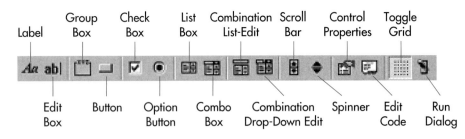

Edit Box   Button   Option Button   Combo Box   Combination Drop-Down Edit   Spinner   Edit Code   Run Dialog

Drawing Canvas Toolbar

Fit Drawing to Canvas   Scale Drawing

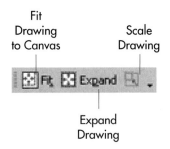

Expand Drawing

Formula Auditing Toolbar

Error Checking   Erase Precedent Arrows   Erase Dependent Arrows   Trace Error   Circle Invalid Data   Show Watch Window

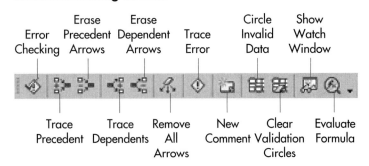

Trace Precedent   Trace Dependents   Remove All Arrows   New Comment   Clear Validation Circles   Evaluate Formula

Shadow Settings Toolbar

Shadow On/Off   Nudge Shadow Down   Nudge Shadow Right

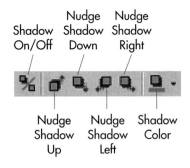

Nudge Shadow Up   Nudge Shadow Left   Shadow Color

Organization Chart Toolbar

Insert Shape   Select

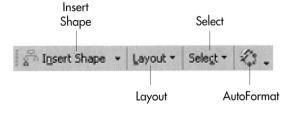

Layout   AutoFormat

Text to Speech Toolbar

Speak Cells   By Rows   Speak on Enter

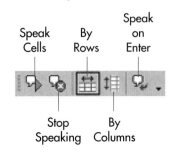

Stop Speaking   By Columns

FIGURE A.1   *Toolbars (continued)*

Drawing Toolbar

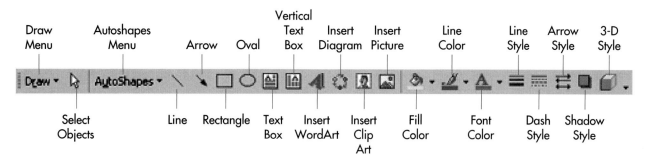

Draw Menu — Autoshapes Menu — Arrow — Oval — Vertical Text Box — Insert Diagram — Insert Picture — Line Color — Line Style — Arrow Style — 3-D Style

Select Objects — Line — Rectangle — Text Box — Insert WordArt — Insert Clip Art — Fill Color — Font Color — Dash Style — Shadow Style

Picture Toolbar

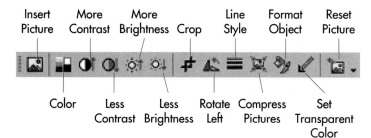

Insert Picture — More Contrast — More Brightness — Crop — Line Style — Format Object — Reset Picture

Color — Less Contrast — Less Brightness — Rotate Left — Compress Pictures — Set Transparent Color

Exit Design Mode Toolbar

Design Mode

Pivot Table Toolbar

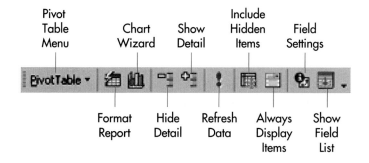

Pivot Table Menu — Chart Wizard — Show Detail — Include Hidden Items — Field Settings

Format Report — Hide Detail — Refresh Data — Always Display Items — Show Field List

Protection Toolbar

Lock Cell — Protect Sheet — Protect Sharing

Allow Users to Edit — Protect Workbook

Reviewing Toolbar

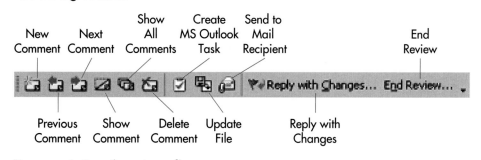

New Comment — Next Comment — Show All Comments — Create MS Outlook Task — Send to Mail Recipient — End Review

Previous Comment — Show Comment — Delete Comment — Update File — Reply with Changes

Stop Recording Toolbar

Stop Macro

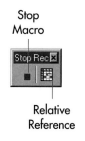

Relative Reference

FIGURE A.1   *(continued)*

Visual Basic Toolbar

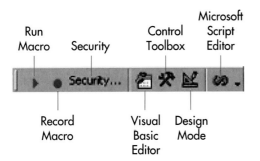

Watch Window Toolbar

Web Toolbar

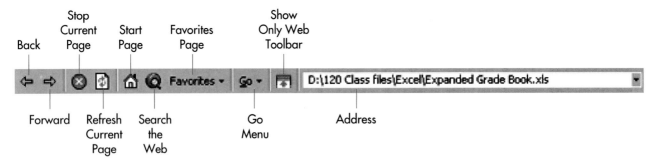

WordArt Toolbar

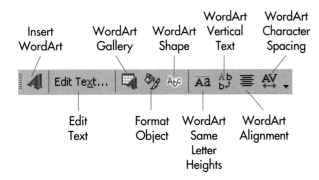

FIGURE A.1   *(continued)*

Solver: A Tool for Optimization

OVERVIEW

The use of a spreadsheet in decision making has been emphasized throughout the text. We showed you how to design a spreadsheet based on a set of initial conditions and assumptions, then see at a glance the effect of changing one or more of those values. We introduced the Scenario Manager to store sets of assumptions so that they could be easily recalled and reevaluated. We discussed the Goal Seek command, which enables you to set the value of a target cell, then determine the input needed to arrive at that target value. However, the Goal Seek command, as useful as it is, is limited to a *single* input variable. This appendix discusses *Solver*, a powerful add-in that is designed for problems involving *multiple* variables.

Solver is an optimization and resource allocation tool that helps you achieve a desired goal. You specify a goal, such as maximizing profit or minimizing cost. You indicate the constraints (conditions) that must be satisfied for the solution to be valid, and you specify the cells whose values can change to reach that goal. Solver will then determine the values for the adjustable cells (i.e., it will tell you how to allocate your resources) to reach the desired goal.

This appendix provides an introduction to Solver through two different examples. The first example shows how to maximize profit. The second example illustrates how to minimize cost. Both examples are accompanied by a hands-on exercise.

EXAMPLE 1—MAXIMIZE PROFIT

Assume that you are the production manager for a company that manufactures computers. Your company divides its product line into two basic categories—desktop computers and laptops. Each product is sold under two labels, a discount line and a premium line. As production manager you are to determine how many computers of each type, and of each product line, to make each week.

Your decision is subject to various constraints that must be satisfied during the production process. Each computer requires a specified number of hours for assembly. Discount and premium-brand desktops require two and three hours, respectively. Discount and premium-brand laptops use three and five hours, respectively. The factory is working at full capacity, and you have only 4,500 hours of labor to allocate among the various products.

Your production decision is also constrained by demand. The marketing department has determined that you cannot sell more than 800 desktop units, nor more than 900 laptops, per week. The total demand for the discount and premium lines is 700 and 1,000 computers, respectively, per week.

Your goal (objective) is to maximize the total profit, which is based on a different profit margin for each type of computer. A desktop and a laptop computer from the discount line have unit profits of $600 and $800, respectively. The premium desktop and laptop computers have unit profits of $1,000 and $1,300, respectively. How many computers of each type do you manufacture each week to maximize the total profit?

This is a complex problem, but one that can be easily solved provided you can design a spreadsheet that is equivalent to Figure B.1. The top half of the spreadsheet contains the information about the individual products. There are three numbers associated with each product—the quantity that will be produced, the number of hours required, and the unit profit. The bottom half of the spreadsheet contains the information about the available resources such as the total number of labor hours that are available. The spreadsheet also contains various formulas that relate the resources to the quantities that are produced. Cell E8, for example, will contain a formula that computes the total number of hours used that is based on the quantity of each computer and the associated hourly requirements.

The problem is to determine the values of cells B2 through B5, which represent the quantity of each computer to produce. You might be able to solve the problem manually through trial and error, by substituting different values and seeing the impact on profit. That is exactly what Solver will do for you, only it will do it much more quickly. (Solver uses various optimization techniques that are beyond the scope of this discussion.)

Once Solver arrives at a solution, assuming that it can find one, it creates a report such as the one shown in Figure B.2. The solution shows the value of the target cell (the profit in this example), based on the values of the adjustable cells (the quantity of each type of computer). The solution that will maximize profit is to manufacture 700 discount laptops and 800 premium desktops for a profit of $1,270,000.

The report in Figure B.2 also examines each constraint and determines whether it is binding or not binding. A ***binding constraint*** is one in which the resource is fully utilized (i.e., the slack is zero). The number of available hours, for example, is a binding constraint because every available hour is used, and hence the value of the target cell (profit) is limited by the amount of this resource (the number of hours). Or stated another way, any increase in the number of available hours (above 4,500) will also increase the profit.

A ***nonbinding constraint*** is just the opposite. It has a nonzero slack (i.e., the resource is not fully utilized), and hence it does not limit the value of the target cell. The laptop demand, for example, is not binding because a total of only 700 laptops were produced, yet the allowable demand was 900 (the value in cell E13). In other words, there is a slack value of 200 for this constraint, and increasing the allowable demand will have no effect on the profit. (The demand could actually be decreased by up to 200 units with no effect on profit.)

FIGURE B.1 *The Initial Worksheet*

Annotations (left margin):
- Need to determine values for cells B2:B5 (quantity to produce)
- Will contain a formula to compute total hours

Worksheet contents:

	A	B	C	D	E
1		Quantity	Hours	Unit Profit	
2	**Discount desktop**		2	$600	
3	**Discount laptop**		3	$800	
4	**Premium desktop**		3	$1,000	
5	**Premium laptop**		5	$1,300	
6					
7	Constraints				
8	Total number of hours used				
9	Labor hours available				4,500
10	Number of desktops produced				
11	Total demand for desktop computers				800
12	Number of laptops produced				
13	Total demand for laptop computers				900
14	Number of discount computers produced				
15	Total demand for discount computers				700
16	Number of premium computers produced				
17	Total demand for premium computers				1,000
18	Hourly cost of labor				$20
19	**Profit**				

FIGURE B.2 *The Solution*

Annotations (left margin):
- Value of target cell (E19)
- Quantities to be produced (B2:B5)
- Indicates whether or not constraint is binding

Target Cell (Max)

Cell	Name	Original Value	Final Value
$E$19	Profit	$0	$1,270,000

Adjustable Cells

Cell	Name	Original Value	Final Value
$B$2	Discount desktop Quantity	0	0
$B$3	Discount laptop Quantity	0	700
$B$4	Premium desktop Quantity	0	800
$B$5	Premium laptop Quantity	0	0

Constraints

Cell	Name	Cell Value	Formula	Status	Slack
$E$8	Total number of hours used	4500	$E$8<=$E$9	Binding	0
$E$10	Number of desktops produced	800	$E$10<=$E$11	Binding	0
$E$12	Number of laptops produced	700	$E$12<=$E$13	Not Binding	200
$E$14	Number of discount computers produce	700	$E$14<=$E$15	Binding	0
$E$16	Number of premium computers produce	800	$E$16<=$E$17	Not Binding	200
$B$2	Discount desktop Quantity	0	$B$2>=0	Binding	0
$B$3	Discount laptop Quantity	700	$B$3>=0	Not Binding	700
$B$4	Premium desktop Quantity	800	$B$4>=0	Not Binding	800
$B$5	Premium laptop Quantity	0	$B$5>=0	Binding	0

The information required by Solver is entered through the ***Solver Parameters dialog box*** as shown in Figure B.3. The dialog box is divided into three sections: the target cell, the adjustable cells, and the constraints. The dialog box in Figure B.3 corresponds to the spreadsheet shown earlier in Figure B.1.

The ***target cell*** identifies the goal (or objective function)—that is, the cell whose value you want to maximize, minimize, or set to a specific value. Our problem seeks to maximize profit, the formula for which is found in cell E19 (the target cell) of the underlying spreadsheet.

The ***adjustable cells*** (or decision variables) are the cells whose values are adjusted until the constraints are satisfied and the target cell reaches its optimum value. The changing cells in this example contain the quantity of each computer to be produced and are found in cells B2 through B5.

The ***constraints*** specify the restrictions. Each constraint consists of a cell or cell range on the left, a relational operator, and a numeric value or cell reference on the right. (The constraints can be entered in any order, but they always appear in alphabetical order.) The first constraint references a cell range, cells B2 through B5, and indicates that each of these cells must be greater than or equal to zero. The remaining constraints reference a single cell rather than a cell range.

The functions of the various command buttons are apparent from their names. The Add, Change, and Delete buttons are used to add, change, or delete a constraint. The Options button enables you to set various parameters that determine how Solver attempts to find a solution. The Reset All button clears all settings and resets all options to their defaults. The Solve button begins the search for a solution.

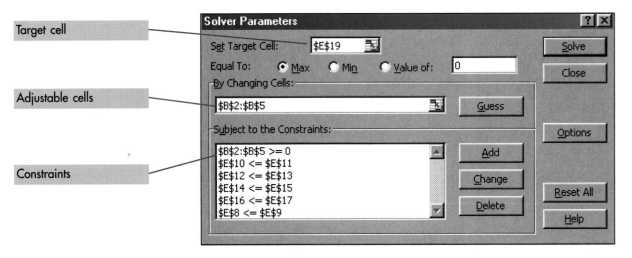

FIGURE B.3   *Solver Parameters Dialog Box*

THE GREATER-THAN-ZERO CONSTRAINT

One constraint that is often overlooked is the requirement that the value of each adjustable cell be greater than or equal to zero. Physically, it makes no sense to produce a negative number of computers in any category. Mathematically, however, a negative value in an adjustable cell may produce a higher value for the target cell. Hence the ***nonnegativity*** (greater than or equal to zero) ***constraint*** should always be included for the adjustable cells.

MAXIMIZE PROFIT

Objective To use Solver to maximize profit; to create a report containing binding and nonbinding constraints. Use Figure B.4 as a guide in the exercise.

Step 1: **Enter the Cell Formulas**

➤ Start Excel. Open the **Optimization workbook** in the **Exploring Excel folder**. Save the workbook as **Finished Optimization** so that you can return to the original workbook if necessary.

➤ If necessary, click the tab for the **Production Mix** worksheet, then click **cell E8** as shown in Figure B.4a.

➤ Enter the formula shown in Figure B.4a to compute the total number of hours used in production.

➤ Enter the remaining cell formulas as shown below:
- Cell E10 (Number of desktops produced) **=B2+B4**
- Cell E12 (Number of laptops produced) **=B3+B5**
- Cell E14 (Number of discount computers produced) **=B2+B3**
- Cell E16 (Number of premium computers produced) **=B4+B5**
- Cell E19 (Profit) **=B2*D2+B3*D3+B4*D4+B5*D5−E18*E8**

➤ Save the workbook.

(a) Enter the Cell Formulas (step 1)

FIGURE B.4 *Hands-on Exercise 1*

Step 2: **Set the Target and Adjustable Cells**

➤ Check that the formula in cell E19 is entered correctly as shown in Figure B.4b. Pull down the **Tools menu**. Click **Solver** to display the Solver Parameters dialog box shown in Figure B.4b.

➤ If necessary, click in the text box for Set Target cell. Click in **cell E19** to set the target cell. The Max option button is selected by default.

➤ Click in the **By Changing Cells** text box. Click and drag **cells B2** through **B5** in the worksheet to select these cells.

➤ Click the **Add command button** to add the first constraint as described in step 3.

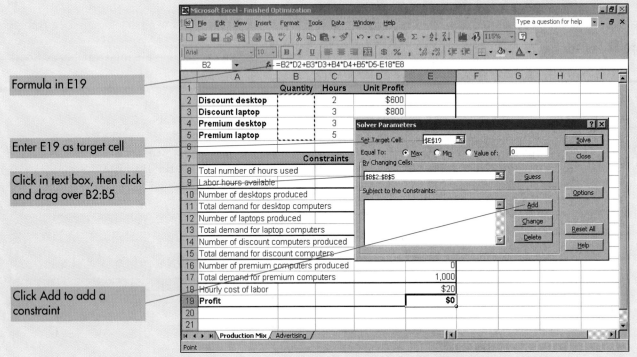

Formula in E19

Enter E19 as target cell

Click in text box, then click and drag over B2:B5

Click Add to add a constraint

(b) Set the Target and Adjustable Cells (step 2)

FIGURE B.4 *Hands-on Exercise 1 (continued)*

MISSING SOLVER

Solver is an optional component of Microsoft Excel, and hence it may not be installed on your system. If you are working on a computer at school, your instructor should be able to notify the network administrator to correct the problem. If you are working on your own machine, pull down the Tools menu, click the Add-Ins command, check the box for Solver, then click OK to close the Add-Ins dialog box. Click Yes when asked to install Solver. You will need the Microsoft Office XP CD.

Step 3: **Enter the Constraints**

➤ You should see the Add Constraint dialog box in Figure B.4c with the insertion point (a flashing vertical line) in the Cell Reference text box.
  • Click in **cell E8** (the cell containing the formula to compute the total number of hours used). The <= constraint is selected by default.
  • Click in the **Constraint** text box, which will contain the value of the constraint, then click **cell E9** in the worksheet to enter the cell reference.
  • Click **Add** to complete this constraint and add another.
➤ You will see a new (empty) Add Constraint dialog box, which enables you to enter additional constraints. Use pointing to enter each of the constraints shown below. (Solver automatically enters each reference as an absolute reference.)
  • Enter the constraint **E10<=E11**. Click **Add**.
  • Enter the constraint **E12<=E13**. Click **Add**.
  • Enter the constraint **E14<=E15**. Click **Add**.
  • Enter the constraint **E16<=E17**. Click **Add**.
➤ Add the last constraint. Click and drag to select **cells B2** through **B5**. Click the drop-down arrow for the relational operators and click the **>=** operator. Type **0** in the text box to indicate that the production quantities for all computers must be greater than or equal to zero. Click **OK**.

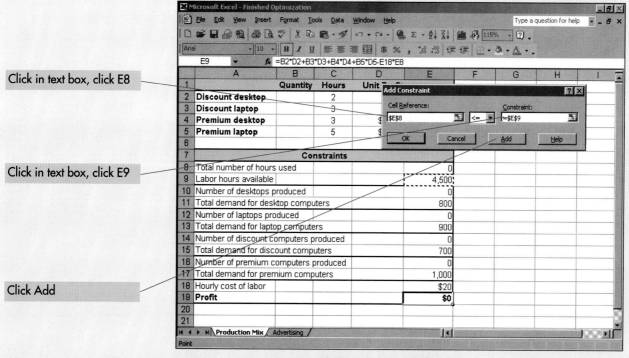

Click in text box, click E8

Click in text box, click E9

Click Add

(c) Enter the Constraints (step 3)

FIGURE B.4   *Hands-on Exercise 1 (continued)*

ADD VERSUS OK

Click the Add button to complete the current constraint and display an empty dialog box to enter another constraint. Click OK only when you have completed the last constraint and want to return to the Solver Parameters dialog box to solve the problem.

Step 4: Solve the Problem

➤ Check that the contents of the Solver Parameters dialog box match those of Figure B.4d. (The constraints appear in alphabetical order rather than the order in which they were entered.)
  - To change the Target cell, click the **Set Target Cell** text box, then click the appropriate target cell in the worksheet.
  - To change (edit) a constraint, select the constraint, then click the **Change button**.
  - To delete a constraint, select the constraint and click the **Delete button**.
➤ Click the **Solve button** to solve the problem.
➤ You should see the Solver Results dialog box, indicating that Solver has found a solution. The maximum profit is $1,270,000. The option button to Keep Solver Solution is selected by default.
➤ Click **Answer** in the Reports list box, then click **OK** to generate the report. You will see the report being generated, after which the Solver Results dialog box closes automatically.
➤ Save the workbook.

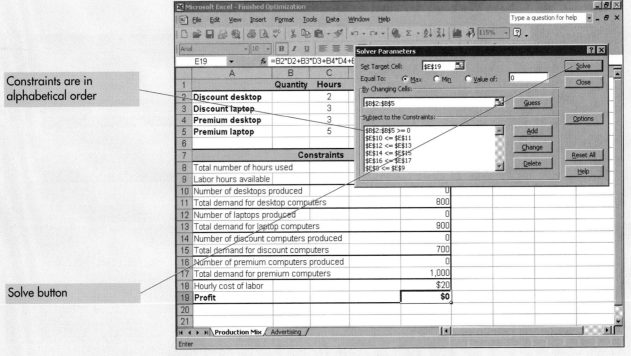

Constraints are in alphabetical order

Solve button

(d) Solve the Problem (step 4)

FIGURE B.4 *Hands-on Exercise 1 (continued)*

Step 5: **View the Report**

➤ Click the **Answer Report 1 worksheet tab** to view the report as shown in Figure B.4e. Click in **cell A4**, the cell immediately under the entry showing the date and time the report was created. (The gridlines and row and column headings are suppressed by default for this worksheet.)

➤ Enter your name in boldface as shown in the figure, then press **enter** to complete the entry. Print the answer sheet and submit it to your instructor as proof you did the exercise.

➤ Save the workbook. Exit Excel if you do not wish to continue with the next exercise at this time.

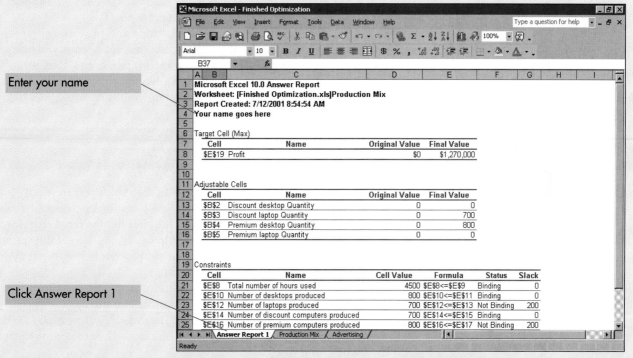

(e) View the Report (step 5)

FIGURE B.4 *Hands-on Exercise 1 (continued)*

VIEW OPTIONS

Any worksheet used to create a spreadsheet model will display gridlines and row and column headers by default. Worksheets containing reports, however, especially reports generated by Excel, often suppress these elements to make the reports easier and more appealing to read. To suppress (display) these elements, pull down the Tools menu, click Options, click the View tab, then clear (check) the appropriate check boxes under Window options.

EXAMPLE 2—MINIMIZE COST

The example just concluded introduced you to the basics of Solver. We continue now with a second hands-on exercise, to provide additional practice, and to discuss various subtleties that can occur. This time we present a minimization problem in which we seek to minimize cost subject to a series of constraints. The problem will focus on the advertising campaign that will be conducted to sell the computers you have produced.

The director of marketing has allocated a total of $125,000 in his weekly advertising budget. He wants to establish a presence in both magazines and radio, and requires a minimum of four magazine ads and ten radio ads each week. Each magazine ad costs $10,000 and is seen by one million readers. Each radio commercial costs $5,000 and is heard by 250,000 listeners. How many ads of each type should be placed to reach at least 10 million customers at minimum cost?

All of the necessary information is contained within the previous paragraph. You must, however, display that information in a worksheet before you can ask Solver to find a solution. Accordingly, reread the previous paragraph, then try to set up a worksheet from which you can call Solver. (Our worksheet appears in step 1 of the following hands-on exercise. Try, however, to set up your own worksheet before you look at ours.)

FINER POINTS OF SOLVER

Figure B.5 displays the **Solver Options dialog box** that enables you to specify how Solver will approach the solution. The Max Time and Iterations entries determine how long Solver will work on finding the solution. If either limit is reached before a solution is found, Solver will ask whether you want to continue. The default settings of 100 seconds and 100 iterations are sufficient for simpler problems, but may fall short for complex problems with multiple constraints.

The Precision setting determines how close the computed values in the constraint cells come to the specified value of the resource. The smaller the precision, the longer Solver will take in arriving at a solution. The default setting of .0000001 is adequate for most problems and should not be decreased. The remaining options are beyond the scope of our discussion.

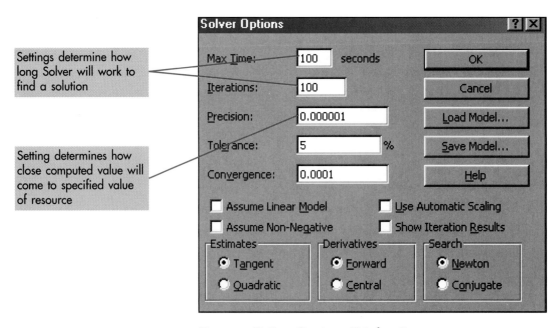

Settings determine how long Solver will work to find a solution

Setting determines how close computed value will come to specified value of resource

FIGURE B.5 *Options Dialog Box*

MINIMIZE COST

Objective   To use Solver to minimize cost; to impose an integer constraint and examine its effect on the optimal solution; to relax a constraint in order to find a feasible solution. Use Figure B.6 as a guide in the exercise.

Step 1:   **Enter the Cell Formulas**

➤ Open the **Finished Optimization workbook** from the previous exercise.
➤ Click the tab for the **Advertising** worksheet, then click in **cell E6**. Enter the formula **=B2*C2+B3*C3** as shown in Figure B.6a.
➤ Click in **cell E10**. Enter the formula **=B2*D2+B3*D3** to compute the size of the audience. Save the workbook.

Click in E6 and enter formula

Click Advertising tab

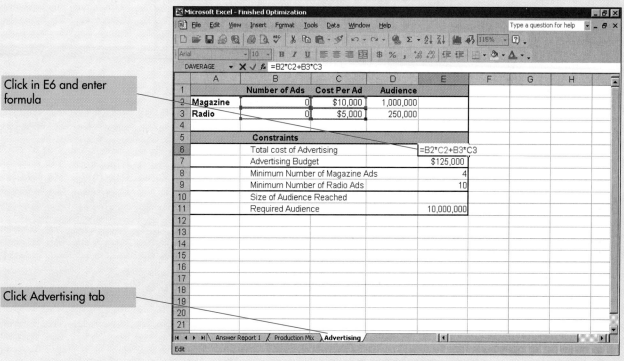

(a) Enter the Cell Formulas (step 1)

FIGURE B.6   *Hands-on Exercise 2*

USE THE TASK PANE

The easiest way to reopen a recently used workbook is to use the task pane. Pull down the View menu and toggle the Task Pane command on so that the task pane is displayed in the right side of the application window. Click the name of the workbook in the Open a workbook area to reopen the workbook. You can also open a recently used workbook from the list that appears at the bottom of the File menu. Another way is to click the Windows Start button, click the Documents command, then click the name of the workbook when it appears in the Documents submenu.

Step 2: **Set the Target and Adjustable Cells**

➤ Pull down the **Tools menu**. Click **Solver** to display the Solver Parameters dialog box shown in Figure B.6b.

➤ Set the target cell to **cell E6**. Click the **Min (Minimize) option button**. Click in the **By Changing Cells** text box.

➤ Click and drag **cells B2** and **B3** in the worksheet to select these cells as shown in Figure B.6b.

➤ Click the **Add command button** to add the first constraint as described in step 3.

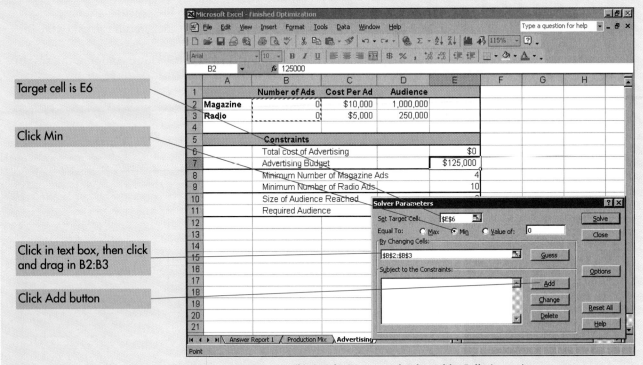

Target cell is E6

Click Min

Click in text box, then click and drag in B2:B3

Click Add button

(b) Set the Target and Adjustable Cells (step 2)

FIGURE B.6 *Hands-on Exercise 2 (continued)*

REVIEW THE TERMINOLOGY

Solver is an optimization technique that allows you to maximize or minimize the value of an objective function, such as profit or cost, respectively. The formula to compute the objective function is stored in the target cell within the worksheet. Other cells in the worksheet contain the variables or adjustable cells. Another set of cells contains the value of the available resources or constraints. This type of optimization problem is referred to as linear programming.

Step 3: **Enter the Constraints**

➤ You should see the Add Constraint dialog box in Figure B.6c with the insertion point (a flashing vertical line) in the Cell Reference text box.
  • Click in **cell E6** (the cell containing the total cost of advertising).
  • The <= constraint is selected by default.
  • Click in the text box to contain the value of the constraint, then click **cell E7** to enter the cell reference in the Add Constraint dialog box. Click **Add**.
➤ You will see a new (empty) Add Constraint dialog box, which enables you to enter additional constraints. Use pointing to enter each of the constraints shown below. (Solver converts each reference to an absolute reference.)
  • Enter the constraint **E10>=E11**. Click **Add**.
  • Enter the constraint **B2>=E8**. Click **Add**.
  • Enter the constraint **B3>=E9**. Click **OK** since this is the last constraint.

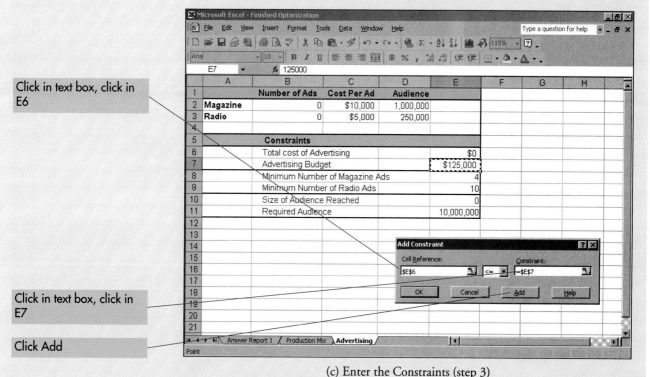

(c) Enter the Constraints (step 3)

FIGURE B.6 *Hands-on Exercise 2 (continued)*

SHOW ITERATION RESULTS

Solver uses an iterative (repetitive) approach in which each iteration (trial solution) is one step closer to the optimal solution. It may be interesting, therefore, to examine the intermediate solutions, especially if you have a knowledge of optimization techniques, such as linear programming. Click the Options command button in the Solver Parameters dialog box, check the Show Iterations Results box, click OK to close the Solver Options dialog box, then click the Solve command button in the usual fashion. A Show Trial Solutions dialog box will appear as each intermediate solution is displayed in the worksheet. Click Continue to move from one iteration to the next until the optimal solution is reached.

Step 4:   **Solve the Problem**

➤ Check that the contents of the Solver Parameters dialog box match those in Figure B.6d. (The constraints appear in alphabetical order rather than the order in which they were entered.)

➤ Click the **Solve button** to solve the problem. The Solver Results dialog box appears and indicates that Solver has arrived at a solution.

➤ The option button to Keep Solver Solution is selected by default. Click **OK** to close the Solver Results dialog box and display the solution.

➤ Save the workbook.

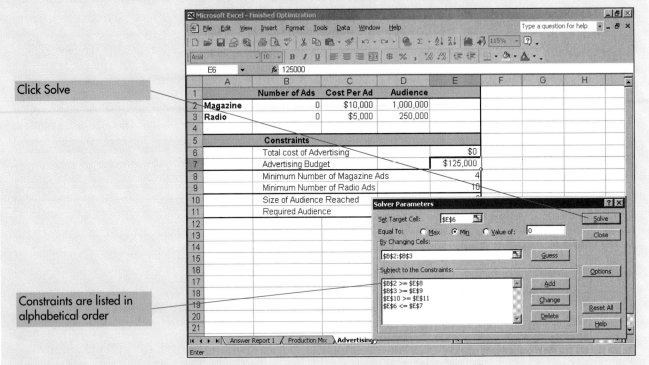

(d) Solve the Problem (step 4)

FIGURE B.6   *Hands-on Exercise 2 (continued)*

USE POINTING TO ENTER CELL FORMULAS

A cell reference can be typed directly into a formula, or it can be entered more easily through pointing. To use pointing, select (click) the cell to contain the formula, type an equal sign to begin entering the formula, then click (or move to) the cell containing the value to be used. Type any arithmetic operator to place the cell reference into the formula, then continue pointing to additional cells. Press the enter key (instead of typing an arithmetic operator) to complete the formula.

Step 5: **Impose an Integer Constraint**

➤ The number of magazine ads in the solution is 7.5 as shown in Figure B.6e. This is a noninteger number, which is reasonable in the context of Solver but not in the "real world" as one cannot place half an ad.

➤ Pull down the **Tools menu**. Click **Solver** to once again display the Solver Parameters dialog box. Click the **Add button** to display the Add Constraint dialog box in Figure B.6e.

➤ The insertion point is already positioned in the Cell Reference text box. Click and drag to select **cells B2** through **B3**. Click the **drop-down arrow** in the Constraint list box and click **int** (for integer).

➤ Click **OK** to accept the constraint and close the Add Constraint dialog box.

➤ The Solver Parameters dialog box appears on your monitor with the integer constraint added. Click **Solve** to solve the problem.

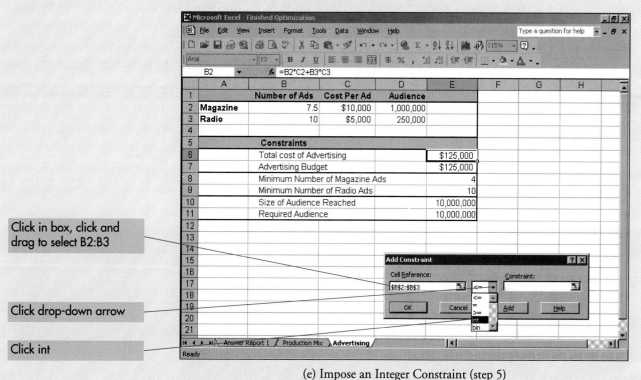

(e) Impose an Integer Constraint (step 5)

FIGURE B.6 *Hands-on Exercise 2 (continued)*

DO YOU REALLY NEED AN INTEGER SOLUTION?

It seems like such a small change, but specifying an integer constraint can significantly increase the amount of time required for Solver to reach a solution. The examples in this chapter are relatively simple and did not take an inordinate amount of time to solve. Imposing an integer constraint on a more complex problem, however, especially on a slower microprocessor, may challenge your patience as Solver struggles to reach a solution.

Step 6: **The Infeasible Solution**

> ➤ You should see the dialog box in Figure B.6f, indicating that Solver could *not* find a solution that satisfied the existing constraints. This is because the imposition of the integer constraint would raise the number of magazine ads from 7.5 to 8, which would increase the total cost of advertising to $130,000, exceeding the budget of $125,000.
> ➤ The desired audience can still be reached but only by relaxing one of the binding constraints. You can, for example, retain the requisite number of magazine and radio ads by increasing the budget. Alternatively, the budget can be held at $125,000, while still reaching the audience by decreasing the required number of radio ads.
> ➤ Click **Cancel** to exit the dialog box and return to the worksheet.

7.5 is not an integer, and thus no solution can be reached

No solution is found

Click Cancel

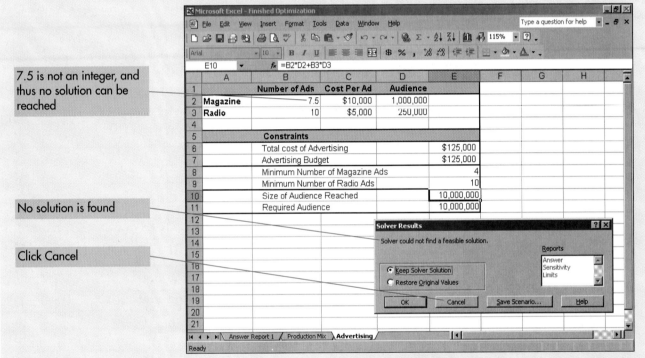

(f) The Infeasible Solution (step 6)

FIGURE B.4   *Hands-on Exercise 2 (continued)*

UNABLE TO FIND A SOLUTION

Solver is a powerful tool, but it cannot do the impossible. Some problems simply do not have a solution because the constraints may conflict with one another, and/or because the constraints exceed the available resources. Should this occur, and it will, check your constraints to make sure they were entered correctly. If Solver is still unable to reach a solution, it will be necessary to relax one or more of the constraints.

Step 7: **Relax a Constraint**

➤ Click in **cell E9** (the cell containing the minimum number of radio ads). Enter **9** and press **enter**.

➤ Pull down the **Tools menu**. Click **Solver** to display the Solver Parameters dialog box. Click **Solve**. This time Solver finds a solution as shown in Figure B.6g.

➤ Click **Answer** in the Reports list box, then click **OK** to generate the report. You will see the report being generated, after which the Solver Results dialog box closes automatically.

➤ Click the **Answer Report 2 worksheet tab** to view the report. Add your name to the report, boldface your name, print the answer report, and submit it to your instructor.

➤ Save the workbook.

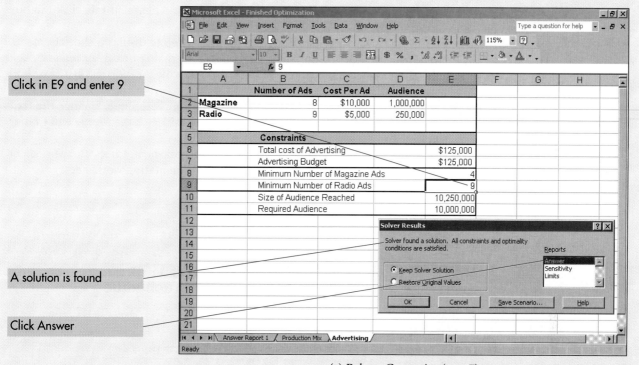

Click in E9 and enter 9

A solution is found

Click Answer

(g) Relax a Constraint (step 7)

FIGURE B.6   *Hands-on Exercise 2 (continued)*

SENSITIVITY, BINDING, AND NONBINDING CONSTRAINTS

A sensitivity report shows the effect of increasing resources associated with the binding and nonbinding constraints within the optimization problem. A binding constraint has a limiting effect on the objective value; that is, relaxing a binding constraint by increasing the associated resource will improve the value of the objective function. Conversely, a nonbinding constraint does not have a limiting effect, and increasing its resource has no effect on the value of the objective function.

Step 8: **Add the Documentation Worksheet**

➤ This step creates a documentation worksheet similar to the one in Chapter 6. Pull down the **Insert menu** and click the **Worksheet command**.

➤ Double click the **tab** of the newly inserted worksheet. Enter **Documentation** as the new name and press **enter**. If necessary, click and drag the worksheet tab to move it to the beginning of the workbook.

➤ Enter the descriptive entries in **cells A3**, **A4**, and **A6** as shown in Figure B.6h. Use boldface as shown. Increase the width of column A.

➤ Enter your name in **cell B3**. Enter =**Today( )** in **cell B4**. Press **enter**. Click the **Left Align button** to align the date as shown in the figure.

➤ Increase the width of column B, then click in **cell B6** and enter the indicated text. Do not press the enter key until you have completed the entry.

➤ Click in **cell B6**, then pull down the **Format menu** and click the **Cells command** to display the Format Cells dialog box. Click the **Alignment tab**, click the box to **Wrap Text**, then click **OK**.

➤ Point to cell **A6**, then click the **right mouse button** to display a shortcut menu. Click **Format Cells** to display the Format Cells dialog box. If necessary, click the **Alignment tab**, click the **drop-down arrow** in the Vertical list box, and select **Top**. Click **OK**.

➤ Click in **cell A1**. Enter **Solver - An Optimization Technique**. Change the font size to **18**. Click and drag to select **cells A1** and **B1**. Click the **Merge and Center button** to center the title across cells A1 and B1.

➤ Complete the entries in the remainder of the worksheet. Check the worksheet for spelling. Save the workbook. Print the documentation worksheet.

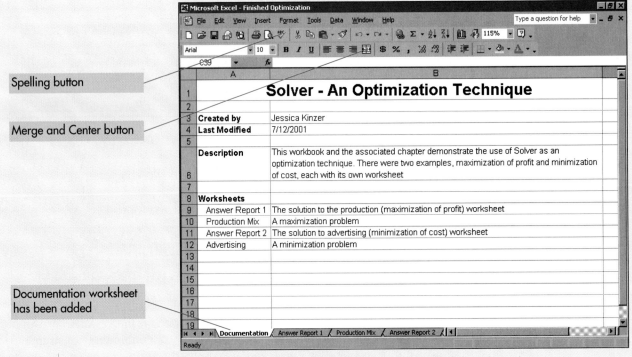

(h) Add the Documentation Worksheet (step 8)

FIGURE B.6 *Hands-on Exercise 2 (continued)*

Solver is an optimization and resource allocation tool that helps you achieve a desired goal, such as maximizing profit or minimizing cost. The information required by Solver is entered through the Solver Parameters dialog box, which is divided into three sections: the target cell, the adjustable cells, and the constraints.

The target cell identifies the goal (or objective function), which is the cell whose value you want to maximize, minimize, or set to a specific value. The adjustable cells are the cells whose values are changed until the constraints are satisfied and the target cell reaches its optimum value. The constraints specify the restrictions. Each constraint consists of a comparison containing a cell or cell range on the left, a relational operator, and a numeric value or cell reference on the right.

The Solver Options dialog box lets you specify how Solver will attempt to find a solution. The Max Time and Iterations entries determine how long Solver will work on finding a solution. If either limit is reached before a solution is found, Solver will ask whether you want to continue. The default settings of 100 seconds and 100 iterations are sufficient for simpler problems, but may not be enough for complex problems with multiple constraints.

KEY TERMS

Adjustable cells (p. 440)
Answer Report (p. 445)
Binding constraint (p. 438)
Constraint (p. 440)
Infeasible solution (p. 452)

Integer constraint (p. 451)
Iteration (p. 446)
Nonbinding constraint (p. 438)
Nonnegativity constraint (p. 440)
Solver (p. 437)

Solver Options dialog box (p. 446)
Solver Parameters dialog box (p. 440)
Target cell (p. 440)

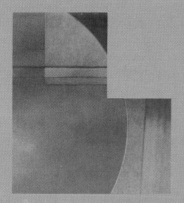

A VBA Primer: Extending Microsoft® Office XP

OBJECTIVES

AFTER READING THIS SUPPLEMENT YOU WILL BE ABLE TO:

1. Describe the relationship of VBA to Microsoft Office XP; explain how to open the VBA editor within an Office application.
2. Distinguish between key words, statements, procedures, and modules; use the Office Assistant to obtain detailed information about any VBA statement.
3. Explain how to create, edit, and run a VBA procedure; explain how the Quick Info and Complete Word tools facilitate VBA coding.
4. Explain how to continue a VBA statement from one line to the next; add and remove comments from a procedure.
5. Distinguish between the MsgBox and InputBox statements; describe at least two arguments for each statement.
6. Explain how to debug a procedure by stepping through its statements; describe the role of the Local and Immediate windows in debugging.
7. Use the If . . . Then . . . Else statement to implement a decision; explain the advantage of the Case statement over multiple ElseIf clauses.
8. Create a custom toolbar with buttons corresponding to the VBA procedures you have developed.
9. Describe several statements used to implement a loop; explain the difference between placing a condition at the beginning or end of a loop.
10. Distinguish between event-driven and traditional programming; create event procedures associated with opening and closing an Excel workbook and with an Access database.

OVERVIEW

Visual Basic for Applications (VBA) is a powerful programming language that is accessible from all major applications in Microsoft Office XP. You do not have to know VBA in order to use Office effectively, but even a basic understanding will help you to create more powerful documents. Indeed, you may already have been exposed to VBA through the creation of simple macros in Word or Excel. A *macro* is a set of instructions (i.e., a program) that simplifies the execution of repetitive tasks. It is created through the *macro recorder* that captures commands as they are executed, then converts those commands to a VBA program. (The macro recorder is present in Word, Excel, and PowerPoint, but not in Access.) You can create and execute macros without ever looking at the underlying VBA, but you gain an appreciation for the language when you do.

The macro recorder is limited, however, in that it captures only commands, mouse clicks, and/or keystrokes. As you will see, VBA is much more than just recorded keystrokes. It is a language unto itself, and thus, it contains all of the statements you would expect to find in any programming language. This lets you enhance the functionality of any macro by adding extra statements as necessary—for example, an InputBox function to accept data from the user, followed by an If . . . Then . . . Else statement to take different actions based on the information supplied by the user.

This supplement presents the rudiments of VBA and is suitable for use with any Office application. We begin by describing the VBA Editor and how to create, edit, and run simple procedures. The examples are completely general and demonstrate the basic capabilities of VBA that are found in any programming language. We illustrate the MsgBox statement to display output to the user and the InputBox function to accept input from the user. We describe the For . . . Next statement to implement a loop and the If . . . Then . . . Else and Case statements for decision making. We also describe several debugging techniques to help you correct the errors that invariably occur. The last two exercises introduce the concept of event-driven programming, in which a procedure is executed in response to an action taken by the user. The material here is application-specific in conjunction with Excel and Access, but it can be easily extended to Word or PowerPoint.

One last point before we begin is that this supplement assumes no previous knowledge on the part of the reader. It is suitable for someone who has never been exposed to a programming language or written an Office macro. If, on the other hand, you have a background in programming or macros, you will readily appreciate the power inherent in VBA. VBA is an incredibly rich language that can be daunting to the novice. Stick with us, however, and we will show you that it is a flexible and powerful tool with consistent rules that can be easily understood and applied. You will be pleased at what you will be able to accomplish.

INTRODUCTION TO VBA

VBA is a programming language, and like any other programming language its programs (or procedures, as they are called) are made up of individual statements. Each *statement* accomplishes a specific task such as displaying a message to the user or accepting input from the user. Statements are grouped into *procedures*, and procedures, in turn, are grouped into *modules*. Every VBA procedure is classified as either public or private. A *private procedure* is accessible only from within the module in which it is contained. A *public procedure*, on the other hand, can be accessed from any module.

The statement, however, is the basic unit of the language. Our approach throughout this supplement will be to present individual statements, then to develop simple procedures using those statements in a hands-on exercise. As you read the discussion, you will see that every statement has a precise *syntax* that describes how the statement is to be used. The syntax also determines the *arguments* (or parameters) associated with that statement, and whether those arguments are required or optional.

The **MsgBox statement** displays information to the user. It is one of the most basic statements in VBA, but we use it to illustrate several concepts in VBA programming. Figure 1a contains a simple procedure called MsgBoxExamples, consisting of four individual MsgBox statements. All procedures begin with a **procedure header** and end with the **End Sub statement**.

The MsgBox statement has one required argument, which is the message (or prompt) that is displayed to the user. All other arguments are optional, but if they are used, they must be entered in a specified sequence. The simplest form of the MsgBox statement is shown in example 1, which specifies a single argument that contains the text (or prompt) to be displayed. The resulting message box is shown in Figure 1b. The message is displayed to the user, who responds accordingly, in this case by clicking the OK button.

Example 2 extends the MsgBox statement to include a second parameter that displays an icon within the resulting dialog box as shown in Figure 1c. The type of icon is determined by a VBA **intrinsic** (or predefined) **constant** such as vbExclamation, which displays an exclamation point in a yellow triangle. VBA has many such constants that enable you to simplify your code, while at the same time achieving some impressive results.

Example 3 uses a different intrinsic constant, vbInformation, to display a different icon. It also extends the MsgBox statement to include a third parameter that is displayed on the title bar of the resulting dialog box. Look closely, for example, at Figures 1c and 1d, whose title bars contain "Microsoft Excel" and "Grauer/Barber", respectively. The first is the default entry (given that we are executing the procedure from within Microsoft Excel). You can, however, give your procedures a customized look by displaying your own text in the title bar.

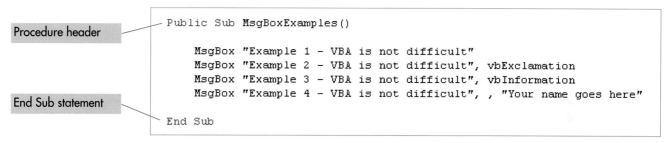

Procedure header

End Sub statement

```
Public Sub MsgBoxExamples()

    MsgBox "Example 1 - VBA is not difficult"
    MsgBox "Example 2 - VBA is not difficult", vbExclamation
    MsgBox "Example 3 - VBA is not difficult", vbInformation
    MsgBox "Example 4 - VBA is not difficult", , "Your name goes here"

End Sub
```

(a) VBA Code

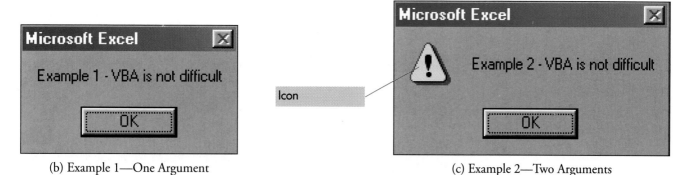

Icon

(b) Example 1—One Argument

(c) Example 2—Two Arguments

FIGURE 1   *The MsgBox Statement*

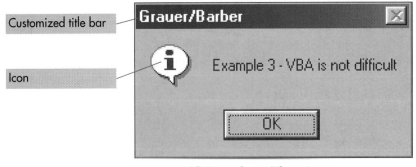

Customized title bar

Icon

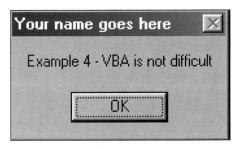

(d) Example 3—Three Arguments   (e) Example 4—Omitted Parameter

FIGURE 1   *The MsgBox Statement (continued)*

Example 4 omits the second parameter (the icon), but includes the third parameter (the entry for the title bar). The parameters are positional, however, and thus the MsgBox statement contains two commas after the message to indicate that the second parameter has been omitted.

THE INPUTBOX FUNCTION

The MsgBox statement displays a prompt to the user, but what if you want the user to respond to the prompt by entering a value such as his or her name? This is accomplished using the ***InputBox function***. Note the subtle change in terminology in that we refer to the InputBox *function*, but the MsgBox *statement*. That is because a function returns a value, in this case the user's name, which is subsequently used in the procedure. In other words, the InputBox function asks the user for information, then it stores that information (the value returned by the user) for use in the procedure.

Figure 2 displays a procedure that prompts the user for a first and last name, after which it displays the information using the MsgBox statement. (The Dim statement at the beginning of the procedure is explained shortly.) Let's look at the first InputBox function, and the associated dialog box in Figure 2b. The InputBox function displays a prompt on the screen, the user enters a value ("Bob" in this example), and that value is stored in the variable that appears to the left of the equal sign (strFirstName). The concept of a variable is critical to every programming language. Simply stated, a ***variable*** is a named storage location that contains data that can be modified during program execution.

The MsgBox statement then uses the value of strFirstName to greet the user by name as shown in Figure 2c. This statement also introduces the ampersand to ***concatenate*** (join together) two different character strings, the literal "Good morning", followed by the value within the variable strFirstName.

The second InputBox function prompts the user for his or her last name. In addition, it uses a second argument to customize the contents of the title bar (VBA Primer in this example) as can be seen in Figure 2d. Finally, the MsgBox statement in Figure 2e displays both the first and last name through concatenation of multiple strings. This statement also uses the ***underscore*** to continue a statement from one line to the next.

VBA is not difficult, and you can use the MsgBox statement and InputBox function in conjunction with one another as the basis for several meaningful procedures. You will get a chance to practice in the hands-on exercise that follows shortly.

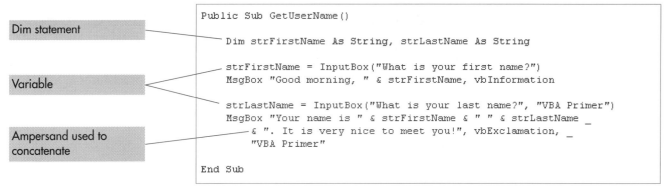

Dim statement

Variable

Ampersand used to concatenate

```
Public Sub GetUserName()

    Dim strFirstName As String, strLastName As String

    strFirstName = InputBox("What is your first name?")
    MsgBox "Good morning, " & strFirstName, vbInformation

    strLastName = InputBox("What is your last name?", "VBA Primer")
    MsgBox "Your name is " & strFirstName & " " & strLastName _
        & ". It is very nice to meet you!", vbExclamation, _
        "VBA Primer"

End Sub
```

(a) VBA Code

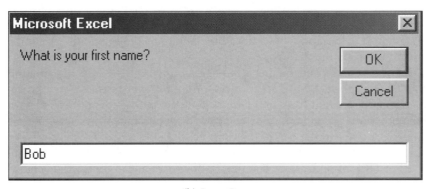

(b) InputBox

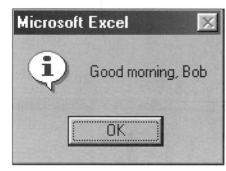

(c) Concatenation

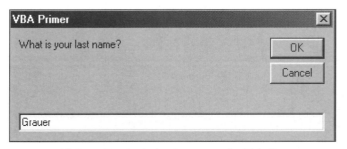

(d) InputBox includes Argument for Title Bar

(e) Concatenation and Continuation

FIGURE 2 *The InputBox Statement*

Declaring Variables

Every variable must be declared (defined) before it can be used. This is accomplished through the ***Dim*** (short for Dimension) ***statement*** that appears at the beginning of a procedure. The Dim statement indicates the name of the variable and its type (for example, whether it will hold characters or numbers), which in turn reserves the appropriate amount of memory for that variable.

A variable name must begin with a letter and cannot exceed 255 characters. It can contain letters, numbers, and various special characters such as an underscore, but it cannot contain a space or the special symbols !, @, &, $, or #. Variable names typically begin with a prefix to indicate the type of data that is stored within the variable such as "str" for a character string or "int" for integers. The use of a prefix is optional with respect to the rules of VBA, but it is followed almost universally.

All VBA procedures are created using the ***Visual Basic Editor*** as shown in Figure 3. You may already be familiar with the editor, perhaps in conjunction with creating and/or editing macros in Word or Excel, or event procedures in Microsoft Access. Let's take a moment, however, to review its essential components.

The left side of the editor displays the ***Project Explorer***, which is similar in concept and appearance to the Windows Explorer, except that it displays the objects associated with the open document. If, for example, you are working in Excel, you will see the various sheets in a workbook, whereas in an Access database you will see forms and reports.

The VBA statements for the selected module (Module1 in Figure 3) appear in the code window in the right pane. The module, in turn, contains declarations and procedures that are separated by horizontal lines. There are two procedures, MsgBoxExamples and GetUserName, each of which was explained previously. A ***comment*** (nonexecutable) statement has been added to each procedure and appears in green. It is the apostrophe at the beginning of the line, rather than the color, that denotes a comment.

The ***Declarations section*** appears at the beginning of the module and contains a single statement, ***Option Explicit***. This option requires every variable in a procedure to be explicitly defined (e.g., in a Dim statement) before it can be used elsewhere in the module. It is an important option and should appear in every module you write (see exercise 5 at the end of the chapter).

The remainder of the window should look reasonably familiar in that it is similar to any other Office application. The title bar appears at the top of the window and identifies the application (Microsoft Visual Basic) and the current document (VBA Examples.xls). The right side of the title bar contains the Minimize, Restore, and Close buttons. A menu bar appears under the title bar. Toolbars are displayed under the menu bar. Commands are executed by pulling down the appropriate menu, via buttons on the toolbar, or by keyboard shortcuts.

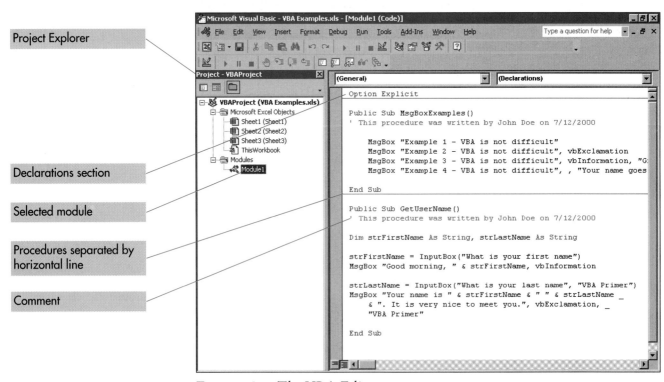

FIGURE 3   *The VBA Editor*

INTRODUCTION TO VBA

Objective   To create and test VBA procedures using the MsgBox and InputBox statements. Use Figure 4 as a guide in the exercise. You can do the exercise in any Office application.

Step 1a: **Start Microsoft Excel**

> ➤ We suggest you do the exercise in either Excel or Access (although you could use Word or PowerPoint just as easily). Go to step 1b for Access.
> ➤ Start **Microsoft Excel** and open a new workbook. Pull down the **File menu** and click the **Save command** (or click the **Save button** on the Standard toolbar) to display the Save As dialog box. Choose an appropriate drive and folder, then save the workbook as **VBA Examples**.
> ➤ Pull down the **Tools menu**, click the **Macro command**, then click the **Visual Basic Editor command** as shown in Figure 4a. Go to step 2.

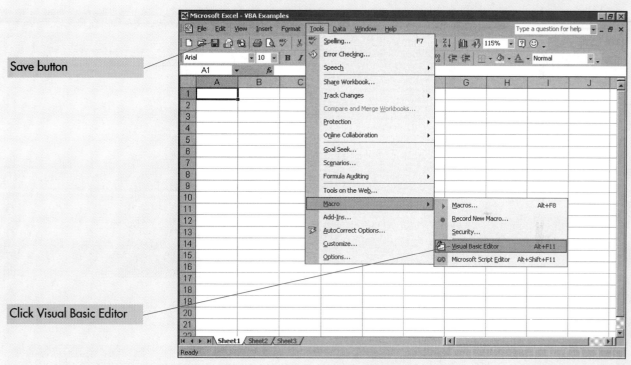

(a) Start Microsoft Excel (step 1a)

FIGURE 4   *Hands-on Exercise 1*

Step 1b: **Start Microsoft Access**

> ➤ Start **Microsoft Access** and choose the option to create a **Blank Access database**. Save the database as **VBA Examples**.
> ➤ Pull down the **Tools menu**, click the **Macro command**, then click the **Visual Basic Editor command**. (You can also use the **Alt+F11** keyboard shortcut to open the VBA editor without going through the Tools menu.)

Step 2: **Insert a Module**

➤ You should see a window similar to Figure 4b, but Module1 is not yet visible. Close the Properties window if it appears.

➤ If necessary, pull down the **View menu** and click **Project Explorer** to display the Project Explorer pane at the left of the window. Our figure shows Excel objects, but you will see the "same" window in Microsoft Access.

➤ Pull down the **Insert menu** and click **Module** to insert Module1 into the current project. The name of the module, Module1 in this example, appears in the Project Explorer pane.

➤ The Option Explicit statement may be entered automatically, but if not, click in the code window and type the statement **Option Explicit**.

➤ Pull down the **Insert menu** a second time, but this time select **Procedure** to display the Add Procedure dialog box in Figure 4b. Click in the **Name** text box and enter **MsgBoxExamples** as the name of the procedure. (Spaces are not allowed in a procedure name.)

➤ Click the option buttons for a **Sub procedure** and for **Public scope**. Click **OK**. The sub procedure should appear within the module and consist of the Sub and End Sub statements.

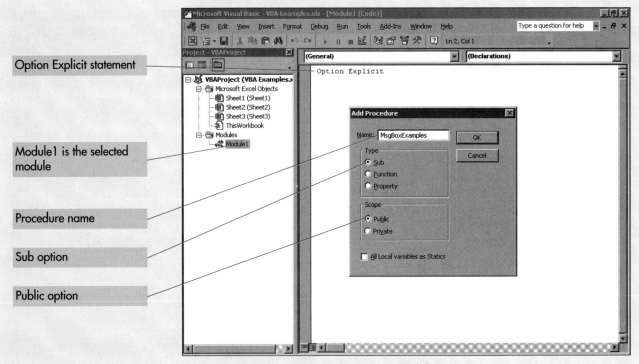

(b) Insert a Module (step 2)

FIGURE 4 *Hands-on Exercise 1 (continued)*

OPTION EXPLICIT

We say more about this important statement later on, but for now be sure that it appears in every module. See exercise 5 at the end of the chapter.

Step 3: **The MsgBox Statement**

> ➤ The insertion point (the flashing cursor) appears below the first statement. Press the **Tab key** to indent, type the key word **MsgBox**, then press the **space bar**. VBA responds with Quick Info that displays the syntax of the statement as shown in Figure 4c.
> ➤ Type a **quotation mark** to begin the literal, enter the text of your message, **This is my first VBA procedure**, then type the closing **quotation mark**.
> ➤ Click the **Run Sub button** on the Standard toolbar (or pull down the **Run menu** and click the **Run Sub command**) to execute the procedure. You should see a dialog box, containing the text you entered, within the Excel workbook (or other Office document) on which you are working.
> ➤ After you have read the message, click **OK** to return to the VBA Editor.

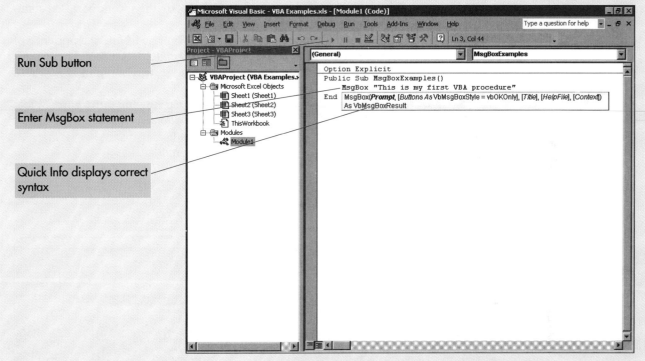

Run Sub button

Enter MsgBox statement

Quick Info displays correct syntax

(c) The MsgBox Statement (step 3)

FIGURE 4 *Hands-on Exercise 1 (continued)*

QUICK INFO—HELP WITH VBA SYNTAX

Press the space bar after entering the name of a statement (e.g., MsgBox), and VBA responds with a Quick Info box that displays the syntax of the statement. You see the arguments in the statement and the order in which those arguments appear. Any argument in brackets is optional. If you do not see this information, pull down the Tools menu, click the Options command, then click the Editor tab. Check the box for Auto Quick Info and click OK.

Step 4: **Complete the Procedure**

➤ You should be back within the MsgBoxExamples procedure. If necessary, click at the end of the MsgBox statement, then press **enter** to begin a new line. Type **MsgBox** and press the **space bar** to begin entering the statement.

➤ The syntax of the MsgBox statement will appear on the screen. Type a **quotation mark** to begin the message, type **Add an icon** as the text of this message, then type the closing **quotation mark**. Type a **comma**, then press the **space bar** to enter the next parameter.

➤ VBA automatically displays a list of appropriate parameters, in this case a series of intrinsic constants that define the icon or command button that is to appear in the statement.

➤ You can type the first several letters (e.g., **vbi**, for vbInformation), then press the **space bar**, or you can use the **down arrow** to select **vbInformation** and then press the **space bar**. Either way you should complete the second MsgBox statement as shown in Figure 4d. Press **enter**.

➤ Enter the third MsgBox statement as shown in Figure 4d. Note the presence of the two consecutive commas to indicate that we omitted the second parameter within the MsgBox statement. Enter your name instead of John Doe where appropriate. Press **enter**.

➤ Enter the fourth (and last) MsgBox statement following our figure. Select **vbExclamation** as the second parameter, type a **comma**, then enter the text of the title bar, as you did for the previous statement.

➤ Click the **Save button** to save the changes to the module.

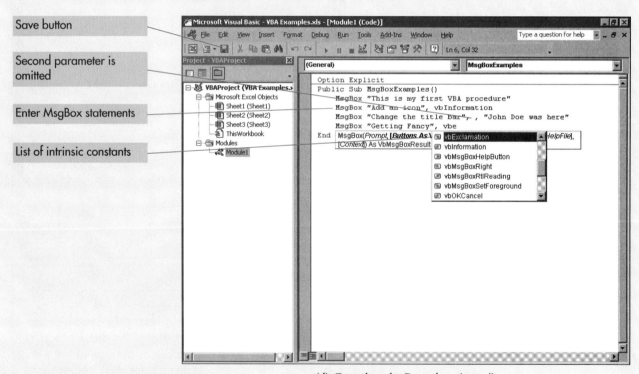

(d) Complete the Procedure (step 4)

FIGURE 4 *Hands-on Exercise 1 (continued)*

Step 5: **Test the Procedure**

➤ It's convenient if you can see the statements in the VBA procedure at the same time you see the output of those statements. Thus we suggest that you tile the VBA Editor and the associated Office application.

• Minimize all applications except the VBA Editor and the Office application (e.g., Excel).

• Right click the taskbar and click **Tile Windows Horizontally** to tile the windows as shown in Figure 4e. (It does not matter which window is on top. (If you see more than these two windows, minimize the other open window, then right click the taskbar and retile the windows.)

• Click anywhere in the VBA procedure, then click the **Run Sub button** on the Standard toolbar.

• The four messages will be displayed one after the other. Click **OK** after each message.

➤ Maximize the VBA window to continue working.

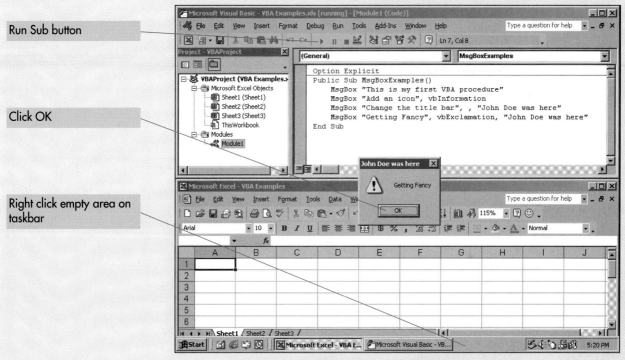

(e) Test the Procedure (step 5)

FIGURE 4 *Hands-on Exercise 1 (continued)*

HIDE THE WINDOWS TASKBAR

You can hide the Windows taskbar to gain additional space on the desktop. Right click any empty area of the taskbar to display a context-sensitive menu, click Properties to display the Taskbar properties dialog box, and if necessary click the Taskbar Options tab. Check the box to Auto Hide the taskbar, then click OK. The taskbar disappears from the screen but will reappear as you point to the bottom edge of the desktop.

Step 6: **Comments and Corrections**

➤ All VBA procedures should be documented with the author's name, date, and other comments as necessary to explain the procedure. Click after the procedure header. Press the **enter key** to leave a blank line.

➤ Press **enter** a second time. Type an **apostrophe** to begin the comment, then enter a descriptive statement similar to Figure 4f. Press **enter** when you have completed the comment. The line turns green to indicate it is a comment.

➤ The best time to experiment with debugging is when you know your procedure is correct. Go to the last MsgBox statement and delete the quotation mark in front of your name. Move to the end of the line and press **enter**.

➤ You should see the error message in Figure 4f. Unfortunately, the message is not as explicit as it could be; VBA cannot tell that you left out a quotation mark, but it does detect an error in syntax.

➤ Click **OK** in response to the error. Click the **Undo button** twice, to restore the quotation mark, which in turn corrects the statement.

➤ Click the **Save button** to save the changes to the module.

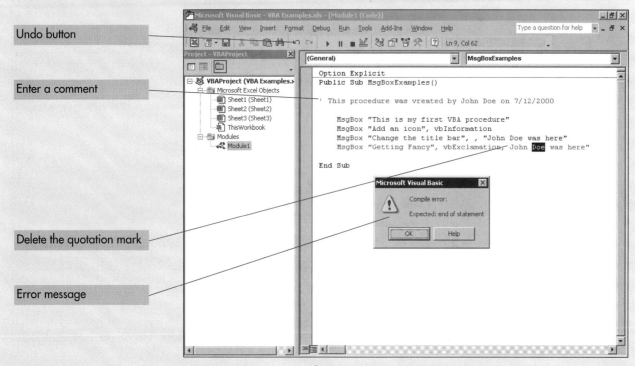

(f) Comments and Corrections (step 6)

FIGURE 4 *Hands-on Exercise 1 (continued)*

RED, GREEN, AND BLUE

Visual Basic for Applications uses different colors for different types of statements (or a portion of those statements). Any statement containing a syntax error appears in red. Comments appear in green. Key words, such as Sub and End Sub, appear in blue.

Step 7: **Create a Second Procedure**

➤ Pull down the **Insert menu** and click **Procedure** to display the Add Procedure dialog box. Enter **InputBoxExamples** as the name of the procedure. (Spaces are not allowed in a procedure name.)

➤ Click the option buttons for a **Sub procedure** and for **Public scope**. Click **OK**. The new sub procedure will appear within the existing module below the existing MsgBoxExamples procedure.

➤ Enter the statements in the procedure as they appear in Figure 4g. Be sure to type a space between the ampersand and the underscore in the second MsgBox statement. Click the **Save button** to save the procedure before testing it.

➤ You can display the output of the procedure directly in the VBA window if you minimize the Excel window. Thus, **right click** the Excel button on the taskbar to display a context-sensitive menu, then click the **Minimize command**. There is no visible change on your monitor.

➤ Click the **Run Sub button** to test the procedure. This time you see the Input box displayed on top of the VBA window because the Excel window has been minimized.

➤ Enter your first name in response to the initial prompt, then click **OK**. Click **OK** when you see the message box that says "Hello".

➤ Enter your last name in response to the second prompt and click **OK**. You should see a message box similar to the one in Figure 4g. Click **OK**.

➤ Return to the VBA procedure to correct any mistakes that might occur. Save the module.

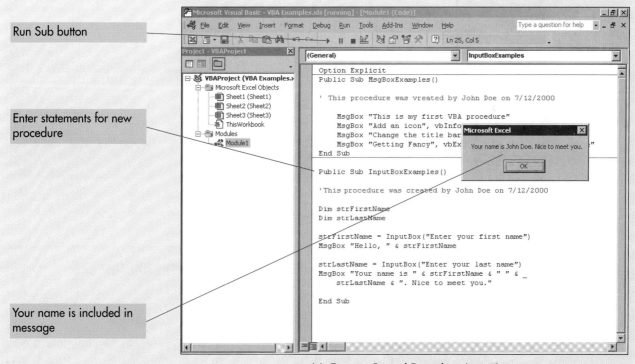

Run Sub button

Enter statements for new procedure

Your name is included in message

(g) Create a Second Procedure (step 7)

FIGURE 4   *Hands-on Exercise 1 (continued)*

Step 8: **Create a Public Constant**

➤ Click after the Options Explicit statement and press **enter** to move to a new line. Type the statement to define the constant, **ApplicationTitle**, as shown in Figure 4h, and press **enter**.

➤ Click anywhere in the MsgBoxExamples procedure, then change the third argument in the last MsgBox statement to ApplicationTitle. Make the four modifications in the InputBoxExamples procedure as shown in Figure 4h.

➤ Click anywhere in the InputBoxExamples procedure, then click the **Run Sub button** to test the procedure. The title bar of each dialog box will contain a descriptive title corresponding to the value of the ApplicationTitle constant.

➤ Change the value of the ApplicationTitle constant in the General Declarations section, then rerun the InputBoxExamples procedure. The title of every dialog box changes to reflect the new value. Save the procedure.

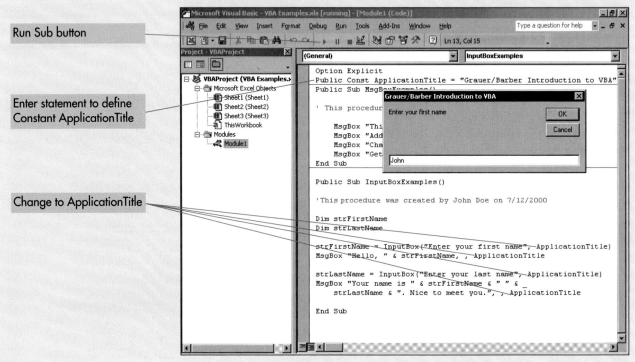

(h) Create a Public Constant (step 8)

FIGURE 4 *Hands-on Exercise 1 (continued)*

CONTINUING A VBA STATEMENT—THE & AND THE UNDERSCORE

A VBA statement can be continued from one line to the next by typing a space at the end of the line to be continued, typing the underscore character, then continuing on the next line. You may not, however, break a line in the middle of a literal (character string). Thus, you need to complete the character string with a closing quotation mark, add an ampersand (as the concatenation operator to display this string with the character string on the next line), then leave a space followed by the underscore to indicate continuation.

Step 9: **Help with VBA**

> ➤ You should be in the VBA editor. If necessary, pull down the **Help menu** and click **Microsoft Visual Basic Help** (or press the **F1 key**) to display the Office Assistant.
> ➤ Click the **Assistant**, type **InputBox**, then click the **Search button** in the Assistant's balloon for a list of topics pertaining to this entry. Click the first entry, **InputBox function**, to display the Help window.
> ➤ Click the **down arrow** on the Options button in the Help window, then click **Show tabs** to expand the Help window to include the Contents, Answer Wizard, and Index tabs as shown in Figure 4i.
> ➤ Take a minute to explore the information that is available. The Office Assistant functions identically in VBA as it does in all other Office applications. Close the Help window.
> ➤ Pull down the **File menu** and click the **Close command** (or click the **Close button** on the VBA title bar) to close the VBA window and return to the application. Click **Yes** if asked whether to save the changes to Module1.
> ➤ You should be back in the Excel (or Access) application window. Close the Office application if you do not want to continue with the next hands-on exercise at this time.
> ➤ Congratulations! You have just completed your first VBA procedure. Remember to use Help anytime you have a question.

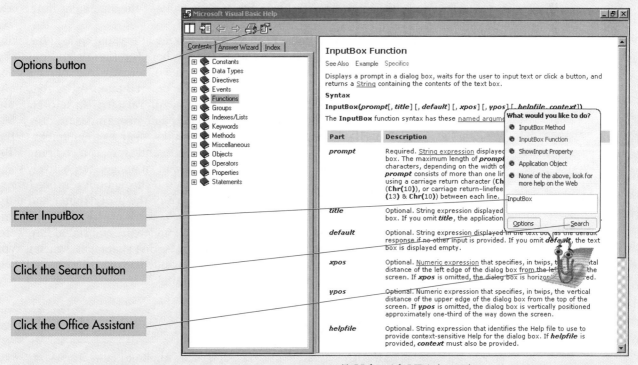

(i) Help with VBA (step 9)

FIGURE 4   *Hands-on Exercise 1 (continued)*

The ability to make decisions within a program, and then execute alternative sets of statements based on the results of those decisions, is crucial to any programming language. This is typically accomplished through an *If statement*, which evaluates a condition as either true or false, then branches accordingly. The If statement is not used in isolation, however, but is incorporated into a procedure to accomplish a specific task as shown in Figure 5a. This procedure contains two separate If statements, and the results are displayed in the message boxes shown in the remainder of the figure.

The InputBox statement associated with Figure 5b prompts the user for the name of his or her instructor, then it stores the answer in the variable strInstructorName. The subsequent If statement then compares the user's answer to the literal "Grauer". If the condition is true (i.e., Grauer was entered into the input box), then the message in Figure 5c is displayed. If, however, the user entered any other value, then the condition is evaluated as false, the MsgBox is not displayed, and processing continues with the next statement in the procedure.

The second If statement includes an optional *Else clause*. Again, the user is asked for a value, and the response is compared to the number 50. If the condition is true (i.e., the value of intUserStates equals 50), the message in Figure 5d is displayed to indicate that the response is correct. If, however, the condition is false (i.e., the user entered a number other than 50), the user sees the message in Figure 5e. Either way, true or false, processing continues with the next statement in the procedure. That's it—it's simple and it's powerful, and we will use the statement in the next hands-on exercise.

You can learn a good deal about VBA by looking at existing code and making inferences. Consider, for example, the difference between literals and numbers. *Literals* (also known as *character strings*) are stored differently from numbers, and this is manifested in the way that comparisons are entered into a VBA statement. Look closely at the condition that references a literal (strInstructorName = "Grauer") compared to the condition that includes a number (intUserStates = 50). The literal ("Grauer") is enclosed in quotation marks, whereas the number (50) is not. (The prefix used in front of each variable, "str" and "int", is a common VBA convention to indicate the variable type—a string and an integer, respectively.)

Note, too, that indentation and spacing are used throughout a procedure to make it easier to read. This is for the convenience of the programmer and not a requirement for VBA. The If, Else, and End If key words are aligned under one another, with the subsequent statements indented under the associated key word. We also indent a continued statement, such as a MsgBox statement, which is typically coded over multiple lines. Blank lines can be added anywhere within a procedure to separate blocks of statements from one another.

THE MSGBOX FUNCTION—YES OR NO

A simple MsgBox statement merely displays information to the user. MsgBox can also be used as a function, however, to accept information from the user such as clicking a Yes or No button, then combined with an If statement to take different actions based on the user's input. In essence, you enclose the arguments of the MsgBox function in parentheses (similar to what is done with the InputBox function), then test for the user response using the intrinsic constants vbYes and vbNo. See exercise 10 at the end of the chapter.

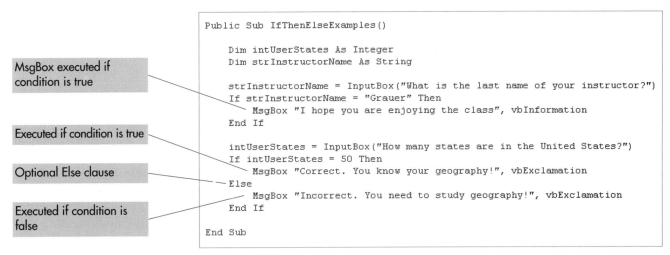

MsgBox executed if condition is true

Executed if condition is true

Optional Else clause

Executed if condition is false

```
Public Sub IfThenElseExamples()

    Dim intUserStates As Integer
    Dim strInstructorName As String

    strInstructorName = InputBox("What is the last name of your instructor?")
    If strInstructorName = "Grauer" Then
        MsgBox "I hope you are enjoying the class", vbInformation
    End If

    intUserStates = InputBox("How many states are in the United States?")
    If intUserStates = 50 Then
        MsgBox "Correct. You know your geography!", vbExclamation
    Else
        MsgBox "Incorrect. You need to study geography!", vbExclamation
    End If

End Sub
```

(a) VBA Code

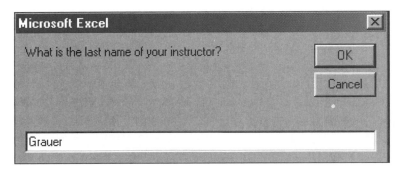

(b) Input Box Prompts for User Response

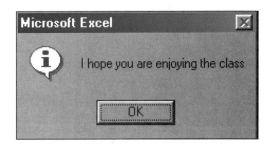

(c) Condition Is True

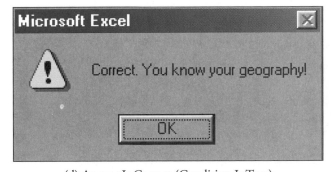

(d) Answer Is Correct (Condition Is True)

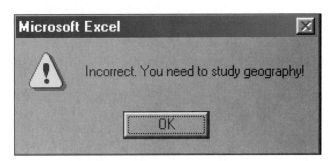

(e) Answer Is Wrong (Condition Is False)

FIGURE 5   *The If Statement*

The If statement is ideal for testing simple conditions and taking one of two actions. Although it can be extended to include additional actions by including one or more ElseIf clauses (If . . . Then . . . ElseIf . . . ElseIf . . .), this type of construction is often difficult to follow. Hence, the **Case statement** is used when multiple branches are possible.

The procedure in Figure 6a accepts a student's GPA, then displays one of several messages, depending on the value of the GPA. The individual cases are evaluated in sequence. Thus, we check first to see if the GPA is greater than or equal to 3.9, then 3.75, then 3.5, and so on. If none of the cases is true, the statement following the Else clause is executed.

Note, too, the format of the comparison in that numbers (such as 3.9 or 3.75) are not enclosed in quotation marks because the associated variable (sngUserGPA) was declared as numeric. If, however, we had been evaluating a string variable (such as, strUserMajor), quotation marks would have been required around the literal values (e.g., Case Is = "Business", Case Is = "Liberal Arts", and so on.) The distinction between numeric and character (string) variables is important.

Numbers are not enclosed in quotes

Executed if none of the cases is true

```
Public Sub CaseExample()

    Dim sngUserGPA As Single

    sngUserGPA = InputBox("What is your GPA?")
    Select Case sngUserGPA
        Case Is >= 3.9
            MsgBox "Congratulations! You are graduating Summa Cum Laude!"
        Case Is >= 3.75
            MsgBox "Well Done! You are graduating Magna Cum Laude!"
        Case Is >= 3.5
            MsgBox "Congratulations! You are graduating Cum Laude!"
        Case Is >= 1.8
            MsgBox "You made it"
        Case Else
            MsgBox "Check the schedule for Summer School"
    End Select

End Sub
```

(a) VBA Code

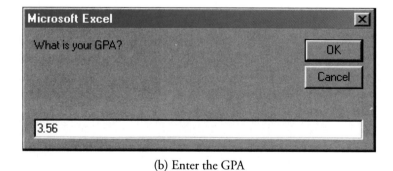

(b) Enter the GPA

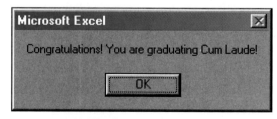

(c) Third Option Is Selected

FIGURE 6   *The Case Statement*

A VBA procedure can be executed in several different ways. It can be run from the Visual Basic Editor, by pulling down the Run menu, clicking the Run Sub button on the Standard toolbar, or using the F5 function key. It can also be run from within the Office application (Word, Excel, or PowerPoint, but not Access), by pulling down the Tools menu, clicking the Macro command, then choosing the name of the macro that corresponds to the name of the procedure.

Perhaps the best way, however, is to create a *custom toolbar* that is displayed within the application as shown in Figure 7. The toolbar has its own name (Bob's Toolbar), yet it functions identically to any other Office toolbar. You have your choice of displaying buttons only, text only, or both buttons and text. Our toolbar provides access to four commands, each corresponding to a procedure that was discussed earlier. Click the Case Example button, for example, and the associated procedure is executed, starting with the InputBox statement asking for the user's GPA.

A custom toolbar is created via the Toolbars command within the View menu. The new toolbar is initially big enough to hold only a single button, but you can add, move, and delete buttons following the same procedure as for any other Office toolbar. You can add any command at all to the toolbar; that is, you can add existing commands from within the Office application, or you can add commands that correspond to VBA procedures that you have created. Remember, too, that you can add more buttons to existing office toolbars.

Once the toolbar has been created, it is displayed or hidden just like any other Office toolbar. It can also be docked along any edge of the application window or left floating as shown in Figure 7. It's fun, it's easy, and as you may have guessed, it's time for the next hands-on exercise.

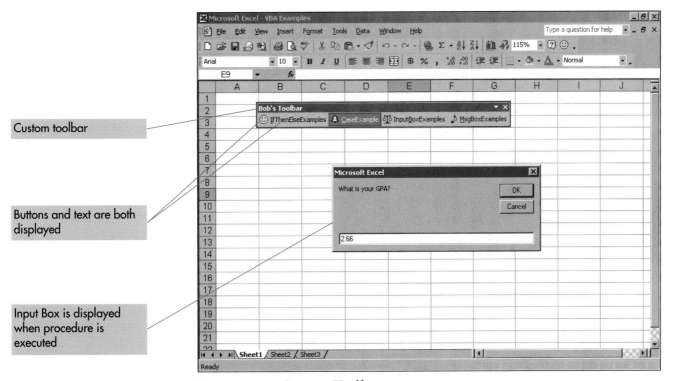

Custom toolbar

Buttons and text are both displayed

Input Box is displayed when procedure is executed

FIGURE 7   *Custom Toolbars*

Objective   To create procedures with If . . . Then . . . Else and Case statements, then create a custom toolbar to execute those procedures. Use Figure 8 as a guide in the exercise.

Step 1:   **Open the Office Document**

> ➤ Open the **VBA Examples workbook** or Access database from the previous exercise. The procedure differs slightly, depending on whether you are using Access or Excel. In Access, you simply open the database. In Excel, however, you will be warned that the workbook contains a macro as shown in Figure 8a. Click the button to **Enable Macros**.
> ➤ Pull down the **Tools menu**, click the **Macro command**, then click the **Visual Basic Editor command**. You can also use the **Alt+F11** keyboard shortcut to open the VBA Editor without going through the Tools menu.

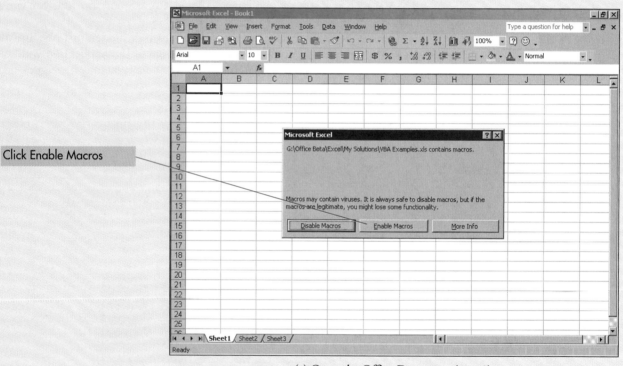

(a) Open the Office Document (step 1)

FIGURE 8   *Hands-on Exercise 2*

MACRO VIRUSES AND VBA PROCEDURES

An Excel macro is always associated with a VBA procedure. Thus, whenever Excel detects a procedure within a workbook, it warns you that the workbook contains a macro, which in turn may carry a macro virus. If you are confident the workbook is safe, click the button to Enable macros; otherwise open the workbook with the macros disabled.

Step 2:   **Insert a New Procedure**

➤ You should be in the Visual Basic Editor as shown in Figure 8b. If necessary, double click **Module1** in the Explorer Window to open this module. Pull down the **Insert menu** and click the **Procedure command** to display the Add Procedure dialog box.

➤ Click in the **Name** text box and enter **IfThenElseExamples** as the name of the procedure. Click the option buttons for a **Sub procedure** and for **Public scope**. Click **OK**. The sub procedure should appear within the module and consist of the Sub and End Sub statements.

➤ Click within the newly created procedure, then click the **Procedure View button** at the bottom of the window. The display changes to show just the current procedure.

➤ Click the **Save button** to save the module with the new procedure.

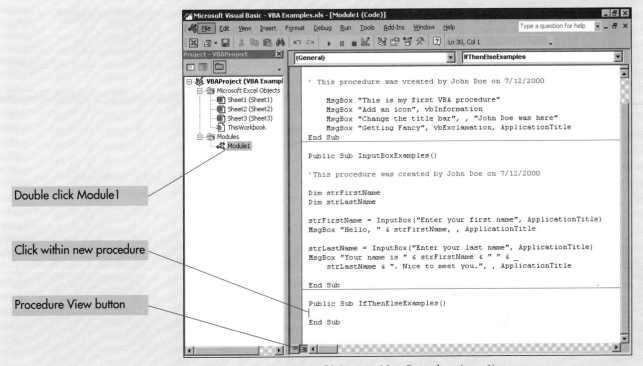

(b) Insert a New Procedure (step 2)

FIGURE 8   *Hands-on Exercise 2 (continued)*

PROCEDURE VIEW VERSUS FULL MODULE VIEW

The procedures within a module can be displayed individually, or alternatively, multiple procedures can be viewed simultaneously. To go from one view to the other, click the Procedure View button at the bottom of the window to display just the procedure you are working on, or click the Full Module View button to display multiple procedures. You can press Ctrl+PgDn and Ctrl+PgUp to move between procedures in either view.

Step 3:   **Create the If ... Then ... Else Procedure**

➤ Enter the IfThenElseExamples procedure as it appears in Figure 8c, but use your instructor's name instead of Bob's. Note the following:

- The Dim statements at the beginning of the procedure are required to define the two variables that are used elsewhere in the procedure.
- The syntax of the comparison is different for string variables versus numeric variables. String variables require quotation marks around the comparison value (e.g., strInstructorName = "Grauer"). Numeric variables (e.g., intUserStates = 50) do not.
- Indentation and blank lines are used within a procedure to make the code easier to read, as distinct from a VBA requirement. Press the **Tab key** to indent one level to the right.

➤ Save the procedure.

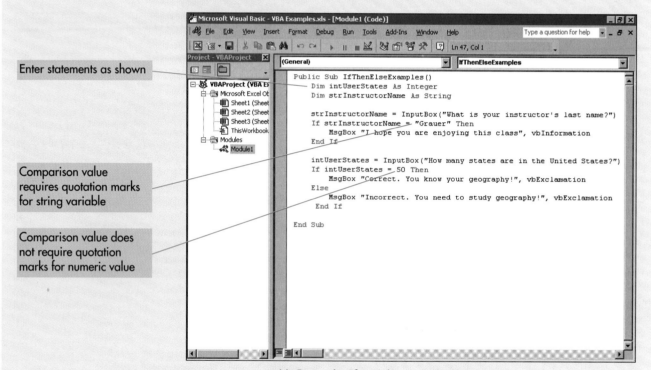

Enter statements as shown

Comparison value requires quotation marks for string variable

Comparison value does not require quotation marks for numeric value

```
Public Sub IfThenElseExamples()
    Dim intUserStates As Integer
    Dim strInstructorName As String

    strInstructorName = InputBox("What is your instructor's last name?")
    If strInstructorName = "Grauer" Then
        MsgBox "I hope you are enjoying this class", vbInformation
    End If

    intUserStates = InputBox("How many states are in the United States?")
    If intUserStates = 50 Then
        MsgBox "Correct. You know your geography!", vbExclamation
    Else
        MsgBox "Incorrect. You need to study geography!", vbExclamation
    End If

End Sub
```

(c) Create the If ... Then ... Else Procedure (step 3)

FIGURE 8   *Hands-on Exercise 2 (continued)*

THE COMPLETE WORD TOOL

It's easy to misspell a variable name within a procedure, which is why the Complete Word tool is so useful. Type the first several characters in a variable name (e.g., "intU" or "strI" in the current procedure), then press Ctrl+Space. VBA will complete the variable for you, if you have already entered a sufficient number of letters for a unique reference. Alternatively, it will display all of the elements that begin with the letters you have entered. Use the down arrow to scroll through the list until you find the item, then press the space bar to complete the entry.

Step 4: **Test the Procedure**

➤ The best way to test a procedure is to display its output directly in the VBA window (without having to switch back and forth between that and the application window). Thus, right click the Excel button on the taskbar to display a context-sensitive menu, then click the **Minimize command**.

➤ There is no visible change on your monitor. Click anywhere within the procedure, then click the **Run Sub button**. You should see the dialog box in Figure 8d.

➤ Enter your instructor's name, exactly as it was spelled within the VBA procedure. Click **OK**. You should see a second message box that hopes you are enjoying the class. This box will be displayed only if you spell the instructor's name correctly. Click **OK**.

➤ You should see a second input box that asks how many states are in the United States. Enter **50** and click **OK**. You should see a message indicating that you know your geography. Click **OK** to close the dialog box.

➤ Click the **Run Sub button** a second time, but enter a different set of values in response to the prompts. Misspell your instructor's name, and you will not see the associated message box.

➤ Enter any number other than 50, and you will be told to study geography. Continue to test the procedure until you are satisfied it works under all conditions.

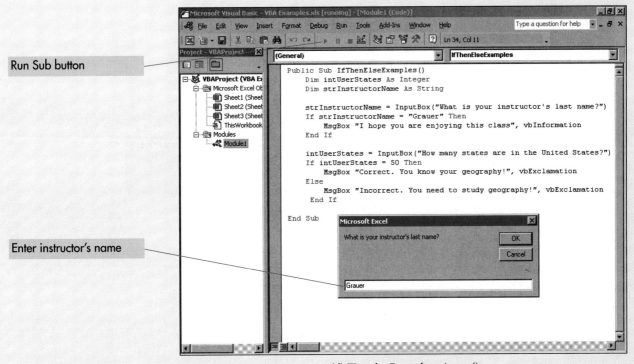

(d) Test the Procedure (step 4)

FIGURE 8 *Hands-on Exercise 2 (continued)*

Step 5: **Create and Test the CaseExample Procedure**

➤ Pull down the **Insert menu** and create a new procedure called **CaseExample**, then enter the statements exactly as they appear in Figure 8e. Note:
  - The variable sngUserGPA is declared to be a single-precision floating-point number (as distinct from the integer type that was used previously). A floating-point number is required in order to maintain a decimal point.
  - You may use any editing technique with which you are comfortable. You could, for example, enter the first case, copy it four times in the procedure, then modify the copied text as necessary.
  - The use of indentation and blank lines is for the convenience of the programmer and not a requirement of VBA.

➤ Click the **Run Sub button**, then test the procedure. Be sure to test it under all conditions; that is, you need to run it several times and enter a different GPA each time to be sure that all of the cases are working correctly.

➤ Save the procedure.

Enter statements for new procedure

Single-precision variable can contain a decimal point

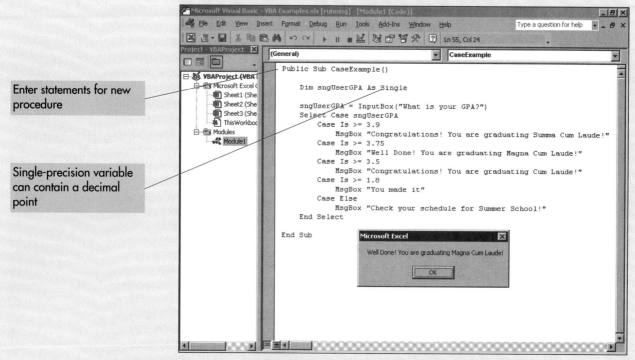

(e) Create and Test the CaseExample Procedure (step 5)

FIGURE 8 *Hands-on Exercise 2 (continued)*

RELATIONAL OPERATORS

The condition portion of an If or Case statement uses one of several relational operators. These include =, <, and > for equal to, less than, or greater than, respectively. You can also use >=, <=, or <> for greater than or equal to, less than or equal to, or not equal. This is basic, but very important, information if you are to code these statements correctly.

Step 6:   **Create a Custom Toolbar**

➤ Click the **Excel** (or **Access**) **button** to display the associated application window. Pull down the **View menu**, click (or point to) the **Toolbars command**, then click **Customize** to display the Customize dialog box in Figure 8f. (Bob's toolbar is not yet visible.) Click the **Toolbars tab**.

➤ Click the **New button** to display the New Toolbar dialog box. Enter the name of your toolbar—e.g., **Bob's toolbar**—then click **OK** to create the toolbar and close the dialog box.

➤ Your toolbar should appear on the screen, but it does not yet contain any buttons. If necessary, click and drag the title bar of your toolbar to move the toolbar within the application window.

➤ Toggle the check box that appears next to your toolbar within the Customize dialog box on and off to display or hide your toolbar. Leave the box checked to display the toolbar and continue with this exercise.

Custom toolbar

New button

Click to display/hide toolbar

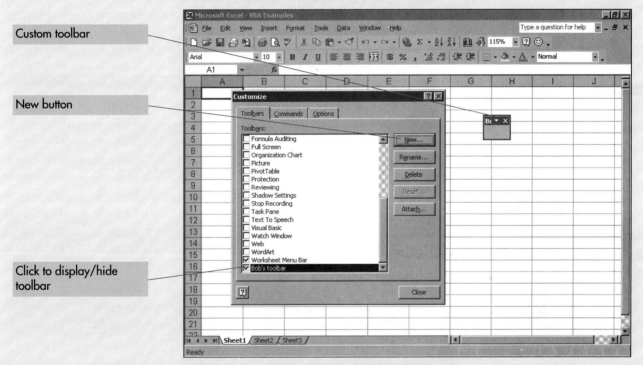

(f) Create a Custom Toolbar (step 6)

FIGURE 8   *Hands-on Exercise 2 (continued)*

FIXED VERSUS FLOATING TOOLBARS

A toolbar may be docked (fixed) along the edge of the application window, or it can be displayed as a floating toolbar anywhere within the window. You can switch back and forth by dragging the move handle of a docked toolbar to move the toolbar away from the edge. Conversely, you can drag the title bar of a floating toolbar to the edge of the window to dock the toolbar. You can also click and drag the border of a floating toolbar to change its size.

Step 7:   **Add Buttons to the Toolbar**

➤ Click the **Commands tab** in the Customize dialog box, click the **down arrow** in the Categories list box, then scroll until you can select the **Macros category**. (If you are using Access and not Excel, you need to select the **File category**, then follow the steps as described in the boxed tip on the next page.)

➤ Click and drag the **Custom button** to your toolbar and release the mouse. A "happy face" button appears on the toolbar you just created. (You can remove a button from a toolbar by simply dragging the button from the toolbar.)

➤ Select the newly created button, then click the **Modify Selection command button** (or right click the button to display the context-sensitive menu) in Figure 8g. Change the button's properties as follows:
  • Click the **Assign Macro command** at the bottom of the menu to display the Assign Macro dialog box, then select the **IfThenElseExamples** macro (procedure) to assign it to the button. Click **OK**.
  • Click the **Modify Selection button** a second time.
  • Click in the **Name Textbox** and enter an appropriate name for the button, such as **IfThenElseExamples**.
  • Click the **Modify Selection button** a third time, then click **Text Only (Always)** to display text rather than an image.

➤ Close the Customize dialog box when you have completed the toolbar. Save the workbook.

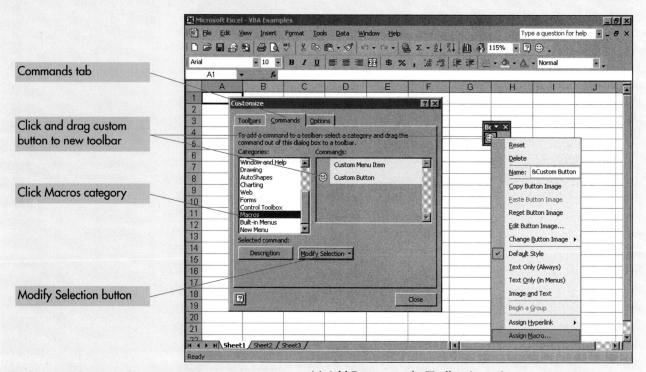

(g) Add Buttons to the Toolbar (step 7)

FIGURE 8   *Hands-on Exercise 2 (continued)*

Step 8: **Test the Custom Toolbar**

> ➤ Click any command on your toolbar as shown in Figure 8h. We clicked the **InputBoxExamples button**, which in turn executed the InputBoxExamples procedure that was created in the first exercise.
> ➤ Enter the appropriate information in any input boxes that are displayed. Click **OK**. Close your toolbar when you have completed testing it.
> ➤ If this is not your own machine, you should delete your toolbar as a courtesy to the next student. Pull down the **View menu**, click the **Toolbars command**, click **Customize** to display the Customize dialog box, then click the **Toolbars tab**. Select (highlight) the toolbar, then click the **Delete button** in the Customize dialog box. Click **OK** to delete the button. Close the dialog box.
> ➤ Exit Office if you do not want to continue with the next exercise.

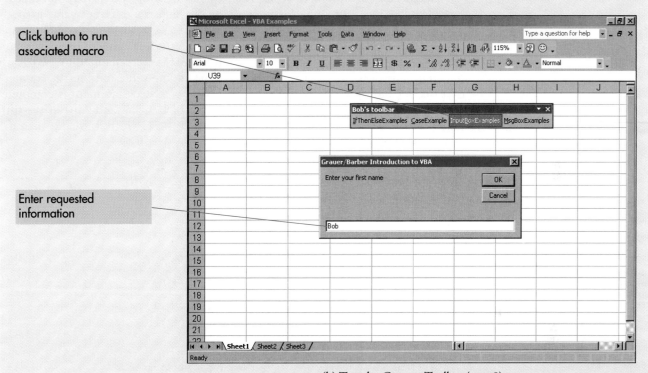

(h) Test the Custom Toolbar (step 8)

FIGURE 8   *Hands-on Exercise 2 (continued)*

ACCESS IS DIFFERENT

The procedure to create a custom toolbar in Access is different from the procedure in Excel. Select the File category within the Customize dialog box, then click and drag the Custom command to the newly created toolbar. Select the command on the toolbar, then click the Modify Selection command button in the dialog box. Click Properties, click the On Action text box, then type the name of the procedure you want to run in the format, =procedurename(). Close the dialog boxes, then press Alt+F11 to return to the VBA Editor. Change the key word "Sub" that identifies the procedure to "Function". Return to the database window, then test the newly created toolbar.

The *For . . . Next statement* executes all statements between the words For and Next a specified number of times, using a counter to keep track of the number of times the statements are executed. The simplest form of the statement, For intCounter = 1 To N, executes the statements within the loop N times.

The procedure in Figure 9 contains two For . . . Next statements that sum the numbers from 1 to 10, counting by one and two, respectively. The Dim statements at the beginning of the procedure declare two variables, intSumofNumbers to hold the sum and intCounter to hold the value of the counter. The sum is initialized to zero immediately before the first loop. The statements in the loop are then executed 10 times, each time incrementing the sum by the value of the counter. The result (the sum of the numbers from 1 to 10) is displayed after the loop in Figure 9b.

The second For . . . Next statement increments the counter by two rather than by one. (The increment or step is assumed to be one unless a different value is specified.) The sum of the numbers is reset to zero prior to entering the second loop, the loop is entered, and the counter is initialized to the starting value of one. Each subsequent time through the loop, however, the counter is incremented by two. Each time the value of the counter is compared to the ending value, until it (the counter) exceeds the ending value, at which point the For . . . Next statement is complete. Thus the second loop will be executed for values of 1, 3, 5, 7, and 9. After the fifth time through the loop, the counter is incremented to 11, which is greater than the ending value of 10, and the loop is terminated.

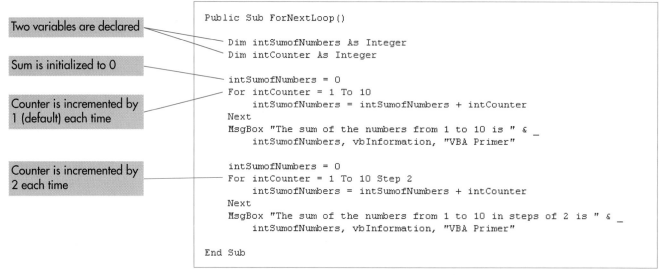

Two variables are declared

Sum is initialized to 0

Counter is incremented by 1 (default) each time

Counter is incremented by 2 each time

```
Public Sub ForNextLoop()

    Dim intSumofNumbers As Integer
    Dim intCounter As Integer

    intSumofNumbers = 0
    For intCounter = 1 To 10
        intSumofNumbers = intSumofNumbers + intCounter
    Next
    MsgBox "The sum of the numbers from 1 to 10 is " & _
        intSumofNumbers, vbInformation, "VBA Primer"

    intSumofNumbers = 0
    For intCounter = 1 To 10 Step 2
        intSumofNumbers = intSumofNumbers + intCounter
    Next
    MsgBox "The sum of the numbers from 1 to 10 in steps of 2 is " & _
        intSumofNumbers, vbInformation, "VBA Primer"

End Sub
```

(a) VBA Code

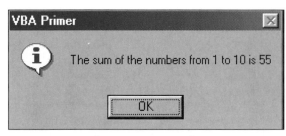

(b) In Increments of 1

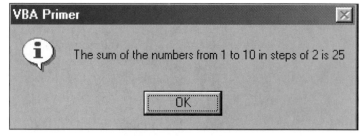

(c) In Increments of 2

FIGURE 9 *For . . . Next Loops*

The For ... Next statement is ideal when you know in advance how many times you want to go through a loop. There are many instances, however, when the number of times through the loop is indeterminate. You could, for example, give a user multiple chances to enter a password or answer a question. This type of logic is implemented through a Do loop. You can repeat the loop as long as a condition is true (Do While), or until a condition becomes true (Do Until). The choice depends on how you want to state the condition.

Regardless of which key word you choose, Do While or Do Until, two formats are available. The difference is subtle and depends on whether the key word (While or Until) appears at the beginning or end of the loop. Our discussion will use the Do Until statement, but the Do While statement works in similar fashion.

Look closely at the procedure in Figure 10a, which contains two different loops. In the first example, the Until condition appears at the end of the loop, which means the statements in the loop are executed, and then the condition is tested. This ensures that the statements in the loop will be executed at least once. The second loop, however, places the Until condition at the beginning of the loop, so that it (the condition) is tested prior to the loop being executed. Thus, if the condition is satisfied initially, the second loop will never be executed. In other words, there are two distinct statements ***Do ... Loop Until*** and ***Do Until ... Loop***. The first statement executes the loop, then tests the condition. The second statement tests the condition, then enters the loop.

```
Public Sub DoUntilLoop()

    Dim strCorrectAnswer As String, strUserAnswer As String

    strCorrectAnswer = "Earth"

    Do
        strUserAnswer = InputBox("What is the third planet from the sun?")
    Loop Until strUserAnswer = strCorrectAnswer
    MsgBox "You are correct, earthling!", vbExclamation

    strUserAnswer = InputBox("What is the third planet from the sun?")
    Do Until strUserAnswer = strCorrectAnswer
        strUserAnswer = InputBox("Your answer is incorrect. Try again.")
    Loop
    MsgBox "You are correct, earthling!", vbExclamation

End Sub
```

Until appears at end of loop

Until appears at beginning of loop

(a) VBA Code

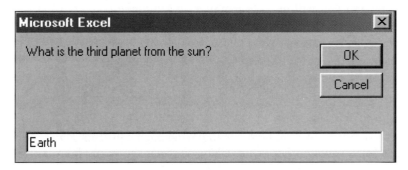

(b) Input the Answer

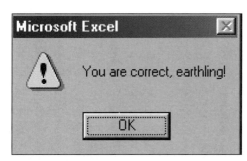

(c) Correct Response

FIGURE 10   *Do Until Loops*

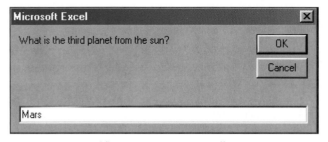

(d) Wrong Answer Initially

(e) Second Chance

FIGURE 10 *Do Until Loops (continued)*

It's tricky, but stay with us. In the first example, the user is asked the question within the loop, and the loop is executed repeatedly until the user gives the correct answer. In the second example, the user is asked the question outside of the loop, and the loop is bypassed if the user answers it correctly. The latter is the preferred logic because it enables us to phrase the question differently, before and during the loop. Look carefully at the difference between the InputBox statements and see how the question changes within the second loop.

DEBUGGING

As you learn more about VBA and develop more powerful procedures, you are more likely to make mistakes. The process of finding and correcting errors within a procedure is known as *debugging* and it is an integral part of programming. Do not be discouraged if you make mistakes. Everyone does. The important thing is how quickly you are able to find and correct the errors that invariably occur. We begin our discussion of debugging by describing two types of errors, *compilation errors* and *execution* (or *run-time*) *errors*.

A compilation error is simply an error in VBA syntax. (Compilation is the process of translating a VBA procedure to machine language, and thus a compilation error occurs when the VBA Editor is unable to convert a statement to machine language.) Compilation errors occur for many reasons, such as misspelling a key word, omitting a comma, and so on. VBA recognizes the error before the procedure is run and displays the invalid statement in red together with an associated error message. The programmer corrects the error and then reruns the procedure.

Execution errors are caused by errors in logic and are more difficult to detect because they occur without any error message. VBA, or for that matter any other programming language, does what you tell it to do, which is not necessarily what you want it to do. If, for example, you were to compute the sales tax of an item by multiplying the price by 60% rather than 6%, VBA will perform the calculation and simply display the wrong answer. It is up to you to realize that the results of the procedure are incorrect, and you will need to examine its statements and correct the mistake.

So how do you detect an execution error? In essence, you must decide what the expected output of your procedure should be, then you compare the actual results of the procedure to the intended result. If the results are different, an error has occurred, and you have to examine the logic in the procedure to find the error. You may see the mistake immediately (e.g., using 60% rather than 6% in the previous example), or you may have to examine the code more closely. And as you might expect, VBA has a variety of tools to help you in the debugging process. These tools are accessed from the *Debug toolbar* or the *Debug menu* as shown in Figure 11.

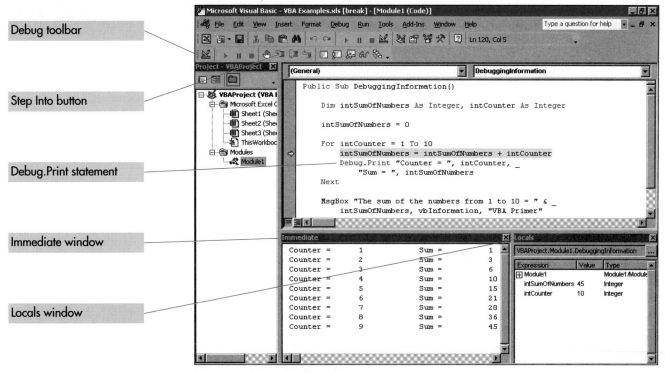

Debug toolbar

Step Into button

Debug.Print statement

Immediate window

Locals window

FIGURE 11 *Debugging*

The procedure in Figure 11 is a simple For . . . Next loop to sum the integers from 1 to 10. The procedure is correct as written, but we have introduced several debugging techniques into the figure. The most basic technique is to step through the statements in the procedure one at a time to see the sequence in which the statements are executed. Click the ***Step Into button*** on the Debug toolbar to enter (step into) the procedure, then continue to click the button to move through the procedure. Each time you click the button, the statement that is about to be executed is highlighted.

Another useful technique is to display the values of selected variables as they change during execution. This is accomplished through the ***Debug.Print statement*** that displays the values in the ***Immediate window***. The Debug.Print statement is placed within the For . . . Next loop so that you can see how the counter and the associated sum change during execution.

As the figure now stands, we have gone through the loop nine times, and the sum of the numbers from 1 to 9 is 45. The Step Into button is in effect so that the statement to be executed next is highlighted. You can see that we are back at the top of the loop, where the counter has been incremented to 10, and further, that we are about to increment the sum.

The ***Locals window*** is similar in concept except that it displays only the current values of all the variables within the procedure. Unlike the Immediate window, which requires the insertion of Debug.Print statements into a procedure to have meaning, the Locals window displays its values automatically, without any effort on the part of the programmer, other than opening the window. All three techniques can be used individually, or in conjunction with one another, as the situation demands.

We believe that the best time to practice debugging is when you know there are no errors in your procedure. As you may have guessed, it's time for the next hands-on exercise.

LOOPS AND DEBUGGING

Objective To create a loop using the For . . . Next and Do Until statements; to open the Locals and Immediate windows and illustrate different techniques for debugging. Use Figure 12 as a guide in the exercise.

Step 1: **Insert a New Procedure**

➤ Open the **VBA Examples workbook** or the Access database from the previous exercise. Either way, pull down the **Tools menu**, click the **Macro command**, then click **Visual Basic Editor** (or use the **Alt+F11** keyboard shortcut) to start the VBA editor.

➤ If necessary, double click **Module1** within the Project Explorer window to open this module. Pull down the **Insert menu** and click the **Procedure command** to display the Add Procedure dialog box.

➤ Click in the **Name** text box and enter **ForNextLoop** as the name of the procedure. Click the option buttons for a **Sub procedure** and for **Public scope**. Click **OK**. The sub procedure should appear within the module and consist of the Sub and End Sub statements.

➤ Click the **Procedure View button** at the bottom of the window as shown in Figure 12a. The display changes to show just the current procedure, giving you more room in which to work.

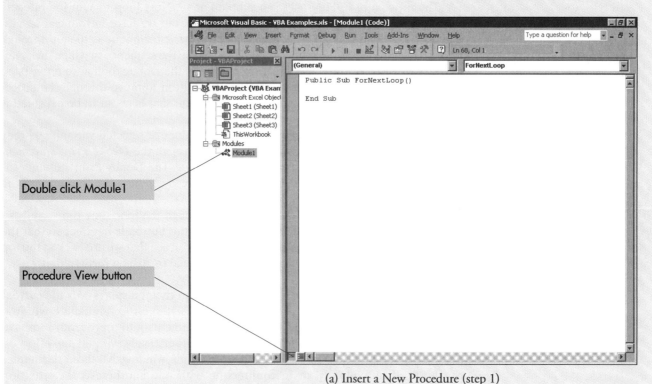

(a) Insert a New Procedure (step 1)

FIGURE 12   *Hands-on Exercise 3*

Step 2:   **Test the For . . . Next Procedure**

➤ Enter the procedure exactly as it appears in Figure 12b. Note the following:
- A comment is added at the beginning of the procedure to identify the author and the date.
- Two variables are declared at the beginning of the procedure, one to hold the sum of the numbers and the other to serve as a counter.
- The sum of the numbers is initialized to zero. The For . . . Next loop varies the counter from 1 to 10.
- The statement within the For . . . Next loop increments the sum of the numbers by the current value of the counter. The equal sign is really a replacement operator; that is, replace the variable on the left (the sum of the numbers) by the expression on the right (the sum of the numbers plus the value of the counter.
- Indentation and spacing within a procedure are for the convenience of the programmer and not a requirement of VBA. We align the For and Next statements at the beginning and end of a loop, then indent all statements within a loop.
- The MsgBox statement displays the result and is continued over two lines.

➤ Click the **Save button** to save the module. Right click the **Excel button** on the Windows taskbar to display a context-sensitive menu, then click the **Minimize command**.

➤ Click the **Run Sub button** to test the procedure, which should display the MsgBox statement in Figure 12b. Correct any errors that may occur.

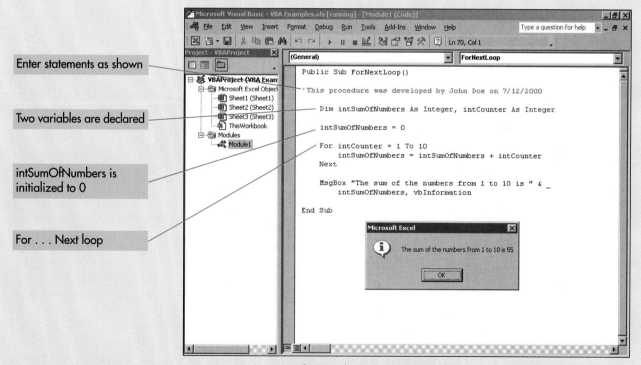

(b) Test the For . . . Next Procedure (step 2)

FIGURE 12   *Hands-on Exercise 3 (continued)*

Step 3: **Compilation Errors**

➤ The best time to practice debugging is when you know that the procedure is working properly. Accordingly, we will make some deliberate errors in our procedure to illustrate different debugging techniques.

➤ Pull down the **View menu**, click the **Toolbars command**, and (if necessary) toggle the Debug toolbar on, then dock it under the Standard toolbar.

➤ Click on the statement that initializes intSumOfNumbers to zero and delete the "s" at the end of the variable name. Click the **Run Sub button**.

➤ You will see the message in Figure 12c. Click **OK** to acknowledge the error, then click the **Undo button** to correct the error.

➤ The procedure header is highlighted, indicating that execution is temporarily suspended and that additional action is required from you to continue testing. Click the **Run Sub button** to retest the procedure.

➤ This time the procedure executes correctly and you see the MsgBox statement indicating that the sum of the numbers from 1 to 10 is 55. Click **OK**.

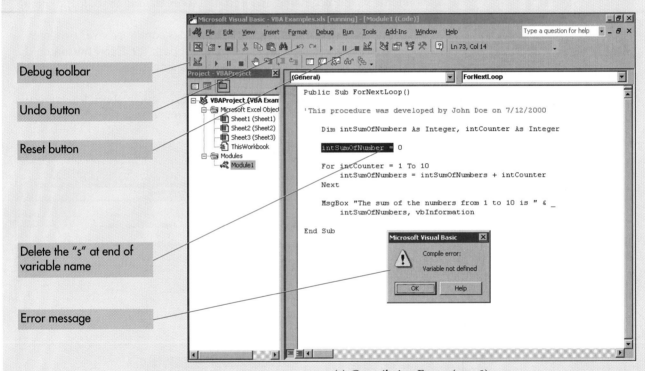

Debug toolbar

Undo button

Reset button

Delete the "s" at end of
variable name

Error message

(c) Compilation Errors (step 3)

FIGURE 12 *Hands-on Exercise 3 (continued)*

USE HELP AS NECESSARY

Pull down the Help menu at any time (or press the F1 key) to access the VBA Help facility to explore at your leisure. You can also obtain context-sensitive help by clicking the Help button when it appears within a dialog box. Click the Help button in Figure 12c, for example, and you will be advised to correct the spelling of the variable.

Step 4: **Step Through a Procedure**

➤ Pull down the **View menu** a second time and click the **Locals Window command** (or click the **Locals Window button** on the Debug toolbar).

➤ If necessary, click and drag the top border of the Locals window to size the window appropriately as shown in Figure 12d.

➤ Click anywhere within the procedure. Pull down the **Debug menu** and click the **Step Into command** (or click the **Step Into button** on the Debug toolbar). The first statement (the procedure header) is highlighted, indicating that you are about to enter the procedure.

➤ Click the **Step Into button** (or use the **F8** keyboard shortcut) to step into the procedure and advance to the next executable statement. The statement that initializes intSumOfNumbers to zero is highlighted, indicating that this statement is about to be executed.

➤ Continue to press the **F8 key** to step through the procedure. Each time you execute a statement, you can see the values of intSumOfNumbers and intCounter change within the Locals window. (You can click the **Step Out button** at any time to end the procedure.)

➤ Correct errors as they occur. Click the **Reset button** on the Standard or Debug toolbars at any time to begin executing the procedure from the beginning.

➤ Eventually you exit from the loop, and the sum of the numbers (from 1 to 10) is displayed within a message box.

➤ Click **OK** to close the message box. Press the **F8 key** a final time, then close the Locals window.

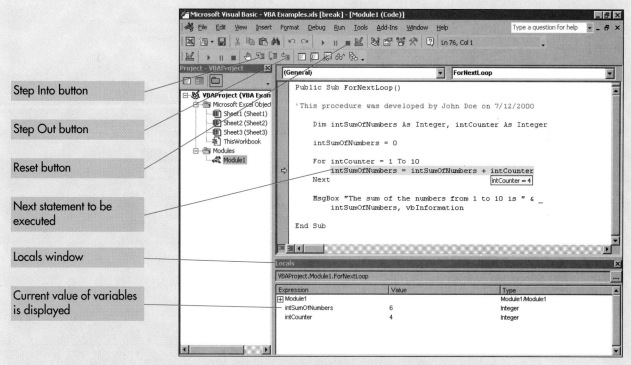

(d) Step Through a Procedure (step 4)

FIGURE 12 *Hands-on Exercise 3 (continued)*

Step 5: **The Immediate Window**

➤ You should be back in the VBA window. Click immediately to the left of the Next statement and press **enter** to insert a blank line. Type the **Debug.Print** statement exactly as shown in Figure 12e. (Click **OK** if you see a message indicating that the procedure will be reset.)

➤ Pull down the **View menu** and click the **Immediate Window command** (or click the **Immediate Window button** on the Debug toolbar). The Immediate window should be empty, but if not, you can click and drag to select the contents, then press the Del key to clear the window.

➤ Click anywhere within the For ... Next procedure, then click the **Run Sub button** on the Debug toolbar to execute the procedure. You will see the familiar message box indicating that the sum of the numbers is 55. Click **OK**.

➤ You should see 10 lines within the Immediate window as shown in Figure 12e, corresponding to the values displayed by the Debug.Print statement as it was executed within the loop.

➤ Close the Immediate window.

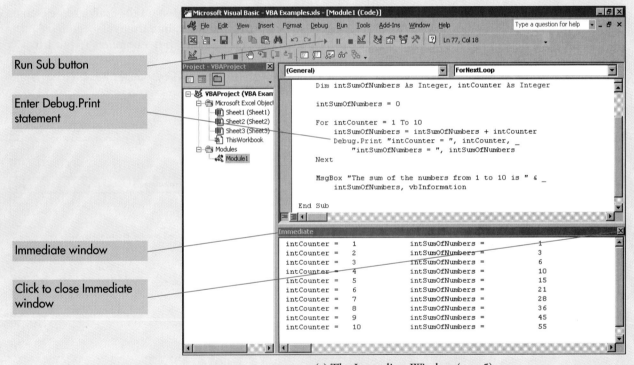

Run Sub button

Enter Debug.Print statement

Immediate window

Click to close Immediate window

(e) The Immediate Window (step 5)

FIGURE 12   *Hands-on Exercise 3 (continued)*

INSTANT CALCULATOR

Use the Print method (action) in the Immediate window to use VBA as a calculator. Press Ctrl+G at any time to display the Immediate window. Click in the window, then type the statement Debug.Print, followed by your calculation, for example, Debug.Print 2+2, and press enter. The answer is displayed on the next line in the Immediate window.

Step 6: **A More General Procedure**

➤ Modify the existing procedure to make it more general; for example, to sum the values from any starting value to any ending value:

- Click at the end of the existing Dim statement to position the insertion point, press **enter** to create a new line, then add the second Dim statement as shown in Figure 12f.
- Click before the For statement, press **enter** to create a blank line, press **enter** a second time, then enter the two InputBox statements to ask the user for the beginning and ending value.
- Modify the For statement to execute from **intStart** to **intEnd** rather than from 1 to 10.
- Change the MsgBox statement to reflect the values of intStart and intEnd, and a customized title bar. Note the use of the ampersand and the underscore, to indicate concatenation and continuation, respectively.

➤ Click the **Save button** to save the module.

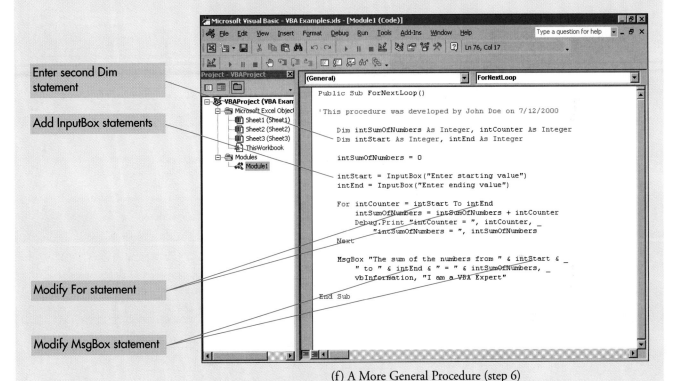

Enter second Dim statement

Add InputBox statements

Modify For statement

Modify MsgBox statement

```
Public Sub ForNextLoop()

    'This procedure was developed by John Doe on 7/12/2000

    Dim intSumOfNumbers As Integer, intCounter As Integer
    Dim intStart As Integer, intEnd As Integer

    intSumOfNumbers = 0

    intStart = InputBox("Enter starting value")
    intEnd = InputBox("Enter ending value")

    For intCounter = intStart To intEnd
        intSumOfNumbers = intSumOfNumbers + intCounter
        Debug.Print "intCounter = ", intCounter, _
            "intSumOfNumbers = ", intSumOfNumbers
    Next

    MsgBox "The sum of the numbers from " & intStart & _
        " to " & intEnd & " = " & intSumOfNumbers, _
        vbInformation, "I am a VBA Expert"

End Sub
```

(f) A More General Procedure (step 6)

FIGURE 12   *Hands-on Exercise 3 (continued)*

USE WHAT YOU KNOW

Use the techniques acquired from other applications such as Microsoft Word to facilitate editing within the VBA window. Press the Ins key to toggle between the insert and overtype modes as you modify the statements within a VBA procedure. You can also cut, copy, and paste statements (or parts of statements) within a procedure and from one procedure to another. The Find and Replace commands are also useful.

Step 7:   **Test the Procedure**

➤ Click the **Run Sub button** to test the procedure. You should be prompted for a beginning and an ending value. Enter any numbers you like, such as 10 and 20, respectively, to match the result in Figure 12g.

➤ The value displayed in the MsgBox statement should reflect the numbers you entered. For example, you will see a sum of 165 if you entered 10 and 20 as the starting and ending values.

➤ Look carefully at the message box that is displayed in Figure 12g. Its title bar displays the literal "I am a VBA expert", corresponding to the last argument in the MsgBox statement.

➤ Note, too, the spacing that appears within the message box, which includes spaces before and after each number. Look at your results and, if necessary, modify the MsgBox statement so that you have the same output. Click **OK**.

➤ Save the procedure.

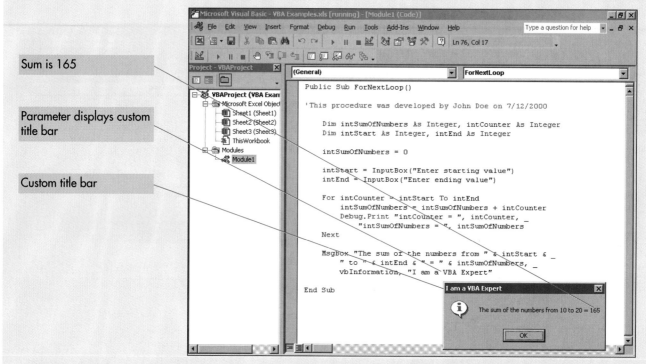

Sum is 165

Parameter displays custom title bar

Custom title bar

(g) Test the Procedure (step 7)

FIGURE 12   *Hands-on Exercise 3 (continued)*

CHANGE THE INCREMENT

The For ... Next statement can be made more general by supplying an increment within the For statement. Try For intCount = 1 To 10 Step 2, or more generally, For intCount = intStart to intEnd Step intStepValue. "Step" is a Visual Basic key word and must be entered that way. intCount, intEnd, and intStepValue are user-defined variables. The variables must be defined at the beginning of a procedure and can be initialized by requesting values from the user through the InputBox statement.

Step 8: **Create a Do Until Loop**

➤ Pull down the **Insert menu** and click the **Procedure command** to insert a new procedure called **DoUntilLoop**. Enter the procedure as it appears in Figure 12h. Note the following:

- Two string variables are declared to hold the correct answer and the user's response, respectively.
- The variable strCorrectAnswer is set to "Earth", the correct answer for our question.
- The initial InputBox function prompts the user to enter his/her response to the question. A second InputBox function appears in the loop that is executed if and only if the user enters the wrong answer.
- The Until condition appears at the beginning of the loop, so that the loop is entered only if the user answers incorrectly. The loop executes repeatedly until the correct answer is supplied.
- A message to the user is displayed at the end of the procedure after the correct answer has been entered.

➤ Click the **Run Sub button** to test the procedure. Enter the correct answer on your first attempt, and you will see that the loop is never entered.

➤ Rerun the procedure, answer incorrectly, then note that a second input box appears, telling you that your answer was incorrect.

➤ Save the procedure.

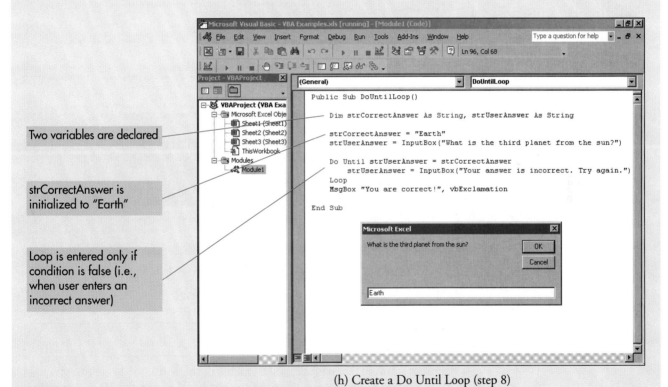

(h) Create a Do Until Loop (step 8)

FIGURE 12   *Hands-on Exercise 3 (continued)*

Step 9: **A More Powerful Procedure**

➤ Modify the procedure as shown in Figure 12i to include the statements to count and print the number of times the user takes to get the correct answer.
  • The variable intNumberOfAttempts is declared as an integer and is initialized to 1 after the user inputs his/her initial answer.
  • The Do loop is expanded to increment intNumberOfAttempts by 1 each time the loop is executed.
  • The MsgBox statement after the loop is expanded prints the number of attempts the user took to answer the question.
➤ Save the module, then click the **Run Sub button** to test the module. You should see a dialog box similar to the one in Figure 12i. Click **OK**.
➤ Pull down the **File menu** and click the **Print command** to display the Print dialog box. Click the option button to print the current module. Click **OK**.
➤ Exit Office if you do not want to continue at this time.

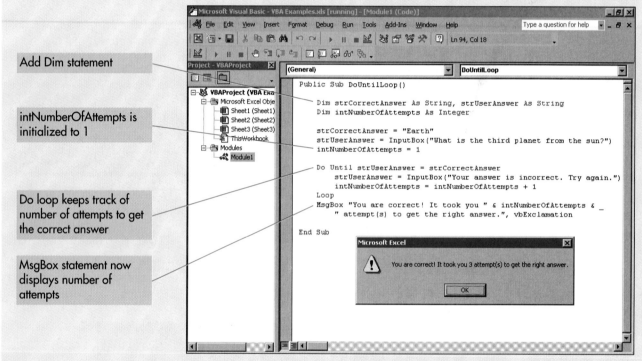

Add Dim statement

intNumberOfAttempts is initialized to 1

Do loop keeps track of number of attempts to get the correct answer

MsgBox statement now displays number of attempts

(i) A More Powerful Procedure (step 9)

FIGURE 12 *Hands-on Exercise 3 (continued)*

IT'S NOT EQUAL, BUT REPLACE

All programming languages use statements of the form N = N + 1, in which the equal sign does not mean equal in the literal sense; that is, N cannot equal N + 1. The equal sign is really a replacement operator. Thus, the expression on the right of the equal sign is evaluated, and that result replaces the value of the variable on the left. In other words, the statement N = N + 1 increments the value of N by one.

Our approach thus far has focused on VBA as an independent entity that can be run without specific reference to the applications in Microsoft Office. We have covered several individual statements, explained how to use the VBA editor to create and run procedures, and how to debug those procedures, if necessary. We hope you have found the material to be interesting, but you may be asking yourself, "What does this have to do with Microsoft Office?" In other words, how can you use your knowledge of VBA to enhance your ability in Microsoft Excel or Access? The answer is to create *event procedures* that run automatically in response to events within an Office application.

VBA is different from traditional programming languages in that it is event-driven. An *event* is defined as any action that is recognized by an application such as Excel or Access. Opening or closing an Excel workbook or an Access database is an event. Selecting a worksheet within a workbook is also an event, as is clicking on a command button on an Access form. To use VBA within Microsoft Office, you decide which events are significant, and what is to happen when those events occur. Then you develop the appropriate event procedures.

Consider, for example, Figure 13, which displays the results of two event procedures in conjunction with opening and closing an Excel workbook. (If you are using Microsoft Access instead of Excel, you can skip this discussion and the associated exercise, and move to the parallel material for Access that appears after the next hands-on exercise.) The procedure associated with Figure 13a displays a message that appears automatically after the user executes the command to close the associated workbook. The procedure is almost trivial to write, and consists of a single MsgBox statement. The effect of the procedure is quite significant, however, as it reminds the user to back up his or her work after closing the workbook. Nor does it matter how the user closes the workbook—whether by pulling down the menu or using a keyboard shortcut—because the procedure runs automatically in response to the Close Workbook event, regardless of how that event occurs.

The dialog box in Figure 13b prompts the user for a password and appears automatically when the user opens the workbook. The logic here is more sophisticated in that the underlying procedure contains an InputBox statement to request the password, a Do Until loop that is executed until the user enters the correct password or exceeds the allotted number of attempts, then additional logic to display the worksheet or terminate the application if the user fails to enter the proper password. The procedure is not difficult, however, and it builds on the VBA statements that were covered earlier.

The next hands-on exercise has you create the two event procedures that are associated with Figure 13. As you do the exercise, you will gain additional experience with VBA and an appreciation for the potential event procedures within Microsoft Office.

HIDING AND UNHIDING A WORKSHEET

Look carefully at the workbooks in Figures 13a and 13b. Both figures reference the identical workbook, Financial Consultant, as can be seen from the title bar. Look at the worksheet tabs, however, and note that two worksheets are visible in Figure 13a, whereas the Calculations worksheet is hidden in Figure 13b. This was accomplished in the Open workbook procedure and was implemented to hide the calculations from the user until the correct password was entered. See exercise 7 at the end of the chapter.

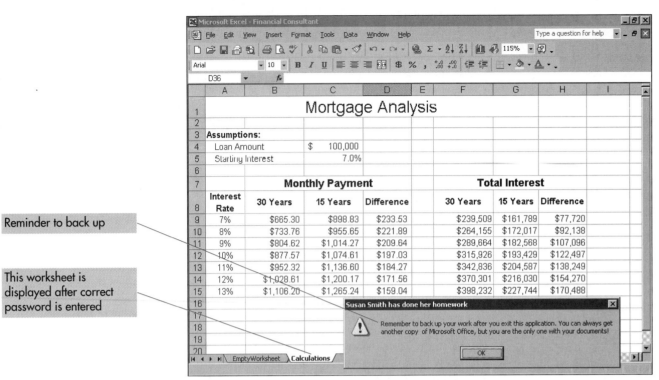

Reminder to back up

This worksheet is displayed after correct password is entered

(a) Message to the User (Close Workbook event)

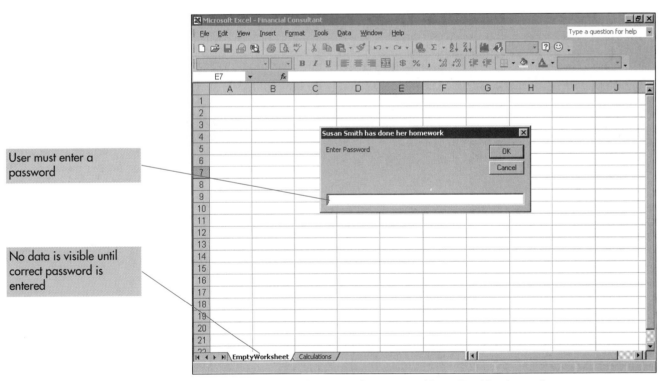

User must enter a password

No data is visible until correct password is entered

(b) Password Protection (Open Workbook event)

FIGURE 13   *Event-Driven Programming*

EVENT-DRIVEN PROGRAMMING (MICROSOFT EXCEL)

Objective To create an event procedure to implement password protection that is associated with opening an Excel workbook; to create a second event procedure that displays a message to the user upon closing the workbook. Use Figure 14 as a guide in the exercise.

Step 1: **Create the Close Workbook Procedure**

> ➤ Open the **VBA Examples workbook** you have used for the previous exercises and enable the macros. If you have been using Access rather than Excel, start Excel, open a new workbook, then save the workbook as **VBA Examples**.
> ➤ Pull down the **Tools menu**, click the **Macro command**, then click the **Visual Basic Editor command** (or use the **Alt+F11** keyboard shortcut).
> ➤ You should see the Project Explorer pane as shown in Figure 14a, but if not, pull down the **View menu** and click the **Project Explorer**. Double click **ThisWorkbook** to create a module for the workbook as a whole.
> ➤ Enter the **Option Explicit statement** if it is not there already, then press **enter** to create a new line. Type the statement to declare the variable, **Application-Title**, using your name instead of Susan Smith.
> ➤ Click the **down arrow** in the Object list box and select **Workbook**, then click the **down arrow** in the Procedure list box and select the **BeforeClose event** to create the associated procedure. (If you choose a different event by mistake, click and drag to select the associated statements, then press the **Del key** to delete the procedure.)
> ➤ Enter the MsgBox statement as it appears in Figure 14a. Save the procedure.

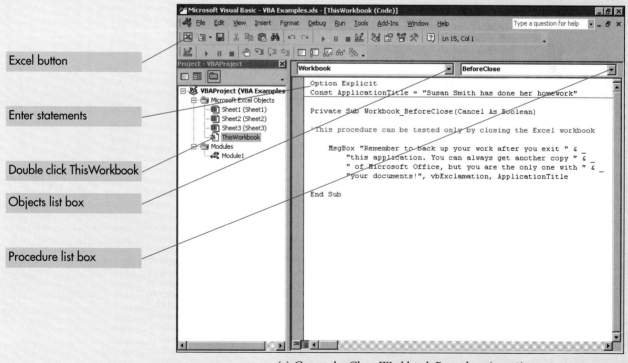

Excel button

Enter statements

Double click ThisWorkbook

Objects list box

Procedure list box

(a) Create the Close Workbook Procedure (step 1)

FIGURE 14 *Hands-on Exercise 4*

Step 2: **Test the Close Workbook Procedure**

> ➤ Click the **Excel button** on the Standard toolbar or on the Windows taskbar to view the Excel workbook. The workbook is not empty; that is, it does not contain any cell entries, but it does contain multiple VBA procedures.
> ➤ Pull down the **File menu** and click the **Close command**, which runs the procedure you just created and displays the dialog box in Figure 14b. Click **OK** after you have read the message, then click **Yes** if asked to save the workbook.
> ➤ Pull down the **File menu** and reopen the **VBA Examples workbook**, enabling the macros. Press **Alt+F11** to return to the VBA window to create an additional procedure.
> ➤ Double click **ThisWorkbook** from within the Projects Explorer pane to return to the BeforeClose procedure and make the necessary corrections, if any.
> ➤ Save the procedure.

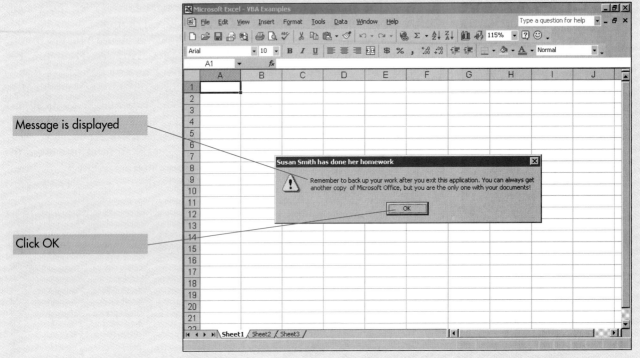

(b) Test the Close Workbook Procedure (step 2)

FIGURE 14   *Hands-on Exercise 4 (continued)*

THE MOST RECENTLY OPENED FILE LIST

One way to open a recently used workbook is to select the workbook directly from the File menu. Pull down the File menu, but instead of clicking the Open command, check to see if the workbook appears on the list of the most recently opened workbooks located at the bottom of the menu. If so, just click the workbook name, rather than having to make the appropriate selections through the Open dialog box.

Step 3:   **Start the Open Workbook Event Procedure**

➤ Click the **Procedure View button** at the bottom of the Code window. Click the **down arrow** in the Procedure list box and select the **Open event** to create an event procedure.

➤ Enter the VBA statements as shown in Figure 14c. Note the following:
- Three variables are required for this procedure—the correct password, the password entered by the user, and the number of attempts.
- The user is prompted for the password, and the number of attempts is set to one. The user is given two additional attempts, if necessary, to get the password correct. The loop is bypassed, however, if the user supplies the correct password on the first attempt.

➤ Minimize Excel. Save the procedure, then click the **Run Sub button** to test it. Try different combinations in your testing; that is, enter the correct password on the first, second, and third attempts. The password is **case-sensitive**.

➤ Correct errors as they occur. Click the **Reset button** at any time to begin executing the procedure from the beginning. Save the procedure.

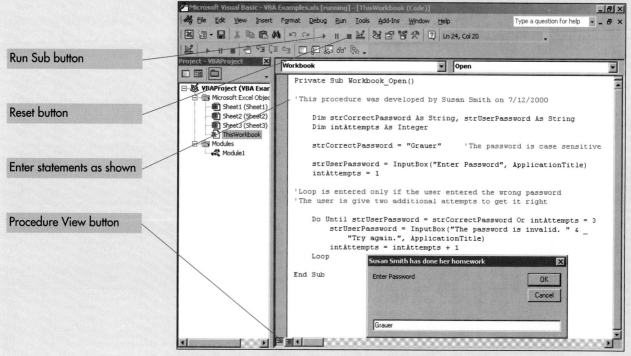

(c) Start the Open Workbook Event Procedure (step 3)

FIGURE 14   *Hands-on Exercise 4 (continued)*

THE OBJECT AND PROCEDURE BOXES

The Object box at the top of the code window displays the selected object such as an Excel workbook, whereas the Procedure box displays the name of the events appropriate to that object. Events that already have procedures appear in bold. Clicking an event that is not bold creates the procedure header and End Sub statements for that event.

Step 4:   **Complete the Open Workbook Event Procedure**

➤ Enter the remaining statements in the procedure as shown in Figure 14d. Note the following:

- The If statement determines whether the user has entered the correct password and, if so, displays the appropriate message.
- If, however, the user fails to supply the correct password, a different message is displayed, and the workbook will close due to the **Workbooks.Close statement** within the procedure.
- As a precaution, put an apostrophe in front of the Workbooks.Close statement so that it is a comment, and thus it is not executed. Once you are sure that you can enter the correct password, you can remove the apostrophe and implement the password protection.

➤ Save the procedure, then click the **Run Sub button** to test it. Be sure that you can enter the correct password (**Grauer**), and that you realize the password is case-sensitive.

➤ Delete the apostrophe in front of the Workbooks.Close statement. The text of the statement changes from green to black to indicate that it is an executable statement rather than a comment. Save the procedure.

➤ Click the **Run Sub button** a second time, then enter an incorrect password three times in a row. You will see the dialog box in Figure 14d, followed by a message reminding you to back up your workbook, and then the workbook will close.

➤ The first message makes sense, the second does not make sense in this context. Thus, we need to modify the Close Workbook procedure when an incorrect password is entered.

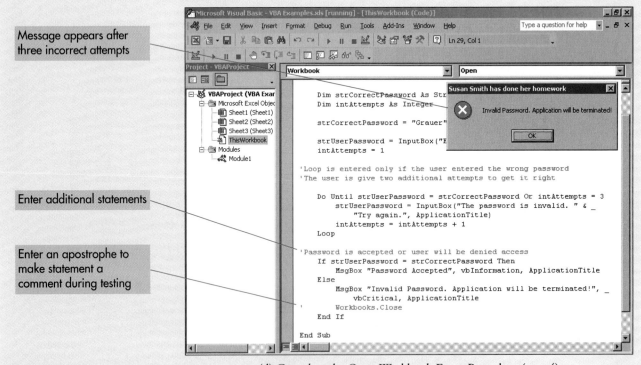

(d) Complete the Open Workbook Event Procedure (step 4)

FIGURE 14   *Hands-on Exercise 4 (continued)*

Step 5: **Modify the Before Close Event Procedure**

➤ Reopen the **VBA Examples workbook**. Click the button to **Enable Macros**.
➤ Enter the password, **Grauer** (the password is case-sensitive), press **enter**, then click **OK** when the password has been accepted.
➤ Press **Alt+F11** to reopen the VBA Editor, and (if necessary) double click **ThisWorkbook** within the list of Microsoft Excel objects.
➤ Click at the end of the line defining the ApplicationTitle constant, press **enter**, then enter the statement to define the **binNormalExit** variable as shown in Figure 14e. (The statement appears initially below the line ending the General Declarations section, but moves above the line when you press enter.)
➤ Modify the BeforeClose event procedure to include an If statement that tests the value of the binNormalExit variable as shown in Figure 14e. You must, however, set the value of this variable in the Open Workbook event procedure as described in step 6. Save the procedure.

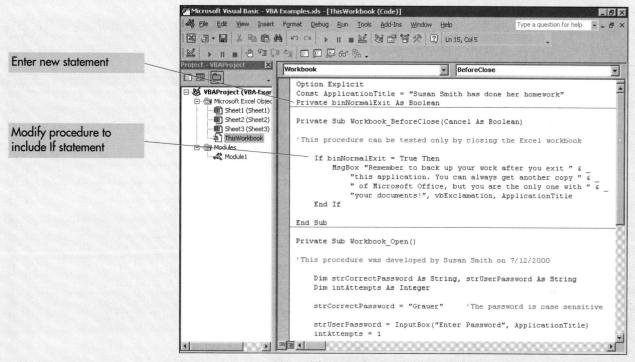

Enter new statement

Modify procedure to include If statement

(e) Modify the Before Close Event Procedure (step 5)

FIGURE 14 *Hands-on Exercise 4 (continued)*

SETTING A SWITCH

The use of a switch (binNormalExit, in this example) to control an action within a procedure is a common programming technique. The switch is set to one of two values according to events that occur within the system, then the switch is subsequently tested and the appropriate action is taken. Here, the switch is set when the workbook is opened to indicate either a valid or invalid user. The switch is then tested prior to closing the workbook to determine whether to print the closing message.

Step 6:   **Modify the Open Workbook Event Procedure**

➤ Scroll down to the Open Workbook event procedure, then modify the If statement to set the value of binNormExit as shown in Figure 14f:

- Take advantage of the Complete Word tool to enter the variable name. Type the first few letters, "binN", then press Ctrl+Space, and VBA will complete the variable name.
- The indentation within the statement is not a requirement of VBA per se, but is used to make the code easier to read. Blank lines are also added for this purpose.
- Comments appear throughout the procedure to explain its logic.
- Save the modified procedure.

➤ Click the **Run Sub button**, then enter an incorrect password three times in a row. Once again, you will see the dialog box indicating an invalid password, but this time you will not see the message reminding you to back up your workbook. The workbook closes as before.

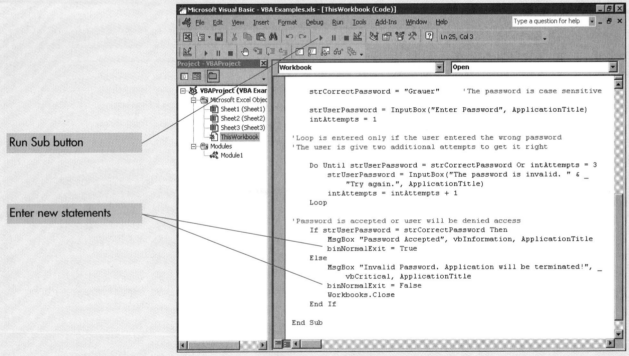

(f) Modify the Open Workbook Event Procedure (step 6)

FIGURE 14   *Hands-on Exercise 4 (continued)*

TEST UNDER ALL CONDITIONS

We cannot overemphasize the importance of thoroughly testing a procedure, and further, testing it under all conditions. VBA statements are powerful, but they are also complex, and a misplaced or omitted character can have dramatic consequences. Test every procedure completely at the time it is created, so that the logic of the procedure is fresh in your mind.

Step 7: **Open a Second Workbook**

➤ Reopen the **VBA Examples workbook**. Click the button to **Enable Macros**.
➤ Enter the password, **Grauer**, then press **enter**. Click **OK** when you see the second dialog box telling you that the password has been accepted.
➤ Pull down the **File menu** and click the **Open command** (or click the **Open button** on the Standard toolbar) and open a second workbook. We opened a workbook called **Financial Consultant**, but it does not matter which workbook you open.
➤ Pull down the **Window menu**, click the **Arrange command**, click the **Horizontal option button**, and click **OK** to tile the workbooks as shown in Figure 14g. The title bars show the names of the open workbooks.
➤ Pull down the **Tools menu**, click **Macro**, then click **Visual Basic Editor**.

Financial Consultant workbook

VBA Examples workbook

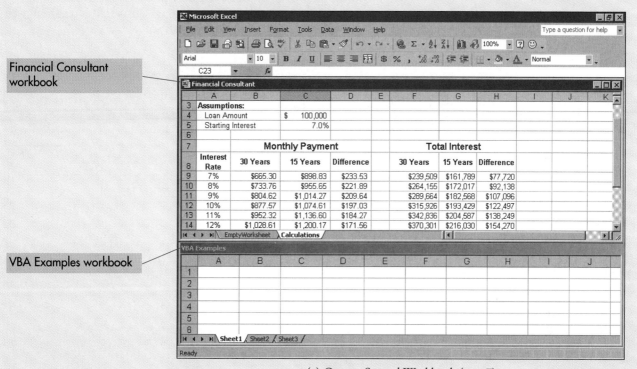

(g) Open a Second Workbook (step 7)

FIGURE 14 *Hands-on Exercise 4 (continued)*

THE COMPARISON IS CASE-SENSITIVE

Any literal comparison (e.g., strInstructorName = "Grauer") is case-sensitive, so that the user has to enter the correct name and case in order for the condition to be true. A response of "GRAUER" or "grauer", while containing the correct name, will be evaluated as false because the case does not match. You can, however, use the UCase (uppercase) function to convert the user's response to uppercase, and test accordingly. In other words, UCase(strInstructorName) = "GRAUER" will be evaluated as true if the user enters "Grauer" in any combination of upper or lowercase letters.

Step 8: **Copy the Procedure**

➤ You should be back in the Visual Basic Editor as shown in Figure 14h. Copy the procedures associated with the Open and Close Workbook events from the VBA Examples workbook to the other workbook, Financial Consultant.
  • Double click **ThisWorkbook** within the list of Microsoft Excel objects under the VBA Examples workbook.
  • Click and drag to select the definition of the ApplicationTitle constant in the General Declarations section plus the two procedures (to open and close the workbook) in their entirety.
  • Click the **Copy button** on the Standard toolbar.
  • If necessary, expand the Financial Consultant VBA Project, then double click **ThisWorkbook** with the list of Excel objects under the Financial Consultant workbook. Click underneath the **Option Explicit command**.
  • Click the **Paste button** on the Standard toolbar. The VBA code should be copied into this module as shown in Figure 14h.
➤ Click the **Save button** to save the module.

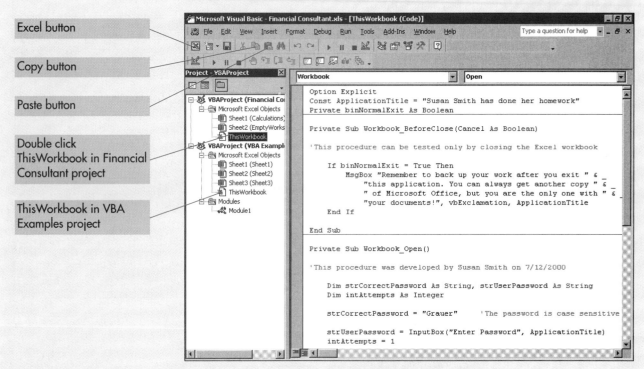

(h) Copy the Procedure (step 8)

FIGURE 14   *Hands-on Exercise 4 (continued)*

KEYBOARD SHORTCUTS—CUT, COPY, AND PASTE

Ctrl+X, Ctrl+C, and Ctrl+V are shortcuts to cut, copy, and paste, respectively, and apply to all applications in the Office suite as well as to Windows applications in general. (The shortcuts are easier to remember when you realize that the operative letters X, C, and V are next to each other at the bottom left side of the keyboard.)

Step 9: **Test the Procedure**

➤ Click the **Excel button** on the Standard toolbar within the VBA window (or click the **Excel button** on the Windows taskbar) to view the Excel workbook. Click in the window containing the Financial Consultant workbook (or whichever workbook you are using), then click the **Maximize button**.

➤ Pull down the **File menu** and click the **Close command**. (The dialog box in Figure 14i does not appear initially because the value of binNormalExit is not yet set; you have to open the workbook to set the switch.) Click **Yes** if asked whether to save the changes to the workbook.

➤ Pull down the **File menu** and reopen the workbook. Click the button to **Enable Macros**, then enter **Grauer** when prompted for the password. Click **OK** when the password has been accepted.

➤ Close this workbook, close the **VBA Examples workbook**, then pull down the **File menu** and click the **Exit command** to quit Excel.

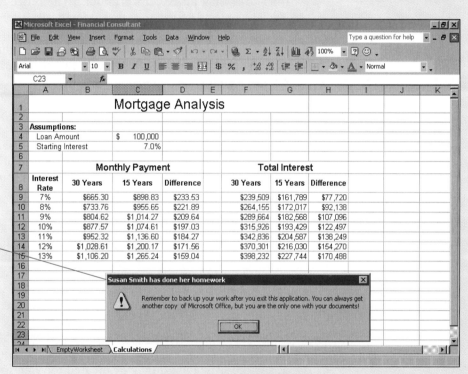

Title bar has been customized

(i) Test the Procedure (step 9)

FIGURE 14   *Hands-on Exercise 4 (continued)*

SCREEN CAPTURE

Prove to your instructor that you have completed the hands-on exercise correctly by capturing a screen, then pasting the screen into a Word document. Do the exercise until you come to the screen that you want to capture, then press the PrintScreen key at the top of the keyboard. Click the Start button to start Word and open a Word document, then pull down the Edit menu and click the Paste command to bring the captured screen into the Word document. See exercise 1 at the end of the chapter.

The same VBA procedure can be run from multiple applications in Microsoft Office, despite the fact that the applications are very different. The real power of VBA, however, is its ability to detect events that are unique to a specific application and to respond accordingly. An event is defined as any action that is recognized by an application. Opening or closing an Excel workbook or an Access database is an event. Selecting a worksheet within a workbook is also an event, as is clicking on a command button on an Access form. To use VBA within Microsoft Office, you decide which events are significant, and what is to happen when those events occur. Then you develop the appropriate *event procedures* that execute automatically when the event occurs.

Consider, for example, Figure 15, which displays the results of two event procedures in conjunction with opening and closing an Access database. (These are procedures similar to those we created in the preceding pages in conjunction with opening and closing an Excel workbook.) The procedure associated with Figure 15a displays a message that appears automatically after the user clicks the Switchboard button to exit the database. The procedure is almost trivial to write, and consists of a single MsgBox statement. The effect of the procedure is quite significant, however, as it reminds the user to back up his or her work. Indeed, you can never overemphasize the importance of adequate backup.

The dialog box in Figure 15b prompts the user for a password and appears automatically when the user opens the database. The logic here is more sophisticated in that the underlying procedure contains an InputBox statement to request the password, a Do Until loop that is executed until the user enters the correct password or exceeds the allotted number of attempts, then additional logic to display the switchboard or terminate the application if the user fails to enter the proper password. The procedure is not difficult, however, and it builds on the VBA statements that were covered earlier.

The next hands-on exercise has you create the event procedures that are associated with the database in Figure 15. The exercise references a switchboard, or user interface, that is created as a form within the database. The switchboard displays a menu that enables a nontechnical person to move easily from one object in the database (e.g., a form or report) to another.

The switchboard is created through a utility called the Switchboard Manager that prompts you for each item you want to add to the switchboard, and which action you want to be taken in conjunction with that menu item. You could do the exercise with any database, but we suggest you use the database we provide to access the switchboard that we created for you. The exercise begins, therefore, by having you download a data disk from our Web site.

EVENT-DRIVEN VERSUS TRADITIONAL PROGRAMMING

A traditional program is executed sequentially, beginning with the first line of code and continuing in order through the remainder of the program. It is the program, not the user, that determines the order in which the statements are executed. VBA, on the other hand, is event-driven, meaning that the order in which the procedures are executed depends on the events that occur. It is the user, rather than the program, that determines which events occur, and consequently which procedures are executed. Each application in Microsoft Office has a different set of objects and associated events that comprise the application's object model.

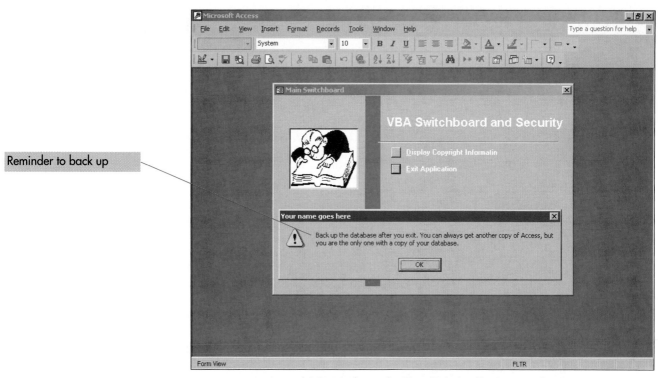

Reminder to back up

(a) Reminder to the User (Exit Application event)

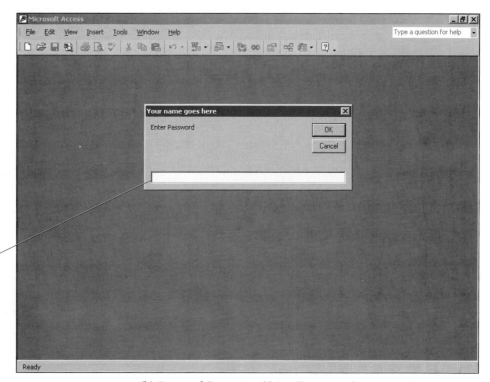

User must enter a
password

(b) Password Protection (Open Form event)

FIGURE 15   *Event-Driven Programming (Microsoft Access)*

EVENT-DRIVEN PROGRAMMING (MICROSOFT ACCESS)

Objective To implement password protection for an Access database; to create a second event procedure that displays a message to the user upon closing the database. Use Figure 16 as a guide in the exercise.

Step 1: **Open the Access Database**

> ➤ You can do this exercise with any database, but we suggest you use the database we have provided. Go to **www.prenhall.com/grauer**, click the **Office 2000 book**, click the **Student Resources tab**, then click the link to download the data disk.
> ➤ Scroll until you can select the disk for the **VBA Primer**. Download the file to the Windows desktop, then double click the file once it has been downloaded to your PC.
> ➤ Double click the file and follow the onscreen instructions to expand the self-extracting file that contains the database.
> ➤ Go to the newly created **Exploring VBA folder** and open the **VBA Switchboard and Security database** as shown in Figure 16a.
> ➤ Pull down the **Tools menu**, click the **Macro command**, then click the **Visual Basic Editor command**. Maximize the VBA Editor window.

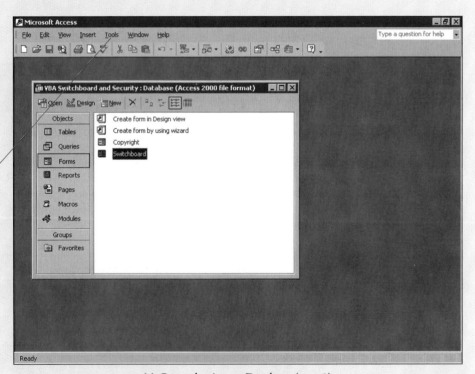

Pull down Tools menu

(a) Open the Access Database (step 1)

FIGURE 16   *Hands-on Exercise 5*

Step 2: **Create the ExitDatabase Procedure**

➤ Pull down the **Insert menu** and click **Module** to insert Module1. Complete the **General Declarations section** by adding your name to the definition of the ApplicationTitle constant as shown in Figure 16b.

➤ Pull down the **Insert menu** and click **Procedure** to insert a new procedure called **ExitDatabase**. Click the option buttons for a **Sub procedure** and for **Public scope**. Click **OK**.

➤ Complete the ExitDatabase procedure by entering the **MsgBox** and **DoCmd.Quit** statements. The DoCmd.Quit statement will close Access, but it is entered initially as a comment by beginning the line with an apostrophe.

➤ Click anywhere in the procedure, then click the **Run Sub button** to test the procedure. Correct any errors that occur, then when the MsgBox displays correctly, **delete the apostrophe** in front of the DoCmd.Quit statement.

➤ Save the module. The next time you execute the procedure, you should see the message box you just created, and then Access will be terminated.

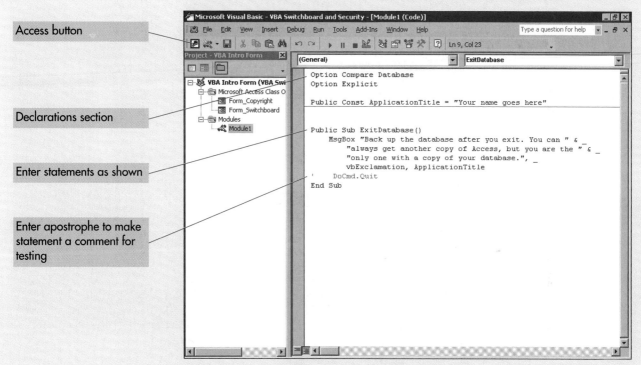

(b) Create the ExitDatabase Procedure (step 2)

FIGURE 16   *Hands-on Exercise 5 (continued)*

CREATE A PUBLIC CONSTANT

Give your application a customized look by adding your name or other identifying message to the title bar of the message and/or input boxes that you use. You can add the information individually to each statement, but it is easier to declare a public constant from within a general module. That way, you can change the value of the constant in one place and have the change reflected automatically throughout your application.

Step 3: **Modify the Switchboard**

➤ Click the **Access button** on the Standard toolbar within the VBA window to switch to the Database window (or use the **F11** keyboard shortcut).

➤ Pull down the **Tools menu**, click the **Database Utilities command**, then choose **Switchboard Manager** to display the Switchboard Manager dialog box in Figure 16c.

➤ Click the **Edit button** to edit the Main Switchboard and display the Edit Switchboard Page dialog box. Select the **&Exit Application command** and click its **Edit button** to display the Edit Switchboard Item dialog box.

➤ Change the command to **Run Code**. Enter **ExitDatabase** in the Function Name text box. Click **OK**, then close the two other dialog boxes. The switchboard has been modified so that clicking the Exit button will run the VBA procedure you just created.

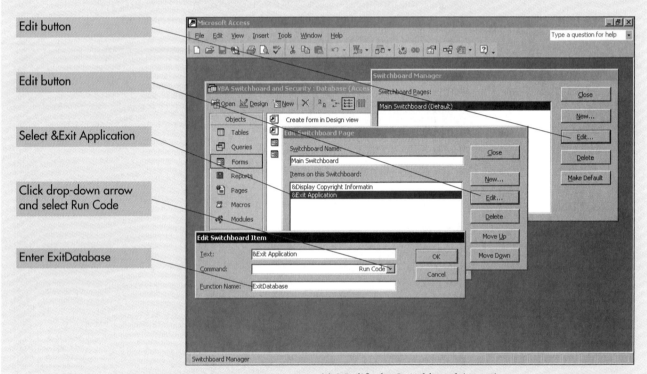

Edit button

Edit button

Select &Exit Application

Click drop-down arrow and select Run Code

Enter ExitDatabase

(c) Modify the Switchboard (step 3)

FIGURE 16 *Hands-on Exercise 5 (continued)*

CREATE A KEYBOARD SHORTCUT

The & has special significance when used within the name of an Access object because it creates a keyboard shortcut to that object. Enter "&Exit Application", for example, and the letter E (the letter immediately after the ampersand) will be underlined and appear as "Exit Application" on the switchboard. From there, you can execute the item by clicking its button, or you can use the Alt+E keyboard shortcut (where "E" is the underlined letter in the menu option).

Step 4:   **Test the Switchboard**

➤ If necessary, click the **Forms tab** in the Database window. Double click the **Switchboard form** to open the switchboard as shown in Figure 16d. The switchboard contains two commands.

➤ Click the **Display Copyright Information command** to display a form that we use with all our databases. (You can open this form in Design view and modify the text to include your name, rather than ours. If you do, be sure to save the modified form, then close it.)

➤ Click the **Exit Application command** (or use the **Alt+E** keyboard shortcut). You should see the dialog box in Figure 16d, corresponding to the MsgBox statement you created earlier. Click **OK** to close the dialog box.

➤ Access itself will terminate because of the DoCmd.Quit statement within the ExitDatabase procedure. (If this does not happen, return to the VBA Editor and remove the apostrophe in front of the DoCmd statement.)

Double click Switchboard form

Forms tab

Click Exit Application button

Click OK

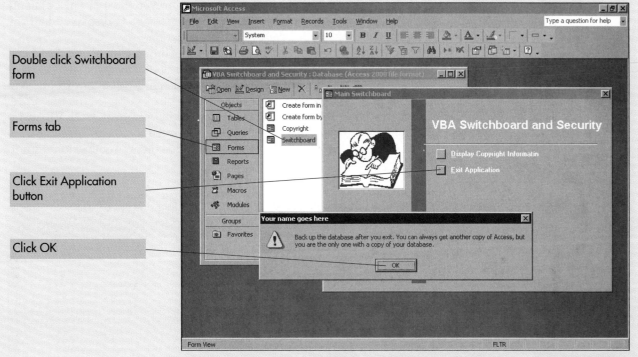

(d) Test the Switchboard (step 4)

FIGURE 16   *Hands-on Exercise 5 (continued)*

BACK UP IMPORTANT FILES

It's not a question of if it will happen, but when—hard disks die, files are lost, or viruses may infect a system. It has happened to us and it will happen to you, but you can prepare for the inevitable by creating adequate backup before the problem occurs. The essence of a backup strategy is to decide which files to back up, how often to do the backup, and where to keep the backup. Do it!

Step 5:   **Complete the Open Form Event Procedure**

➤ Start Access and reopen the **VBA Switchboard and Security database**. Press **Alt+F11** to start the VBA Editor. Click the **plus sign** next to Microsoft Access Class objects, double click the module called **Form_Switchboard**, then look for the **Form_Open procedure** as shown in Figure 16e.

➤ The procedure was created automatically by the Switchboard Manager. You must, however, expand this procedure to include password protection. Note the following:

- Three variables are required—the correct password, the password entered by the user, and the number of attempts.

- The user is prompted for the password, and the number of attempts is set to one. The user is given two additional attempts, if necessary, to get the correct password.

- The If statement at the end of the loop determines whether the user has entered the correct password, and if so, it executes the original commands that are associated with the switchboard. If, however, the user fails to supply the correct password, an invalid password message is displayed and the **DoCmd.Quit** statement terminates the application.

- We suggest you place an **apostrophe** in front of the statement initially so that it becomes a comment, and thus it is not executed. Once you are sure that you can enter the correct password, you can remove the apostrophe and implement the password protection.

➤ Save the procedure. You cannot test this procedure from within the VBA window; you must cause the event to happen (i.e., open the form) for the procedure to execute. Click the **Access button** on the Standard toolbar to return to the Database window.

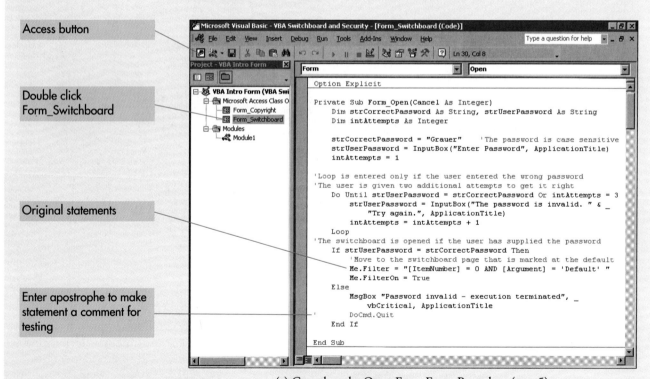

(e) Complete the Open Form Event Procedure (step 5)

FIGURE 16   *Hands-on Exercise 5 (continued)*

Step 6:   **Test the Procedure**

➤ Close all open windows within the Access database except for the Database window. Click the **Forms tab**, then double click the **Switchboard Form**.

➤ You should be prompted for the password as shown in Figure 16f. The password (in our procedure) is **Grauer**.

➤ Test the procedure repeatedly to include all possibilities. Enter the correct password on the first, second, and third attempts to be sure that the procedure works as intended. Each time you enter the correct password, you will have to close the switchboard, then reopen it.

➤ Test the procedure one final time, by failing to enter the correct password. You will see a message box indicating that the password is invalid and that execution will be terminated. Termination will not take place, however, because the DoCmd.Quit statement is currently entered as a comment.

➤ Press **Alt+F11** to reopen the VBA Editor. Delete the apostrophe in front of the DoCmd.Quit statement. The text of the statement changes from green to black to indicate that it is an executable statement. Save the procedure.

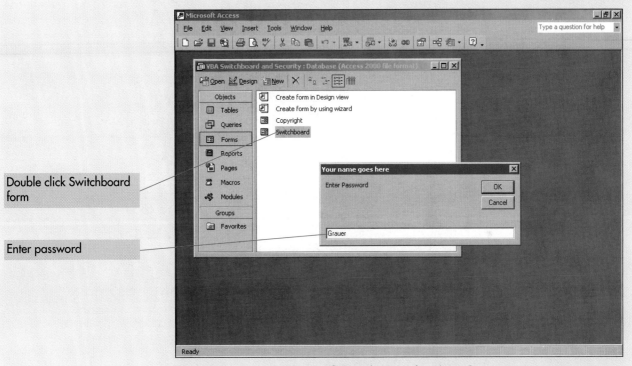

Double click Switchboard form

Enter password

(f) Test the Procedure (step 6)

FIGURE 16   *Hands-on Exercise 5 (continued)*

TOGGLE COMMENTS ON AND OFF

Comments are used primarily to explain the purpose of VBA statements, but they can also be used to "comment out" code as distinct from deleting the statement altogether. Thus you can add or remove the apostrophe in front of the statement, to toggle the comment on or off.

Step 7: **Change the Startup Properties**

➤ Click the **Access button** on the VBA Standard toolbar to return to the Database window. Pull down the **Tools menu** and click **Startup** to display the Startup dialog box as shown in Figure 16g.

➤ Click in the **Application Title** text box and enter the title of the application, **VBA Switchboard and Security** in this example.

➤ Click the **drop-down arrow** in the Display Form/Page list box and select the **Switchboard form** as the form that will open automatically in conjunction with opening the database.

➤ Clear the check box to display the Database window. Click **OK** to accept the settings and close the dialog box. The next time you open the database, the switchboard should open automatically, which in turn triggers the Open Form event procedure that will prompt the user to enter a password.

➤ Close the Switchboard form.

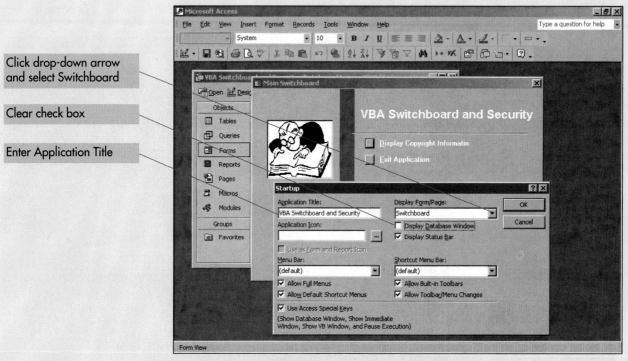

Click drop-down arrow and select Switchboard

Clear check box

Enter Application Title

(g) Change the Startup Properties (step 7)

FIGURE 16 *Hands-on Exercise 5 (continued)*

HIDE THE DATABASE WINDOW

Use the Startup property to hide the Database window from the novice user. You avoid confusion and you may prevent the novice from accidentally deleting objects in the database. Of course, anyone with some knowledge of Access can restore the Database window by pulling down the Window menu, clicking the Unhide command, then selecting the Database window from the associated dialog box. Nevertheless, hiding the Database window is a good beginning.

Step 8: **Test the Database**

➤ Close the database, then reopen the database to test the procedures we have created in this exercise. The sequence of events is as follows:

- The database is loaded and the switchboard is opened but is not yet visible. The Open Form procedure for the switchboard is executed, and you are prompted for the password as shown in Figure 16h.
- The password is entered correctly and the switchboard is displayed. The Database window is hidden, however, because the Startup Properties have been modified.

➤ Click the **Exit Application command** (or use the **Alt+E** keyboard shortcut). You will see the message box reminding you to back up the system, after which the database is closed and Access is terminated.

➤ Testing is complete and you can go on to add the other objects to your Access database. Congratulations on a job well done.

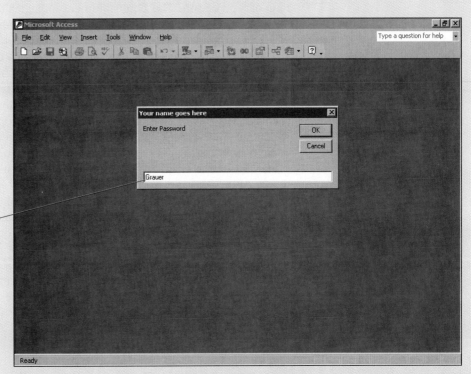

Enter password

(h) Test the Database (step 8)

FIGURE 16   *Hands-on Exercise 5 (continued)*

HIDE MENUS AND TOOLBARS

You can use the Startup property to hide menus and/or toolbars from the user by clearing the respective check boxes. A word of caution, however—once the menus are hidden, it is difficult to get them back. Start Access, pull down the File menu, and click Open to display the Open dialog box, select the database to open, then press and hold the Shift key when you click the Open button. This powerful technique is not widely known.

Visual Basic for Applications (VBA) is a powerful programming language that is accessible from all major applications in Microsoft Office XP. A VBA statement accomplishes a specific task such as displaying a message to the user or accepting input from the user. Statements are grouped into procedures, and procedures in turn are grouped into modules. Every procedure is classified as either private or public.

The MsgBox statement displays information to the user. It has one required argument, which is the message (or prompt) that is displayed to the user. The other two arguments, the icon that is to be displayed in the dialog box and the text of the title bar, are optional. The InputBox function displays a prompt to the user requesting information, then it stores that information (the value returned by the user) for use later in the procedure.

Every variable must be declared (defined) before it can be used. This is accomplished through the Dim (short for Dimension) statement that appears at the beginning of a procedure. The Dim statement indicates the name of the variable and its type (for example, whether it will hold a character string or an integer number), which in turn reserves the appropriate amount of memory for that variable.

The ability to make decisions within a procedure, then branch to alternative sets of statements is implemented through the If . . . Then . . . Else or Case statements. The Else clause is optional, but may be repeated multiple times within an If statement. The Case statement is preferable to an If statement with multiple Else clauses.

The For . . . Next statement (or For . . . Next loop as it is also called) executes all statements between the words For and Next a specified number of times, using a counter to keep track of the number of times the loop is executed. The Do . . . Loop Until and/or Do Until . . . Loop statements are used when the number of times through the loop is not known in advance.

VBA is different from traditional programming languages in that it is event-driven. An event is defined as any action that is recognized by an application, such as Excel or Access. Opening or closing an Excel workbook or an Access database is an event. Selecting a worksheet within a workbook is also an event, as is clicking on a command button on an Access form. To use VBA within Microsoft Office, you decide which events are significant, and what is to happen when those events occur. Then you develop the appropriate event procedures.

KEY TERMS

Argument (p. 2)
Case statement (p. 18)
Character string (p. 16)
Comment (p. 6)
Compilation error (p. 30)
Complete Word tool (p. 22)
Concatenate (p. 4)
Custom toolbar (p. 19)
Debug menu (p. 30)
Debug toolbar (p. 30)
Debug.Print statement (p. 31)
Debugging (p. 30)
Declarations section (p. 6)
Dim statement (p. 5)
Do Loops (p. 29)
Else clause (p. 16)
End Sub statement (p. 3)
Event (p. 41)

Event procedure (Access) (p. 52)
Event procedure (Excel) (p. 41)
Execution error (p. 30)
For . . . Next Statement (p. 28)
Full Module view (p. 21)
Help (p. 15)
If statement (p. 16)
Immediate window (p. 31)
InputBox function (p. 4)
Intrinsic constant (p. 3)
Literal (p. 16)
Locals window (p. 31)
Macro (p. 2)
Macro recorder (p. 2)
Module (p. 2)
MsgBox statement (p. 3)
Object box (p. 45)
Option Explicit (p. 6)

Private procedure (p. 2)
Procedure (p. 2)
Procedure box (p. 45)
Procedure header (p. 3)
Procedure view (p. 21)
Project Explorer (p. 6)
Public procedure (p. 2)
Quick Info (p. 9)
Run-time error (p. 30)
Statement (p. 2)
Step Into button (p. 31)
Syntax (p. 2)
Underscore (p. 4)
Variable (p. 4)
VBA (p. 1)
Visual Basic Editor (p. 6)
Visual Basic for Applications (p. 2)

1. Which of the following applications in Office XP has access to VBA?
   (a) Word
   (b) Excel
   (c) Access
   (d) All of the above

2. Which of the following is a valid name for a VBA variable?
   (a) Public
   (b) Private
   (c) strUserFirstName
   (d) int Count Of Attempts

3. Which of the following is true about an If statement?
   (a) It evaluates a condition as either true or false, then executes the statement(s) following the keyword "Then" if the condition is true
   (b) It must contain the keyword Else
   (c) It must contain one or more ElseIf statements
   (d) All of the above

4. Which of the following lists the items from smallest to largest?
   (a) Module, procedure, statement
   (b) Statement, module, procedure
   (c) Statement, procedure, module
   (d) Procedure, module, statement

5. Given the statement, MsgBox "Welcome to VBA" , , "Bob was here", which of the following is true?
   (a) "Welcome to VBA" will be displayed within the resulting message box
   (b) "Welcome to VBA" will appear on the title bar of the displayed dialog box
   (c) The two adjacent commas will cause a compilation error
   (d) An informational icon will be displayed with the message

6. Where are the VBA procedures associated with an Office document stored?
   (a) In the same folder, but in a separate file
   (b) In the Office document itself
   (c) In a special VBA folder on drive C
   (d) In a special VBA folder on the local area network

7. The Debug.Print statement is associated with the:
   (a) Locals window
   (b) Immediate window
   (c) Project Explorer
   (d) Debug toolbar

8. Which of the following is the proper sequence of arguments for the MsgBox statement?
   (a) Text for the title bar, prompt, button
   (b) Prompt, button, text for the title bar
   (c) Prompt, text for the title bar, button
   (d) Button, prompt, text for the title bar

9. Which of the following is a true statement about Do loops?
   (a) Placing the Until clause at the beginning of the loop tests the condition prior to executing any statements in the loop
   (b) Placing the Until clause at the end of the loop executes the statements in the loop, then it tests the condition
   (c) Both (a) and (b)
   (d) Neither (a) nor (b)

10. Given the statement, For intCount = 1 to 10 Step 3, how many times will the statements in the loop be executed (assuming that there are no statements in the loop to terminate the execution)?
    (a) 10
    (b) 4
    (c) 3
    (d) Impossible to determine

11. Which of the following is a *false* statement?
    (a) A dash at the end of a line indicates continuation
    (b) An ampersand indicates concatenation
    (c) An apostrophe at the beginning of a line signifies a comment
    (d) A pair of quotation marks denotes a character string

12. What is the effect of deleting the apostrophe that appears at the beginning of a VBA statement?
    (a) A compilation error will occur
    (b) The statement is converted to a comment
    (c) The color of the statement will change from black to green
    (d) The statement is made executable

13. Which of the following If statements will display the indicated message if the user enters a response other than "Grauer" (assuming that "Grauer" is the correct password)?
    (a) If strUserResponse <> "Grauer" Then MsgBox "Wrong password"
    (b) If strUserResponse = "Grauer" Then MsgBox "Wrong password"
    (c) If strUserResponse > "Grauer" Then MsgBox "Wrong password"
    (d) If strUserResponse < "Grauer" Then MsgBox "Wrong password"

14. Which of the following will execute the statements in the loop at least once?
    (a) Do ... Loop Until
    (b) Do Until ..... Loop
    (c) Both (a) and (b)
    (d) Neither (a) nor (b)

15. The copy and paste commands can be used to:
    (a) Copy statements within a procedure
    (b) Copy statements from a procedure in one module to a procedure in another module within the same document
    (c) Copy statements from a module in an Excel workbook to a module in an Access database
    (d) All of the above

ANSWERS

1. d	6. b	11. a
2. c	7. b	12. d
3. a	8. b	13. a
4. c	9. c	14. a
5. a	10. b	15. a

BUILDS ON

HANDS-ON
EXERCISE 4
PAGES 43–51

1. **Screen Capture:** The ability to capture a screen, then print the captured screen as part of a document, is very useful. The Word document in Figure 17, for example, captures the Excel screen as a workbook is opened, with the dialog box in place.

    Open the completed workbook from the fourth hands-on exercise. Press the PrintScreen key when prompted for the password to copy the screen to the Windows clipboard, an area of memory that is accessible to any Windows application. Next, start (or switch to) a Word document, and then execute the Paste command in the Edit menu to paste the contents of the clipboard into the current document. That's all there is to it. The screen is now part of the Word document, where it can be moved and sized like any other Windows object. Print the Word document for your instructor.

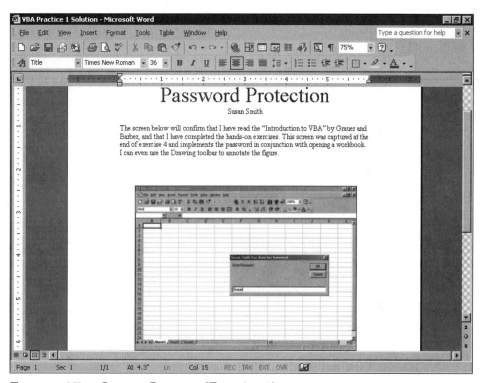

FIGURE 17 *Screen Capture (Exercise 1)*

2. **VBA in a Word Document:** Everything that you have learned with respect to creating VBA event procedures in Excel or Access is also applicable to Microsoft Word. Accordingly, start Microsoft Word and create the document in Figure 18. Read the document carefully, then create the Document_Close event procedure to display the indicated message box, adding your name to the title bar. Prove to your professor that you have completed this assignment by capturing the screen in Figure 18, as described in the previous exercise.

BUILDS ON

HANDS-ON
EXERCISE 4
PAGES 43–51

3. **The Before Print Event:** Open the Excel workbook that you used in the fourth hands-on exercise to create an event procedure associated with the Before_Print event. The procedure is to contain a MsgBox statement to remind the user to print a workbook with both displayed values and cell contents as shown in Figure 19.

    The easiest way to switch between the two views is to press Ctrl+~. (The tilde is located at the upper-left of the keyboard.) Prove to your professor that you have completed this assignment by capturing the screen in Figure 19.

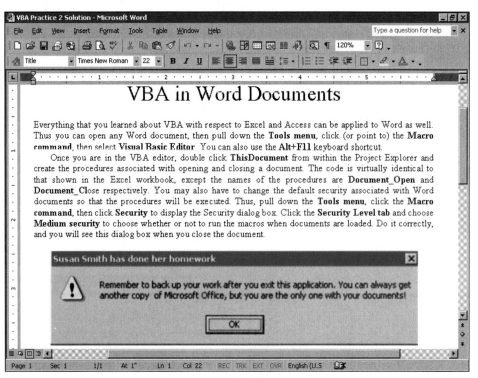

FIGURE 18 *VBA in a Word Document (Exercise 2)*

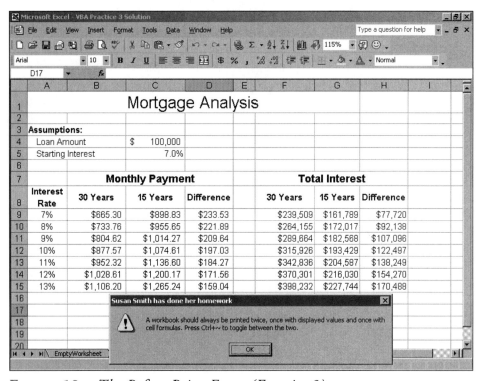

FIGURE 19 *The Before Print Event (Exercise 3)*

BUILDS ON

HANDS-ON
EXERCISE 5
PAGES 54–61

4. **The On Click Event:** Open the Access database that you used in the fifth hands-on exercise to create an event procedure associated with the On Click event for the indicated command button.

   a. Open the Copyright form from the switchboard, then change to the Design view. Modify the form so that it contains your name rather than ours.

   b. Right click the Technical Support button to display a context-sensitive menu, click Properties, click the Event tab, then select the On Click event. Click the Build button, select Code Builder as shown in Figure 20, and click OK.

   c. The VBA Editor will position you within the On Click event procedure for the command button. All you need to do is add a single MsgBox statement to identify yourself as "Tech Support". Be sure to include the parameter to display your name on the title bar of the message box.

   d. Save the form, then go to form view and click the button to view the message box you just created. Prove to your professor that you have completed this assignment by capturing the associated screen, as described in exercise 1.

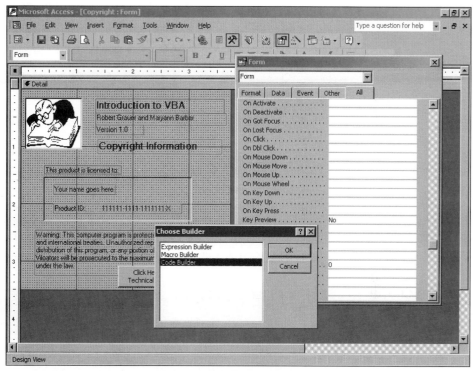

FIGURE 20 *The On Click Event (Exercise 4)*

5. **The Option Explicit Statement:** The Option Explicit statement should appear at the beginning of every module, but this is not a VBA requirement, only a suggestion from the authors. Omitting the statement can have serious consequences in that the results of a procedure are incorrect, a point that is illustrated in Figure 21.

   a. What is the answer that is displayed in the message box of Figure 21? What is the answer that should be displayed?

   b. Look at the statements within the For ... Next loop to see if you can detect the reason for the error. (*Hint:* Look closely at the variable names.)

   c. What does the Option Explicit statement do? How would including the statement in the procedure of Figure 21 help to ensure the correct result?

   d. Summarize your answers in a note to your instructor.

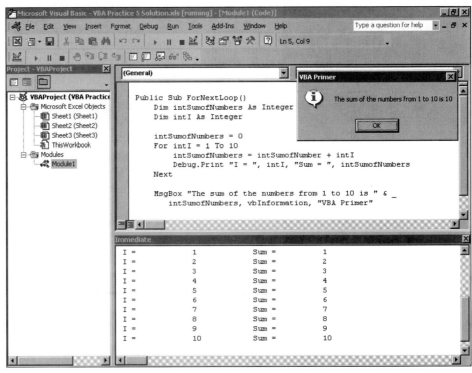

FIGURE 21   *The Option Explicit Statement (Exercise 5)*

6. String Processing: The procedure in Figure 22 illustrates various string processing functions to validate a user's e-mail address. Answer the following:
   a. What are the specific checks that are implemented to check the user's
      e-mail address? Are these checks reasonable?
   b. What does the VBA Len function do? What does the InStr function do? (Use
      the VBA Help menu to learn more about these functions.)
   c. What is the purpose of the variable binValidEmail within the procedure?

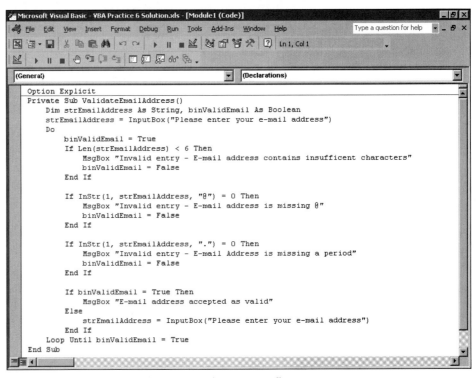

FIGURE 22   *String Processing (Exercise 6)*

BUILDS ON

HANDS-ON
EXERCISE 4
PAGES 43–51

7. Hiding a Worksheet: Figure 23 expands on the procedure to implement password protection in an Excel workbook by hiding the worksheet until the correct password has been entered.

a. What additional statements have been added to the procedure in Figure 23 that were not present in Hands-on Exercise 4? What is the purpose of each statement?

b. What statement could you add to the procedure to hide the empty worksheet after the correct password has been entered?

c. Summarize your answers in a note to your instructor.

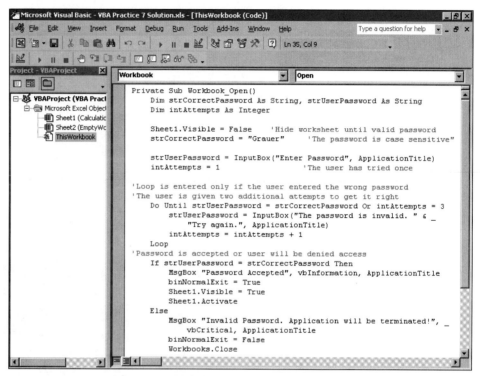

FIGURE 23   *Hiding a Worksheet (Exercise 7)*

8. Help with VBA: Help is just a mouse click away and it is invaluable. Use the Help facility to look up detailed information that expands a topic that was discussed in the chapter. The screen in Figure 24, for example, explains the integer data type and its use within a Dim statement. The information is quite detailed, but if you read carefully, you will generally find the answer. Print three different Help-screens for your instructor.

9. Invoking a Procedure: The same statement (or set of statements) is often executed from many places within a single procedure or from multiple procedures within an application. You can duplicate the code as necessary, but it is far more efficient to create a single procedure that contains the repeated statements, and then invoke that procedure. The advantage to this approach is that you have to write (or modify) the procedure only once.

The module in Figure 25 illustrates how this is accomplished. The History-Quiz procedure asks the user multiple questions, then displays one of two messages, depending on whether the response is correct. These messages are contained in two separate procedures, then the appropriate procedure (CorrectAnswer or IncorrectAnswer) is called from within the HistoryQuiz procedure, depending on whether the user's answer is right or wrong. Create and test the module in Figure 25 to be sure you understand this technique.

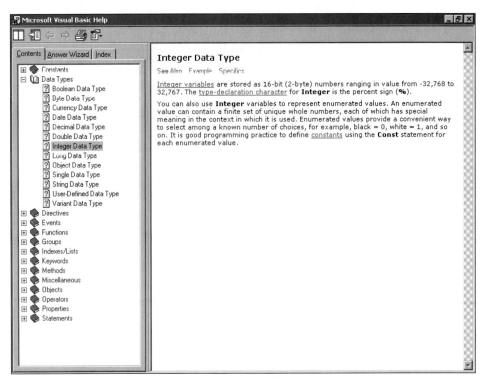

FIGURE 24   *Help with VBA (Exercise 8)*

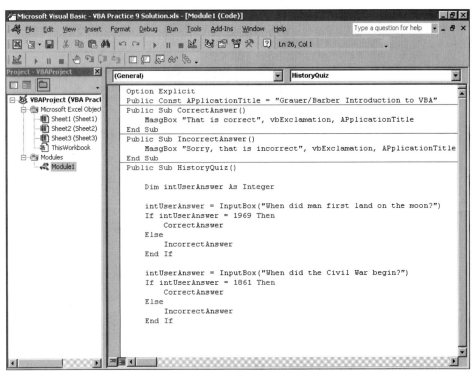

FIGURE 25   *Invoking a Procedure (Exercise 9)*

10. The MsgBox Function: The procedure in Figure 26 shows how the MsgBox statement can accept information from the user and branch accordingly. A simple MsgBox statement merely displays a message. If, however, you enclose the parameters of the MsgBox statement in parentheses, it becomes a function and returns a value (in this example, a mouse click indicating whether the user clicked yes or no). The use of parentheses requires that you include a second parameter such as vbYesNo to display the Yes and No command buttons. You then embed the MsgBox function within an If statement that tests for the intrinsic contstants, vbYes and vbNo, respectively.

You can concatenate the vbYesNo intrinsic constant with another constant such as vbQuestion to display an icon next to the buttons as shown in Figure 26. You can also use other intrinsic constants such as vbOKCancel to display different sets of command buttons.

Add the procedure in Figure 26 to the VBA Examples workbook (or Access database) that you created in the chapter. Print the procedure for your instructor.

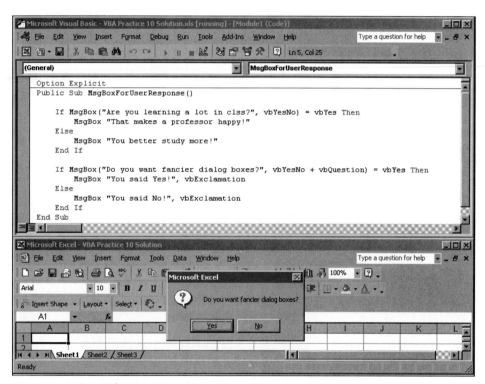

FIGURE 26 *The MsgBox Function (Exercise 10)*

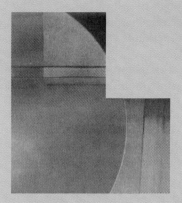

Essentials of
Microsoft® Windows®

OBJECTIVES

AFTER READING THIS SUPPLEMENT YOU WILL BE ABLE TO:

1. Describe the objects on the Windows desktop; use the icons on the desktop to start the associated applications.
2. Explain the significance of the common user interface; identify the elements that are present in every window.
3. Explain in general terms the similarities and differences between various versions of Windows.
4. Use the Help command to learn about Windows.
5. Format a floppy disk.
6. Differentiate between a program file and a data file; explain the significance of the icons that appear next to a file in My Computer and Windows Explorer.
7. Explain how folders are used to organize the files on a disk; use the View menu and/or the Folder Options command to change the appearance of a folder.
8. Distinguish between My Computer and Windows Explorer with respect to viewing files and folders; explain the advantages of the hierarchical view available within Windows Explorer.
9. Use Internet Explorer to download a file; describe how to view a Web page from within Windows Explorer.
10. Copy and/or move a file from one folder to another; delete a file, then recover the deleted file from the Recycle Bin.

OVERVIEW

Microsoft® Windows is a computer program (actually many programs) that controls the operation of a computer and its peripherals. The Windows environment provides a common user interface and consistent command structure for every application. You have seen the interface many times, but do you really understand it? Can

1

you move and copy files with confidence? Do you know how to back up the Excel spreadsheets, Access databases, and other Office documents that you work so hard to create? If not, now is the time to learn. This section is written for you, the computer novice, and it assumes no previous knowledge.

We begin with an introduction to the Windows desktop, the graphical user interface that enables you to work in intuitive fashion by pointing at icons and clicking the mouse. We identify the basic components of a window and describe how to execute commands and supply information through different elements in a dialog box. We introduce you to My Computer, an icon on the Windows desktop, and show you how to use My Computer to access the various components of your system. We also describe how to access the Help command.

The supplement concentrates, however, on disk and file management. We present the basic definitions of a file and a folder, then describe how to use My Computer to look for a specific file or folder. We introduce Windows Explorer, which provides a more efficient way of finding data on your system, then show you how to move or copy a file from one folder to another. We discuss other basic operations, such as renaming and deleting a file. We also describe how to recover a deleted file (if necessary) from the Recycle Bin.

There are also four hands-on exercises, which enable you to apply the conceptual discussion in the text at the computer. The exercises refer to a set of practice files (data disk) that we have created for you. You can obtain these files from our Web site (www.prenhall.com/grauer) or from a local area network if your professor has downloaded the files for you.

THE DESKTOP

Windows 95 was the first of the so-called "modern Windows" and was followed by Windows NT, Windows 98, Windows 2000, Windows Me (Millennium edition), and most recently, by Windows XP. Each of these systems is still in use. Windows 98 and its successor, Windows Me, are geared for the home user and provide extensive support for games and peripheral devices. Windows NT, and its successor Windows 2000, are aimed at the business user and provide increased security and reliability. Windows XP is the successor to all current breeds of Windows. It has a slightly different look, but maintains the conventions of its various predecessors. Hence we have called this module "Essentials of Microsoft Windows" and refer to Windows in a generic sense. (The screens were taken from Windows 2000 Professional, but could just as easily have been taken from other versions of the operating system.)

All versions of Windows create a working environment for your computer that parallels the working environment at home or in an office. You work at a desk. Windows operations take place on the *desktop* as shown in Figure 1. There are physical objects on a desk such as folders, a dictionary, a calculator, or a phone. The computer equivalents of those objects appear as icons (pictorial symbols) on the desktop. Each object on a real desk has attributes (properties) such as size, weight, and color. In similar fashion, Windows assigns properties to every object on its desktop. And just as you can move the objects on a real desk, you can rearrange the objects on the Windows desktop.

Figure 1a displays the typical desktop that appears when Windows is installed on a new computer. It has only a few objects and is similar to the desk in a new office, just after you move in. This desktop might have been taken from any of five systems—Windows 95, Windows NT, Windows 98, Windows 2000, or Windows Me—and is sometimes called "Classic Windows." The icons on this desktop are opened by double clicking. (It is possible to display an alternate desktop with underlined icons that are opened by single clicking, but that option is rarely used.) Figure 1b shows the new Windows XP desktop as it might appear on a home computer, where individual accounts are established for different users.

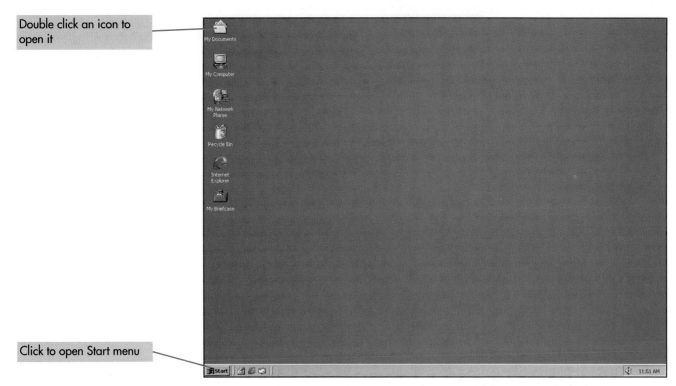

Double click an icon to open it

Click to open Start menu

(a) Windows 95, Windows NT, Windows 98, Windows Me, and Windows 2000

Individual desktops are established for different users

(b) Windows XP

FIGURE 1   *The Different Faces of Windows*

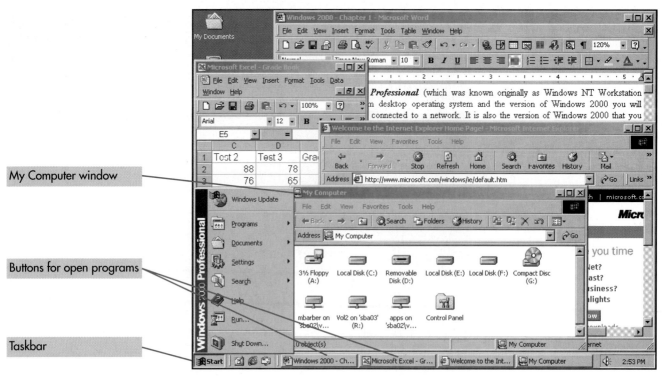

My Computer window

Buttons for open programs

Taskbar

(c) A Working Desktop (all versions of Windows)

FIGURE 1   *The Different Faces of Windows (continued)*

Do not be concerned if your desktop is different from ours. Your real desk is arranged differently from those of your friends, just as your Windows desktop will also be different. Moreover, you are likely to work on different systems—at school, at work, or at home, and thus it is important that you recognize the common functionality that is present on all desktops. The *Start button*, as its name suggests, is where you begin. Click the Start button and you see a menu that lets you start any program installed on your computer.

Look now at Figure 1c, which displays an entirely different desktop, one with four open windows that is similar to a desk in the middle of a working day. Each window in Figure 1c displays a program that is currently in use. The ability to run several programs at the same time is known as *multitasking*, and it is a major benefit of the Windows environment. Multitasking enables you to run a word processor in one window, create a spreadsheet in a second window, surf the Internet in a third window, play a game in a fourth window, and so on. You can work in a program as long as you want, then change to a different program by clicking its window.

You can also change from one program to another by using the taskbar at the bottom of the desktop. The *taskbar* contains a button for each open program, and it enables you to switch back and forth between those programs by clicking the appropriate button. The taskbar in Figure 1a does not contain any buttons (other than the Start button) since there are no open applications. The taskbar in Figure 1c, however, contains four additional buttons, one for each open window.

The icons on the desktop are used to access programs or other functions. The *My Computer* icon is the most basic. It enables you to view the devices on your system, including the drives on a local area network to which you have direct access. Open My Computer in either Figure 1a or 1b, for example, and you see the objects in the My Computer window of Figure 1c. The contents of My Computer depend on the hardware of the specific computer system. Our system, for example, has one floppy drive, three local (hard or fixed) disks, a removable disk (an Iomega Zip drive), a CD-ROM, and access to various network drives. The My Computer window also contains the Control Panel folder that provides access to functions that control other elements of your computing environment. (These capabilities are not used by beginners, are generally "off limits" in a lab environment, and thus are not discussed further.)

The other icons on the desktop are also noteworthy. The *My Documents* folder is a convenient place in which to store the documents you create. *My Network Places* extends the view of your computer to include the other local area networks (if any) that your computer can access, provided you have a valid username and password. The *Recycle Bin* enables you to restore a file that was previously deleted. The Internet Explorer icon starts *Internet Explorer*, the Web browser that is built into the Windows operating system.

THE DOJ (DEPARTMENT OF JUSTICE) VERSUS MICROSOFT

A simple icon is at the heart of the multibillion dollar lawsuit brought by 19 states against Microsoft. In short, Microsoft is accused of integrating its Internet Explorer browser into the Windows operating system with the goal of dominating the market and eliminating the competition. Is Internet Explorer built into every current version of Microsoft Windows? Yes. Can Netscape Navigator run without difficulty under every current version of Microsoft Windows? The answer is also yes. As of this writing the eventual outcome of the case against Microsoft has yet to be determined.

THE COMMON USER INTERFACE

All Windows applications share a *common user interface* and possess a consistent command structure. This means that every Windows application works essentially the same way, which provides a sense of familiarity from one application to the next. In other words, once you learn the basic concepts and techniques in one application, you can apply that knowledge to every other application. Consider, for example, Figure 2, which shows open windows for My Computer and My Network Places, and labels the essential elements in each.

The contents of the two windows are different, but each window has the same essential elements. The *title bar* appears at the top of each window and displays the name of the window, My Computer and My Network Places in Figure 2a and 2b, respectively. The icon at the extreme left of the title bar identifies the window and also provides access to a control menu with operations relevant to the window such as moving it or sizing it. The *minimize button* shrinks the window to a button on the taskbar, but leaves the window in memory. The *maximize button* enlarges the window so that it takes up the entire desktop. The *restore button* (not shown in either figure) appears instead of the maximize button after a window has been maximized, and restores the window to its previous size. The *close button* closes the window and removes it from memory and the desktop.

The *menu bar* appears immediately below the title bar and provides access to *pull-down menus*. One or more *toolbars* appear below the menu bar and let you execute a command by clicking a button as opposed to pulling down a menu. The *status bar* at the bottom of the window displays information about the window as a whole or about a selected object within a window.

A vertical (or horizontal) *scroll bar* appears at the right (or bottom) border of a window when its contents are not completely visible and provides access to the unseen areas. A scroll bar does not appear in Figure 2a since all of the objects in the window are visible at the same time. A vertical scroll bar is found in Figure 2b, however, since there are other objects in the window.

Title bar

Menu bar

Toolbars

Minimize button

Maximize button

Close button

Status bar

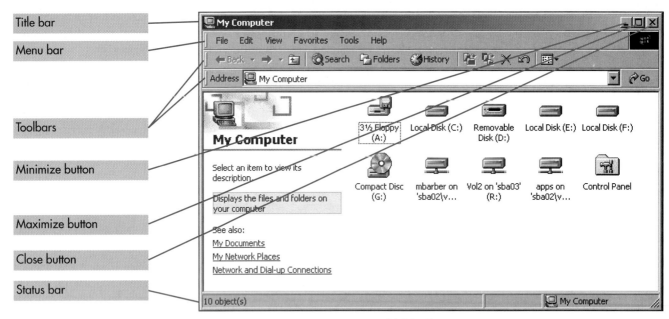

(a) My Computer

Title bar

Menu bar

Toolbars

Minimize button

Maximize button

Close button

Scroll bar

Status bar

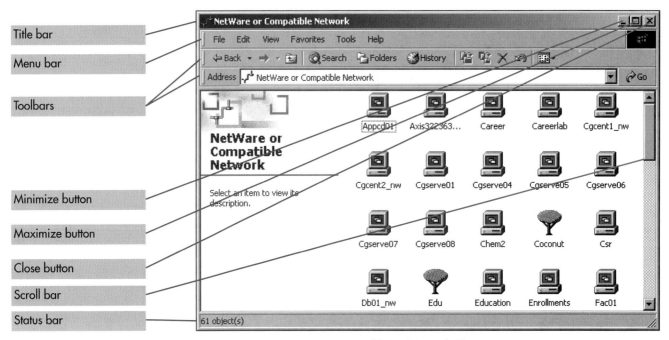

(b) My Network Places

FIGURE 2   *Anatomy of a Window*

ESSENTIALS OF MICROSOFT WINDOWS

Moving and Sizing a Window

A window can be sized or moved on the desktop through appropriate actions with the mouse. To *size a window*, point to any border (the mouse pointer changes to a double arrow), then drag the border in the direction you want to go—inward to shrink the window or outward to enlarge it. You can also drag a corner (instead of a border) to change both dimensions at the same time. To *move a window* while retaining its current size, click and drag the title bar to a new position on the desktop.

Pull-Down Menus

The menu bar provides access to *pull-down menus* that enable you to execute commands within an application (program). A pull-down menu is accessed by clicking the menu name or by pressing the Alt key plus the underlined letter in the menu name; for example, press Alt+V to pull down the View menu. (You may have to press the Alt key in order to see the underlines.) Three pull-down menus associated with My Computer are shown in Figure 3.

Commands within a menu are executed by clicking the command or by typing the underlined letter. Alternatively, you can bypass the menu entirely if you know the equivalent keystrokes shown to the right of the command in the menu (e.g., Ctrl+X, Ctrl+C, or Ctrl+V to cut, copy, or paste as shown within the Edit menu). A dimmed command (e.g., the Paste command in the Edit menu) means the command is not currently executable; some additional action has to be taken for the command to become available.

An ellipsis (. . .) following a command indicates that additional information is required to execute the command; for example, selection of the Format command in the File menu requires the user to specify additional information about the format-

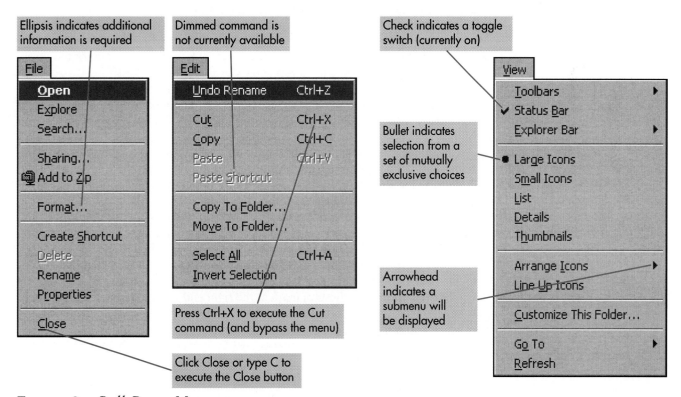

FIGURE 3   *Pull-Down Menus*

ting process. This information is entered into a dialog box (discussed in the next section), which appears immediately after the command has been selected.

A check next to a command indicates a toggle switch, whereby the command is either on or off. There is a check next to the Status Bar command in the View menu of Figure 3, which means the command is in effect (and thus the status bar will be displayed). Click the Status Bar command and the check disappears, which suppresses the display of the status bar. Click the command a second time and the check reappears, as does the status bar in the associated window.

A bullet next to an item (e.g., Large Icons in Figure 3) indicates a selection from a set of mutually exclusive choices. Click another option within the group (e.g., Small Icons) and the bullet will disappear from the previous selection (Large Icons) and appear next to the new selection (Small Icons).

An arrowhead after a command (e.g., the Arrange Icons command in the View menu) indicates that a submenu (also known as a cascaded menu) will be displayed with additional menu options.

Dialog Boxes

A *dialog box* appears when additional information is necessary to execute a command. Click the Print command in Internet Explorer, for example, and you are presented with the Print dialog box in Figure 4, requesting information about precisely what to print and how. The information is entered into the dialog box in different ways, depending on the type of information that is required. The tabs at the top of the dialog box provide access to different sets of options. The General and Paper tabs are selected in Figures 4a and 4b, respectively.

Option (Radio) buttons indicate mutually exclusive choices, one of which must be chosen, such as the page range in Figure 4a. You can print all pages, the selection (highlighted text), the current page, or a specific set of pages (such as pages 1–4), but you can choose one and only one option. Click a button to select an option, which automatically deselects the previously selected option.

A *text box* enters specific information such as the pages that will be printed in conjunction with selecting the radio button for pages. A flashing vertical bar (an I-beam) appears within the text box when the text box is active, to mark the insertion point for the text you will enter.

A *spin button* is another way to enter specific information such as the number of copies. Click the Up or Down arrow to increase or decrease the number of pages, respectively. You can also enter the information explicitly by typing it into a spin box, just as you would a text box.

Check boxes are used instead of option buttons if the choices are not mutually exclusive or if an option is not required. The Collate check box is checked in Figure 4a, whereas the Print to file box is not checked. Individual options are selected and cleared by clicking the appropriate check box, which toggles the box on and off.

A *list box* such as the Size is list box in Figure 4b displays some or all of the available choices, any one of which is selected by clicking the desired item. Just click the Down arrow on the list box to display the associated choices such as the paper source in Figure 4b. (A scroll bar appears within an open list box if all of the choices are not visible and provides access to the hidden choices.)

The *Help button* (a question mark at the right end of the title bar) provides help for any item in the dialog box. Click the button, then click the item in the dialog box for which you want additional information. The Close button (the X at the extreme right of the title bar) closes the dialog box without executing the command.

Tabs provide access to
different sets of options

Spin buttons

Check box is clear if
option is not required

Option buttons indicate
mutually exclusive choices

Text box enters
specific information

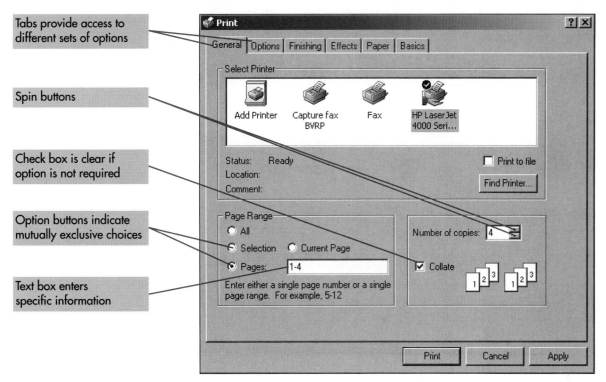

(a) General Tab

Help button

Close button

List box displays some
or all available choices

Click down arrow to
display associated choices

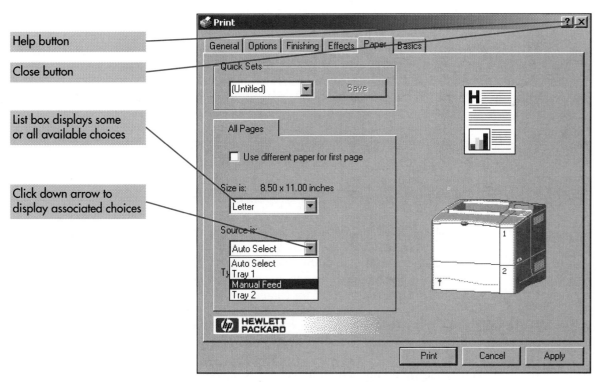

(b) Paper Tab

FIGURE 4   *Dialog Boxes*

All dialog boxes also contain one or more ***command buttons***, the function of which is generally apparent from the button's name. The Print button, in Figure 4a, for example, initiates the printing process. The Cancel button does just the opposite, and ignores (cancels) any changes made to the settings, then closes the dialog box without further action. An ellipsis (three dots) on a command button indicates that additional information will be required if the button is selected.

THE MOUSE

The mouse is indispensable to Windows and is referenced continually in the hands-on exercises throughout the text. There are five basic operations with which you must become familiar:

- To ***point*** to an object, move the mouse pointer onto the object.
- To ***click*** an object, point to it, then press and release the left mouse button.
- To ***right click*** an object, point to the object, then press and release the right mouse button. Right clicking an object displays a context-sensitive menu with commands that pertain to the object.
- To ***double click*** an object, point to it and then quickly click the left button twice in succession.
- To ***drag*** an object, move the pointer to the object, then press and hold the left button while you move the mouse to a new position.

You may also encounter a mouse with a wheel between the left and right buttons that lets you scroll through a document by rotating the wheel forward or backward. The action of the wheel, however, may change, depending on the application in use. In any event, the mouse is a pointing device—move the mouse on your desk and the mouse pointer, typically a small arrowhead, moves on the monitor. The mouse pointer assumes different shapes according to the location of the pointer or the nature of the current action. You will see a double arrow when you change the size of a window, an I-beam as you insert text, a hand to jump from one help topic to the next, or a circle with a line through it to indicate that an attempted action is invalid.

The mouse pointer will also change to an hourglass to indicate Windows is processing your command, and that no further commands may be issued until the action is completed. The more powerful your computer, the less frequently the hourglass will appear.

The Mouse versus the Keyboard

Almost every command in Windows can be executed in different ways, using either the mouse or the keyboard. Most people start with the mouse and add keyboard shortcuts as they become more proficient. There is no right or wrong technique, just different techniques, and the one you choose depends entirely on personal preference in a specific situation. If, for example, your hands are already on the keyboard, it is faster to use the keyboard equivalent. Other times, your hand will be on the mouse and that will be the fastest way. Toolbars provide still other ways to execute common commands.

In the beginning, you may wonder why there are so many different ways to do the same thing, but you will eventually recognize the many options as part of Windows' charm. It is not necessary to memorize anything, nor should you even try; just be flexible and willing to experiment. The more you practice, the faster all of this will become second nature to you.

All versions of Windows include extensive documentation with detailed information about virtually every function in Windows. It is accessed through the ***Help command*** on the Start menu, which provides different ways to search for information.

The ***Contents tab*** in Figure 5a is analogous to the table of contents in an ordinary book. The topics are listed in the left pane and the information for the selected topic is displayed in the right pane. The list of topics can be displayed in varying amounts of detail, by opening and closing the various book icons that appear. (The size of the left pane can be increased or decreased by dragging the border between the left and right pane in the appropriate direction.)

A closed book such as "Troubleshooting and Maintenance" indicates the presence of subtopics, which are displayed by opening (clicking) the book. An open book, on the other hand, such as "Internet, E-mail, and Communications," already displays its subtopics. Each subtopic is shown with one of two icons—a question mark to indicate "how to" information, or an open book to indicate conceptual information. Either way, you can click any subtopic in the left pane to view its contents in the right pane. Underlined entries in the right pane (e.g., Related Topics) indicate a hyperlink, which in turn displays additional information. Note, too, that you can print the information in the right pane by pulling down the Options menu and selecting the Print command.

The ***Index tab*** in Figure 5b is analogous to the index of an ordinary book. You enter the first several letters of the topic to look up, such as "floppy disk," choose a topic from the resulting list, and then click the Display button to view the information in the right pane. The underlined entries in the right pane represent hyperlinks, which you can click to display additional topics. And, as in the Contents window, you can print the information in the right pane by pulling down the Options menu and selecting the Print command.

The ***Search tab*** (not shown in Figure 5) displays a more extensive listing of entries than does the Index tab. It lets you enter a specific word or phrase and then it returns every topic containing that word or phrase.

The ***Favorites tab*** enables you to save the information within specified help topics as bookmarks, in order to return to those topics at a later date, as explained in the following hands-on exercise.

FORMATTING A FLOPPY DISK

You will soon begin to work on the computer, which means that you will be using various applications to create different types of documents. Each document is saved in its own file and stored on disk, either on a local disk (e.g., drive C) if you have your own computer, or on a floppy disk (drive A) if you are working in a computer lab at school.

All disks have to be formatted before they can hold data. The formatting process divides a disk into concentric circles called tracks, and then further divides each track into sectors. You don't have to worry about formatting a hard disk, as that is done at the factory prior to the machine being sold. You typically don't even have to format a floppy disk, since most floppies today are already formatted when you buy them. Nevertheless, it is very easy to format a floppy disk and it is a worthwhile exercise. Be aware, however, that formatting erases any data that was previously on a disk, so be careful not to format a disk with important data (e.g., one containing today's homework assignment). Formatting is accomplished through the ***Format command***. The process is straightforward, as you will see in the hands-on exercise that follows.

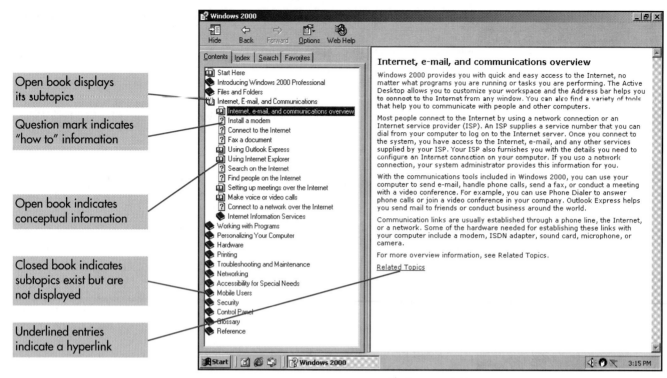

Open book displays its subtopics

Question mark indicates "how to" information

Open book indicates conceptual information

Closed book indicates subtopics exist but are not displayed

Underlined entries indicate a hyperlink

(a) Contents Tab

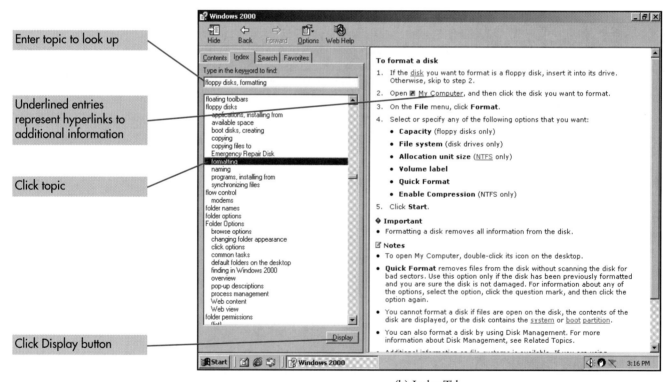

Enter topic to look up

Underlined entries represent hyperlinks to additional information

Click topic

Click Display button

(b) Index Tab

FIGURE 5   *The Help Command*

WELCOME TO WINDOWS

Objective   To turn on the computer, start Windows, and open My Computer; to move and size a window; to format a floppy disk and use the Help command. Use Figure 6 as a guide in the exercise.

Step 1:   **Open My Computer**

➤ Start the computer by turning on the various switches appropriate to your system. Your system will take a minute or so to boot up, after which you may be asked for a **user name** and **password**.

➤ Enter this information, after which you should see the desktop in Figure 6a. It does not matter if you are using a different version of Windows.

➤ Close the Getting Started with Windows 2000 window if it appears. Do not be concerned if your desktop differs from ours.

➤ The way in which you open My Computer (single or double clicking) depends on the options in effect as described in step 2. Either way, however, you can **right click** the **My Computer icon** to display a context-sensitive menu, then click the **Open command**.

➤ The My Computer window will open on your desktop, but the contents of your window and/or its size and position will be different from ours. You are ready to go to work.

Right click My Computer and click Open from the context-sensitive menu

Click to close Getting Started with Windows 2000 window

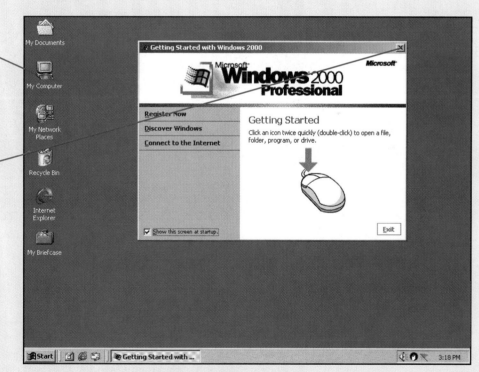

(a) Open My Computer (step 1)

FIGURE 6   *Hands-on Exercise 1*

Step 2:   **Set the Folder Options**

> ➤ Pull down the **Tools menu** and click the **Folder Options command** to display the Folder Options dialog box. Click the **General tab**, then set the options as shown in Figure 6b. (Your network administrator may have disabled this command, in which case you will use the default settings.)
>   • The Active desktop enables you to display Web content directly on the desktop. We suggest that you disable this option initially.
>   • Enabling Web content in folders displays the template at the left side of the window. The Windows classic option does not contain this information.
>   • Opening each successive folder within the same window saves space on the desktop as you browse the system. We discuss this in detail later on.
>   • The choice between clicking underlined items and double clicking an icon (without the underline) is personal. We prefer to double click.
> ➤ Click **OK** to accept the settings and close the Folder Options dialog box. The My Computer window on your desktop should be similar to ours.

General tab

Set the options as shown

Click OK

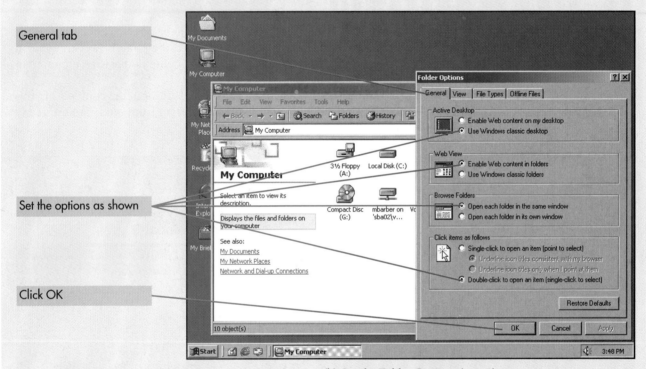

(b) Set the Folder Options (step 2)

FIGURE 6   *Hands-on Exercise 1 (continued)*

IT'S DIFFERENT IN WINDOWS 98

The Folder Options command is under the View menu in Windows 98, whereas it is found in the Tools menu in Windows 2000. Thus, to go from clicking to double clicking in Windows 98, pull down the View menu, click Folder Options, click the General tab, then choose Web style or Classic style, respectively. The procedure to display Web content in a folder is also different in Windows 98; you need to pull down the View menu and toggle the As Web Page command on.

Step 3: **Move and Size a Window**

> ➤ If necessary, pull down the **View menu** and click **Large Icons** so that your My Computer window more closely resembles the window in Figure 6c.
> ➤ Move and size the My Computer window on your desktop to match the display in Figure 6c.
>   • To change the width or height of the window, click and drag a border (the mouse pointer changes to a double arrow) in the direction you want to go.
>   • To change the width and height at the same time, click and drag a corner rather than a border.
>   • To change the position of the window, click and drag the title bar.
> ➤ Click the **minimize button** to shrink the My Computer window to a button on the taskbar. My Computer is still active in memory, however. Click the **My Computer button** on the taskbar to reopen the window.
> ➤ Click the **maximize button** so that the My Computer window expands to fill the entire screen. Click the **restore button** (which replaces the maximize button and is not shown in Figure 6c) to return the window to its previous size.

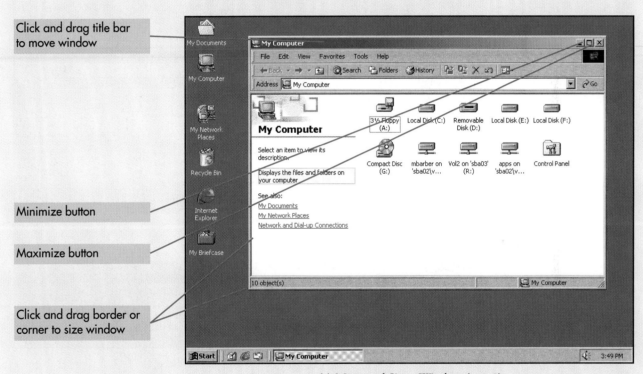

Click and drag title bar to move window

Minimize button

Maximize button

Click and drag border or corner to size window

(c) Move and Size a Window (step 3)

FIGURE 6 *Hands-on Exercise 1 (continued)*

MINIMIZING VERSUS CLOSING AN APPLICATION

Minimizing an application leaves the application open in memory and available at the click of the taskbar button. Closing it, however, removes the application from memory, which also causes it to disappear from the taskbar. The advantage of minimizing an application is that you can return to the application immediately. The disadvantage is that leaving too many applications open simultaneously may degrade performance.

Step 4:   **Use the Pull-Down Menus**

➤ Pull down the **View menu**, then click the **Toolbars command** to display a cascaded menu as shown in Figure 6d. If necessary, check the commands for the **Standard Buttons** and **Address Bar**, and clear the commands for Links and Radio.

➤ Pull down the **View menu** to make or verify the following selections. (You have to pull down the View menu each time you make an additional change.)
  • The **Status Bar command** should be checked. The Status Bar command functions as a toggle switch. Click the command and the status bar is displayed; click the command a second time and the status bar disappears.)
  • Click the **Details command** to change to this view. Notice that the different views are grouped within the menu and that only one view at a time can be selected.

➤ Pull down the **View menu** once again, click (or point to) the **Explorer Bar command**, and verify that none of the options is checked.

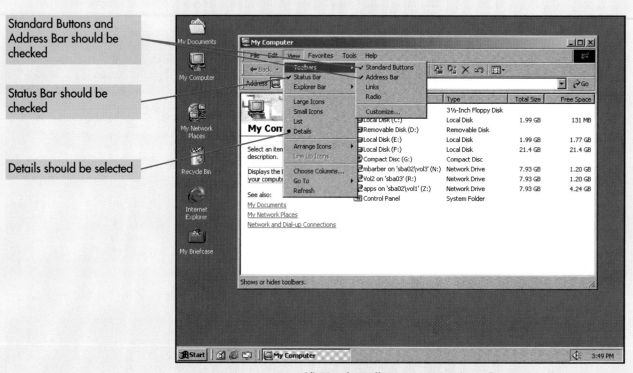

Standard Buttons and Address Bar should be checked

Status Bar should be checked

Details should be selected

(d) Use the Pull-Down Menus (step 4)

FIGURE 6   *Hands-on Exercise 1 (continued)*

DESIGNATING THE DEVICES ON A SYSTEM

The first (usually only) floppy drive is always designated as drive A. (A second floppy drive, if it were present, would be drive B.) The first hard (local) disk on a system is always drive C, whether or not there are one or two floppy drives. Additional local drives, if any, a Zip (removable storage) drive, a network drive, and/or the CD-ROM are labeled from D on.

Step 5: **Format a Floppy Disk**

➤ Place a floppy disk in drive A. Select (click) drive A, then pull down the **File menu** and click the **Format command** to display the dialog box in Figure 6e.
- Set the **Capacity** to match the floppy disk you purchased (1.44MB for a high-density disk and 720KB for a double-density disk).
- Click the **Volume label text box** if it's empty or click and drag over the existing label. Enter a new label (containing up to 11 characters).
- You can check the **Quick Format box** if the disk has been previously formatted, as a convenient way to erase the contents of the disk.

➤ Click the **Start button**, then click **OK** after you have read the warning. The formatting process erases anything that is on the disk, so be sure that you do not need anything on the disk you are about to format.

➤ Click **OK** after the formatting is complete. Close the Format dialog box, then save the formatted disk for use with various exercises later in the text.

➤ Close the My Computer window.

Click to select
appropriate capacity

Enter a Volume label

Quick Format box

Click OK

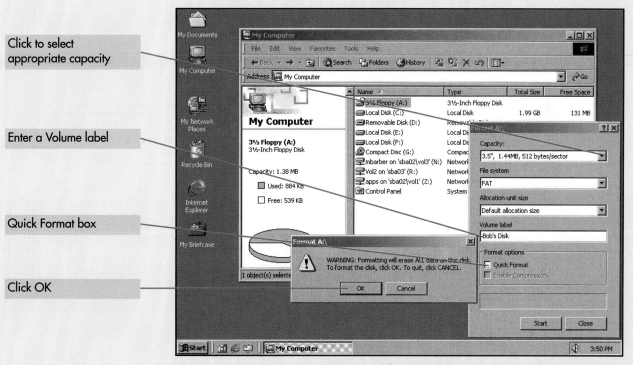

(e) Format a Floppy Disk (step 5)

FIGURE 6   *Hands-on Exercise 1 (continued)*

THE HELP BUTTON

The Help button (a question mark) appears in the title bar of almost every dialog box. Click the question mark, then click the item you want information about (which then appears in a pop-up window). To print the contents of the pop-up window, click the right mouse button inside the window, and click Print Topic. Click outside the pop-up window to close the window and continue working.

Step 6: **The Help Command**

➤ Click the **Start button** on the taskbar, then click the **Help command** to display the Help window in Figure 6f. Maximize the Help window.

➤ Click the **Contents tab**, then click a closed book such as **Hardware** to open the book and display the associated topics. Click any one of the displayed topics such as **Hardware overview** in Figure 6f.

➤ Pull down the **Options menu** and click the **Print command** to display the Print Topics dialog box. Click the option button to print the selected topic, click **OK**, then click the **Print button** in the resulting dialog box.

➤ Click the **Index tab**, type **format** (the first several letters in "Formatting disks," the topic you are searching for). Double click the subtopic "overview". Pull down the **Options menu** and click the **Print command** to print this information as well.

➤ Submit the printed information to your instructor. Close the Help window.

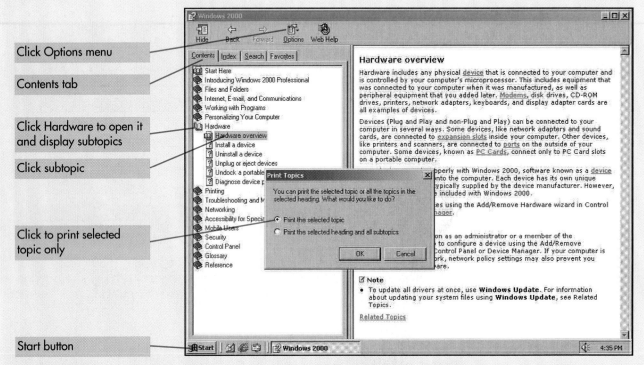

(f) The Help Command (step 6)

FIGURE 6   *Hands-on Exercise 1 (continued)*

THE FAVORITES TAB

Do you find yourself continually searching for the same Help topic? If so, you can make life a little easier by adding the topic to a list of favorite Help topics. Start Help, then use the Contents, Index, or Search tabs to locate the desired topic. Now click the Favorites tab in the Help window, then click the Add button to add the topic. You can return to the topic at any time by clicking the Favorites tab, then double clicking the bookmark to display the information.

Step 7:   **Shut Down the Computer**

➤ It is very important that you shut down your computer properly as opposed to just turning off the power. This enables Windows to properly close all of its system files and to save any changes that were made during the session.

➤ Click the **Start button**, click the **Shut Down command** to display the Shut Down Windows dialog box in Figure 6g. Click the **drop-down arrow** to display the desired option, then click **OK**.

 • Logging off ends your session, but leaves the computer running at full power. This is the typical option you select in a laboratory setting.

 • Shutting down the computer ends the session and also closes Windows so that you can safely turn the power off. (Some computers will automatically turn the power off for you if this option is selected.)

 • Restarting the computer ends your sessions, then closes and restarts Windows to begin a new session.

➤ Welcome to Windows 2000!

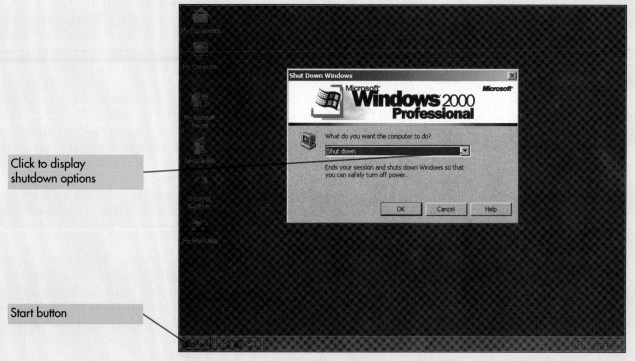

Click to display
shutdown options

Start button

(g) Shut Down the Computer (step 7)

FIGURE 6   *Hands-on Exercise 1 (continued)*

THE TASK MANAGER

The Start button is the normal way to exit Windows. Occasionally, however, an application may "hang"—in which case you want to close the problem application but leave Windows open. Press Ctrl+Alt+Del to display the Windows Security dialog box, then click the Task Manager command button. Click the Applications tab, select the problem application, and click the End Task button.

A *file* is a set of instructions or data that has been given a name and stored on disk. There are two basic types of files, *program files* and *data files*. Microsoft Word and Microsoft Excel are examples of program files. The documents and workbooks created by these programs are examples of data files.

A *program file* is an executable file because it contains instructions that tell the computer what to do. A *data file* is not executable and can be used only in conjunction with a specific program. As a typical student, you execute (run) program files, then you use those programs to create and/or modify the associated data files.

Every file has a *file name* that identifies it to the operating system. The file name may contain up to 255 characters and may include spaces. (File names cannot contain the following characters: \, /, :, *, ?, ", <, >, or |. We suggest that you try to keep file names simple and restrict yourself to the use of letters, numbers, and spaces.) Long file names permit descriptive entries such as *Term Paper for Western Civilization* (as distinct from a more cryptic *TPWCIV* that was required under MS-DOS and Windows 3.1).

Files are stored in *folders* to better organize the hundreds (thousands, or tens of thousands) of files on a hard disk. A Windows folder is similar in concept to a manila folder in a filing cabinet into which you put one or more documents (files) that are somehow related to each other. An office worker stores his or her documents in manila folders. In Windows, you store your files (documents) in electronic folders on disk.

Folders are the keys to the Windows storage system. Some folders are created automatically; for example, the installation of a program such as Microsoft Office automatically creates one or more folders to hold the various program files. Other folders are created by the user to hold the documents he or she creates. You could, for example, create one folder for your word processing documents and a second folder for your spreadsheets. Alternatively, you can create a folder to hold all of your work for a specific class, which may contain a combination of word processing documents and spreadsheets. The choice is entirely up to you, and you can use any system that makes sense to you. Anything at all can go into a folder—program files, data files, even other folders.

Figure 7 displays the contents of a hypothetical Homework folder with six documents. Figure 7a enables Web content, and so we see the colorful logo at the left of the folder, together with links to My Documents, My Network Places, and My Computer. Figure 7b is displayed without the Web content, primarily to gain space within the window. The display or suppression of the Web content is determined by a setting in the Folder Options command.

Figures 7a and 7b are displayed in different views. Figure 7a uses the *Large Icons view*, whereas Figure 7b is displayed in the *Details view*, which shows additional information for each file. (Other possible views include Small Icons, List, and Thumbnail.) The file icon, whether large or small, indicates the *file type* or application that was used to create the file. The History of Computers file, for example, is a Microsoft Word document. The Grade Book is a Microsoft Excel workbook.

Regardless of the view and options in effect, the name of the folder (Homework) appears in the title bar next to the icon of an open folder. The minimize, maximize, and Close buttons appear at the right of the title bar. A menu bar with six pull-down menus appears below the title bar. The Standard Buttons toolbar appears below the menu, and the Address Bar (indicating the drive and folder) appears below the toolbar. A status bar appears at the bottom of both windows, indicating that the Homework folder contains six objects (documents) and that the total file size is 525KB.

Folder name

Menu bar

Standard Buttons toolbar

Address bar

Web content view
displays colorful logo

Status bar

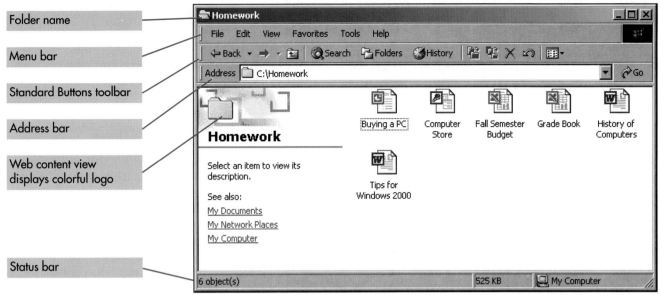

(a) Large Icons View with Web Content Enabled

Folder name

Menu bar

Standard Buttons toolbar

Address bar

Icon indicates an Excel file

Icon indicates a Word
document

Status bar

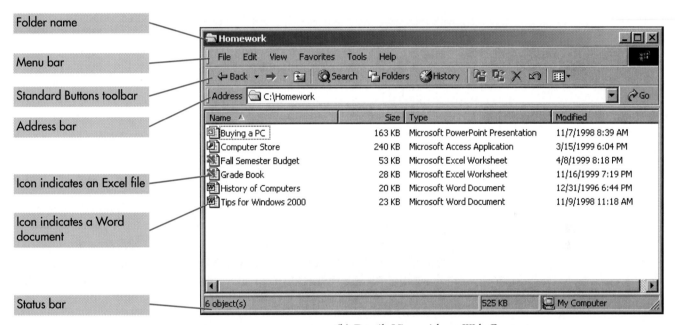

(b) Details View without Web Content

FIGURE 7   *The Homework Folder*

CHANGE THE VIEW

Look closely at the address bar in Figures 7a and 7b to see that both figures
display the Homework folder on drive C, although the figures are very different in appearance. Figure 7a displays Web content to provide direct links to
three other folders, and the contents of the Homework folder are displayed in
the Large Icons view to save space. Figure 7b suppresses the Web content and
uses the Details view to provide the maximum amount of information for each
file in the Homework folder. You are free to choose whichever options you
prefer.

My Computer enables you to browse through the various drives and folders on a system in order to locate a document and go to work. Let's assume that you're looking for a document called "History of Computers" that you saved previously in the Homework folder on drive C. To get to this document, you would open My Computer, from where you would open drive C, open the Homework folder, and then open the document. It's a straightforward process that can be accomplished in two different ways, as shown in Figure 8.

The difference between the two figures is whether each drive or folder is opened in its own window, as shown in Figure 8a, or whether the same window is used for every folder, as in Figure 8b. (This is another option that is set through the Folder Options command.) In Figure 8a you begin by double clicking the My Computer icon on the desktop to open the My Computer window, which in turn displays the devices on your system. Next, you double click the icon for drive C to open a second window that displays the folders on drive C. From there, you double click the icon for the Homework folder to open a third window containing the documents in the Homework folder. Once in the Homework folder, you can double click the icon of an existing document, which starts the associated application and opens the document.

The process is identical in Figure 8b except that each object opens in the same window. The Back arrow on the Standard Buttons toolbar is meaningful in Figure 8b because you can click the button to return to the previous window (drive C), then click it again to go back to My Computer. Note, however, that the button is dimmed in all three windows in Figure 8a because there is no previous window, since each folder is opened in its own window.

THE EXPLORING OFFICE PRACTICE FILES

There is only one way to master the file operations inherent in Windows and that is to practice at the computer. To do so requires that you have a series of files with which to work. We have created these files for you, and we reference them in the next several hands-on exercises. Your instructor will make these files available to you in a variety of ways:

- The files can be downloaded from our Web site, assuming that you have access to the Internet and that you have a basic proficiency with Internet Explorer. Software and other files that are downloaded from the Internet are typically compressed (made smaller) to reduce the amount of time it takes to transmit the file. In essence, you will download a *compressed file* (which may contain multiple individual files) from our Web site and then uncompress the file onto a local drive as described in the next hands-on exercise.
- The files might be on a network drive, in which case you can use My Computer (or Windows Explorer, which is discussed later in the chapter) to copy the files from the network drive to a floppy disk. The procedure to do this is described in the third hands-on exercise.
- There may be an actual "data disk" in the computer lab. Go to the lab with a floppy disk, then use the Copy Disk command (on the File menu of My Computer) to duplicate the data disk and create a copy for yourself.

It doesn't matter how you obtain the practice files, only that you are able to do so. Indeed, you may want to try different techniques in order to gain additional practice with Windows.

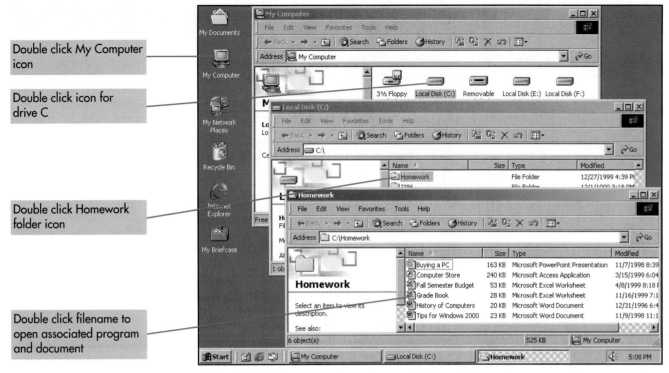

Double click My Computer icon

Double click icon for drive C

Double click Homework folder icon

Double click filename to open associated program and document

(a) Multiple Windows

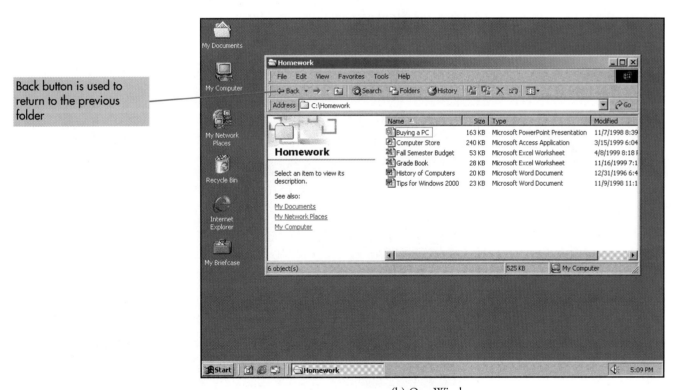

Back button is used to return to the previous folder

(b) One Window

FIGURE 8   *Browsing My Computer*

THE PRACTICE FILES VIA THE WEB

Objective To download a file from the Web. The exercise requires a formatted floppy disk and access to the Internet. Use Figure 9 as a guide in the exercise.

Step 1: **Start Internet Explorer**

> Start Internet Explorer, perhaps by double clicking the **Internet Explorer icon** on the desktop, or by clicking the **Start button**, clicking the **Programs command**, then locating the command to start the program. If necessary, click the **maximize button** so that Internet Explorer takes the entire desktop.
> Enter the address of the site you want to visit:
> • Pull down the **File menu**, click the **Open command** to display the Open dialog box, and enter **www.prenhall.com/grauer** (the http:// is assumed). Click **OK**.
> • *Or,* click in the **Address bar** below the toolbar, which automatically selects the current address (so that whatever you type replaces the current address). Enter the address of the site you want to visit, **www.prenhall.com/grauer** (the http:// is assumed). Press **enter**.
> You should see the *Exploring Office Series* home page as shown in Figure 9a. Click the book for **Office XP**, which takes you to the Office XP home page.
> Click the **Student Resources link** (at the top of the window) to go to the Student Resources page.

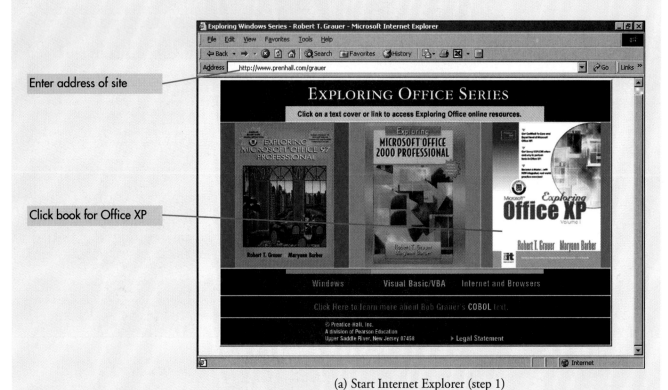

Enter address of site

Click book for Office XP

(a) Start Internet Explorer (step 1)

FIGURE 9   *Hands-on Exercise 2*

Step 2: **Download the Practice Files**

➤ Click the link to **Student Data Disk** (in the right frame), then scroll down the page until you can see **Essentials of Microsoft Windows**.

➤ Click the indicated link to download the practice files. The Save As dialog box is not yet visible.

➤ You will see the File Download dialog box asking what you want to do. Click **Save**. The Save As dialog box appears as shown in Figure 9b.

➤ Place a formatted floppy disk in drive A, click the **drop-down arrow** on the Save in list box, and select (click) **drive A**. Click **Save** to begin downloading the file.

➤ The File Download window will reappear on your screen and show you the status of the downloading operation. If necessary, click **Close** when you see the dialog box indicating that the download is complete.

➤ Close Internet Explorer.

Click link to Student
Resources

Click to select drive A

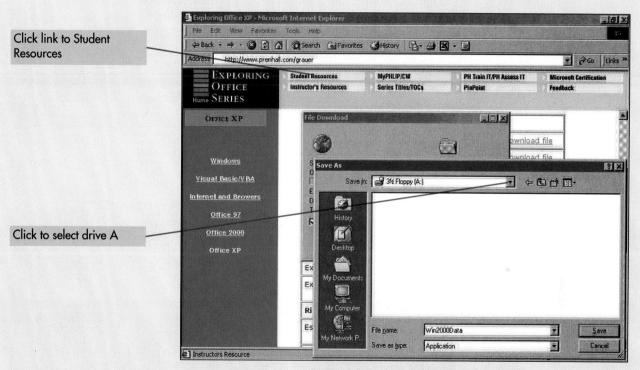

(b) Download the Practice Files (step 2)

FIGURE 9 *Hands-on Exercise 2 (continued)*

REMEMBER THE LOCATION

It's easy to download a file from the Web. The only tricky part, if any, is remembering where you have saved the file. This exercise is written for a laboratory setting, and thus we specified drive A as the destination, so that you will have the file on a floppy disk at the end of the exercise. If you have your own computer, however, it's faster to save the file to the desktop or in a temporary folder on drive C. Just remember where you save the file so that you can access it after it has been downloaded.

Step 3:   **Open My Computer**

➤ Double click the My Computer icon on the desktop to open My Computer. If necessary, customize My Computer to match Figure 9c.
  • Pull down the **View menu** and change to the **Details view**.
  • Pull down the **View menu** a second time, click (or point to) the **Toolbars command**, then check the **Standard buttons** and **Address Bar** toolbars.
➤ Pull down the **Tools menu** and click the **Folder Options command** to verify the settings in effect so that your window matches ours. Be sure to **Enable Web content in folders** (in the Web View area), to **Open each folder in the same window** (in the Browse Folders area), and **Double Click to open an item** (in the Click Items area). Click **OK**.
➤ Click the icon for **drive A** to select it. The description of drive A appears at the left of the window.
➤ Double click the icon for **drive A** to open this drive. The contents of the My Computer window are replaced by the contents of drive A.

Double click to open
My Computer

Click icon for drive A
to select it; double click
icon to open it

Description of drive A

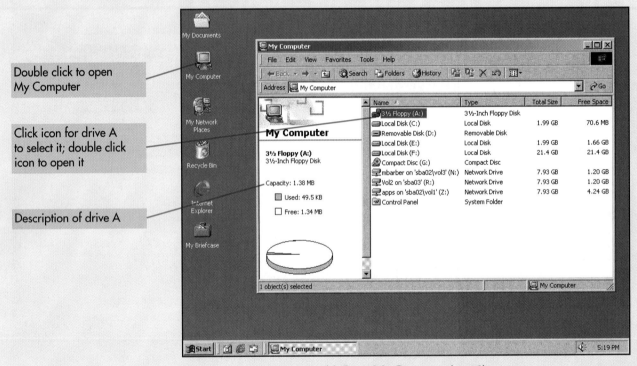

(c) Open My Computer (step 3)

FIGURE 9   *Hands-on Exercise 2 (continued)*

THE RIGHT MOUSE BUTTON

Point to any object on the Windows desktop or within an application window, then click the right mouse button to see a context-sensitive menu with commands pertaining to that object. You could, for example, right click the icon for drive A, then select the Open command from the resulting menu. The right mouse button is one of the most powerful Windows shortcuts and one of its best-kept secrets. Use it!

Step 4: **Install the Practice Files**

➤ You should see the contents of drive A as shown in Figure 9d. (If your desktop displays two windows rather than one, it is because you did not set the folder options correctly. Pull down the **Tools menu**, click the **Folder Options command**, and choose the option to **Open each folder in the same window**.)

➤ Double click the **Win2000data file** to install the data disk. You will see a dialog box thanking you for selecting the *Exploring Windows* series. Click **OK**.

• Check that the Unzip To Folder text box specifies **A:** to extract the files to the floppy disk. (You may enter a different drive and/or folder.)

• Click the **Unzip button** to extract the practice files and copy them onto the designated drive. Click **OK** after you see the message indicating that the files have been unzipped successfully. Close the WinZip dialog box.

➤ The practice files have been extracted to drive A and should appear in the Drive A window. If you do not see the files, pull down the **View menu** and click the **Refresh command.**

Double click icon for Win2000data file

A:\ should be specified as Unzip To Folder

Click Unzip

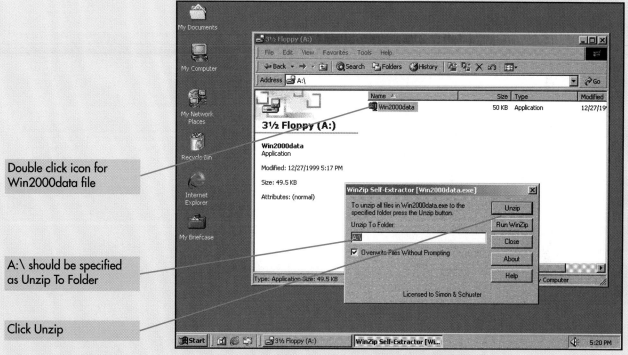

(d) Install the Practice Files (step 4)

FIGURE 9   *Hands-on Exercise 2 (continued)*

DOWNLOADING A FILE

Software and other files are typically compressed to reduce the amount of storage space the files require on disk and/or the time it takes to download the files. In essence, you download a compressed file (which may contain multiple individual files), then you uncompress (expand) the file on your local drive in order to access the individual files. After the file has been expanded, it is no longer needed and can be deleted.

Step 5: **Delete the Compressed File**

➤ If necessary, pull down the **View menu** and click **Details** to change to the Details view in Figure 9e. (If you do not see the descriptive information about drive A at the left of the window, pull down the **Tools menu**, click the **Folder Options command**, and click the option button to **Enable Web content in folders.**)

➤ You should see a total of six files in the Drive A window. Five of these are the practice files on the data disk. The sixth file is the original file that you downloaded earlier. This file is no longer necessary, since it has been already been expanded.

➤ Select (click) the **Win2000data file**. Pull down the **File menu** and click the **Delete command**, or click the **Delete button** on the toolbar. Pause for a moment to be sure you want to delete this file, then click **Yes** when asked to confirm the deletion as shown in Figure 9e.

➤ The Win2000Data file is permanently deleted from drive A. (Items deleted from a floppy disk or network drive are not sent to the Recycle Bin, and cannot be recovered.)

Delete button

Click to select Win2000data

Double click Windows 2000 Overview to open it

Click Yes

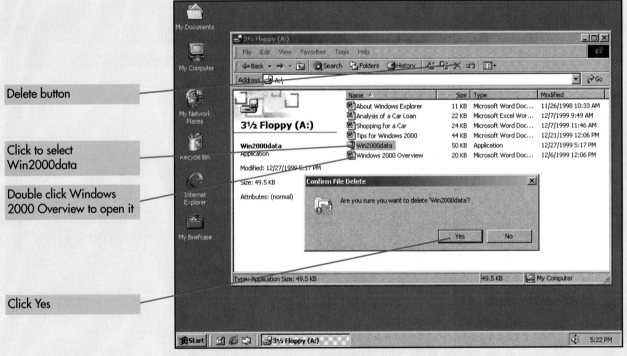

(e) Delete the Compressed File (step 5)

FIGURE 9 *Hands-on Exercise 2 (continued)*

SORT BY NAME, DATE, FILE TYPE, OR SIZE

Files can be displayed in ascending or descending sequence by name, date modified, file type, or size by clicking the appropriate column heading. Click Size, for example, to display files in the order of their size. Click the column heading a second time to reverse the sequence; that is, to switch from ascending to descending, and vice versa.

Step 6: **Modify a Document**

➤ Double click the **Windows 2000 Overview** document from within My Computer to open the document as shown in Figure 9f. (The document will open in the WordPad accessory if Microsoft Word is not installed on your machine.) If necessary, maximize the window for Microsoft Word.

➤ If necessary, click inside the document window, then press **Ctrl+End** to move to the end of the document. Add the sentence shown in Figure 9h followed by your name.

➤ Pull down the **File menu**, click **Print**, then click **OK** to print the document and prove to your instructor that you did the exercise.

➤ Pull down the **File menu** and click **Exit** to close the application. Click **Yes** when prompted to save the file.

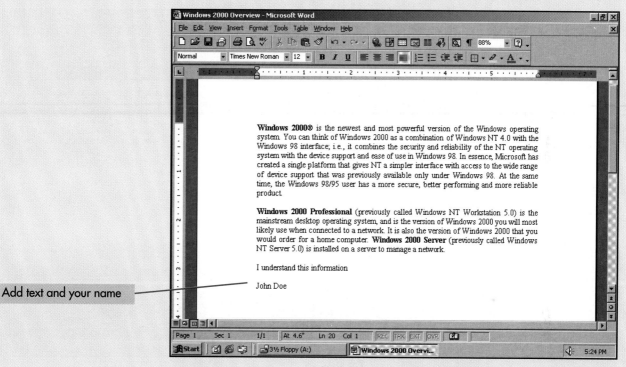

Add text and your name

(f) Modify a Document (step 6)

FIGURE 9 *Hands-on Exercise 2 (continued)*

THE DOCUMENT, NOT THE APPLICATION

All versions of Windows are document oriented, meaning that you are able to think in terms of the document rather than the application that created it. You can still open a document in traditional fashion by starting the application that created the document, then using the File Open command in that program to retrieve the document. It's often easier, however, to open the document from within My Computer (or Windows Explorer) by double clicking its icon. Windows then starts the application and opens the data file. In other words, you can open a document without explicitly starting the application.

Step 7: **Check Your Work**

➤ You should be back in the My Computer window as shown in Figure 9g. If necessary, click the **Views button** to change to the Details view.
➤ Look closely at the date and time that is displayed next to the Windows 2000 Overview document. It should show today's date and the current time (give or take a minute) since that is when the document was last modified.
➤ Look closely and see that Figure 9g also contains a sixth document, called "Backup of Windows 2000 Overview". This is a backup copy of the original document that will be created automatically by Microsoft Word if the appropriate options are in effect. (See the boxed tip below.)
➤ Exit Windows or, alternatively, continue with steps 8 and 9 to return to our Web site and explore additional resources.

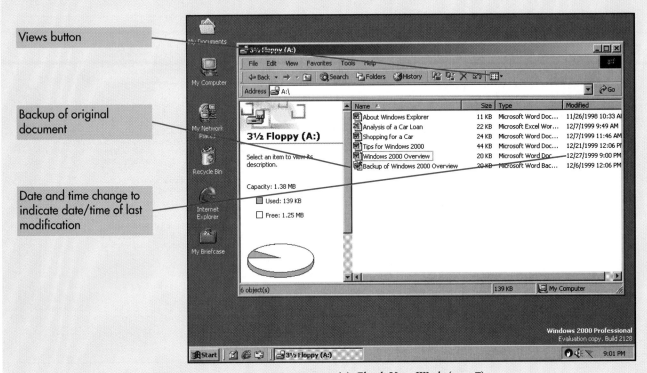

Views button

Backup of original document

Date and time change to indicate date/time of last modification

(g) Check Your Work (step 7)

FIGURE 9   *Hands-on Exercise 2 (continued)*

USE WORD TO CREATE A BACKUP COPY

Microsoft Word enables you to automatically create a backup copy of a document in conjunction with the Save command. The next time you are in Microsoft Word, pull down the Tools menu, click the Options command, click the Save tab, then check the box to always create a backup copy. Every time you save a file from this point on, the previously saved version is renamed "Backup of document," and the document in memory is saved as the current version. The disk will contain the two most recent versions of the document, enabling you to retrieve the previous version if necessary.

Step 8: **Download the PowerPoint Lecture**

➤ Restart Internet Explorer and connect to **www.prenhall.com/grauer**. Click the book for **Office XP**, click the link to **Student Resources**, then choose **PowerPoint Lectures** to display the screen in Figure 9h.

➤ Click the down arrow until you can click the link to the PowerPoint slides for **Essentials of Windows 2000**. The File Download dialog box will appear. Click **Save**.

➤ Click the **drop-down arrow** on the Save in list box, and select **drive A**. Be sure that the floppy disk is still in drive A, then click **Save** to begin downloading the file. Click **OK** when you see the dialog box indicating that the download is complete.

➤ Click the taskbar button to return to the **My Computer window** for drive A. You should see all of the files that were previously on the floppy disk plus the file you just downloaded.

➤ Double click the **Win2000ppt file**, then follow the onscreen instructions to unzip the file to drive A.

Click the Student Resources tab

Click the link to PowerPoint Lectures

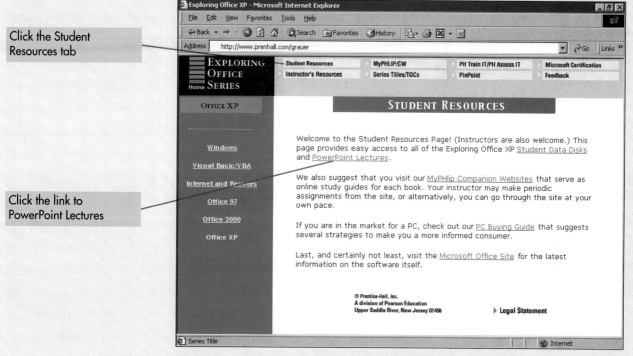

(h) Download the PowerPoint Lecture (step 8)

FIGURE 9   *Hands-on Exercise 2 (continued)*

THE MyPHLIP WEB SITE

The MyPHLIP (Prentice Hall Learning on the Internet Partnership) Web site is another resource that is available for the Exploring Office series. Click the MyPHLIP tab at the top of the screen, which takes you to www.prenhall.com/myphlip, where you will register and select the text you are using. See exercise 3 at the end of the chapter.

Step 9:   **Show Time**

> ➤ Drive A should now contain a PowerPoint file in addition to the self-extracting file. (Pull down the **View menu** and click the **Refresh command** if you do not see the PowerPoint file.)
> ➤ Double click the PowerPoint file to open the presentation, then click the button to Enable Macros (if prompted). You should see the PowerPoint presentation in Figure 9i. (You must have PowerPoint installed on your computer in order to view the presentation.)
> ➤ Pull down the **View menu** and click **Slide Show** to begin the presentation, which is intended to review the material in this supplement. Click the left mouse button (or press the **PgDn key**) to move to the next slide.
> ➤ Click the left mouse button continually to move from one slide to the next. Close PowerPoint at the end of the presentation.
> ➤ Exit Windows if you do not want to continue with the next exercise at this time.

Pull down the View menu and click the Slide Show command

The presentation reviews the material on Windows

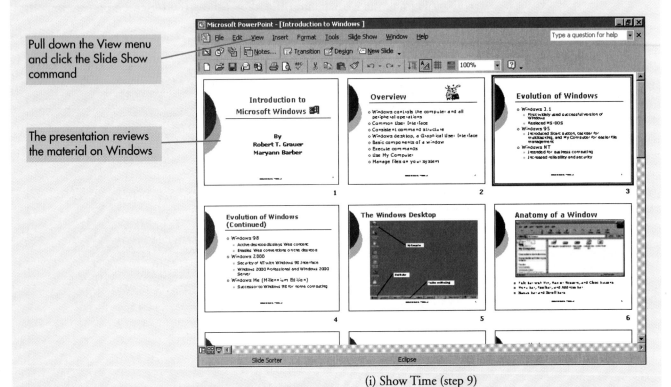

(i) Show Time (step 9)

FIGURE 9   *Hands-on Exercise 2 (continued)*

MISSING POWERPOINT—WHICH VERSION OF OFFICE DO YOU HAVE?

You may have installed Microsoft Office on your computer, but you may not have PowerPoint. That is because Microsoft has created several different versions of Microsoft Office, each with a different set of applications. Unfortunately, PowerPoint is not included in every configuration and may be missing from the suite that is shipped most frequently with new computers.

Windows has two different programs to manage the files and folders on a system, My Computer and Windows Explorer. My Computer is intuitive, but less efficient, as you have to open each folder in succession. Windows Explorer is more sophisticated, as it provides a hierarchical view of the entire system in a single window. A beginner might prefer My Computer, whereas a more experienced user will most likely opt for Windows Explorer.

Assume, for example, that you are taking four classes this semester, and that you are using the computer in each course. You've created a separate folder to hold the work for each class and have stored the contents of all four folders on a single floppy disk. Assume further that you need to retrieve your third English assignment so that you can modify the assignment, then submit the revised version to your instructor. Figure 10 illustrates how Windows Explorer could be used to locate your assignment.

The Explorer window in Figure 10a is divided into two panes. The left pane contains a tree diagram (or hierarchical view) of the entire system showing all drives and, optionally, the folders in each drive. The right pane shows the contents of the active drive or folder. Only one object (a drive or folder) can be active in the left pane, and its contents are displayed automatically in the right pane.

Look carefully at the icon for the English folder in the left pane of Figure 10a. The folder is open, whereas the icon for every other folder is closed. The open folder indicates that the English folder is the active folder. (The name of the active folder also appears in the title bar of Windows Explorer and in the Address bar.) The contents of the active folder (three Word documents in this example) are displayed in the right pane. The right pane is displayed in Details view, but could just as easily have been displayed in another view (e.g., Large Icons).

As indicated, only one folder can be open (active) at a time in the left pane. Thus, to see the contents of a different folder such as Accounting, you would open (click on) the Accounting folder, which automatically closes the English folder. The contents of the Accounting folder would then appear in the right pane. You should organize your folders in ways that make sense to you, such as a separate folder for every class you are taking. You can also create folders within folders; for example, a correspondence folder may contain two folders of its own, one for business correspondence and one for personal letters.

Windows Explorer can also be used to display a Web page, as shown in Figure 10b. All you do is click the icon for Internet Explorer in the left pane to start the program and display its default home page. Alternatively, you can click in the Address bar and enter the address of any Web page directly; for example, click in the Address bar and type www.microsoft.com to display the home page for Microsoft. Once you are browsing pages on the Web, it's convenient to close the left pane so that the page takes the complete window. You can reopen the Folders window by pulling down the View menu, clicking the Explorer Bar command, and toggling Folders on.

THE SMART TOOLBAR

The toolbar in Windows Explorer recognizes whether you are viewing a Web page or a set of files and folders, and changes accordingly. The icons that are displayed when viewing a Web page are identical to those in Internet Explorer and include the Search, Favorites, and History buttons. The buttons that are displayed when viewing a file or folder include the Undo, Delete, and Views buttons that are used in file management.

Name of active folder

Minus indicates object is expanded

Active folder

Plus sign indicates object is collapsed

Contents of active folder

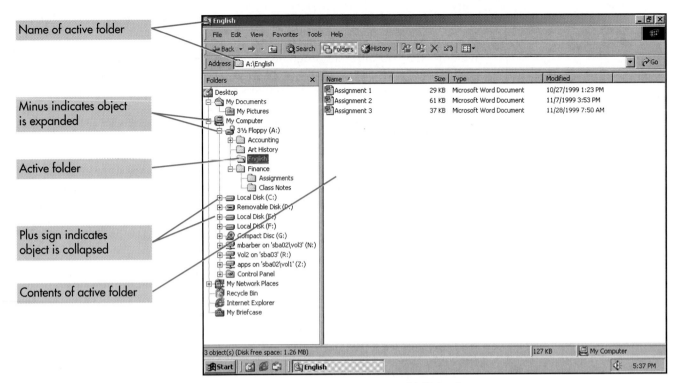

(a) Drive A

Enter address of desired site

Click to close left pane

Click icon for Internet Explorer

Web page is displayed

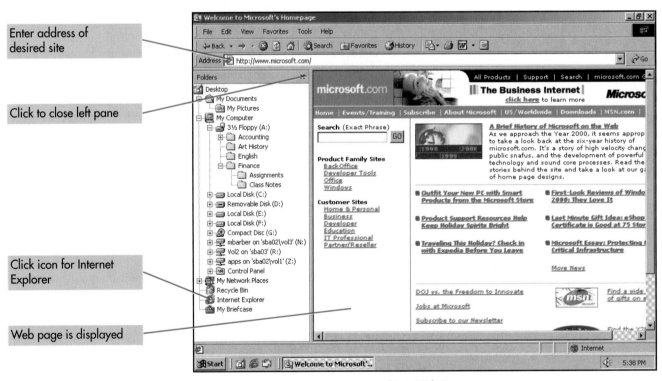

(b) A Web Page

FIGURE 10   *Windows Explorer*

Expanding and Collapsing a Drive or Folder

The tree diagram in Windows Explorer displays the devices on your system in hierarchical fashion. The desktop is always at the top of the hierarchy, and it contains icons such as My Computer, the Recycle Bin, Internet Explorer, and My Network Places. My Computer in turn contains the various drives that are accessible from your system, each of which contains folders, which in turn contain documents and/or additional folders. Each object may be expanded or collapsed by clicking the plus or minus sign, respectively. Click either sign to toggle to the other. Clicking a plus sign, for example, expands the drive, then displays a minus sign next to the drive to indicate that its subordinates are visible.

Look closely at the icon next to My Computer in either Figure 10a or 10b. It is a minus sign (as opposed to a plus sign) and it indicates that My Computer has been expanded to show the devices on the system. There is also a minus sign next to the icon for drive A to indicate that it too has been expanded to show the folders on the disk. Note, however, the plus sign next to drives C and D, indicating that these parts of the tree are currently collapsed and thus their subordinates (in this case, folders) are not visible.

Any folder may contain additional folders, and thus individual folders may also be expanded or collapsed. The minus sign next to the Finance folder, for example, indicates that the folder has been expanded and contains two additional folders, for Assignments and Class Notes, respectively. The plus sign next to the Accounting folder, however, indicates the opposite; that is, the folder is collapsed and its subordinate folders are not currently visible. A folder with neither a plus nor a minus sign, such as Art History, does not contain additional folders and cannot be expanded or collapsed.

The hierarchical view within Windows Explorer, and the ability to expand and collapse the various folders on a system, enables you to quickly locate a specific file or folder. If, for example, you want to see the contents of the Art History folder, you click its icon in the left pane, which automatically changes the display in the right pane to show the documents in that folder. Thus, Windows Explorer is ideal for moving or copying files from one folder or drive to another. You simply select (open) the folder that contains the files, use the scroll bar in the left pane (if necessary) so that the destination folder is visible, then click and drag the files from the right pane to the destination folder.

The Folder Options command functions identically in Windows Explorer and in My Computer. You can decide whether you want to single or double click the icons and/or whether to display Web content within a folder. You can also use the View menu to select the most appropriate view. Our preferences are to double click the icons, to omit Web content, and to use the Details view.

CONVERGENCE OF THE EXPLORERS

Windows Explorer and Internet Explorer are separate programs, but each includes some functionality of the other. You can use Windows Explorer to display a Web page by clicking the Internet Explorer icon within the tree structure in the left pane. Conversely, you can use Internet Explorer to display a local drive, document, or folder. Start Internet Explorer in the usual fashion, click in the Address bar, then enter the appropriate address, such as C:\ to display the contents of drive C.

THE PRACTICE FILES VIA A LOCAL AREA NETWORK

Objective   To use Windows Explorer to copy the practice files from a network drive to a floppy disk. The exercise requires a formatted floppy disk and access to a local area network. Use Figure 11 as a guide in the exercise.

Step 1:   **Start Windows Explorer**

➤ Click the **Start Button**, click **Programs**, click **Accessories**, then click **Windows Explorer**. Click the **maximize button** so that Windows Explorer takes the entire desktop as shown in Figure 11a. Do not be concerned if your desktop is different from ours.

➤ Make or verify the following selections using the **View menu**. You have to pull down the View menu each time you choose a different command.
  • The **Standard buttons** and **Address bar** toolbars should be selected.
  • The **Status Bar command** should be checked.
  • The **Details view** should be selected.

➤ Click (select) the **Desktop icon** in the left pane to display the contents of the desktop in the right pane. Your desktop may have different icons from ours, but your screen should almost match Figure 11a. We set additional options in the next step.

Standard buttons toolbar

Address bar

Click Desktop icon to select it

Details view

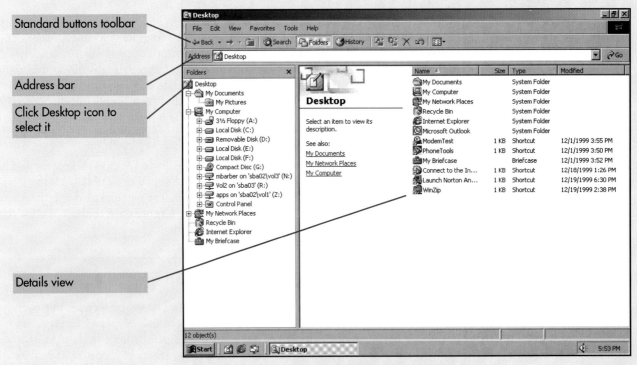

(a) Start Windows Explorer (step 1)

FIGURE 11   *Hands-on Exercise 3*

Step 2:   **Change the Folder Options**

- ➤ Click the **minus** (or the **plus**) **sign** next to My Computer to collapse (or expand) My Computer and hide (or display) the objects it contains. Toggle the signs back and forth a few times for practice. End with a minus sign next to My Computer as shown in Figure 11b.
- ➤ Place a newly formatted floppy disk in drive A. Click the drive icon next to drive A to select the drive and display its contents in the right pane. The disk does not contain any files since zero bytes are used.
- ➤ Displaying Web content at the left of a folder (as is done in Figure 11b) is fine when a drive or folder does not contain a large number of files. It is generally a waste of space, however, and so we want to change the folder options.
- ➤ Pull down the **Tools menu** and click the **Folder Options command** to display the Folder Options dialog box in Figure 11a. Click the option to **Use Windows classic folders**. Click **OK**.

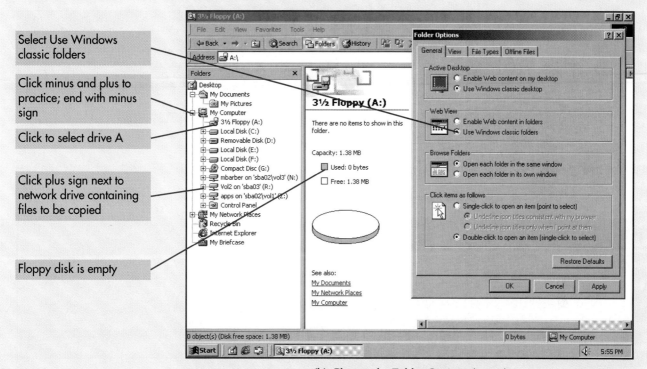

Select Use Windows classic folders

Click minus and plus to practice; end with minus sign

Click to select drive A

Click plus sign next to network drive containing files to be copied

Floppy disk is empty

(b) Change the Folder Options (step 2)

FIGURE 11   *Hands-on Exercise 3 (continued)*

THE PLUS AND MINUS SIGN

Any drive, be it local or on the network, may be expanded or collapsed to display or hide its folders. A minus sign indicates that the drive has been expanded and that its folders are visible. A plus sign indicates the reverse; that is, the device is collapsed and its folders are not visible. Click either sign to toggle to the other. Clicking a plus sign, for example, expands the drive, then displays a minus sign next to the drive to indicate that the folders are visible. Clicking a minus sign has the reverse effect.

Step 3:   **Select the Network Drive**

➤ Click the **plus sign** for the network drive that contains the files you are to copy (e.g., drive **R** in Figure 11c). Select (click) the **Exploring Windows 2000 folder** to open this folder.

➤ You may need to expand other folders on the network drive (such as the Datadisk folder on our network) as per instructions from your professor. Note the following:

• The Exploring Windows 2000 folder is highlighted in the left pane, its icon is an open folder, and its contents are displayed in the right pane.

• The status bar indicates that the folder contains five objects and the total file size is 119KB.

➤ Click the icon next to any other folder to select the folder, which in turn deselects the Exploring Windows 2000 folder. (Only one folder in the left pane is active at a time.) Reselect (click) the **Exploring Windows 2000 folder**.

Expand other folders as necessary

Click Exploring Windows 2000

Status bar

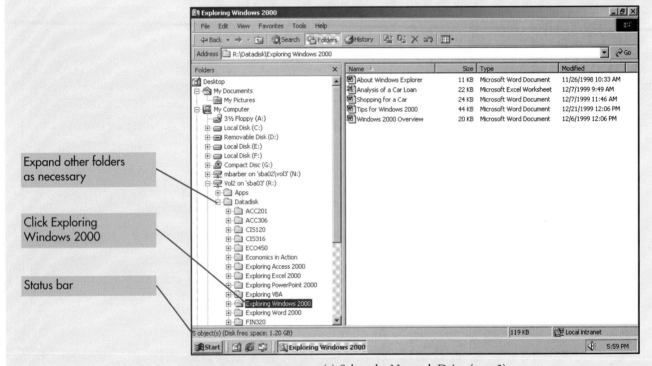

(c) Select the Network Drive (step 3)

FIGURE 11   *Hands-on Exercise 3 (continued)*

CUSTOMIZE WINDOWS EXPLORER

Increase or decrease the size of the left pane within Windows Explorer by dragging the vertical line separating the left and right panes in the appropriate direction. You can also drag the right border of the various column headings (Name, Size, Type, and Modified) in the right pane to increase or decrease the width of the column. And best of all, you can click any column heading to display the contents of the selected folder in sequence by that column. Click the heading a second time and the sequence changes from ascending to descending and vice versa.

Step 4:   **Copy the Individual Files**

➤ Select (click) the file called **About Windows Explorer**, which highlights the file as shown in Figure 11d. Click and drag the selected file in the right pane to the **drive A icon** in the left pane:
  • You will see the ⊘ symbol as you drag the file until you reach a suitable destination (e.g., until you point to the icon for drive A). The ⊘ symbol will change to a plus sign when the icon for drive A is highlighted, indicating that the file can be copied successfully.
  • Release the mouse to complete the copy operation. You will see a pop-up window, which indicates the status of the copy operation.

➤ Select (click) the file **Tips for Windows 2000** after the pop-up window disappears. Copy the selected file to drive A by dragging its icon from the right pane to the drive A icon in the left pane.

➤ Copy the three remaining files to drive A as well. Select (click) drive **A** in the left pane, which in turn displays the contents of the floppy disk in the right pane. You should see the five files you have copied to drive A.

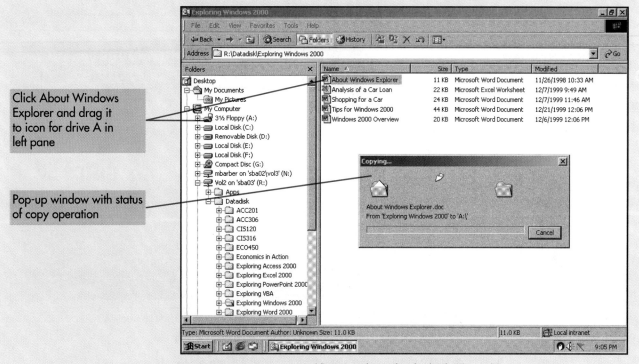

Click About Windows Explorer and drag it to icon for drive A in left pane

Pop-up window with status of copy operation

(d) Copy the Individual Files (step 4)

FIGURE 11   *Hands-on Exercise 3 (continued)*

SELECT MULTIPLE FILES

Selecting one file automatically deselects the previously selected file. You can, however, select multiple files by clicking the first file, then pressing and holding the Ctrl key as you click each additional file. Use the Shift key to select multiple files that are adjacent to one another by clicking the first file, then pressing and holding the Shift key as you click the last file.

Step 5: **Display a Web Page**

➤ This step requires an Internet connection. Click the **minus sign** next to the network drive to collapse that drive. Click the **minus sign** next to any other expanded drive so that the left pane is similar to Figure 11e.

➤ Double click the **Internet Explorer icon** to start Internet Explorer and display the starting page for your configuration. The page you see will be different from ours, but you can click in the Address bar near the top of the window to enter the address of any Web site.

➤ Look closely at the icons on the toolbar, which have changed to reflect the tools associated with viewing a Web page. Click the **Back button** to return to drive A, the previously displayed item in Windows Explorer. The icons on the toolbar return to those associated with a folder.

➤ Close Windows Explorer. Shut down the computer if you do not want to continue with the next exercise at this time.

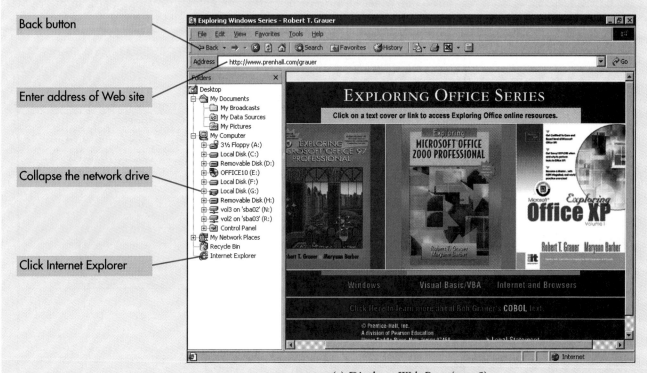

Back button

Enter address of Web site

Collapse the network drive

Click Internet Explorer

(e) Display a Web Page (step 5)

FIGURE 11 *Hands-on Exercise 3 (continued)*

SERVER NOT RESPONDING

Two things have to occur in order for Internet Explorer to display the requested document—it must locate the server on which the document is stored, and it must be able to connect to that computer. If you see a message similar to "Server too busy or not responding", it implies that Internet Explorer has located the server but was unable to connect because the site is busy or is temporarily down. Try to connect again, in a minute or so, or later in the day.

As you grow to depend on the computer, you will create a variety of files using applications such as Microsoft Word or Excel. Learning how to manage those files is one of the most important skills you can acquire. The previous hands-on exercises provided you with a set of files with which to practice. That way, when you have your own files you will be comfortable executing the various file management commands you will need on a daily basis. This section describes the basic file operations you will need, then presents another hands-on exercise in which you apply those commands.

Moving and Copying a File

The essence of file management is to move and copy a file or folder from one location to another. This can be done in different ways, most easily by clicking and dragging the file icon from the source drive or folder to the destination drive or folder, within Windows Explorer. There is one subtlety, however, in that the result of dragging a file (i.e., whether the file is moved or copied) depends on whether the source and destination are on the same or different drives. Dragging a file from one folder to another folder on the same drive moves the file. Dragging a file to a folder on a different drive copies the file. The same rules apply to dragging a folder, where the folder and every file in it are moved or copied as per the rules for an individual file.

This process is not as arbitrary as it may seem. Windows assumes that if you drag an object (a file or folder) to a different drive (e.g., from drive C to drive A), you want the object to appear in both places. Hence, the default action when you click and drag an object to a different drive is to copy the object. You can, however, override the default and move the object by pressing and holding the Shift key as you drag.

Windows also assumes that you do not want two copies of an object on the same drive, as that would result in wasted disk space. Thus, the default action when you click and drag an object to a different folder on the same drive is to move the object. You can override the default and copy the object by pressing and holding the Ctrl key as you drag. It's not as complicated as it sounds, and you get a chance to practice in the hands-on exercise, which follows shortly.

Deleting a File

The **Delete command** deletes (erases) a file from a disk. The command can be executed in different ways, most easily by selecting a file, then pressing the Del key. It's also comforting to know that you can usually recover a deleted file, because the file is not (initially) removed from the disk, but moved instead to the Recycle Bin, from where it can be restored to its original location. Unfortunately, files deleted from a floppy disk are not put in the Recycle Bin and hence cannot be recovered.

The **Recycle Bin** is a special folder that contains all files that were previously deleted from any hard disk on your system. Think of the Recycle Bin as similar to the wastebasket in your room. You throw out (delete) a report by tossing it into a wastebasket. The report is gone (deleted) from your desk, but you can still get it back by taking it out of the wastebasket as long as the basket wasn't emptied. The Recycle Bin works the same way. Files are not deleted from the hard disk per se, but moved instead to the Recycle Bin from where they can be restored to their original location.

The Recycle Bin will eventually run out of space, in which case the files that have been in the Recycle Bin the longest are permanently deleted to make room for additional files. Accordingly, once a file is removed from the Recycle Bin it can no longer be restored, as it has been physically deleted from the hard disk. Note, too, that the protection afforded by the Recycle Bin does not extend to files deleted from a floppy disk. Such files can be recovered, but only through utility programs outside of Windows 2000.

Renaming a File

Every file or folder is assigned a name at the time it is created, but you may want to change that name at some point in the future. Point to a file or a folder, click the right mouse button to display a menu with commands pertaining to the object, then click the **Rename command**. The name of the file or folder will be highlighted with the insertion point (a flashing vertical line) positioned at the end of the name. Enter a new name to replace the selected name, or click anywhere within the name to change the insertion point and edit the name.

Backup

It's not a question of if it will happen, but when—hard disks die, files are lost, or viruses may infect a system. It has happened to us and it will happen to you, but you can prepare for the inevitable by creating adequate backup *before* the problem occurs. The essence of a **backup strategy** is to decide which files to back up, how often to do the backup, and where to keep the backup. Once you decide on a strategy, follow it, and follow it faithfully!

Our strategy is very simple—back up what you can't afford to lose, do so on a daily basis, and store the backup away from your computer. You need not copy every file, every day. Instead, copy just the files that changed during the current session. Realize, too, that it is much more important to back up your data files than your program files. You can always reinstall the application from the original disks or CD, or if necessary, go to the vendor for another copy of an application. You, however, are the only one who has a copy of your term paper.

Write Protection

A floppy disk is normally **write-enabled** (the square hole is covered with the movable tab) so that you can change the contents of the disk. Thus, you can create (save) new files to a write-enabled disk and/or edit or delete existing files. Occasionally, however, you may want to **write-protect** a floppy disk (by sliding the tab to expose the square hole) so that its contents cannot be modified. This is typically done with a backup disk where you want to prevent the accidental deletion of a file and/or the threat of virus infection.

Our Next Exercise

Our next exercise begins with the floppy disk containing the five practice files in drive A. We ask you to create two folders on drive A (step 1) and to move the various files into these folders (step 2). Next, you copy a folder from drive A to the My Documents folder (step 3), modify one of the files in the My Documents folder (step 4), then copy the modified file back to drive A (step 5). We ask you to delete a file in step 6, then recover it from the Recycle Bin in step 7. We also show you how to write-protect a floppy disk in step 8. Let's get started.

FILE MANAGEMENT

Objective Use Windows Explorer to move, copy, and delete a file; recover a deleted file from the Recycle Bin; write-protect a floppy disk. Use Figure 12 as a guide in the exercise.

Step 1: **Create a New Folder**

> ➤ Start Windows Explorer, maximize its window, and if necessary, change to **Details view**. Place the floppy disk from Exercise 2 or 3 in drive A.
> ➤ Select (click) the icon for **drive A** in the left pane of the Explorer window. Drive A should contain the files shown in Figure 12a.
> ➤ You will create two folders on drive A, using two different techniques:
>   • Point to a blank area anywhere in the **right pane**, click the **right mouse button** to display a context-sensitive menu, click (or point to) the **New command**, then click **Folder** as the type of object to create.
>   • The icon for a new folder will appear with the name of the folder (New Folder) highlighted. Type **John Doe's Documents** (use your own name) to change the name of the folder. Press **Enter**.
>   • Click the icon for **drive A** in the left pane. Pull down the **File menu**, click (or point to) the **New command**, and click **Folder** as the type of object to create. Type **Automobile** to change the name of the folder. Press **Enter**. The right pane should now contain five documents and two folders.
> ➤ Pull down the **View menu**. Click the **Arrange icons command**, then click the **By Name command** to display the folders in alphabetical order.

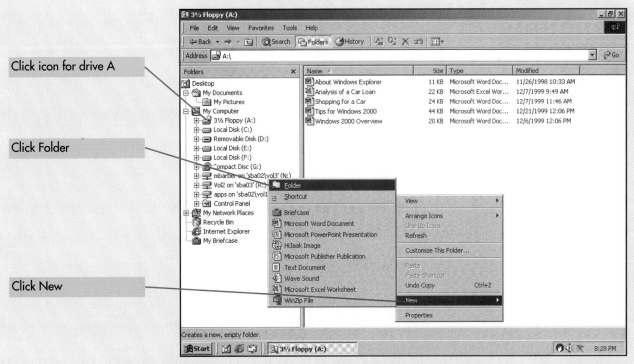

(a) Create a New Folder (step 1)

FIGURE 12 *Hands-on Exercise 4*

Step 2: **Move a File**

➤ Click the **plus sign** next to drive A to expand the drive as shown in Figure 12b. Note the following:
- The left pane shows that drive A is selected. The right pane displays the contents of drive A (the selected object in the left pane).
- There is a minus sign next to the icon for drive A in the left pane, indicating that it has been expanded and that its folders are visible. Thus, the folder names also appear under drive A in the left pane.

➤ Click and drag the icon for the file **About Windows Explorer** from the right pane, to the **John Doe's Documents folder** in the left pane, to move the file into that folder.

➤ Click and drag the **Tips for Windows 2000** and **Windows 2000 Overview** documents to the **John Doe's Documents folder** in similar fashion.

➤ Click the **John Doe's Documents folder** in the left pane to select the folder and display its contents in the right pane. You should see the three files that were just moved.

➤ Click the icon for **Drive A** in the left pane, then click and drag the remaining files, **Analysis of a Car** and **Shopping for a Car**, to the **Automobile folder**.

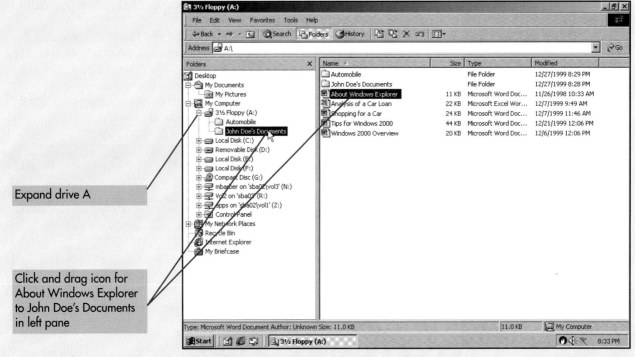

(b) Move a File (step 2)

FIGURE 12 *Hands-on Exercise 4*

RIGHT CLICK AND DRAG

Click and drag with the right mouse button to display a shortcut menu asking whether you want to copy or move the file. This simple tip can save you from making a careless (and potentially serious) error. Use it!

Step 3: **Copy a Folder**

➤ Point to **John Doe's Documents folder** in either pane, click the **right mouse button**, and drag the folder to the **My Documents folder** in the left pane, then release the mouse to display a shortcut menu. Click the **Copy Here command**.
  • You may see a Copy files message box as the individual files within John Doe's folder are copied to the My Documents folder.
  • If you see the Confirm Folder Replace dialog box, it means that you already copied the files or a previous student used the same folder when he or she did this exercise. Click the **Yes to All button** so that your files replace the previous versions in the My Documents folder.

➤ Click the **My Documents folder** in the left pane. Pull down the **View menu** and click the **Refresh command** (or press the **F5 key**) so that the tree structure shows the newly copied folder. (Please remember to delete John Doe's Documents folder at the end of the exercise.)

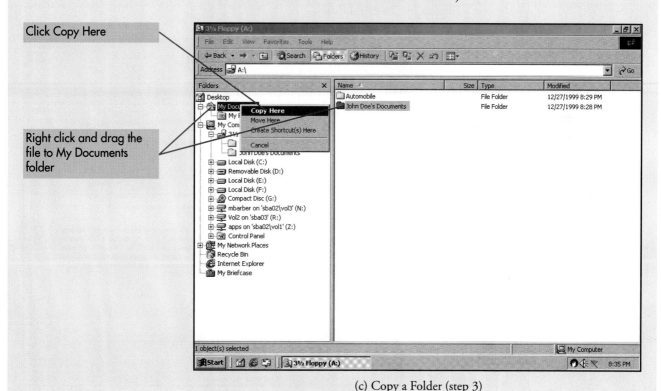

(c) Copy a Folder (step 3)

FIGURE 12   *Hands-on Exercise 4 (continued)*

THE MY DOCUMENTS FOLDER

The My Documents folder is created by default with the installation of Microsoft Windows. There is no requirement that you store your documents in this folder, but it is convenient, especially for beginners who may lack the confidence to create their own folders. The My Documents folder is also helpful in a laboratory environment where the network administrator may prevent you from modifying the desktop and/or from creating your own folders on drive C, in which case you will have to use the My Documents folder.

Step 4: **Modify a Document**

➤ Click **John Doe's Documents folder** within the My Documents folder to make it the active folder and to display its contents in the right pane. Change to the **Details view**.

➤ Double click the **About Windows Explorer** document to start Word and open the document. Do not be concerned if the size and/or position of the Microsoft Word window are different from ours.

➤ If necessary, click inside the document window, then press **Ctrl+End** to move to the end of the document. Add the sentence shown in Figure 12d.

➤ Pull down the **File menu** and click **Save** to save the modified file (or click the **Save button** on the Standard toolbar). Pull down the **File menu** and click **Exit**.

➤ Pull down the **View menu** in Windows Explorer and click **Refresh** (or press the **F5 key**) to update the contents of the right pane. The date and time associated with the About Windows Explorer file has been changed to indicate that the file has just been modified.

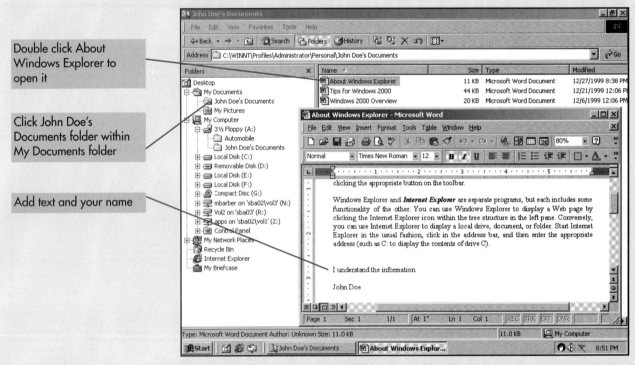

Double click About Windows Explorer to open it

Click John Doe's Documents folder within My Documents folder

Add text and your name

(d) Modify a Document (step 4)

FIGURE 12 *Hands-on Exercise 4 (continued)*

KEYBOARD SHORTCUTS

Ctrl+B, Ctrl+I, and Ctrl+U are shortcuts to boldface, italicize, and underline, respectively. Ctrl+X (the X is supposed to remind you of a pair of scissors), Ctrl+C, and Ctrl+V correspond to Cut, Copy, and Paste, respectively. Ctrl+Home and Ctrl+End move to the beginning or end of a document. These shortcuts are not unique to Microsoft Word, but are recognized in virtually every Windows application. See practice exercise 11 at the end of the chapter.

Step 5: **Copy (Back Up) a File**

➤ Verify that **John Doe's folder** within My Documents is the active folder, as denoted by the open folder icon. Click and drag the icon for the **About Windows Explorer** file from the right pane to John Doe's Documents folder on **Drive A** in the left pane.

➤ You will see the message in Figure 12e, indicating that the folder (on drive A) already contains a file called About Windows Explorer and asking whether you want to replace the existing file. Click **Yes** because you want to replace the previous version of the file on drive A with the updated version from the My Documents folder.

➤ You have just backed up the file; in other words, you have created a copy of the file on the disk in drive A. Thus, you can use the floppy disk to restore the file in the My Documents folder should anything happen to it.

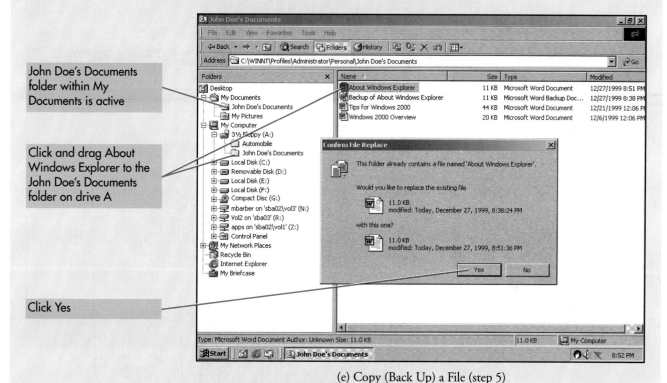

John Doe's Documents folder within My Documents is active

Click and drag About Windows Explorer to the John Doe's Documents folder on drive A

Click Yes

(e) Copy (Back Up) a File (step 5)

FIGURE 12 *Hands-on Exercise 4 (continued)*

FILE EXTENSIONS

Long-time DOS users remember a three-character extension at the end of a file name to indicate the file type; for example, DOC or XLS to indicate a Word document or Excel workbook, respectively. The extensions are displayed or hidden according to a setting in the Folder Options command. Pull down the Tools menu, click the Folder Options command to display the Folder Options dialog box, click the View tab, then check (or clear) the box to hide (or show) file extensions for known file types. Click OK to accept the setting and exit the dialog box.

Step 6: **Delete a Folder**

➤ Select (click) **John Doe's Documents folder** within the My Documents folder in the left pane. Pull down the **File menu** and click **Delete** (or press the **Del key**).

➤ You will see the dialog box in Figure 12f asking whether you are sure you want to delete the folder (i.e., send the folder and its contents to the Recycle Bin). Note the recycle logo within the box, which implies that you will be able to restore the file.

➤ Click **Yes** to delete the folder. The folder disappears from drive C. Pull down the **Edit menu**. Click **Undo Delete**. The deletion is cancelled and the folder reappears in the left pane. If you don't see the folder, pull down the **View menu** and click the **Refresh command**.

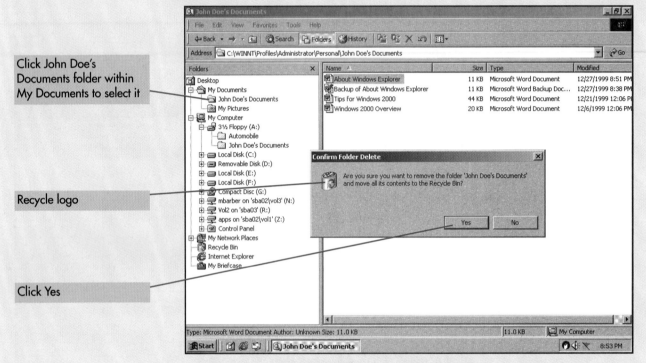

Click John Doe's Documents folder within My Documents to select it

Recycle logo

Click Yes

(f) Delete a Folder (step 6)

FIGURE 12   *Hands-on Exercise 4 (continued)*

THE UNDO COMMAND

The Undo command is present not only in application programs such as Word or Excel, but in Windows Explorer as well. You can use the Undo command to undelete a file provided you execute the command immediately (within a few commands) after the Delete command. To execute the Undo command, right-click anywhere in the right pane to display a shortcut menu, then select the Undo action. You can also pull down the Edit menu and click Undo to reverse (undo) the last command. Some operations cannot be undone (in which case the command will be dimmed), but Undo is always worth a try.

Step 7: **The Recycle Bin**

> ➤ Select John Doe's Documents folder within the My Documents folder in the left pane. Select (click) the **About Windows Explorer** file in the right pane. Press the **Del key**, then click **Yes**.
> ➤ Click the **Down arrow** in the vertical scroll bar in the left pane until you see the icon for the **Recycle Bin**. Click the icon to make the Recycle Bin the active folder and display its contents in the right pane.
> ➤ You will see a different set of files from those displayed in Figure 12g. Pull down the **View menu**, click (or point to) **Arrange icons**, then click **By Delete Date** to display the files in this sequence.
> ➤ Click in the **right pane**. Press **Ctrl+End** or scroll to the bottom of the window. Point to the **About Windows Explorer** file, click the **right mouse button** to display the shortcut menu in Figure 12g, then click **Restore**.
> ➤ The file disappears from the Recycle bin because it has been returned to John Doe's Documents folder.

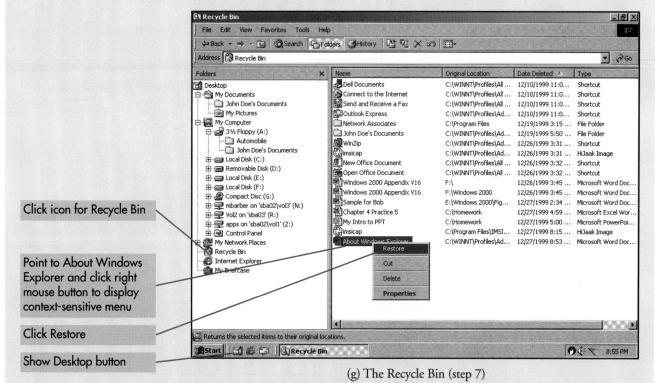

Click icon for Recycle Bin

Point to About Windows Explorer and click right mouse button to display context-sensitive menu

Click Restore

Show Desktop button

(g) The Recycle Bin (step 7)

FIGURE 12 *Hands-on Exercise 4 (continued)*

THE SHOW DESKTOP BUTTON

The Show Desktop button on the taskbar enables you to minimize all open windows with a single click. The button functions as a toggle switch. Click it once and all windows are minimized. Click it a second time and the open windows are restored to their positions on the desktop. If you do not see the Show Desktop button, right click a blank area of the taskbar to display a context-sensitive menu, click Toolbars, then check the Quick Launch toolbar.

Step 8: **Write-Protect a Floppy Disk**

➤ Remove the floppy disk from drive A, then move the built-in tab on the disk so that the square hole on the disk is open. Return the disk to the drive.

➤ If necessary, expand drive A in the left pane, select the **Automobile folder**, select the **Analysis of a Car Loan document** in the right pane, then press the **Del key**. Click **Yes** when asked whether to delete the file.

➤ You will see the message in Figure 12h indicating that the file cannot be deleted because the disk has been write-protected. Click **OK**. Remove the write-protection by moving the built-in tab to cover the square hole.

➤ Repeat the procedure to delete the **Analysis of a Car Loan document**. Click **Yes** in response to the confirmation message asking whether you want to delete the file.

➤ The file disappears from the right pane, indicating it has been deleted. The **Automobile folder** on drive A should contain only one file.

➤ Delete **John Doe's Documents folder** from My Documents as a courtesy to the next student. Exit Windows Explorer. Shut down the computer.

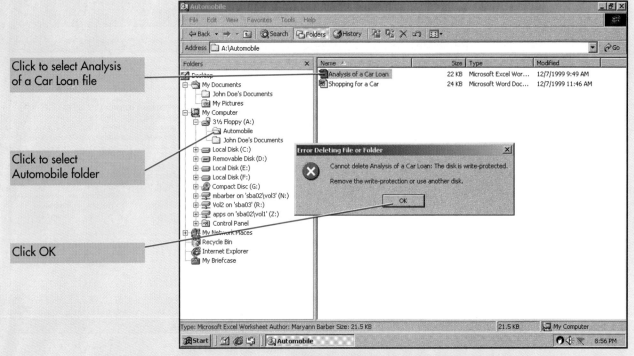

(h) Write-Protect a Floppy Disk (step 8)

FIGURE 12   *Hands-on Exercise 4 (continued)*

BACK UP IMPORTANT FILES

We cannot overemphasize the importance of adequate backup and urge you to copy your data files to floppy disks and store those disks away from your computer. You might also want to write-protect your backup disks so that you cannot accidentally erase a file. It takes only a few minutes, but you will thank us, when (not if) you lose an important file and don't have to wish you had another copy.

Microsoft Windows controls the operation of a computer and its peripherals. Windows 98 and its successor, Windows Me, are geared for the home user and provide extensive support for games and peripheral devices. Windows NT and its successor, Windows 2000, are aimed at the business user and provide increased security and reliability. Windows XP replaces all current versions of Windows. All versions of Windows follow the same conventions and have the same basic interface.

All Windows operations take place on the desktop. Every window on the desktop contains the same basic elements, which include a title bar, a control-menu box, a minimize button, a maximize or restore button, and a close button. Other elements that may be present include a menu bar, vertical and/or horizontal scroll bars, a status bar, and various toolbars. All windows may be moved and sized. The Help command in the Start menu provides access to detailed information.

Multitasking is a major benefit of the Windows environment as it enables you to run several programs at the same time. The taskbar contains a button for each open program and enables you to switch back and forth between those programs by clicking the appropriate button.

A dialog box supplies information needed to execute a command. Option buttons indicate mutually exclusive choices, one of which must be chosen. Check boxes are used if the choices are not mutually exclusive or if an option is not required. A text box supplies descriptive information. A (drop-down or open) list box displays multiple choices, any of which may be selected. A tabbed dialog box provides access to multiple sets of options.

A floppy disk must be formatted before it can store data. Formatting is accomplished through the Format command within the My Computer window. My Computer enables you to browse the disk drives and other devices attached to your system. The contents of My Computer depend on the specific configuration.

A file is a set of data or set of instructions that has been given a name and stored on disk. There are two basic types of files, program files and data files. A program file is an executable file, whereas a data file can be used only in conjunction with a specific program. Every file has a file name and a file type. The file name can be up to 255 characters in length and may include spaces.

Files are stored in folders to better organize the hundreds (or thousands) of files on a disk. A folder may contain program files, data files, and/or other folders. There are two basic ways to search through the folders on your system, My Computer and Windows Explorer. My Computer is intuitive but less efficient than Windows Explorer, as you have to open each folder in succession. Windows Explorer is more sophisticated, as it provides a hierarchical view of the entire system.

Windows Explorer is divided into two panes. The left pane displays all of the devices and, optionally, the folders on each device. The right pane shows the contents of the active (open) drive or folder. Only one drive or folder can be active in the left pane. Any device, be it local or on the network, may be expanded or collapsed to display or hide its folders. A minus sign indicates that the drive has been expanded and that its folders are visible. A plus sign indicates that the device is collapsed and its folders are not visible.

The result of dragging a file (or folder) from one location to another depends on whether the source and destination folders are on the same or different drives. Dragging the file to a folder on the same drive moves the file. Dragging the file to a folder on a different drive copies the file. It's easier, therefore, to click and drag with the right mouse button to display a context-sensitive menu from which you can select the desired operation.

The Delete command deletes (removes) a file from a disk. If, however, the file was deleted from a local (fixed or hard) disk, it is not really gone, but moved instead to the Recycle Bin from where it can be subsequently recovered.

Backup strategy (p. 42)
Check box (p. 8)
Close button (p. 5)
Command button (p. 10)
Common user interface (p. 5)
Compressed file (p. 22)
Contents tab (p. 11)
Copy a file (p. 47)
Data file (p. 20)
Delete a file (p. 41)
Desktop (p. 2)
Details view (p. 20)
Dialog box (p. 8)
Favorites tab (p. 18)
File (p. 20)
Filename (p. 20)
File type (p. 20)
Folder (p. 20)
Folder Options command (p. 14)
Format command (p. 17)
Help command (p. 18)

Index tab (p. 14)
Internet Explorer (p. 40)
List box (p. 8)
Maximize button (p. 5)
Menu bar (p. 5)
Minimize button (p. 5)
Mouse operations (p. 10)
Move a file (p. 44)
Move a window (p. 15)
Multitasking (p. 4)
My Computer (p. 22)
My Documents folder (p. 45)
My Network Places (p. 5)
New command (p. 43)
Option button (p. 8)
Program file (p. 20)
Pull-down menu (p. 7)
Radio button (p. 8)
Recycle Bin (p. 49)
Rename command (p. 42)
Restore a file (p. 5)

Restore button (p. 5)
Scroll bar (p. 5)
Size a window (p. 15)
Spin button (p. 8)
Start button (p. 4)
Status bar (p. 5)
Taskbar (p. 4)
Text box (p. 8)
Task Manager (p. 19)
Title bar (p. 5)
Toolbar (p. 5)
Undo command (p. 48)
Windows 2000 (p. 2)
Windows 95 (p. 2)
Windows 98 (p. 2)
Windows Explorer (p. 33)
Windows Me (p. 2)
Windows NT (p. 2)
Windows XP (p. 2)
Write-enabled (p. 42)
Write-protected (p. 42)

MULTIPLE CHOICE

1. Which versions of the Windows operating system were intended for the home computer?
   (a) Windows NT and Windows 98
   (b) Windows NT and Windows XP
   (c) Windows NT and Windows 2000
   (d) Windows 98 and Windows Me

2. What happens if you click and drag a file from drive C to drive A?
   (a) The file is copied to drive A
   (b) The file is moved to drive A
   (c) A menu appears that allows you to choose between moving and copying
   (d) The file is sent to the recycle bin

3. Which of the following is *not* controlled by the Folder Options command?
   (a) Single or double clicking to open a desktop icon
   (b) The presence or absence of Web content within a folder
   (c) The view (e.g., using large or small icons) within My Computer
   (d) Using one or many windows when browsing My Computer

4. What is the significance of a faded (dimmed) command in a pull-down menu?
   (a) The command is not currently accessible
   (b) A dialog box will appear if the command is selected
   (c) A Help window will appear if the command is selected
   (d) There are no equivalent keystrokes for the particular command

5. Which of the following is true regarding a dialog box?
   (a) Option buttons indicate mutually exclusive choices
   (b) Check boxes imply that multiple options may be selected
   (c) Both (a) and (b)
   (d) Neither (a) nor (b)

6. Which of the following is the first step in sizing a window?
   (a) Point to the title bar
   (b) Pull down the View menu to display the toolbar
   (c) Point to any corner or border
   (d) Pull down the View menu and change to large icons

7. Which of the following is the first step in moving a window?
   (a) Point to the title bar
   (b) Pull down the View menu to display the toolbar
   (c) Point to any corner or border
   (d) Pull down the View menu and change to large icons

8. How do you exit from Windows?
   (a) Click the Start button, then click the Shut Down command
   (b) Right click the Start button, then click the Shut Down command
   (c) Click the End button, then click the Shut Down command
   (d) Right click the End button, then click the Shut Down command

9. Which button appears immediately after a window has been maximized?
   (a) The close button
   (b) The minimize button
   (c) The maximize button
   (d) The restore button

10. What happens to a window that has been minimized?
    (a) The window is still visible but it no longer has a minimize button
    (b) The window shrinks to a button on the taskbar
    (c) The window is closed and the application is removed from memory
    (d) The window is still open but the application is gone from memory

11. What is the significance of three dots next to a command in a pull-down menu?
    (a) The command is not currently accessible
    (b) A dialog box will appear if the command is selected
    (c) A Help window will appear if the command is selected
    (d) There are no equivalent keystrokes for the particular command

12. The Recycle Bin enables you to restore a file that was deleted from:
    (a) Drive A
    (b) Drive C
    (c) Both (a) and (b)
    (d) Neither (a) nor (b)

13. The left pane of Windows Explorer may contain:
    (a) One or more folders with a plus sign
    (b) One or more folders with a minus sign
    (c) Both (a) and (b)
    (d) Neither (a) nor (b)

14. Which of the following was suggested as essential to a backup strategy?
    (a) Back up all program files at the end of every session
    (b) Store backup files at another location
    (c) Both (a) and (b)
    (d) Neither (a) nor (b)

ANSWERS

1. d	**5.** c	**9.** d	**13.** c
2. a	**6.** c	**10.** b	**14.** b
3. c	**7.** a	**11.** b	
4. a	**8.** a	**12.** b	

1. My Computer: The document in Figure 13 is an effective way to show your instructor that you understand the My Computer window, and further that you have basic proficiency in Microsoft Word.
   a. Open My Computer to display the contents of your configuration. Pull down the View menu and switch to the Details view. Size the window as necessary. Press Alt + Print Screen to capture the copy of the My Computer window to the Windows clipboard. (The Print Screen key captures the entire screen. Using the Alt key, however, copies just the current window.)
   b. Click the Start menu, click Programs, then click Microsoft Word.
   c. Pull down the Edit menu. Click the Paste command to copy the contents of the clipboard to the document you are about to create. The My Computer window should be pasted into your document.
   d. Press Ctrl+End to move to the end of your document. Press Enter two or three times to leave blank lines as appropriate. Type a modified form of the memo in Figure 13 so that it conforms to your configuration.
   e. Finish the memo and sign your name. Pull down the File menu, click the Print command, then click OK in the dialog box to print the document.

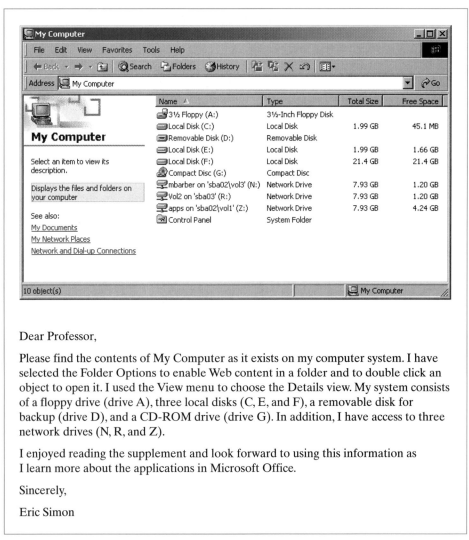

Dear Professor,

Please find the contents of My Computer as it exists on my computer system. I have selected the Folder Options to enable Web content in a folder and to double click an object to open it. I used the View menu to choose the Details view. My system consists of a floppy drive (drive A), three local disks (C, E, and F), a removable disk for backup (drive D), and a CD-ROM drive (drive G). In addition, I have access to three network drives (N, R, and Z).

I enjoyed reading the supplement and look forward to using this information as I learn more about the applications in Microsoft Office.

Sincerely,

Eric Simon

FIGURE 13   *My Computer (exercise 1)*

2. Windows Explorer: Prove to your instructor that you have completed the fourth hands-on exercise by creating a document similar to the one in Figure 14. Use the technique described in the previous problem to capture the screen and paste it into a Word document.

Compare the documents in Figures 13 and 14 that show My Computer and Windows Explorer, respectively. My Computer is intuitive and preferred by beginners, but it is very limited when compared to Windows Explorer. The latter displays a hierarchical view of your system, showing the selected object in the left pane and the contents of the selected object in the right pane. We urge you, therefore, to become comfortable with Windows Explorer, as that will make you more productive.

Dear Professor,

This document shows that I have completed the last hands-on exercise and that I have a basic proficiency in Windows Explorer. I can now create a folder and move and copy files with confidence. These skills will become increasingly important as I use various applications throughout the semester.

I also understand the role of the Windows clipboard, an area of memory that is available to every application. I simply press the Print Screen key to capture a screen to the clipboard, and then I use the Paste button to copy the contents of the clipboard into the Word document.

Sincerely,

Alex Rogers

FIGURE 14 *Windows Explorer (exercise 2)*

3. MyPHLIP Web Site: Every text in the *Exploring Office XP* series has a corresponding MyPHLIP (Prentice Hall Learning on the Internet Partnership) Web site, where you will find a variety of student resources as well as online review questions for each chapter. Go to www.prenhall.com/myphlip and follow the instructions. The first time at the site you will be prompted to register by supplying your e-mail address and choosing a password. Next, you choose the discipline (CIS/MIS) and a book (e.g., *Exploring Microsoft Office XP, Volume 1*), which in turn will take you to a page similar to Figure 15.

Your professor will tell you whether he or she has created an online syllabus, in which case you should click the link to find your professor after adding the book. Either way, the next time you return to the site, you will be taken directly to your text. Select any chapter, click "Go", then use the review questions as directed.

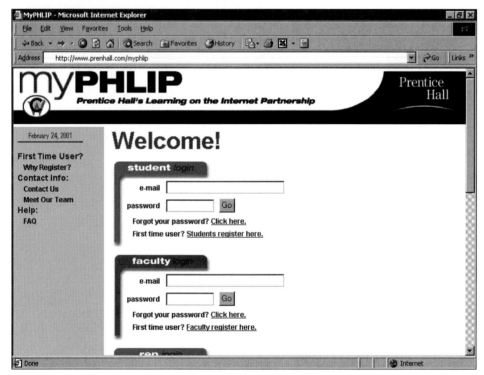

FIGURE 15   *MyPHLIP Web Site (Windows module) (exercise 3)*

4. Organize Your Work: A folder may contain documents, programs, or other folders. The My Classes folder in Figure 16, for example, contains five folders, one folder for each class you are taking this semester. Folders help you to organize your files, and you should become proficient in their use. The best way to practice with folders is on a floppy disk, as was done in Figure 16. Accordingly:
   a. Format a floppy disk or use the floppy disk you have been using throughout the chapter.
   b. Create a Correspondence folder. Create a Business and a Personal folder within the Correspondence folder.
   c. Create a My Courses folder. Within the My Courses folder create a separate folder for each course you are taking.
   d. Use the technique described in problems 1 and 2 to capture the screen in Figure 16 and incorporate it into a document. Add a short paragraph that describes the folders you have created, then submit the document.

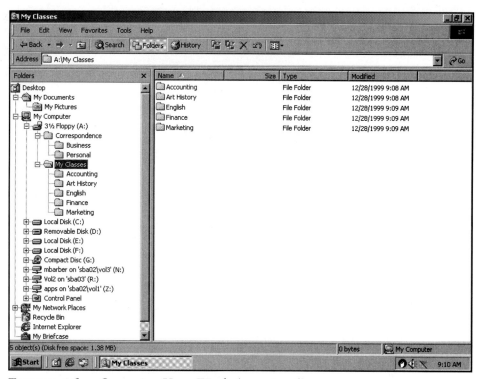

FIGURE 16 *Organize Your Work (exercise 4)*

5. **The Windows Web Site:** The Web is the best source for information on any application. Go to the Windows home page (www.microsoft.com/windows) as shown in Figure 17, then write a short note to your instructor summarizing the contents of that page and the associated links. Similar pages exist for all Microsoft applications such as www.microsoft.com/office for Microsoft Office.

6. **Implement a Screen Saver:** A screen saver is a delightful way to personalize your computer and a good way to practice with Microsoft Windows. This is typically not something you can do in a laboratory setting, but it is well worth doing on your own machine. Point to a blank area of the desktop, click the right mouse button to display a context-sensitive menu, then click the Properties command to open the Display Properties dialog box in Figure 18. Click the Screen Saver tab, click the Down arrow in the Screen Saver list box, and select Marquee Display. Click the Settings command button, enter the text and other options for your message, then click OK to close the Options dialog box. Click OK a second time to close the Display Properties dialog box.

7. **The Active Desktop:** The Active Desktop displays Web content directly on the desktop, then updates the information automatically according to a predefined schedule. You can, for example, display a stock ticker or scoreboard similar to what you see on television. You will need your own machine and an Internet connection to do this exercise, as it is unlikely that the network administrator will let you modify the desktop:
   a. Right click the Windows desktop, click Properties to show the Display Properties dialog box, then click the Web tab. Check the box to show Web content on the Active desktop.
   b. Click the New button, then click the Visit Gallery command button to go to the Active Desktop Gallery in Figure 19 on page 59. Choose any category, then follow the onscreen instructions to display the item on your desktop. We suggest you start with the stock ticker or sports scoreboard.
   c. Summarize your opinion of the active desktop in a short note to your instructor. Did the feature work as advertised? Is the information useful to you?

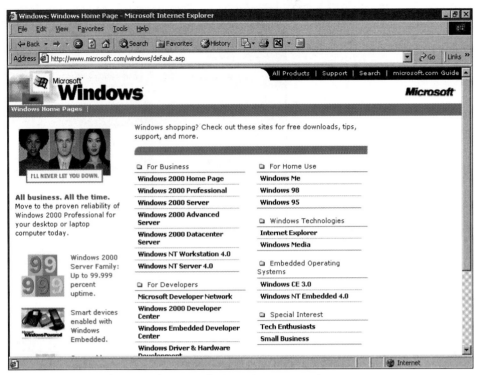

FIGURE 17 *The Windows Web Site (exercise 5)*

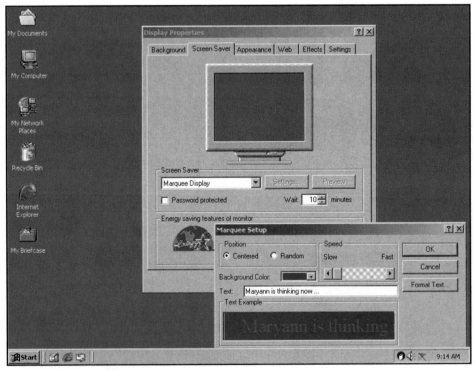

FIGURE 18 *Implement a Screen Saver (exercise 6)*

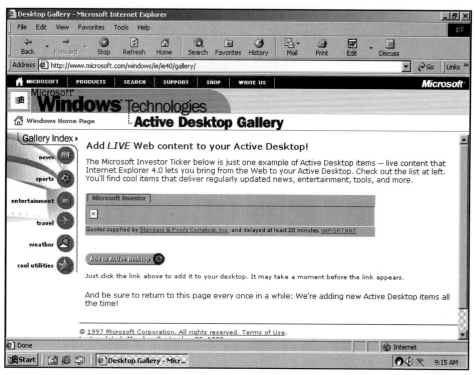

FIGURE 19   *The Active Desktop (exercise 7)*

8. The Control Panel: The Control Panel enables you to change the hardware or software settings on your system. You will not have access to the Control Panel in a lab environment, but you will need it at home if you change your configuration, perhaps by installing a new program. Click the Start button, click Settings, then select Control Panel to display the Control Panel window. Click the down arrow on the Views button to change to the Details view as shown in Figure 20. (The Control Panel can also be opened from My Computer.)

   Write a short report (two or three paragraphs is sufficient) that describes some of the capabilities within Control Panel. *Be careful about making changes, however, and be sure you understand the nature of the new settings before you accept any of the changes.*

9. Users and Passwords: Windows 2000 enables multiple users to log onto the same machine, each with his or her own user name and password. The desktop settings for each user are stored individually, so that all users have their own desktop. The administrator and default user is created when Windows 2000 is first installed, but new users can be added or removed at any time. Once again you will need your own machine:
   a. Click the Start button, click Settings, then click Control Panel to open the Control Panel window as shown in Figure 21. The Control Panel is a special folder that allows you to modify the hardware and/or software settings on your computer.
   b. Double click the Users and Passwords icon to display the dialog box in Figure 20. *Be very careful about removing a user or changing a password, because you might inadvertently deny yourself access to your computer.*
   c. Summarize the capabilities within the users and passwords dialog box in a short note to your instructor. Can you see how these principles apply to the network you use at school or work?

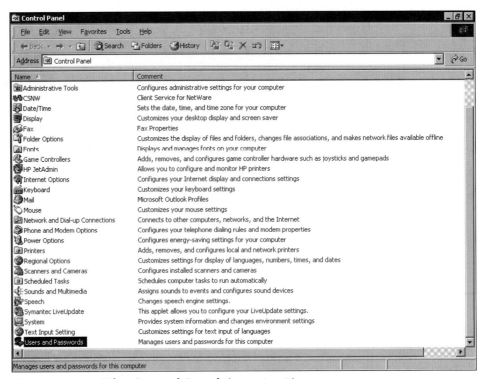

FIGURE 20   *The Control Panel (exercise 8)*

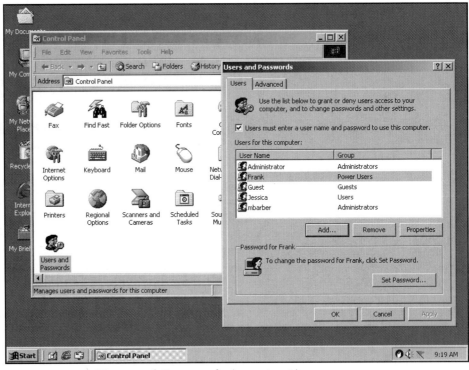

FIGURE 21   *Users and Passwords (exercise 9)*

10. The Fonts Folder: The Fonts folder within the Control Panel displays the names of the fonts available on a system and enables you to obtain a printed sample of any specific font. Click the Start button, click (or point to) the Settings command, click (or point to) Control Panel, then double click the Fonts icon to open the Fonts folder and display the fonts on your system.

   a. Double click any font to open a Fonts window as shown in Figure 22, then click the Print button to print a sample of the selected font.

   b. Open a different font. Print a sample page of this font as well.

   c. Locate the Wingdings font and print this page. Do you see any symbols you recognize? How do you insert these symbols into a document?

   d. How many fonts are there in your fonts Folder? Do some fonts appear to be redundant with others? How much storage space does a typical font require? Write the answers to these questions in a short paragraph.

   e. Start Word. Create a title page containing your name, class, date, and the title of this assignment (My Favorite Fonts). Center the title. Use boldface or italics as you see fit. Be sure to use a suitable type size.

   f. Staple the various pages together (the title page, the three font samples, and the answers to the questions in part d). Submit the assignment to your instructor.

FIGURE 22   *The Fonts Folder (exercise 10)*

11. Keyboard Shortcuts: Microsoft Windows is a graphical user interface in which users "point and click" to execute commands. As you gain proficiency, however, you will find yourself gravitating toward various keyboard shortcuts as shown in Figures 23a and 23b. There is absolutely no need to memorize these shortcuts, nor should you even try. A few, however, have special appeal and everyone has his or her favorite. Use the Help menu to display this information, pick your three favorite shortcuts, and submit them to your instructor. Compare your selections with those of your classmates.

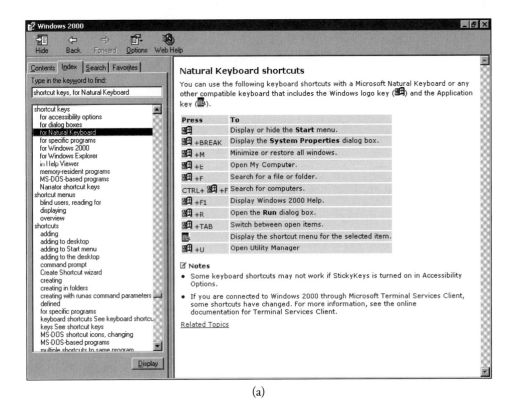

(a)

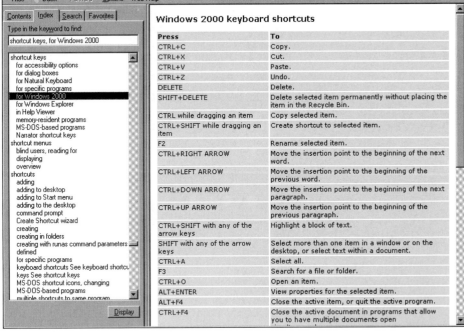

(b)

FIGURE 23 *Shortcut Keys for Natural Keyboard (Exercise 11)*

Planning for Disaster

Do you have a backup strategy? Do you even know what a backup strategy is? You had better learn, because sooner or later you will wish you had one. You will erase a file, be unable to read from a floppy disk, or worse yet suffer a hardware failure in which you are unable to access the hard drive. The problem always seems to occur the night before an assignment is due. The ultimate disaster is the disappearance of your computer, by theft or natural disaster. Describe, in 250 words or less, the backup strategy you plan to implement in conjunction with your work in this class.

Your First Consultant's Job

Go to a real installation such as a doctor's or attorney's office, the company where you work, or the computer lab at school. Determine the backup procedures that are in effect, then write a one-page report indicating whether the policy is adequate and, if necessary, offering suggestions for improvement. Your report should be addressed to the individual in charge of the business, and it should cover all aspects of the backup strategy; that is, which files are backed up and how often, and what software is used for the backup operation. Use appropriate emphasis (for example, bold italics) to identify any potential problems. This is a professional document (it is your first consultant's job), and its appearance should be perfect in every way.

File Compression

You've learned your lesson and have come to appreciate the importance of backing up all of your data files. The problem is that you work with large documents that exceed the 1.44MB capacity of a floppy disk. Accordingly, you might want to consider the acquisition of a file compression program to facilitate copying large documents to a floppy disk in order to transport your documents to and from school, home, or work. (A Zip file is different from a Zip drive. The latter is a hardware device, similar in concept to a large floppy disk, with a capacity of 100MB or 250MB.)

You can download an evaluation copy of the popular WinZip program at www.winzip.com. Investigate the subject of file compression and submit a summary of your findings to your instructor.

The Threat of Virus Infection

A computer virus is an actively infectious program that attaches itself to other programs and alters the way a computer works. Some viruses do nothing more than display an annoying message at an inopportune time. Most, however, are more harmful, and in the worst case, erase all files on the disk. Use your favorite search engine to research the subject of computer viruses in order to answer the following questions. When is a computer subject to infection by a virus? What precautions does your school or university take against the threat of virus infection in its computer lab? What precautions, if any, do you take at home? Can you feel confident that your machine will not be infected if you faithfully use a state-of-the-art antivirus program that was purchased in January 2001?

The Briefcase

It is becoming increasingly common for people to work on more than one machine. Students, for example, may alternate between machines at school and home. In similar fashion, an office worker may use a desktop and a laptop, or have a machine at work and at home. In every instance, you need to transfer files back and forth between the two machines. This can be done using the Copy command from within Windows Explorer. It can also be done via the Briefcase folder. Your instructor has asked you to look into the latter capability and to prepare a brief report describing its use. Do you recommend the Briefcase over a simple Copy command?

Cut, Copy, and Paste

The Cut, Copy, and Paste commands are used in conjunction with one another to move and copy data within a document, or from one Windows document to another. The commands can also be executed from within My Computer or Windows Explorer to move and copy files. You can use the standard Windows shortcuts of Ctrl+X, Ctrl+C, and Ctrl+V to cut, copy, and paste, respectively. You can also click the corresponding icons on the Standard Buttons toolbar within Windows Explorer or My Computer.

Experiment with this technique, then write a short note to your instructor that summarizes the various ways in which files can be moved or copied within Windows 2000.

Register Now

It is good practice to register every program you purchase, so that the vendor can notify you of new releases and/or other pertinent information. Windows provides an online capability whereby you can register via modem. To register your copy of Windows, click the Start button, click Programs, click Accessories, click Welcome to Windows, then click the Registration Wizard. Follow the directions that are displayed on the screen. (Registering a program does carry the risk of having unwanted sales messages sent to you by e-mail. At the Web site, look for a check box in which you choose whether to receive unsolicited e-mail.) You can do this exercise only if you are working on your own computer.

INDEX